The Spontaneous Brain

The Spontaneous Brain

From the Mind–Body to the World–Brain Problem

Georg Northoff

The MIT Press
Cambridge, Massachusetts
London, England

This book was set in ITC Stone Sans Std and ITC Stone Serif Std by Toppan Best-set Premedia Limited. Printed and bound in the United States of America.

Library of Congress Cataloging-in-Publication Data

Names: Northoff, Georg, author.
Title: The spontaneous brain : from the mind–body to the world–brain problem / Georg Northoff.
Description: Cambridge, MA : The MIT Press, [2018] | Includes bibliographical references and index.
Identifiers: LCCN 2017053687 | ISBN 9780262038072 (hardcover : alk. paper)
Subjects: LCSH: Brain—Physiology. | Mind and body. | Neurosciences—Philosophy.
Classification: LCC QP376 .N679 2018 | DDC 612.8/2—dc23 LC record available at https://lccn.loc.gov/2017053687

10 9 8 7 6 5 4 3 2 1

Contents

Preface

How can we address the question of the existence and reality of mental features? Philosophers have long argued about the existence and reality of the mind when raising the metaphysical question for its relation to the body, the mind–body problem. This conundrum, especially in recent times, is complemented by the neuroscientists' search for empirical answers, that is, neuronal mechanisms in the brain with the neural correlates of such mental features as consciousness, self, free will, and others—for the neuroscientists the mind is nothing but the brain. Despite the conjoint efforts of both philosophy and neuroscience, no conclusive answer to the question of the existence and reality of mental features has yet been proposed.

I do not aim here to provide yet another answer to the question of the mind–body problem as such by making yet another suggestion regarding how the mind is related to the body. Instead, I question the question itself. I argue that the question regarding the mind and its relationship to the body is simply the wrong question to address the existence and reality of mental features: the question of the mind and its relation to body is wrong, as it is implausible on empirical, ontological, and epistemological-methodological grounds. Therefore, I consider the mind–body problem to be the wrong path by which to tackle the question for the existence and reality of mental features.

How can we raise the question about mental features in a more plausible way? I argue that it would be better to raise the question of the existence and reality of mental features in terms of the brain's relation to the world, the world–brain relation, as I call it. Empirical evidence suggests that the brain's spontaneous activity and its spatiotemporal structure are central for aligning and integrating the brain within the world—the world–brain relation; hence, the main title of this book. Moreover, I argue that that very same relation, the world–brain relation, can also address the question of the existence and reality of mental features such as consciousness in an empirically, ontologically, conceptually more plausible way than the mind–body problem.

The ideas and arguments in this book have a long history in my search for introducing the relevance of the brain into philosophy without rendering the latter merely empirical. My first attempts in this endeavor were published in German (*The Brain: A Neurophilosophical State of Art*, Northoff, 1999) and followed up in English in *Philosophy of Brain: The Brain Problem* (Northoff, 2004). Since then, brain imaging technology has strongly advanced, which has allowed me to explore the brain and its relationship to mental features like the self and consciousness in empirical terms—these subjects and the development of a novel model of brain in terms of its coding and spontaneous activity as well as a neurophenomenal account of consciousness are well documented in various papers (see www.georgnorthoff.com) as well as in my two-volume work *Unlocking the Brain*, vol. 1, *Coding*, and vol. 2, *Consciousness* (Northoff, 2014a, 2014b).

On the philosophical side, I reread Kant's *Critique of Pure Reason* (Kant, 1781/1998) and considered it in the context of the brain—this, modifying Kant's famous quote with respect to Hume, "awakened me from the dogmatic slumbers of the mind and its chains" by means of which it constrains philosophy. In conjunction with the empirical data and the development of a novel model of brain (*Unlocking the Brain*), I became more and more convinced that the mind–body problem is an ill-posed problem if not altogether a nonsensical one. That possibility was raised rather implicitly in my textbook *Minding the Brain* (Northoff, 2014d) especially in the critical reflection sections of the volume.

This neuro-philosophical reevaluation sent me searching for a viable alternative. Any rejection of a framework is only complete when one can provide a better alternative. For that reason, I ventured into different philosophical territories including process philosophy, phenomenological philosophy, philosophy of science, and philosophy of mind (and even Chinese philosophy as in the Chinese translation of my textbook *Minding the Brain*). I found such an alternative in what I describe as the world–brain problem, which is mentioned briefly for the first time in my more popular and general audience book *Neurophilosophy and the Healthy Mind. Learning from the Unwell Brain* (Northoff, 2016e). The present book now presents a more detailed philosophical elaboration of the world–brain problem as a basic ontological problem and then posits how it can replace the metaphysical mind–body problem as paradigm for the existence and reality of mental features.

I am grateful to several people. Lucas Jurkovics (Ottawa, Canada) was very helpful in editing chapters 1–3 and parts of chapters 5 and 6. Beni Majid (Iran) deserves great credit for introducing me to structural realism and extrapolating my empirical work on the self to a philosophical context. He must also be thanked for helpful criticism of chapters 15. I am also very thankful to Kathinka Evers (Uppsala, Sweden) for her excellent critique of chapters 13–15 and the suggestion of replacing "vantage point from *without* brain" with "vantage point from *beyond* brain." Moreover, Takuya Niikawa (Sapporo, Japan) deserves a great thank you for reading and amending chapters 9–11 in an extremely nice, constructive, and very helpful way, part of which we discussed during a wonderful day of hiking in Hokkaido, Japan. I am also grateful for excellent help by Ivar Kolvaart and Federico Zilio in correcting the proofs.

The various members of my research group in Ottawa, Canada (most notably Zirui Huang, Pengmin Qin, Niall Duncan, Paola Magioncalda, Matteo Martino, Jianfeng Zhang, Takashi Nakao, Annemarie Wolf, Marcello Costandino, Diana Ghandi, Stefano Damiano, and Fransesca Ferri as well as colleagues Heinz Boeker, Kai Cheng, Szu-Ting, Tim Lane, Peter Hartwich, Andre Longtin, Hsiu-Hau Lin, and Maia Fraser) on brain imaging of mental features and psychiatry must also be thanked for providing wonderful data and inspiring discussion about how the brain works and how it is related to mental features such as consciousness and self. Thank you also to the Institute of Mental Health Research and its director Dr. Zul Merali as well as the Canada Research Chair, Michael Smith Chair for Neuroscience and Mental Health, and the Institute of Mind and Brain Research at the University of Ottawa for providing both resources and time to enable me to write this book.

Some of the material of this book has been probed in several talks and discussions at Zhejiang University in Hangzhou, China; the University of Uppsala, Sweden; the Center for Process Studies in Claremont, California, USA; the Human Brain Project of the European Union in Paris, France; Collège de France in Paris, France; University of Istanbul, Turkey; Taipei Medical University in Taipei, Taiwan; Kyoto University, Kyoto, Japan; Tokyo

University, Tokyo, Japan; Hokkaido University, Sapporo, Japan; Yang Ming University in Taipei, Taiwan; and Tsinghua University in Taiwan. I am very grateful to Philip Laughlin from the MIT Press for taking on this project. I am also grateful to my helpful and patient editor Judith Feldmann and to Elissa Schiff and Regina Gregory for providing excellent support—thank you so much! Finally, I am indebted to my partner John Sarkissian who has to endure my philosophical and mental withdrawal from the world in his relationship to somebody who claims the world–brain relation to be the basis of consciousness.

Introduction

From Mind to World

What are mental features? Mental features such as consciousness, self, free will, and sense of the other determine our relation to the world and thus our very existence and reality within the world. If, for instance, we lose consciousness, as in sleep or in a vegetative state, our relation to the world is disrupted. Since mental features are central to our existence within the world, we have an urgent need to understand their origin and mechanisms. Accordingly, to unravel the existence and reality of mental features, we need to understand their relation to the world.

Neuroscientists investigate the brain in empirical terms and search for neuronal mechanisms underlying mental features including consciousness, self, free will, and others. They mainly focus on the brain and its neural activity—however, that focus leaves out consideration of the world. Philosophers, in contrast, associate mental features with the mind. They subsequently raise the question of the existence and reality of mind and how it is related to the existence of the body, or what we may term the mind–body problem. In the shift of focus from brain to mind, however, once again any relation to the world is left out.

The central argument of this book is that we need to consider the world in both neuroscientific and philosophical investigation of mental features such as consciousness. Specifically, I argue that the need to include the world in our neuroscientific and philosophical investigation of mental features will change and shift our focus from brain and mind to world–brain relation as a necessary condition of mental features, specifically consciousness. We are then no longer confronted with the mind–body problem in our quest for the existence and reality of mental features. Instead, we may then need to shift our focus to what I describe as the "world–brain problem"—this requires nothing less than a Copernican revolution in neuroscience and philosophy. This is the central thesis and argument in this book hence its title and subtitle.

From Mind–Body Problem to World–Brain Problem

The mind–body problem is one of the most basic and pressing questions in our time. However, a definite answer remained elusive so far in both neuroscience and philosophy. Descartes famously assumed that mind and body are related to different substances, that is, mental and physical—this established mind–body dualism. Since his time various answers ranging from interactive dualism over materialism and physicalism to panpsychism have been suggested to address the metaphysical question of the relationship between mind and body (Searle, 2004). However, despite the wide variety of different suggestions, no answer is considered definite.

Others even contested that the mind–body problem is a metaphysical problem at all. Instead, they provide epistemological (Stoljar, 2006), conceptual (Bennett & Hacker, 2003), or empirical (P. S. Churchland, 2002; Dennett, 1981; Snowdon, 2015) answers to the mind–body problem. Even worse, some consider the mind–body problem as mysterious and thus altogether insolvable (McGinn, 1991; Nagel, 2000, 2012). Taken all together, we are confronted with a deadlock. None of the current answers to the mind–body problem is conclusive. While, at the same time, attempts of shifting, eliminating, or declaring unknowable the mind–body problem are not convincing either. The mind–body problem thus remains a stubbornly resisting "knot" in our understanding of ourselves and the world that we have not untangled so far.

I here do not aim to provide yet another answer to the mind–body problem. Instead, I question the question itself. I argue that the question itself, that is, how the mind is related to body and brain, is simply not plausible on different grounds: empirical (parts I and II), ontological (part III), and epistemic-methodological (part IV). We therefore have to abandon the mind–body problem as the "right" approach to answer our question of the existence and reality of mental features.

What is the alternative to the mind–body problem? I argue that that alternative can be found in what I describe as the "world–brain problem."

The world–brain problem is an ontological problem, which distinguishes it from the mind–body problem, which is metaphysical (rather than ontological) (see chapters 9 and 14 for my distinction between ontology and metaphysics). As such, the world–brain problem focuses on the ontological relation between world and brain including its relevance for mental features: How is the world related to the brain; and how can that relation account for the existence and reality of mental features, foremost, consciousness?

The world–brain problem requires us to consider the brain in an ontological rather than merely an empirical context. To develop a plausible ontological model of brain, we may want to consider some of its empirical features. One such empirical feature consists of the brain's spontaneous activity. In addition to neural activity related to specific tasks or stimuli, specifically, stimulus-induced or task-related activity, the brain shows an intrinsic activity, that is, a spontaneous activity (see discussion in next section for details).

I argue that that very same spontaneous activity is central for the brain's ontological determination including its relation to world, that is, the world–brain relation and for mental features. Therefore, I consider the brain's spontaneous activity central for shifting from the mind–body problem to a world–brain problem—hence the title and subtitle of this book. Such a shift from mind–body to world–brain problem is possible, however only when we shift our current pre-Copernican to a truly post-Copernican vantage point—this amounts to nothing less than a Copernican revolution in neuroscience and philosophy (see chapters 12–14 for further discussion).

Model of Brain I—The Spontaneous Brain

How can we characterize the brain by itself, independent of mental features? The brain can empirically be characterized by neural activity that includes both spontaneous or resting-state activity and task-evoked or stimulus-induced activity (Northoff, 2014a; Raichle, 2015a,b). Although much attention in both neuroscience and philosophy has been devoted to the brain's stimulus-induced or task-evoked activity and related sensory and cognitive functions, the central role of the brain's spontaneous or resting-state activity has only recently been considered.

Historically, Hans Berger, who introduced the EEG (Berger, 1929), observed spontaneous activity in the brain that remained independent of any external tasks or stimuli. This theory was further advanced by Bishop (1933) and Lashley (1951) and has recently gained more traction in neuroscience with the observation of spontaneous oscillations (Buzsáki, 2006; Llinas, 1988; Yuste et al., 2005), spontaneous coherence or connectivity between neural activities in different regions of the brain (Biswal et al., 1995; Greicius et al. 2003), and the default-mode network (DMN) (Greicius et al., 2003; Raichle, 2015a,b; Raichle et al., 2001). These and other observations all point to a central role of the brain's spontaneous activity for its neural activity including both resting state and task-evoked or stimulus-induced activity (see Northoff, 2014a,b; Northoff et al., 2010; as well as Huang et al., 2015, for an extensive discussion).

The observation of the brain's spontaneous activity has profoundly shifted our model of brain. Instead of considering the brain as a purely extrinsically driven device, the spontaneous activity observed suggests what Raichle has described as an "intrinsic model of brain" (Raichle, 2009, 2010). This is reminiscent of a Kantian-like model of mind that, applied to the brain, suggests the brain's spontaneous activity to structure and organize its own task-evoked or stimulus-induced activity and the related sensory and cognitive functions (Fazelpour & Thompson, 2015; Northoff, 2012a,b, 2014a,b).

The Kantian-like view of the brain carries important ramifications for our model of brain. Traditional models of brain are largely neurosensory and/or neurocognitive in that they focus on the brain's sensory and/or cognitive functions as mostly mediated by its stimulus-induced or task-evoked activity (P. M. Churchland, 2012; Northoff, 2016a; Thagard, 2012a,b). The observation of spontaneous activity may put the brain's neurosensory and neurocognitive functions into a larger empirical context—precisely what kind of model of brain this requires, however, remains unclear (Klein, 2014; Northoff, 2012a,b). Therefore, the first part of the present book investigates different models of brain and how these models can incorporate the brain's spontaneous activity and its relation to stimulus-induced activity.

Model of Brain II—The Brain's Spontaneous Activity and Its Spatiotemporal Structure

Why and how is the brain's spontaneous activity relevant? Several investigations show that the spontaneous activity is relevant for mental features such as consciousness and self (Huang, Dai, et al., 2014; Huang, Zhang, Wu, et al. 2015, 2016; Northoff, 2014b; Qin & Northoff, 2011; Qin et al., 2015; and many others; see chapters 4–8 for a more thorough discussion of this topic and its implications). Importantly, mental features seem to be specifically related in an as yet unclear way to the spatiotemporal structure of the brain's spontaneous activity. Let us briefly describe that spatiotemporal structure.

The brain's spontaneous activity can spatially be characterized by various neural networks that consist of regions showing close functional connectivity with each other. There is for instance the DMN that includes mainly the cortical midline structures (Andrews-Hanna et al., 2016; Northoff et al., 2006), which show strong low-frequency fluctuations (Northoff, 2014a; Raichle, 2009; Raichle et al., 2001).

Other neural networks include the sensorimotor network, the salience network, the ventral and dorsal attention network, the cingulum–operculum network, and the central executive network (Menon, 2011, for a review). These neural networks are related to each other in continuously and dynamically changing constellations (de Pasquale et al., 2010, 2012), resulting in what may be described as spatial structure that, through its functional nature, supersedes the anatomical structure.

In addition to such spatial structure on the functional level, the spontaneous activity can also be characterized by a rich temporal structure. The temporal structure consists in fluctuations in its neural activity in different frequency bands ranging from infraslow (0.0001–0.1 Hz) over delta (1–4 Hz), theta (5–8 Hz), alpha (8–12 Hz) and beta (12–30 Hz) to gamma (30–180 Hz). Most importantly, these different frequency bands are coupled with each other, with for instance the phase of lower frequency bands being coupled to the phase or power of higher ones (Buzsáki, 2006; Buzsáki, Logothetis, & Singer, 2013; Northoff, 2014a). The coupling between different frequencies, that is, cross-frequency coupling, yields a complex temporal structure in the brain's intrinsic activity that, as shown most recently, is related in some still unclear ways to the spatial structure and the brain's various neural networks (e.g., Ganzetti & Mantini, 2013; Northoff, 2014a).

Model of Consciousness—From World–Brain Relation to Consciousness

Why and how is the spontaneous activity's spatiotemporal structure relevant for consciousness and mental features in general? The spontaneous activity's spatiotemporal structure does not end at the boundaries of the brain. Instead, it transgresses the boundaries of brain and skull by extending to both body and world. For instance, recent investigations show that the temporal structure of the body in the heart (Babo-Rebelo, Richter, et al., 2016, Babo-Rebelo, Wolpert, et al., 2016) and the stomach (Richter et al., 2017) is coupled and linked to the temporal structure of the brain's spontaneous activity (Park & Tallon-Baudry, 2014). The brain's spontaneous activity and its temporal structure seem to align themselves to the temporal structure of the body—one can thus speak of *spatiotemporal alignment* of the brain to the body (see chapter 8 of this volume and Northoff & Huang, in press, for further discussion).

The same holds, analogously, with regard to the world—the brain's spontaneous activity and its spatiotemporal structure align themselves to the world. This is most apparent when we listen to music and dance to its rhythm—we align our brain's temporal structure of its neural activity (as in its frequencies and synchronization) to the temporal structure of the music and, more generally, the world (see chapter 8 for details on spatiotemporal alignment; Schroeder & Lakatos, 2008; Schroeder at el., 2008). One can thus speak of spatiotemporal alignment of the brain to the world (chapter 8; Northoff & Huang, 2017).

Most important, empirical data suggest that such spatiotemporal alignment of brain to body and world is central for consciousness (see the section on spatiotemporal alignment in chapter 8; Lakatos et al., 2013; Park et al., 2014). The better our brain aligns us to body and world, the more likely we can become conscious of the respective contents in body and world (see discussion in chapters 7 and 8). Hence, spatiotemporal alignment of brain to body and world is central for mental features such as consciousness. I therefore argue for a spatiotemporal model of consciousness (and mental features in general) (chapters 7 and 8; see also Northoff, 2014b, 2017a,b; Huang & Northoff, in press).

Such spatiotemporal model of consciousness conceives the relation of brain to world (with the body being part of the world) (see the section on spatiotemporal alignment in chapter 8), that is, the world–brain relation, as a core nucleus of mental features. The brain and its spatiotemporal features must be related to the spatiotemporal features of the world to make consciousness possible. If, in contrast, the brain and its spontaneous activity remain unable, for whatever reason, to constitute such spatiotemporal relation to the world, consciousness (and mental features in general) are lost. This is, for example, the case in altered states of consciousness such as unresponsive wakefulness, sleep, and anesthesia (see discussion throughout chapters 4–5).

In sum, empirical data suggest that the brain's spontaneous activity shows an elaborate spatiotemporal structure that extends beyond the brain itself to body and world. I therefore speak of the world–brain relation, which, as I argue, is central for mental features such as consciousness.

World–Brain Relation I—Ontic Structural Realism

How can we account for the existence and reality of mental features? Descartes attributed mental features such as consciousness to mind, whose existence and reality he characterized by a mental substance whereas the reality of the body is characterized by physical substance. Such *substance-based metaphysics* has since been replaced by *property-based metaphysics*. Property-based metaphysics suggests specific properties, physical or mental, to determine the existence and reality of body or mind. The properties are intrinsic to body or mind since without those very same properties, the physical or the mental, body or mind, would not exist. Properties are thus the basic units of existence and reality in property-based metaphysics (see chapter 9).

Although property-based metaphysics dominates the discussion around the mind–body problem, other approaches have been suggested as well. One such approach is, for instance, the *capacity-based metaphysics* advanced by McDowell (1994, 2009). Instead of supposing mental (or physical) properties, McDowell characterizes the mind by capacities that are conceptual and actualized and realized in mental features such as thinking and knowing (see also Schechtman, 1997, for a capacity-based approach although presented in a more empirical rather than conceptual sense).

A still different approach may be found in the *process-based metaphysics* of, for instance, Alfred North Whitehead (Griffin, 1998; Northoff, 2016a,b; Rescher, 2000; Whitehead 1929/1978). Processes as the basic units of existence and reality are here proposed to underlie mental features such as consciousness (Griffin, 1998; Northoff, 2016a,b). Such a process-based approach is, for instance, often associated with panpsychism when offered as a solution to the mind–body problem (Griffin, 1998; Strawson, 2006).

How, then, may we characterize the brain—can we even characterize its existence and reality by properties, capacities, or processes? I argue that, as based on empirical evidence alone, characterization of neither is plausible. The existence and reality of the brain cannot be found in properties, processes, or capacities. Instead, based on the spontaneous activity and its spatiotemporal structure, we need to ontologically determine the brain's existence and reality by structure and relation (chapter 9). More specifically, the brain's structure and its relation to the world, the world–brain relation as I call it, determines the brain's existence and reality (chapter 9). Therefore, ontologically considered, the world–brain relation replaces the physical or mental properties, capacities, or processes that all supposedly reside inside the brain. Note the concept of world–brain relation is now understood in an ontological rather than empirical sense.

Ontologically, this presupposes what is described as structural realism (SR) and, more specifically, its ontological variant *ontic structural realism* (OSR) (Beni, 2016, in press; Esfeld & Lam, 2010; Isaac, 2014; Ladyman, 1998; see chapters 12–14 on OSR of world–brain relation). Thus, OSR claims that structure and relation are the most basic units of existence and reality. The ontological claim of SR draws empirically mainly on physics (Esfeld & Lam, 2010). I here extend OSR to the brain, that is, to the world–brain relation and mental features (see Beni, 2016; Isaac, 2014; and chapters 10–11 in this volume for SR of mental features).

World–Brain Relation II—Ontological Predisposition of Consciousness

How does the world–brain relation, as defined in terms of OSR, stand in relation to mental features? I will argue that the world–brain relation, as defined by OSR, is a necessary condition of possible consciousness, that is, it is an ontological predisposition of consciousness (OPC) (chapters 10 and 11). The world–brain relation establishes a necessary and, relying on Nagel

(2000), a posteriori (rather than a priori) connection between brain and consciousness through the ontological definition of brain: the world–brain relation serves as OPC, and the brain, as based on its spatiotemporal relation to the world, is necessarily and a posteriori (rather than a priori) connected to mental features such as consciousness (see the section on Thomas Nagel in chapter 10 for details; see also Nagel, 2000, for discussion of the necessary and a posteriori [rather than a priori] connection between brain and mental features).

The characterization of world–brain relation as OPC with necessary and a posteriori connection between the brain and mental features allows me to take a novel view to a classic question. The classic question concerns the very existence or reality of mental features such as consciousness. This question is traditionally addressed in terms of the mind–body problem: mental features are supposed to be necessarily and a priori connected to the mind, which, in turn, raises the question of the mind's relationship to the body, what we have termed the mind–body problem.

I argue that the role of the mind can be replaced by the world–brain relation. Like the mind, the world–brain relation allows for necessary (although a posteriori rather than a priori connection) connection to mental features. This makes it possible to trace the existence and reality of mental features to the world–brain relation. Most important, we then no longer need to assume the mind to account for the necessary connection of mental features to their underlying ontological origin. This renders the mind superfluous, and thus also the question of its relation to the body, the mind–body problem. If the mind is superfluous, it is nonsensical to even raise the question of the mind–body problem. The mind–body problem thereby also becomes superfluous and ultimately nonsensical.

Accordingly, instead of discussing different forms of a mind–body relation, we can better focus on the problem of explaining how world and brain are ontologically related to each other and how that relation can account for the existence and reality of mental features. This in essence is what I describe as the world–brain problem that can then replace the mind–body problem (chapters 10 and 11). For this reason I conclude that the world–brain problem offers a novel answer (one that is different from the mind–body problem) to an old question regarding the existence and reality of mental features. In short, I postulate that the mind–body problem can be replaced by the world–brain problem.

World–Brain Relation III—Eliminative Materialism or Identity Theory?

Without going into too much detail, I want to briefly flesh out some features that substantially distinguish the world–brain problem from other approaches in current philosophy of mind.

First and foremost, the suggestion to replace the concept of mind in favor of a world–brain relation seems to be reminiscent of eliminative materialism (EM) (Churchland, 1988, 2002). Roughly, EM claims that we can eliminate the concept of mind as well as mental features such as consciousness in favor of the brain and its neural activity. Although such elimination of mind seems to be well in accordance with the present approach, the similarity is only superficial at best (see chapter 13 for more detailed discussion). There are several important differences for us to consider.

First, there is methodological difference. EM pursues a reductive strategy in that it infers ontological assumptions from empirical observation; this stands counter to the approach that only claims compatibility between empirical and ontological realms while it considers any kind of inference to be fallacious (see the second section in chapter 9). Second, EM and my approach differ in their ontological presupposition: EM still presupposes property-based ontology with physical properties (although it denies mental properties), whereas my approach rejects exactly that when it favors relation-based ontology such as OSR (see the third section in chapter 9).

Finally, EM draws the radical conclusion that mental features such as consciousness do not exist and are not real because they can be eliminated and replaced by neuronal features. This stands counter to what I posit here. I claim that consciousness and its phenomenal features and, more generally, mental features cannot be eliminated but are real and existent in very much the same way as Earth's water is real and exists. Moreover, in the same way that water can be traced to H_2O as an ontological predisposition, consciousness and mental features can be traced to a world–brain relation as their ontological predispositions, or OPC.

Does my approach amount to an identity theory between the brain's physical features and the mind's mental features? The similarity is superficial at best. I no longer presuppose mind as a possible ontological substrate of mental features. However, it does not mean that I discard mental features such as consciousness. Contrary to the current philosophy of mind, I dissociate or disentangle mental features such as consciousness from the concept of mind (chapter 9): once we can draw the necessary (and a posteriori rather than a priori) connection of mental features to the world–brain relation as an underlying ontological predisposition, we no longer need the concept of mind, which thereby simply becomes superfluous.

That the assumption of the mind's existence is simply superfluous in my approach marks a central distinction of identity theory. Identity theory claims a direct identity between brain and mental features with a necessary connection that remains somewhat obscure (see Searle, 2004, for discussion). I also postulate that brain and consciousness are necessarily (a priori) connected; however, such necessary connection is not direct but indirect as it is based on a world–brain relation as the underlying ontological predisposition (see the second part in chapter 9) that renders it less intuitive and more plausible on logical–conceptual grounds. Therefore, my approach with the world–brain problem must be distinguished from identity theory and related approaches.

World–Brain Relation IV—Neutral Monism or Panpsychism?

One may also sense some similarity to neutral monism (NM) as first put forward by Bertrand Russell. The theory of NM claims the existence and reality of a third neutral ontological substrate to which both mind (i.e., mental features) and body (i.e., physical features) can be traced. Such a neutral ontological substrate is neither physical nor mental but, as the name suggests, neutral as regards both. The assumption of such a third neutral ontological substrate seems to resemble what I describe as world–brain relation as an ontological predisposition of mental features. However, unlike NM, I no longer presuppose the concept of mind; this relieves me of tracing the mind to an underlying neutral ontological substrate that it shares with the body.

Moreover, the fact that I no longer need to find an ontological substrate of mind allows me to replace the triangular relation among the third neutral substance, body, and mind in NM by a much more simple and straightforward relation or necessary connection of world–brain relation to consciousness and mental features. The triple ontology of body, mind, and neutral substrate in NM can subsequently be replaced by an ontology that postulates structure and relation as sole and only ontological substrate. This does not only avoid the logical–conceptual complexities of NM but is also empirically rather plausible since it is in full accordance with the empirical data.

My approach also needs to be clearly distinguished from panpsychism in its various forms (Strawson, 2006). There are no psychic properties or processes—structure and relation as basic units of existence and reality are not psychic or mental by themselves. That would be to confuse the OPC, that is, the world–brain relation, with what it predisposes, consciousness (chapter 10). Whether the characterization of world–brain relation as OPC amounts to some structuralist–realist form of protopanpsychism (Chalmers, 1996) may well need to be discussed in the future.

In sum, the present approach must be distinguished from the various mind–body theories as it does not share the basic presuppositions of these theories, that is, the (possible existence and reality of) mind and property-based ontology. This does not only apply to the theories here discussed but to all mind–body theories in general.

World–Brain Relation versus Mind—Copernican Revolution

The proponent of mind may now want to argue that even if we can replace the mind–body relation by a world–brain relation on ontological grounds, our "intuition" of the mind (Dennett, 2013; Nagel, 1974; Papineau, 2002) nevertheless remains. Due to the pulling forces of the intuition of mind, we cannot but assume the existence and reality of mind (even if later we argue that its existence and reality consist in body or brain). Put in a slightly different way, even if rendered implausible on empirical and ontological grounds, the concept of mind nevertheless remains an option for our intuition, or intuition of mind as I have termed it (chapters 12–14).

How can we rule out and ultimately eliminate concept of intuition of mind? I argue that we need to shift our vantage point or viewpoint (see section 1 in chapter 12 for definition of the concept of vantage point). Copernicus shifted the world's geocentric vantage point from Earth to a heliocentric vantage point beyond earth—this allowed him to take into view how Earth (including ourselves) is part of the universe and is related to the universe by revolving around the sun (chapter 12), generally described as the "Copernican revolution" in physics and cosmology.

Analogous to Copernicus (albeit in a weak rather than strong sense), I argue that we need to replace our current vantage point from within mind (or within brain) (chapter 13) to a vantage point from beyond brain (chapter 14). Such a vantage point from beyond brain will allow us to take the view that the brain is part of the world by being related to it, that is, by a world–brain relation comprising structure and relation as the basic units of existence and reality (and thus presupposing OSR). Most important, this shift in vantage point allows us to encompass that the very same world–brain relation is a necessary condition of possible mental features, thereby allowing for an ontological predisposition of consciousness.

To sum up, the shift in vantage point from within mind or brain to a vantage point from beyond brain renders transparent the necessary (and a posteriori rather than a priori) connection between brain and consciousness that hitherto has remained opaque to us. As we can now take into view how consciousness is necessarily connected to the brain, that is, through world–brain relation, we no longer need to posit or intuit a mind to allow for a necessary connection of consciousness to its underlying ontological substrate. The posit or intuition of mind thus becomes unnecessary and may be replaced by our view of the world–brain relation with its necessary connection to mental features that is now rendered transparent by our novel viewpoint presented above (chapter 14).

In the same way that an intuition of Earth as being the center of the universe was rendered impossible by the dramatic shift in vantage point of Copernicus, the vantage point from beyond brain now makes impossible the intuition of mind as the center of mental features, ourselves, and the world (chapter 17). This enormous paradigm shift allows us to replace the mind–body problem by the world–brain problem—this shift in viewpoint amounts to a Copernican-like revolution in the spheres of both neuroscience and philosophy.

World–Brain Problem I—Main Argument of the Book

The main argument of the book is that the world–brain problem is a more plausible problem than the mind–body problem when one addresses the question of the existence and reality of mental features. This argument is fleshed out for the reader in three different ways in the volume, empirically (Parts I and II), ontologically (Part III), and in epistemic–methodological terms (Part IV) terms (see figure 0.1).

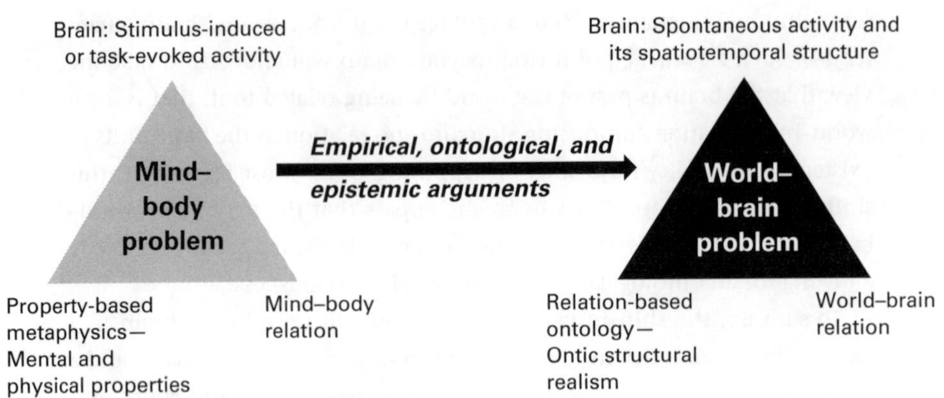

Figure 0.1
From the mind–body problem to the world–brain problem.

Empirically this argument is based on the brain's spontaneous activity and, more specifically, its spatiotemporal structure. That very same spatiotemporal structure makes it possible for the brain to extend beyond itself to body and world, thus constituting what I term the *world–brain relation*. The world–brain relation, in turn, is central for mental features such as consciousness.

Ontologically, the central empirical roles of the world–brain relation and spatiotemporal structure imply a novel ontology of brain and mental features, that is, one that is based on structure and relation—this leads us to ontic structural realism (OSR). OSR allows us to determine the existence and reality of the brain by a world–brain relation, which, in turn, serves as ontological predisposition of consciousness (OPC). Since mental features can be traced to the world–brain relation, I speak of the world–brain problem. Given all the evidence both empirical and ontological, I argue that we can replace the mind–body problem by the world–brain problem when we address that basic question regarding the existence and reality of mental features.

World–Brain Problem II—Overview and Structure of the Book

The book is divided into four parts: (I) "Models of Brain"; (II) "Models of Consciousness"; (III) "World–Brain Problem"; and (IV) "Copernican Revolution." A glossary contains definitions to key terms.

The first part discusses different models of brain as they are implied in the current neuroscientific discussion. This ranges from the spectrum model (chapter 1) over the interaction model (chapter 2) to the prediction model (chapter 3) of brain. These different models of brain are assessed with regard to the currently available empirical evidence. I remain within the purely empirical and, more specifically, neuronal realm without touching on ontological and mental issues at all. However, I propose that a proper model of brain is central for tackling ontological issues revolving around mental features.

The second part of the book extends the discussion of the first part from brain to consciousness. I now consider consciousness in empirical terms. Specifically, I now apply the different models of brain, including the spectrum model (chapter 4), the interaction model (chapter 5), and the prediction model (chapter 6), as discussed in the first part, to recent data on the neuronal features underlying consciousness. This is followed by elaboration of a spatiotemporal theory of consciousness (chapter 7) that highlights the central role of the brain's alignment to both body and world (chapter 8). Note that such spatiotemporal theory of consciousness remains purely empirical at this point in the book—hence it is here understood as a neuroscientific theory of consciousness.

The third part focuses on the ontological characterization of brain (chapter 9), mental features (chapter 10), and world itself (chapter 11) with regard to mental features. I first develop an ontology of brain in which the brain's existence and reality are defined by spatiotemporal relation and structure presupposing structural realism (chapter 9). That ontology of brain provides the foundation for an ontology of mental features with the world–brain relation as ontological predisposition of consciousness (chapter 10). Finally, I suggest the spatiotemporal ontology of world as being central for mental features (chapter 11). I conclude that world–brain relation and consecutively the world–brain problem, as I say, can well account for the existence and reality of mental features. The world–brain problem can thus replace the mind–body problem.

The fourth part of the book focuses on the epistemic-methodological presuppositions of both the mind–body and the world–brain problem. Specifically, I argue that we need to take a specific viewpoint or vantage point in order to be able to view how the world–brain relation can account for mental features and replace the mind–body problem. Drawing on the analogy of the Copernican revolution in physics and cosmology (chapter 12), I argue that we need to change our ontological vantage point. Instead of presupposing a vantage point from within the mind or brain (chapter 13), we need to shift to a vantage point from beyond brain (chapter 14). This permits us to take into view the necessary connection between the world–brain relation and mental features, a paradigm shift that ultimately allows us to replace the mind–body with the world–brain problem. I therefore conclude that we require nothing less than a twenty-first-century Copernican-like revolution in the fields of neuroscience and philosophy.

I Models of Brain

1 Beyond the Passive/Active Dichotomy: A Spectrum Model of the Brain's Neural Activities

Introduction

General Background

The way in which investigators think about the brain can have a deep impact on the empirical investigations of neuroscience as well as on the interpretation of their philosophical implications. One model of the brain, favored by the early British neurologist Sir Charles Sherrington (1857–1952), proposed that the brain and the spinal cord were primarily reflexive. *Reflexive* in this model means that the brain reacts in predefined and automatic ways to sensory stimuli such as auditory or visual stimuli. Stimuli from outside the brain, originating externally in either the body or the environment, are assumed to determine completely and exclusively the subsequent neural activity. The resulting stimulus-induced activity, and more generally, any neural activity, in the brain is then traced back to the external stimuli to which the brain merely passively reacts. One may therefore speak of what I describe as the *passive model* of the brain.

An alternative view, however, had already been suggested by one of Sherrington's students, Thomas Graham Brown. In contrast to his teacher, Brown suggested that the brain's neural activity—that is, within the spinal cord and brain stem—is not primarily driven and sustained by external stimuli from outside the brain. Instead, Brown held that the spinal cord and brain stem do show spontaneous activity that originates internally within the brain itself. Hans Berger, who introduced the electroencephalogram (EEG) early on (Berger, 1929), also observed spontaneous activity in the brain that remained independent of any external tasks or stimuli.

Other neuroscientists, including Bishop (1933), Lashley (1951), and Goldstein (2000), followed Brown's line of thought and proposed that the brain actively generates its own activity internally, that is, it generates spontaneous activity—or resting-state activity as it is also called in its operational-behavioral version (see Northoff, 2014a; Raichle, 2015a,b; as well as discussion below). Recently, the view of central or spontaneous activity has gained more traction in neuroscience with the observation of spontaneous oscillations (Buzsáki, 2006; Llinás, 1988; Yuste, MacLean, Smith, & Lansner, 2005), spontaneous coherence or connectivity between different regions' neural activities (Biswal et al., 1995; Greicius, Krasnow, Reiss, & Menon, 2003), and the default-mode network (DMN) (Greicius et al., 2003; Raichle, 2015b; Raichle et al., 2001).

These and other observations point out the central role of the brain's spontaneous activity for its neural activity including both resting state and task-evoked or stimulus-induced activity (see Huang, Zhang, Longtin, et al., 2017; Northoff, 2014a,b; Northoff, Qin, & Nakao, 2010 for an extensive discussion). This leads me to speak of an *active model* of the brain. Such an active model of the brain is nicely illustrated in the following quote by the early German neurologist Kurt Goldstein in his book *The Organism*, which appeared originally in 1934 (Goldstein, 2000):

> The system is never at rest, but in a continual state of excitation. The nervous system has often been considered as an organ at rest, in which excitation arises only as a response to stimuli. … It was not recognized that events that follow a definite stimulus are only an expression of a change of excitation in the nervous system, that they represent only a special pattern of the excitation process. This assumption of a system at rest was especially favored by the fact that only the external stimuli were considered. Too little attention was given to the fact that the organism is continuously exposed, even in the apparent absence of outward stimuli, to the influence of internal stimuli—influences that may be of highest importance for its activity, for example, the effect of stimuli issuing from the blood, the importance of which was particularly pointed out by Thomas Graham Brown. (Goldstein, 2000, pp. 95–96)

Recently, the issue of how to model the brain has gained increased traction given the discovery of the DMN (Raichle et al., 2001). The DMN is a neural network that covers various regions predominantly in the middle of the brain, the so-called cortical midline structures (Northoff & Bermpohl, 2004; Northoff et al., 2006). The DMN shows particularly high levels of metabolism and neural activity in the absence of any specific external stimuli, which condition has been termed the *resting state* (Logothetis et al., 2009; Raichle, 2015a,b; Raichle et al., 2001; see also Klein, 2014, for an excellent discussion in a more philosophical context).

Since its initial discovery, the high levels of resting state or spontaneous activity (for the sake of simplicity I use both terms here interchangeably) in the DMN have been associated with different mental features such as self, consciousness, mind wandering, episodic memory retrieval, time prospection and retrospection, and random thoughts (Christoff, 2012; D'Argembeau et al., 2010a, 2010b; Fazelpour & Thompson, 2015; Northoff, 2012a–c, 2014b; Northoff et al., 2006; Smallwood & Schooler, 2015; Spreng, Mar, & Kim, 2009). Because it is apparently implicated in a wide range of different functions, the exact role of the DMN remains unclear at this point in time.

What is clear, however, is that the nature of the DMN's activity supports an active model of the brain. Put into a more philosophical context, some authors (Churchland, 2012; Fazelpour & Thompson, 2015; Hohwy, 2014; Northoff, 2012a) have compared the active model of the brain to the model of mind developed by Kant (1781/1998). Briefly, Kant argued against a passive model of mind wherein its activity would be completely determined by external stimuli, which was the view of David Hume. Instead, Kant conceived of the mind as exhibiting spontaneity, entailing an active rather than passive model of mind. The old dispute between Hume and Kant about passive versus active models of mind has thus resurfaced in the form of a quandary in theoretical neuroscience.

Main Aim and Argument

The main focus in this chapter is on discussing empirical evidence in favor of different models of the relationship between spontaneous and stimulus-induced activity. This serves to develop an empirically plausible model of brain activity, the spectrum model (see parts I–III). I argue that the disjunction of passive (part I) and active (part II) models of brain is ill conceived. The brain neither generates its neural activity in a completely passive way as driven by the external stimuli nor in an exclusively active way, that is, entirely driven by its spontaneous activity. Instead, based on empirical evidence, we need to accept a model of brain that undermines the passive/active dichotomy and integrates both in a spectrum that allows for categorizing different forms of neural activity according to the degree of the brain's participation in generating that activity (part III).

Note that this claim is purely neuronal: I argue that different sorts of neural activity involve resting-state activity to different degrees, with some being more active while others remain rather passive. The spectrum model of brain is not directly concerned with mental features and how they are related to the spectrum of neural activities, although such work may eventually become viable once the relevant neuronal features are more deeply understood. Instead, I here focus exclusively on the brain's neuronal features, specifically on how its neural activity falls on a continuum or spectrum between purely active and passive modes. I leave open the spectrum model's relation to mental features such as consciousness, which is discussed in chapter 4.

Definition and Clarification of Concepts

Before continuing, we need to shed a brief light on some terminological issues. First, there is the distinction among different forms of neural activity, spontaneous activity, resting-state activity, and stimulus-induced activity. *Spontaneous activity* refers to the neural activity that is generated within the brain itself independent of any external stimuli from outside the brain, that is, interoceptive stimuli from the body and exteroceptive stimuli from the world (see Northoff, 2014a; Raichle, 2015a,b). The term spontaneous activity thus denotes the origin of neural activity and is meant in a purely neuronal sense.

This is different from the concept of *resting state*, which describes a particular behavioral condition: eyes closed or open with fixation and the absence of any specific stimuli or tasks (see Northoff, 2014a; Raichle, 2015a,b). The resting state is often taken as the operational condition that measures the brain's spontaneous activity. For the sake of simplicity I here use the terms "resting state" and "spontaneous activity" in an interchangeable way to denote the absence of any stimuli from outside the brain (including both interoceptive stimuli from the body and exteroceptive stimuli from the world).

In addition, we also need to distinguish the term *stimulus-induced* or *task-evoked* activity. Operationally both resting state/spontaneous activity and stimulus-induced/task-evoked activity can well be distinguished: the resting state is measured with eyes closed or open in the absence of specific stimuli or tasks, whereas stimulus-induced activity is tested for by applying specific stimuli or tasks.

However, the distinction between those two forms of neural activity may no longer be as clear cut when taken in a more physiological sense because it may be that external stimuli simply modulate the ongoing spontaneous activity. This would make the distinction between the forms of activity rather relative (in at least operational terms) if not superfluous (in physiological terms) (see Klein, 2014; Northoff, 2014b; Raichle, 2009, 2015a,b; as well as below for details). The main aim of this volume is to discuss different possible relations between resting-state/spontaneous activity and stimulus-induced/task-evoked activity and to assess their viability according to available empirical data.

Finally, we also need to clarify the concepts of active and passive. In this context the concepts of active and passive concern the degree to which the brain itself provides a contribution to its own neural activity. The passive end of the spectrum would apply to neural activity that is determined by external stimuli, whereas the active end of the spectrum applies when the brain itself exhibits neural activity prior to and independent of external stimuli.

Part I: Passive Model of the Brain

The passive model describes the brain's neural activity as being dependent on external stimuli it receives from body and environment. The resulting neural activity, *stimulus-induced activity*, is taken to be determined entirely by the external stimulus; the brain itself just passively processes the external stimuli and does not actively participate in constituting its own neural activity. A passive model of brain can come in two extreme versions, strong and weak, and an intermediate version, the moderate version. I here sketch briefly the two extreme versions.

The strong passive model argues that the brain has no impact at all on how it responds to stimuli. The weak passive model of brain could acknowledge spontaneous activity in the brain but assign it just a modulatory but not a causal role. A causal impact of spontaneous activity on stimulus-induced activity would involve the former causing the latter, so that that there would be no stimulus-induced activity without spontaneous activity even in the presence of external stimuli. In the case of a modulatory impact, stimulus-induced activity would still be present even in the absence of spontaneous activity, which, if present, serves just to modulate the degree of stimulus-induced activity. Based on recent empirical evidence, I argue in the chapters that follow that both versions, weak and strong, as well as the moderate version of the passive model of brain are to be rejected.

Passive Model of Brain Ia: Strong Model—Absence of Resting-State Activity

The strong passive model claims that stimulus-induced activity in the brain can be accounted for entirely by external stimuli. Moreover, a strong passive model of the brain would claim that there is no neural activity at all in the brain unless there is stimulus-induced activity. However, empirical evidence conflicts with these claims. Accordingly, the strong passive model is not empirically tenable and thus merely logically conceivable; a discussion of why it is not tenable, however, is helpful for understanding the other more tenable views.

How can we characterize the brain's resting state? One should be aware that the concept of the brain's intrinsic or resting-state activity or spontaneous activity (I use all three terms interchangeably) is a rather heterogeneous one and raises several questions (see also Cabral, Kringelbach, & Deco, 2013; Mantini, Corbetta, Romani, Orban, & Vanduffel, 2013; Morcom & Fletcher, 2007a,b; Northoff, 2014a).

Terminologically, different concepts are used to describe the resting state. In addition to resting-state activity, other terms including baseline, spontaneous activity, or intrinsic activity are also used to describe the internally generated activity in the brain (see Deco, Jirsa, & McIntosh, 2013; Mantini et al., 2013; Northoff, 2014a). Importantly, the brain's resting-state activity is not restricted or limited to a particular region or network in the brain (Northoff, 2014a; Raichle, 2009). Instead, it is pervasive throughout the whole brain.

The brain is an energy-hungry system. It consumes 20 percent of the whole body's overall glucose and oxygen budget while accounting for only 2 percent of the body's weight (Shulman, Hyder, & Rothman, 2014). Most importantly, all that energy is mainly invested into the spontaneous activity itself; neural activity in response to external stimuli, that is, stimulus-induced activity, only uses a tiny fraction of that, amounting to 5 percent of the overall energy budget of the brain (Raichle, 2015a,b). What does the brain's resting state do with all that energy? The high amounts of glucose and oxygen seem to be mainly invested in neuronal signaling and activity, with 75–80 percent accounting for the latter (Rothman, De Feyter, Graaf, Mason, & Behar, 2011).

These data suggest close coupling between metabolism and neuronal activity, which then is only slightly modified during stimulus-induced activity (considered from an energetic perspective). Metabolic activity can be measured by the cerebral metabolism rates of glucose or oxygen (CMRglc or $CMRO_2$), whereas neuronal activity can be accounted for by measuring the cycles between glutamate and glutamine (as between neurons and glia with the former being converted into the latter by the enzyme glutamine synthetase) as well as between glutamine and GABA (with the latter being synthesized out of the former via glutamate by the enzyme GAD67) (see Hyder et al., 2006; Shulman et al., 2014).

Investigations in both animals (rats) and humans indicate close coupling between metabolic and neuronal activity: the higher the metabolism in the brain, the higher its neural activity, as in spontaneous or resting-state activity, whereas the metabolism is only marginally increased, if at all, during stimulus-induced activity (Hyder, Fulbright, Shulman, & Rothman, 2013; Hyder et al., 2006; Hyder, Rothman, & Bennett, 2013; Shulman et al., 2014).

Taken together, the strong passive model would need to argue that there is no spontaneous activity internally generated by the brain independent of any external stimuli from outside the brain. This is not compatible at all with the empirical data as reflected in the brain's metabolism and its close coupling to neural activity. Importantly, the high metabolism and its transformation into neural activity are not related to any external stimuli from outside the brain. These factors speak strongly against the strong passive model of brain.

Moreover, a strong passive model of brain would need to presuppose a principally different design of the brain without any metabolism and neural activity independent of external stimuli. Both metabolism and its coupling to resting-state activity would consequently remain absent. This makes it clear that the strong passive model is merely conceivable (on logical grounds) but not a tenable paradigm (on empirical grounds). However, despite being empirically nontenable, the strong passive model can nevertheless teach us about the central relevance of the brain's metabolism and its coupling to neural activity for the brain's operation and functioning (even if the empirical details of such neuro-metabolic coupling remain yet to be explored).

Passive Model of Brain Ib: Moderate Model—No Impact of Resting-State Activity on Stimulus-Induced Activity

The advocate of the passive model of brain may now want to argue that the presence of the brain's resting-state activity even in sensory cortices can well be acknowledged without undermining the basic assumption of the passive processing of stimuli. Specifically, even if resting-state activity is present in sensory cortices, the stimulus-induced activity in these regions can nevertheless be sufficiently and exclusively related to the external stimuli themselves. Resting-state and stimulus-induced activity would then operate in a parallel and segregated way with no interaction (whether causal or modulatory) between them. In that case the resting-state activity in the sensory cortices should have no impact at all on stimulus-induced activity in the same regions entailing that the former is not necessary at all for the latter. That amounts to a moderate version of the passive model of brain, which again is not supported by empirical evidence.

One functional magnetic resonance imaging (fMRI) study focused on the auditory cortex (Sadaghiani, Hesselmann, & Kleinschmidt, 2009). These researchers let subjects perform an auditory detection task and presented broadband noise stimuli in unpredictable intervals of 20–40 ms. The subjects had to press a button when, and only when, they thought they heard the target sound; otherwise, they did not hit the button. This allowed the researchers to compare the neural activity preceding hits with the activity preceding instances where subjects did not hear the target sound.

Interestingly, successful detection was preceded by significantly higher prestimulus activity, for example, resting-state activity, in auditory cortex, when compared to missed detection. Thus, the level of resting-state activity in auditory cortex impacted the degree of perception, such as whether subjects could hear the auditory stimuli.

But what about rest–stimulus interaction in a sensory modality other than the auditory? The same group also investigated rest–stimulus interaction in the visual modality (Hesselmann, Kell, Eger, & Kleinschmidt, 2008). Higher pre-stimulus resting-state activity levels in the fusiform face area were related to subsequent perception of a face rather than a vase in the Rubin ambiguous vase–face figure. Therefore, higher resting-state activity in the fusiform face biases the subsequent perceptual content toward seeing the face, rather than the vase.

Analogous findings were observed with another visual stimulus such as visual motion: the resting-state activity in the visual motion area in the middle temporal cortex (V5/MT) predicted the degree of the subsequent perception of coherent motion (Hesselmann et al., 2008). Hesselmann and colleagues also related pre-stimulus resting-state activity and peak stimulus-induced activity with behavioral performance: the less prestimulus resting-state activity and peak stimulus-induced activity correlated each other, the better the subjects' subsequent behavioral performance, for example, the motion perception. Hence, better behavioral performance went along with increased distinction of stimulus-induced activity from the preceding resting-state activity.

Does rest–stimulus interaction also hold in regions other than the sensory cortex? Coste, Sadaghiani, Friston, and Kleinschmidt (2011) conducted a Stroop task wherein the names of colors interfered with the color in which the respective color names were presented (the word "green" was, for instance, presented in the color "red"). Subjects had to push a button to determine the color and whether it was congruent or incongruent.

This study again showed that the prestimulus activity in relevant regions such as the anterior cingulate cortex (ACC) and the dorsolateral prefrontal cortex (DLPFC) predicted subsequent behavioral performance, that is, reaction times. The higher the prestimulus resting-state activity in the ACC and the DLPFC, the faster the subsequent reaction times in response to the stimuli.

Whereas this concerns cognitive regions like the ACC and the DLPLFC, the reverse relation was observed in sensory regions involved in color and word processing: the higher the prestimulus resting-state activity in the right color-sensitive area and the visual word-form area, the slower the subsequent reaction times. These data clearly show that rest–stimulus interaction is mediated by both higher-order cognitive and lower-order sensory regions but in different ways: higher prestimulus activity leads to faster reaction times in cognitive regions, whereas it induces slower reaction times in sensory regions. Since it is one and the same stimulus that both sensory and cognitive regions process, the differential impact of high prestimulus activity levels on reaction times can only be due to differential impacts of the regions themselves, for example, cognitive and sensory, on the external stimulus. This entails different forms of rest–stimulus interaction.

What do these findings imply for our argument against the strong passive model? They demonstrate that stimulus-induced activity in sensory cortices and other regions such as the prefrontal cortex is not sufficiently and exclusively related to the external stimulus itself (as either sensory or cognitive stimulus). Instead, the prestimulus resting-state activity level seems to impact the degree or amplitude of stimulus-induced activity. This means that the external stimulus itself is only necessary, but it is not sufficient by itself for determining stimulus-induced activity.

Accordingly, the empirical evidence from these and other studies (see Northoff, 2014a; Northoff, Qin, & Nakao, 2010, for review) speaks against such exclusive determination of stimulus-induced activity by the external stimulus and thus against the moderate passive model of brain. One should be aware that the stimulus being necessary but not sufficient for stimulus-induced activity would still allow for resting activity to have a merely modulatory impact on stimulus-induced activity. That leads us to the weak passive model of brain as it shall be discussed below.

Passive Model of Brain IIa: Weak Model—No Causal Impact of Resting-State Activity on Stimulus-Induced Activity

The proponent of the passive model of brain may nevertheless not yet be ready to relinquish his or her view of the brain as passive. He may strengthen his argument by weakening his claim, stating that the resting-state activity may indeed modulate stimulus-induced activity, whereas it does not causally impact such activity in the same way that the external stimulus does. Only the external stimulus has a causal impact on stimulus-induced activity— meaning that without external stimuli there would be no stimulus-induced activity.

In that case the resting state has at best mere modulatory impact. Modulatory impact means that the resting state does not cause stimulus-induced activity, which therefore would still persist even in the absence of the resting state; the resting state can only modulate or vary the degree of stimulus-induced activity, whereas the latter's occurrence remains independent of the former. Accordingly, the resting state is not a necessary condition of stimulus-induced activity when it exerts only modulatory impact. This amounts to a weak passive model of brain, which, like its more extreme siblings, conflicts with the empirical data. The data show that the resting-state activity's impact is not only modulatory but causal.

How can we experimentally demonstrate that resting-state activity causally impacts the stimulus-induced activity? One strategy here may be to vary the overall global level of resting-state activity and then to see how that impacts stimulus-induced activity during particular tasks. This was done in animals in a study by the group led by Robert Shulman. He tested how the baseline or resting-state metabolism impacts subsequent stimulus-induced activity in an animal study (Maandag et al., 2007).

Maandag et al. (2007) induced pharmacologically high and low levels of resting-state activity in rats and measured their neural activity in fMRI during forepaw stimulation. The high level of resting activity condition was associated with widespread activity across the cortex and rather weak evoked activity in sensorimotor cortex during the forepaw movement. This pattern was reversed in the low resting-state activity condition wherein neural activity was stronger in the sensorimotor cortex but more or less absent in other cortical regions. These results demonstrate that the level of resting-state activity causally impacts stimulus-induced activity (see also G. Shulman et al., 2009; R. Shulman, Hyder, & Rothman, 2009; van Eijsden, Hyder, Rothman, & Shulman, 2009, for a discussion of the results by Maandag et al. on a conceptual level).

Passive Model of Brain IIb: Weak Model—Causal Impact of Resting-State Activity on Stimulus-Induced Activity

The empirical data show the causal impact of the resting state on stimulus-induced activity in animals. Is there empirical evidence for analogous causal relationship between resting state and stimulus-induced activity in humans? For that, Qin et al. (2013) devised a clever experimental design by taking advantage of the distinctions between different baselines. They delivered the same auditory stimuli once during eyes open and once during eyes closed. This allowed them to test for the causal impact of two different resting states, that is, eyes open and closed, on the stimulus-induced activity related to the same stimulus.

First, based on a special acquisition technique in fMRI called sparse sampling, Qin et al. determined the impact of the scanner noise on the auditory cortex and compared that condition to the complete absence of any scanner noise. *Sparse sampling* is an experimental scenario in which the scanner noise is shut down for some seconds while the neural activity, that is, the blood oxygenation level dependent signal (BOLD) response during the period can be recorded after the scanner is turned on again (because the BOLD response shows temporal delay). As expected, this yielded strong activity changes in the bilateral auditory cortex in the comparison of noise versus no noise. These activity changes during the comparison of noise versus non-noise served to determine and locate the auditory cortex's resting-state activity, albeit indirectly, via the comparison of noise versus no noise. Qin and colleagues then used the auditory cortex as the region of interest for the subsequent analyses.

In a second step, Qin et al. (2013) conducted data acquisition in fMRI during eyes open and closed to investigate the resting-state activity in visual cortex and its modulation by a very basic stimulus, eyes open. Analogous to the noise in auditory cortex, the eyes open condition served to determine the visual cortex's resting-state activity; this region was then used as a region of interest in subsequent analyses. Data in both eyes-open and -closed conditions were acquired in two different modes, in 20-s periods (block design), which allowed for the generation of BOLD changes, that is, neural activity, and in 6-min periods to determine functional connectivity of the visual cortex to other regions, for instance, the auditory cortex.

Finally, in a third step, Qin (Qin et al., 2012) investigated auditory name perception in two conditions, eyes open and closed, by letting subjects listen to the same names during both conditions: with closed and open eyes. This strategy served to investigate the impact of eyes open and closed, mirroring different baselines (i.e., eyes closed and open), on stimulus-induced activity associated with the same stimulus.

How did the different resting states, that is, eyes closed and open, modulate stimulus-induced activity? During eyes closed, the subject's own name induced significantly stronger activity in auditory cortex than other persons' names. Such response difference between one's own and other names disappeared, however, when the names were presented during eyes open. Because the stimuli were the same in both cases, the absence of any difference in signal change between one's own and other names during eyes open is most likely to be due to the difference between eyes open and close in the spontaneous activity itself (although an impact from the body and its interoceptive stimuli cannot be completely excluded).

Therefore, the spontaneous activity in the auditory cortex must have undergone some changes when the eyes were opened, thereby apparently changing its sensitivity, especially to the stimuli of the others' names.

Although we currently do not know what exactly changed in the resting state itself during the transition from eyes closed to eyes open, our data nevertheless demonstrate the causal impact of the resting-state activity level on subsequent stimulus-induced activity in auditory cortex.

Our data indicate that there must be some causal interaction between the resting-state activity and the stimulus-induced activity in auditory cortex. Hence, the amount or degree of stimulus-induced activity is determined not only by the stimulus itself but also by the level of the resting-state activity. However, the exact neuronal mechanisms underlying the resting state's causal impact on stimulus-induced activity remain unclear at this point in time (see also He, 2013; Huang, Ferri, Longtin, Dumont, & Northoff, 2016; Northoff, 2014b; Huang, Zhang, Longtin, et al., 2017).

Different modes of rest-stimulus interaction are plausible. For instance, the stimulus-induced activity may just be added on top of the ongoing resting state activity. Alternatively, the stimulus may elicit a degree of stimulus-induced activity that is either weaker or stronger than the mere addition between the resting-state activity level and the stimulus-induced activity in which case one would speak of nonadditive interaction. Which model holds, the additive or nonadditive model? This determination is subject to ongoing investigation (see chapter 2 for details).

Passive Model of Brain IIc: Causal versus Modulatory Impact of Resting-State Activity on Stimulus-Induced Activity

Taken together, these findings suggest that the resting state has an active causal impact on stimulus-induced activity. The resting-state activity causally interacts with the stimulus, especially a subject's own name, and becomes therefore a necessary (although nonsufficient) condition of the resulting stimulus-induced activity.

However, a proponent of a weak passive model may be tempted to argue that this example only shows the modulatory, rather than causal, impact of the resting state on stimulus-induced activity. In that case, one would expect the resting state to impact, that is, to modulate all three names in the same unspecific way; but the data do not show this because there are strong differences in how the resting-state activity interacts with the three names. These differences speak in favor of a specific causal impact of the resting state on specific stimuli rather than a nonspecific modulatory effect that remains unspecific to the type of stimulus.

We should, however, be aware that the data presented leave many questions open. One issue is the exact nature of the interaction; even a weak causal interaction must be explained by specific underlying neurophysiological mechanisms. Hence, at this point we cannot be fully clear about the causal nature of the rest-stimulus interaction. The kind of rest-stimulus causality I claim occurs in the example of Qin et al. (2013) is obviously a weaker form of causality than the one that claims a complete absence of stimulus-induced activity in the absence of resting-state activity. Hence, one may want to investigate different forms of causality (e.g., the four forms of causality as distinguished by Aristotle) in the future.

Another issue to consider is that the psychological implications of such rest-stimulus interaction are left completely open. The study by Qin et al. (2013) only focused on the neuronal differences of the stimulus-induced activity related to the own (and familiar and other) name during two different resting-state conditions, eyes closed and eyes open. In contrast, Qin and colleagues did not consider whether the differential neuronal reactivity of the resting state during eyes closed and open to the own name also impacted the psychological features, for example, perception.

For instance, subjects may have heard their own name in a more intense and attentive way during eyes closed when compared to eyes open (due to the additional visual-attentional distraction in the latter condition); this could be probed by reaction times in response to the own name which should then be faster during eyes closed than eyes open. The possible presence of such additional psychological differences may further support the assumption of causal rest-stimulus interaction.

What do these data imply with regard to the characterization of the brain as either passive or active? They suggest that the brain itself, through its resting-state activity level seems to provide an active contribution (that may come in different degrees) to its own neural activity. Such empirically grounded evidence speaks against a passive model of brain in all its versions, strong, moderate, and weak. We therefore shift our focus now to the active model of brain.

Part II: Active Model of Brain

Active Model of Brain Ia: Spatial Structure of Resting-State Activity

Early neuroimaging investigation using techniques such as fMRI and EEG focused on stimulus-induced activity including the brain's response to sensorimotor, cognitive, affective or social stimuli or tasks. Recently, neuroimaging has shifted focus to the brain's spontaneous activity and to its spatial and temporal structure. Initially, it was thought that spontaneous activity was contained to a particular neural network, the DMN (see also Klein, 2014). However, it soon became clear that spontaneous activity is pervasive throughout the whole brain.

Spontaneous activity has been observed in many different neural networks including the central executive network, the salience network, and the sensorimotor network (see Klein, 2014). Even in regions as dependent on external stimuli as the sensory cortices, there is spontaneous activity. The continuous neural activity occurring throughout the brain is spatially structured. Specific regions coordinate their ongoing resting-state activity, as measured in functional connectivity, thereby forming neural networks. This suggests that the brain's resting-state activity can be characterized by a particular spatial structure, which when indexed by functional connectivity describes how two or more regions' neural activities are synchronized and coordinated across time.

Active Model of Brain Ib: Temporal Structure of Resting-State Activity

In addition to its spatial structure, there appears to be quite an elaborate temporal structure in the brain's intrinsic activity, which is manifest in its fluctuations in different frequency ranges. In the DMN, spontaneous fluctuations are characterized predominantly by low frequencies (<0.1 Hz). However, low- and high-frequency fluctuations in neural activity have been observed in sensory cortices, motor cortex, insula, and subcortical regions, such as the basal ganglia and thalamus (see Buckner, Andrews-Hanna, & Schacter, 2008; Freeman, 2003; Hunter et al., 2006; G. Shulman et al., 2009; R. Shulman et al., 2009; R. Shulman, Rothman, Behar, & Hyder, 2004; Wang, Duratti, Samur, Spaelter, & Bleuler, 2007).

How are low and high frequencies related to each other in the brain's resting state? The empirical data suggest that low and high frequencies modulate each other (see the recent reviews by Canolty & Knight, 2010; Fell & Axmacher, 2011; Fries, 2009; Sauseng & Klimesch, 2008). For instance, Vanhatalo et al. (2004) conducted an EEG study of healthy and epileptic subjects during sleep. They used direct-current EEG to record low-frequency oscillations. All subjects showed infraslow oscillations (0.02–0.2 Hz) that were much stronger than during the awake resting state and even stronger than during stimulus-induced activity; these oscillations were detected across all electrodes—and thus the whole brain—without any specific, visually obvious spatial distribution evident.

Most interestingly, Vanhatalo et al. (2004) observed phase-locking or phase synchronization between the slow (0.02–0.2 Hz) oscillations and the amplitudes of the faster (1–10 Hz) oscillations. The amplitudes of the faster frequency oscillations (1–10 Hz) were highest during the negative phases of the slow oscillations (0.02–0.2 Hz). Such phase-locking of fast frequency oscillations' amplitude to the phases of slower ones can also be described as *phase-power coupling* (see Canolty & Knight, 2010; Sauseng & Klimesch, 2008, for reviews). Generally, the coupling seems to occur in the direction from slow- to fast-frequency fluctuations (see Buzsáki, 2006; Buzsáki, Logothetis, & Singer, 2013). Such coupling from slow-frequency phase to faster-frequency amplitude represents one of the ways that different oscillatory patterns in neural activity can be related to one another. Such phenomena comprise the temporal structure of spontaneous activity.

Active Model of Brain Ic: Spatiotemporal Structure of Resting-State Activity

How is such temporal structure related to the spatial structure of the brain's intrinsic activity? In a recent study, de Pasquale et al. (2012) observed that the DMN (and especially the posterior cingulate cortex) shows the highest degree of correlation with other networks in specifically the beta frequency range. The DMN seems to interact much more with the other networks than the latter do with each other. The reasons for that remain unclear but may be due, in part, to the central position of the DMN (and its midline structures) in the middle of the brain.

This fact likely makes the DMN prone to higher degrees of cross-network interaction than the other more laterally situated networks (e.g., the executive network or the sensorimotor networks; see Northoff, 2014a). Such cross-network interaction is dynamic and transient, and therefore it continuously changes. There are, for instance, alternate periods of low and high synchronization between DMN and other networks implying that cross-network synchronization and desynchronization go hand in hand.

These findings suggest that the spatial structure is closely linked to temporal dynamics, that is, oscillations in different frequency ranges (reviewed by Ganzetti & Mantini, 2013). Specifically, different neural networks may show different frequency ranges. For instance, Hipp, Hawellek, Corbetta, Siegel, and Engel (2012) observed that the medial temporal lobe is mainly characterized by theta frequency range, 4–6 Hz; the lateral parietal regions are rather featured by alpha to beta frequency range, 8–23 Hz; and the sensorimotor areas show even higher frequencies, 32–45 Hz. These findings demonstrate the close link between spatial and temporal dimensions in the spontaneous activity.

The tight link between the temporal and spatial structures is well reflected in the empirically informed theories of "nested oscillations" and "nested synchrony," as observed in the resting-state activity by Monto (2012) using magnetoencephalography. Following him, *nested oscillations* describe the phase-phase/power coupling between low- and high-frequency fluctuations within one particular region. *Neural synchrony* extends beyond that, as it refers to the interregional coordination of nested oscillations in one particular region: the phase of a low-frequency fluctuation in one region may mediate the coupling of a high-frequency fluctuation in that region with a high-frequency fluctuation in another region.

In sum, these data show spatial and temporal structure in resting-state activity. The exact mechanisms and features of this spatiotemporal structure remain unclear, but we know that such spatiotemporal structure is highly dynamic rather than static, that is, its spatial and temporal configurations are subject to continuous change.

Active Model of Brain Id: An Active Rather Than Passive Model of Brain?

What do these findings of a dynamic spatiotemporal structure in the brain's resting state tell us with regard to the model of brain? Let us start with the structure and organization of resting-state activity. I propose, based on empirical data, that in order to be processed, an external stimulus must interact with the resting state and its spatiotemporal structure. The external stimulus is integrated within the resting state and its spatial and temporal features. This allows the single discrete point in time and space of the stimulus to be linked with and integrated within the different time scales of the brain and its spontaneous activity.

How such rest-stimulus integration is related to mental features including consciousness of the respective stimulus remains unclear at this point. Therefore, the current chapter focuses exclusively on the brain and its neural activity independent of its role in mental features such as consciousness, which requires future elaboration in both neuroscientific and philosophical arenas.

At this point one may want to raise the issue of the model of a purely active brain that is not impacted at all by external stimuli . In such a case the spontaneous activity's spatial and temporal structure should show exactly the same neuronal features during both a resting state and exposure to stimuli and tasks. Such a radical case would mean that the brain and its neural activity would be "self-evidencing" (Hohwy, 2014) rather than "world-evidencing" (as one might say analogously). However, that is not in accordance with the empirical data, which clearly show stimulus-induced or task-evoked activity to differ from the ongoing spontaneous activity.

A more moderate proposal would be to allow for stimulus-induced or task-evoked activity but in such way that the spontaneous activity is not altered. In that case one would for instance expect that the neural networks and the various frequency fluctuations, such as the spontaneous activity's spatiotemporal structure, would remain the same during both resting state and exposure to stimuli and tasks. That is not the case, however.

Although present during sleep, rest, and tasks, the different neural networks and the frequency fluctuations change their relations with each other. For instance, as indicated above, the infraslow frequency fluctuations are particularly strong during sleep, less strong during awake rest, and even less strong during awake tasks. This suggests that one cannot really account for the brain and its spontaneous activity in terms of a purely active model in either a radical or even moderate form. For that reason I now propose what I call the spectrum model of brain.

Part III: Spectrum Model of Brain

Spectrum Model of Brain Ia: From Passive and Active Models to a Spectrum Model of Brain

Where do these findings leave us in our search for an empirically plausible model of brain? The data clearly do not support a passive model of brain nor are they in favor of an active model. We may thus need to opt for a third model in which the brain can be featured as both active and passive at the same time. I call such model the "spectrum model" of brain.

What do I mean by the concept of *spectrum model*? Neither the brain's spontaneous activity alone nor the external stimuli by themselves determine stimulus-induced activity in the brain. Instead, it is their relation and thus their balance, that is, how they stand in relation to each other, that determines stimulus-induced activity. Since there is a spectrum or continuum of different possible balances or relations between spontaneous activity and external stimuli, I speak of a spectrum model of brain.

Specifically, such spectrum or continuum assumes that neural activity in the brain can result from different constellations or balances between internally and externally generated activity. Neural activity is consequently characterized as hybrid, stemming from both internal and external sources. The spectrum model concerns how the brain's neural activity can involve different degrees of resting-state activity and, still, be shaped by external stimuli. One and the same neural activity level may be constituted by different degrees of resting-state activity at different times.

For instance, if the resting-state activity is rather strong and the external stimuli are weak, as for instance with a very low sound or weak visual feature, neural activity will be predominantly determined by the resting-state activity. If, in contrast, the resting-state activity is rather weak, the external stimuli (even if not that strong themselves) will have a stronger impact in shaping and constituting the brain's neural activity.

Accordingly, the spectrum model of the brain suggested here is about the balance between the contributions of resting-state activity and external stimuli to the brain's neural activity. Since various constellations in the balance between the resting state and external stimuli are possible, the brain's neural activity can best be captured by a spectrum model that has room for configurations between the purely active and purely passive models discussed above.

Spectrum Model of Brain Ib: Middle and Extreme Cases in the Spectrum

The spectrum model carries major implications regarding how we can and cannot bring high-resolution definition to the concepts of resting-state and stimulus-induced activity. Within the context of the spectrum model, both are at best relative (rather than absolute) distinctions. The context of discussion can impact these issues. Whether one is speaking about operationalized concepts deployed in empirical investigations or trying to do justice to the basic physiological facts of the brain can make a difference to how one uses these concepts.

Operationally, we clearly need to distinguish between resting-state and stimulus-induced activities: resting-state activity is measured in a particular behavioral state, for example, eyes closed or open without any specific tasks or stimuli, whereas stimulus-induced activity is tested for by applying specific tasks or stimuli. In contrast, in a physiological context, the distinction between resting-state and stimulus-induced activity seems to evaporate. There is simply neural activity in the brain that may originate from different constellations of different sources.

According to the spectrum model, the brain's neural activity is by default a hybrid or mixture between resting state and stimulus-induced activity. Neural activity is thus never determined 100 percent by either the resting state alone or by external stimuli alone. Neither extreme case occurs. The healthy brain operates apparently within the middle range of the spectrum or the continuum between different constellations of resting-state and stimulus-induced activity. This leaves open the more extreme cases of the spectrum. I suggest that we can find those in psychiatric disorders: here the constellation or balance between resting-state and stimulus-induced activity seems to shift from the middle of the spectrum toward its more extreme ends.

Let us consider schizophrenia and especially the auditory hallucinations that often occur with this disorder. Auditory hallucinations can be characterized by an abnormal increase in the level and functional connectivity of resting-state activity in the auditory cortex (see Alderson-Day et al., 2016; Northoff, 2014c, for recent reviews). In contrast, external stimuli such as auditory stimuli barely induce any activity change anymore in the auditory cortex of these patients. Neural activity in the auditory cortex in these patients is thus predominantly determined by the resting-state activity. Even during external stimulus processing, auditory cortical activity is predominantly constituted by the resting state rather than the external stimulus (see Alderson-Day et al., 2016; Northoff, 2014c; Northoff & Qin, 2011).

Another example occurs with depression. In depression, resting-state activity is abnormally elevated in the ACC. Symptomatically this is apparently related to ruminations and increased focus on the self and internal mental contents at the expense of external mental contents (see Northoff & Sibille, 2014a). Additionally, studies have demonstrated that the degree of activity change elicited by external stimuli is significantly reduced (if it can be observed at all) in depressed patients. The elevated resting-state activity is simply no longer as reactive to change related to external stimuli (see Grimm, Boesiger, et al., 2009; Grimm, Ernst, et al., 2009; Northoff, Wiebking, Feinberg, & Panksepp, 2011). Accordingly, as in the case of the auditory cortex in schizophrenia, neural activity in ACC during depression seems to be predominantly determined by the resting state rather than by the external stimuli.

Let us now consider the opposite extreme, neural activity being determined predominantly by external stimuli with relatively minor impact from the resting state. In healthy subjects this may, for instance, be the case in the presence of an abnormally strong external stimulus such as an extremely loud noise. The extremely strong stimulus will then override the impact of the resting state and determine the neural activity. A pathological instance of such a scenario may be the case of mania, the opposite of depression. In such a condition resting-state activity in ACC is reduced when compared to healthy subjects (Magioncalda et al., 2014; Martino et al., 2016), which seems to predispose it to react abnormally strongly to external stimuli.

What do these cases tell us for the spectrum model? In the case of elevated resting-state activity, the brain itself is highly active and determines its own neural activity, even in response to external stimuli. The opposite is the case when the external stimuli are extremely strong and/or the resting state is rather weak. In that case the external (or internal or neuronal) stimuli predominate in the brain, which by itself is then rather passive with a high degree of receptivity. Accordingly, these instances are cases that are shifted from the middle range of the spectrum toward being closer to the extreme ends of the spectrum between activity and passivity (see figure 1.1).

It is worth emphasizing that these extreme cases are not the norm. They are exceptions and can lead to major mental and psychological changes as in depression and schizophrenia. The healthy brain's neural activity, in contrast, usually occupies a middle range in the spectrum where neural activity is codetermined by both resting state and external stimuli. The fluctuations in the degrees to which the resting state and external stimuli contribute to neural activity are consequently much more modest if not minor when compared to the major changes observed in the cases that shift more toward the extreme ends of the spectrum as in psychiatric disorders.

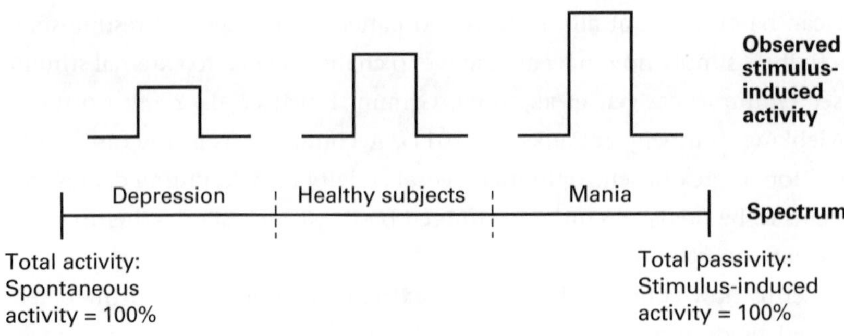

Figure 1.1
Spectrum model of neural activity.

In sum, our brain's neural activity is neither purely active nor completely passive. Instead, we may best account for the brain's neural activity in terms of a spectrum model where neural activity is assumed to be codetermined by both the resting state and external stimuli in varying degrees and balances. Such a spectrum model entails a continuum between different degrees of activity and passivity in the brain's neural activity.

Conclusion

In this chapter, we have discussed different models of the brain, passive, active, and spectrum, in the light of recent empirical findings in neuroscience as well as theoretical evidence as presented in the philosophy of science. The passive model of brain assumes that neural activity in general and stimulus-induced activity in particular are accounted for sufficiently (if not exclusively) by external stimuli themselves. Such a brain would only passively receive and process external stimuli but would not really contribute to shaping and constituting the resulting stimulus-induced activity. However, recent empirical evidence does not support such a model since the brain's own activity, its resting state or spontaneous activity, causally impacts stimulus-induced activity.

The let us turn toward an active model of brain. In this case the brain itself is characterized by neural activity that occurs prior to and independent of external stimuli, the brain's spontaneous or resting-state activity. Moreover, recent empirical evidence suggests that the brain's spontaneous or resting-state activity exhibits a certain spatial and temporal structure as, for instance, in its different neural networks and frequency fluctuations.

Does the brain's resting state or spontaneous activity determine stimulus-induced activity? As I demonstrate in the third section above, stimulus-induced activity seems to result from codetermination by both external stimuli and spontaneous activity, that is, world and brain. Stimulus-induced activity may then be determined by the spectrum or continuum of different possible relationships or balances between spontaneous activity, or brain, and external stimuli, world.

Beyond its empirical and theoretical plausibility, the spectrum model of brain carries far-reaching implications. The brain can no longer be regarded as merely passive in a purely empirical sense. Nor can the brain be regarded as purely active in an idealistic or constructivist sense. The spectrum model of brain builds on both ideas by integrating them into a spectrum or continuum of different relationships or balances between passive and active features. These relations or balances between passive and active features will prove central in our understanding of how the brain can yield consciousness, as is discussed in the second part of this book.

2 Relation between Spontaneous and Stimulus-Induced Activity: Interaction Model of Brain

Introduction

General Background

What does it mean to be in a resting state? This is one of the central questions in neuroscience where the brain's spontaneous activity has been the subject of intense debate (see, for instance, Cabral et al., 2013; Northoff, 2014a,b; Raichle, 2001, 2010; Shulman et al., 2014). This question has also become a subject for philosophy (see the recent excellent paper by Klein, 2014). Because its exact meaning, role, and purpose all remain unclear, the brain's spontaneous activity is typically defined in purely operational terms by the absence of specific external stimuli (see Logothetis et al., 2009). The brain's spontaneous activity, then, often acts as a baseline, especially in functional brain imaging (such as fMRI) (see Klein, 2014; Morcom & Fletcher, 2007a,b). In other words, the brain's spontaneous activity serves as a reference for determining the contours of task-evoked or stimulus-induced activity (these terms are used interchangeably throughout this volume). Whether it is feasible for the spontaneous to serve as such a baseline has been debated in both neuroscience (Morcom & Fletcher, 2007a,b) and philosophy (Klein, 2014).

One reason for doubt about the use of spontaneous activity as a reference for task-evoked activity is the dynamic character of spontaneous activity. Specifically, the way that spontaneous activity appears to change in ways that trace back to task-evoked activity calls into question the use of the former as a way of demarcating the latter. The stimuli or task may impact spontaneous activity by changing its level, degree of functional connectivity, or variability, which has been called stimulus-rest interaction (see Northoff et al., 2010; Schneider et al., 2008). Additionally, data for the converse scenario, the spontaneous activity impacting the subsequent stimulus-induced or task-evoked activity, that is, rest–stimulus interaction, has been reported (see He, 2013; Northoff et al., 2010; Sadaghinai, Hesselmann, et al., 2010).

The two kinds of interaction between spontaneous and stimulus-induced activity just discussed provide reason for skepticism regarding whether the spontaneous can serve as absolute and independent reference for stimulus-induced activity. The apparent impossibility of a clean-cut segregation of spontaneous and stimulus-induced activity suggests that shifting focus to their relation could be heuristically valuable. Klein (2014), for instance, suggested that the two types of neural activity involve different temporal dimensions: the spontaneous activity can operate on long-term time scales across hours, days, and months if not years, whereas the stimulus-induced activity is limited to the very short-term time scales in which particular stimuli are processed. This is a promising hypothesis, but Klein does not explain the exact nature of their relation, that is, how long- and short-time scales interact and are integrated with each other.

I suggest that there are at least two plausible ways that spontaneous and task-evoked activity could be related to one another. It could be that they operate in parallel or that they interact with one another. Parallelism is the view that spontaneous and task-evoked activities are decidedly independent neural phenomena. An interactionist view, in contrast, claims either that stimulus-induced activity is unilaterally dependent on the spontaneous or that there is a mutual dependence between them.

Importantly, one could distinguish between strong and weak forms of both parallelism and interactionism. Strong parallelism would not allow for any kind of relation such as spatial or temporal overlap between spontaneous and task-evoked activity. In contrast, weak parallelism may posit a spatial or temporal overlap between spontaneous and task-evoked activity but without the latter changing the ongoing levels or features of the former, or vice versa. In other words, weak parallelism posits independence in the levels (and features) of both forms of activity: spontaneous activity remains the same irrespective of whether task-evoked activity is present or not, and task-evoked activity remains the same independent of the level of spontaneous activity.

There could also be weak and strong forms of interactionism. Weak interactionism could be signified by a relation such as additive interaction, that is, mere superposition between spontaneous and task-evoked activity without mutual change. Taken in this sense, weak interactionism may overlap to a significant degree with weak parallelism. For this reason I will focus my discussion only on the former (while neglecting the latter). Strong interactionism, in contrast, does not only allow for mere superposition like spatiotemporal overlap and additive interaction but goes further by postulating reciprocal dependence and change in the levels of spontaneous and task-evoked activity.

Focusing on the discussion of parallelism versus interactionism, the present chapter can be regarded as an extension and specification of the first chapter. There I endorsed a spectrum model of the brain that considers stimulus-induced activity to result from a continuum or balance between spontaneous activity and stimuli. As pointed out, this presupposes direct interaction and reciprocal modulation between spontaneous activity and stimuli. The exact nature of this interaction, however, was left open. Clarifying the character of the interaction between spontaneous and stimulus-induced activity as well as their underlying mechanisms and principles is the overarching goal of the present chapter.

Main Aim and Argument

The aims of this chapter are to discuss these two models, parallelism and interactionism and to provide arguments for and against each based on available empirical data and theoretical accounts of scientific reasoning. The first part focuses on parallelism in its strong form, whereas the second part investigates interactionism in both forms, weak and strong. To do this, I must avoid worries about how exactly to determine what counts as spontaneous activity. The empirical data that are most probative with respect to the relation between spontaneous and task-invoked activity are concerned purely with neural activity.

I therefore need to clarify a number of potentially important ways in which the pertinent phenomena can be characterized. For discussion about the viability of studying spontaneous activity in metabolic, biochemical, spatial, temporal, or psychological terms, see Northoff (2014a). Focusing on the purely neuronal level allows me to target the relation between spontaneous and stimulus-induced activity as indexed by spatial (i.e., functional connectivity) and temporal (i.e., fluctuations in different frequency ranges) measures.

In addition to empirical evidence, I also discuss theoretical evidence as stemming from philosophy of science (third section in this chapter: "Fundamental Principle of Brain Activity—Difference-Based Coding"). Relying on the philosopher of science R. Giere and his concept of fundamental principle, I propose that a particular coding strategy by the brain, namely difference-based coding, allows for interaction between spontaneous activity and stimuli. Therefore, I argue that difference-based coding can be regarded as a fundamental principle (or bridge principle) in the sense of Giere.

Conceptual Definitions and Clarifications

Before we go ahead, we should make a couple of clarifications. The concept of spontaneous activity is usually understood in an operational sense that denotes a behavioral state—both eyes closed and eyes open with a visual fixation cross are common examples used in neuroimaging (Logothetis et al., 2009; Northoff, 2014a,b; Raichle, 2015a,b). Psychologically, the spontaneous activity may be characterized by mind wandering, random thoughts, or stimulus-unrelated thoughts (Fox et al., 2015; Smallwood & Schooler, 2015). In contrast, I use the concept of spontaneous activity to refer to neuronal activity irrespective of any operational, psychological, or behavioral concerns (Raichle, 2015a,b). It is the spontaneous activity of the brain that Raichle termed "default-mode function" of the brain (Buckner et al., 2008; Llinás, 2001; Northoff, 2014a,b; Raichle, 2009; Raichle et al., 2001); it is this sense of the term "spontaneous activity" that I presuppose here.

It is also worth noting that one might judge the claim about strong interaction between spontaneous and stimulus-induced activity to be almost trivially true. The baseline state against which deviations are measured, whether a true neuronal resting state or a particular cognitive state can be assumed to impact the subsequent processing of and behavior resulting from any stimuli or task. This means that interactionism is almost trivially true, which could be interpreted to mean that there is nothing special about the brain's spontaneous activity.

However, the main focus here is not so much on the psychological and behavioral implications but exclusively on the neuronal mechanisms underlying such interaction. Rather than focusing on behavioral or psychological states, I exclusively focus on the neuronal mechanisms that underlie interaction on the behavioral and psychological level. For that purpose I discuss different neural models of interaction between spontaneous activity and stimulus-induced activity.

One of those models, specifically, the parallel model may be considered a straw man from an empirical perspective given the observed behavioral and psychological interactions. However, taken in a purely logical context in terms of conceivability, parallelism nevertheless must be considered an option; my aim is thus to refute such parallelism on empirical grounds and show that it is simply not in accordance with the empirical data. It is useful to learn what it is about the design of the brain that accounts for strong parallelism not being a tenable option from an empirical perspective.

Part I: Parallelism Model between Spontaneous and Stimulus-Induced Activity

Roughly, *parallelism* is the view that spontaneous activity and stimulus-induced activity operate in parallel without any direct interaction. In order for empirical evidence about neural activity to be relevant to this claim, it needs to be made more precise. One way to do this is to consider parallelism to entail that spontaneous activity and task-evoked activity are neurally segregated from one another. This segregation could occur in one of two ways. Spontaneous activity and task-evoked activity might be spatially segregated, in which case they would transpire in distinct neuronal systems, or they could be temporally segregated, in which case they would be constituted respectively by forms of neural activity that have distinct profiles in terms of amplitude fluctuation across different frequency ranges.

Parallelism Ia: Spatial Segregation and Parallel Processing

The default-mode network (DMN) includes medial regions in the brain such as the anterior and posterior cingulate cortex and the medial prefrontal cortex as well as the inferior parietal cortex. The DMN has gotten its name due to its high levels of spontaneous activity (Buckner et al., 2008; Raichle, 2015a,b; Raichle et al., 2001) and is contrasted with other neural regions/networks such as the sensory or lateral prefrontal cortices and their respective, sensorimotor and control-executive networks (SMN, CEN). According to this rubric, regions outside the DMN are not related to spontaneous activity. This view ascribes spatial segregation to spontaneous activity and stimulus-induced activity because each is taken to transpire in distinct neural neighborhoods. Klein (2014) describes this as the "standard thesis," which I rephrase as the "standard view."

Still, there are reasons to question the significance of the data in support of these claims for spatial segregation. Already in some of the early work on spontaneous activity, Simpson, Drevets, Snyder, Gusnard, and Raichle (2001) and Gusnard and Raichle (2001), showed that the DMN underwent deactivation during task-evoked activity whenever the task involved either self-referential (personally relevant stimuli such as the subject's own name) or cognitive-attentional elements. Such deactivation indicates responsiveness to the stimulus and can therefore be taken as evidence for the claim that the DMN can in fact be operative during stimulus-induced or task-evoked activity, even if it provides little indication as to what sorts of operations it is performing.

In addition, functional connectivity within the DMN (roughly, the degree to which activity changes across time in different parts of the DMN can be said to correlate with one another) has been shown to change during exposure to tasks or stimuli. This phenomenon has been described as "background functional connectivity" (Smith et al., 2009) and serves as strong indication that spontaneous activity in the DMN is preserved during and, at the same time, modulated by stimulus-induced or task-evoked activity. If the two were entirely independent, one would expect that task-invoked activity would fail to disturb the DMN. Unless one maintains that changes in the DMN's functional connectivity during the performance of tasks constitute a coincidence, this finding is reason to doubt the parallelism thesis even if one accepts the spatial segregation hypothesis of the "standard view."

Additionally, the parallelist view of resting state/task-evoked activity can be undermined by resisting the spatial segregation hypothesis. If it is the case that spontaneous activity occurs outside the DMN, then it would no longer be viable to endorse parallelism on the basis of claims about spatial segregation between spontaneous activity and task-evoked activity. A number of studies have begun to illuminate the presence of spontaneous activity in neural regions outside the DMN. In fact, it has been shown that regions of the brain often thought to be dedicated to stimulus-induced and task-evoked activity, like the CEN and SMN, can themselves be characterized as involving spontaneous activity (see Klein 2014; Northoff, 2014a; Shulman et al., 2014).

Note however that the findings considered so far just speak against spatial parallelism in particular but not parallelism in general. There could still be parallel processing between spontaneous activity and stimulus-induced activity within one and the same region or network. It is conceivable that both forms of activity occur in various regions/networks but that they remain completely independent of each other in each region. In order to evaluate the prospects for this form of parallelism, the temporal features of spontaneous activity and task-invoked activity need to be investigated.

Parallelism Ib: Temporal Segregation and Parallel Processing

Parallelism is not necessarily ruled out by the above arguments against the spatial segregation hypothesis. If it could be shown that spontaneous activity and task-evoked activity are constituted by fluctuations in completely different frequency ranges, parallelism might still be vindicated. For instance, it could be that infraslow frequency fluctuations occur only in spontaneous activity, whereas higher frequency fluctuations only occur during stimulus-induced activity. This would provide some evidence for parallelism.

To evaluate the hypothesis that spontaneous activity and task-evoked activity are temporally segregated along these lines, a brief recap of the temporal features of neural activity is needed. The brain's neural activity can be characterized by fluctuations in different frequency ranges. Infraslow frequency fluctuations are in the range between 0.001 to 0.1 Hz (as measured with fMRI) and are complemented by slow (0.01 to 4 Hz: slow and delta) and faster frequency ranges between 5 and 8 Hz (theta), 8–12 Hz (alpha), 12–30 Hz (beta), and 30–180 Hz (gamma) (as measured with EEG) (Buzsáki, 2006; Engel, Gerloff, Hilgetag, & Nolte, 2013; Northoff, 2014a). Importantly, these different frequency ranges occur throughout the whole brain in various regions and networks, although there are some differences that result from the degree of spatial extension in the networks. Due to their longer phase durations, the infraslow frequency fluctuations are spatially more extended, that is, spread over more regions than the more localized higher frequency fluctuations such as gamma (Buzsáki, 2006; Northoff, 2014a).

Spontaneous activity in the DMN shows infraslow frequency fluctuations (0.001 to 0.1Hz) that are slower, stronger in their power, and more variable than in other networks such as SMN and CEN (Lee, Northoff, & Wu, 2014). This provides some reason to suspect that infraslow frequency fluctuations are specific to spontaneous activity, but this claim does not withstand empirical scrutiny. As demonstrated by Smith et al. (2009), infraslow frequency fluctuations in DMN are preserved and modulated during task-evoked activity as manifest in "background functional connectivity."

In addition to the spatial features already discussed, functional connectivity also includes a strong temporal component in that it is calculated on the basis of the statistically based correlation, that is, synchronization of signal changes from different regions across different time points (see Fingelkurts et al. 2004a–c). The data by Smith et al. (2009) suggest that infraslow frequency fluctuations do not only occur in the spontaneous activity but also during stimulus-induced activity. Hence, infraslow frequency fluctuations overlap between spontaneous activity and stimulus-induced activity, which weakens the case for temporal segregation.

So far, I have demonstrated that empirical evidence speaks against the hypothesis of infraslow frequency fluctuations being involved in spontaneous activity but not in stimulus-induced activity. However, temporal segregation could still be viable if it were shown that high-frequency fluctuations such as gamma do not occur in the spontaneous activity but only during stimulus-induced activity. Once again however, this is not supported by empirical evidence. Even in the spontaneous activity, high-frequency fluctuations such as gamma can be observed (see Northoff, 2014a, for details).

To be sure, different regions and networks show different profiles or patterns in the relations between infraslow (0.01–0.1 Hz), slow (0.1–1 Hz) and fast (1–180 Hz) frequency fluctuations. The sensory regions such as the visual cortex may show rather strong higher frequency fluctuations (such as gamma), whereas their infraslow frequency fluctuations may not be as strong (Engel et al, 2013; Lee et al., 2014). This pattern is reversed in, for instance, the DMN where infraslow frequency fluctuations are rather strong and higher frequency ranges are relatively weak (Buzsáki, 2006). However, the case for parallelism as a model of the relation between spontaneous activity and stimulus-induced activity requires more than this. The temporal segregation hypothesis would require that certain forms of fluctuation are only present during spontaneous activity and others only present in stimulus-induced activity, which possibility has been disproven by the findings reviewed in this section.

However, the refutation of the temporal segregation hypothesis does not fully clinch the case against parallelism. Although it has been shown that spontaneous and stimulus-induced activity cannot be inferred to be independent on the basis of broad spatial or temporal features, it could still be the case that each form of neural activity has a kind of cerebral autonomy. The different frequency fluctuations may take place in multiple neural regions but still run in parallel in the sense that they do not influence one another.

The argumentative burden on this hypothesis is severe, however. It would be difficult to conclusively show that spontaneous and stimulus-induced activity have no influence on one another, especially considering that the two forms of neural activity overlap in both spatial and temporal ways. Thus, the final refutation of parallelism must await the vindication of its rival, interactionism. Fortunately, there is ample empirical evidence in support of interactionism.

Part II: Interaction Model between Spontaneous and Stimulus-Induced Activity

Having discarded the spatial and temporal segregation hypotheses, our investigation of the relation between spontaneous and stimulus-induced activity must now explore the possibility that, despite their spatial and temporal overlap, these forms of neural activity are independent. If it can be shown that one of these is predictive of the other, or that one modulates the other (see chapter 1 for empirical support), the fate of parallelism will be sealed, and focus should be shifted to the nature and significance of their interaction.

This part of the investigation will be concerned with whether spontaneous activity and stimulus-induced activity are related to one another in an additive or nonadditive way. In a nutshell, additive interaction entails that stimulus-induced activity is merely added to the ongoing spontaneous activity without there being changes in either one that can be traced to the other. There would be nonadditive interaction, on the other hand, if it could be shown that features of the spontaneous activity are explanatory with respect to some features of stimulus-induced activity, or that there are features of stimulus-induced activity that explain changes in subsequent spontaneous activity. We will see that although there is some empirical evidence for additive interaction, the case for nonadditive interaction is stronger.

Interaction Model Ia: Additive Interaction between Spontaneous and Stimulus-Induced Activity

From the previous sections, we know that the only remaining way for parallelism to be considered viable as a model of the relation between spontaneous and stimulus-induced activity is for there to be only additive interaction between the two. This would require that, even though both recruit the same spatial and temporal features of neural activity, they nevertheless do not directly impact or modulate each other. Because spontaneous activity is ongoing in the brain and stimulus-induced activity occurs only when prompted by particular sensory episodes, the prospects for their interaction being merely additive can be illuminated by investigating whether the degree of stimulus-induced activity depends completely and exclusively on the stimulus alone. Unless this can be shown, parallelism must be discarded in favor of interactionism.

There have been studies on both cellular (Arieli, Sterkin, Grinvald, & Aertsen, 1996; Azouz & Gray, 1999) and regional (Becker, Reinacher, Freyer, Villringer, & Ritter, 2011; Fox et al., 2006) features of neural activity that have provided evidence for a stimulus-related signal being merely superimposed on ongoing spontaneous activity. For instance, Fox et al. (2006) showed that signal changes in motor cortex induced by a movement remained independent of the ongoing spontaneous activity in the very same region, the motor cortex. More specifically, the activity level in the motor cortex at stimulus onset, which signifies the spontaneous activity, did not exert any impact on subsequent stimulus-induced activity in the motor cortex. Hence, in this case the stimulus-induced activity seems to be added to or superimposed on top of the spontaneous activity independent of the amplitude of the latter (see left part in figures 2.1A and 2.1B).

Since the degree of stimulus-evoked activity in these studies is not disturbed by differences in the amount of spontaneous activity occurring at stimulus onset, the interaction between the two is additive. Thus, in some

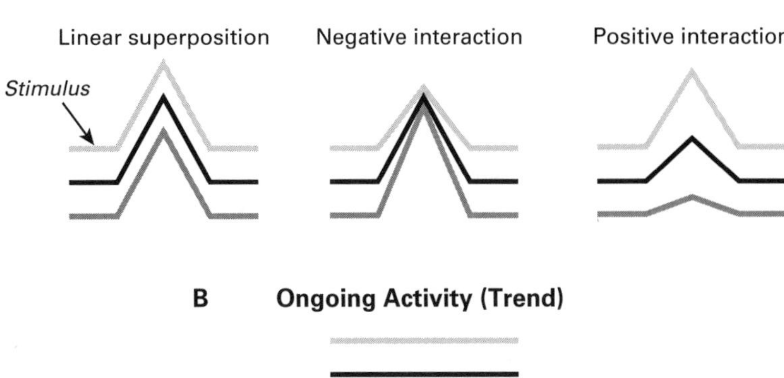

Figure 2.1
Nonadditive interaction (A) at three different levels of resting state (or ongoing) activity (B).

cases at least, spontaneous and stimulus-induced activities are processed independently.

A similar superposition of stimulus-induced activity on spontaneous activity was demonstrated by Engel et al. (2013). They showed that stimulus-induced activity can be simply added to spontaneous activity by elevating the power of high-frequency fluctuations such as gamma. Importantly, in these studies spontaneous gamma power did not predict stimulus-induced gamma power. Thus, there is reason to believe that stimulus-induced activity can run parallel to spontaneous activity, independently recruiting similar spatial (regions) and temporal (amplitude of frequency fluctuations) features of neural activity.

The studies reviewed in this section provide some hope for the weak interactionist or parallelist model, but they are far from decisive. As mentioned earlier, if we find instances of dependence, for example, interaction between spontaneous and stimulus-induced activity, that is enough to shed doubt on parallelism (in at least its strong version; see introduction of this chapter). The findings of Fox et al. (2005) and Engel et al. (2013) do not confirm this claim. They are just indications that sometimes stimulus-induced activity is merely superimposed on spontaneous activity. Parallelism (in at least its strong version) remains vulnerable to evidence for any nonadditive interactions between them. The next section reviews studies that provide this.

Interaction Model Ib: Nonadditive Interaction between Spontaneous and Stimulus-Induced Activity

One measure often used to indicate stimulus-induced activity is trial-to-trial variability (TTV) which, roughly described, refers to the differences in amplitude of neural activity between different trials related to the repeated presentation of one and the same stimulus or task (Churchland et al., 2010). Importantly, TTV is measured in reference to the degree of variability at the onset of the stimulus or task, which reflects the variability of the spontaneous activity at the time of stimulus onset. This means that TTV is not a purely stimulus-related measure but one where the trial-based effects of the stimuli on variability are measured against the resting state's level of ongoing variability.

Nor can TTV be regarded as mere noise that is related to technical artifacts rather than being physiological, that is, neural by itself: neural activity in the spontaneous activity continuously changes its levels as indexed by temporal variance (He, 2013). The incoming stimulus impinges on the spontaneous activity by reducing its ongoing temporal variance transiently, which we measure as TTV on both cellular and regional levels of neural activity (Churchland et al., 2010; He, 2013).

The use of TTV as a measure of stimulus-induced activity carries implications regarding the relation between spontaneous activity and stimulus-induced activity. The data from Fox et al. (2005) and Engel et al. (2013) reviewed above only addressed stimulus-induced activity in terms of its amplitude without considering TTV. When stimulus-induced activity is investigated in terms of TTV, it becomes more difficult to maintain that it fails to interact with spontaneous activity.

Many studies on cellular and regional features of neural activity have shown reduction in the degree of ongoing variability in neural activity related to repeated stimuli or tasks, that is, reduction in TTV (see Churchland et al., 2010; He, 2013; White, Abbot, & Fiser, 2012). Recently, Huang, Zhang, Longtin, et al. (2017) demonstrated that the degree of stimulus-related reduction in TTV depends on the level of spontaneous activity at stimulus onset: higher levels of spontaneous activity at stimulus onset lead to higher reduction in stimulus-induced TTV, whereas lower levels of spontaneous activity at stimulus onset have resulted in lower TTV reduction (see also Ponce-Alvarez et al., 2015, for confirmation from the side of computational modeling). This is strong evidence that the degree of TTV is dependent on the resting state, which speaks against parallelism and in favor of interactionism.

Huang, Zhang, Longtin, et al. (2017) also performed studies on the saturation effect, which refers to the maximum possible level of neural activity the brain can generate (in a particular region or network or the whole brain) independent of whether that activity is related to spontaneous activity or stimulus-induced activity. If, for instance, the level of spontaneous activity is already high by itself, it may be close to the saturation level and hence will not leave much room for additional increases in the level of neural activity due to stimulus-induced activity. The stimulus can then no longer induce the degree of activity it would if the spontaneous activity were further from the saturation point (see also Ponce-Alvarez et al., 2015, for supporting such neuronal claims on the basis of computational modeling).

Thus, the brain's biophysical limitations on the degree of activity it can generate creates a link between spontaneous activity and stimulus-induced activity. Since there is a finite amount of neural activity that the brain can perform, the degree of spontaneous activity affects stimulus-induced activity by leaving more or less neural activity for a stimulus to induce. This is more evidence in favor of interactionism.

The saturation effect is just one way that spontaneous activity can have an impact on subsequent stimulus-induced activity. Another stream of research has shown that different levels of spontaneous activity can have considerable impact on subsequent stimulus-induced activity without the saturation effect being a factor (He, 2013; Hesselmann, Kell, Eger, et al., 2008, Hesselmann, Kell, & Kleinschmidt 2008; Huang, Zhang, Longtin, et al., 2017; Sadaghiani et al., 2009; Sadaghiani, Hesselmann, et al., 2010; see Northoff , Qin, Nakao, 2010, and Northoff, Duncan, & Hayes, 2010, for review). For instance, Hesselmann, Kell, Eger, et al. (2008) showed that when the level of prestimulus activity was low in the fusiform face area (FFA), a region that is strongly implicated in processing faces, subsequent stimulus-induced activity was rather high in the same region, and this even had clear behavioral consequences. Subjects with low spontaneous activity were more likely to subsequently see an ambivalent stimulus as a face (rather than a vase).

Analogous results were observed in the neural structures involved in other sensory modalities such as the auditory cortex (see Sadaghiani et al., 2009). This Sadaghiani et al. study showed that certain auditory tones could be detected only when the stimulus-induced activity was preceded by high amplitude levels of prestimulus spontaneous activity in the auditory cortex. Higher prestimulus spontaneous activity levels correlated with both higher subsequent stimulus-induced activity and subjects being more likely to detect the tones. In another study (Hesselmann et al., 2008), they showed that low prestimulus activity levels in fusiform face area lead to high poststimulus amplitude with high recognition of faces. Based on these findings, they assume nonadditive interaction between ongoing spontaneous activity and stimulus-induced activity (Sadaghiani, Hesselmann et al., 2010).

The likelihood of such nonadditive interaction was further bolstered by He (2013), who observed that both amplitude and TTV during stimulus-induced activity were inversely proportional to prestimulus levels of spontaneous activity. This means that lower levels of prestimulus activity predicted higher amplitudes and higher reduction in TTV during exposure to the stimulus.

That finding was further extended by Huang, Zhang, Longtin, et al. (2017) who showed that interaction between rest and stimuli-related neural activity is affected by the phase of ongoing infraslow frequency fluctuations. It was shown that if the ongoing infraslow frequency fluctuation finds itself in its positive phase (corresponding to low excitability in response to external stimuli), subsequent stimulus-related amplitude and TTV reduction will be low. Likewise, if the ongoing infraslow frequency fluctuation finds itself in its negative phase (corresponding to high excitability in response to external stimuli), subsequent stimulus-related amplitude and TTV reduction will be high. The degree of rest–stimulus interaction in a particular region or network is thus directly dependent on the phase of the prestimulus spontaneous activity at stimulus onset.

Taken together, these results suggest that stimulus-related phenomena such as amplitude and degree of TTV are directly dependent on the level of spontaneous activity at stimulus onset or prestimulus. These data speak in favor of nonadditive (rather than additive) interaction between spontaneous and stimulus-induced activity and thus form the beginnings of a positive case for strong interactionism (see middle and right parts in figure 2.1A).

Contrary to some of the studies explored earlier, stimulus-induced activity is not merely superimposed on spontaneous activity. Instead, it is clear that there is at least one direction of influence between them. The findings reviewed in this section establish that spontaneous activity is influential with respect to stimulus-induced activity in many ways. This is known as *rest–stimulus interaction* (Northoff et al., 2010), and although it would be sufficient for claiming that parallelism is flawed, there is still more to be said in support of an interactionist model. The next section shows that there is also the reversed relation, that is, stimulus–rest interaction in the brain.

Interaction Model Ic: Stimulus–Rest Interaction

So far, I have only explored one-half of interactionism, the influence of spontaneous activity on subsequent stimulus-induced activity, that is, the rest–stimulus interaction. The other half, the influence of stimulus-induced activity on subsequent spontaneous activity, that is, stimulus–rest interaction, remains to be addressed. The findings reviewed so far are compatible with there being nonadditive rest–stimulus interaction but only additive stimulus–rest interaction. This could support claims for a hybrid model in which interactionism characterizes the influence of spontaneous on stimulus-induced activity, whereas parallelism characterizes the influence of stimulus-induced on spontaneous activity.

If this were the case, spontaneous activity could be ascribed a degree of neural autonomy because its essential features would not change throughout stimulus-induced activity. This possibility is significant because it would mean that despite there being interaction between spontaneous and stimulus-induced activity, spontaneous activity could still serve as a reference against which stimulus-induced activity is defined. That would resolve the aforementioned controversy concerning the use of spontaneous activity as a baseline for demarcating task-evoked activity (see Klein, 2014; Morcom & Fletcher, 2007a,b).

However, empirical evidence speaks against such a scenario. Several studies have demonstrated that stimuli or tasks and their related stimulus-induced or task-evoked activities do have an impact on subsequent spontaneous activity (see Northoff, Qin, Nakao 2010, for a review). For instance, high self-related or personally relevant stimuli induced higher activity levels in the midline DMN regions associated with spontaneous activity during the subsequent period (the intertrial interval) when compared to low self-related or personally irrelevant stimuli (Schneider et al., 2008). Additionally, emotional stimulation and working memory have been observed to change the subsequent spontaneous activity in the amygdala after emotional stimuli and in the dorsolateral prefrontal cortex after working memory tasks (see Northoff, Duncan, Hayes, 2010, for review).

Taken together, these findings suggest that spontaneous activity is just as sensitive to preceding stimulus-induced activity as the latter is sensitive to the former. It can be concluded that the rest–stimulus interaction established in the previous section is complemented by stimulus–rest interaction and that both are nonadditive. Although many empirical details still need to be worked out, the evidence currently available strongly suggests that spontaneous and stimulus-induced activity are mutually dependent on each other in several ways. It is therefore reasonable to reject all forms of parallelism and embrace interactionism.

Part III: Fundamental Principle of Brain Activity—Difference-Based Coding

I so far have described different models of brain, parallelism versus interaction, with empirical evidence tilting the balance in favor of the latter. This leaves open, however, how such interaction, especially the nonadditive interaction, takes place. The explanation leads us to take a deeper look into the mechanisms that operate behind our observations. Specifically, this makes it necessary to investigate the brain's coding strategy and the fundamental principles underlying the constitution and generation of its neural activity.

Fundamental Principle Ia: Encoding of Natural Statistics

How is the nonadditive interaction between spontaneous activity and the stimulus possible? There must be direct interaction between spontaneous activity and stimulus since otherwise the two could not contribute in varying degrees to one and the same neural activity, that is, stimulus-induced activity. Additionally, both must be able to reciprocally modulate each other: a strong spontaneous activity might weaken the impact of the stimulus on stimulus-induced activity, whereas a strong stimulus would weaken the influence of ongoing spontaneous activity on ensuing stimulus-induced activity.

At a glance one may think that spontaneous activity and stimuli are too different to allow for the sort of direct interaction described above. The stimulus can be characterized by a particular event or object at a specific point in time and space entailing a small spatiotemporal range or scale. In contrast, the spatiotemporal scale of the spontaneous activity is much larger than that of typical stimuli ranging from the infraslow (0.01–1 Hz) to the ultrafast gamma (180 Hz) fluctuations. These differences in spatiotemporal range or scale between spontaneous and stimulus-induced activity pose a challenge for explaining how the two can directly interact with one another.

The interaction between spontaneous activity and stimuli can occur because the two share something like a common code or "common currency" that underlies their differences. One way to construct the needed bridge would be to code stimuli and spontaneous activity in direct relation to each other on the basis of their different statistical frequency distribution across time and space, that is, in terms of spatiotemporal structure. Spontaneous activity shows continuous change, which results in a certain statistical frequency distribution that I describe as "neuronal statistics" (Northoff, 2014a). The stimuli themselves follow and occur in a certain statistical frequency distribution, that is, their "natural statistics" (Barlow, 2001).

What exactly is meant by "natural statistics"? Rather than coding each stimulus by itself, Barlow suggests that the brain codes and represents "chunks of stimuli" and their details together. He calls the results of this process "gathered details" (Barlow, 2001, p. 603). Let us take the example of a complex scene with a breakfast table covered with various items of food and plates, and so on. In this case our glance first falls on the big teapot in the middle; then we wander to the bread basket, and from there to the cheese plate, the jams, and the various other plates. All items are located at different spatial positions on the table and are not perceived simultaneously by us—rather, we perceive them sequentially by letting our glance wander around the table and its various items.

If one were encoding each single stimulus by itself, one would not connect all items together and consider them to belong to one and the same table, the breakfast table. Moreover one would not render the connection that categorizes each as relevant for breakfast. Despite their spatial and temporal differences, the different stimuli (and hence the different items) must be encoded in conjunction. Once they are put together during encoding, they come to constitute what Barlow describes as "chunks of stimuli" and "gathered details."

Yet another example is the perception of a melody. We do not hear any single tone in isolation but perceive the present tone in relation to the previous one and often make predictions about the next forthcoming tone. This is only possible if we encode the present tone in relation to the previous one thus putting both together as "chunks of tones" with "gathered details." (See Northoff, 2014b, chs. 13–15.) This is only possible, according to Barlow, if our brain encodes the occurrence of the tones (and stimuli in general) in terms of their statistical occurrence in time and space. The closer temporally the tone follows the preceding one, the more likely both tones are encoded and processed together as "chunks of tones." The same principle holds obviously for the spatial dimension: in the case of the breakfast table, the various items are spatially near to one another and are therefore highly likely to be encoded together as "chunks of stimuli."

How can we specify the encoding strategy that results in gathered details? Let us start with what is *not* encoded into neural activity, since that will make it easier for us to better understand the brain's actual encoding strategy. When perceiving a melody, for example, Barlow proposes that the sensory cortex does not encode each tone by itself. Instead of encoding single stimuli by themselves, the brain seems to encode the distribution of the stimulus.

Within a bird's song, for example, the bird's brain will encode the distribution of a particular tone across discrete points in physical time. And the brain may also encode the spatial position of the bird's tone relative to, for instance, a nearby rustling of leaves. What is encoded into neural activity is thus the statistical frequency distribution of stimuli across different discrete points in physical time and space. This is what Barlow describes as the encoding of the stimuli's "natural statistics," the statistical frequency distribution of a stimulus across discrete positions in time and space.

Fundamental Principle Ib: Difference-Based Coding and Nonadditive Interaction

Having described natural statistics, it is now imperative to clarify the nature of "neuronal statistics." Externally generated events in the environment are encoded in terms of their statistical frequency distributions, or natural statistics, into the brain's neural activity, the result of which is stimulus-induced activity. The same holds, analogously, for the brain's spontaneous activity itself. Internally generated events within the brain are encoded in terms of their statistical frequency distributions, or neuronal statistics, the result of which is spontaneous activity.

This phenomenon has major implications. The encoding of the external stimuli's natural statistics into neural activity is only possible through interaction with the neuronal statistics that characterize spontaneous activity. The interaction between external stimulus and spontaneous activity can consequently be sketched as an interaction between two different statistics, natural and neuronal.

Let us recount the interaction between stimulus and spontaneous activity and their respective statistics in more detail. The brain and its spontaneous activity's neuronal statistics encode stimuli as statistical frequency distributions across different points in time and space. The resulting neural activity, the stimulus-induced activity, then reflects the statistically based differences between the spontaneous activity's neuronal statistics and the stimuli's natural statistics—this amounts to *difference-based coding* (see Northoff, 2014a, for empirical detail). Thus, statistically based differences provide the "common currency" between spontaneous activity's neuronal statistics and stimuli's natural statistics. This common currency, I contend, constitutes the relation that brains bear to the wider world in which they exist—this phenomenon amounts to what I describe in chapter 3 as the *world–brain relation* (see figures 2.2A and 2.2B).

We can now explain how difference-based coding makes the nonadditive interaction between spontaneous and stimulus-induced activity possible. Nonadditive interaction is possible only if the spontaneous activity can directly interact with the stimulus and impact the degree to which it elicits stimulus-induced activity in the brain. Different degrees of nonadditive interaction are mediated by different degrees of statistical–difference-based matching between the spontaneous activity's neuronal statistics and the stimuli's natural statistics. This means that the better their respective statistics match in their statistically based differences, the more strongly the spontaneous activity's neuronal statistics can impact the stimulus and its natural statistics, and the higher the degree of nonadditive interaction.

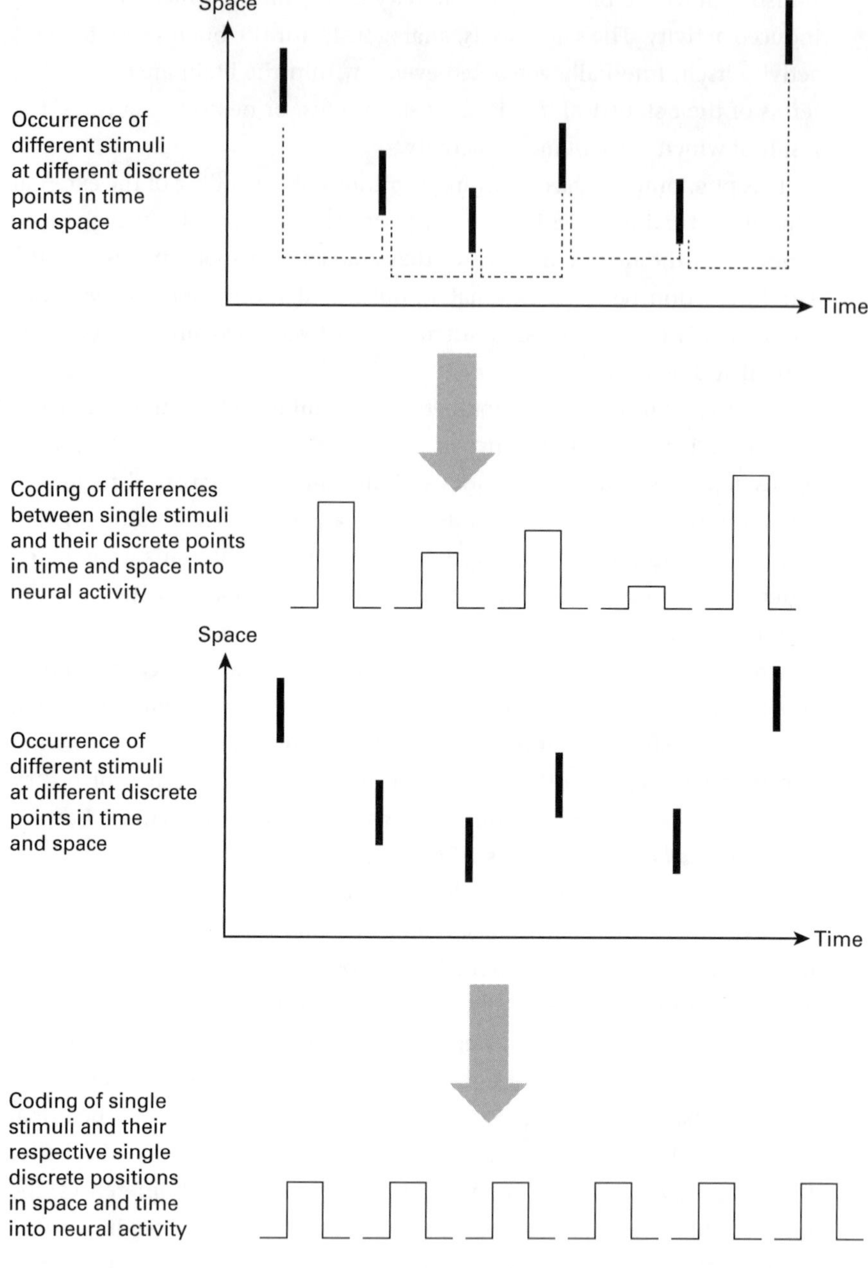
Space
Occurrence of different stimuli at different discrete points in time and space
Time
Coding of differences between single stimuli and their discrete points in time and space into neural activity
Space
Occurrence of different stimuli at different discrete points in time and space
Time
Coding of single stimuli and their respective single discrete positions in space and time into neural activity

Let us conceive a thought experiment. Imagine there were stimulus- rather than difference-based coding. In such a case, the stimulus would only be encoded in an isolated way, in its discrete point in time and space, remaining untethered by any statistically based relation to other stimuli or to the brain's spontaneous activity. This would make any direct interaction (e.g., reciprocal modulation) between spontaneous activity and stimuli less likely. Stimulus-induced activity would supervene on the ongoing spontaneous activity in a merely additive way. In short, stimulus-based coding precludes nonadditive interaction. This suggests that difference-based coding may be what underlies nonadditive interaction.

How would such stimulus-based coding affect the person's perception and cognition of external events in the environment? Temporally separate stimuli could no longer be integrated and linked. For instance, one starts looking at the eyes in the face of a person and then continues to the nose and the mouth. Difference-based coding allows for encoding the statistically based temporal differences among eyes, nose, and mouth as incidences of natural statistics, which makes possible their integration and relation as is present when we perceive them as part of one face.

Figure 2.2

Different models of neural coding. The figure depicts two different models of neural coding, difference-based coding (A) and stimulus-based coding (B). The upper part in each figure illustrates the occurrence of stimuli across time and space as indicated by the vertical lines. The lower part in each figure with the bars stands for the action potentials as elicited by the stimuli with the blue arrow describing the link between stimuli and neural activity. (A) In the case of difference-based coding, the stimuli and their respective temporal and spatial positions are compared, matched, and integrated with each other. In other terms, the differences between the different stimuli across space and time are computed as indicated by the dotted lines. The degree of difference between the different stimuli's spatial and temporal positions does in turn determine the resulting neural activity. The different stimuli are thus dependent on each other when encoded into neural activity. Hence, there is no longer one-to-one matching between stimulus and neural activity. (B) This is different in the case of stimulus-based coding. Here each stimulus, including its respective discrete position in space and time, is encoded in the brain's neural activity. Most importantly, in contrast to difference-based coding, each stimulus is encoded by itself independent of the respective other stimuli. This results in one-to-one matching between stimuli and neural activity.

Fundamental Principle IIa: Models and Fundamental Principles

In the previous section I argued that the interaction model requires a particular coding strategy, namely, difference-based coding. There is still more to say about the relation between the interaction model and difference-based coding. To clarify the nature of this relation, we may look into the philosopher of science R. Giere's thoughts on the determination of models and fundamental principles.

What are models?

Models posit particular relations between different events or features we observe. The human sensory system is far better at observing certain events or features than it is at clarifying the relation that holds between things perceived. For understanding and capturing the relation between the different observed events or features, we construct models. These models can then, in turn, be tested experimentally.

Let us consider the relation between the Earth and sun as a paradigmatic example. The Ptolemaic geocentric model took the Earth as the center of the universe around which the sun revolves. Copernicus, with the Copernican revolution (see chapter 15 for the application of that revolution to philosophy), reversed that relation and suggested a different model, a heliocentric model: now the earth revolves around the sun, which is the center of the universe. Slowly, investigators elaborated ever more precise ways to test the relative empirical plausibility of both models. As we all know, the brilliant scientific observations of both Galileo and Newton shifted the pendulum toward the Copernican model.

Let us apply this to our interaction model. The interaction model establishes a relation between spontaneous activity and stimuli and addresses the question of how they interact with each other. As discussed above, the interaction model is supported by empirical investigation. For instance, investigators have directly compared additive and nonadditive interaction models by checking to see which model made better predictions about the prestimulus amplitude and phase dependence of stimulus-induced activity (He, 2013; Huang, Zhang, Longtin, et al. 2017).

A close relation to observed reality distinguishes models from fundamental principles. Following Giere (1999, 2004, 2008a, 2008b), fundamental principles refer to "abstract entities or objects" that structure and provide templates for subsequent development of models that target more concrete and specific features. Importantly, unlike laws, principles do not result from empirical universalization, nor can they be traced to (or subsumed under) some logicolinguistic structure or formalism (which distinguishes them from the propositions of logic and mathematics). Instead, principles must be conceived as constructions developed by the scientist to explain her or his models and data. Taken in this way, principles may be regarded as "vehicles for making empirical claims" (Giere, 2004, p. 745).

Fundamental principles are highly abstract in that they are far removed from any specific aspect or feature in the world itself (Cartwright and Giere also distinguish between fundamental and bridge principles; see below). Examples of fundamental principles include, for instance, principles of mechanics (Newton), principle of electromagnetism (Maxwell), principle of relativity (Einstein), principle of uncertainty and quantum mechanism (Bohr, Heisenberg), principle of thermodynamics (Prigogine), principle of natural selection (Darwin), the principles of genetics (Mendel), etc. (Giere, 1999, p. 7, 2004, pp. 744–745). These are fundamental principles that guide our scientific investigation of the world and its nature in physics, chemistry, and biology. Each fundamental principle is posited to make sense of observations; the principles thus remain abstract insofar as they are distinct from the observations themselves.

Fundamental Principle IIb: Difference-Based Coding as Fundamental Principle

As indicated above, Giere (1999, 2004, 2008a) characterizes principles by their (1) abstract objects or entities and (2) high degree of abstraction with no direct physical realization and no specific values of the supposed variables (like "drawings of an architect that were never built") (Giere, 2004, p. 745, 2008a, p. 5). Both criteria are met by difference-based coding. Difference-based coding makes ontological commitment to abstract objects, namely statistically based differences. These underlie the events or objects we perceive, but we do not directly perceive them. Statistically based differences can thus be compared to the force of gravity that we do not observe as such, but which is inferred from the effects we do observe.

The same holds of the differences implicated in difference-based coding. We can only observe stimuli, single and isolated stimuli separated from each other in terms of their location or position in time and space. In contrast, we do not directly perceive the statistically based differences between the different stimuli and their temporal and spatial differences. On a more general level this amounts to an inability to perceive the statistically based differences that constitute spatiotemporal relations between different stimuli, that is, their natural statistics. Our perceptual inability has an empirical analogue in neuroscientists' inability to link and relate spontaneous and stimulus-induced activity through direct observation of neural activity.

We are here focusing on the first inability, our principal inability to perceive the statistically based spatiotemporal differences between different stimuli. I postulate that this inability causes major reverberations regarding how to conceive difference-based coding. The best we can do is to indirectly perceive and grasp the statistically based differences by, for instance, using computational modeling (and mathematical formalization). Difference-based coding thus refers to an abstraction, the process of comparing and matching different difference-based statistical frequency distributions between spontaneous activity's neuronal statistics and stimuli's natural statistics.

There is no direct physical realization of differences; they are just statistical relations, which compare well to other examples of fundamental principles provided by Giere, such as numerical relations, geometrical figures, or square roots (Giere, 2008a, p. 5). Moreover, the differences are spatiotemporal. The differences are temporal: at various points in time they could refer to statistical differences between the occurrence of dynamic changes in spontaneous activity or stimuli. Additionally, the differences are also spatial: they refer to statistical differences between the occurrence of stimuli on the one hand and spontaneous activity's dynamic changes on the other at different points in space.

Accordingly, difference-based coding is intrinsically spatiotemporal: it consists of the detection of spatiotemporal differences across events and objects through their influence on ongoing spatiotemporal differences in the brain's spontaneous activity. Since we cannot directly access or observe statistically based spatiotemporal differences, the concept of difference presupposed therein is highly abstract and thus an ideal candidate for a fundamental principle (in the sense of Giere).

What is the role and function of fundamental principles? Giere argues that fundamental principles serve as a "general template" for organizing and structuring the features or aspects in a model including their relations (Giere, 2004, p. 745, 2008a, p. 5). Difference-based coding can serve to structure and organize models of the brain's neural activity such as the interaction model. I have made a case for the claim that difference-based coding provides insight into the neuronal mechanisms underlying the nonadditive interaction between spontaneous activity and stimuli.

Essentially the concept is that this nonadditive interaction is the result of statistically based spatiotemporal differences between the spontaneous activity's neuronal statistics and the stimuli's natural statistics. This analysis is not a generalization from empirical data but, rather, an attempt to infer how the relevant empirical data could accumulate in support of the interaction model. As Giere might describe it, difference-based coding results from tracing our model of the data, the interaction model, to some underlying principle that can serve as general umbrella and "vehicle for making empirical claims" (Giere, 2004, p. 745).

Despite the case I have presented, it could still be that difference-based coding is *not* a fundamental principle of the brain's neural activity. To be sure, one would need to demonstrate that all neural activity in the brain including nonadditive interaction is constituted by difference-based coding. Moreover, I would need to demonstrate on either empirical or theoretical grounds that without difference-based coding there would be no nonadditive interaction at all, indeed, in the most extreme of all cases, no neural activity at all. Only if all this were shown to be the case would it be assured that difference-based coding is a fundamental principle of the brain's neural activity.

Future investigation may demonstrate that difference-based coding underlies all forms of stimulus-induced activity and spontaneous activity. That would lend further empirical support to the supposition that difference-based coding really underlies neural activity in general and can therefore be conceived as a fundamental principle of the brain's neural activity (see chapter 4 and especially Northoff, 2014a, for additional support in this direction).

Conclusion

I have discussed different models of the relation between the brain's spontaneous and stimulus-induced activity. I distinguished between parallelist and interactionist accounts and considered empirical evidence for and against each. On several points, the evidence is clear. First, I have shown that despite the appeal of the standard view that localizes spontaneous activity entirely within the slower fluctuations that occur in the DMN's neural activity, spontaneous and stimulus-induced activity are neither spatially nor temporally segregated from one another. Second, it was shown that spontaneous and stimulus-induced activity do have effects on one another and that these transpire in a nonadditive fashion.

Third, venturing into the philosophy of science, I opted for difference-based coding as a fundamental principle (or bridge principle) to underlie the interaction model. Although this is sufficient to accept interactionism and reject parallelism, much more empirical investigation is required to illuminate the ways that these forms of neural activity interact. There are also important conceptual issues that the foregoing argument barely touches on.

For example, it is not clear what the implications of the empirical evidence being on the side of interactionism are for a proposal such as the one advanced by Klein. Klein (2014) argues that spontaneous and stimulus-induced activity may involve very different time scales. He argues that spontaneous activity may cover a much larger or long-term time scale than stimulus-induced activity. If Klein is right, one could conceive of the interactionist model of spontaneous and stimulus-induced activity in temporal terms. This raises the possibility that the nonadditive interaction between them may serve the purpose of integrating the information contained in short-term stimulus-induced activity into the longer-term spontaneous activity. This is an empirically tractable possibility.

Further investigation could, for example, investigate whether the nonadditive interaction between spontaneous and stimulus-induced activity is related to the coupling of long-term infraslow and short-term high-frequency fluctuations, that is, cross-frequency coupling. By coupling different frequencies, the spontaneous activity constructs a certain temporal structure, a sort of grid of temporal continuities in neural activity across different time scales, that is, in the different coupled frequencies. This temporal structure may be central for processing stimuli and providing the kind of nonadditive interaction effects discussed in the first two sections of this chapter. However, the exact relation between cross-frequency coupling and rest–stimulus interaction remains to be explored.

Future investigation may also reveal whether the integration of information contained in different temporal scales has either behavioral or phenomenal significance. As indicated in the first two sections of this chapter, the nonadditive interaction may strengthen stimulus-induced activity which in turn may make it more likely that we can detect the respective stimulus. Furthermore, the integration of different time scales, that is, long- and short-term may be particularly relevant for subjective consciousness wherein we experience fleeting short-term contents that appear to depend on a contrast with a relatively stable long-term background in order to reach awareness.

One would consequently expect the degree of nonadditive rest–stimulus interaction to be directly proportional to the degree of consciousness associated with that respective stimulus and its contents (see Northoff, 2014b). Thus, although it is important to have set the record straight regarding the problems of parallelism and the promise of interactionism, the fact that empirical evidence comes down on the side of interactionism ought to be seen as just a small early step toward understanding how the brain's spontaneous and stimulus-induced activities conspire to manifest human mindedness.

Finally, the interaction model of brain raises questions of underlying fundamental principle. Based on empirical evidence, I proposed that a particular coding strategy, namely difference-based coding, may be an abstract fundamental principle. Difference-based coding is an empirically plausible statistically based coding strategy that allows for direct interaction between the spontaneous activity's neuronal statistics and the stimuli's natural statistics.

3 Is Our Brain an Open or Closed System? Prediction Model of Brain and World–Brain Relation

Introduction

General Background

How can we be confident in rejecting the possibility of a Cartesian demon that is working to ensure that we are deceived about the real nature of objects and events in the world? If our mind is an open system and thus closely coupled with the world, possible deception about the objects and events within that very same world is unlikely. If, in contrast, our mind remains a closed or self-evidencing system that is inferentially secluded from the world, the door to skepticism and hence for a possible Cartesian demon must be left ajar (see, e.g., Hohwy, 2007, 2013, 2014). Accordingly, the question of whether to characterize the mind as an open or closed system has major epistemic implications.

As do many other philosophers, I believe that mind and its features have their basis in the brain and its neural operations. Although this position is not without opposition, this chapter is not an occasion to adjudicate the metaphysical controversy concerning the relation between the mind and the brain. Here, I am exploring the epistemic implications of a widespread and important conception of how the brain interacts with the world: predictive coding. Given how many neuroscientists are working on predictive coding, and the way that philosophical appeals to neuroscience are increasingly common, thoroughly exploring the epistemic implications of predictive coding should be useful to several scholarly communities. This chapter is about how the brain and its neural operations are related to the world—that amounts to what I conceptually describe as the "world–brain relation."

Recent work in neuroscience seems to indicate that predictive coding is the main and overarching informational strategy of the brain (Friston, 2010). *Predictive coding* argues that the neural activity we observe in the brain in response to specific stimuli or tasks does not exclusively result from the stimulus or input alone but, rather from the comparison between the actual input and a predicted input. The brain itself generates a prediction or anticipation of an input, which is then matched and compared with the actual input. The difference between these is called the *prediction error*, which is taken to be the primary determinant of stimulus-induced activity in the brain.

Predictive coding is thus an empirical theory about how the brain operates and generates stimulus-induced or task-evoked activity thereby presupposing a prediction model of brain. The relevance of predictive coding and its prediction model of brain extends beyond the merely empirical domain of neuroscience, however. It is commonly taken to have significant epistemic implications. The main issue is whether allegiance to the empirical doctrine of predictive coding entails that the brain be construed as an inferentially secluded system.

Jacob Hohwy (2013, 2014) argues that predictive coding entails a self-evidencing brain that has no direct contact with the world and is therefore closed to and inferentially secluded from the world. Others disagree. For instance, Andy Clark (2012, 2013), argues that predictive coding is compatible with a conception of the brain as an open system. This is a tricky issue. One and the same neuronal mechanism, predictive coding, is associated with different and seemingly contradictory characterizations of the brain.

The first aim of this chapter is to argue that the brain can and should be characterized as both an open and closed system. These need not be taken to be contradictory descriptions if sufficient attention is paid to the differences between spontaneous (or resting state) and stimulus-induced activity in the brain. I use the concepts of spontaneous activity and resting state more or less interchangeably (see chapters 1 and 2 for more details on this point). The term *resting state* is usually used as an operational term denoting a behavioral condition, that is, the state of the brain in the absence of any specific tasks or stimuli. The term *spontaneous activity* emphasizes that such resting-state activity is not just independent of external stimuli but also generated by the brain itself.

Main Aims and Arguments

It is commonplace to think of the brain as subject to *stimulus-induced activity*—neural responses to events in the external world. That the brain is also subject to neural activity that is not related to specific stimuli or tasks but rather originates spontaneously within the brain itself, is less well known and too often neglected in discussions about the philosophical implications of neuroscience. I argue that this latter form of neural activity, so-called resting state, or spontaneous activity, is a means by which the brain references its own activity to elements of the external world—this provides the basis for a description of the brain as in part an open and world-evidencing system that includes the world–brain relation and the prediction model of brain.

The second aim of the chapter is to present some empirical facts about an extreme case wherein the resting state's alignment to the world is altered in an abnormal way. This extreme case is the brain of a schizophrenic, which can serve as an apparent counter-example to the description of the brain as an open system. The main question is whether some symptoms of schizophrenia, such as delusions and hallucinations, should be interpreted as complicating the picture of the brain as an open system with world–brain relation.

In the first part of the chapter, I show that the brain's resting state aligns to the world in a statistical way. Although I take this to be sufficient permission for deeming the brain an open system, it does entail that different brains can display different degrees of alignment to the world, that is, different types of world–brain relation.

In extreme cases such as schizophrenia, the resting state's statistically based alignment to the world can break down dramatically. The resulting hallucinations and delusions can be usefully investigated as a clinical analogue to the systematic deception that Descartes imagined perpetrated by an "evil demon" and that appears in the debate between Hohwy and Clark. I conclude that because schizophrenia is an abnormal condition involving abnormal brains, there is good reason not to generalize such epistemic worries across the class of brains in general. In contrast, I suggest that the occurrence of schizophrenic hallucinations and delusions be interpreted as indicative of the fact that the brain's openness to the world is a highly intricate and therefore delicate phenomenon.

Part I: Predictive Coding and Stimulus-Induced Activity

Predictive Coding Ia: Actual and Predicted Inputs and the Prediction Error

Many early neuroscientists tended to conceive of the brain as mainly in the business of responding to stimulations from the outside world. This resulted in an emphasis on stimulus-induced or task-evoked activity (see also Raichle, 2009, for an overview). One of the things that functional imaging techniques such as electroencephalography (EEG), magnetoencephalography (MEG), positron emission tomography scan (PET), or functional magnetic resonance imaging (fMRI) can do even in the absence of sophisticated theories about neural activity is indicate how the brain responds to stimuli. Thus, many imaging studies seek to show how the brain's activity changes in response to particular conditions, such as the presence of a visual stimulus in the form of a picture. It was commonly assumed that such stimulus-induced activity was determined mainly, if not entirely by the features of the relevant stimulus. Raichle (2009, 2015a,b) described this framework as an "extrinsic view of the brain" (see also Northoff, 2014a).

This traditional view of the brain's stimulus-induced or task-evoked activity has been placed into doubt by predictive coding. Specific stimuli or tasks are no longer considered sufficient by themselves to account for the activity changes associated with the brain's response to stimuli. Instead, what we observe as activity change during stimulus-induced or task-evoked activity results from a process whereby the brain generates predictions of impending input and compares this content to the actual input it receives from the world.

The predicted input is called the *empirical prior.* Once the actual stimulus arrives, it is set and compared against the empirical prior; if the actual stimulus is identical to the predicted one, the former will not induce any activity change; if in contrast, the actual stimulus diverges from the predicted one, the former will induce strong activity change. The resulting activity change, that is, stimulus-induced or task-evoked activity, thus reflects *prediction error*, the degree to which the actual input deviates from the predicted input.

Some of the clearest examples of predictive coding occur in the visual cortex (see, e.g., Alink, Schwiedrzik, Kohler, Singer, & Muckli, 2010; Egner, Monti, & Summerfield, 2010; Langner et al., 2011; Rauss, Schwartz, &

Pourtois, 2011; Spratling, 2010, 2012a,b). I discuss here one representative study by Rao and Ballard (1999). They approached the question of whether higher visual cortical regions carry predictions for lower ones in terms of *feedback connections*. The basic idea is that when neural activity in a lower visual area is dependent on that of a higher region, one can safely assume that the latter carries a predicted input for the former. In order to test this assumption, Rao and Ballard applied a computational simulation model of neural activity in lower and higher visual regions.

This allowed them to test the mathematical description of predictive coding. At the time, it would not have been possible to carry out a comparable investigation using functional brain imaging and nonsimulated data. Rao and Ballard (1999) (see also Doya et al., 2011, for an interesting extension concerning decision making) demonstrated that feedback connections from higher to lower cortical areas carry predictions of visual input, which is processed by lower regions' activities. *Lower regions* refer to those regions that are more proximally responsive to stimuli whereas *higher regions* refer to parts of the visual cortex that are more distally responsive.

The lower regions include the primary visual cortex, or V1, where information is received from subcortical regions, such as the lateral geniculate nucleus. This process is followed by subsequent processing of the same visual stimulus in the secondary visual cortex, or V2, a "higher" region. These higher visual regions seem to carry signals that aim at anticipating the incoming visual stimuli processed in the lower regions, for example, V1. The "anticipations" generated in the higher regions are a part of *feedforward* connections, which are involved in processing discrepancy between the predictions and the actual sensory input.

These findings from the visual cortex show that the brain generates predicted input that is then compared with actual input. This should clarify the sense in which the doctrine of predictive coding takes actual stimuli from the environment as insufficient to account for stimulus-induced or task-evoked activity. The actual stimulus is a necessary but nonsufficient condition that has to be complemented by a predicted input (or stimulus or task) to generate stimulus-induced or task-evoked activity.

Predictive Coding Ib: Predicted Input and Rest–Stimulus Interaction

The study described above just investigated the visual cortex. Karl Friston (2010) proposes a more general hierarchical architecture that posits bottom-up processing of the actual sensory input in the sensory cortex and top-down processing of the same by more cognitive regions in the prefrontal cortex. In addition to the lowermost and uppermost regions of the sensory and the prefrontal cortex, there are many other regions sandwiched in between, whose interrelations need to be explained.

Friston argues that particular regions can serve as both lower and higher nodes in the hierarchy relative to other levels. One region may serve as a higher level of processing relative to another by contributing predictions concerning activation patterns in the latter. The same region may serve as a lower processing level to another region that generates predictions concerning the former's operations. Since the same region's neural activity serves as both predicted input (for the next-lower one) and actual input (for the next-higher one), continuous matching and comparison processes occur between lower and higher regions' neural activities (Friston, 2010).

These continuous matching and comparison processes occur throughout the whole brain enabling the generation of prediction errors at each processing level (Friston, 2010). Clearly, this makes predictive coding a hugely complicated process. At least one thing is clear, however. The anticipated inputs must be generated prior to processing of the actual input or they would not be in place to function as predictions. This means that the level of activity prior to the onset of a stimulus, the prestimulus resting-state activity, must encode the predicted input. The interaction between predicted and actual input may consequently be described as interaction between prestimulus resting state and the actual stimulus. This has been described as rest–stimulus interaction (Northoff, 2014a; Northoff, Qin, & Nakao, 2010). Although the exact neuronal mechanisms underlying such rest–stimulus interaction are currently far from understood (Huang, Zhang, Longtin et al., 2017; Northoff, 2014a, for first steps), that there is some such interaction and that it is important for predictive coding are well-supported claims.

Predictive Coding IIa: Rest–Stimulus Interaction

Various spatial and temporal metrics can be used to measure resting-state activity. Spatial measures such as fMRI target different neural networks, allowing for measurements based of functional connectivity within the networks themselves as well as between different networks (Cabral,

Kringelbach, & Deco, 2013; Menon, 2011; Raichle et al., 2001). Temporally, resting-state activity can be measured in electrophysiological or magnetic activity as with EEG or MEG. These techniques target neural activity changes in different frequency ranges, as well as the phenomenon of *cross-frequency coupling,* which refers to cases of activity in one frequency range being causally related to activity in another frequency range (Cabral et al., 2013; Engel, Gerloff, Hilgetag, & Nolte, 2013; Ganzetti & Mantini, 2013).

One can also measure the brain's resting-state activity in psychological terms. The brain's resting-state activity (especially in the default-mode network, or DMN) has been shown to be associated with mind wandering (Mason et al., 2007), random thoughts (Doucet et al., 2012), or self-generated thoughts (Smallwood & Schooler, 2015). Psychologically, resting-state activity seems to specialize in internally generated mental activity (such as thoughts or imagery) as distinguished from externally generated mental contents (such as perceptions).

A recent fMRI study focusing on the auditory cortex (Sadaghiani, Hesselmann, & Kleinschmidt, 2009) shows that resting-state activity impacts stimulus-induced activity and associated perception of objects and events in the world. The investigators had subjects perform an auditory detection task and presented broadband noise stimuli in unpredictable intervals of 20–40 ms. The subjects had to press a button when, and only when, they thought they heard the target sound; otherwise, they were not to hit the button. This allowed the researchers to compare the neural activity preceding hits with the neural activity preceding instances of subjects failing to detect the target sound.

Interestingly, successful detection was preceded by significantly higher prestimulus activity in the auditory cortex in comparison to misses. This was complemented by another analysis of the same data (Sadaghiani, Poline, Kleinschmidt, & D'Esposito, 2015) wherein it was indicated that certain neural networks such as the DMN showed enhanced functional connectivity prior to the onset of those auditory stimuli that were detected.

Taken together, these studies and others (see Northoff, 2014a; Northoff et al., 2010) show that the resting state exerts a strong impact on the contents of our perception. The resting state's prestimulus activity level seems to be central in determining the contents that we subsequently perceive (see Hohwy, 2013, 2014, for more details).

Sadaghiani, Hesselmann, et al. (2010) explain that their findings concerning prestimulus activity are compatible with predictive coding. The higher the levels of prestimulus activity, the more likely that a specific predicted input (as distinguished from others) is generated. In contrast, lower levels of prestimulus activity may then be assumed to reflect the generation of ambiguous or vague predicted inputs.

The resulting stimulus-induced activity may then be traced to the interaction between the predicted input, as reflected in the prestimulus activity levels, and the actual input, the auditory tone. The better subjects predicted the auditory tone, the higher their levels of prestimulus resting-state activity, and the more likely they were to detect the tone. This makes it clear that stimulus-induced activity (and its associated behavioral and phenomenal effects) is dependent on the level of prestimulus resting-state activity, which provides one example of rest–stimulus interaction.

Predictive Coding IIb: Predicted Input—Brain as a Self-Evidencing and Closed System

One aspect of the traditional view of stimulus-induced activity mentioned above is the idea that the stronger the actual stimulus, the stronger the degree or amplitude of the resultant stimulus-induced activity. According to this traditional picture, since stimulus-induced activity is exclusively determined by the stimulus itself, the brain and its stimulus-induced activity can be regarded as an open system. Being an open system involves the brain setting or referencing its stimulus-induced activity against the actual stimulus and thus, more generally, the environment or the world. The scenario changes though once one accepts predictive coding.

In the case of predictive coding, stimulus-induced activity is no longer exclusively determined by the actual stimulus but also by the predicted input. Predictive coding entails that stimulus-induced activity depends on the degree to which actual and predicted input match or converge: the more predicted and actual input differ from each other, the stronger the resulting stimulus-induced activity.

If, in contrast, they do not diverge from each other, the degree of stimulus-induced activity will be rather low irrespective of the degree or intensity of the actual input itself. The stimulus-induced activity is consequently no longer set or referenced against the actual input and the environment or world but, rather, against the brain's activity itself. The brain may consequently be characterized as a closed system.

There is therefore something right about Hohwy's (2013, 2014) claim that the brain is a self-evidencing system. The degree to which the brain reacts to stimuli related to events and objects in the world is mitigated by the brain itself. The brain's ongoing resting-state activity is as important a contributor as the objects or events of perception themselves.

Thus, if the case made above for the claim that resting-state activity constitutes the predicted input is accepted, then there is reason to believe that the brain is indeed a self-evidencing system that is operationally closed to and inferentially secluded from the world. If we were to stop here, it would seem fair to say that the world's objects and events can at best impact the brain in an indirect way.

Predictive Coding IIc: Predicted Input—Auditory Hallucination

This characterization of the brain as a closed and self-evidencing system has major epistemic implications. The fact that the brain's predictive coding is based on closed and inferentially secluded processes opens the door for skepticism. It remains impossible for us to rule out the possibility that the objects or events we perceive are more related to the predicted input and hence to the brain's resting state (and its spatiotemporal structure) rather than directly to the objects or events themselves. Such an internalist model of knowledge may be most visible in extreme cases where the predicted input completely overrides the impact of the actual input.

The overriding of the actual input by the predicted input seems to occur for instance in patients with schizophrenia who suffer from delusions and hallucinations. The events or objects in both delusions and hallucinations are internally generated in the brain's resting state in the form of predicted inputs that seem to be abnormally strong such that they override (and ultimately preempt) the would-be impact of the actual input (Adams, Stephan, Brown, Frith, & Friston, 2013; Corlett, Taylor, Wang, Fletcher, & Krystal, 2010; Corlett, Honey, Krystal, & Fletcher, 2011; Fletcher & Frith, 2009; Fogelson, Litvak, Peled, Fernandez-del-Olmo, & Friston, 2014; Ford et al., 2014; Horga, Schatz, Abi-Dargham, & Peterson, 2014; Jardri & Denève, 2013; Notredame, Pins, Deneve, & Jardri, 2014).

For instance, in the case of auditory hallucination there is solid empirical evidence for increased resting-state activity in the auditory cortex (Northoff, 2014b; Northoff & Qin, 2011). Such increased resting-state activity may lead to the constitution of abnormally strong predicted inputs that are no longer impacted by any actual input anymore. The internally generated predicted inputs may be so strong as to operate as quasi-actual input with the result that subjects hear illusionary voices, that is, experience auditory hallucinations. The brains of schizophrenics, thus, confuse predicted and actual input, taking the former for the latter. These patients no longer react much to externally occurring inputs, paying low amounts of attention to external sounds while preserving a keen focus on the hallucinated voices.

This theory is supported empirically by the observation that stimulus-induced activity related to external auditory stimuli is abnormally low in some schizophrenics (Northoff, 2014b; Northoff & Qin, 2011). In this situation, the resting state itself constitutes a rather strong predicted input that cannot be modulated anymore by external auditory input. The resulting prediction error, that is, the "stimulus-induced activity" in the auditory cortex, consequently reflects mainly the predicted input with just a marginal contribution from external auditory stimuli. The subjects therefore perceive contents encoded by predicted input, rather than from the external auditory input.

What does such aberrant predictive coding in schizophrenia imply for characterizing the brain? The brain in schizophrenia may indeed be closed to the world (in their world–brain relation) to a higher degree than in healthy subjects. This involves a breakdown of the normally functioning indirect inference of events and objects carried out through predictive coding. For schizophrenic patients, the balance between internally generated predicted inputs and externally generated actual input is shifted abnormally toward the former.

What in the normal case serves as an internally generated reference, for example, the predicted input, against which the externally generated events and objects, including the actual input, is matched and compared, operates now as actual input by itself. The brain's neural activity is consequently closed to the world to a higher degree than in healthy subjects where the predicted input can still be modulated and impacted by the actual input.

Part II: Prediction Model and the Spontaneous Activity's Statistically Based Alignment to the World

Prediction Model Ia: Spontaneous Activity and the World–Brain Relation

I have so far traced the predicted input back to the resting state and its specific spatial (e.g., relations between networks) and temporal (e.g., relations between low and high frequencies) features. But how are the resting state itself and its spatiotemporal structure generated and shaped? It is important to address this question since the predicted input is generated by the resting state. The resting state's spatiotemporal structure including its origin should consequently surface in the predicted input itself.

Although the resting state's various spatial and temporal features are present in the adult brain, they are only present as predispositions in the infant brain. This means that the resting state's spatiotemporal structure is strongly experience-dependent one (see also Duncan et al., 2015; Nakao, Bai, Nashiwa, & Northoff, 2013; Sadaghiani & Kleinschmidt, 2013). The concept of experience-dependence means that features of the resting state and its spatiotemporal structure are shaped by the experiences of subjects. For instance, early developmental experiences may have a major impact on the spatiotemporal structure of the resting state.

A recent study showed the resting state's spatiotemporal structure in adulthood to be predictive of subjects having incurred childhood trauma (Duncan et al., 2015; Nakao et al., 2013). Specifically, the degree of entropy (i.e., the degree of disorder in neural activity across time) in the resting state of adults predicted the degree of early childhood trauma: the higher the degree of early childhood trauma, the higher degree of entropy in the resting state's spatiotemporal structure in adulthood (Duncan et al., 2015).

This shows that early experiences can be encoded into the resting state's spatiotemporal structure and can persist thereafter for rather long time frames. The resting state and its spatiotemporal structure may consequently be likened to a mirror of our experience with the world and may therefore be characterized as "experience-dependent." Such "experience-dependence" of the brain's spontaneous activity is possible only when it is continuously linked or coupled and thus related to the world. This phenomenon constitutes what I describe as the "world–brain relation."

Prediction Model Ib: The Spontaneous Activity's Statistically Based Alignment to the World

In order to encode life events into its spatiotemporal structure, the brain's resting-state activity must somehow align to these events. What are the neural mechanisms of such alignment? To discuss this, I will focus on a study by Stefanics et al. (2010). These authors conducted an EEG study in healthy human subjects. Subjects were presented with target tones to which they had to react by pressing a button, thus yielding a reaction time.

Preceding the target tone, the investigators presented different cue stimuli (also tones, although with a different frequency than the target tone) that indicated the probability of the subsequent target tone's occurrence. In the first experiment four different cue tones were presented, one indicating 10 percent; the second, 37 percent; the third, 64 percent; and the fourth a 91 percent probability of the target tone's occurrence. Depending on the degree of probability indicated by the cue tone, it was followed either by a target tone or by another cue tone a certain percentage of the time.

Following previous data from Schroeder and Lakatos (2009a,b), the authors focused on slow-frequency oscillations in the delta range and their entrainment of faster-frequency oscillations (such as gamma). This approach was adopted because the investigators suspected the slow-fast-frequency entrainment to be related to the statistical probability of the stimulus's occurrence across time.

What were the findings of Stefanics and colleagues (2010)? As expected, they demonstrated that the reaction time (time needed for the response to target tones) was significantly faster in those trials (target tones) where the preceding cue tones correlated with higher probability. The higher the probability indicated by the cue tone, the faster subjects were able to react. This pattern was observed in both experiments. The subjects thus had been able to learn the probability of the tones.

Does this entail predictive coding with the generation of a predicted input? In order to demonstrate that, one would need to omit the tone at some instances. If the subjects then still showed the same behavioral and neural reaction as in the presence of the tone, those reactions must then be based on a predicted input (since there would be no actual input). The data do indeed confirm that assumption as is discussed below. First, I want to briefly discuss the EEG data.

The EEG data show that the phase of delta oscillation was significantly shifted and aligned, or *entrained* as is said in neuroscience, to the onset of the target tone as manifest in a significant phase preference. The target tone's onset was especially locked to the negative phase, that is, the negative deflection in the ongoing cycle of the fluctuations in the delta range. The phase locking was much higher in response to the cue tones indicating higher probability of subsequent target tones.

How is such phase locking possible? It is possibly only if the phases of the delta oscillations actively shift their onsets toward the predicted or expected onsets of the target tone. This is indeed confirmed by the data that showed that higher predictability of the target tone's onset as indicated by the cue tone induced higher degrees of phase shifting of the delta oscillation's phase onset. Such a relation between the phase shifting and the predictability of the target tone suggests that the phase onsets are aligned, that is, entrained by the probability of the target tone rather than by its actual presence. The higher the probability of the target tone, the more likely the phase shift occurs irrespective of whether the target tone turns out to occur or not.

However, how is it possible that the phase shift is dependent on the probability rather than the presence of the tone? It is possible because the phase shift reflects the prediction of the actual input, the predicted input, rather than presence of the actual input itself. By indicating higher probability of the target tone, the cue tone makes it easier for the brain to generate a proper prediction, the predicted input, which neurally is manifested in the observed phase shift (see van Atteveldt, Murray, Thut, & Schroeder, 2014).

More generally, one may say that the phase onset of the delta oscillations followed the expected natural statistics of the target tone. Different probabilities of the target tone's occurrence led consequently to different degrees of phase shifting. These results thus provide empirical support for the claim that the resting state encodes the probability of stimuli in the world and as such accounts for the world–brain relation.

By shifting the phase onsets of especially low-frequency fluctuations such as delta oscillations, the resting-state activity can encode the statistically based temporal (and spatial) differences between different stimuli (see van Atteveldt et al., 2014, for an overview of other pertinent results). If that is true, one would expect that a high probability cue tone without the subsequent presence of the actual tone should lead to the same behavioral and neural reaction as occurs on those occasions when the target tone does occur. This is indeed the case as demonstrated by a second experiment in the study by Stefanics et al. (2010), which is discussed below.

Prediction Model IIa: Brain's Resting State as Open and World-Evidencing System—Stochastically Based World–Brain Relation

Empirically, one may consider the delta phase shifting to be an example of stimulus-induced activity rather than resting-state activity. Each auditory tone induces stimulus-induced activity that can be traced to rest–stimulus interaction between predicted and actual input and the resulting prediction error (see van Atteveldt et al., 2014, for such an interpretation). If so, delta phase shifting would not add anything new to the interpretation of the brain's predictive coding activity as exemplary of a closed system. However, this sort of phase shifting is related to the resting state rather than stimulus-induced activity.

The results described above were demonstrated in the first experiment by Stefanics et al. (2010), where the prediction and thus the expected stimulus onset fell together with the onset of the presentation of the target tone. Hence, it remains impossible to disentangle the effects of the resting state from those induced by the target tone itself. To address this, the investigators conducted a second experiment.

The second experiment presented the same target tone but now varied its temporal relation to the cue tones by presenting the target tone either early, right after the cue tone, or rather late. Both early and late target presentations were preceded by two different cue tones that either indicated 20 percent or 80 percent target-tone occurrence. This allowed the experimenters to investigate especially the late-target tone trials when an early target tone was expected (with especially high probability of 80 percent) but not delivered.

In those trials where a cue tone indicating high probability (80 percent) was followed by a late target tone, delta oscillations were locked in their phase to the expected onset of the target even though it was not delivered (because it was a late–target tone trial). Such delta-phase entrainment was observed in conditions where cue tones (20 percent, 80 percent) were followed by late target trials (rather than early target trials). And as in experiment 1, the phase locking to the expected target tone onset was significantly higher in those trials with high-probability cue tones (80 percent) when compared to those with low-probability cues (20 percent). The delta oscillations' phase onsets were thus shifted to the expected target-tone onsets, even if they were not actually delivered.

What does this experiment tell us about the predicted input? By being exposed to the prior cue tones, the resting state generates a predicted input which, if sufficiently strong in the degree to which the input is predicted, will be exerted even in the absence of an actual tone. Neuronally, this is realized by the delta phase shift in the in those trials where the target tone is actually not presented.

Most importantly, this and other studies (see Northoff, 2014b, as well as van Atteveldt et al., 2014, for details) support the view that the resting state's spatiotemporal structure (as for instance its delta phase onsets) are statistically based (rather than one single stimulus). The resting state's delta phase in particular and its temporal structure in general are based on the statistical occurrence of myriad stimuli across time in the environment rather than based on the occurrence of a single stimulus at one particular point in time. This amounts to a stochastically based world–brain relation.

Prediction Model IIb: Brain's Resting State as Open and World-Evidencing System—Empirical and Conceptual Confusion?

The data about delta phase shifting can only be obtained by considering several stimuli and, more specifically, their statistical frequency (probability) distribution across time. A longer time scale such as this differs significantly from those presupposed in the data by Stefanics et al. (2010) and the other data about prestimulus effects described earlier. There, the time scale is extremely short covering only single stimuli while neglecting the impact of different stimuli in the brain's neuronal activity across time.

Quite generally, studies of stimulus-induced activity focus on the neural activity related to single stimuli at a particular point in time thus neglecting resting-state activity, the study of which requires observing the brain's response to several stimuli over time. Due to its dependence on the statistically based occurrence of stimuli across time, phase shifting in general and delta-phase shifting in particular should be associated with resting-state activity (see also Klein, 2014).

Single stimuli are usually presented for several milliseconds or seconds that impact neural activity within this rather short time frame. Resting-state activity, in contrast, presupposes a much longer time scale. As we have seen in the previous section, resting state is not restricted to one particular brief stimulus mimicking a single auditory tone at one particular point in time. Instead, resting-state activity seems to encode information concerning a much longer time scale that extends over several tones (as in the experiment by Stefanics et al., 2010) or even years (as in the childhood trauma data). This makes it clear that neural activity in resting state and stimulus-induced activity operate on different time scales.

What does this imply for our characterization of the brain in general? The resting state aligns itself in terms of an "extra-neuronal loop" (Clark, 2013) to the statistically based temporal and spatial structure of objects and events in the world. It is not, therefore, closed and inferentially secluded when referring to and measuring its own resting-state activity against input from actual stimuli. Andy Clark, one of the main proponents of the view of the brain as an open system, also emphasizes the statistical nature of the brain's neural activity and bases his account of predictive coding on it (Clark, 2013, pp.4 and 8). He does not yet make the distinction, however, between resting state and stimulus-induced activity, which puts his account of predictive coding in direct opposition and seemingly logical contradiction to that of Hohwy (2013, 2014) (see figure 3.1).

It may be odd, but it is not contradictory for me to have characterized the brain as both open and closed to the world. This is not contradictory once one embraces the distinction between resting state and stimulus-induced activity. The brain's stimulus-induced or task-evoked activity as its response to specific stimuli or tasks is indeed closed to and inferentially secluded from the world: it is generated in relation to the brain's predicted input and its prestimulus resting-state activity level reflecting an "*intra*neuronal loop."

In contrast, this does not apply to the brain's resting-state activity that is aligned to the world in a statistically and spatiotemporally based way. The brain's resting-state activity is consequently aligned and open to the world because it is part of an "*extra*neuronal loop" as Clark (2013) describes it.

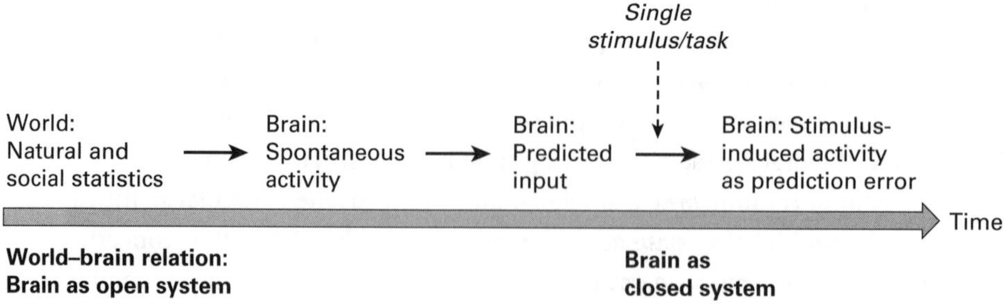

Figure 3.1
Brain as an open and closed system.

By looping outside itself into the world, the brain (and its resting state as I would add to Clark's case) becomes open to the world.

Prediction Model IIIa: The Brain's Openness to the World—Empirical and Epistemological Meanings of "Open"

Why is the encoding of the statistical occurrence of stimuli by resting-state activity important in this context of interpreting predictive coding? The predicted input is generated by the resting state and, more specifically, the prestimulus resting state. That by itself can lead to the adoption of the view that the brain is a closed and self-evidencing system. However, if the resting state itself encodes the statistical occurrence of stimuli, perhaps it should not be conceived of as a closed system. Instead, the resting state may then be considered an open system that references or sets its own activity level against the statistical occurrence or probability of stimuli in the world or in the environment.

However, we have to be careful here with what exactly we mean by "open." The concept of "open" can be taken in an empirical or epistemological sense. If taken in a purely empirical way, it simply means that the brain's resting-state activity by itself has direct access to the external world in that it encodes the statistical frequency distributions of external stimuli from the world. The question guiding the empirical meaning of "open" is: "How is the brain's spontaneous or resting-state activity related to external stimuli in the world?"

This purely empirical meaning of "open" is much weaker than its epistemological sibling. The epistemological meaning of "open" entails not only direct contact (as in the empirical meaning) but, much stronger, that what is encoded into the brain's resting-state activity reflects the truth. The question guiding the epistemological sense of "open" is: To what extent should a process of statistical alignment between the predicted inputs of the brain and events in the world be taken to confirm the world–brain relation as truth preserving?

The distinction between empirical and epistemological meanings of "open" is especially important in the philosophical context. The philosopher concerned by the Cartesian demon might reject the openness of the mind, in the epistemological sense of "open." The empirical and epistemological meanings of "open" can dissociate from each other, however. The case of schizophrenia already described is an instance where a degree of empirical openness is accompanied by seemingly more pressing epistemological closedness. The brain, despite being empirically open, can fail to be world-evidencing in severe schizophrenia. Although empirically open, the schizophrenic's brain may nevertheless be closed epistemologically. This complication is explored below.

Prediction Model IIIb: The Brain's Openness to the World in Schizophrenia—Exclusion of the Cartesian Demon?

I pointed out that delta phase locking is central in aligning the brain's spontaneous activity to external stimuli in the world. However, what if the described phase locking and thus the resting state's "extra-neuronal loop" do not function properly anymore? That seems to be the case in schizophrenia (Lakatos, Schroeder, Leitman, & Javitt, 2013). Using essentially the same design as Stefanics et al. (2010), Lakatos et al. (2013) recently conducted an EEG study in schizophrenic patients to whom they presented a stream of auditory stimuli (i.e., tones) with regular, that is, rhythmic interstimulus intervals (1500 ms). The stream of auditory stimuli included some deviant stimuli (20 percent) that were distinguished in their frequency. Healthy and schizophrenic subjects had either to listen passively (passive task), detect the easily detectable deviant stimuli (easy task), or detect the more difficult (variation by frequency) detectable stimuli (difficult task).

Schizophrenic patients did show a much lower degree of delta phase locking in response to the onsets in the stream of auditory stimuli when compared to healthy subjects. Moreover, the degree to which delta phase locking was impaired correlated with the severity of a subject's psychopathological symptoms of hallucinations and delusions. This strongly suggests that the degree of phase alignment or entrainment is closely related to the kind of objects or events one perceives. If the resting state can properly align itself to the statistically based temporal (and spatial) structure of objects and events in the world, the latter form the content in one's perception. In that case the looming threats of the actual occurrence of a Cartesian demon and skepticism are more or less (that is, in a statistically based way) excluded.

If, in contrast, the resting state can for some yet unclear reason no longer properly align itself to the objects and events in the world, the contents in perception and cognition become detached and dissociated from the events and objects in the world resulting in delusions and hallucinations as in schizophrenia. In that case the danger of a Cartesian demon resurfaces. This means that due to the statistically and spatiotemporally based nature of the resting state's alignment to the world, we remain unable to principally exclude the possibility of a Cartesian demon-like drift away from the world's objects and events. However, this only applies to extreme cases as in schizophrenia. In the "normal and healthy" case, our brain's resting state can align us to the world in a statistically and spatiotemporally based way: this amounts to a stochastically based world–brain relation.

Importantly, this means that the characterization of the brain's resting state in particular and the brain in general by openness to the world due to an "extraneuronal loop" does not necessarily exclude the remote possibility of a Cartesian demon-based skepticism. Still, we may consider the skepticism issue in a statistically based way. Statistically our brain's spontaneous activity or resting state aligns us to the world and keeps us open to its events and objects in most instances. Thus, taken in a statistical sense, our cognition and knowledge of the world can be secured in the majority of instances. This may be relevant for future epistemological discussion that then may also determine the concept of skepticism in a more detailed and sophisticated way.

The possibility of both the Cartesian demon and skepticism (in whatever epistemological–philosophical version) consequently rests ultimately on the statistically based degree to which our brain's resting-state activity is aligned with and open to the world. If the resting state's degree of statistically based alignment to the world tends toward zero as in the case of schizophrenia (with, for instance, low degrees or absent delta-phase shifting), the predicted inputs generated by the resting state no longer carry predictive value but are, instead, neurally mistaken for actual inputs. If, in contrast, our brain's spontaneous activity or resting state aligns us well to the world (with for instance high degrees of delta-phase shifting), our predicted inputs generated by our resting state carry a high degree of fidelity that minimizes the possible basis for Cartesian skepticism.

How does this affect our knowledge? Our knowledge of the world depends on the brain and its statistically based relation to the world, for example, the world–brain relation. On the basis of such a world–brain relation, we can generate models about the world including the world–brain relation. Those very same models (see chapters 2 as well as 9 and 10) are based on both brain, that is, brain-model dependent, and world, that is, world–model dependent (see chapters 9 and 10).

If our knowledge were only and exclusively dependent on the brain itself, for example, brain-model dependent, independent of world–brain relation and concurrent world-model dependence, the door for skepticism would be wide open. This is not the case however. Our brain's spontaneous or resting-state activity aligns itself to the world's statistical frequency distributions, or, the world–brain relation, which entails world-model dependence (see chapter 10 for details). That closes the door for skepticism and keeps it only minimally open, that is, in a statistical sense with low probability. This hinges strongly on the relationship between ontological and epistemological assumptions, an issue that will be central for reformulating the mind–body problem as the world–brain problem (see chapters 12–15).

Conclusion

I introduced predictive coding with predicted input and prediction error as one of the major models of the brain's neural activity in current neuroscience. On the level of model, this entails a prediction model of brain. The prediction model of brain raises the question whether the brain's neural activity is closed with respect to itself and thus self-evidencing, or, alternatively, whether the brain's neural activity is open to the world and thus world- rather than self-evidencing. The empirical data support the view of the brain as an open and world-evidencing system: these show that the brain's spontaneous or resting-state activity is aligned in a statistically based way to the statistical frequency distributions of events in the world, the world–brain relation.

Does our brain, with world–brain relation and the prediction model, open the door for the Cartesian demon and skepticism (in whatever version) in our cognition and knowledge of the world? The empirically informed philosopher may say that in the normal or healthy case, our cognition and knowledge reflect more or less, that is, in a statistically based way, the world as it is by itself. This is due to the brain and its spontaneous activity's or resting-state's statistically based alignment to the world. That however, so the traditional philosopher might claim, does not exclude the theoretical possibility of skepticism.

Accordingly, to reconcile both the empirically informed and the traditional philosopher, we cannot exclude in principal that our cognition and knowledge are infected by the Cartesian demon and skepticism. This however is exceedingly unlikely in the "normal" case but possibly prevalent in extreme cases such as those of schizophrenia. Accordingly, we cannot exclude the Cartesian demon and skepticism in an absolute sense. However, we can nevertheless say that, on statistical grounds, the probability of such a Cartesian demon and its skepticism is rather low if not minimal, except when one is in an extreme state such as schizophrenia.

II Models of Consciousness

4 Spectrum Model of Brain and Consciousness

Introduction

The spectrum model of brain refers to the hybrid nature of stimulus-induced activity as resulting from the impacts of both spontaneous activity and stimulus (see chapter 1). Although the spectrum model describes the neural activity in the brain including the relation between spontaneous and stimulus-induced activity, I left open whether that very same relation is also relevant for consciousness. That subject is the focus of this chapter.

Consciousness is not a homogenous entity. Instead, it is rather heterogeneous in that it includes different dimensions. One such dimension is the contents of consciousness such as the computer of which we are conscious (see Koch & Crick, 2003). Yet another dimension is the level of consciousness that refers to the arousal or the state of wakefulness of a person (see Laureys, 2005; see also Northoff, 2014b). The level of consciousness is often investigated in an indirect way. Patients who lose their level of consciousness as in disorders of consciousness such as sleep, anesthesia, or vegetative state (VS) may serve to reveal the neural correlates of the level of consciousness in an indirect way. I also pursue such indirect strategies in this chapter to investigate the relevance of the spectrum model of brain for the level of consciousness.

The general and overarching aim in this chapter is to investigate the relevance of both spectrum and interaction models of brain for the level of consciousness. My central argument is that the spectrum model of brain, on the basis of empirical evidence stemming from disorders of consciousness, is relevant for the level of consciousness. Specifically, I argue that the loss of the hybrid nature of stimulus-induced activity leads to loss of the level of consciousness in disorders of consciousness; this shifts these patients' stimulus-induced activities from the "hybrid middle" toward the passive pole of the spectrum.

Part I: Stimulus-Induced Activity and the Level of Consciousness

Empirical Findings Ia: Preservation of Stimulus-Induced Activity during the Loss of Consciousness

Adrian Owen (Owen et al., 2006) scanned a patient in VS as featured by loss of consciousness in functional magnetic resonance imaging (fMRI) and let him perform specific cognitive tasks. While lying in the scanner, the VS patient was instructed to perform motor and visual imagery tasks (Owen et al., 2006): the patient was asked to imagine playing tennis. Surprisingly this yielded neural activity in the supplementary motor area (SMA), a region typically associated with the initiation of either physical or imaginary movements, in the VS patient. This region is related to movements as one would imagine or would perform them when playing tennis either mentally or physically. Most interestingly, the same region was activated in more or less the same way in healthy subjects. Hence, the VS patient was apparently able to perform a cognitive task as complex as imagining playing tennis. The same holds, analogously, in yet another task, spatial navigation when imaging walking through the rooms of your house. As in the case of the motor imagery task, the spatial navigation task activated the same region, the parahippocampal gyrus, in the patient as in the healthy subjects). The fact that both patient and healthy subjects recruited and activated the same regions during the two tasks suggests that the patient was able to perform the tasks in the same way as the conscious healthy subjects. Therefore, one can conclude that the patient herself must be conscious since otherwise she could not have performed the tasks and activated the same regions as the healthy subjects. The results were recently replicated in a larger sample by Monti et al. (2010). Analogous paradigms were here conducted in a larger group of fifty-four patients, of whom twenty-three were diagnosed with VS and thirty-one with minimally conscious state (MCS) (Monti et al., 2010). They had to perform the same tasks, imagining playing tennis and imagining walking from room to room in their own house. Five patients (four VS, one MCS) were indeed able to willfully modulate their neural activity during the tasks in a proper way: imagining playing tennis led to activation in the SMA in all five patients.

Moreover, as in the single patient study, imagining walking and spatially navigating in the own house induced neural activity changes in the parahippocampal gyrus in three VS patients and in one MCS patient. These neural patterns were again similar to those in the healthy control subjects. Since then, other investigations of cognitive tasks requiring task-related efforts and willful modulation have been conducted in VS and MCS—they have all demonstrated some preserved neural activity in the relevant regions in these patients (see table 3 in Laureys & Schiff, 2012, for an overview).

Taken together, these findings show that stimulus-induced activity seems to be still present during the loss of consciousness as in VS and MCS (see also Laureys & Schiff, 2012). This is further supported by other findings in anesthesia where, despite the loss of consciousness, subjects still show stimulus-induced activity in response to sensory stimuli and cognitive tasks (see MacDonald et al., 2015, for review).

Empirical Findings Ib: Abnormal Stimulus-Induced Activity during the Loss of Consciousness

The above described studies applied mainly cognitive tasks (and sensory stimuli) in order to elicit stimulus-induced or task-evoked activity. One may also apply a different kind of stimulus, a magnetic stimulus as applied by transcranial magnetic stimulation (TMS), to probe stimulus-induced activity. This was done by Rosanova et al. (2012), who combined TMS-based application of a magnetic pulse with continuous electrophysiological recording through electroencephalography (EEG).

Rosanova et al. combined TMS and EEG in five patients with VS, five patients with MCS, and two patients with locked-in syndrome (LIS) (patients with LIS, who are conscious but cannot communicate with the outside world) (Rosanova et al., 2012). Five of these patients were investigated several times in different stages of improvement, VS, MCS, and a fully conscious state (with only three patients in the last stage). Magnetic impulses were applied via TMS on the right and left medial frontal (superior frontal gyrus) and parietal (superior parietal gyrus) cortex to probe these regions' neural activity changes in the resting state. The neural effects and especially the temporal and spatial spread and propagation of the magnetic stimulation were measured with simultaneous high-density, 264-channel EEG.

How did the VS patients' resting state react to the TMS pulse? The VS patients showed a simple positive–negative EEG response that remained local, short, and did not change at all. This contrasted with the MCS patients, for whom the TMS impulse triggered a more complex EEG response that spread both spatially and temporally and also changed over time. The pattern in MCS resembled more closely the pattern in the two LIS patients than the pattern in VS patients. A similar pattern was observed in the longitudinal investigation of the five patients who were investigated several times throughout improvement. Their response patterns became more complex and thus spatially and temporally more propagated in the three patients who recovered from VS over MCS to the fully conscious state. In contrast, neither the more-extended spatial and temporal propagation nor more-complex response patterns could be observed in the two patients who remained in VS.

Taken together, as in the case of sensory and cognitive stimuli or tasks, the findings demonstrate that the TMS pulse still elicits stimulus-induced activity during the loss of consciousness. This is further corroborated by analogous TMS-EEG findings in both anesthesia and sleep (see chapter 15 in Northoff, 2014b, for an overview). However, stimulus-induced activity in response to the magnetic pulse is abnormal in that it lacks proper spatial and temporal distribution: there is neither spatial expansion nor temporal propagation of stimulus-induced activity across different regions and in time. Accordingly, stimulus-induced activity by itself is still present. However, the spatiotemporal features of stimulus-induced activity including its degree of spatial expansion (see chapter 7 for details) change and become abnormal, that is, they are reduced and local rather than expanded and global, during the loss of consciousness.

Empirical Findings IIa: Integrated Information Theory

Before discussing the above described results, I want to introduce briefly the two main theories of consciousness as discussed in current neuroscience, the integrated information theory (IIT) (Tononi et al., 2016) and the global neuronal workspace theory (GNWT) (Dahaene & Changeux, 2011; Dahaene et al., 2014). Both consider a specific neuronal mechanism, either information integration or globalization of neuronal activity, to be central, that is sufficient, for consciousness (see Koch et al., 2016, for an overview).

Edelman (2003, 2004) and Seth, Izhikevict, Reeke, and Edelman (2006) consider cyclic processing and thus circularity within the brain's neural organization central for constituting consciousness (see also Llinás et al., 1998, 2002). Cyclic processing describes the reentrance of neural activity in the same region after looping and circulating in other regions via so-called reentrant (or feedback) circuits. This is, for instance, the case in primary visual cortex (V1): the initial neural activity in V1 is transferred to higher visual regions such as the inferotemporal cortex (IT) in feed-forward connections. From there it is conveyed to the thalamus, which relays the information back to V1 and the other cortical regions, implying thalamocortical reentrant connections (see also Tononi & Koch, 2008; as well as Lamme, 2006; Lamme & Roelfsema, 2000; van Gaal & Lamme, 2012). Consciousness and its contents are supposedly constituted on the basis of such feedback or reentrant connections that allow for cyclic processing (see also Edelman & Tononi, 2000).

What is the exact neuronal mechanism of the feedback or reentrant circuits? Reentrant circuits integrate information from different sources as associated with the neural activity in different regions and networks. This leads Tononi to emphasize the integration of information as the central neuronal mechanism in yielding and constituting the contents of consciousness. He consequently developed what he calls the "integrated information theory" (IIT; Tononi, 2004; Tononi & Koch, 2008; Tononi et al., 2016).

The IIT proposes the degree of information (as understood in a formal sense as in information theory rather than in common sense) that is linked and integrated central for consciousness: if the degree of integration of different information is low due to, for instance, disruption in functional connectivity between different regions, consciousness remains impossible. This is supported by experimental data that indeed show disruption of functional connectivity between different regions in various disorders of consciousness such as VS (Rosanova et al., 2012), non-REM (NREM) sleep (Qin et al., in revision; Tagliazucchi et al., 2013), and anesthesia (see Ferrarelli, Massimini et al., 2010).

To measure the degree of information integration across, for instance, different regions in the brain, Tononi and others (Seth et al., 2006, 2008; Seth, Barrett, & Barnett, 2011) developed specific quantifiable measures. Neurobiologically, Tononi postulates the integration of information to be particularly related to the thalamocortical reentrant connections. These reentrant connections process all kinds of stimuli from different sources and regions, thus remaining unspecific with regard to the selected content.

Such integration of different contents from different sources and regions is proposed to make possible the contents of consciousness and ultimately even their particular phenomenal quality, that is, qualia. In contrast, unconscious contents do not undergo such cyclic processing through the thalamus and the respectively associated information integration.

Empirical Findings IIb: Global Neuronal Workspace Theory

Another suggestion for the neural correlate of the contents of consciousness comes from Baars (Baars, 2005; Baars & Franklin, 2007) and others including Dehaene (Dehaene & Changeux, 2005, 2011; Dehaene, Changeux, Naccache, Sackur, & Sergent, 2006, for excellent overviews). They postulate global distribution of neural activity across many brain regions in a so-called global workspace central for yielding consciousness. If extended to the neuronal level, that very same global workspace may be found in specific circuits in the brain such as prefrontal and parietal cortex—Dehaene et al. (2014) therefore speak of a "neuronal global workspace theory," the GNWT (see below in this section and the next).

The information and its contents processed in the brain must be distributed globally across the whole brain in order for them to become associated with consciousness. If, inversely, information is only processed locally within particular regions but no longer globally throughout the whole brain, it cannot be associated with consciousness anymore. The main distinction between unconsciousness and consciousness is then supposed to be manifest in the difference between local and global distribution of neural activity. Hence, the global distribution of neural activity is here considered a sufficient condition and thus neural correlate of consciousness (NCC).

Dehaene and Changeux (2005, 2011) take the assumption of a global workspace of consciousness as starting point and determine it in more neuronal detail when suggesting what they call the global neuronal workspace theory (GNWT). They postulate that neural activity in the prefrontal–parietal cortical network is central for yielding consciousness. More specifically, the prefrontal–parietal cortical network has to be recruited by the single stimulus in order to link and recruit its cognitive function that is central for instantiating consciousness: that makes possible the global distribution and processing of the stimulus, which, in turn, is supposed to be central for constituting the contents of consciousness.

The global workspace theory must be distinguished from other cognitive theories of consciousness. Some accounts link attention and/or working memory closely to consciousness and its contents (see, e.g., Lamme, 2006; Lamme & Roelfsema, 2000; van Gaal & Lamme, 2011). However, recent investigations have shed some doubt on attention and/or working memory being implicated in selecting the contents of consciousness (see Graziano & Kastner, 2011; van Boxtel et al., 2010a,b). This is supported by recent analyses that demonstrated consciousness and attention (and other cognitive functions) to occur independently of each other (see Faivre et al., 2014; Koch et al., 2016; Koch & Tsuchiya, 2012; Lamme, 2010; Tononi & Koch, 2015; Tsuchiya et al., 2015; van Boxtel et al., 2010a,b).

Stimulus-Induced Activity Ia: Spatiotemporal Expansion versus Spatiotemporal Constriction

We are now ready to discuss the above-described results on stimulus-induced activity and the neuroscientific theories of consciousness with regard to the spectrum model of brain. The first question I raise is the following: What do these results tell us about the role of stimulus-induced activity for the level of consciousness? The findings show that stimulus-induced activity as elicited by either cognitive or magnetic stimuli is still present in subjects who have lost their consciousness. This leaves us with two choices with regard to the relation between brain and mental features.

Either one assumes that the presence of stimulus-induced activity is simply not relevant for consciousness—the presence of stimulus-induced activity does not entail the presence of consciousness. Stimulus-induced activity can therefore not be conceived a sufficient condition, that is, an NCC. One would consecutively need to search for other neuronal features beyond stimulus-induced activity that are sufficient for constituting consciousness. Supposing that the patients are indeed unconscious, these neuronal features may then be impaired in disorders of consciousness.

Or, alternatively, one may suppose that the subjects showing stimulus-induced activity are conscious rather than unconscious—the presence of stimulus-induced activity entails the presence of consciousness. The presence of stimulus-induced activity especially in response to cognitive tasks such as motor imagery or spatial navigation (of the patient's own house) can then be considered a neural correlate of consciousness, that is, NCC: the subjects must have understood the task requirement in order to elicit the observed stimulus-induced or task-evoked activity since otherwise, that is, in case they were unconscious and did not understand the instruction, they could not have elicited the observed neural activity changes.

The assumption that the patients must have understood the task instructions carries major clinical implications. The clinical diagnosis of the loss of consciousness and thus of VS in those patients showing the presence of stimulus-induced activity is simply wrong—neuronal evidence would then override clinical observation. This is indeed the conclusion current neuroscientists such as Adrian Owen and Stephen Laureys, two of the main investigators in the domain of VS, draw. They consider the presence of stimulus-induced or task-evoked activity in response to cognitive stimuli a neuronal marker for the presence of consciousness (see Bayne et al., 2016; Laureys & Schiff, 2012; Monti et al., 2010; Owen et al., 2006).

However, the data on TMS-induced stimulus-induced activity show that matters are not as clear-cut. Stimulus-induced activity is present here too. Does one therefore need to infer the presence of consciousness? Despite the presence of stimulus-induced activity in both conscious and unconscious subjects, there are nevertheless some differences between both groups. These differences concern mainly the spatiotemporal features of stimulus-induced activity.

The stimulus-induced activity in unconscious patients is neither as spatially extended (as to other regions and networks) nor as temporally propagated (as to more distal time points) in unconscious subjects. More generally, this means that stimulus-induced activity operates on a much more limited, that is, a more constricted, spatiotemporal range in the unconscious subjects—there is spatiotemporal constriction rather than spatiotemporal expansion.

Stimulus-Induced Activity Ib: Spatiotemporal versus Cognitive Features

What do I mean by "spatiotemporal expansion and constriction"? Roughly, the concept of spatiotemporal expansion describes the degree to which the stimulus-induced or task-evoked activity goes, that is, reaches, extends, or expands, beyond the specific discrete point in time and space at which the stimulus or task occurs and enters the brain.

Given that the stimulus-induced or task-evoked activity may extend, or expand, beyond the presence of the stimulus or tasks—the actual stimulus-induced or task-evoked activity may still be present even if the stimulus or task itself is already absent (see chapter 7 for more details on the concept of spatiotemporal expansion). If, in contrast, the presence of stimulus-induced or task-evoked activity is more limited in that it is tied and limited to the presence of the stimulus or task itself, one may speak of "spatiotemporal constriction."

What do the concepts of spatiotemporal expansion and constriction imply for consciousness? The above described TMS-EEG findings suggest that the spatiotemporal features of stimulus-induced activity rather than its mere presence or absence are central for constituting the level of consciousness. Stimulus-induced activity must show a certain yet unclear degree of spatiotemporal expansion in order to allow for assigning a certain level of consciousness to the stimulus. In contrast, spatiotemporal constriction of stimulus-induced activity, even if present, leads to the absence of consciousness. The sufficient condition of consciousness, that is, its neural correlate or NCC, can then be found in the degree of spatiotemporal expansion of stimulus-induced activity rather than in the latter's mere presence.

The advocate of stimulus-induced activity as NCC may now want to argue that such spatiotemporal characterization neglects its cognitive features. If the subjects can elicit stimulus-induced activity in response to cognitive tasks (see above), the subjects must have understood the cognitive demands, which is possible only if they are conscious. Stimulus-induced activity is taken here as index of cognitive function (Bayne et al., 2016) whose operation is possible only on the basis of consciousness being present.

That inference from the presence of cognitive function and operation to the presence of consciousness, as I say, a "cognitive–phenomenal inference," is, however, an assumption that is not supported by empirical data. Cognitive functions, even complex ones, can still be present even in the absence of consciousness thus operating in an unconscious rather than conscious mode (see Faivre et al., 2014, Mudrik et al., 2014, for strong empirical support in this direction). One can therefore not infer from the presence of cognitively based stimulus-induced activity the actual presence of consciousness.

The cognitive–phenomenal inference may thus be fallacious, a cognitive–phenomenal fallacy. This puts the supposed attribution of consciousness to those vegetative patients showing cognitively based stimulus-induced activity on rather shaky if not implausible empirical grounds. We must consequently search for neuronal features other than those related to the cognitive features of stimulus-induced activity to reveal the NCC.

Stimulus-Induced Activity IIa: Spatiotemporal Framing of GNWT and IIT

The data suggest that the spatiotemporal features of stimulus-induced activity are central for consciousness. Specifically, stimulus-induced activity must show a certain yet unclear degree of spatiotemporal expansion (as distinguished from spatiotemporal constriction) to serve as NCC. Where and how is the spatiotemporal expansion of stimulus-induced activity coming from? This leads us back to the different neuroscientific theories of consciousness most notably the theories of integrated information theory (IIT) and the global neuronal workspace (GNWT).

The GNWT presupposes spatial expansion of stimulus-induced activity when postulating the need for prefrontal and parietal cortical recruitment during stimulus-induced activity. Moreover, it presupposes temporal propagation when suggesting a later event-related potential such as the P300 to signify the presence of consciousness (Dehaene et al., 2014; Dehaene & Changeux, 2011). Because globalization of neural activity is based on spatiotemporal features, for example the expansion to prefrontal-parietal regions and later potentials such as P300, I speak of *spatiotemporal globalization*. Importantly, it may be the degree of expansion in both space, that is, to other regions, and time, to later time periods such as P300, that may be central for instantiating consciousness. Instead of the cognitive functions associated with neuronal globalization, I suppose the underlying spatiotemporal features central for consciousness.

The same holds analogously in the IIT. The above described results on the magnetically based stimulus-induced activity serve Tononi to support his IIT (Koch et al., 2016; Tononi & Koch, 2015). Specifically, he supposes that the spatiotemporally constricted stimulus-induced activity in unconscious subjects' indexes decreased integration of information. I now suppose that the decrease in spatiotemporal extension, that is, spatiotemporal constriction, is central for the loss of consciousness.

What Tononi and the IIT describe as decreased information integration may then be traced to decreased expansion of the spatial and temporal features of stimulus-induced activity, or the activity elicited by the TMS pulse. I thus suppose that information integration is about integration of spatial and temporal features as related to spatiotemporal expansion of stimulus-induced activity. In short, information integration is spatiotemporal integration (see chapter 7 for more details on this point).

Taken together, both GNWT and IIT are well compatible with the here-suggested spatiotemporal characterization of stimulus-induced activity as marker of consciousness. What they describe as globalization and information integration, as based on data, can be framed in terms of the spatiotemporal features of stimulus-induced or task-evoked activity. Therefore, I speak of spatiotemporal globalization and spatiotemporal integration to characterize GNWT and IIT in spatiotemporal terms. This leads me to a spatiotemporal model of consciousness, which will be developed in the second part of the book (chapters 7–8).

Stimulus-Induced Activity IIb: "Argument of Triviality"

The proponent of IIT and GNWT may now want to argue that the spatiotemporal framing is rather trivial. Given that any neural activity operates in time and space, both information integration and neuronal globalization are spatiotemporal by default. The assumption of globalization and information integration consecutively does not add any additional and novel information—the concepts of spatiotemporal globalization and spatiotemporal integration are trivial. This amounts to what I call the *argument of triviality*.

However, I reject the argument of triviality. The concepts of spatiotemporal expansion and spatiotemporal constriction show that one and the same stimulus or task can be processed in different ways, that is, expanded and constricted. The different ways can be distinguished on spatiotemporal grounds: the stimulus-induced activity can last longer or shorter and be spatially more or less distributed. Such spatiotemporal characterization of stimulus-induced activity seems to remain more or less independent of the stimulus or task itself. Instead, it seems to be dependent on the brain itself and, more specifically, what the brain itself adds and contributes to its own processing of the stimulus or tasks. Let me explicate this in the following way.

I propose that the brain's own addition to the neural processing of stimuli or tasks consists in the spatiotemporal features of stimulus-induced or task-evoked activity. Specifically, the brain's spontaneous activity adds a spatiotemporal dimension to its own processing of stimuli or tasks, tasks which then can be processed in either a spatiotemporally more expanded or more constricted way.

By adding the spatiotemporal dimension, the resulting stimulus-induced or task-evoked activity becomes more or less independent of the actual presence of the respective stimulus or task itself—the presence of stimulus-induced or task-evoked activity may then be well compatible with the absence of the actual stimulus or task itself. How is that related to consciousness? Based on the findings above, I postulate that the degree of spatiotemporal expansion of the stimulus-induced or task-evoked activity beyond the actual presence of the stimulus or task itself is directly related, that is, proportional to the level of consciousness.

The argument of triviality can thus be rejected. The brain can process one and the same stimulus in different ways that can be distinguished on spatiotemporal grounds, either constricted or expanded. The possibility of different ways of spatiotemporal processing of one and the same stimulus or task makes the spatiotemporal characterization of stimulus-induced or task-evoked activity anything but trivial. Moreover, the different ways of spatiotemporal processing provide a low-level dynamic neuronal mechanism for what IIT describes as integration (on an informational level) and GNWT as globalization (on a cognitive level). To neglect such a basic underlying level is to neglect that their difference, that is, whether constricted or expanded, leads to different behavioral outcomes (see chapter 7 for the argument of triviality).

Stimulus-Induced Activity IIc: From the "Spectrum Model" of Brain to Consciousness

Where and how does such spatiotemporal expansion of stimulus-induced activity originate if not in the stimulus or task itself? I indicated that the brain's spontaneous activity contributes the spatiotemporal dimension, which I propose is central for consciousness. One would consequently expect differences in the brain's spontaneous activity during the presence and absence of consciousness.

We recall that the spectrum model of brain (chapter 1) conceived stimulus-induced activity in a hybrid way. Stimulus-induced activity is neither exclusively and sufficiently associated with the stimulus itself (either a cognitive or a magnetic stimulus) nor with the spontaneous activity. Instead, the spectrum model postulates that stimulus-induced activity must be considered hybrid, that is, a mixture between the impact of the spontaneous activity and the impact of the stimulus.

What does the spectrum model of brain imply for consciousness? Following the spectrum model of brain, we need to search for the spontaneous activity and how it is altered in those unconscious subjects that show spatiotemporally constricted stimulus-induced activity in response to either cognitive or magnetic stimuli. This leads us back to the brain's spontaneous activity and its temporal structure and how they are altered in disorders of consciousness.

Part II: Spontaneous Activity and the Level of Consciousness

Empirical Findings Ia: Spontaneous Activity and Its Temporal Structure—Power Law Exponent and Cross-Frequency Coupling

We have already discussed that the brain's spontaneous activity can be characterized by an elaborate spatiotemporal structure (chapter 1). I now point out two temporal features, namely the power law exponent (PLE) and cross-frequency coupling (CFC) that, as we discuss below, will prove relevant for consciousness.

He (He, Zempel, Snyder, & Raichle, 2010) analyzed electrocorticographic data, measuring local field potentials of patients with epilepsy who underwent surgery. She analyzed data during REM sleep, slow- wave sleep (SWS), and in the awake state. First, she analyzed the power spectra (plotted in log-log coordinates) thus showing the PLE that refers to the relation in power between slower and faster frequency fluctuations; it followed the typical distribution with faster frequencies showing higher power and lower frequencies exhibiting lower power than slower frequencies. She also observed different peaks of power during SWS (0.8 Hz, 12 Hz) and the awake state (alpha, beta, theta).

Second, the PLE was estimated for five different subjects in the three conditions (awake, REM, SWS) for low (< 0.1 Hz) and high (>1–100 Hz) frequency ranges. Interestingly, no significant differences in the PLE could be yielded among the three different states (awake, REM, SWS, as calculated by effect of arousal state on the PLE).

Next, He (He et al., 2010) investigated the phase-amplitude coupling between slow and fast frequencies; the strength of such CFC was formalized by a modulation index (MI). The MI was obtained for all possible frequency pairs for all electrodes in 1-Hz frequency steps. Significant values of the MI, and thus nested frequencies (signifying cross-frequency, phase-amplitude coupling), were obtained for all three states (wakefulness, REM, SWS) across the entire frequency range.

She then demonstrated that the preferred phase in the slower frequency for coupling to the amplitude of the higher frequency clustered around the peak and the trough of the phase. The peak and trough reflect the most positive and most negative parts of the phase or cycle duration where it shows the highest and the lowest degrees of excitability.

Taken together, the data show that the brain's spontaneous activity is not random but rather highly structured by showing strong CFC with multiple phase-amplitude coupling from slow to fast frequency fluctuations. He (He et al., 2010) consequently assumed that this temporal structure operates in the background, against which any subsequent changes in neural activity, as for instance by external stimuli or tasks, occur and can be measured. Moreover, it seemed that the spontaneous activity's temporal structure as indexed by both PLE and CFC is more or less preserved during the loss of consciousness, as in sleep.

Empirical Findings Ib: PLE and CFC in Sleep and Anesthesia

Is the spontaneous activity's temporal structure as indexed by PLE and CFC really preserved during the loss of consciousness? Tagliazucchi et al. (2013) conducted an fMRI study in sixty-three subjects during the different stages of NREM sleep. Here the power spectrum as the relation between different frequencies was measured with the Hurst exponent (in a voxel-based analysis) during the transition from wakefulness to the different stages of NREM sleep (N1–N3 with the latter being the deepest).

Interestingly, they observed significant decay of the global Hurst exponent of the whole brain from wakefulness (where it was the highest) over N1 and N2 to N3, the deepest stage of NREM sleep. This means that the power spectrum and thus the degree of scale-free activity (as measured by PLE/DFA) significantly and progressively decrease during the different stages of NREM sleep. Such global decrease of the power spectrum was also observed in anesthesia using fMRI (Zhang et al., 2017). Zhang et al. (2017)

observed a global decrease of the PLE across the whole brain in the anesthetic state when compared to the awake state in the same subjects. This went along with a decrease in neuronal variability in the whole brain—the spontaneous activity thus did no longer exhibit as many spontaneous changes anymore in the anesthetic state.

What about the spatial and temporal features of the power spectrum decrease during the loss of consciousness? Let us start with the spatial dimension. More regionally specific effects were tested in a second step in the study by Tagliazucchi et al. (2013). Voxelwise comparison of the four stages (wakefulness, N1–N3) showed significant regional differences in the Hurst exponent in the frontal and parietal regions (that are associated with neural networks such as the DMN and the attention network) during N2 and N3 when compared to wakefulness (and N1). The deepest sleep stage, that is, N3, was associated with more widespread global decrease in the Hurst exponent in the frontal and parietal regions as well as in the occipital cortex and the visual network. In contrast, no major differences in the Hurst exponent could be detected in N1 when compared to wakefulness.

In addition, they also focused on the temporal dimension and, more specifically, on the different frequency ranges. The fMRI measures mainly infraslow frequency fluctuations (IFF) in the range between 0.01 to 0.1 Hz, whereas the EEG records faster frequencies ranging from 1 to 4 Hz (delta) to gamma (30–180 Hz). Tagliazucchi et al. (2013) now related the Hurst exponent as obtained in the infraslow range of fMRI (0.01–0.1 Hz) to the power of the delta frequency band (1–4 Hz) as recorded in a simultaneous EEG. The Hurst index (from fMRI) in the frontoparietal regions associated with DMN and attention networks correlated negatively with delta power (from EEG as averaged across all channels): the lower the Hurst index in the infraslow range (0.01–0.1 Hz), the higher the delta power (1–4 Hz).

These findings suggest a specific significance of the IFF, that is, 0.01 to 0.1Hz, for the level of consciousness (see also Northoff, 2017a, for a recent review). The decrease in the power spectrum (as measured with Hurst) indicates a power decrease in the very slow frequency ranges, such as 0.01 to 0.027 Hz that is featured as slow-5. Is slow-5 power specifically decreased during the loss of consciousness? This was indeed observed in anesthesia by Zhang et al. (2017), who found significant decrease in the power of slow-5 variability (rather than in slow-4, e.g., 0.027–0.073 Hz) during the anesthetic state.

In sum, these studies in sleep and anesthesia show significantly decreased power spectrum with specific power decrease in the infraslow ranges of 0.01 to 0.1 Hz in the whole brain during the loss of consciousness. However, the findings suggest that there is some grading from more local to global neuronal changes in both spatial and temporal dimensions during the transition from the awake to the deeply unconscious state. Most notably, the findings indicate special significance of especially the very slow fluctuations, the IFF as featured by their long cycle durations (with up to 100s), for the level of consciousness (see Northoff, 2017a, for more details).

Spontaneous Activity Ia: Temporal Relation and Integration

What do these findings tell us about the spontaneous activity and its spatiotemporal structure with regard to the level of consciousness? The spatiotemporal structure of the spontaneous activity can by itself be characterized by spatiotemporal relation and integration. We now explore the exact nature of these findings below.

The spontaneous activity shows an elaborate temporal structure. This temporal structure can be measured by the PLE that indexes the temporal relation in the power between infraslow, slow, and faster frequencies. The strongest power can be observed in the very lowest frequency ranges, that is, the IFF, whereas slow and faster frequency ranges show less power. Together, this results in the typical power spectrum that can be characterized as scale-free activity (He, 2011, 2014).

This temporal relation in the power among infraslow, slow, and faster frequencies is changed in altered states of consciousness. The above-described findings suggest that the power in the IFF in general and specifically in their slowest frequency range such as the slow-5 (0.01–0.027 Hz) is diminished in unconscious states such as anesthesia or deep sleep. That leads to decrease in PLE: the decrease in the power of the infraslow frequencies weakens the "temporal basement" upon which neural activity related to faster frequencies stands. The data suggest that that temporal basement is central for consciousness.

Taken together, these findings show that the spontaneous activity's temporal power relation among infraslow, slow, and faster frequencies is relevant for the level of consciousness. One may now want to argue that these findings only show the relevance of *temporal relation* but not of *temporal integration*. The relation in the power among the different frequencies is altered, but that does not yet tell us anything about temporal integration, that is, how the different frequencies are linked and integrated with each other.

For that, we need to investigate how the different frequencies are coupled and linked to each other as in cross-frequency coupling (CFC). The above described data show that there is indeed major CFC in the conscious brain that speaks in favor of temporal integration (that extends beyond simple temporal relation). Is such temporal integration as indexed by CFC also relevant for the level of consciousness? Abnormal, such as decreased CFC within the faster frequency ranges between 1 Hz and 60 Hz has been reported in anesthesia (see Lewis et al., 2012; Mukamel et al., 2011, 2014; Purdon et al., 2013, 2015). This leaves open, however, CFC between the infraslow and slow/faster frequency ranges. That has been tested in multiple simultaneous fMRI-EEG studies in conscious subjects that most often demonstrated a relation between infraslow frequencies (as in fMRI) on the one hand and delta and alpha frequencies (as in EEG) on the other (see Sadaghiani, Scherringa, et al., 2010).

As described above, unconscious subjects in sleep show IFF-delta power–power relationship though in an inverse, that is, negative way (see discussion directly above). However, whether that power–power relation between IFF and delta can be traced to the IFF-phase–delta-amplitude relation as usually measured in CFC remains unclear at this point. If so, one would suppose not just abnormal temporal relation but also a decrease in temporal integration in unconscious subjects. Such decrease in temporal integration may limit and thus constrict temporal continuity of the spontaneous activity across its different frequency ranges. This amounts to what I describe as *temporal constriction*. That very same temporal constriction of the spontaneous activity's temporal continuity may be central for the loss of consciousness as the authors of the above study suggest themselves (Tagliazucchi et al., 2013).

Spontaneous Activity Ib: Spatial Relation and Integration

What about spatial relation and integration? Spatial relation is usually indexed by functional connectivity that is based on a statistically based correlation between two (or more) regions' time series during the resting state. Several investigations have demonstrated reduced functional connectivity in disorders of consciousness such as sleep, anesthesia, and VS (see, e.g., Huang et al., 2014a,b, 2016; Qin et al., submitted; Vanhaudenhuyse et al., 2011). This suggests reduced spatial relation in spontaneous activity during the unconscious state.

Moreover, the findings in both sleep and anesthesia as described above clearly demonstrate the global nature of the PLE/Hurst reduction occurring across all regions and networks during the fully unconscious state. This suggests reduced spatial relation and integration of spontaneous activity in unconsciousness. The findings in sleep demonstrate that these changes in spatial integration occur in a graded way with more local reduction in N2 and stronger more globalized reduction in N3 (see discussion in the previous section).

Overall, the spontaneous activity shows decreased spatiotemporal integration in disorders of consciousness such as sleep, anesthesia, and VS. This suggests that the spontaneous activity's spatiotemporal relation and integration are relevant for the level of consciousness.

Spontaneous Activity Ic: Spatiotemporal Integration of Stimulus-Induced Activity within Spontaneous Activity

How are the spontaneous activity's spatiotemporal relation and integration related to the spatiotemporal expansion (or constriction) of stimulus-induced activity? Unfortunately, spontaneous activity and stimulus-induced activity have rarely been investigated together in conjunction in unconscious subjects.

One notable exception is presented by Huang et al. (2014a). They observed that the significant decrease in functional connectivity between the anterior (such as, perigenual anterior cingulate cortex) and posterior (such as, posterior cingulate cortex) cortical midline regions is related to the reduced stimulus-induced activity in response to self-related stimuli (see chapter 4 for details). This suggests decreased interaction and thus decreased spatiotemporal integration of stimulus-induced activity within the spontaneous activity and its spatiotemporal structure.

This assumption of direct relation of impairments in the spontaneous activity's spatiotemporal relation and integration with changes in stimulus-induced activity is further supported by additional data. These data show decreased nonadditive rest–stimulus interaction in disorders of consciousness (Huang et al., 2017) (see chapter 2 for details on nonadditive interaction). Although rather tentative, these data suggest that the changes in the spontaneous activity's spatiotemporal relation and integration impact the stimulus-induced activity including its spatiotemporal expansion (or constriction).

One may want to suggest the following hypothesis: the more spatiotemporal relation and integration are reduced in the spontaneous activity, the lower the degree to which the stimulus-induced activity can be spatiotemporally expanded (and the higher the degree of its spatiotemporal constriction). I therefore propose that the low degrees of spatial expansion and temporal propagation of the magnetically based–stimulus-induced activity (during TMS-EEG) in unconscious subjects may be traced to changes in their spontaneous activity's spatiotemporal relation and integration.

How can we investigate this hypothesis? One could, for instance, investigate the PLE/Hurst and CFC in the EEG resting state and prestimulus periods (e.g., prior to the magnetic pulse/stimulus); they could then be correlated with the degrees of spatial expansion and temporal propagation of the magnetically based–stimulus-induced activity. Lower values in the spontaneous and prestimulus activity's PLE and CFC should lead to lower degrees of spatial expansion and temporal propagation of the subsequent magnetically based–stimulus-induced activity. Demonstration of that, however, remains to be done in the future.

In sum, I hypothesize that spontaneous and stimulus-induced activity are closely related to and integrated within each other on spatiotemporal grounds. I therefore speak of spatiotemporal integration between spontaneous and stimulus-induced activity that is ultimately based on the spatiotemporal relation and integration within the spontaneous activity itself. Most important, the data suggest that such spatiotemporal integration between spontaneous and stimulus-induced activity is relevant for and, even stronger, proportional to the level of consciousness.

Spontaneous Activity IIa: Spectrum Model of Brain and Consciousness—Passive Model

What does the need for spatiotemporal integration between spontaneous and stimulus-induced activity imply for the relevance of the spectrum model of brain for the level of consciousness? The main point of the spectrum model of brain is the hybrid nature of stimulus-induced activity that supposedly results from the impact of both spontaneous activity and stimulus. The data suggest that the hybrid nature of stimulus-induced activity seems to be central for constituting the level of consciousness. Let us specify that in the following discussion.

Stimulus-induced activity is still present in the absence of consciousness. What, in contrast, is not present during the absence of consciousness is the spatiotemporal expansion of stimulus-induced activity. That very same spatiotemporal expansion seems to be based on the spontaneous activity and its spatiotemporal relation and integration. If the latter two are altered, as seems to be the case in disorders of consciousness, stimulus-induced activity can no longer be spatiotemporally extended; this, apparently, makes it impossible to assign consciousness to the respective stimulus (as either cognitive, magnetic, or otherwise).

The changes in the spontaneous activity in the disorders of consciousness entail that its (altered) spatiotemporal structure cannot impact subsequent stimulus-induced activity anymore. There is less spatiotemporal integration in spontaneous activity, which makes stimulus-induced activity less hybrid during the loss of consciousness. Instead of being codetermined by both spontaneous activity and stimulus, stimulus-induced activity is solely (and exclusively in most extreme cases) determined by the stimulus itself: the hybrid balance between spontaneous activity and stimulus is shifted toward the latter, which makes stimulus-induced activity less hybrid and less spatiotemporally extended.

How does that relate to the spectrum model of brain? The spectrum model of brain postulates that stimulus-induced activity consists of different components including contributions from both stimulus and the brain's spontaneous activity. Hence, stimulus-based coding is hybrid by default. However, the balance between both components, stimulus and spontaneous activity, may vary. If the contribution from the stimulus predominates, the resulting stimulus-induced activity shifts more toward the passive pole of the spectrum. If, in contrast, the contribution of the spontaneous activity predominates, the stimulus-induced activity can be located more on the active end of the spectrum.

I distinguished among different models on the passive end of the spectrum of stimulus-induced activity: (1) the weakly passive model supposes modulatory but not causal impact of spontaneous activity on stimulus-induced activity; (2) the moderately passive model suggests no impact of spontaneous activity on stimulus-induced activity; and (3) the strongly passive model assumes that there is no spontaneous activity at all any more (see chapter 1 for a generalized discussion).

I now postulate that the different passive models of stimulus-induced activity are well in accordance with the data on the different degrees of spatiotemporal expansion (as in the TMS-EEG study) stages during the loss of consciousness as experienced in MCS, VS, and coma. The above-described TMS-EEG results show that magnetically based–stimulus-induced activity is more spatiotemporally expanded in the MCS subjects and less so in the VS patients. Stimulus-induced activity in the MCS subjects may thus correspond to the weakly passive model.

In contrast, stimulus-induced activity in VS subjects may rather presuppose the moderately passive model. Finally, the even more extreme cases of coma and especially of brain death show no spatiotemporal expansion of stimulus-induced activity at all anymore resulting in spatiotemporal constriction or total absence of stimulus-induced activity—they may thus come close to the strongly passive model.

What does this tell us about the level of consciousness in the healthy subject? The hybrid nature of stimulus-induced activity and ultimately the spectrum model of brain are relevant for the level of consciousness: the more hybrid the stimulus-induced activity as resulting from the impact and spatiotemporal integration between spontaneous activity and stimulus, the higher the level of consciousness (see figure 4.1).

Spontaneous Activity IIb: Spectrum Model of Brain and Consciousness—Active Model

One may now want to argue, however, that the assumption of the hybrid nature of stimulus-induced activity neglects the opposite end, the active pole of the spectrum model. In that case, stimulus-induced activity is determined solely by the spontaneous activity itself without any impact by the stimulus anymore. One then reverts to the opposite extreme and neglects the middle ground, which, as I suggest, is central for consciousness.

Analogously to the passive pole, one may want to distinguish among different stages or degrees on the active end of the spectrum. In the case of a weakly active model, the spontaneous activity can no longer be affected by stimulus-induced activity in a causal way; however, the former can still

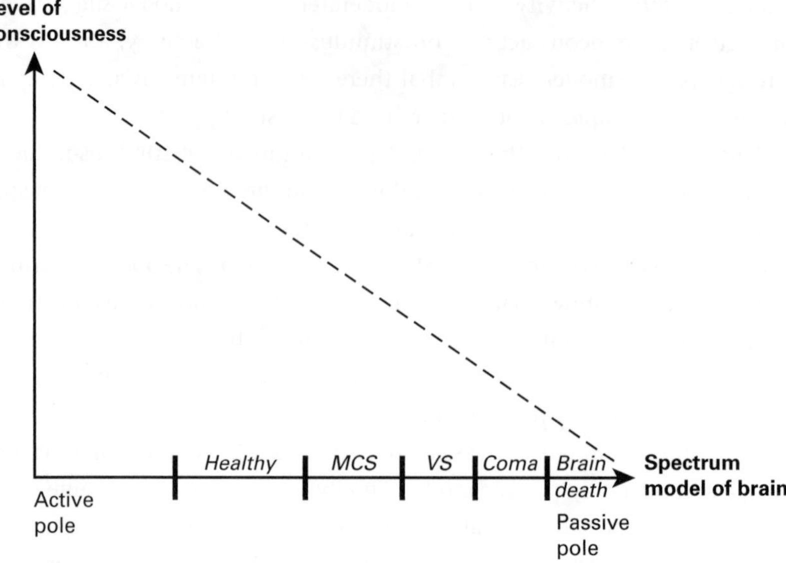

Figure 4.1
Spectrum model of brain and the level of consciousness.

be modulated by the former in a modulatory way. That very same modulation disappears in the moderately active model: the spontaneous activity can no longer be modulated by stimulus-induced activity even in a noncausal way. Finally, the strongly active model postulates the absence of any stimulus-induced activity with the spontaneous activity taking over its role (see figure 4.2).

How can we relate the different active models to specific disorders? We have seen that the disorders of consciousness entail a passive model where the impact of the spontaneous activity on subsequent stimulus-induced activity decreases and vanishes—this, as I suppose, is directly proportional to the degree to which consciousness is lost. What about the opposite end, the active models? I postulate that psychiatric disorders are a perfect test case here.

Depression can be characterized by increased spontaneous activity, specifically in the midline regions and the DMN (see Northoff, 2015a, 2016a,b, for review), but the stimulus-induced activity in these regions is decreased and, it can be hypothesized, may no longer affect the spontaneous activity in these regions in a causal way. One may thus want to assume a weakly

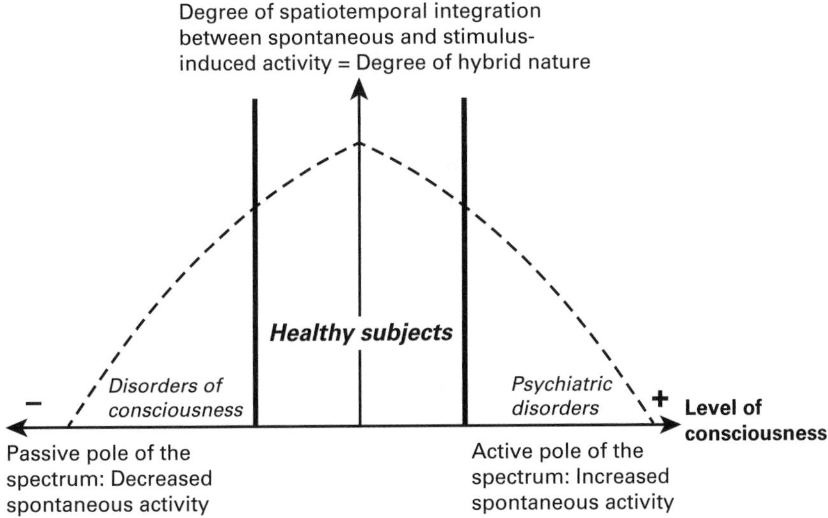

Figure 4.2
Spectrum model of brain and its relation to consciousness.

active model in depression. Symptomatically, the lacking causal impact of stimulus-induced activity on spontaneous activity may, for instance, be reflected in the fact that, behaviorally, these patients no longer react properly to external stimuli and continue ruminating on their own thoughts (even when confronted with external stimulation).

Bipolar disorder can be characterized by mania and depression that show opposite motor behavior with psychomotor retardation in depression and psychomotor agitation in mania. The manic patient runs around, whereas the depressed patient sits in the corner. That seems to be related to neuronal variability in the sensorimotor network: manic patients show increased resting state neuronal variability in this network, whereas the same measure is decreased in depressed subjects (Martino et al., 2016; Northoff et al., 2017). Importantly, the psychomotor behavior cannot be modulated by any external stimuli at all. Neuronally, this may be related to the fact that the depressed patients' spontaneous activity in the sensorimotor network is no longer modulated in either a causal or noncausal way by the external stimuli. The depressed patients' spontaneous sensorimotor cortical neuronal variability may thus correspond to the moderately active model of stimulus-induced activity.

Yet another example is displayed in schizophrenia. Here the patients can experience auditory hallucinations that are related to increased activity in the resting state (Alderson-Day et al., 2016; Northoff & Duncan, 2016). Despite the absence of any stimulus-induced activity, patients nevertheless experience voices in the external world, which, in the healthy subjects, are usually associated with stimulus-induced activity. Hence, the schizophrenic patients' spontaneous activity takes over the role of stimulus-induced activity. This corresponds to the strongly active model of stimulus-induced activity where it disappears while its role is taken over by the spontaneous activity itself.

One may now want to argue that the psychiatric examples fit well with the active end of the spectrum model of brain. In contrast, they are not relevant for consciousness because it is the case at the opposite end of the spectrum, its passive pole. However, such supposition is to neglect that psychiatric disorders also show changes in consciousness. Depressed patients show increased awareness of their own inner thoughts and beliefs, and the same holds for schizophrenic patients with regard to their auditory hallucinations.

One may therefore tentatively suggest that the level of consciousness in these patients is increased (rather than decreased). Hence, rather than rejecting the relevance of the spectrum model of brain for consciousness, psychiatric disorders support the model by showing the opposite extreme in the level of consciousness (Northoff, 2013, 2014b).

Conclusion

Is the spectrum model of brain relevant for the level of consciousness? I have demonstrated that stimulus-induced activity shows decreased spatiotemporal expansion during the loss of consciousness. That, as it may be hypothesized, is closely related to changes in the spontaneous activity and its degree of spatiotemporal relation and integration. Therefore, the spontaneous activity can no longer impact stimulus-induced activity any more as in the healthy subject.

The resulting stimulus-induced activity consequently shifts more toward the passive pole of the spectrum: it is more strongly dominated by the stimulus itself than by the brain's spontaneous activity. Different models of stimulus-induced activity on the passive end of the spectrum, weak, moderate, and strong, may thus correspond to different degrees in the loss of consciousness such as MCS, VS, and coma. Accordingly, the spectrum model of brain conforms well to the data during the loss of consciousness and can therefore be considered relevant for consciousness.

Finally, the data and their explanation by the spectrum model of brain suggest that stimulus-induced activity and spontaneous activity take on different roles for consciousness. The stimulus-induced activity and its underlying nonadditive rest–stimulus interaction may serve as a sufficient neural condition of actual consciousness, that is, as NCC. In contrast, the spontaneous activity may rather provide the necessary condition of possible consciousness, a neural predisposition of consciousness (Northoff, 2013, 2014b; Northoff & Heiss, 2015, Northoff & Huang, 2017). That neural predisposition of consciousness, however, needs to be explained in greater detail. For that, we now shift our focus to yet another model of brain, the interaction model and how it relates to consciousness.

5 Interaction Model of Brain and Consciousness

Introduction

In the second part of chapter 2, I introduced the interaction model of brain that concerns the nature of the interaction between spontaneous activity and stimuli as being nonadditive rather than merely additive or parallel. The interaction model describes the neural activity in the brain including the relation between spontaneous and stimulus-induced activity. In contrast, I left open whether the interaction model is also relevant for consciousness; that is the focus in this chapter.

The general and overarching aims of this chapter are to investigate the relevance of the interaction models of brain for consciousness. The argument is that the interaction model of brain is indeed relevant for consciousness.

Our first specific aim is to discuss the interaction of model of brain and most notably the nonadditive rest–stimulus interaction in the context of recent findings from disorders of consciousness. Based on empirical evidence, I propose that the degree of nonadditive interaction between spontaneous and stimulus–induced activity is directly relevant for the spatiotemporal expansion of stimulus-induced activity, including its association with consciousness. Even stronger, the empirical data suggest that the degree of nonadditive interaction may serve as a neural signature and thus as a neural correlate of consciousness (NCC).

The second specific aim of this chapter entails showing the central role of spontaneous activity for nonadditive rest–stimulus interaction and its relation to consciousness. I argue that the spontaneous activity is a necessary condition of possible consciousness and thus a neural predisposition of consciousness (NPC). Conceptually, the NPC can be enriched by the concept of capacities as understood by Nancy Cartwright—I thus argue for a capacity-based approach (rather than a law-based approach) to the brain and its relation to consciousness.

Part I: Interaction Model and Consciousness

Empirical Findings Ia: Stimulus Differentiation and the Level of Consciousness

Building on a recent study by Qin et al. (2010), Huang (Huang et al. 2014, 2017a,b) from our group investigated stimulus–induced activity in the vegetative state (VS) (i.e., unresponsive wakefulness [URWS] as it is called these days) during self- and non-self-related stimuli. Instead of letting subjects listen to their own (and other) name(s) (as in Qin et al., 2010), subjects now had to perform an active self-referential task wherein they had to refer to themselves, that is, each to his or her own self.

Two types of questions, autobiographical and common sense, were presented via audio. The autobiographical questions asked for real facts in the subjects' lives as obtained from their relatives. This required subjects to actively link the question to their own selves, a self-referential task. The control condition consisted of common-sense questions whereby subjects were asked for basic facts such as whether one minute is sixty seconds. Instead of giving a real response via button click (because it was impossible with these patients), the subjects were asked to answer (mentally not behaviorally) with "yes" or "no."

Huang first compared autobiographical and common-sense questions in healthy subjects. As expected on the basis of previous findings about the involvement of midline regions in self-relatedness (Northoff, 2016c,d, 2017a,b; Northoff et al., 2006), this yielded significant signal changes in the midline regions, including the anterior regions such as the perigenual anterior cingulate cortex (PACC) extending to ventromedial prefrontal cortex and the posterior regions such as the posterior cingulate cortex (PCC): the activity changes were significantly stronger in the self-related condition when compared to the non-self-related condition.

What did the brains in the VS patients now show in the very same regions? They showed signal changes in these regions that were reduced compared to those in healthy subjects. More specifically, the degree of neural differentiation between self- and non-self-related conditions was much lower.

How are these signal changes now related to consciousness? As in the study by Qin et al. (2010), a significant correlation in anterior midline regions was observed. The midline regions' activity including the PACC, dorsal anterior cingulate cortex, and PCC correlated with the degree of consciousness (as measured with the Coma Recovery Scale–Revised). It seems that the more signal changes in these regions differentiated neuronally between self- and non-self-referential conditions, the higher the levels of consciousness that patients exhibited. Thus we have observed a direct relation between the degree of neuronal self–nonself differentiation and the level of consciousness in anterior and posterior midline regions.

Empirical Findings Ib: From Spontaneous to Stimulus-Induced Activity

What about the resting-state activity in the same patients? For our purposes, one wants to know whether the diminished responses to self-specific stimuli are related to changes in the resting state in the relevant midline regions. For that, Huang, Dai, et al. (2014) also investigated the resting state, for example, its functional connectivity and low-frequency fluctuations, in exactly those regions that showed diminished signal differentiation, that is, stimulus-induced activity, during the self-referential task.

As in the previous studies, the VS patients showed significantly reduced functional connectivity from the PACC to the PCC in the resting state. In addition, the neuronal variability of the amplitude in the slowest frequency range (i.e., slow-5 as from 0.01 to 0.027 Hz) was significantly lower in both PACC and PCC in VS when compared to healthy subjects.

Given that we investigated exactly the same regions during both resting state and task, this strongly suggests that the resting-state abnormalities in these regions are somehow related to the earlier described changes during the self-referential task. This was further supported by correlation analysis: the higher the neuronal variability in the slow frequency range (i.e., slow-5) in PACC and PCC, the higher the degree of neuronal signal differentiation between self- and non-self-related conditions in the same regions during stimulus-induced activity.

Taken together, these findings suggest that the stimulus-induced activity is mediated by spontaneous activity and thus affected by the latter's changes during the loss of consciousness. What remains unclear is their exact interaction, that is, rest–stimulus interaction during, for instance, the loss of consciousness. We discussed in the interaction model that spontaneous activity and stimulus may interact in a nonadditive way. If such nonadditive interaction is central for consciousness, one would expect it to be altered, that is, decreased and ultimately as additive during the loss of consciousness. This is indeed the case, as is supported by additional empirical data that we discuss in the next section.

Interaction Model Ia: Stimulus-Induced Activity and Rest-Stimulus Interaction

What do these findings tell us with regard to stimulus-induced activity and its relevance for the level of consciousness? Let us start with the neuronal side of things. The findings by Huang, Dai, et al. (2014) show the following: (1) there are changes in stimulus-induced activity in VS subjects who are unable to properly differentiate between self- and non-self-related stimuli, in specifically midline regions such as PACC and PCC; (2) changes in the resting state's spatial structure of VS subjects as reflected in reduced PACC–PCC functional connectivity; (3) changes in the resting state's temporal structure of VS patients as in decreased neuronal variability in PACC and PCC; (4) correlation of the resting state's reduced neuronal variability with the decreased neuronal self–nonself differentiation during stimulus-induced activity; (5) correlation of decreased neuronal self–nonself differentiation with the level of consciousness.

Taken together, these findings suggest that the abnormally reduced neuronal variability in spontaneous activity is related to the decreased neuronal self–nonself differentiation during stimulus-induced activity. This suggests abnormal interaction between spontaneous activity and self- and non-self-related stimuli. That, in turn, seems to make impossible the association of stimulus-induced activity with consciousness; this is supported by the correlation between self-related activity and the level of consciousness as observed by Huang, Dai, et al. (2014).

However, my thesis on the effect of abnormal interaction on the loss of consciousness so far relies solely on correlational evidence. Correlation itself does not prove interaction let alone causal relation between spontaneous activity and stimulus-induced activity (as for instance required by both the spectrum and interaction models of brain). The argument of abnormal direct and most likely causal interaction thus rests on rather questionable empirical grounds, that is, correlation. Therefore, we cannot really suppose abnormal interaction between spontaneous and stimulus-induced activity in VS.

In order to support the assumption of abnormal interaction, we therefore need neuronal measures that directly index the interaction between spontaneous and stimulus-induced activity. One such neuronal measure is trial-to-trial variability (TTV). TTV measures the degree of changes in ongoing neuronal variability during stimulus-induced activity in relation to the degree of variability at stimulus onset (or the preceding prestimulus period). By measuring the relative change in neuronal variability, TTV accounts for how the stimulus (and stimulus-induced activity) causally impacts and changes the ongoing variability of the spontaneous activity. Therefore, TTV can be considered an indirect index of causal interaction between the resting state and stimulus.

Let us now consider the TTV in the above discussed data on self–nonself differentiation? Huang et al. (2017a) first investigated a healthy sample with the same paradigm of self and nonself stimuli as in VS. This yielded significantly stronger TTV reduction in specifically PACC and PCC during self-related stimuli when compared to non-self-related stimuli. The same finding was confirmed in a second data set on healthy subjects using the same paradigm. This suggests that self–nonself differentiation is directly related to the interaction between spontaneous and stimulus-induced activity with regard to variability, for example, in TTV. That subject is the focus of the next section.

Interaction Model Ib: Nonadditive Rest–Stimulus Interaction and Consciousness

How is the TTV as an index of rest–stimulus interaction related to the level of consciousness? The data by Huang, Dai, et al. (2014) show that stimulus-induced activity as based on decreased neuronal self–nonself differentiation is related to the level of consciousness by showing correlation (see section directly above). This leaves open, however, the role of TTV and thus of the rest–stimulus interaction itself in consciousness.

That interaction was tested for in the subsequent study in VS and anesthesia subjects (Huang et al., 2017b). Applying the same self–nonself paradigm to VS patients, Huang et al. (2017b) demonstrated significantly reduced TTV reduction in PACC and PCC in VS patients that also correlated with their level of consciousness. The VS patients basically did not show any stimulus-induced change in the ongoing variability—there was no TTV reduction after stimulus onset as is typical in healthy subjects. This was further confirmed in a separate sample of anesthetized subjects who, similar to the VS patients, did not show any reduction in their TTV (see Huang et al., 2017b; see also Schurger et al., 2015, for additional support of lacking global TTV reduction in magnetoencephalography (MEG) in VS).

Taken together, these findings suggest that the direct interaction between spontaneous and stimulus-induced activity as indexed by TTV is not only relevant for self–nonself differentiation but, more important, for indexing the level of consciousness. We need to be more precise however. We have already distinguished between additive and nonadditive interaction between spontaneous and stimulus-induced activity (see part II in chapter 2 for details).

Additive interaction means that the stimulus-induced activity simply supervenes on the ongoing spontaneous activity without showing any direct causal interaction. In that case, stimulus-induced activity is just added on top of the ongoing resting-state activity without the latter impacting the former. In contrast, nonadditive interaction refers to direct causal interaction of the former by the latter (see part II in chapter 2 for details). Here, the stimulus-induced activity is not simply added onto the ongoing spontaneous activity; hence the amplitude resulting from a nonadditive interaction is either higher or lower than the sum total of both spontaneous activity and stimulus-related effects (see part II in chapter 2).

As demonstrated by Huang, Zhang, Longtin, et al. (2017) in a separate study, the degree of nonadditive interaction can be indexed by the degree of TTV reduction: the stronger the TTV reduction, the higher the degree of nonadditive interaction. If conversely, there is no TTV reduction, interaction remains rather additive than nonadditive (see part II in chapter 2). That exactly seems to be the case during the loss of consciousness as in VS and anesthesia: both show lack of TTV reduction in PACC and PCC as well as throughout the whole brain (Huang, Zhang, Longtin, et al., 2017; see also Schurger et al., 2015, for additional support coming from magnetoencephalography.

Consequently, I postulate that the degree of nonadditive interaction between spontaneous and stimulus-induced activity (as measured by TTV) can provide a neural signature of the level of consciousness. Nonadditive interaction can thus be conceived as sufficient neural condition of consciousness, that is, as the NCC (Koch et al., 2016). Loss of consciousness, then, may be related to additive rather than nonadditive rest–stimulus interaction as can be seen in the data. Ultimately, both spontaneous and stimulus-induced activity may operate in parallel in patients who have lost their consciousness—nonadditive interaction is then replaced by parallelism as may be the case in coma. This conclusion remains to be tested in the future however (see figure 5.1).

How sensitive is TTV to different degrees in the level of consciousness? This was explicitly tested by Huang et al. (2017b) in anesthesia when he compared three different levels of consciousness in awake, sedated (e.g., 50% of anesthetic dose), and anesthesia (e.g., 100% of anesthetic dose) states. Again he applied a self–nonself paradigm that elicited strong TTV changes, that is, TTV reduction, in specifically the PCC in the awake state especially during self-related stimuli (and less strong during non-self-related stimuli).

What about the TTV in the sedated and anesthetized state? Most interestingly, lack of TTV reduction in PCC was already observed during the sedated state and did not deteriorate further during the anesthetic state:

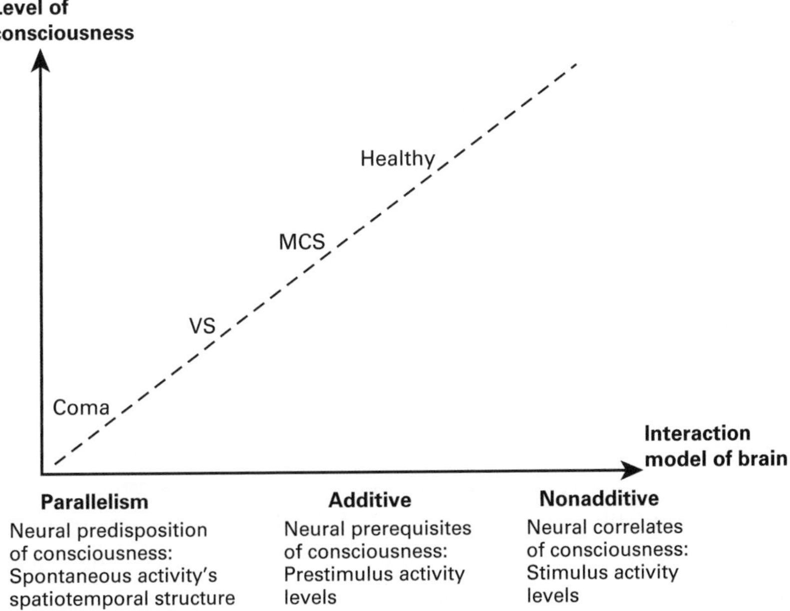

Figure 5.1
Interaction model of brain and the level of consciousness. MCS indicates minimally conscious state; VS, vegetative state.

difference in the degree of TTV was observed in PCC in the sedated state when compared to the awake state. In contrast, the comparison between the sedated and anesthetized states did not show any difference in TTV in PCC any longer. That suggests TTV as an index of nonadditive rest–stimulus interaction, which also seems to be related to the level of consciousness.

Interaction Model IIa: Neural Correlates versus Neural Predispositions of the Level of Consciousness

How are nonadditive rest–stimulus interaction and its relevance for consciousness related to the spontaneous activity? Findings in healthy subjects show direct relation between the spontaneous activity's temporal structure and the degree of nonadditive interaction (see part II in chapter 2 and Huang, Zhang, Longtin, et al., 2017). How is that related to the level of consciousness? As described in the first part of chapter 4, the spontaneous activity's temporal structure (as indexed by PLE and neuronal variability) is impaired, that is, reduced during the loss of consciousness.

Huang et al. (2017b) now investigated the PLE and functional connectivity (FC) (i.e., the degree of connection or synchronization between different regions' neural activities) in the same three stages of anesthesia, awake, sedated, and anesthetic, where he also measured the TTV. Unlike in the TTV, this demonstrated no difference in the spontaneous activity's PLE and FC during the sedated state when compared to the awake state. In contrast, the findings showed major differences in the spontaneous activity's global PLE and FC between sedated and anesthetic states (see also Qin et al., in revision; Zhang et al., 2017).

In sum, these findings suggest neuronal dissociation between rest–stimulus interaction and TTV on the one hand and the spontaneous activity's PLE and FC on the other. During the sedated state and its slightly impaired level of consciousness, the rest–stimulus interaction with TTV is already reduced, whereas the spontaneous activity's temporal structure (e.g., PLE and FC) is still preserved. The latter only changes once one becomes fully and deeply unconscious as in the anesthetic state. Accordingly, rest–stimulus interaction/TTV and spontaneous activity/PLE–FC seem to take on differential roles for consciousness: rest–stimulus interaction as indexed by TTV seems to be a sensitive and fine-grained marker that is reduced already in sedated states. In contrast, the spontaneous activity's temporal structure seems to be more robust and immune against such a change—only in the deeply unconscious state as in anesthesia or VS does it change but remains preserved during sedated states.

Taken together, these findings, suggest, albeit tentatively, differential roles of rest–stimulus interaction and spontaneous activity for consciousness. Rest–stimulus interaction as indexed by TTV may be a sufficient neural condition of the level of consciousness and thus be an NCC (Koch, 2004; Koch et al., 2016, for the concept of NCC). Rest–stimulus interaction may thus be central and sufficient for realizing actual consciousness.

In contrast, the spontaneous activity's spatiotemporal structure (the PLE, neuronal variability, and FC) may be regarded as what recently has been described as NPC (Northoff, 2013, 2014b; Northoff & Heiss, 2015). The concept of NPC refers to those neural conditions that make possible or predispose consciousness while not actually realizing it (as in the case of the NCC). I now propose that the spatiotemporal structure of the spontaneous activity itself predisposes and thus makes possible consciousness. If that very same spatiotemporal structure is altered by itself, consciousness becomes impossible; this is, as suggested by the empirical data, the case in disorders of consciousness (see figure 5.1).

Part II: Capacities and Consciousness

Capacity-Based Approach Ia: Capacities and Causal Structures

What exactly do we mean by the concept of predisposition in NPC? For that, I now turn to a more conceptual discussion about the concept of capacities as introduced and understood by Cartwright (1989, 1997, 2007, 2009); she contrasts capacities and laws that are described briefly in the following paragraphs (without much discussion of philosophical detail).

The traditional view of laws usually focuses on the derivability of theories toward the phenomenon. From this criterion of derivability, observing regularities is essential for the establishment of laws. Regularities of an event can then help scientists to form a hypothesis to explain the causes of the phenomenon. Therefore, laws capable of describing what actually happens are considered fundamental by empiricists. However, Cartwright claims that the capacities of an entity are more basic than laws. Instead of depicting the actual event, capacities indicate the properties of entities that can be fully instantiated without disturbances. Due to the complicated context of the environment, these capacities may not be directly observable in the natural world. Hence, they are abstract and hypothetical in some sense.

Although both regularists and causal structuralists develop their hypotheses from observation, they endow the laws different status. The regularists consider the laws governing the phenomenon: without laws the phenomenon would not exist. But the causal structuralists consider laws the final product of a stable causal structure, being the end point of explanation. The laws are only the attempt of describing the event in an analytic sense, not understanding the essence of the world.

Despite the fact that capacities are not as intuitive as laws during observation, they are not purely logical terms but real causal powers and thus ontological (rather than merely logical) features. Cartwright proposes that these causal powers are the smallest units with which to analyze the phenomenon. They are the subject of the minimal models, and often expressed with the ceteris paribus clause.

When a capacity is put into the context of the environment, it works together with other capacities to form a phenomenon—the phenomenon is the net effect of the causal powers. The combination of different capacities is a composite model. Within it the causal powers form a causal structure. By manipulating each of the capacities in the causal structure, whether removing or adding it to the model, one can understand more about its causal power and its relation with other capacities.

What about causal structure? Causal structure is not only the basis of an event, but a nomological machine to generate laws. The concept of nomological machine regards the law structural and secondary. This contradicts with the regularists' view, which regards the laws as regular and fundamental. Although one may argue there are regularities in the actual world, they are produced by a stable causal structure, not by themselves as universal laws. These dissimilar views of laws also affect their attitude to their disturbances.

We cannot completely avoid the disturbing factors during experiments in most cases. For the regularists, disturbances are their enemies that interfere with the reproducibility of laws; whereas in the case of a causal structure, disturbances are the factors not yet included in the model. They are part of the environmental background and have their own capacities. Rather than interrupting, they help the researchers to build a more complete causal structure that can better explain a particular phenomenon.

Capacity-Based Approach Ib: Three-Level Model of Nature

In her research, Cartwright comes to a three-level model of nature. There are first the *capacities* or *causal powers*. They are the smallest and most basic and fundamental units characterizing nature; we cannot delve any deeper or further in nature. Capacities refer to the most basic existence and reality in nature. Beyond capacities there is nothing that exists and is real in nature. This makes it clear that the concept of capacities is an ontological one that signifies existence and reality in nature, that is, the world.

Such ontological determination of capacities entails that, in our methodological investigation of nature, capacities appear as rather abstract. There is no direct method of observing or measuring them but only an indirect mechanism through the resulting causal structure and the target phenomena. Capacities are consequently the most basic and fundamental units of nature that are revealed once one strips off or subtracts (or abstracts from) all the resulting effects (as manifested in causal structure and target phenomena) of the natural world.

This is reflected in the following quote with regard to capacities in economics: "In methodology, the term of 'capacities' is used to mark out the abstract fact of an economic factor: what would be the factor's effect if it were unimpeded" (Cartwright, 2007, p. 45). Analogously applied to the brain, capacities will mark out a most basic and fundamental factor on which subsequent and directly observable neural activity relies and is based on. We find as we progress in our investigation and discussion that the brain's spontaneous activity harbors certain capacities that shape and impact subsequent stimulus-induced activity in certain ways rather than in others.

Capacities with their causal power constitute a particular causal structure that results from the interaction between different causal powers (or capacities). This means that due to the capacities different components are arranged in a particular way, thereby forming a causal structure: "A causal structure is a fixed (enough) arrangement of components with stable (enough) capacities that can give rise to the kind of regular behavior that we describe in our scientific laws" (Cartwright, 1989, p. 349; see also Cartwright, 1997). Importantly, without these underlying capacities, such causal structure would not be present at all (or at least would be principally different).

Finally, there is a third level that concerns the target phenomena such as the regular behavior that can be directly observed in empirical–experimental investigation. As indicated in the above quote on causal structure, the target phenomena, such as consciousness for one example, directly result from the causal structure that, by itself, is based on the capacities. How then can we measure and test for whether the target phenomena result from the causal structure? For such determinations, we can use external perturbations such as provoking events to unfold the causal structure and test whether it yields a target phenomenon, for example, consciousness, as in our case (see figure 5.2).

The three-level model distinguishes Cartwright's capacity-based model of nature from a law-driven model. The law-driven model does not see any need to assume causal structure as a mediating factor: instead there is a direct law-driven relation between the causal powers (that Cartwright attributes to capacities) and the target phenomenon. The causal powers themselves no longer reflect mere capacities but causes, meaning efficient causes that directly (rather than indirectly as in capacities) cause the target phenomenon. The law-driven model thus postulates direct relation between cause and target phenomenon without any mediating causal structure (see figure 5.3).

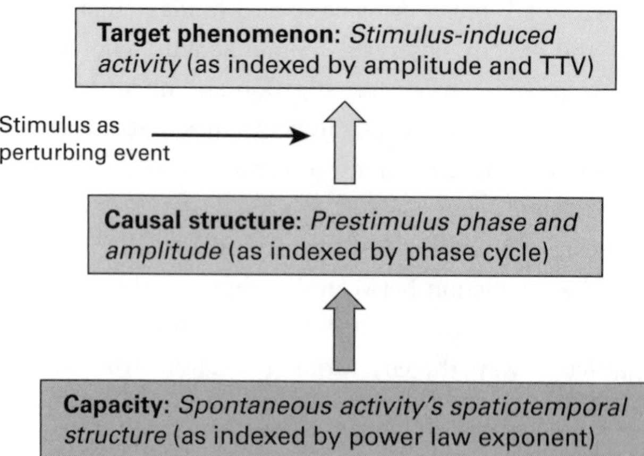

Figure 5.2
Capacity-based model of nonadditive rest–stimulus interaction. TTV indicates trial-to-trial variability.

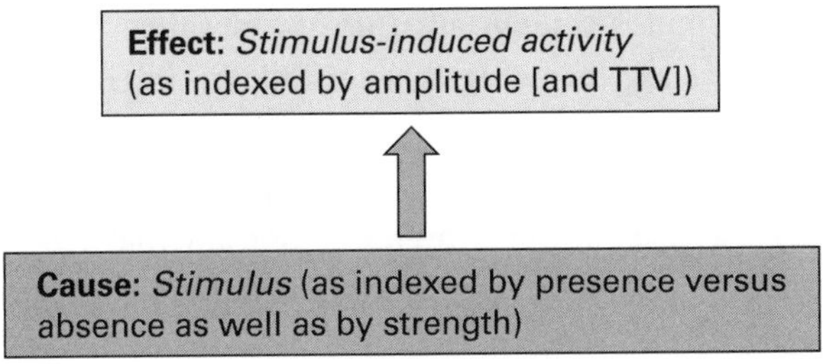

Figure 5.3
Law-driven model of nonadditive rest–stimulus interaction. TTV indicates trial-to-trial variability.

To understand a capacity-based model of nature and how it distinguishes from a law-driven model, we consequently need to understand how capacities (or causal powers) constitute a causal structure that in turn gives rise to the target phenomenon in question. Importantly, we need to make clear that, without such mediating causal structure, the target phenomenon in question would remain impossible. We are now ready to apply such capacity-based model to the brain and consciousness; this subject constitutes the focus for the remainder of this chapter.

Capacity-Based Approach IIa: Nonadditive Rest–Stimulus Interaction—Causal Structure and Consciousness

How is the example of nonadditive rest–stimulus interaction related to the capacity and the three-level model? The data by He (2013) and especially Huang, Zhang, Longtin, et al. (2017) show that the degree of stimulus-induced amplitude and TTV are dependent on the prestimulus resting-state activity levels in a nonadditive way: lower prestimulus activity levels lead to higher poststimulus-related amplitude and lower TTV. Most importantly, this, as shown by Huang, Zhang, Longtin, et al. (2017), was dependent on the ongoing phase cycle of the resting state at stimulus onset: a negative phase, that is, a trough, led to higher amplitudes and lower TTV than a positive phase, that is, a peak.

The phase and its cycling between positive and negative phases, peaks and troughs, are the means or tools by which the ongoing resting state can impact subsequent stimulus-induced activity: if the stimulus happens to be timed in such a way that it falls into the positive phase, subsequent amplitude will be low and TTV reduction rather high, whereas the opposite pattern occurs when the stimulus timing falls into the negative phase. Finally, the phase and its cycling including the nonadditive interaction itself and its measurement in terms of stimulus-induced activity and TTV were dependent on, that is, they correlated with, the temporal structure of the spontaneous activity itself (as measured by the power law that signifies the relation between lower and higher frequency fluctuations and their power across time) (Huang, Zhang, Longtin, et al., 2017).

How now can we relate these findings to the three-level model of capacities? Let us start from the top, the target phenomenon. The target phenomenon consists here of the observed stimulus-induced activity: this is the neuronal activity we directly observe in response to a stimulus and that we measure in terms of amplitude and TTV. Hence, the amplitude of stimulus-induced activity and its TTV together constitute the target phenomenon.

The target phenomenon is supposed to result from an underlying causal structure that in turn is based on a capacity. Let us start with the causal structure itself. The causal structure consists here of the levels of prestimulus activity. The amplitude at stimulus onset can be either high or low, which directly impacts the target phenomenon, the amplitude and TTV of stimulus induced activity. More importantly, there is the specific phase of the slower ongoing oscillations at stimulus onset (trough or peak) which yield a higher amplitude and stronger TTV reduction when it is a trough compared to when the phase at onset is a peak. Accordingly, prestimulus amplitude and phase and their manifestation at stimulus onset account for the causal structure underlying the target phenomenon.

We demonstrated that the causal structure, as accounted for by prestimulus phase and stimulus-induced amplitude, yields the target phenomenon, the stimulus-induced activity as measured by amplitude and TTV. In contrast, we did not discuss the perturbing event that impinged on and interacted with the causal structure in such a way that it yielded stimulus-induced activity in a nonadditive way. This concerns the external stimulus and its timing with regard to the ongoing phase of resting-state activity, which accounts for the nonadditive nature of rest–stimulus interaction. If in contrast there were no such causal structure with different phase cycles, the interaction would no longer be nonadditive but merely additive.

Imagine if there were to be no phase cycles either positive and negative with low and high excitability, respectively. In that case the causal structure of the prestimulus interaction would no longer yield nonadditive rest–stimulus interaction but merely additive rest–stimulus interaction: the amplitude of the stimulus-induced activity would be merely added on top of the ongoing resting-state activity, and, even more important, the latter's ongoing variability would probably not be reduced as measured by the TTV. This makes it clear that the underlying causal structure, the prestimulus amplitude and phase cycle, has indeed a direct causal effect on the target phenomenon, the rest–stimulus interaction that consists in its nonadditive nature. Without the causal structure, the prestimulus amplitude and phase cycling, the perturbing event, that is, the stimulus, could only yield additive but no nonadditive rest–stimulus interaction. That, as we have just demonstrated, leads to the absence of consciousness. Hence, the causal structure as second level is central for associating stimulus-induced activity with consciousness.

Capacity-Based Approach IIb: Nonadditive Rest–Stimulus Interaction—Capacities and Consciousness

What about the third level, the capacities underlying the causal structure? The capacity consists in the spontaneous activity itself and more specifically its temporal structure. Huang, Zhang, Longtin, et al. (2017) observed that the temporal structure of the spontaneous activity (as measured in a separate session with the power law exponent [PLE]) that signifies the relation between higher and lower frequency fluctuations and their power across time, specifically, across six minutes as measured) predicted both the prestimulus amplitude and phase cycling and subsequently the degree of nonadditive interaction including the amplitude and TTV of stimulus-induced activity.

How can we account for these findings in terms of capacities? One would assume that the spontaneous activity's temporal structure, specifically its nestedness/scale-free nature (measured by PLE), provides a capacity for nonadditive rest-stimulus interaction. Specifically, the spontaneous activity's temporal structure makes possible or predisposes the nonadditive nature of rest—stimulus interaction. This means that without such temporal structure, as for instance, without lower- and higher-frequency fluctuations being related to each other as measured in PLE, rest–stimulus interaction could possibly not be nonadditive anymore but merely additive.

That seems to be, for instance, the case in disorders of consciousness, which demonstrate the dramatic consequences of a lack of nonadditive interaction, namely the loss of consciousness. Consciousness can thus not only be related to nonadditive rest–stimulus interaction itself but also to its underlying capacities as related to the spontaneous activity's spatiotemporal structure. We would leave out half of the neuronal mechanisms if we were considering only nonadditive rest–stimulus interaction.

More generally, I here suggest a capacity-based approach to consciousness. This helps us to better understand the distinction between NCC and NPC. The NCC reflect a particular not-yet-fully clear causal structure that allows for nonadditive rest–stimulus interaction and thereby yields the target phenomenon, the association of stimulus-induced activity with consciousness.

In contrast, the NPC concern the capacities, that is, the causal power of the spontaneous activity that first and foremost make possible nonadditive rest–stimulus interaction (and the subsequent association of stimulus-induced activity with consciousness). We saw that that very same capacity, the NPC of the spontaneous activity and its spatiotemporal structure, is lost in disorders of consciousness.

This carries clinical relevance. Changes in the NPC make consciousness impossible so that clinical recovery with return to consciousness is rather unlikely if not impossible—this is, for instance, the case in full-blown coma. Change in NPC must be distinguished from isolated changes in NCC. Isolated changes in NCC still allow for the recovery of consciousness since the underlying NPCs are still preserved. Such isolated change in NCC (and concurrent preservation of NPC) may, for instance, be the case in the minimally conscious state (MCS) and in those VS patients who subsequently wake up (Northoff & Heiss, 2015).

Capacity-Based Approach IIIa: Law-Driven Model of Nonadditive Rest–Stimulus Interaction—Stimulus as Cause

The proponent of a law-driven model of brain may now want to argue that the nonadditive rest–stimulus interaction can be explained in direct causal terms: an underlying cause can directly and sufficiently account for the target phenomenon itself without assuming the mediating effect of a causal structure. Such direct and sufficient cause may be presented in three different scenarios as possible arguments against a capacity-based model of nonadditive rest–stimulus interaction.

The first scenario would be one where everything that I attributed to the resting state could all be related to the stimulus itself with the consecutive assumption of only stimulus-induced activity operating in the brain without any spontaneous activity; the second scenario would acknowledge spontaneous activity but would not attribute any causal relevance to it for rest–stimulus interaction; the third scenario would be one where the cause of nonadditive rest–stimulus interaction would be directly related to the resting state itself, the spontaneous activity.

Let us start with the first scenario. One may assume that the brain itself can only be characterized by stimulus-induced activity while there is no spontaneous activity at all. What is described as spontaneous activity may then be assumed to result from stimuli as well, thus being an instance of stimulus-induced activity rather than reflecting a truly distinct form of neural activity such as spontaneous activity (see, for instance, Morcom & Fletcher, 2007a,b). Although it may seem weird, one could indeed take such a view since the spontaneous activity itself is malleable by external stimuli and thus experience-dependent, as, for instance, reflected in the spontaneous activity's relation to earlier childhood trauma (see Duncan et al., 2015). However, one can nevertheless distinguish spontaneous and stimulus-induced activity by their different spatiotemporal ranges and scales (see e.g., Klein, 2014, as well as below for details). Let us nevertheless assume for the sake of the argument that there is no distinction between stimulus-induced activity and spontaneous activity so that the brain's neural operations can exclusively be characterized by stimulus-induced activity.

How would rest–stimulus interaction look in such a case? There would simply be no rest–stimulus interaction since there is no resting state anymore which makes its interaction with the stimulus simply impossible. The observed nonadditive effects could then only be attributed to the stimuli themselves. Different stimuli may elicit different degrees of amplitudes and trial-based variability, for example, TTV, in their stimulus-induced activity. However, due to the absence of the prestimulus amplitude and phase cycle as underlying causal structure, one and the same stimulus should then always elicit the same amplitude and TTV.

This was not the case in our data however, where one and the same stimulus elicited different degrees of amplitude and TTV depending on prestimulus amplitude and phase cycle. The assumption of the law-driven model of directly and causally relating the nonadditive nature of stimulus-induced activity (rather than of rest–stimulus interaction) to the direct causal impact of the stimulus itself is simply empirically implausible and thus argues against a direct and sufficient causal effect of the stimulus itself in a law-driven way.

Moreover, I would argue that, even if the nonadditive nature of stimulus-induced activity is preserved, there would nevertheless be consciousness associated with that stimulus-induced activity. The stimulus must interact with the spontaneous activity and its spatiotemporal structure in order for the nonadditive interaction to be associated with consciousness. Why? Because by interacting nonadditively with the spontaneous activity, the stimulus gets access to the latter's larger spatiotemporal scale; that, in turn, is important for spatiotemporal expansion and thus for consciousness (see Northoff & Huang, 2017, and part II in chapter 7, for details on the latter point).

What about the second scenario that acknowledges the spontaneous activity but renders it causally impotent? In that case there would be a resting state but its prestimulus amplitude and phase cycles would have no impact on the subsequent processing of the stimulus. The different phase cycles would then no longer reflect different degrees of excitability for the stimulus, which consequently would make impossible the nonadditive nature of the rest–stimulus interaction. Stimulus-induced activity would consequently merely be added on the ongoing resting-state activity with the rest–stimulus interaction being additive rather than nonadditive. This makes impossible associating consciousness to stimulus-induced activity.

The stimulus would still be the sole and sufficient cause for the observed stimulus-induced activity, for example, its amplitude and TTV indicating direct and sufficient causal relation between stimulus and stimulus-induced activity in a law-driven way. That however is not empirically plausible given that the data show clear impact of the prestimulus amplitude and phase cycle on subsequent stimulus-induced activity that is central for consciousness. Accordingly, the second scenario of the law-driven advocate remains empirically implausible as well.

Capacity-Based Approach IIIb: Law-Driven Model of Nonadditive Rest–Stimulus Interaction—"Spatiotemporal Capacities"

What about the third scenario where the resting state is conceived as the sole, direct, and sufficient cause for nonadditive rest–stimulus interaction? In that case one would expect that the degree of nonadditivity would remain always the same during different stimuli, which would then show analogous degrees of amplitudes and TTV. For instance, self- and non-self-related stimuli (as one's own and other names or auto- and heterobiographical events as phrased in sentences) should then induce the same degree of stimulus-related amplitude and TTV in the same regions.

The last, however, is not the case as a subsequent study by Huang et al. (2016) has demonstrated. He showed that self- and non-self-related stimuli induced different degrees of nonadditive rest–stimulus interaction with subsequently different degrees of amplitudes and TTV's especially in cortical midline regions (such as the medial prefrontal cortex and posterior cingulate cortex) even though the prestimulus resting state's distribution of positive and negative, or peak and trough, phase cycles at stimulus onset was the same for self- and non-self-related stimuli.

These data show that the degree of nonadditive interaction is not only upon the resting state itself, that is, its capacity (as reflected in its temporal structure that can be measured with PLE and its ongoing phase cycle at stimulus onset), but also on the content of the stimuli themselves (self- vs. non-self-related, such as one's own vs. others' names) and their timing relative to the ongoing phase cycles). The resting state's temporal structure is consequently not sufficient by itself in a law-driven way as proposed by the advocate of a law-driven model; it is only necessary but not sufficient for nonadditive rest-stimulus interaction.

I therefore propose different roles for resting state activity and stimulus in nonadditive rest–stimulus interaction. The resting state, specifically its temporal structure, provides the capacity for yielding a particular causal structure, that is, its prestimulus amplitude and phase cycle. The resting state's causal structure has the capacity to interact with different kinds of perturbing events, that is, different stimuli. However, the degree of the actual interaction, that is, the observed degree of nonadditivity, depends not only on the resting state itself but also on the stimulus itself, that is, its content and timing. Together, resting state and stimulus and, more specifically, the degree of their nonadditive interaction yield the target phenomenon, for example, stimulus-induced activity with amplitude and TTV.

What is the role of the stimulus? The stimulus, that is, its content and timing, provides the context for the resting state activity and its capacity—this amounts to what, relying on Cartwright, can be described as "contextual modulation or dependence" (of the resting state's capacity on the stimulus as context). The assumption of such contextual modulation of the resting state's capacity by the stimulus is not compatible with and therefore stands opposite to the notion of laws. In the context of a law-driven model, one may want to presume a law that specifically refers to the resting state's degree of non-additive interaction with stimuli. That law would describe how the resting state itself can mediate different degrees of nonadditive interaction by itself (rather than describing the resting state's capacity for a certain range of different degrees of nonadditive interaction as in the capacity-based model). Specifically, different degrees in the resting state's temporal structure would then "translate" one-to-one into different degrees of nonadditive rest–stimulus interaction. Put more philosophically, the resting state itself would exert direct causal impact on rest–stimulus interaction as the resting state itself would then be the sufficient (rather than necessary nonsufficient) condition.

Importantly, such a law describing direct causal impact of the resting state itself on subsequent stimulus-induced activity would exclude possible contextual modulation of the degree of nonadditive rest–stimulus interaction by the stimuli themselves. Such contextual dependence of the resting state's nonadditive rest–stimulus interaction can only be accounted for by capacities but not by laws. Accordingly, although conceivable on logical grounds, the characterization of the resting state by a law-based model rather than a capacity-based model for nonadditive rest–stimulus interaction must be rebutted on empirical grounds as related to the contextual, stimulus-related dependence of nonadditive rest–stimulus interaction. In sum, the empirical data argue in favor of a capacity-based rather than a law-driven model of brain underlying its propensity for nonadditive rest–stimulus interaction.

Most important, such a capacity-based approach to the brain is central for consciousness. We have seen that the exclusive consideration of stimulus-induced activity as NCC leaves out something crucial, namely the spontaneous activity as neural predisposition of consciousness. The need to consider NPC in addition to NCC urges us to shift from a law-based approach to a capacity-based approach in our explanation of the relation between brain and consciousness. Only when we consider the capacities as described in the NPC, can we understand why and how the brain's neural activity can be associated with consciousness. The empirical data show that those very same capacities, that is, the NPC, consist in the spontaneous activity's spatiotemporal structure. Therefore, one may specify the notion of capacities as "spatiotemporal capacities" in the context of brain and consciousness.

Conclusion

I have demonstrated here that the interaction model is not only relevant for the brain (chapter 2) but also for consciousness. There must be non-additive rather than merely additive interaction between spontaneous activity and stimuli in order for associating stimulus-induced activity with consciousness. Conceptually, the central role of the spontaneous activity is described as "neural predisposition of consciousness." The NPC concern the necessary condition of possible consciousness as distinguished from the sufficient conditions of actual consciousness, the NCC.

The role of the spontaneous activity of NPC is described further in conceptual terms by the notion of capacities that entail a capacity-based approach. Relying on Cartwright (1989, 1997, 2007, 2009), I attribute such a capacity-based approach to the brain and its relation to consciousness. Specifically, I postulated that the spontaneous activity can be characterized by capacities that predispose consciousness. These capacities seem to exist in the spontaneous activity's spatiotemporal structure; for that reason, one may specify the brain's capacities as "spatiotemporal capacities." I propose that the brain's spatiotemporal capacities are central for consciousness and further develop and explicate this spatiotemporal model of consciousness in chapters 7 and 8.

6 Prediction Model of Brain and Consciousness

Introduction

We have already touched on a discussion of the prediction model of brain that is based on predictive coding (see the first part in chapter 3 for details; see also Friston, 2010; Hohwy, 2013, 2014). Specifically, the prediction model postulates that stimulus-induced activity results from the interaction between the predicted (or anticipated) input and the actual input, which constitutes the prediction error. Importantly, the prediction error is supposed to determine the content associated with stimulus-induced activity; depending on the degree of the prediction error, the underlying content may either be more similar to the one encoded by the predicted input or, alternatively, resemble more the one related to the incoming stimulus, that is, the actual input.

Predictive coding extends the originally sensory model of stimulus-induced activity as based on the actual input itself to a more cognitive model that includes prediction, that is, the predicted input. This raises two questions with regard to consciousness: (1) Can the cognitive model of stimulus-induced activity and its contents account for the selection of contents in consciousness? (2) Is predictive coding sufficient by itself to associate any given content with consciousness? If the prediction model of brain can address both questions, we can extend the cognitive model of stimulus-induced activity as in predictive coding to a cognitive model of consciousness.

The main and overarching aim in this chapter is to investigate the relevance of the prediction model of brain and, more specifically, predictive coding for both the contents of consciousness and for consciousness itself. Based on empirical data on prestimulus prediction of subsequent conscious contents, I argue that the prediction model of brain can well account for the selection of contents in consciousness, thus addressing the first question (see section beginning part I, below). In contrast, predictive coding remains insufficient to answer the second question, that is, how any given content can be associated with consciousness (see section beginning part II, below).

We therefore cannot extend the cognitive model of stimulus-induced activity and its contents to a cognitive model of the contents of consciousness. I thus conclude that consciousness is different from and extends beyond its contents. Instead of coming with the contents themselves, consciousness is associated to the contents thus requiring a neuronal mechanism that is separate from the one underlying the selection of contents.

Part I: Prediction Model and Contents—Selection of Contents in Consciousness

Empirical Findings Ia: Prestimulus Activity and Bistable Perception—Sensory Cortex

How can we investigate the contents of consciousness? The group around Andreas Kleinschmidt (Hesselmann, Kell, Eger, et al., 2008) investigated human subjects in functional magnetic resonance imaging (fMRI) during the Rubin face-stimulus illusion. Although subjects are presented one stimulus, they perceive two different contents such as a vase or a face in response—hence, the content of the stimulus is the same even though the subjects perceive two distinct perceptual contents. This phenomenon that describes changing contents in consciousness is called *bistable* or *multistable perception*.

Hesselmann, Kell, Eger, et al. (2008) first analyzed stimulus-related activity and thus those epochs where the stimulus was presented; these epochs were distinguished according to whether the subjects perceived a face or a vase. Since the fusiform face area (FFA) is well known to be related to the processing of faces specifically, the focus was here on the FFA during both face and vase percepts.

What results did Hesselmann and colleagues obtain? The FFA showed greater stimulus-induced signal changes in those trials where subjects perceived a face compared with the ones where subjects had perceived a vase. The authors then went further ahead and sampled the signal changes in the FFA immediately prior to the onset of the stimulus defining a prestimulus baseline (or resting state) phase. Interestingly, this yielded significantly higher prestimulus signal changes in the right FFA during those trials where subjects had perceived a face.

In contrast, such prestimulus signal changes were not observed in the same region, the right FFA, when subjects perceived a vase rather than a face. In addition to such perceptual specificity, there was also regional specificity displayed. The prestimulus resting-state signal change increases were only observed in the right FFA; they did not occur in other regions such as the visual or prefrontal cortex. This displays what may be described as spatial specificity.

In addition to *perceptual and regional spatial specificity*, Hesselmann Kell, Eger, et al. (2008) also investigated *temporal specificity*. They conducted an ANOVA (analysis of variance) for the interaction between time point (early and late prestimulus resting-state signal changes in the FFA) and percept (vase, face). This revealed statistically significant interaction between time point and percept. The late resting-state signal changes were more predictive of the subsequent percept, that is, face or vase, than the early ones. The prestimulus resting-state's neural activity at the time point immediately preceding the stimulus thus seems to contain the most information about the subsequent percept and its underlying stimulus-induced activity; this entails what can be described as temporal specificity.

What does such temporal specificity imply? The authors themselves remark that the immediate prestimulus resting-state FFA signal changes contain as much information about the subsequent perceptual content as the stimulus-induced activity in FFA itself (Hesselmann Kell, Eger, et al., 2008). Hence the observed spatial and temporal specificities tell us about which content is selected and dominates in subsequent perception, that is, the perceptual specificity of phenomenal content.

One may now want to argue that the observed FFA differences during stimulus-induced activity between the two percepts may stem from the preceding prestimulus resting-state differences rather than from the stimulus itself. The prestimulus resting-state differences may thus simply be carried forth into the stimulus period and the stimulus-induced activity. If so, one would expect mere addition and thus linear interaction between the prior resting state and the neural activity induced by the stimulus itself. The assumption of such merely additive and linear interactions between resting state and stimulus is not in accordance, however, with the data, as will become clear in the discussion directly below.

The data show that the prestimulus resting-state differences disappeared almost completely in the signal, that is, the stimulus-induced activity, once the stimulus set in. This argues against a simple carryover effect, in which case one would expect the differences in the preceding resting-state activity to persist during the onset of the subsequent stimulus. Instead, the results suggest an interaction between prestimulus resting state and stimulus along the lines of a nonlinear and thus nonadditive (rather than additive) interaction (see He, 2013; Huang, Zhang, Longtin, et al., 2017; as well as the second part in chapter 2 in this volume for more details on the nonadditive rest–stimulus interaction).

Empirical Findings Ib: Prestimulus Activity and Bistable Perception—Prefrontal Cortex

Increased prestimulus resting-state signal changes in stimulus-specific regions and nonadditive rest–stimulus interaction could also be observed in other bi- or multistable perception tasks in both visual and auditory sensory modalities (see Sadaghiani, Hesselmann, et al., 2010, for an overview). The tasks showing changes in prestimulus resting-state activity included an ambiguous auditory perception task in which increased prestimulus resting-state changes could be observed in an auditory cortex. Increases in auditory cortical prestimulus resting-state activity predicted the hits (as distinguished from the misses) in an auditory detection task near the auditory threshold (Sadaghiani et al., 2009; Sadaghiani, Hesselmann et al. 2010; Sterzer, Kleinschmidt, & Rees, 2009).

Analogously, the coherent percept in a motion decision task could also be predicted by increased prestimulus resting-state activity in a motion-sensitive area (hMT+) in the occipitotemporal cortex (see Hesselmann, Kell, & Kleinschmidt, 2008). In addition to the predictive effects of increased prestimulus resting-state activity in hMT+, nonadditive interaction between prestimulus and stimulus-induced activity could be observed along the lines described earlier. These findings argue against simple propagation or carryover of preceding prestimulus resting-state differences into subsequent stimulus-induced activity. Instead, they let the authors propose complex, that is, nonadditive, interaction between resting-state and stimulus-induced activity.

Can multistable perception thus be sufficiently explained by prestimulus resting-state changes and nonlinear rest–stimulus interaction in early sensory regions? No, because in addition to these lower-level sensory regions, higher-level cognitive regions such as the prefrontal cortex also show differences in prior resting-state activity that also predict the subsequent percept. This has been demonstrated by Sterzer et al. (2009) as well as Sterzer and Kleinschmidt (2007). They applied an ambiguous motion stimulus and showed increased resting-state signal changes in the right inferior prefrontal cortex prior to stimulus onset.

Most important, chronometric analysis (i.e., signal amplitude at different time points) of fMRI data have revealed that such increased right inferior prefrontal cortical prestimulus activity occurred prior to the onset of neural activity differences in motion-sensitive extrastriate visual cortex. An analogous finding was made in an electroencephalographic (EEG) study during visual presentation of the Neckar cube (Britz, Landis, & Michel, 2009). Here, the right inferior parietal cortex showed increased prestimulus resting-state activity 50 ms prior to the reversal of the perceptual content that predicted the subsequent percept.

Taken together, the data suggest that prestimulus resting-state activity in higher regions such as the prefrontal or parietal cortex may be crucial in predicting the subsequent content in perception, that is, the phenomenal content of consciousness.

This may be possible by higher regions modulating the resting-state activity in lower sensory regions (see also Sterzer et al., 2009, for such interpretation as well as the papers by Lamme, 2006; Lamme & Roelfsma, 2000; Summerfield et al., 2008; van Gaal & Lamme, 2011). Accordingly, prestimulus resting-state activity changes are central on both lower-order sensory and higher-order cognitive regions with both determining and selecting the contents in subsequent perception (as in bistable perception).

Prediction Model and Content Ia: Predictive Coding and Stimulus-Induced Activity

What does the example of bistable perception tell us about contents and their role in consciousness? The example of bistable perception tells us that there is no direct relation between the content related to the input and the content in perception, that is, consciousness. One and the same input and its associated content can be associated with different contents in perception. How is that possible? The empirical data show that prestimulus activity changes in lower sensory regions, FFA, and prefrontal cortex impact which content will be perceived in consciousness: the prestimulus resting state activity levels add something and manipulate the actual input (and its content) in such way that the contents of perception are not identical to the actual input's content.

What exactly does this addition contributed by the prestimulus resting state consist of? That question may be split into two distinct aspects concerning first stimulus-induced activity itself and second its associated contents. The prestimulus activity level seems to impact and manipulate both stimulus-induced activity and its respective contents in such way that the latter can be associated with consciousness. Let us start with the first aspect, the manipulation of stimulus-induced activity itself.

The prediction model of brain claims that prediction, that is, the predicted input, as supposed in predictive coding, makes the difference (Clark, 2012, 2013; Friston, 2010; Hohwy, 2013; Northoff, 2014a). Put in a nutshell (see the first part in chapter 3 for more details), predictive coding supposes that the neural activity observed in response to specific stimuli or tasks, known as stimulus-induced or task-evoked activity, does not exclusively result from the stimulus alone, that is, from the actual input but, rather, from the balance or better comparison between actual and predicted inputs (see Clark, 2013; Friston, 2008, 2010; Hohwy, 2013, 2014; Northoff, 2014a, chapters 7–9).

Specifically, the degree to which actual and predicted input match with each other is described as the prediction error that indexes the error in the anticipated or predicted input when compared to the actual input. A low prediction error signals that the actual input was predicted well by the predicted or anticipated input—this leads to low amplitude in subsequent stimulus-induced activity. In contrast, a high prediction error indicates large discrepancy or error, in the predicted input—this yields high amplitude in subsequent stimulus- or task-induced activity.

Taken together, the prediction model of brain supposes that prestimulus resting-state activity levels impact and modulate the amplitude of subsequent stimulus-induced activity. This concerns the stimulus-induced activity itself—but what about the impact of the predicted input on the contents associated with that very same stimulus-induced activity? That is our focus in the next section.

Prediction Model and Content Ib: Predictive Coding and the Content of Consciousness

How does such a prediction model of brain stand in relation to the above reported prestimulus findings? The group (Sadaghiani, Hesselmann et al., 2010) around Kleinschmidt interprets its above-described findings on the contents of consciousness during bistable perception in terms of predictive coding. If the prestimulus activity levels are high, the predicted input is strong and can therefore not be overridden by the actual input, the stimulus—this results in a low prediction error.

The content of perception is then predominantly shaped by the predicted input rather than the actual input itself. For instance, high prestimulus activity levels in the FFA will tilt the content that is associated with subsequent stimulus-induced activity during bistable perception toward faces. One then perceives the contents one expects or anticipates rather than the contents that are actually presented in the actual input or stimulus.

If, in contrast, prestimulus activity levels are low, the predicted input is not as strong; this allows the actual input to exert stronger impact on subsequent stimulus-induced activity resulting in higher prediction error. This is the case in those trials where FFA prestimulus activity levels are low. One then perceives the content related to the actual input itself as based on the sensory input rather than the content associated with the predicted input, that is, the anticipated content. Thus predictive coding seems to account well for different contents associated with high and low prestimulus activity levels in FFA.

Taken together, the balance between prestimulus activity levels and actual input determines the content during subsequent perception. High prestimulus activity levels signal strong predicted input, or anticipation, which associated content may then override the content related to the actual input during subsequent perception. Conversely, weak prestimulus activity levels may allow the content associated with the actual input to predominate in subsequent perception. On the neuronal level this balance between prestimulus activity and actual input may be mediated by nonadditive interaction. The prediction model of brain (see the first and second parts in chapter 3) is thus well in tune with the interaction model of brain (see the second part in chapter 2) with regard to the contents in consciousness (see also the second part in chapter 5).

Prediction Model and Content IIa: Selection of Contents in Consciousness versus Association of Contents with Consciousness

We have seen that predictive coding can well account for the content of consciousness, that is, whether, for instance, we perceive a face or vase during bistable perception. This concerns the contents themselves. However, it leaves open how and why a particular content such as a vase or a face is associated with consciousness at all rather than remaining within the unconscious. True, the FFA shows high prestimulus activity levels. But, importantly, that does not mean that the high prestimulus activity in FFA encodes a specific content by itself, that is, a specific face. In contrast, the high prestimulus activity in FFA only means that it can impact the subsequent processing of a specific stimulus and tilt or shift perceptual content in a certain direction, for instance, toward a face or vase. Most importantly, the high prestimulus activity in FFA tells us nothing about whether that content will be associated with consciousness. Accordingly, high FFA activity level does not yet explain why that very same content, the face or the vase, is associated with consciousness rather than unconsciousness.

We thus need to distinguish two different questions. First, there is the question about the specific contents of consciousness, that is, whether consciousness is characterized by content a or b: What is the specific content in consciousness and how is it selected? I therefore speak of *selection of contents in consciousness*. The relevance of such selection of contents has been recognized and discussed by the group around Kleinschmidt in the context of predictive coding (Sadaghiani, Hesselmann et al., 2010).

Second, there is the dual-pronged question about why and how any given content, irrespective of whether it is content a or b, can be associated with consciousness at all. The question for associating contents with consciousness is not trivial at all given that any content (such as content a or b) can be processed in an unconscious way without ever being associated with consciousness. The question can thus be formulated in the following way: Why and how can any given content be associated with consciousness rather than remaining in the unconscious? I therefore speak of *association of contents with consciousness* as distinguished from the selection of contents in consciousness.

The answer to the second question is even more fundamental given that basically all contents ranging from simple sensory contents to complex cognitive contents can be processed in an unconscious way rather than a conscious one (for empirical evidence, see Faivre et al., 2014; Koch et al., 2016; Lamme, 2010; Northoff, 2014b; Northoff et al., 2017; Tsuchiya et al., 2015; Tsuchiya & Koch, 2012). The fact that all contents can be processed in an unconscious way raises the question of whether consciousness comes really with the selected contents themselves or, as hypothesized in the second question, is associated to the contents. Therefore, the second question becomes our focus in the discussion that follows.

If predictive coding can also provide an answer to the second question, the prediction model of brain is indeed relevant for consciousness. If, in contrast, the prediction model of brain cannot provide a proper answer, we need to search for a different neuronal mechanism to account for consciousness itself independent of its respective contents. Thus, the nature and importance of the role played by the prediction model together become the next focus of our interest.

Prediction Model and Content IIb: Predictive Coding and Selection of Contents in Consciousness

Predictive coding is about content. There is strong empirical evidence that predictive coding occurs throughout the whole brain and is therefore implicated in the processing of all contents. The relevant prediction processes can be observed at different levels (regional and cellular levels), during different functions (action, perception, attention, motivation, memory, etc.), and in various regions (cortical and subcortical) (see den Ouden, Friston, Daw, McIntosh, & Stephan, 2012; Mossbridge et al., 2014). Given the apparent centrality of predictive coding for neural activity, one should regard it as a basic and most fundamental computational feature of neural processing in general that allows the brain to process any kind of content (Hohwy, 2014).

More specifically, predictive coding aims to explain the processing of various contents including sensory, motor, affective, cognitive, social (Kilner et al., 2007), perceptual (Alink et al., 2010; Hohwy, 2013; Doya et al., 2011; Rao & Ballard, 1999; Seth, 2015; Summerfield et al., 2006), attentional (Clark, 2013; den Ouden, Kok, & de Lange, 2012), interoceptive, and emotional (Seth, 2013; Seth, Suzuki, & Critchley, 2012) contents. Recently, predictive coding has also been suggested to account for mental contents including the self (Apps & Tsakiris, 2013, 2014; Limanowski & Blankenburg,

2013; Seth, 2013, 2015; Seth, Suzuki, & Critchley, 2012), intersubjectivity (Friston & Frith, 2015), dreams (Hobson & Friston, 2012, 2014), and consciousness (Hohwy, 2013, 2017).

Given its ubiquitous involvement in the processing of any content, predictive coding is well suited to address the first question we posed, the one regarding the selection of contents in consciousness (see previous section): What contents are selected and constituted in consciousness? The answer here, as we have discussed, consists in referring to the balance between predicted and actual input, *the prediction error,* which is central for selecting the respectively associated content. If the prediction error is high, the content selected will conform to the one related to the actual input. If, in contrast, the prediction error is low, the selected content will be more related to the one of the predicted input. Accordingly, I consider predictive coding a sufficient condition of the selection of content in consciousness.

That leaves open whether predictive coding can also sufficiently account for the second, two-tiered question: Why and how is any given content associated with consciousness at all rather than remaining in the unconscious? More specifically, one may want to raise the question of whether it is the predicted input itself that makes the difference between association and nonassociation of a given content (as related to either the predicted or actual input) with consciousness during subsequent stimulus-induced activity. Importantly, that association remains independent of the selected content as related to either the predicted or actual input. Hence, the question for the association of contents with consciousness remains independent of the question for the selection of content in consciousness.

Part II: Prediction Model and Consciousness—Association of Contents with Consciousness

Empirical Findings Ia: Predicted Input—Unconscious or Conscious?

Can predictive coding account for the association of contents with consciousness? Traditional models of stimulus-induced activity (such as neurosensory models; see chapter 1, part I, and chapter 3, part I) that hold the actual input, that is, the stimulus itself, to be sufficient cannot properly account for consciousness. Consciousness itself does not come with the stimulus itself (the actual input) and therefore cannot be found in such (supposedly) purely sensory-based stimulus-induced activity.

Predictive coding, however, presupposes a different model of stimulus-induced activity. Rather than being sufficiently determined by the actual input, specifically, the sensory input, stimulus-induced activity is also codetermined by the predicted input of the prestimulus activity levels. The neurosensory model of stimulus-induced activity is thus replaced by a neurocognitive model (part II in chapter 5).

Can the neurocognitive model of stimulus-induced activity as in predictive coding account for the association of any given content with consciousness? If so, the cognitive component itself, the predicted input, should allow for associating contents with consciousness. The predicted input itself including its content should then be associated with consciousness rather than unconsciousness. The prediction model of brain and its neurocognitive model of stimulus-induced activity would thus be extended to consciousness entailing a cognitive model of consciousness (see, e.g., Hohwy, 2013; Mossbridge et al., 2014; Palmer, Seth, & Hohwy, 2015; Seth, Suzuki, & Critchley, 2012; Yoshimi & Vinson, 2015).

In contrast, if dissociation between predicted input and consciousness is possible, that is, allows for an unconscious predicted input, empirical evidence would not support the supposed relevance of the predicted input for associating contents with consciousness. Even if it held true for the brain's neural processing of contents, the prediction model of brain and its cognitive model of stimulus-induced activity could then no longer be extended to consciousness. The crucial question thus is whether the predicted input and its contents are associated with consciousness by default, that is, automatically, which would make impossible unconscious processing. Or, alternatively, whether predicted input and its contents can also be processed in an unconscious way—in that case, consciousness would not be associated in an automatic way. We take up this question in the next section.

Empirical Findings Ib: Predicted Input—Unconscious Processing

Vetter et al. (2014) conducted a behavioral study in which they separated the predicted percept in a visual motion paradigm from the actually presented stimulus and the subsequently perceived content or percept. The authors exploited the fact that conscious perception of apparent motion varies with motion frequencies (those frequencies in which we perceive the movement or motion of a stimulus) with each subject preferring a specific frequency. The respective individual's preferred motion frequency must reflect the predicted input, that is, the predicted motion percept.

To serve as prediction of a specific actual input, the predicted input must be *in time with* the frequency in order to serve as predicted input, whereas, if it is not in accordance with the respective frequency or *out of time*, it cannot serve as predicted input. Vetter, Sanders, and Muckli (2014) consequently distinguished between predicted percepts as being in time with the subsequent actual input and unpredicted percepts as being out of time with the subsequent actual input.

The authors presented the subjects with three different kinds of actual inputs, intermediate, high, and low motion frequencies. They observed that the in-time predicted input worked well and thus predicted actual input in the intermediate motion frequencies, which was also associated with conscious awareness of the predicted input itself. In contrast, the low motion frequencies neither took on the role as predicted input nor was either associated with consciousness.

That was different in high motion frequencies, however. In this case the in-time predicted input still functioned and operated as prediction but was no longer associated with conscious illusory motion perception (despite the fact that it predicted well the subsequent actual input). There is a dissociation between the high frequencies serving as predicted input and their association with consciousness: they take on the role as predicted input but are not associated with consciousness. Hence, predicted input/predictive coding and consciousness can dissociate from each other with both not being coupled with each other by default, that is, in a necessary way.

The study by Vetter et al. (2014) shows three different scenarios: (1) predicted input with consciousness (as in intermediate-motion frequencies); (2) predicted input without consciousness (as in high-motion frequencies); (3) no predicted input at all (as in low-motion frequencies). Together, these data by Vetter et al. (2014) suggest that predictive coding is not necessarily coupled with consciousness—the presence of predictive coding is well compatible with the absence of consciousness.

The assumption of unconscious processing of the predicted input is further supported by others (see den Ouden et al., 2009; Kok, Brouwer, van Gerven, & de Lange, 2013; Wacongne et al., 2011). One can consequently infer that empirical evidence does not support the claim that the predicted input is associated with and thus sufficient by itself for consciousness. Note that my claim does not contest that there are unconscious elements in the predicted inputs. My claim concerns only that the predicted input itself can be processed in a completely unconscious way without entailing consciousness. This speaks against the predicted input being a sufficient neural condition of consciousness.

In contrast, it leaves open whether the predicted input may at least be a necessary (but nonsufficient) neural condition of consciousness. In either case we need to search for a yet different neuronal mechanism that allows for associating consciousness to contents as either related to predicted or to actual input. How can we describe the requirements for such an additional neuronal mechanism in more detail? We consider this question in the section that follows.

Empirical Findings IIa: From the Predicted Input to Consciousness

How does the requirement for an additional neuronal mechanism stand in relation to the cognitive model of consciousness? It means that the neurocognitive model of stimulus-induced activity as based on the predicted input and its modulation of the actual input cannot sufficiently account for associating any given content with consciousness. The predicted input itself can remain unconscious; that is, it cannot be associated with consciousness.

How and from where, then, is consciousness coming from if not from the predicted input itself? One may now revert to the actual input. However, as stated in the previous section, consciousness does not come with the actual input, that is, the sensory stimulus, either. We thus remain in the dark as to where and how consciousness can be associated with any given content independent of whether it originates in either the predicted input or the actual input.

Where does this leave us? The extension of the neurosensory to a neurocognitive model of stimulus-induced activity as in predictive coding only concerns the selection of contents in consciousness. In contrast, the neurocognitive model as presupposed by predictive coding remains insufficient by itself to address the question for the association of contents with consciousness. The prediction model of brain and its neurocognitive model of stimulus-induced activity therefore cannot be simply extended to a cognitive model of consciousness. Instead, we require a model of consciousness that is not primarily based on the neurocognitive model of stimulus-induced activity as in the prediction model of brain.

Put differently, we require a noncognitive model of stimulus-induced activity with its ultimate extension into a noncognitive model of consciousness (see Lamme, 2010; Northoff & Huang, in press; Tsuchiya et al., 2015, for first steps in this direction within the context of neuroscience) in order to account for our second two-part question of why and how consciousness can be associated with contents. Such a model is put forth and developed in the second part of this volume (chapters 7–8) where I present a spatiotemporal model of consciousness. Before considering such a spatiotemporal model, however, we should discuss some counterarguments by the advocate of predictive coding.

The advocate of predictive coding may now want to argue that the predicted input is only half of the story. The other half consists of the prediction error. Even if the predicted input itself may remain unconscious, the prediction error may nevertheless allow for associating contents with consciousness. In that case the prediction error itself and, more specifically, its degree (whether high or low) may allow for associating contents with consciousness. For example, a high degree of prediction error, as based on strong discrepancy between predicted and actual input, may favor the association of the respective content with consciousness. Conversely, if the prediction error is low, the content may not be associated with consciousness. Is such association between prediction error and consciousness supported on empirical grounds? We investigate this further in the next section.

Empirical Findings IIb: Interoceptive Sensitivity versus Interoceptive Accuracy and Awareness

The model of predictive coding has been mainly associated with exteroceptive stimulus processing: the processing of inputs to neural activity that originate from the environment. However, recently Seth (2013, 2014; Seth, Suzuki, & Critchley, 2012) suggests extending the model of predictive coding from extero- to interoceptive stimulus processing, thus applying it to stimuli generated within the body itself. As with exteroceptive stimulus processing, the stimulus-induced activity resulting from interoceptive stimuli is supposed by Seth to result from a comparison between predicted and actual interoceptive input.

Seth and Critchley (2013) (see also Hohwy, 2013) argue that the predicted input is closely related to what is described as agency, the multimodal integration between intero- and exteroceptive inputs. Neuronally, agency is related to higher-order regions in the brain such as the lateral prefrontal cortex where statistically based models of the possible causes underlying an actual input are developed.

Seth observes that comparison between predicted interoceptive input and actual interoceptive input takes place in a region on the lateral surface of the brain, the insula. The anterior insula may be central here because it is where intero- and exteroceptive pathways cross such that intero- and exteroceptive stimuli can be linked and integrated (see Craig, 2003, 2009, 2011); such intero-exteroceptive integration allows the insula to generate interoceptive–exteroceptive predictions of, for instance, pain, reward, and emotions (as suggested by Seth, Suzuki, & Critchley, 2012; Seth & Critchley, 2013; as well as Hohwy, 2013).

Is the processing of the interoceptive–exteroceptive predicted input associated with consciousness? One way to test this is to investigate conscious awareness of the heartbeat. We do need to distinguish between interoceptive accuracy and awareness since they may dissociate from each other. One can, for instance, be inaccurate about one's heart rhythm while being highly aware of one's own heartbeat (Garfinkel et al., 2015) as, for instance, is the case in anxiety disorder. Let us start with interoceptive accuracy. We may be either less or more accurate in our perception of our own heartbeat (Garfinkel et al., 2015). Such inaccuracy in the awareness of our heartbeat leads us to the concept of interoceptive accuracy (which, analogously, may also apply to exteroceptive stimuli, or exteroceptive accuracy).

The concept of *interoceptive accuracy* (or, alternatively, interoceptive inaccuracy) describes the degree to which the subjective perception of the number of heartbeats deviates from the number of objective heartbeats (as measured for instance with EEG) or, more generally "the objective accuracy in detecting internal bodily sensations" (Garfinkel et al., 2015). The less deviation between objective and subjective heartbeat numbers, the higher the degree of interoceptive accuracy. In contrast, the more deviation between objective and subjective heartbeat numbers, the higher the degree of interoceptive inaccuracy.

Interoceptive accuracy must be distinguished from interoceptive awareness. Interoceptive awareness describes the consciousness or awareness of one's own heartbeat. One may well be aware of one's own heartbeat even if one remains inaccurate about it. In other terms, interoceptive awareness and interoceptive accuracy may dissociate from each other. Recently, Garfinkel et al. (2015) also distinguished between interoceptive sensibility and awareness. Following Garfinkel et al. (2015), interoceptive sensibility concerns the "self-perceived dispositional tendency to be internally self-focused and interoceptively cognizant" (using self-evaluated assessment of subjective interoception).

Taken in this sense, interoceptive sensibility includes the subjective report of the heartbeat (whether accurate or inaccurate), which entails consciousness; interoceptive sensibility can thus be considered an index of consciousness (in an operational sense as measured by the subjective judgment). Interoceptive sensibility must be distinguished from interoceptive awareness, which concerns the metacognitive awareness of interoceptive (in)accuracy of the heartbeat.

Put more simply, interoceptive sensibility can be described as consciousness of the heartbeat itself, whereas interoceptive awareness refers to the cognitive reflection on one's own sensibility, thus entailing a form of metaconsciousness: awareness. Accordingly, the question of consciousness with regard to interoceptive stimuli from the heart comes down to interoceptive sensitivity (as distinguished from both interoceptive accuracy and awareness). For that reason, I focus in the following on interoceptive sensitivity as paradigmatic instance of consciousness.

Prediction Model and Consciousness Ia: Contents—Accurate versus Inaccurate

The example of interoception makes clear that we need to distinguish between the association of contents with consciousness on the one hand and the accuracy/inaccuracy in our detection and awareness of contents. Put somewhat differently, we need to distinguish the cognitive process of detection/awareness of contents as accurate or inaccurate from the phenomenal or experiential processes of consciousness of those contents irrespective of whether they are accurate or inaccurate in our awareness.

The distinction between consciousness and detection/awareness does not apply only to interoceptive stimuli from one's own body, such as one's own heartbeat, but also to exteroceptive stimuli from the environment. We may be accurate or inaccurate in our reporting and judgment of exteroceptive stimuli such as when we misperceive a face as a vase. Moreover, we may remain unaware of our inaccuracy in our judgment; the unawareness of the inaccuracy in our judgment may guide our subsequent behavior. Therefore, both exteroceptive accuracy/inaccuracy and awareness need to be distinguished from exteroceptive sensitivity, that is, consciousness itself: the latter refers to the association of exteroceptive contents with consciousness independent of whether that very same content is detected. Moreover, the association of consciousness of exteroceptive contents remains independent of whether the subject is aware of its own accuracy or inaccuracy.

First and foremost, the preceding reflections culminate in a useful distinction between two different concepts of contents: accurate and inaccurate. The accurate concept of content refers exclusively to accurate registering and processing of events or objects within the body and/or world in the brain. Conceived in an accurate way, content is supposed to reflect objects and events as they are (entailing realism).

In contrast, the inaccurate concept of content covers improper or inaccurate registering and processing of events or objects in the body and/or world in the brain. If content only existed in an accurate way, intero- and exteroceptive (in)accuracy should remain impossible. However, that premise is not endorsed by empirical reality since, as we have seen, we can perceive our own heartbeat inaccurately, and we are all familiar with misperceiving elements of our environments.

The virtue of predictive coding is that it can account for the inaccuracies in content far better than can be done with a naïve conception of the brain as a passive receiver and reproducer of inputs. By combining predicted input/output with actual input/output, predictive coding can account for the selection of inaccurate contents in our interoception, perception, attention, and so forth. In a nutshell, predictive coding is about contents, and its virtue lies in the fact that it can account for accurate and inaccurate as well as internally and externally generated contents.

In sum, predictive coding can well account for the selection of contents as well as our awareness of those contents as accurate or inaccurate. In contrast, predictive coding remains insufficient when it comes to explain how those very same contents can be associated with consciousness in the first place.

Prediction Model and Consciousness Ib: Contents and Consciousness

Can predictive coding also extend beyond contents, that is both the accurate and inaccurate, to their association with consciousness? For his example of interoceptive stimuli, Seth supposes that predictive coding accounts for interoceptive sensitivity, that is, the association of interoceptive stimuli with consciousness. More specifically, Seth (2013; Seth, Suzuki, & Critchley, 2012) infers from the presence of predictive coding of interoceptive stimuli in terms of predicted input and prediction error within the insula specifically to the presence of consciousness, that is, consciousness of one's own heartbeat, which results in what he describes as "conscious presence" (Seth, Suzuki, & Critchley, 2012).

Since he infers from the presence of predictive coding the presence of consciousness, I here speak of a *prediction inference*. The concept of prediction inference refers to the assumption that one infers from the neural processing of contents in terms of predicted and actual inputs the actual presence of consciousness. Is the prediction inference justified? I argue that such inference is justified for contents including the distinction between accurate and inaccurate contents: we can infer from the neural processing of predicted and actual input to accurate and inaccurate contents—I call such inference *prediction inference*.

In contrast, that very same inference is not justified when it comes to consciousness: we cannot infer from the neural processing of predicted and actual input to the association of content (including both accurate and inaccurate contents) with consciousness—I call such inference *prediction fallacy*. From this, I argue that Seth can make his assumption of the presence of consciousness only on the basis of committing such a prediction fallacy. We analyze this fallacy in detail in the next section.

Prediction Model and Consciousness IIa: Prediction Inference versus Prediction Fallacy

Seth infers, from the fact that predictive coding operates in interoceptive stimulus processing, the presence of consciousness in the form of interoceptive sensibility. Specifically, he infers from the presence of interoceptive predicted inputs (as generated in the insula) the presence of conscious interoceptive contents, for example, the heartbeat during subsequent stimulus-induced activity as based on the prediction error. That inference, however, overlooks the fact that interoceptive contents can nevertheless remain within the realm of unconsciousness. The presence of interoceptive predicted input and the subsequent prediction error in stimulus-induced activity may account for the presence of interoceptive contents, for example, our own heartbeat, including our subsequent judgment of these interoceptive contents as either accurate or inaccurate.

In contrast, the interoceptive contents themselves do not yet entail the association of contents with consciousness—they can well remain as unconscious (as is most often the case in daily life) irrespective of whether they are (judged and detected and become aware as) accurate or inaccurate. The conceptual distinction between consciousness of contents on the one hand and accurate/inaccurate contents on the other is supported on empirical grounds given data that show how interoceptive accuracy can dissociate from interoceptive sensitivity, that is, consciousness (and also from interoceptive awareness) and can thus remain unconscious (rather than conscious) (see Garfinkel et al., 2015).

The same holds analogously for exteroceptive contents as originating in the external world rather than in one's own internal body. These exteroceptive contents may be accurate or inaccurate with respect to the actual event in the world; that remains independent of whether they are associated with consciousness. This independence is supported by empirical data (see Faivre et al., 2014; Koch et al., 2016; Lamme, 2010; Northoff, 2014b; Northoff et al., 2017; Tsuchiya et al., 2015; Koch & Tsuchiya, 2012). Therefore, the conceptual distinction between consciousness of contents and the contents themselves including whether they are accurate or inaccurate is supported on empirical grounds for both intero- and exteroceptive contents, or, put another way, from body and the world.

The distinction between consciousness of contents and contents themselves carries far-reaching implications for the kind of inference we can make from the presence of contents to the presence of consciousness. Seth's prediction inference accounts well for the interoceptive contents and their accuracy or inaccuracy. In contrast, that very same prediction inference cannot answer the questions of why and how the interoceptive contents, as based on predicted input and prediction error, are associated with consciousness rather than remaining within the unconscious.

Hence, to account for the association of the interoceptive contents with consciousness, Seth (2013) requires an additional step, the step from unconscious interoceptive contents (including both accurate and inaccurate) to conscious interoceptive content (irrespective of whether these contents are detected/judged as accurate or inaccurate). This additional step is neglected, however, when he directly infers from the presence of predictive coding of contents in terms of predicted input and prediction error to their association with consciousness.

What does this mean for the prediction inference? The prediction inference can well account for interoceptive accuracy/inaccuracy and, thus, more generally, for the selection of contents. Predictive coding allows us to differentiate between inaccurate and accurate intero-/exteroceptive contents. Thus, the prediction inference remains nonfallacious when it comes to the contents themselves including their accuracy or inaccuracy. However, this contrasts with intero-/exteroceptive sensitivity and, more generally, with consciousness. But the prediction inference cannot account for the association of intero-/exteroceptive contents including both accurate and inaccurate contents with consciousness. When it comes to consciousness, then, the prediction inference must thus be considered fallacious, which renders it what I describe as *prediction fallacy* (see figures 6.1a and 6.1b).

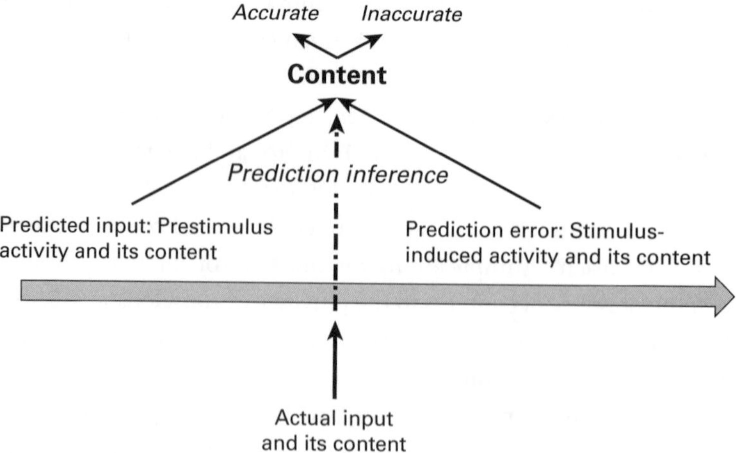

Figure 6.1a
Prediction inference.

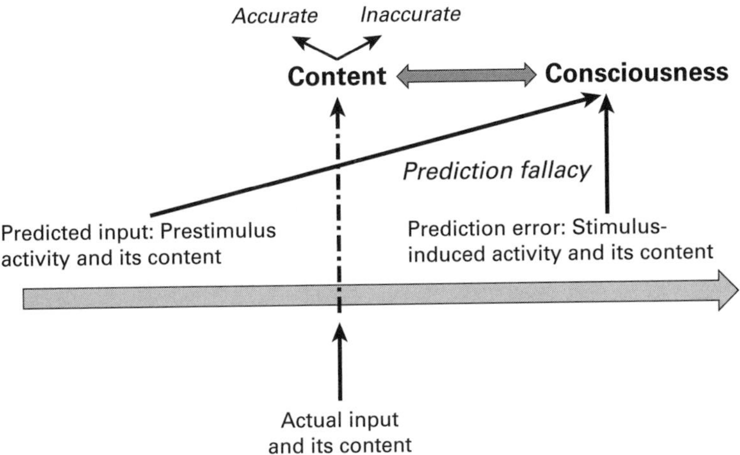

Figure 6.1b
Prediction fallacy.

Prediction Model and Consciousness IIb: Consciousness Extends beyond Contents and Cognition

What is the take-home message from this discussion? Both predicted input and prediction error themselves do not entail any association of their respective contents with consciousness. The empirical data show that both predicted input and prediction error can remain unconscious. There are contents from the environment that remain unconscious in our perception and cognition. We, for instance, plan and execute many of our actions in an unconscious way. Given the framework of predictive coding, planning of action is based on generating a predicted input, while the execution of action is related to prediction error. As both planning and execution of action can remain unconscious, neither predicted input nor prediction output is associated with consciousness. Hence, the example of action supports the view that predictive coding does not entail anything about whether contents are associated with consciousness.

Let us consider the following example. When we drive our car along familiar routes, much of our perception of the route including the landscape along it will remain an unconscious element. That changes once some unknown not yet encountered obstacle, such as a street blockade due to an accident, occurs. In such a case, we may suddenly perceive the houses along the route in a conscious way and become aware that, for instance, there are some beautiful mansions. Analogous to driving along a familiar route, most of the time the contents from our body, such as our heartbeat, remain unconscious entities.

The prediction fallacy simply ignores that the contents associated with both predicted input and prediction error can remain unconscious by us. The fallacy rests on the confusion between selection of contents (which may be accurate or inaccurate) and consciousness of contents. Predictive coding and the prediction model of brain can well or sufficiently account for the distinction between accuracy and inaccuracy of contents. In contrast, they cannot sufficiently account for why and how the selected contents (accurate and inaccurate) can be associated with consciousness rather than remaining as unconscious contents. In sum, the prediction inference remains nonfallacious with regard to the selected contents (as accurate or inaccurate), whereas it becomes fallacious when it comes to the association of contents with consciousness.

What does the prediction fallacy entail for the cognitive model of consciousness? The cognitive model of consciousness is based first on contents and second on the processing of selected contents in terms of predictive coding with predicted input and prediction error. The cognitive model tacitly presupposes a hidden inference from the the selection of contents (as accurate or inaccurate) to the association of those contents with consciousness.

However, the distinction between the selected contents as accurate or inaccurate on the basis of predictive coding does not entail anything for their association with consciousness. The inference from prediction to consciousness is thus fallacious, what we may term a prediction fallacy. Empirical data show that any selected contents (accurate or inaccurate as well as predicted input or prediction error) can remain unconscious and do therefore not entail their association with consciousness.

In conclusion, the cognitive model of stimulus-induced activity and the brain in general as based solely on contents as in the prediction model of brain remain insufficient to account for consciousness. For that reason, we need to search for an additional dimension beyond contents and prediction that determines consciousness. Put simply, consciousness extends beyond contents and our cognition of them.

Conclusion

I have discussed here the relevance of the prediction model of brain for consciousness. The prediction model of brain focuses on content and a cognitive model of stimulus-induced activity. We saw that the prediction model can well account for the contents in consciousness, encompassing the selection of contents as accurate or inaccurate. We can indeed infer from the neural processing of contents in terms of predicted and actual input to the selection of contents that can be accurate or inaccurate. Such prediction inference, as I describe it, addresses our first question, the one for the selection of contents in consciousness, rather well.

In contrast, the second question for the association of contents with consciousness has remained open. The only way to address that question on the basis of the prediction model of brain is to commit what I have described as the prediction fallacy wherein one infers from the processing of contents in terms of predicted and actual input their actual association with consciousness. However, no empirical evidence supports the association of the contents related to predicted input or prediction error (predictive coding) with consciousness.

Nor can a direct inference be made from the processing of contents to their association with consciousness without committing the prediction fallacy. More generally, the prediction fallacy suggests that the cognitive model of stimulus-induced activity as presupposed on the basis of the prediction model of brain cannot be extended to consciousness. A cognitive model of consciousness thus remains insufficient on both empirical and conceptual grounds.

What do the prediction fallacy and the insufficiency of the cognitive model of consciousness imply for the characterization of consciousness? Consciousness cannot be sufficiently determined by contents alone. Consciousness is more than its contents; for that reason, any model of consciousness must extend beyond contents and cognition. Therefore, consciousness cannot be sufficiently determined by cognitive functions such as anticipation or prediction (as in predictive coding), or by others including attention, working memory, executive function, and additional functions. This finding is also empirically supported by showing that the neural mechanisms underlying these various cognitive functions do not sufficiently account for associating the cognitive functions and their contents with consciousness (see Faivre et al., 2014; Koch et al., 2016; Lamme, 2010; Northoff, 2014b; Northoff et al., 2017; Tsuchiya et al., 2015; Tsuchiya & Koch, 2012).

Put simply, consciousness does not come with the contents but extends beyond contents and our cognition of them. There must be an additional factor that allows associating contents with consciousness rather than having them remain in the unconscious. This requires us to develop and search for a model of consciousness, a noncognitive model, such as the "noncognitive consciousness" proposed by Cerullo et al. (2015), that introduces an additional dimension and thereby extends beyond the cognitive model. I postulate that such additional dimension can be found in spatiotemporal features. This leads me to suggest a spatiotemporal model of consciousness that is developed in detail in the next several chapters.

7 Spatiotemporal Model of Consciousness I: Spatiotemporal Specificity and Neuronal-Phenomenal Correspondence

Introduction

General Background

Consciousness is a complex phenomenon that includes different dimensions. The initial characterization of consciousness by contents (Crick & Koch, 2003; Koch, 2004) has been complemented by the level or state of consciousness (Bachmann & Hudetz, 2014; Koch et al., 2016; Laureys, 2005). Recently, additional dimensions have been suggested. One such dimension is the distinction between phenomenal/experiential and cognitive aspects of consciousness (Cerullo, Metzinger, & Mangun, 2015; Northoff, 2014b). Another dimension was introduced with the form (or structure) of consciousness (Northoff, 2013, 2014b). The form of consciousness pertains to the grouping and ultimately the organization of different contents, which, neuronally, is supposedly associated with the spontaneous activity and its spatiotemporal structure. The exact neuronal mechanisms underlying the different dimensions of consciousness, for example, level/state, content/form, phenomenal/experiential, cognitive/reporting, including their relations, remain an open question.

Many studies in healthy subjects sought to associate consciousness with stimulus-induced or task-evoked brain activity. Specifically, the stimulus-induced or task-evoked activities refer to those neural activity changes that are related to and sufficient for the contents of consciousness (Koch et al., 2016). We therefore speak of content–neural correlates of consciousness (NCC). Temporally, the content–NCC is associated with event-related potentials such as the N100, P300 (Bachmann & Hudetz, 2014; Dehaene & Changeux, 2011; Koch et al., 2016). Spatially, stimulus-induced or task-evoked activity in higher-order brain regions such as the prefrontal cortex and posterior cortical "hot zones" may be the NCC for mediating conscious content (Dehaene et al., 2014; Dehaene & Changeux, 2011; Koch et al., 2016).

More recently, different components of stimulus-induced activity have been identified including the distinction between early and late stimulus-induced activity, as well as the interaction between pre- and poststimulus activity. Early stimulus-induced activity, as tested for in "no-report" paradigms may be related to the phenomenal features of consciousness (e.g., experience), whereas late stimulus-induced activity is supposedly more related to its cognitive components (e.g., reporting and awareness of contents) (Koch et al., 2016; Lamme, 2010a,b; Northoff, 2014b; Tononi et al., 2016; Tsuchiya et al., 2015). On the other end, prior to stimulus onset, several studies have demonstrated that the level of prestimulus spontaneous activity impacts both stimulus-induced activity and the respectively associated content of consciousness (Boly et al., 2007; Hesselmann, Kell, & Kleinschmidt, 2008; Mathewson et al., 2009; Ploner et al., 2010; Qin et al., 2016; Sadaghiani, Hesselmann, Friston, & Kleinschmidt, 2010, Sadaghiani et al., 2015; Schölvinck et al., 2012; van Dijk et al., 2008; Yu et al., 2015). The relevance of prestimulus activity level suggests a central role of the brain's spontaneous activity for consciousness. This is also supported by other studies in subjects with altered states of consciousness, such as unresponsive wakefulness state (UWRS), sleep, and anesthesia; these subjects showed major changes in the brain's spontaneous activity (Bayne, Hohwy, & Owen, 2016).

Why and how are these different forms of neural activity (i.e., spontaneous, prestimulus, early, and late stimulus-induced activity) related to consciousness and its different dimensions? To date, this subject has not yet been thoroughly examined. I here propose that these different forms of neural activity reflect different ways of how the brain constructs its own inner time and space, that is, its *intrinsic time and space* (see the section below titled "Definition of Time and Space"). This hypothesis comprises what I describe as the *spatiotemporal theory of consciousness* (STC).

Time and Space

Time and space are the central and most basic building blocks of nature. Time and space can be constructed in different ways. Although the different ways of constructing time and space have been investigated extensively in the field of physics, their relevance for the brain's neural activity and, even more importantly, to consciousness remains largely unknown. Current neuroscientific views focus mainly on information, behavioral, affective, or cognitive features of brain and consciousness such as integrated information theory (IIT) (Tononi et al., 2016), or cognitive theory such as the global neuronal workspace theory (GNWT) (Dehaene et al., 2014; Dehaene & Changeux, 2011), and predictive coding (see chapters 3 and 6 of this volume for details, as well as Friston, 2010; Hohwy, 2013; Seth, 2014). Whereas these views presuppose and implicitly touch on the brain's own time and space, they do not consider time and space themselves—central dimensions of the brain's neural activity—in an explicit way, that is, they do not consider how the brain itself constructs time and space in its own neural activity.

Given that (1) time and space are most basic features of nature and (2) that the brain itself is part of nature, we here consider the brain and its neural activity in explicitly temporal and spatial terms. In other words, we conceive the brain's different forms of neural activity (spontaneous, prestimulus, early and late stimulus-induced activity) in primarily spatiotemporal terms rather than in informational, behavioral, cognitive, or affective terms. I postulate that such a spatiotemporal view of the brain's neural activity is central for understanding how the brain can generate consciousness with its different dimensions. In this sense, then, consciousness may be understood as a spatiotemporal phenomenon of the brain's neural activity.

Aim and Overview

The main and overarching aim of this chapter is to provide a unified hypothesis that directly links and thus integrates the different forms of neural activity with the different dimensions of consciousness. Such an integrative, coherent framework is suggested to consist of temporal and spatial features of the brain's neural activity (across all forms of neural activity) comprising what I describe as the *spatiotemporal theory of consciousness* (STC; see also Northoff & Huang, 2017). Based on various lines of empirical evidence, I postulate here that the four dimensions of consciousness (level/state, content/form, phenomenal/experience, cognitive/reporting) are mediated by four corresponding spatiotemporal neuronal mechanisms: (1) the neuronal mechanism of *spatiotemporal nestedness* accounts for the level or state of consciousness; (2) the neuronal mechanism of *spatiotemporal alignment* accounts for selecting the content and constituting the structure, or, as I say, the form of consciousness (Northoff, 2013, 2014b); (3) the neuronal mechanism of *spatiotemporal expansion* accounts for the phenomenal dimension of consciousness, for example, experience with qualia; (4) the neuronal mechanism of *spatiotemporal globalization* accounts for the cognitive dimension of consciousness, that is, the reporting of its contents (see a summary in figure 7.1). The STC is primarily a neuroscientific theory of brain and consciousness, which carries major philosophical implications of a novel view of consciousness (see also Northoff, 2014b, 2016a–d, 2017a,b). Most importantly, the spatiotemporal view of consciousness entails a paradigm shift from a mind–body problem to a world–brain problem, which will be explicated in chapters 9–11 of this book (figure 7.1).

Three of these mechanisms (1, 3, and 4) I discuss in detail in the present chapter and reserve a detailed analysis of the fourth, spatiotemporal alignment, for the next chapter (chapter 8) in the volume. Conceptually, I also discuss two arguments in the third part of the present chapter that may be raised against such a spatiotemporal model of consciousness. First, the argument of nonspecificity claims that the suggested spatiotemporal mechanisms remain unspecific with respect to consciousness. I will reject that argument by showing that consciousness is based on specific spatiotemporal mechanisms of the brain's neural activity. I therefore characterize consciousness by spatiotemporal specificity, as will be discussed in the first part in this chapter.

Second, the argument of triviality states that the characterization of both brain and consciousness in spatiotemporal terms remains trivial because time and space are the basic ingredients of the world in general and of the brain in particular. I will reject that argument by demonstrating a nontrivial correspondence between neuronal and phenomenal features, that is, a neuronal-phenomenal correspondence, with respect to spatiotemporal features, as will be discussed in the second part of this chapter.

Definition of Time and Space

What do we mean by the terms *time* and *space*? One would argue that the brain's neural activity is by default temporal and spatial. This makes any account of consciousness and its different dimensions in spatiotemporal terms rather self-evident. We do need, however, to clarify what exactly we

Consciousness Dimensions	Level/State	Content	Phenomenology/ Experience	Cognitive Processing/ Reporting
Experimental testing	Task-free/resting-state paradigms	Prestimulus paradigms	Poststimulus no-report paradigms	Poststimulus report paradigms
Types of brain's neural activity	Spontaneous activity	Prestimulus activity	Early stimulus-induced activity	Late stimulus-induced activity
Spatiotemporal features	Infraslow Temporal correlations Cross-frequency coupling Small-worldness Dynamic repertoire	Nonlinear interaction between pre- and post-stimulus-evoked activity Phase-preference	P50 and N100 Posterior cortical hot zones Sensory areas Cortical midline regions	Gamma activity P3b wave Prefrontal-parietal recruitment loops
Neuronal mechanisms	**Spatiotemporal nestedness**	**Spatiotemporal alignment**	**Spatiotemporal expansion**	**Spatiotemporal globalization**
Terminology	Neural predisposition of consciousness (NPC)	Neural prerequisite of consciousness (preNPC)	Neural correlates of consciousness (NCC)	Neural consequence of consciousness (NCCcon)

Figure 7.1
Overview of different spatiotemporal mechanisms and the different dimensions of consciousness.

mean by the concepts of time and space in STC (see also chapter 9 for an ontological definition of time and space).

The STC refers to time and space of the brain; that is, how the brain constructs its own time and space in its neural activity. One may thus speak of time and space of the brain, or the "intrinsic" time and space of its neural activity. The construction of such intrinsic time and space of the brain itself and its neural activity needs to be distinguished from our perception and cognition of time and space including their neural correlates—the latter presupposes the former. The focus in this chapter is not on the neural correlates of our perception and cognition of time and space but rather on how the brain itself constitutes its own time and space, that is, intrinsic time and space (see appendix 2 in Northoff, 2014b, for more details).

The brain's intrinsic time concerns the duration of neuronal activity embedded in specific frequency ranges. These frequency ranges are distinguished from higher frequency ranges such as ultrasound (Nagel, 1974) or lower frequency ranges of other nature phenomena such as seismic earth waves (He et al., 2010). As for the brain's intrinsic space, we speak of the extension of neural activity across different regions and networks in the brain. Briefly, the brain's intrinsic time and space or its "operational time and space" (Fingelkurts, Fingelkurts, & Neves, 2013), can be characterized by temporal duration and spatial extension of its neural activity. Both terms, temporal duration and spatial extension describe how the brain constitutes its self, that is, by "intrinsic" neural activity within the space and time of the anatomostructural brain.

Let us describe the notions of *temporal duration* and *spatial extension* of the brain's neural activity in more empirical detail. First, the temporal duration is related to the temporal ranges or circle durations of neural oscillations or fluctuations. This includes different frequencies ranging from infraslow (0.0001–0.1 Hz), over slow (0.1–1 Hz), delta (1–4 Hz), and theta (5–8 Hz) to faster frequencies of alpha (8–12 Hz), beta (13–30 Hz), and broadband gamma (30–240 Hz) (Buzsáki, 2006; Buzsáki et al., 2013; Buzsáki & Draguhn, 2004). These different frequencies show different functions and, most likely, are associated with different underlying neurophysiological mechanisms that give rise to a wide range of behavioral and functional opportunities (Buzsáki, 2006).

Second, the temporal duration of the brain's neural activity can also be characterized by intrinsic temporal autocorrelation in milliseconds to seconds and minutes range. These time scales can be measured by an "autocorrelation window" (Honey et al., 2012) and scale-free or fractal properties such as the power law exponent or Hurst exponent (He, 2014; He et al., 2010). This characterization of the brain's neural activity by temporal duration across different time scales makes clear that the brain's intrinsic time (i.e., its inner duration) is highly structured and very finely organized. We will see further below that such temporal structure and organization in the brain's neural activity are central for consciousness.

Third, the range of frequencies and the intrinsic temporal organization of the brain's neural activity strongly influence the processing of extrinsic stimuli. The different frequencies with their respective cycle durations provide windows of opportunity, that is, "temporal receptive windows" (Hasson, Chen, & Honey, 2015) to acquire and encode extrinsic stimuli and their temporal sequences (Lakatos et al., 2008, 2013; Schroeder & Lakatos, 2009a,b). Therefore, there appear to exist intrinsic "temporal receptive windows" that match with the physical features of the extrinsic stimuli in hierarchy time scales (Chen, Hasson, & Honey, 2015; Hasson et al., 2015; Honey et al., 2012; Murray et al., 2014).

We may now want to consider the intrinsic space of the brain's neural activity, that is, its spatial extension. The brain shows an extensive structural connectivity that links and connects across neurons, regions, and networks. This structural connectivity provides the hardware through which neurons can functionally communicate (called *functional connectivity*). Although there is strong dependency of functional connectivity on structural connectivity (Honey et al., 2009), the divergence between both forms of connectivity is relevant for consciousness: loss of consciousness is marked by a loss of divergence between structural and functional connectivity (Tagliazucchi et al., 2016). Finally, it should be mentioned that the brain's intrinsic space is also related to its small-world organization (one that is spatially scale-free) with various features including modularity and centrality (Bassett & Sporns, 2017; Sporns & Betzel, 2016).

We have so far described the temporal duration and spatial extension of the brain's neural activity and how together they construct the brain's intrinsic time and space. We also need to consider that the brain and its intrinsic time and space are located in the extrinsic time and space encompassing both the body and the world (Park, Correia, Ducorps, & Tallon-Baudry, 2014; Park & Tallon-Baudry, 2014). Empirical data suggest that the brain's intrinsic time and space align themselves to extrinsic time and space in order to constitute a world–brain relation (see the next section for details of such spatiotemporal alignment). Such world-brain relation allows us to experience ourselves including our body within and our self as part of the spatiotemporally more extended world.

I propose that the brain constitutes the temporal and spatial features of its own neural activity in a most specific way—I therefore speak of what I describe as temporal and spatial mechanisms. Most importantly, I propose that these spatiotemporal mechanisms with their construction of the brain's duration and extension are central for constituting the different dimensions of consciousness, the level/state, content, and form. In a nutshell, the spatiotemporal model of consciousness conceives both brain and consciousness in spatiotemporal terms—I propose that a specific way of constituting time and space by the brain's neural activity is central for transforming neural activity into phenomenal activity, what we call consciousness.

Spatiotemporal Model of Consciousness I: Spatiotemporal Nestedness—Neural Predisposition of Consciousness and Spatiotemporal Specificity

Empirical Findings Ia: Spontaneous Activity—Temporal Nestedness

The brain's spontaneous activity shows a certain temporal structure. This is, for example, reflected in the fact that the spontaneous activity operates across different frequency ranges (as from infraslow/0.01–0.1 Hz) over slow (0.01–1 Hz) and fast (1–180 Hz) ranges (Buzsáki, 2006; Buzsáki et al., 2013). Importantly, neural activity in the different frequencies shows a fractal organization such that the power of slower frequency ranges is higher than that in faster frequency ranges, which can be described as scale-free activity (He, 2014; He et al., 2010; Linkenkaer-Hansen et al., 2001; Palva et al., 2013; Palva & Palva, 2012; Zhigalov et al., 2015).

Scale-free activity has been further characterized by long-range temporal autocorrelation (LRTC) across widespread cortical regions (Bullmore et al., 2001; He 2011; He et al., 2010; Linkenkaer-Hansen, Nikouline, Palva, & Ilmoniemi, 2001; Palva et al., 2013). As fluctuations, the infraslow frequencies have often been conceived as mere noise; however, that 1/f noise-like signal consists of the neural activity itself (rather than to some noise-related activity by our method of measurement). The data as shown below suggest that the structured 1/f noise-like signal is central for the level/state of consciousness.

In addition to their scale-free fractal nature with LRTC, infraslow, slow, and faster frequencies are also coupled to each other as measured by cross-frequency coupling (CFC) (Aru et al., 2015; Bonnefond et al., 2017; He, Zempel, Snyder, & Raichle, 2010; Hyafil et al., 2015). CFC allows for linking the different frequency ranges, typically with the amplitude of the higher-frequency ranges being coupled to and integrated within the phase of the lower-frequency ones. This has been shown in both slow/faster (Aru et al., 2015; Buzsáki & Draguhn, 2004; Buzsáki et al., 2013; Hyafil, Giraud, Fontolan, & Gutkin, 2015) and infraslow ranges (Huang et al., 2016).

To summarize, the brain's spontaneous activity shows an elaborate temporal organization in that different temporal ranges or scales are linked and integrated with each other. This is manifest in scale-free activity with LRTC and fractal nature as well as in CFC. Such organization amounts to what can be described as *temporal nestedness* of the brain's spontaneous activity.

Empirical Findings Ib: Spontaneous Activity—Spatial Nestedness

We may now consider the spatial organization of the brain's spontaneous activity. The faster frequencies are relatively spatially restricted in the brain and temporally regular (Buszaki, 2006). In contrast, the infraslow frequencies are more spatially extended throughout the brain and temporally irregular (Buzsáki, 2006; He, 2014; He et al., 2010). Moreover, spatially, one can observe modularity with small-world properties, which also follows scale-free fractal organizational patter on the spatial level (Sporns & Betzel, 2016)—this allows for *hierarchical modularity* with both integration and segregation of information across the whole brain (Deco et al., 2015).

Moreover, different regions or networks show different time scales. For instance, the sensory regions/networks show rather short time scales, whereas the default-mode network (DMN) seems to exhibit the longest time scales and thus the strongest power in the infraslow frequency range (see Hasson et al., 2015; Lee et al., 2014; He 2011; Huang, Zhang, Longtin, et al. 2017). Therefore, analogous to the temporal side, one may want to speak of spatial nestedness with a hierarchy of time scales (Murray et al., 2014).

Taken together, scale-free activity with LRTC, CFC (as well as other temporal features including variability, complexity, or cross-threshold crossing), and small-worldness with hierarchical modularity establish a specific temporal and spatial structure in the brain's overall or global neural activity (Huang et al., 2014, 2016; Hudetz et al., 2015, Mitra et al., 2015; Palva et al., 2013; Palva & Palva, 2012; see also He et al., 2010).

Due to the nesting of different frequencies/regions in such spatiotemporal structure, we characterize the latter by the term *spatiotemporal nestedness*. Such spatiotemporal nestedness may be described as an "integrated hierarchy of time and spatial scales" (Murray et al., 2014; see also Bonnefond et al., 2017; Florin & Baillet, 2015). We see in the following section that such an integrated hierarchy of time and spatial scales of the brain's neural activity is central for the level/state of consciousness.

Empirical Findings IIa: Spatiotemporal Nestedness and the Level/State of Consciousness

We must also consider the LRTC, CFC, and small-worldness during the loss of consciousness. Scale-free activity (as measured by power law exponent or detrended fluctuation analysis) is progressively reduced during the advancement of sleep stages N1 to N3 in the infraslow frequency range (Mitra et al., 2015; Tagliazucchi et al., 2013; Tagliazucchi & Laufs, 2014; Zhigalov et al., 2015). These studies observed progressive reduction in infraslow scale-free activity globally as well as in specific networks such as a DMN (including midline regions) and an attention network (including the lateral frontoparietal regions).

Whereas fMRI measures infraslow frequency range (<0.1 Hz), EEG usually targets higher-frequency ranges (1–180 Hz). Interestingly, misbalance between lower and higher frequencies, for example, stronger delta (1–4 Hz) with weaker beta and gamma (20–60 Hz), was found in unresponsive wakefulness state (UWS) and anesthesia (Lewis et al., 2012; Purdon et al., 2013; Sarà et al., 2011; Sitt et al., 2014). Studies on anesthesia also showed abnormal coupling of the ongoing phase in slow frequencies (0.01–1Hz) to either spiking rates (Lewis et al., 2012) or faster frequencies like alpha during the loss of consciousness (Mukamel et al., 2014).

Notably, an elegant EEG study by Purdon et al. (2013) showed that alpha amplitudes were maximal at low-frequency peaks during anesthetic-induced unconsciousness, whereas this relation reversed during consciousness and transition period to unconsciousness. Moreover, the phase–amplitude coupling and thus CFC predicted recovery of consciousness (Purdon et al., 2013). Taken together, the findings show that the temporal and spatial organization of the brain's spontaneous activity by LRTS, CFC, scale-free, and small-world is central for the level/state of consciousness. Temporal nestedness of neural activity may thus not only organize and structure our brain's spontaneous activity but also yield the level/state of consciousness (figure 7.1a).

Let us now consider nestedness of neural activity on the spatial side. Barttfeld et al. (2015) showed reduced small-world organization in monkey anesthesia. Analogous findings were observed in human subjects (Uehara et al., 2014). It has been shown that dynamic functional connectivity was reduced in human anesthesia that resembled structural connectivity whereas in the awake state both structural and functional connectivity diverged transiently in specifically sensory regions (Tagliazucchi et al., 2016). Liu et al. (2014) observed reduced functional connectivity in both anesthesia and unresponsive wakefulness state (UWS); however, only UWS showed decreased scale-free properties while the latter were maintained in anesthesia.

Empirical Findings IIb Spatiotemporal Nestedness—Neural Predispositions of the Level/State of Consciousness

How can spatiotemporal nestedness of neural activity account for the level/state of consciousness? Spatiotemporal nestedness is a global feature of neural activity spanning across different time scales, frequencies, and regions or networks. Temporally, it refers to the integration or coupling across infraslow, slow, and fast frequencies, whereas spatially different regions/networks are integrated and organized in terms of small-world properties. Hence, spatiotemporal integration of different temporal and spatial scales allows constituting what we have described as spatiotemporal nestedness of neural activity.

Analogously, the level or state of consciousness can be considered a global feature that integrates and operates across different intrinsic temporal and spatial scales. For instance, the level/state of consciousness remains continuous across both short and longer time intervals, and this applies also to proximal and distal spatial environment. Psychologically, the level/state of consciousness may thus include different time and space scales that are nested within each other and may operate in a scale-free way. As such, the level/state of consciousness may well correspond to the spatiotemporal integration of the brain's global integration of temporal and spatial dimensions. I propose that integration of different temporal and spatial scales is a central mechanism for constituting spatiotemporal nestedness in the level/state of consciousness.

In other words, I propose a correspondence of spatiotemporal scales between the brain's spontaneous activity and the level/state of consciousness: the degree to which different temporal and spatial scales/ranges are integrated may correspond to the degree of temporal and spatial continuity of the level/state of consciousness. One may consequently hypothesize that fluctuations in the degree of spatiotemporal nestedness of the brain's neural activity may correspond to analogous fluctuations in our level/state of consciousness across time and space. Accordingly, I propose a spatiotemporal correspondence between neural activity and the level/state of consciousness.

Moreover, it should be noted that the level/state of consciousness is not about specific contents but concerns "conscious experiences in their entirety, irrespective of their specific contents" (Koch et al., 2016). I maintain that spatiotemporal nestedness represents the brain's neural activity in its entirety irrespective of specific contents. Therefore, spatiotemporal nestedness of the brain's spontaneous activity is a necessary condition of possible consciousness—a neural predisposition of consciousness (NPC) (Northoff & Heiss, 2015).

Note that we here explicitly refer to the global spatiotemporal organization or structure of the brain's spontaneous activity rather than to global activity or global metabolism (Schölvinck et al., 2010; Shulman et al., 2009) per se (or to a specific neural network such as the DMN). Global activity or metabolism may well be present without a specific spatiotemporal structure. We propose that it is the latter, the spatiotemporal structure that constitutes the degree of fractal and scale-free organization of the brain's spontaneous activity, rather than the mere level of global activity or metabolism by itself, that is central for the level or state of consciousness. However, it should be noted that a sufficient metabolism level and thus energy supply may be necessary to constitute complex temporal and spatial structure—what we have termed spatiotemporal nestedness—in the brain's neural activity. This may explain the findings, in specifically in UWRS, that the degree of glucose metabolism is usually the best predictor of the level/state of consciousness in these patients (Stender et al., 2014).

In sum, the studies just discussed demonstrate the central rule of LRTC, CFC, and small-world organization for the level/state of consciousness: LRTC, CFC, and small-world organization are spatiotemporal mechanisms that constitute the spontaneous activity's structure as spatiotemporally nested. The level/state of consciousness is consequently a spatiotemporal phenomenon that can be traced back to the spatiotemporal nestedness of the brain's spontaneous activity.

Let us rephrase the relation between neural activity and the level/state of consciousness. I propose that the spatiotemporal nestedness of the brain's global neural activity is directly manifested in corresponding global features in consciousness, that is, its spatiotemporal nestedness. Consciousness is therefore as scale-free, as cross-frequency coupled, and as small-world organized as the spatiotemporal nestedness of the brain's neural activity. If the brain's neural activity is no longer scale-free, cross-frequency coupled, and small-world organized, as in anesthesia, sleep, and unresponsive wakefulness, then consciousness is lost (as its spatiotemporal nestedness is lost). Therefore, I consider spatiotemporal nestedness of the brain's neural activity to be a distinct neural predisposition of the level/state of consciousness (NPC) (figure 7.2).

Empirical Findings IIc: Spatiotemporal Fragmentation and Isolation—Loss of the Level/State of Consciousness

How can we demonstrate in more detail that spatiotemporal nestedness of neural activity predisposes the level/state of consciousness? In a landmark study Lewis (Lewis et al., 2012) simultaneously investigated spiking in single unit recording and local field potentials (LFP) in three subjects with epilepsy during the loss of consciousness when undergoing anesthesia with propofol (see also Mukamel et al., 2014; Mukamel et al., 2011; Purdon et al., 2013; Purdon, Sampson, Pavone, & Brown, 2015).

During the application of increasing propofol dosage, subjects were stimulated with an auditory task during which they heard their own name (every 4 s) after which they had to respond by clicking a button. The loss of consciousness (LOC) was defined as the time period from 1s before the first missed stimulus to the second missed stimulus (in a sequence) amounting to a 5-s period (1 s + 4 s as interstimulus interval). This allowed Lewis et al. (2012) to compare the time period before the loss of consciousness (pre-LOC) with the time period after the loss of consciousness (post-LOC).

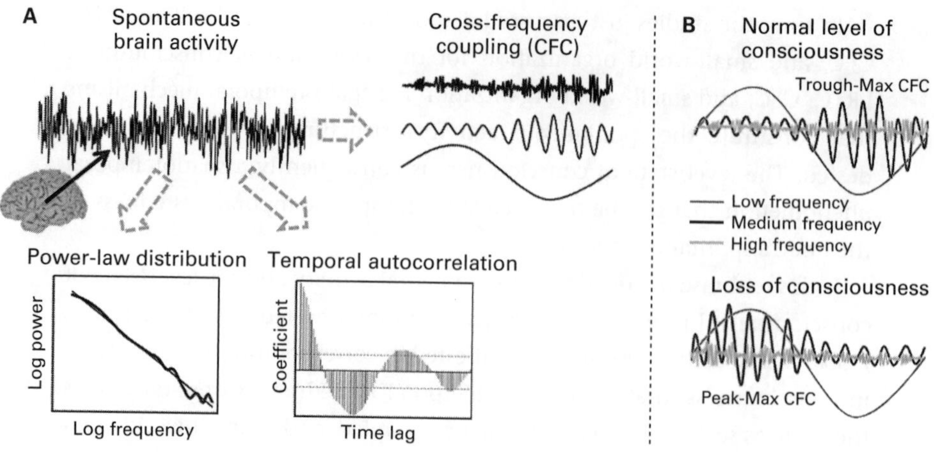

Figure 7.2
Temporal nestedness in the brain's spontaneous activity and its relation to consciousness. (A) Measures of temporal structure in the brain's spontaneous activity. (B) Changes in cross-frequency coupling during the loss of consciousness.

Let us start with a consideration of the spike rates. The spike rates decreased after 0–30 s of LOC with decreases of 81 percent to 92 percent when compared to pre-LOC. However, after around 4 min into the post-LOC state, the spike rates recovered and even increased (30%) when compared to pre-LOC: the spikes occurred in short periods in a highly dense way interrupted by rather long periods of total silence, or, total suppression. Hence spiking is preserved even when consciousness is lost; however, the firing pattern, that is, its temporal structure, changed showing long periods of silence.

What does this tell us about the LFP? The data showed a clear increase in the power of the slow oscillation (0.1–1 Hz), that is, slow cortical potentials (SCP) in post-LOC, which, unlike the spiking rates, remained stable during the entire period (5 min.) during which consciousness was lost. Other frequencies such as delta (increase), theta (decrease), alpha (increase), and gamma (increase) also changed but did not remain stable throughout the whole 5-min period when consciousness was lost. The authors conclude that the increase in the power of lower frequencies, the SCP, indicates the beginning of the loss of consciousness. In contrast, the power in higher frequencies was not directly related to the loss of consciousness (due to their instability in the period when consciousness was lost).

How are the LFP and especially the SCP related to the spiking rates? Lewis et al. (2012) observed that after LOC the spiking rate was significantly coupled to the phase of the SCP: 46.9 percent of the spikes from all recording units occurred near the trough (indexing high excitability as distinguished from the low excitability of the peak) in the phase of the slow oscillation (0.1–1 Hz). Most interestingly, such increased phase-spike coupling developed within seconds (–2.5–7.5 s) of LOC onset and may therefore be regarded as an index of LOC (Lewis et al., 2012).

The increase in phase-spiking coupling during LOC means that the firing is condensed to certain periods, that is, the trough, while the remaining periods, the descending, ascending, and peak parts of the slow oscillations' cycle durations, did not show any firing any longer. Lewis et al. (2012) therefore speak of "on- and off-states" in firing rates and consequently of "temporal fragmentation" during LOC. In contrast, spiking is not as strongly entrained by the SCP phase when consciousness is still present: neurons fire here in all phases of the ongoing SCP including peak and trough as well as in ascending and descending phases.

Lewis et al. (2012) also investigated the relation between different channels and thus the way that the temporal dynamics translates into spatial distribution. For that, Lewis et al. (2012) calculated a phase-locking factor (PLF) between two oscillations in near and distant channels. Whereas the PLF for near channels was the same for pre- and post-LOC, it decreased proportionally with distance: the more distant the channel, the more variable the phase offsets of the respective channels. The same held analogously for the phase-spiking rates: the more distant spiking rates during post-LOC were no longer as strongly associated with a specific part of the ongoing phase, for example, trough, as the local firing rates. The local spatiotemporal dynamics is thus preserved, whereas the more distant or global spatiotemporal dynamics is broken down or fragmented—this suggests impaired communication between distant regions and thus spatial fragmentation with spatial isolation

In sum, the data suggest that the long-distance coupling of the slower frequencies' phase to the faster frequencies' amplitude, that is CFC, is disrupted implying "spatial fragmentation" of neural activity. Given the implications of these data, one can speak of spatiotemporal fragmentation with the loss of spatiotemporal nestedness, which is replaced by spatiotemporal isolation of neural activity during the unconscious state. Spatiotemporal isolation leads to the loss of temporal continuity of neural activity, which entails the loss of the "subjective feeling of continuity" (Tagliazzuchi et al., 2016, p. 10), indexing the breakdown of the level/state of consciousness.

How can we illustrate the importance of temporal continuity? The loss of temporal continuity in both neural activity and level/state of consciousness can be compared to the loss of continuity when one takes out two to three Russian dolls that are nested and contained within each other. Whereas from the outside everything looks the same (as the largest doll is preserved), the inner configuration with the degree of nestedness is altered once two to three of the smaller Russian dolls are removed. In the same way that the inner spatial continuity is no longer preserved in a nest of Russian dolls, the loss of temporal continuity on the neuronal level amounts to temporal fragmentation with the subsequent loss of temporal continuity, which, in turn, leads to the breakdown of the level/state of consciousness.

Spatiotemporal Model Ia: Spatiotemporal Integration versus Content-Based Integration

How can spatiotemporal integration account for the level/state of consciousness? The data of Lewis et al. (2012) show that the disruption of long-distance (cross-regional) temporal integration, that is, temporal fragmentation, leads to the loss of consciousness. Since temporal fragmentation of neural activity is accompanied by its spatial fragmentation, I speak of spatiotemporal fragmentation. The fact that spatiotemporal fragmentation features the loss of consciousness suggests a central role of spatiotemporal integration for consciousness. How can we determine spatiotemporal integration in more detail and distinguish it from other forms of integration?

First, we must consider exactly what is meant here by "integration." One can describe different forms of integration, such as multisensory integration, perceptual integration, semantic integration, cognitive integration, and formal mathematical integration (see Mudrik, Faivre, & Koch, 2014, for an excellent overview). These forms of integration implicate the neural processing of different stimuli (or contents) and how they are related and linked together as in multisensory integration, perceptual integration, semantic integration, and cognitive integration. Moreover, there is also a purely formal form of integration, namely, mathematical integration (Mudrik et al., 2014).

What is the common denominator among these different forms of integration? They all, more or less, concern contents in their various facets and modalities. Different contents, such as sensory, cognitive, affective social, and others, are integrated with each other. One can therefore speak of *content-based integration*. Note that here I use the notion of "content" in a purely empirical way (rather than in a conceptual sense) and, in that sense, in a rather wide way—content-based integration concerns contents we can observe that can include sensory, affective, motor, cognitive, social, and additional contents. Hence, my empirical notion of contents is not restricted to cognitive contents (see part II in chapter 6).

How does such content-based integration stand in relation to the concept of integration as in spatiotemporal integration? Instead of integrating contents, spatiotemporal integration concerns the linkage of space and time by coupling different spatiotemporal scales or ranges in the brain's neural activity. For instance, the temporal features of the spontaneous activity such as the fluctuations in the different frequencies are integrated as resulting in CFC and scale-free activity. Analogously, the spatial features in the brain's neural activity such as the different regions are integrated in terms of cross-regional CFC, functional connectivity, and small-world properties.

Taken together, spatiotemporal integration is about the integration of different temporal and spatial scales or ranges rather than different contents. Therefore, I speak of spatiotemporal integration and distinguish it from content-based integration. I now posit that spatiotemporal integration in this sense characterizes the brain's neural activity: this can be described by its spatiotemporal nestedness and be measured by LRTC, CFC, and small-world properties (and others).

Most importantly, I consider spatiotemporal integration of the different temporal and spatial scales within the brain's neural activity central for consciousness: spatiotemporal integration allows for spatiotemporal nestedness, which can be considered a neural predisposition of the level/state of consciousness. The level/state of consciousness is thus based on spatiotemporal features like integration and nestedness rather than specific contents. Such spatiotemporal view is well compatible with the description of "conscious experiences in their entirety, irrespective of their specific contents" as expressed by Koch et al. (2016).

Spatiotemporal Model Ib: Spatiotemporal Integration without Content-Based Integration

The advocate of content-based integration may now want to argue that contents are associated with different spatiotemporal features. Therefore, the distinction between spatiotemporal and content-based integration will ultimately collapse and will no longer make a difference with regard to consciousness. Spatiotemporal integration is content-based integration, and, for that reason, consciousness is ultimately based on contents and their integration. I reject this argument since it neglects the difference and possible dissociation between spatiotemporal and content-based integration.

How are spatiotemporal and content-based integration related to each other? The advocate of content-based integration assumes that it is a necessary if not sufficient condition of spatiotemporal integration: without content-based integration, spatiotemporal integration and consequently consciousness remain impossible. I argue for the reverse situation. Specifically, I argue first that spatiotemporal integration can occur in the absence of content-based integration; and second, that content-based integration is based on and presupposes spatiotemporal integration. This amounts to the assumption that spatiotemporal integration is a necessary condition of content-based integration, whereas the latter is not a necessary condition of the former.

Can spatiotemporal integration occur in the absence of content-based integration? In that case, one would expect that spatiotemporal integration of neural activity could occur in the absence of and thus remains independent of any specific stimuli. That is, for instance, the case in the resting state in which no specific stimuli or tasks are applied to probe the brain's stimulus-induced or task-evoked activity. The above described measures of LRTC, CFC, and small-world properties are indeed obtained in the resting state during the absence of stimuli or tasks. One can therefore assume that spatiotemporal integration of neural activity occurs in the resting state and remains thus independent of stimuli and their specific contents. Spatiotemporal integration can thus occur in the absence of content-based integration.

The advocate of content-based integration may now want to argue that even in the resting state plenty of stimuli are present. One can imagine, one has spontaneous thoughts, and there is continuous interoceptive input—there is thus no stimulus-free state. This implies that, even if present, spatiotemporal integration cannot be separated from content-based integration—that makes the argument of the independence of the former from the latter futile. The advocate is right. There is indeed continuous stimulus input and thus content-based integration even in the resting state.

However, there are extreme states where the balance between spatiotemporal and content-based integration is shifted toward the former at the expense of the latter. That is, for instance, the situation in meditation. In that case, one detaches the brain's neural activity from the continuous stimulus input and their contents, that is, one's own cognition, and, in extreme cases, also from one's own body's input (Tang & Northoff, 2017 Tang, Holzel, & Posner, 2015). The data suggest that spatiotemporal integration of the brain's spontaneous activity remains and becomes probably even stronger in meditation during the absence of content-based integration (Tang, Holzel, & Posner, 2015, Tang & Northoff, 2017). Accordingly, although not fully detailed here, meditation can be considered an empirical example of spatiotemporal integration without or with minimal content-based integration.

Yet another example of spatiotemporal integration without content-based integration is that of psychiatric disorders. Depressed or manic patients suffering from bipolar disorder often show abnormally slow (depression) or fast (mania) temporal integration that is not accompanied by corresponding contents. They thus experience changes in their inner time consciousness without any related contents (Northoff et al., 2017). Taking both meditation and psychiatric disorders together, I argue that content-based integration is a not a necessary condition of spatiotemporal integration. This allows me to reject the argument that spatiotemporal integration is based on content-based integration or, in a weaker version, cannot be separated from contents.

Spatiotemporal Model Ic: Spatiotemporal Integration as Necessary Condition of Content-Based Integration

Can we consider spatiotemporal integration as a necessary condition of content-based integration? I argue that that is indeed the case and can be illustrated by the examples of multisensory integration (see chapter 10 in Northoff, 2014a, for details; see also Ferri et al., 2015; Stein et al. 2009) and temporal coding. Multisensory integration describes the integration between different sensory stimuli, that is, cross-modal stimuli. Such integration between different sensory stimuli follows certain mechanisms or principles. One such mechanism is the spatial coincidence of the two sensory stimuli, which enables and facilitates their integration: if the two cross-modal stimuli coincide at the same point in space, as for instance in a particular cell population or region, their likelihood of being integrated is much higher than when they do not spatially coincide and are processed in different cells or regions (see Stein et al., 2009; chapter 10 in Northoff, 2014a).

The same holds analogously for temporal coincidence: if the two sensory stimuli temporally coincide and thus occur at the same point in time, they can be much better integrated with each other than when they occur at different points in time. This makes it clear that multisensory stimuli are integrated with each other on the basis of their underlying spatial and temporal features, that is, their spatial and temporal coincidence (as based ultimately on probability distributions) (Northoff, 2014a). Spatiotemporal integration thus underlies and, at the same time, makes possible multisensory integration—the integration between different stimuli and their respective contents is defined by the integration of their underlying spatial and temporal features.

Spatiotemporal integration also underlies what can be described as "temporal coding" that describes the processing of information on the basis of temporal features. (Jensen et al., 2014). Gamma frequency (30–40 Hz) shows shorter cycle duration than alpha frequency (8–12 Hz). Presupposing CFC from alpha phase to gamma amplitude allows us to temporally segment the content that is processed via neural excitation according to the cycle duration of the frequencies: if the phase of the longer alpha cycle duration (100 ms) is coupled to and thereby allows excitation of the gamma amplitude, the contents may be temporally segmented according to the gamma cycles (10–30 ms).

Jensen et al. (2014) therefore speak of "phase coding" or "temporal coding." The integration of contents, that is, which stimuli are integrated into contents and which ones are excluded or segregated, depends on the ongoing phase cycles of gamma and alpha and their CFC. The content is thus integrated on the basis of the temporal features of alpha and gamma—with the result being Jensen's temporal coding. This example clearly reveals how the temporal (and possibly spatial) features of the brain's neural activity allow for integrating contents—spatiotemporal integration with temporal and spatial coding may thus underlie content-based integration.

Because temporal and spatial coding allows for integrating contents, I propose that spatiotemporal integration is the most basic and fundamental form of integration. It already occurs in the spontaneous activity itself and therefore exists prior to stimulus-induced activity including its respective content. Moreover, it concerns the spatial and temporal features rather than the stimuli and their contents by themselves—spatiotemporal integration is therefore more basic than the various forms of integration involving stimuli and contents.

How is spatiotemporal integration related to consciousness? Spatiotemporal integration occurs and operates prior to and independent of consciousness. It occurs automatically and by default—spatiotemporal integration is an in-built mechanism. We are not and, put more strongly, we cannot become aware or conscious of such integration between different frequencies and regions in our brain's neural activity. Nor can we become aware of corresponding integration between different stimuli or contents in our consciousness. Instead, we can only access the ready-made result, that is, spatiotemporal nestedness, that becomes manifest at the level/state of actual consciousness.

Spatiotemporal Model IIa: Argument of Nonspecificity—Specificity of Spatiotemporal Mechanisms for Brain and Consciousness

The critic may now to argue that although spatiotemporal mechanisms, including integration and expansion, are empirically grounded, they remain unspecific when it comes to consciousness. The very same spatiotemporal mechanisms can operate during both consciousness and unconsciousness. This holds especially given that any neuronal mechanisms of the brain is based on the temporal and spatial features of its neural activity regardless of whether it is associated with consciousness. The claim of the argument is thus that spatiotemporal mechanisms do not allow us to distinguish between conscious and unconscious states and therefore remain unspecific. We may thus put forward such nonspecificity against the thesis that spatiotemporal mechanisms characterize consciousness: I therefore speak of an *argument of nonspecificity*.

What are we to make of the argument of nonspecificity? I reject this argument. True, any neural activity in the brain is spatial and temporal, as it takes place in time and space. Therefore, any neural activity in the brain will be spatial and temporal by default—time and space in such a general sense remain indeed too unspecific to distinguish consciousness and unconsciousness. For that reason, the mere temporal and spatial nature of the brain's neural activity does not permit us to distinguish between spatiotemporal mechanisms involved in consciousness as distinguished from unconsciousness.

However, the argument of nonspecificity neglects the fact that the brain can construct the temporal and spatial features of its neural activity in different ways. For instance, the brain's neural activity may show spatiotemporal nestedness with strong LRTC, CFC, and small-world properties. Yet at the same time, neural activity may also show spatiotemporal fragmentation rather than nestedness (see the section on time, space, and the brain, above). Moreover, concerning stimulus-induced activity, there may either be spatiotemporal expansion or, as I propose, spatiotemporal constriction (as in the TMS-EEG presented by Massimini et al. 2005, 2007; Casal et al., 2013; see part II in chapter 4 for details).

These examples demonstrate that the brain's spontaneous and stimulus-induced activity can be constructed in different ways. These different ways may be distinguished from each other on temporal and spatial grounds—they are thus far from being unspecific: the brain's neural activity can construct the temporal and spatial features of its neural activity in distinctive ways that lead to different organization, for example spatiotemporal nestedness versus fragmentation and spatiotemporal expansion versus constriction. We may therefore confidently rebut the argument of nonspecificity with respect to the spatiotemporal characterization of the brain's neural activity: the spatiotemporal mechanisms allow for a specific organization of the brain's neural activity as distinguished from others.

Moreover, the data suggest that such spatiotemporal organization of neural activity allows distinguishing between consciousness and unconsciousness. Based on the data, I propose that spatiotemporal organization of neural activity in a specific way (in this case, spatiotemporal nestedness and expansion rather than fragmentation and constriction) distinguishes consciousness from unconsciousness. Therefore, I rebut the argument of nonspecificity with respect to the spatiotemporal characterization of consciousness and its relation to the brain: the underlying spatiotemporal mechanisms are not nonspecific but rather specific for consciousness, as distinguished from those underlying unconsciousness.

Spatiotemporal Model IIb: Argument of Nonspecificity—Spatiotemporal Mechanisms and Models of Brain

How can we further substantiate the specific nature of the postulated spatiotemporal mechanisms? We have suggested different models of brain including the spectrum model (chapter 1) and the interaction model (chapter 2). To further support the specificity of the supposed spatiotemporal mechanisms, we may also want to link them to the models of brain.

Let us start with a consideration of the spectrum model of brain as presented in chapter 1.

The spectrum model argues for a continuum between passive and active features in neural activity; it therefore constitutes a "hybrid" by default, that is, a mixture of both stimulus-induced and spontaneous activity (chapter 1). Spatiotemporal expansion as associated with consciousness is well compatible with such a model: higher degrees of spatiotemporal expansion make stimulus-induced activity more hybrid and shift it more toward the active pole of the spectrum. The opposite is the case in unconsciousness: high degrees of spatiotemporal constriction lead to less hybrid stimulus-induced activity (as less impacted by the spontaneous activity), which shifts it more toward the passive pole of the spectrum.

Analogously, the same holds true for spatiotemporal nestedness. High degrees of LRTC, CFC, and small-world properties shift the brain's neural activity toward the "active" pole of the spectrum. In contrast, spatiotemporal isolation with low degrees of LRTC, CFC, and small-world properties shifts the brain's neural activity toward the opposite pole, the "passive" pole of the spectrum. The neural distinction between spatiotemporal nestedness and isolation, including their association with consciousness and unconsciousness, is thus well compatible with the spectrum model of brain.

We can make an analogous case for the interaction model of brain that postulates a continuum of different degrees of nonadditive interaction between spontaneous activity and stimuli (chapter 2). Data show that spatiotemporal expansion is related to a higher degree of nonadditive rest-stimulus interaction (Huang et al., 2015), which, in turn, seems to be sufficient for associating stimuli with consciousness (chapter 5). The degree of nonadditivity in rest-stimulus interaction is rather low in cases of spatiotemporal constriction as during unconsciousness. Hence, the distinction between consciousness and unconsciousness by spatiotemporal expansion and constriction is well compatible with the interaction model of brain.

In conclusion, I reject the argument of nonspecificity against the spatiotemporal model of consciousness by arguing for what I describe as spatiotemporal specificity. Yes, the brain's neural activity in general is indeed both spatial and temporal. However, the advocate of this argument ignores the fact that those very same spatiotemporal features of the brain's neural activity can be constructed in different ways as related to different spatiotemporal mechanisms. The different spatiotetmporal mechanisme are central for distinguishing between the presence and absence of consciousness. Accordingly, based on the empirical data reviewed in this section, I argue for spatiotemporal specificity in the relationship between brain and consciousness.

Finally, we should note that the rejection of the argument of nonspecificity concerns the phenomenal features of consciousness and thus noncognitive consciousness as presented in the spatiotemporal model of consciousness. By contrast, we leave open here whether the argument may apply to "cognitive consciousness" as specified in the GNWT. The spatiotemporal characterization, as suggested here, may indeed remain too unspecific when it comes to the cognitive features of consciousness.

Spatiotemporal Model of Consciousness II: Spatiotemporal Expansion—Neural Correlate of Consciousness and Neuronal-Phenomenal Correspondence

Empirical Findings Ia: Stimulus-Induced Activity—Amplitude Increase and Trial-to-Trial Variability Reduction

We have so far discussed that the spatiotemporal nestedness of the brain's spontaneous activity provides a neural predisposition of the level/state of consciousness or NPC. The spatiotemporal alignment of the brain's spontaneous and/or prestimulus activity to single stimuli and long-term stimulus sequences in our body and the world is considered to be a neural prerequisite of consciousness, what we have previously designated as preNCC. This leaves open the neural correlates of consciousness, what we have previously designated as NCC—the neural mechanisms that are sufficient to associate specific contents with consciousness.

How, we may ask, is the stimulus processed in neural terms so that it can be associated with consciousness? Data have revealed that the amplitude of stimulus-evoked neural activity can be considered a marker of consciousness: the higher the amplitude in response to the stimulus, the more likely the stimulus will be associated with consciousness (Koch et al., 2016; Tsuchiya et al., 2015). In addition, data from various studies have shown that, compared to unconsciousness processing, stimulus-induced activity during consciousness lasts longer and is spatially more extended. This has been reviewed extensively in recent papers (Dehaene et al., 2014; Koch et al., 2016); for this reason, we only highlight here some results on temporal duration and spatial extension (figure 7.3).

Li et al. (2014) measured slow cortical potentials in MEG during presentation of near-threshold visual stimuli. The MEG results showed long-lasting event-related magnetic fields (ERMF) between 300 ms and 2–3 s poststimulus during seen trials when compared to unseen ones. The long-lasting ERMF do not resemble oscillations but slow DC-type drift (a slow change in the power of the frequency over longer stretches of time), making them likely reflect slow cortical potentials in the slow frequency range between 0.1 and 5 Hz. Interestingly, the long lasting ERMF were specific for subjective awareness, the seen versus the unseen, whereas they appeared neither in objective performance, for example, as distinction between correct and incorrect trials, nor in confidence judgments. The long-lasting ERMF changes during seen trials were accompanied by widespread activity changes in temporal and frontoparietal cortices. One can therefore suppose that slow cortical potentials shape stimulus-induced activity and its association with consciousness; this view is further supported by the findings revealed in phase and power analysis discussed in the same study (see Li et al., 2014).

The central role of spatiotemporal expansion is impressively demonstrated in the TMS-EEG experiments by the group around Massimini (Casali et al., 2013; Massimini et al., 2010). They applied the same TMS pulse (in premotor and parietal cortical regions) during both conscious and unconscious states in UWRS, anesthesia, and sleep. The degree of spatiotemporal expansion of TMS-induced activity varied considerably between conscious and unconscious states. During the conscious state, the TMS-pulse induced spatially extended activity for long durations. In contrast, both temporal

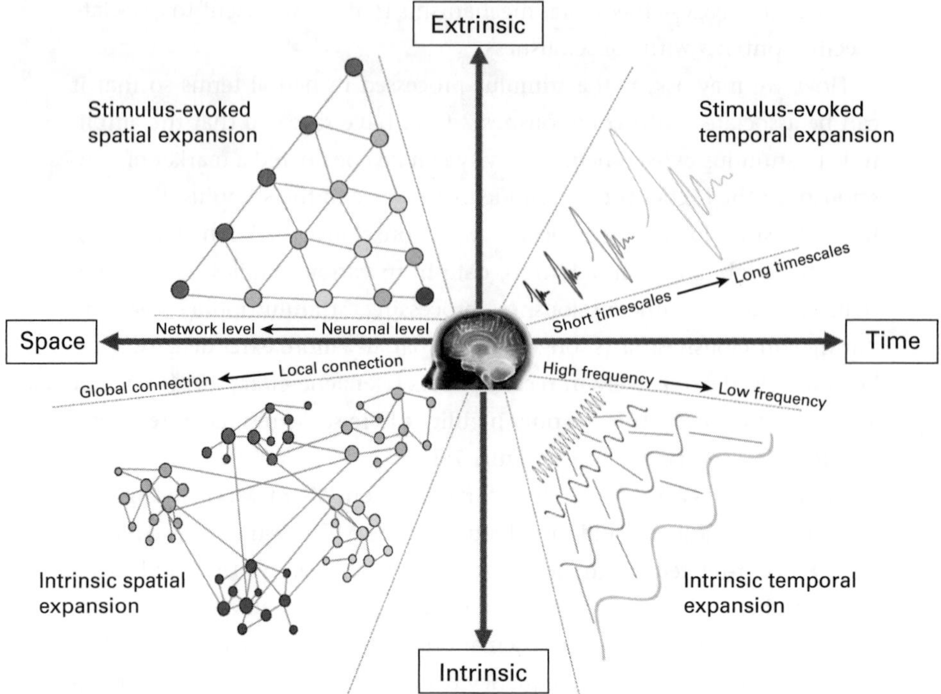

Figure 7.3
Spatiotemporal expansion of neural activity.

duration and spatial extension of TMS-induced activity were extremely restricted during the unconscious state in anesthesia, UWRS, and sleep.

Why and how is it possible that the same TMS pulse leads to different spatiotemporal features of the stimulus-induced activities during conscious versus unconscious states? I posit that this is related to the spontaneous activity itself as well as its neural interaction with the TMS pulse, that is, the rest-stimulus (or rest-pulse) interaction (Huang, Zhang, Longtin, et al., 2017; Northoff et al., 2010). The fact that stimulus-induced activity expands during consciousness suggests that the stimulus can better suppress the ongoing spontaneous activity: the better the stimulus interacts with the spontaneous activity and suppresses its ongoing fluctuations, the more likely the stimulus can expand the temporal duration and spatial extension of the activity it induces. Such suppression of the ongoing spontaneous activity by the stimulus can be measured by trial-to-trial variability, which has been shown on both cellular (Churchland et al., 2010) and regional (Ferri et al., 2015; He, 2013; Huang, Zhang, Longtin, et al., 2017) levels of neural activity. The more the stimulus suppresses the variability of the ongoing spontaneous activity, the more (negative) interaction between spontaneous and stimulus-evoked activity (He, 2013; Huang, Zhang, Longtin, et al., 2017). Although the exact neural mechanisms of such suppression of spontaneous activity fluctuations by the stimulus remain unclear, I would hypothesize that the spatiotemporal expansion of stimulus-induced activity is related to the suppression of ongoing activity and rest-stimulus interactions.

Empirical Findings Ib: Spatiotemporal Expansion: Expansion versus Integration—Integrated Information Theory

How does the supposed spatiotemporal expansion of stimulus-induced activity as NCC stand in relation to integration and the integrated information (IIT) (Tononi et al., 2016; Tononi & Koch, 2015)? Stated simply, the main thesis of the IIT is that consciousness is based on information integration that has been mathematically formalized in the phi index, while, empirically, it has been operationalized by the perturbation complexity index (Casali et al., 2013). One should also note that the concept of information in the IIT does not refer to information in terms of specific contents as traditionally or commonly understood (Tononi & Koch, 2015). Rather, within the context of the IIT, information refers to "how a *system of mechanisms* in *a state*, through its cause-effect power, specifies a *form ('informs' conceptual structure)* in the *space of possibilities*" (Tononi & Koch, 2015, p. 8; emphasis added). Let us explicate that quote in spatiotemporal terms of the STC with further consideration focusing especially on those concepts highlighted by italics.

How do Tononi and Koch's concepts of "form," "space of possibilities," and "state" stand in relation to spatiotemporal expansion advocated here? The data suggest that the stimulus both suppresses and enhances the neuronal features of the brain's spontaneous activity. Spatiotemporal expansion is thus dependent on and ultimately based on spatiotemporal nestedness and alignment: without proper degrees of spatiotemporal nestedness and alignment, the stimulus will not be able to spatiotemporally expand its stimulus-induced activity. One may assume that the constellation of the various spatiotemporal mechanisms (which, as we predict, will be complemented by various other spatiotemporal mechanisms in the future) corresponds to what Tononi and Koch (2015, p. 8) describe as "system of mechanisms." We suggest that such a "system of mechanisms" operates on a spatiotemporal platform, hence our suggestion of the various spatiotemporal mechanisms.

What exactly is meant by "a state"? I suggest that "a state" refers to the brain's spontaneous activity and, more specifically, its degree of spatiotemporal nestedness. The various spatiotemporal mechanisms, as suggested here, operate within the space of the brain's spontaneous activity and its spatiotemporal structure: both spatiotemporal alignment and spatiotemporal expansion are based and dependent on the spontaneous activity's spatiotemporal nestedness. At the same time, however, the very same spatiotemporal nestedness is modulated by increasingly longer stimulus sequences; the "state," that is, the spontaneous activity's spatiotemporal nestedness as we say, is itself not fixed but, rather, highly dynamic and malleable.

How, then, may we conceive the concepts of "form ('informs' conceptual structure)" and "space of possibilities" as raised in IIT in the spatiotemporal context of STC? The STC suggests that spatiotemporal alignment of the brain's neural activity to the spatiotemporal structure of body and world provides a spatiotemporally based form as background and third dimension (in addition to level/state and content) of consciousness. Therefore, we suggest that what the IIT describes as "form" may be traced to the virtual spatiotemporal structure or organization among brain, body, and world that constitutes the form we experience as the third dimension of consciousness. More specifically, what Tononi describes as "conceptual structure" may then be traced to what we describe as "form" characterized by spatiotemporal structure as ranging in a virtual probability-based way between world and brain (i.e., the world-brain relation).

The very same spatiotemporal structure that ranges among brain, body, and the world provides the neural prerequisite (or, to be more precise, a neuro-ecological prerequisite) of consciousness (preNCC). This spatiotemporal structure is probabilistic and renders certain ways of spatiotemporal expansion and stimulus-induced activity possible while it excludes others. If, for instance, the spontaneous activity's various frequencies are already suppressed and nonreactive in the resting state, the stimulus will not be able to enhance them to expand its own stimulus-induced activity; this, in turn, makes it impossible to associate stimulus-induced activity with consciousness. Accordingly, what Tononi and Koch (2015) (see also Tononi et al., 2016) describe as a "space of possibilities" may find its more specific neuronal mechanisms in spatiotemporal nestedness as NPC and spatiotemporal alignment as preNCC. His "space of possibilities" is thus a space of possible spatiotemporal configurations.

In sum, I propose that what we term here the STC or spatiotemporal approach to consciousness is well compatible with the IIT. Integration as in IIT is supposed to occur within a temporal and spatial arena rather than on a sensory or cognitive basis. Moreover, we regard the concrete spatiotemporal determination of specific neuronal mechanisms, spatiotemporal mechanisms, involved in consciousness as complementary to the more abstract notion of information in IIT. Future investigation may want to apply some of the mathematical and operational measures of the IIT in the context of the presumed spatiotemporal mechanisms of STC.

Empirical Findings IIa: Stimulus-Induced Activity—Early versus Late

How can we investigate consciousness? The traditional way is to ask subjects whether they saw or heard something and then to make a judgment; this has recently been described as "report paradigm" (Tsuchiya et al., 2015). However, the judgment or report itself may introduce a cognitive component that as such may not belong to consciousness proper. The neural mechanisms underlying such a judgment or report may thus be a neural consequence of rather than a neural correlate of consciousness (see Aru, Bachmann, Singer, & Melloni, 2012; deGraaf et al., 2012; Li et al., 2014). For this reason, report paradigms have been contrasted with "no-report paradigms" where the subjects do not need to report or to give a judgment (Lamme, 2010a,b; Tsuchiya et al., 2015).

No-report paradigms reveal a different spatial and temporal pattern from report paradigms. Several studies have demonstrated that early components (such as P50 and N100) of stimulus-induced activity (from around 100 ms to 200–300 ms) indicate the presence and experience of a specific content in consciousness even if that very same content may not yet be accessible for subsequent reporting (Andersen, Pedersen, Sandberg, & Overgaard, 2015; Koch et al., 2016; Koivisto et al., 2016; Koivisto & Revensuo, 2010; Palva et al., 2005; Pitts, Metzler, & Hillyard, 2014; Pitts, Padwal, Fennelly, Martínez, & Hillyard, 2014; Rutiku, Martin, Bachmann, & Aru, 2015;

Schurger, Sarigiannidis, Naccache, Sitt, & Dehaene, 2015; Tsuchiya et al., 2015). The presence of these electrophysiological markers of early stimulus-induced activity such as N100 is reduced if not completely absent in altered states of consciousness such as anesthesia, slow-wave sleep, and vegetative state (Bachmann & Hudetz, 2015; Koch et al., 2016; Purdon et al., 2013; Sitt et al., 2014; Schurger et al., 2015).

We now consider the spatial side. The report paradigms of Tsuchiya et al. show extensive involvement of the especially lateral prefrontal and parietal cortical regions (Tsuchiya et al., 2015). In contrast, as reviewed in detail in Tsuchiya et al. (2015) and in Koch et al. (2016), no-report paradigms do not show prefrontal-parietal recruitment but rather posterior cortical regions at the interface between parietal, occipital, and temporal cortex with a specific focus on higher sensory regions, or, "hot zones" as Koch (see Koch et al., 2016) calls them.

Moreover, we need to consider the distinction between medial and lateral prefrontal regions. Lateral prefrontal regions are recruited during judgment, in what may be termed *report paradigms* because they are related to various cognitive functions including working memory (Northoff et al., 2004; Tsuchiya et al., 2015). In contrast, due to the lower cognitive load as related to the absence of judgment, *no-report paradigms* lead to stronger involvement of medial prefrontal regions such as the ventromedial prefrontal cortex that present lower degrees of deactivation in fMRI (Northoff et al., 2004; Shulman et al., 1997a,b). This is well compatible with the involvement of the midline regions in various forms of spontaneous mental activity associated with consciousness such as spontaneous thoughts (Christoff et al., 2016), mental time travel with episodic simulation (Schacter et al., 2012), and self-related processing (Northoff, 2016d; Northoff et al., 2006).

What does the operational distinction between the report and no-report paradigms, and their different neuronal correlates, imply for our characterization of consciousness? The late event-related potentials such as the P300 and lateral prefronto-parietal regions seem to be related to the cognitive functions implicated in judgment of stimuli as conscious (see Silverstein et al., 2015, for providing evidence that the P3b may occur even during unconscious states). Late event-related potentials and lateral prefronto-parietal cortical activity may consequently be associated with awareness of the content of consciousness rather than with consciousness itself. We therefore postulate that these neuronal measures obtained in report paradigms reflect what has been conceptually described as "neural consequence of consciousness" (NCC con) rather than the NCC proper (Aru et al., 2012; deGraaf et al., 2012; Northoff, 2014b).

In contrast to report paradigms, no-report paradigms reveal earlier event-related potentials such as N100 and 200 as well as posterior cortical regions and/or cortical midline regions. I propose that these earlier spatiotemporal features of stimulus-induced activity reflect the NCC as detailed in the previous section. Taken in this sense, the NCC must be distinguished from the NCC con in both operational and neuronal terms.

Empirical Findings IIb: Cognitive Features of Consciousness—Global Neuronal Workspace Theory

Relying on report paradigms, the various findings supporting the global neuronal workspace theory (GNWT) show later components such as P300 and prefrontal cortical involvement (see Baars 2005; Dehaene et al., 2014; Dehaene & Changeux, 2011, for excellent reviews). We do not recapitulate here the various findings that support the GNWT, which have been reviewed in detail elsewhere (Dehaene & Changeux, 2011; Dehaene et al., 2014). Due to the impressive findings it has revealed, however, the question is not so much *whether* late prefrontal activity is related to consciousness in general but, rather, to what feature of consciousness it is related. That distinction is the focus of the discussion that follows.

The GNWT postulates that the environmental stimuli and their respective contents become globally available for cognition. Such globalizing and sharing presumably is made possible by the architecture of the brain, most especially the design of both the lateral prefrontal and parietal cortex as a "global workspace" where the different functional systems of the brain (specifically memory, evaluative/reward, attentional, motor, and perceptual systems) converge and overlap. We describe that confluence as *spatial globalization* of local-regional, stimulus-induced activity that is globalized throughout the whole brain including prefrontal and parietal cortex. Dehaene (Dehaene et al., 2014) and Moutard (Moutard, Dehaene, & Malach, 2015) characterize this as "non-linear ignition": they suggest that the transition from merely local-regional to global prefrontal-parietal activity must be ignited by the stimulus in a nonlinear rather than merely a linear way. The exact neuronal mechanisms of such nonlinear ignition of lateral prefrontal-parietal cortical activity, however, remain unclear.

In addition to its spatial component, the GNWT also considers temporal measures such as late event-related potentials (P300), synchronization between regions, and high-frequency oscillations including gamma as central for consciousness (Dehaene & Changeux, 2011; Dehaene et al., 2014). Analogous to spatial globalization, such extension of neural activity to different temporal domains from the early sensory-based event-related potentials such as N100 (see Bachmann & Hudetz, 2015) to later event-related potentials and higher frequencies such as gamma may be described by the term *temporal globalization*. Such temporal globalization seems to be deficient in altered states of consciousness where the temporal extension to later event-related potentials (as in reduced P300) and higher frequencies (as in reduced gamma power) is no longer present (Koch et al., 2016; Sitt et al., 2014) (see figure 7.4).

Which feature or aspect of consciousness is targeted by the GNWT and, more specifically, by its assumed spatiotemporal globalization of stimulus-induced activity? By relying on report paradigms, the GNWT indexes consciousness by accessing and reporting the contents of consciousness. The access and reporting of contents is experimentally reflected in that the participants are required to access and report the stimulus content by clicking a button with intent that is taken to represent an index of consciousness (Dehaene & Changeux, 2011; Dehaene et al., 2014). The lateral prefrontal-parietal cortex and the late components of stimulus-induced activity from 300 ms to 500 ms such as P300 (or even longer up to 800 ms) are strongly associated with cognitive functions such as selective attention, expectation, self-monitoring, and task planning and, most importantly, accessing and reporting the contents of consciousness (Koch et al., 2016; Tsuchiya et al., 2015, Andersen et al., 2016 Aru et al., 2012; deGraaf et al., 2012; Pitts, Metzler, et al., 2014; Pitts, Padwal, et al., 2014; Rutiku et al., 2015; Schurger et al. 2015; Tsuchiya et al., 2015).

Spatiotemporal globalization of stimulus-induced activity as required for the accessing and reporting of contents in consciousness must be distinguished from consciousness itself. This is supported by the data obtained using nonreport paradigms as discussed in the previous section. I therefore conceive of spatiotemporal globalization as the neural consequence of consciousness or NCC con (see Andersen et al., 2016 Aru et al., 2012; deGraaf,

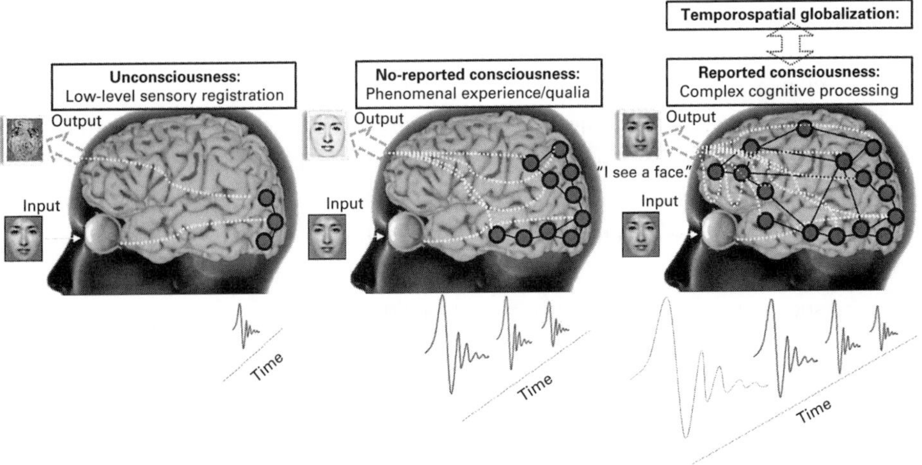

Figure 7.4
Temporospatial globalization of neural activity and consciousness.

Hsieh, & Sack, 2012; Li et al., 2014; Overgaard & Fazekas, 2016; Tononi & Koch, 2015; Tsuchiya et al., 2015).

To summarize, we suggest that spatiotemporal globalization, as postulated in GNWT, allows for late and prefronto-parietal cortical involvement in stimulus-induced activity during consciousness. Late and prefronto-parietal cortical involvement is experimentally related to accessing and reporting of contents. Therefore, I propose that late prefronto-parietal activity and thus spatiotemporal globalization is neural consequence of the phenomenal features consciousness that occur prior to and independent of accessing and reporting contents. As it is related to the access and reporting of contents, spatiotemporal globalization must be distinguished from spatiotemporal expansion of stimulus-induced activity that, as we suggest, is more related to the phenomenal features of consciousness.

Spatiotemporal Model Ia: From Spatiotemporal Expansion to Phenomenal Features

We have so far discussed various neuronal mechanisms such as spatiotemporal expansion and globalization. This leaves open the phenomenal features of consciousness including their relation to these neuronal mechanisms. These subjects are our next focus of consideration.

What are the phenomenal features of consciousness and how are they neuronally instantiated? In essence, this is the central question of both neuroscience and the philosophy of consciousness. *Phenomenal features* refer to experience that is subjective rather than objective. Philosophers often describe phenomenal features by their qualitative character—from *qualia* as the "what it is like" of experience (Nagel, 1974). Other phenomenal features concern the directedness of experience toward a specific content, for example, intentionality (Searle, 2004), self-perceptiveness with first-person perspective, and others (Northoff, 2014b, 2016c,d).

Without going into detail, we recognize that these phenomenal features must be distinguished from the cognitive features of consciousness. Phenomenal features concern the experience of a content as conscious, whereas cognitive features allow one to access and subsequently report that very same content. The distinction between phenomenal and cognitive features of consciousness is more or less mirrored in the conceptual distinction between noncognitive and cognitive consciousness (Cerullo et al., 2015).

How can spatiotemporal expansion of stimulus-induced activity serve as a neural correlate of the phenomenal features of consciousness? Buzsáki contends that "perception goes *beyond* the stimulus" (Buzsáki, 2006). We now suggest that such "*beyond*" is central for the phenomenal features of consciousness and that it consists of spatiotemporal features. The stimulus itself can be characterized in temporal and spatial terms by its duration and extension. That contrasts with the experience or consciousness within which the very same stimulus usually lasts longer and extends beyond its mere physical duration and extension. For instance, even though they may be physically absent, we may still hear the last tones of a melody and may still visualize the last scene of an opera in a more temporally and spatially extended sense. In brief, the spatiotemporal features of the stimulus in consciousness thus expand beyond the ones featuring the stimulus in purely physical terms so that these features show both longer temporal duration and yield more distributed spatial extension.

From where does such spatiotemporal expansion beyond the stimulus's own physical duration and extension in consciousness emerge? We tentatively suggest that it arises from or, put differently, is appended to the stimulus by the brain's spontaneous activity. The brain's spontaneous activity shows a large temporal and spatial scale or range that extends far beyond the range of the single stimulus. For instance, the stimulus may show a duration of 100 ms, which corresponds to alpha frequency or a duration of 1 s as mirroring delta frequency. The spontaneous activity, in contrast, includes a much wider variety of different frequencies ranging from infra-slow frequencies to considerably faster ones.

This carries major implications for how the stimulus is processed by the brain's spontaneous activity, the, "rest-stimulus interaction" (Northoff et al., 2010). When interacting with the spontaneous activity, the stimulus and its more limited spatiotemporal scale during its presentation interact with a much larger spatiotemporal range of the brain's spontaneous activity. This, in turn, makes possible for the brain to integrate, nest, and contain the stimulus and its associated stimulus-induced activity within the spontaneous activity and its larger spatiotemporal scale. This, in turn, expands the stimulus's own temporal duration and spatial extension beyond itself according to the brain's intrinsic temporal duration and spatial extension of its spontaneous activity. Such *nesting* or *embedding* may, for instance, be manifested in the stimulus-induced modulation of the spontaneous activity's scale-free activity, which allows expansion of the stimulus beyond its own original spatiotemporal scales.

In sum, I hypothesize that the degree of spatiotemporal expansion of the stimulus beyond its own or original spatiotemporal features (as during the stimulus' presentation in the experimental situation) is closely related to the association of the stimulus/contents with the phenomenal features. Given such spatiotemporal expansion of the stimulus by the brain's spontaneous activity, the resulting phenomenal features may by themselves be characterized as spatiotemporal in a virtual way: the degree of the stimulus's spatiotemporal expansion on the neuronal level of rest–stimulus interaction may directly correspond to the experience of the spatiotemporal features of the stimulus in consciousness. Therefore, I postulate that consciousness and its phenomenal features are spatiotemporal features.

Spatiotemporal Model Ib: From Spatiotemporal Features to Neuronal-Phenomenal Correspondence

Given the central role of spatiotemporal expansion, one expects correspondence between the spatiotemporal features of the brain's spontaneous activity as modulated by the stimulus on the one hand and the spatiotemporal features during the experience of the stimulus in consciousness on the other. I therefore speak of neuronal-phenomenal correspondence between phenomenal features and the spatiotemporally expanded stimulus-induced activity. Neuronal-phenomenal correspondence as described here yields "the neurophenomenal hypothesis" (Northoff, 2014b), although conceptually it may be described variously as "isomorphism" (Fell, 2004), "operational time-space" (Fingelkurts et al., 2013), or "identity" (Tononi et al., 2016).

Note that such neuronal-phenomenal correspondence exists between the brain's neuronal activity and the phenomenal features of consciousness. In contrast, there is no such correspondence between the stimulus itself, that is, its physical features in terms of time and space and the phenomenal features of consciousness. There is thus a discrepancy between physical and phenomenal features of the stimulus—a physical-phenomenal discrepancy that one may say comes close to what we have described as a *physical-neuronal discrepancy*. There is thus a gap between physical and phenomenal features. This gap can be filled or bridged by the brain's spontaneous activity and its spatiotemporal features.

More specifically, the brain's spontaneous activity provides a spatiotemporal framework that allows us to associate phenomenal features with the otherwise purely physical stimulus. As they are based on the spontaneous activity's spatiotemporal features, phenomenal features must by themselves be characterized as spatiotemporal. Time and space are here understood in the sense of "inner duration" and "inner extension," as discussed above in the section on time, space, and brain. Presupposing such a sense of time and space, phenomenal features can be characterized as spatiotemporal—phenomenal features are spatiotemporal features.

Spatiotemporal features link the brain's neuronal features to the phenomenal features of consciousness. The glue or "common currency" between brain and consciousness and thus between neuronal and phenomenal features consists in spatiotemporal features. Construing spatiotemporal features as common currency allows us to associate phenomenal features with the stimulus by processing and integrating the latter within the brain's spontaneous activity.

Importantly, such integration allows for expanding the spatiotemporal features of the stimulus by the spontaneous activity's spatiotemporal structure; if such spatiotemporal expansion is sufficient and goes beyond the stimulus itself, the resulting stimulus-induced activity can be associated with consciousness and its phenomenal features. The phenomenal features of consciousness can consequently be characterized by spatiotemporal features that correspond to (and ultimately are shared with) the spatiotemporal features of the brain's spontaneous activity and the degree to which the latter expands the stimulus's spatiotemporal features. Accordingly, spatiotemporal expansion can be considered the neuronal mechanism that underlies neuronal-phenomenal correspondence.

Note that the concept of neuronal-phenomenal correspondence is a bridge concept between neuronal, that is, empirical, and phenomenal, that is, experiential, domains. The concept is not purely empirical, as phenomenal features cannot be observed from the third-person perspective in the same way we observe neuronal states in neuroscience. At the same time, neuronal-phenomenal correspondence is not a fully phenomenal concept, either, as such correspondence cannot be experienced in consciousness. Hence, I consider neuronal-phenomenal correspondence a truly "neurophenomenal concept" (Northoff, 2014b).

Finally, note that neuronal-phenomenal correspondence is also not an ontological concept. The concept only claims a correspondence between neuronal and phenomenal states with respect to spatiotemporal features. As such, neuronal-phenomenal correspondence does not imply any assumption about whether phenomenal features exist independent of neuronal features. It also implies nothing about whether the existence of phenomenal features and thus consciousness can be reduced to the existence of neuronal states and the brain. Accordingly, neuronal-phenomenal correspondence remains neutral to any such ontological claims.

Neuronal-phenomenal correspondence may nevertheless carry important implications for the ontological domain. As stated, neuronal-phenomenal correspondence only describes that neuronal and phenomenal features show corresponding spatiotemporal features; this remains independent of any claims of the existence underlying both neuronal and phenomenal features. One may extend the claim of correspondence to the ontological domain, however. In that case, one does not only claim a spatiotemporal correspondence but, what is much stronger, that neuronal and phenomenal features share the same underlying spatiotemporal features. The existence and reality of phenomenal and neuronal features is consequently based on and traced to spatiotemporal features. Such ontological extension of neuronal-phenomenal correspondence requires an ontology that considers space and time as the basic units of existence and reality. I claim that both consciousness and brain, and thus neuronal and phenomenal features, can indeed by characterized such a spatiotemporal ontology that describes their commonly underlying existence and reality. Such a spatiotemporal ontology will be developed in the third part of this book.

Spatiotemporal Model IIa: Argument of Triviality—The Empirical versus the Conceptual-Logical

We may now revisit and reject what I have referred to as the argument of triviality. The *argument of triviality* claims that the characterization of both brain and consciousness by spatiotemporal features is trivial. Briefly, the argument posits that characterizing the brain's neural activity by spatiotemporal features is trivial since neural activity is intrinsically both spatial, that is, it involves different regions, and temporal, it covers different frequencies. The brain's neural activity is consequently spatiotemporal by default because to imply otherwise, for example in the absence of any spatiotemporal features, would be to accept absence of any neural activity whatsoever—the brain would no longer be a brain and thus simply remain absent.

Characterizing the brain's neural activity by spatiotemporal features may consequently be considered trivial because this characterization does not say something novel or add anything to what we already know about the brain and its neural activity. By analogy, the same obvious characterization also applies to consciousness and its spatiotemporal characterization: any behavior including consciousness and other mental states is temporal and spatial by the very nature of the underlying brain and its neural activity. Therefore, much like the spatiotemporal characterization of the brain's neural activity, the spatiotemporal model of consciousness is also trivial. This is what I call the *argument of triviality.*

One may now wonder how the argument of triviality may be distinguished from the argument of nonspecificity. The argument of nonspecificity concerns the specific versus the unspecific nature of spatiotemporal mechanisms, that is, whether the spatiotemporal mechanisms are associated with specific patterns and organization of the brain's neural activity as well as with consciousness as distinguished from unconsciousness (see above in the first part on the spatiotemporal model of consciousness). The argument of nonspecificity can thus be characterized as an empirical argument. It is one that concerns the question for the empirical specificity of spatiotemporal mechanisms.

The argument of triviality, in contrast to the argument of nonspecificity, extends beyond spatiotemporal mechanisms and raises a deeper and more basic question: Does the characterization of brain and consciousness by time and space in general tell us anything at all? The argument is thus no longer merely empirical, as is the argument of unspecificity, but, rather, it entails a strong conceptual–logical (and ultimately also ontological) dimension: it raises the question of the characterization of the basic ingredients underlying the spatiotemporal mechanisms. Therefore, I now provide a rejection of the argument of triviality on conceptual-logical grounds that complements my empirical rejection of the same argument in chapter 4. To address the argument of triviality, we therefore need to venture from the empirical to more conceptual–logical grounds.

Spatiotemporal Model IIb: Argument of Triviality—Spatiotemporal Features versus Spatiotemporal Mechanisms

I argue that the proponent of the argument of triviality neglects the difference between spatiotemporal features on one hand and spatiotemporal mechanisms on the other. Yes, it is true that the brain exhibits spatiotemporal features including different frequency ranges and regions as we can observe them. Therefore, to now characterize the brain by these spatiotemporal features is correct, but it does not say anything beyond what is evident; the spatiotemporal characterization of the brain is thus trivial. The argument of triviality may thus hold for the brain's spatiotemporal features. However, even if this were the case, the argument of triviality for the brain's spatiotemporal features does not imply that the same holds for spatiotemporal mechanisms and thus for consciousness itself.

We may now turn our consideration to the exact nature of the relation between spatiotemporal features and spatiotemporal mechanisms.

How are spatiotemporal features and mechanisms related to each other? The data show that the same spatiotemporal features, such as the same regions and the same frequency range, can be related to two different spatiotemporal mechanisms, such as spatiotemporal integration and fragmentation, with different outcomes or results, exemplified by spatiotemporal nestedness and isolation. I propose, then, that spatiotemporal features and mechanisms can dissociate from each other: the same spatiotemporal features can be associated with different spatiotemporal mechanisms in the same way that different spatiotemporal features can be related to one and the same spatiotemporal mechanism.

What does such possible dissociation between spatiotemporal features and mechanisms indicate for the argument of triviality? The argument of triviality certainly applies to spatiotemporal features. It is indeed trivial to characterize the brain by different regions or different frequencies, since those spatiotemporal features determine the brain as brain. The absence of those spatiotemporal features portends the absence of the brain, that is, brain death. Hence, a proponent of the argument of triviality is correct in stating the trivial nature of spatiotemporal features.

However, this does not imply that the proponent of triviality is also correct when it comes to an analysis of the genesis of spatiotemporal mechanisms. Spatiotemporal mechanisms are not identical with spatiotemporal features. This is well reflected in the fact that the same spatiotemporal features, such as different frequencies, can be associated with different spatiotemporal mechanisms, such as spatiotemporal nestedness or isolation (as demonstrated in the data in the first part of this chapter). We therefore need to describe and specify the spatiotemporal mechanisms in order to understand how, as a result, one and the same set of spatiotemporal features can lead ultimately to different results or outcomes, for example either to spatiotemporal nestedness or isolation.

Given that spatiotemporal features and spatiotemporal mechanisms are not identical, the characterization of the brain's neural activity by spatiotemporal mechanisms adds something novel and is thus no longer to be considered trivial and self-evident. The argument of triviality can consequently be rejected with regard to spatiotemporal mechanisms (while, at the same time, we may accept triviality for spatiotemporal features). Thus, when the proponent of this argument declares the spatiotemporal model of consciousness to be trivial, he or she is confusing spatiotemporal features and mechanisms in the brain's neural activity.

Importantly, the nontrivial characterization of the brain by spatiotemporal mechanisms carries over to consciousness. The data discussed throughout this chapter characterize consciousness by specific spatiotemporal mechanisms: spatiotemporal nestedness, expansion, and globalization. I have showed that deficits in these spatiotemporal mechanisms lead to the absence of consciousness even if the spatiotemporal features of the brain remain the same. Spatiotemporal mechanisms are thus critically relevant for the presence of consciousness. Since spatiotemporal mechanisms are critically relevant, the spatiotemporal characterization of consciousness is not trivial at all.

Spatiotemporal Model IIc: Argument of Triviality—Phenomenal and Ontological Implications

The proponent of the argument of triviality may not yet give in. Even if nontrivial on empirical and conceptual–logical grounds, the spatiotemporal characterization of consciousness nevertheless may appear trivial when it comes to phenomenal and ontological issues. The spatiotemporal characterization simply does not add anything and only accentuates the triviality: consciousness occurs in the space and time of the world and must therefore be characterized as spatiotemporal by default. I, obviously, for the reasons explained in the last three paragraphs, reject that argument.

Regarding phenomenal features, the spatiotemporal model of consciousness is far from trivial. The spatiotemporal model of consciousness carries the implication that phenomenal features such as qualia and intentionality, among others are indeed spatiotemporal rather than nontemporal and nonspatial as is often assumed (explicitly or, more often, implicitly) in philosophy. If the hypothesis of spatiotemporal correspondence between neuronal and phenomenal features is correct, the phenomenal features may, for instance, be characterized by spatiotemporal nestedness of the various contents in consciousness as well as by spatiotemporal expansion of specific contents. In contrast, isolated contents that are not spatiotemporally nested within and expanded by the brain's spatiotemporal structure will then remain impossible in consciousness.

Accordingly, the spatiotemporal model of consciousness leads to the neurophenomenal hypothesis (Northoff, 2014b), which can be experimentally tested to make specific predictions about the relation between neuronal and phenomenal features (see Northoff, 2014b, for full development of this thesis). The spatiotemporal characterization of consciousness is thus far from trivial when it comes to its phenomenal features.

How may we categorize ontological issues? Time and space are presupposed and defined in a certain way pertaining to how the brain's neural activity itself constructs time and space. We saw that the brain relates and links different temporal and spatial scales with each other in a way that results in spatiotemporal integration and nestedness (see first part in this chapter). Such spatiotemporal integration and nestedness presuppose a particular ontological notion of time and space: time and space can no longer be accounted for in terms of discrete points in time and space but, rather, by their relation and structure. This ontologic confluence is what I describe as relational time and space (discussed in greater detail in chapter 9) that presupposes relation and structure rather than elements and properties as the basic units of existence and reality. In essence, this presents as a theory of ontic structural realism, which is the overarching subject of chapters 9–11. Accordingly, the spatiotemporal model of consciousness is far from trivial when it comes to considering ontological matters and presenting major ontological implications for explication of the mind–body problem.

Ultimately, then, I reject the argument of triviality on empirical, conceptual-logical, phenomenal, and ontological grounds. Empirically, spatiotemporal mechanisms are not trivial since they must be distinguished from other mechanisms such as cognitive, sensory, and other mechanisms. Conceptually and logically, we must distinguish spatiotemporal mechanisms from spatiotemporal features with only the latter but not the former being considered as trivial. While taken in the context of experience, that is, in a phenomenological context, the spatiotemporal model implies spatiotemporal characterization of phenomenal features—a process that absolutely cannot be characterized as trivial given that phenomenal features are often determined to be nontemporal and nonspatial. Finally, the spatiotemporal model cannot be considered trivial on ontological grounds, since it presupposes different nontraditional determinations of both time/space and existence and of reality in general.

Conclusion

Time and space are the central and most basic building blocks of nature, and therefore they naturally apply to the brain and how the brain constitutes its neural activity. For this reason, we here propose a conception of the brain's neural activity in primarily spatiotemporal terms that we hypothesize are central for consciousness and that thereby constitute our spatiotemporal theory of consciousness.

How, it is essential for us to ask, can stimuli and their respective contents be associated with consciousness? Consciousness goes *beyond* contents as we have discussed in chapters 5 and 6. Yet what exactly does this "beyond" consist in? In this chapter I have argued that this "beyond" consists of spatiotemporal features: the spatiotemporal mechanisms of the brain's neural activity that allow neural matter to associate stimuli with consciousness. In this chapter we have discussed three such spatiotemporal mechanisms, spatiotemporal nestedness, spatiotemporal expansion, and spatiotemporal globalization. Despite their differences, all mechanisms are intrinsically spatiotemporal, that is, they are spatiotemporal mechanisms, as distinguished from content-based, cognitive, and informational mechanisms. Spatiotemporal mechanisms allow for neural activity and stimuli to be processed according to their spatiotemporal features: they allow stimuli and their respective contents to be processed in a more expanded and nested spatiotemporal context that allows the association of these stimuli with consciousness.

More generally, spatiotemporal expansion and nestedness can be considered as the empirical building blocks of a spatiotemporal model of consciousness (see Northoff & Huang, in press, as well as Northoff, 2017a,b, for more empirical details in what we describe as the spatiotemporal theory of consciousness or STC). In essence, the spatiotemporal theory of consciousness conceives both brain and consciousness in spatiotemporal terms rather than in terms of sensorimotor, cognitive, affective, or social functions and their respective contents. I have demonstrated that such a spatiotemporal model of consciousness can well counter the challenges of the arguments of both nonspecificity and triviality. Most important, as proposed in the concluding section of this chapter, the spatiotemporal model of consciousness is not only empirically relevant but also carries major conceptual, phenomenological, and ontological implications—and these topics become the focus for the next part of this book.

Acknowledgment

I thank Zirui Huang with whom I recently published several parts of this chapter (Northoff & Huang, 2017, in *Neuroscience & Biobehavioral Reviews*).

8 Spatiotemporal Model of Consciousness II: Spatiotemporal Alignment—Neuro-ecological Continuum and World–Brain Relation

Introduction

General Background

Can consciousness be limited and restricted to the brain? I so far pointed out how the spatiotemporal features of the brain and its spontaneous activity are necessary for associating contents with consciousness (chapter 7). I discussed three spatiotemporal mechanisms, spatiotemporal expansion, nestedness, and globalization: the content and its rather small spatiotemporal scale or range (as consisting in specific points in time and space) are expanded and nested within the larger spatiotemporal scale or range of the brain's spontaneous activity. Put more formally, the spatiotemporal scale or range of the brain's spontaneous activity is a necessary condition of consciousness. Taken in such purely neuronal sense, consciousness is indeed limited to the confines and boundaries of the brain.

Consciousness goes beyond the brain and its spatiotemporal scale or range though. More specifically, consciousness *expands beyond the brain to body and world.* This has been postulated in various ways in philosophy as best reflected in the four E's, embodiment, embeddedness, extendedness, and enactment (Clark, 1997, 2008; Clark & Chalmers, 2010; Gallagher, 2005; Lakoff & Johnson, 1999; Noe, 2004; Rowland, 2010; Shapiro, 2014; Thompson, 2007; Varela et al., 1991). However, the detailed characterization of these concepts, including their relationship to the brain's neuronal mechanisms, remains controversial if not unclear.

When considering consciousness itself, the need for including body and world is almost self-evident. We, for instance, experience seismic earth waves whose frequency range is much slower than that of our brain. Or, alternatively, we can become conscious of processes that are much faster than the frequency range of our brain. Consciousness and its spatiotemporal scale or range thus expand beyond those of the brain's spontaneous activity to those of body and world. Hence, when suggesting a spatiotemporal theory of consciousness (STC; chapter 7), we need to include the spatiotemporal ranges or scales of both body and world. The exact mechanisms underlying such inclusion of body and world in consciousness remain unclear, however.

Aim and Argument

The aim in this chapter is to expand the STC beyond the brain to body and world. I will argue that the possible inclusion of the spatiotemporal scales or ranges of both body and world in consciousness is empirically (i.e., neuronally) based on aligning and relating the brain's spatiotemporal features to those of body and world—I thus speak of "spatiotemporal alignment" as a mechanism by means of which the brain interacts with body and world. Such spatiotemporal alignment can, on the conceptual side, be described as a "neuro-ecological continuum" and a "world-brain relation" (see below for the definition of both concepts). Spatiotemporal alignment's allowing for body–brain relation will be the focus in the first part while the brain's spatiotemporal alignment to the world (i.e., world–brain relation) will be discussed in the second part.

Conceptually, I frame the need for including body and world in consciousness under the umbrella which I describe as the "argument of inclusion," which is a conceptual argument that includes two halves. The first half concerns the body: do we need to include the body in our account of the brain and its neuronal (i.e., empirical) mechanisms, and how is that relevant for consciousness?

The second half of the argument of inclusion concerns the world (see below for definition of the concept of world): do we need to include the world in our account of the brain, and how is that relevant for consciousness? Based on empirical evidence, I will argue that the brain's spatiotemporal alignment to the world provides a neuro-ecological continuum, which allows for a world–brain relation. Most important, empirical evidence suggests that spatiotemporal alignment with world–brain relation is a necessary but nonsufficient condition of consciousness (a neural prerequisite of consciousness), as distinguished from sufficient conditions (neural correlates of consciousness; see chapter 7). neural correlates of consciousness (NCCs) that concern actual rather than possible consciousness.

Part I: Body and Consciousness

Empirical Findings Ia: Body and Brain—Spatiotemporal Alignment

How is the brain related to the body? Recent studies have investigated the relationship of the brain to the heart and the stomach. These studies show a close relationship between brain and body in specifically temporal terms.

Chang et al. (2013) demonstrated (using a sliding window approach) that the dynamic functional connectivity from amygdala and anterior cingulate cortex to brain stem, thalamus, putamen, and dorsolateral prefrontal cortex covaried with heart rate variability. The more variability in the heart rate, the more variability in the functional connectivity between these regions. This was confirmed in a subsequent study by Jennings et al. (2016); they observed functional connectivity of medial prefrontal cortex to covary with the heart rate.

These functional magnetic resonance imaging (fMRI) studies show a close relationship (i.e., alignment), between the brain's spontaneous activity and the heartbeat, that is, *cardiocortical coupling*. Such cardiocortical coupling seems to be mediated by temporal features such as variability in both brain and heart. That leaves open the exact mechanisms and the directionality of their alignment. This can be addressed in electroencephalography (EEG) or magnetoencephalography (MEG) studies.

Lechinger (Lechinger, Heib, Gruber, Schabus, & Klimesch, 2015) recently reported an EEG study on the relationship between heart rate and phase locking in the brain's spontaneous activity during awake and asleep states. The phase onset of especially the delta/theta frequency (2–6 Hz) in the brain's spontaneous activity was shifted and thus locked to the onset of the heartbeat. Accordingly, the brain's spontaneous activity actively aligned, that is, shifted its own phase onsets in orientation on and correspondence to the ongoing temporal structure of the heartbeat. One can thus speak of "temporal alignment" that, if extended by the spatial domain, amounts to spatiotemporal alignment.

Most interestingly, the phase locking of the delta/theta frequency to the heartbeat was reduced progressively during the different sleep stages, that is, from N1 to N3, within the non-REM sleep where consciousness is increasingly lost. In contrast, the phase locking pattern during REM sleep, that is, when one dreams, resembled that of the awake state. These data suggest that the brain's spatiotemporal alignment to the heartbeat is relevant for consciousness (i.e., the level of consciousness). If the brain's neural activity no longer is aligned to, and instead is detached from, the temporal structure of the heartbeat, consciousness, as in sleep, seems to be lost. I therefore speak of "temporal detachment" of the brain from the heart/body as distinguished from "temporal alignment" (see below for more details on both terms).

How about the alignment and coupling of the brain to organs of the body other than the heart? A recent study by Richter et al. (2017) investigated the relationship between the infraslow (around 0.05-Hz) rhythm generated by the stomach (as measured by a special device recording the stomach's movements) and the different frequencies in the brain's spontaneous activity (as measured by MEG). They observed that the phase of the stomach's infraslow frequency was coupled with the amplitude in the alpha range (10–11 Hz) in the brain's spontaneous activity. One can thus speak of cross-frequency coupling between body and brain, that is, what I call a *gastrocortical phase–amplitude coupling*.

Neuronally, the gastrocortical phase–amplitude coupling was associated with neural activity in two specific regions of the brain, the anterior insula and the occipital–parietal cortex. Most importantly, Richer et al. (2017) also measured the directionality of the coupling between stomach and heart. They measured the information transfer by using transfer entropy. The data showed information transfer from the stomach to the brain and thus from the former's infraslow frequency phases to the brain's alpha amplitude in anterior insula and occipital cortex. In contrast, reverse information from the neural activity in the two brain regions to the stomach was not observed.

Taken together, the data show a close relationship between brain and body. Specifically, the data suggest that the brain and its spontaneous activity's spatiotemporal structure align themselves to the spatiotemporal structure of the body (as, e.g., to the stomach's movements or the heart's beats). Such spatiotemporal alignment is a central feature of the brain's spontaneous activity that, for instance, can shift its phase onsets in orientation on the onset of external stimuli. Spatiotemporal alignment of the brain to the body must thus be considered an active rather than passive process by means of which the brain's spontaneous activity can conform its own spatiotemporal structure to that of the body.

Empirical Findings Ib: Body and Brain—Spatiotemporal Alignment and Consciousness

Is the spatiotemporal alignment of the body's temporal features to the brain and its neural activity relevant for consciousness? I so far only demonstrated how both body and brain are coupled by means of their temporal features. This left open whether such spatiotemporal alignment is also relevant for consciousness. That shall be the focus in the following; for that, I will discuss a recent study by Park et al. (2014).

Park et al. (2014) used MEG to investigate the impact of the heartbeat on conscious detection of visual stimuli. They investigated visual grating stimuli in a near-threshold way, that is, stimuli were presented at an intensity that was close to the individual limit of conscious perception for each subject. While undergoing MEG and electrocardiogram (heart) recording, the subjects were exposed to these near-threshold visual stimuli and had to make a decision for each stimulus as to whether they perceived and thus detected it or not. The behavioral data showed a detection rate of 46 percent, which indicates conscious perception of approximately half of the stimuli.

How is such conscious detection dependent upon the brain's spontaneous activity and its coupling to the heartbeat? Park et al. (2014) did not observe a direct relation of heartbeat and heartbeat variability to the subjects' hit rate, that is, the conscious detection of stimuli. Hence, the heartbeat itself had no direct impact on conscious detection.

However, when Park et al. (2014) considered the neural correlates of the heartbeats' processing in the brain (the heartbeat-evoked potential [HEP], as can be measured with MEG), they observed that that the amplitude of the HEP predicted conscious detection (i.e., hits): the amplitude of the HEP was significantly different between hits and misses with hits showing higher amplitude than misses. Accordingly, the way the brain processed the heartbeat impacted whether consciousness was associated with the visual stimuli.

The HEP, and its effects on conscious detection, was most predominantly located in anterior midline regions like the perigenual anterior cingulate cortex and ventromedial prefrontal cortex (PACC and VMPFC) where interoceptive stimuli from the body and exteroceptive stimuli are linked and integrated. The very same regions (PACC and VMPFC) also showed fluctuations in the spontaneous activity which were related to the fluctuations in the HEP, that is, heartbeat variability.

These data suggest that the heartbeat affects and modulates the brain's spontaneous activity and its spatiotemporal structure, which is manifested in corresponding fluctuations of the HEP in the spontaneous activity. That very same HEP-related modulation of the brain's spontaneous activity, in turn, impacts whether consciousness can be associated with the external visual stimuli during subsequent stimulus-induced activity. Taken together, this study demonstrates well the impact of the heartbeat on the association of consciousness to external contents, that is, visual consciousness.

Does the same hold, analogously, also for associating internal contents with consciousness? The same group (Babo-Rebelo et al., 2016) tested whether consciousness of internal contents such as one's own self (in terms of "I" and "Me") and the latter's neural correlates in the brain's spontaneous activity (as measured with MEG) are also coupled to the heartbeat. They again observed that spontaneous fluctuations in HEP in the PACC and VMPFC predicted the fluctuations in consciousness of one's self in terms of either "I" (operationalized as "first-person perspective subject or agent of my own thoughts") or "me" (operationalized as "thinking about my own self") (Babo-Rebelo et al., 2016).

In sum, these data demonstrate temporal alignment between heart rate and the brain's neural activity. Most importantly, they show that such temporal alignment is central for associating internal or external contents (such as visual stimuli or one's own self) with consciousness. If temporal alignment is lost and replaced by temporal detachment between body and brain, consciousness is lost.

Therefore, I postulate that spatiotemporal alignment of the brain's spontaneous activity to the body is central for consciousness: the better the brain's spontaneous activity and its spatiotemporal structure are aligned to the body's activity and its spatiotemporal structure, the higher the likelihood that contents including both internal (such as one's own self) and external (such as visual stimuli) can be associated with consciousness. If, in contrast, there is spatiotemporal detachment (as I say), consciousness remains impossible.

Spatiotemporal Model Ia: Body–Brain Relation—Spatiotemporal Alignment

What do these findings imply for the spatiotemporal model of consciousness? I will argue that they require us to expand the spatiotemporal model of consciousness beyond the boundaries of the brain to include the body.

The findings show coupling and a close relationship between brain and body. Though the findings are not abundant as yet, they nevertheless clearly show that the brain and body are aligned to each other on spatiotemporal grounds. The brain and its spontaneous activity's spatiotemporal structure are aligned to the body and its spatiotemporal structure. The spatiotemporal structure of the brain's spontaneous activity is manifest in the different frequencies including its phase onsets while the body's temporal structure is reflected in heartrate variability and the frequency of the stomach's movements.

The data suggest that the temporal structures in the activities of both brain and body can couple and align to each other by, for instance, the phase onsets of their fluctuations. I described such temporal (and ultimately spatial) coupling as *spatiotemporal alignment*. The concept of spatiotemporal alignment is an empirical concept that describes coupling between brain and body on spatiotemporal grounds. That very same coupling aligns body and brain in spatiotemporal terms: the spatiotemporal structure of the brain aligns itself to the spatiotemporal structure of the body. If, in contrast, there is no such alignment, the temporal and spatial structure of body and brain remain detached from each other—I therefore speak of *spatiotemporal detachment*.

The concept of alignment must be distinguished from that of representation. Without going into the myriad details of representation, I here determine representation by specific contents. For instance, a specific content such as the heart or the stomach as such may be modeled and consequently represented in the brain's neural activity. Representation thus entails content-based coupling between brain and body. Alignment, in contrast, refers to time- and space-based coupling, that is, spatiotemporal coupling: brain and heart/stomach are linked and coupled by their temporal and spatial features rather than the contents themselves, that is, stomach or heart as such. I postulate that the empirical data speak in favor of spatiotemporal alignment rather than representation.

Spatiotemporal Model Ib: Body–Brain Relation—Definition

The concept of spatiotemporal alignment also entails directionality. We saw directionality in the coupling between brain and stomach/heart: the brain aligns (i.e., shifts) the phase onsets of its spontaneous activity to the heartbeat or, alternatively, its amplitude is coupled to the phase onset of the stomach. Either case involves the same directionality: the brain's spontaneous activity aligns itself to the body (i.e., heart or stomach) rather than the latter aligning itself to the former. Hence, there is directionality from body to brain (as is supported specifically by the data on the information transfer from stomach to brain). I therefore speak of *body–brain relation.*

What do I mean by the concept of body–brain relation? The notion is conceptual rather than empirical. The concept of body–brain relation describes how the body with its larger spatiotemporal scale is related to the brain with its smaller spatiotemporal scale—this, as will be detailed below, is made possible by the nesting of the brain within the body amounting to *spatiotemporal nestedness*.

Taken in this sense, the concept of body–brain relation must be distinguished from that of brain–body relation in which case one would suppose reverse integration, that is, the body integrates and nests within the brain, with subsequent spatiotemporal alignment of the body to the brain. While certainly conceivable on a purely conceptual level, I argue that the concept of brain–body relation is not empirically plausible given the data presented above.

Note that I do not deny the reverse directionality from brain to body as described in brain–body relation. The way we impact our body by our brain-based action and cognition certainly warrants the concept of brain–body relationship. This pertains to action and cognition, however. Accordingly, I distinguish body–brain relation and brain–body relation not only in merely conceptual terms, that is, by their directionality, but also on functional or behavioral grounds. The body–brain relation (rather than brain–body relation) is central for consciousness while the brain–body relation (rather than the body–brain relation) is central for action and cognition. To confuse the body–brain relation and the brain–body relation would thus be to confuse consciousness and action/cognition.

Spatiotemporal Model IIa: Body–Brain Relation—Embodiment

The proponents of the four E's (i.e., embodiment, extendedness, enactment, and embeddedness) argue that consciousness extends beyond the brain to body and world (Clark, 1997, 2008; Clark & Chalmers, 2010; Gallagher, 2005; Lakoff & Johnson, 1999; Noe, 2004; Rowland, 2010; Shapiro, 2014; Thompson, 2007; Varela et al., 1991). I do not intend to go into the details of this discussion here. Instead, I shed only a brief light on the most basic definition of the four E's. That serves me to argue for a spatiotemporal view on the four E's. Specifically, I will argue that the inclusion of body and world in consciousness as postulated in the four E's is based on what I empirically described as spatiotemporal alignment and, conceptually, as world–brain relation.

Let us focus first on *embodiment*. Roughly, embodiment points out that the body needs to be considered in consciousness: the body is not just an "output device" of the brain but also provides important input in constituting consciousness—the brain and the body may thus have "shared circuits" that are relevant for consciousness (Gallagher, 2005; Lakoff & Johnson, 1999; Shapiro, 2014; Varela et al., 1991). Conceiving embodiment in this sense, the body must be included in our definition of consciousness and may therefore, in addition to the brain, be regarded a necessary condition of possible consciousness.

One may note at first glance that the concept of embodiment is rather close to that of body–brain relation. Why do I then introduce a novel concept (i.e., body–brain relation) rather than using the well-known one (i.e., embodiment)? True, the concept of body–brain relation overlaps with that of embodiment. The concept of body–brain relation can be understood as spatiotemporal specification of the more unspecific and general concept of embodiment. I argue for two such spatiotemporal specifications.

First, the concept of body–brain relation explicitly emphasizes the central role of relation. Spatiotemporal alignment allows us to establish an empirical relation between body and brain. That very same relation is now put into conceptual terms when describing it as body–brain relation. We will see later in Part III of this book that the notion of relation in such empirical and conceptual sense can be brought to an ontological level as when supposing ontic structural realism (chapter 9). Hence, the notion of relation may provide linkage between empirical and ontological levels. For that reason, I want to explicitly use the term *relation*—therefore, I prefer speaking of body–brain relation rather than embodiment.

Second, the concept of relation in body–brain relation is meant in a spatiotemporal way. The relation between body and brain is a spatiotemporal relation as being based on spatiotemporal alignment. Such spatiotemporal relation must be distinguished from other forms of relation such as sensorimotor or cognitive relation (see also chapters 9 and 10 for more details on this point). Especially, sensorimotor relation is often emphasized in embodiment (Merleau-Ponty, 1963; Shapiro, 2014): the brain is integrated within and thus related to the body by means of sensorimotor functions that are initiated in the brain and manifest in the body—that is, in terms of action and perception.

Without providing the details, I here postulate that such sensorimotor relation between body and brain is based on and can ultimately be traced to their spatiotemporal relation (i.e., their spatiotemporal alignment). We therefore need to describe such spatiotemporal relation using concepts that are distinguished from sensorimotor relation as implied by embodiment. That is the moment where the concept of body–brain relation comes in—a concept that can well account for such spatiotemporal rather than merely sensorimotor relation between body and brain.

Spatiotemporal Model IIb: Body–Brain Relation—Consciousness and Argument of Inclusion

As discussed above, embodiment supposes shared circuits between body and brain. Such shared circuits are often assumed to consist in "sensorimotor circuits": sensorimotor functions are initiated in the brain's sensorimotor regions/network while they are realized and manifest in the body's sensory and motor pathways. Spatiotemporal alignment also establishes a shared circuit between body and brain. However, the shared circuit is not sensorimotor.

Instead, the shared circuit consists in a spatiotemporal circuit that, as between heart/stomach and brain, is shared and therefore operates across the boundaries between body and brain. The spatiotemporal circuit, in turn, provides the basis for sensorimotor circuits and their central role in sensorimotor function (i.e., action and perception). Without the underlying spatiotemporal circuit, the sensorimotor circuits would, at best, render possible only movement and sensation but not action and perception.

The difference between movement/sensation and action/perception amounts to the difference between the absence and presence of consciousness. Therefore, I assume that the spatiotemporal circuits are relevant for consciousness. Because of its spatiotemporal alignment to the body with body–brain relation, the single system consisting of body and brain can expand its spatiotemporal scale or range beyond that of the brain itself. One may thus speak of spatiotemporal expansion of the brain beyond itself to body and world. Importantly, I consider such spatiotemporal expansion across the boundaries of brain and body to operate on the basis of the same mechanism as operates in expansion within the brain itself (chapter 7).

Recall that I introduced the mechanism of spatiotemporal expansion in the previous chapter. It described how the brain's spontaneous activity and its spatiotemporal structure can expand the single stimuli or contents beyond their discrete points in time and space to a larger spatiotemporal scale. Put slightly differently, "spatiotemporal expansion" describes the expansion of the stimulus-induced activity's small spatiotemporal scale by the brain's spontaneous activity's larger spatiotemporal scale. Since the brain's spontaneous activity is limited to the brain, spatiotemporal expansion in this sense remains within the spatiotemporal confines or boundaries of the brain.

The current data show that, by aligning to the body, the brain and, more specifically, its spontaneous activity's spatiotemporal structure expands beyond itself to the body. Accordingly, the same mechanism (i.e., spatiotemporal expansion) that operates within the brain itself also operates across brain and body. In the same way that the brain's spontaneous activity expands the spatiotemporal scale of its own stimulus-induced activity, the body expands the spatiotemporal scale of its own brain's spontaneous activity. One may thus assume double spatiotemporal expansion—that is, within brain as well as across brain and body.

Why is such double spatiotemporal expansion relevant for consciousness? We saw in chapter 7 that spatiotemporal expansion of stimulus-induced activity by the brain's spontaneous activity is central for associating contents with consciousness. The current data on both visual consciousness and self-consciousness (as detailed above) show that, analogously, spatiotemporal expansion of the brain's spontaneous activity by the body is equally relevant for consciousness. I therefore postulate that spatiotemporal expansion across the boundaries of body and brain (i.e., the body–brain relation) is necessary for consciousness, as without such spatiotemporal expansion consciousness cannot be realized.

I am now ready to address the first half of the argument of inclusion. The first half of the argument of inclusion raises this question: do we need to include the body in our account of the brain, and how is that relevant for consciousness? Yes, the body must be included in our account of the brain with such inclusion taking place on spatiotemporal grounds (i.e., spatiotemporal inclusion). This specifies the hypothesis of embodiment in spatiotemporal terms by spatiotemporal alignment and body–brain relation.

Most important, I demonstrated that spatiotemporal alignment and body–brain relation are central for—that is, they predispose—consciousness. If, in contrast, there were spatiotemporal detachment of the brain from the body replacing their spatiotemporal alignment, consciousness would be lost. Therefore, I consider spatiotemporal alignment and body–brain relation necessary conditions of possible consciousness (i.e., a neural prerequisite). Taken in such expanded way, that is, from brain to body, the spatiotemporal model of consciousness can well accommodate the first half of the argument of inclusion, that is, the need to include the body in our models of both brain and consciousness.

Part II: World and Consciousness

Empirical Findings Ia: World and Brain—Spatiotemporal Alignment and Perception

How is the brain related to the world? I will now show that spatiotemporal alignment does not only hold for the relationship between body and brain (i.e., body–brain relation), but also for the one between world and brain (i.e., world–brain relation). This, as I will show, is strongly supported by empirical data where the brain's neural activity aligns itself to the temporal (and spatial) structure in the environment.

We are confronted with various types of stimuli in our environment that need to be encoded by our brain. For example, when we hear a music piece that is rhythmic, our brain seems to encode the rhythmic structure of the melody in such way that we are able to align ourselves to the melody. This allows us to participate in the melody's rhythmic structure when, for instance, we swing our arms and legs while dancing. Our brain seems to sample the rhythmic structure of the tone sequence presented, which enables our participation in the rhythmic structure of the environmental events or objects (i.e., the music piece).

What kind of neuronal mechanisms mediate our brain's apparent conforming and aligning to the rhythmic structure of environmental events? This was investigated experimentally in a recent study by Atteveldt et al.

(2015). They presented background tones in either a rhythmic way (i.e., same time intervals between tones) or a random way (i.e., varying time intervals between tones). The rhythmic or random temporal structure of these tones served as background tones in blocks of 30 seconds: a 30 s block with rhythmic tones was followed by a 30 s block of random tones (interspersed by 15 s of baseline with no tones at all), which, in turn, was followed by a 30 s block of rhythmic tones and so on. These tones serving as background tones were combined with target tones (5–10 Hz slower frequency than the background tones) that were interspersed between the background tones; subjects had to detect the target tones and indicate that detection by button click. Subjects were investigated using fMRI with simultaneous EEG to combine both high spatial (fMRI) and temporal (EEG) accuracy.

What were their findings? Behaviorally, they observed significantly lower (i.e., faster) reaction times in response to target tones that were embedded in a rhythmic stream of tones when compared to those presented in the random sequence. Moreover, the hit, or detection, rate (i.e., the number of correctly detected tones) was significantly higher and thus more accurate in the rhythmic condition when compared to the random condition (see figure 2 in Atteveldt et al., 2015). This suggests that the temporal structure of the background condition has a significant impact on the perception and subsequent detection of the target tones: the background tones' mode of presentation (rhythmic vs. random) impacted the detection (i.e., perception) and speed of motor reaction (i.e., reaction time) of the target tones.

Analogous results were obtained on the neuronal level. First, fMRI results showed the involvement of a distributed neural network with superior temporal gyrus (STG, which includes the auditory cortex), the insula, the medial frontal cortex, the thalamus, the brain stem, and the cerebellum when comparing the sound detection (rhythmic and random structure) with a no sound condition. When directly comparing the two sound conditions, higher signal responses were observed in bilateral STG in the random condition relative to the rhythmic condition (see figure 3 in Atteveldt et al., 2015).

Moreover, one could follow the sequence of the blocks in the dynamics of the STG signal: the response signal in STG showed a dynamic high–low pattern in that it was low during rhythmic blocks and high during random blocks (see figure 4 in Atteveldt et al., 2015). Finally, the degree of signal in right STG correlated positively with reaction times: the lower the response signal in right STG during all conditions (including both rhythmic and random), the faster the reaction times in response to the target tones.

Taken together, the behavioral results show that the rhythmic background condition led to faster reaction times in response to single stimuli when compared to the random background condition. However, contrary to expectation, that did not yield higher activity in, for instance, the STG. Instead, the opposite was observed, namely, lower activity changes in the STG during the rhythmic condition when compared to the random presentation. This was further underlined by the observed positive correlation between reaction time and STG activity.

Empirical Findings Ib: World and Brain—Spatiotemporal Alignment and Efficient Encoding

What about the EEG? The authors observed a particular waveform, N100, that is specific for the perception and subsequent detection of auditory tones as, for instance, the target tones in the present experimental paradigm. Interestingly, the amplitude of the N100 in response to the target tones was significantly lower in the rhythmic condition when compared to the target tones in the random condition (see figure 5 in Atteveldt et al., 2015). Moreover, the N100 was initiated earlier or faster (i.e., peak latency) in response to the target during the rhythmic condition relative to the random condition (see figures 6 and 7 in Atteveldt et al., 2015).

Taking both fMRI and EEG together, the results show that the brain seems to encode rhythmic and nonrhythmic (i.e., random) background stimuli sequences in the environment in different ways, which, in turn, impacts subsequent perception and detection of the target stimuli. Detection of target tones within rhythmic and random background tone sequences yielded differences on behavioral, and electrophysiological levels: the rhythmic condition showed more accurate and faster reaction times, decreased STG signals, and faster and lower N100 amplitude.

However, one may now be puzzled about the results. One would have expected higher activity in STG and N100 in the rhythmic condition because of the faster and more accurate reaction times. That was not the case though. Instead, the results showed the opposite, namely, that faster and more accurate reaction times went along with lower STG activity and

N100 amplitude. This suggests, as the authors remark, a more efficient encoding of the rhythmic sequence (as indexed by faster and more accurate reaction times). However, what is meant by "efficient" encoding?

More efficient encoding means that less energy, and consequently less energy-based change by the brain's spontaneous activity (as indexed by lower STG and N100 signals; see also ten Over et al., 2014, for behavioral support), is required to process the stimuli: the better the brain can align its spontaneous activity to the external stimuli (by integrating the latter within the former's spatiotemporal structure), the more minimal the effort the brain has to expend in changing its ongoing spontaneous activity (such as its frequencies and amplitudes), the lower the degree of subsequent stimulus-induced activity (as in STG/fMRI and N100/EEG), and the faster the respectively associated behavior (i.e., the reaction times).

In contrast, the random stimulus sequence does not allow for such efficient encoding. There is no longer a rhythmic tone sequence in the environment to which the brain's spontaneous activity can conform and thus align itself. In that case, the brain may need to recruit and expend a higher amount of energy and change in its ongoing spontaneous activity in order to process the external stimuli.

Taken altogether, the brain's spontaneous activity seems to align itself to the temporal and ultimately to the spatiotemporal structure in its respective environmental context (i.e., the world). In the same way that the brain's spontaneous activity aligns itself to the body, it also, analogously, aligns itself to the world. In both cases, body and world, the brain's alignment is based on spatiotemporal ground, implying spatiotemporal alignment. The present data show that the brain's spatiotemporal alignment to the world also impacts subsequent stimulus-induced activity in response to specific stimuli as well as the latter's association with consciousness (i.e., perception).

Empirical Findings Ic: Rhythmic versus Continuous Modes of Brain Activity

Based on the findings described above and others, Schroeder and Lakatos (Lakatos et al., 2005, 2008, 2009; Schroeder et al., 2008; Schroeder & Lakatos 2009a,b, 2012; Schroeder et al., 2010) distinguish two different spatiotemporal modes of neural activity, that is, a rhythmic and a continuous mode. Let us start with the rhythmic mode.

In the case of a rhythmic mode, the brain's slow-frequency fluctuations can align their phases with the probability distributions of the stimuli, that is, their predicted occurrence across different discrete points in (physical) time and space. The brain's intrinsic activity can *quasi* follow what occurs in the environment. In such a "rhythmic mode" of neural operation, the fast-frequency oscillations during stimulus-induced activity are more or less aligned to the slow-frequency fluctuations and in turn the phases of these slow-frequency fluctuations are aligned to the statistical/likelihood structure of the stimuli in the environment (see also Canolty & Knight, 2010; Canolty et al., 2012; Klimesch et al., 2010; Sauseng & Klimesch, 2008, for excellent and critical reviews of such stimulus–phase coupling).

How can we describe the rhythmic mode of brain activity in more detail? There are two distinct processes in play. First, there is the cross-frequency coupling that allows for coupling and linking—that is, entraining—fast-frequency oscillations and even behavior to the phase of the ongoing slow-frequency oscillation in the spontaneous activity. And second, there is the coupling or alignment of the spontaneous activity's slow-frequency oscillations and especially their phases to the onset of the rhythmic or statistical structure of the stimuli's occurrence in the environment.

However, there are not always rhythmic stimuli in the environment that the brain and its intrinsic activity can align to. The rhythmic mode must therefore be distinguished from a more "continuous mode" of neural operation (Schroeder & Lakatos, 2009a,b). Unlike in the rhythmic mode, there seems to be no specific rhythm or statistical structure in the stimulus presentation to which the spontaneous activity's slow-frequency oscillations (and subsequently the faster frequencies and behavior) can entrain and align their phase onsets. In other words, the brain is now "left to itself" and must therefore by itself actively structure and organize its own spontaneous activity.

How can the brain structure and organize its own spontaneous activity in such continuous mode? The brain can no longer rely on the rhythmic presentation of external stimuli and align itself to them but must become active itself, that is, continuously active. Instead of adapting the fast-frequency oscillations to the slower ones, as in the rhythmic mode, the stimulus-induced fast-frequency oscillations are now "on their own" in the continuous mode. The stimulus-induced fast-frequency oscillations must account for the stimulus independently of the resting-state activity's slow-frequency oscillations and their phase onsets; that is so because the latter are no longer aligned to the statistical structure of the external stimuli. Rather than being helpful by aligning themselves to the extrinsic stimuli, as in the rhythmic mode, the spontaneous activity's slow-frequency oscillations may now stand in the way of eliciting stimulus-induced fast-frequency oscillations.

Increase in the power of faster frequencies such as gamma may therefore be accompanied by their decreased cross-frequency coupling to slower frequencies' phase onsets. This is exactly what has been observed in paradigms where there is no rhythmic presentation of stimuli (see above). The slow-frequency fluctuations (such as infraslow and delta) are consequently suppressed, while the fast-frequency fluctuations (such as gamma) are strengthened in order to process the external stimuli themselves independent of their respective temporal context in the environment. The temporal pattern in the continuous mode is thus reversed when compared to the one in the rhythmic mode, where the slow-frequency fluctuations are (relatively) stronger and the fast-frequency fluctuations remain (relatively) weak.

Empirical Findings IIa: World and Brain—Spatiotemporal Alignment and Social World

Recent neuroscience introduced the simultaneous scanning of two (or more) subjects' neural activities during one and the same task. This procedure, called *hyperscanning*, allows researchers to investigate *brain-to-brain coupling* (Hasson et al., 2012), which entails neuronal and perceptual synchronization between different subjects (see Acquadro et al., 2015; Babiloni & Astolfi, 2015; Hasson & Frith, 2016; Koike et al., 2015; Schoot et al., 2016, for recent reviews). I here focus on one particular study that investigated how the playing of shared music by different players allows for their neuronal and perceptual synchronization (Lindenberger et al., 2009; Saenger et al., 2012).

Lindenberger et al. (2009) investigated, using EEG, eight pairs of guitarists playing one and the same melody together (sixty trials meaning sixty repetitions), a modern jazz fusion piece in E-minor with four quarters per measure. In each of the eight pairs of guitarists, they selected one lead guitarist with the respective other one following (before playing, the two guitarists were given a preparatory period during which they listened to a metronome and its beat). This served to test how much the one subject synchronizes her or his own playing and rhythm to those of the lead guitarist. That is possible only when the following subject's perception of the guitar tones becomes synchronized with the playing and perception of the lead guitarist. The experimental design is thus based on the synchronization of the perceptions between two different subjects, the following and lead guitarist. This amounts to what I describe as "perceptual synchronization."

Is the synchronization between the two subjects' perceptions (e.g., perceptual synchronization) mediated by corresponding synchronization between their brains (e.g., neuronal synchronization)? For that, the investigators measured EEG in both subjects during their guitar playing. Using EEG, they determined the*phase locking index* (PLI); they measured the invariance of phases across different trials from single electrodes within one subject's brain. This served to determine the degree of cortical synchronization between different electrodes within one particular brain related to one subject. More generally, this measures neuronal synchronization within the single brain.

In addition, they determined what they call *interbrain phase coherence* (IPC). The IPC measures the degree of constancy in phase differences across different trials in one and the same electrode from two different brains (of the two subjects in each pair) simultaneously. This served to determine the degree of cortical synchronization between different subjects' brains in one particular electrode reflecting neuronal synchronization between different brains. Specifically, they time locked the periods around the onset of the metronome beat in the preparatory period and the play onset of the lead guitarists (3-s sequences with 1 s before onset and 2 s after). Based on prior considerations, they focused on lower and midrange frequencies up to 20 Hz.

What were the results? Let us start within the neuronal synchronization within brains. They observed an increase in phase synchronization between the different electrodes within each subject as indexed by the PLI. Such locking of the phase onsets between the different electrodes' activities within the subjects' brains was observed in especially fronto-central electrodes in the theta range (4–8 Hz) during both the onset of the metronome beats and the play onset of the lead guitarist. The task thus leads to increased cortical synchronization between the different electrodes within the subjects' brains.

How about the neuronal synchronization between the different subjects' brains? The increase in PLI in the brain of each subject was accompanied by an increase in IPC, the measure of the coherence of the phases between the brains of the two subjects. Especially the fronto-central electrodes showed increased phase coherence in a lower frequency, namely, the delta range (1–4 Hz) between the brains of the two subjects while they were playing the melody.

How are both intra- and intersubject measures of neural activity related to each other? Interestingly, intrasubject phase locking (PLI) and intersubject phase coherence (IPC) were positively correlated with each other: the higher the degree of intrasubject phase locking, the higher the degree of intersubject phase coherence. Both forms of neuronal synchronization, that is, within and between brains, are thus directly related and are apparently dependent upon each other.

Empirical Findings IIb: World and Brain—Spatiotemporal Alignment and Perceptual–Social Synchronization

How are the two forms of neuronal synchronization, for example, within and between brains, related to consciousness as, for instance, in perception of the different subjects—does neuronal synchronization entail perceptual synchronization? Lindenberger et al. (2009) observed that delta phase coherence in the following guitarists occurred in temporal relation to the play onset of the lead guitarist and her or his starting gesture immediately prior to play onset. The neuronal synchronization between the different subjects' brains as indexed by delta phase coherence is thus related to the perceptual synchronization of the following guitarists to the lead guitarists. In short, neuronal synchronization within and between the subjects' brains entails perceptual synchronization between subjects.

One may now want to argue that phase coherence between the different subjects' brains can be traced back to the similarity of stimuli (the guitarists were playing the same piece) rather than their synchronization to each other. For that purpose, the same group conducted another study where they let the guitarist play different segments from the same piece, this time a classical piece, a rondo from an earlier composer (see Saenger et al., 2012). By letting the different guitarists play identical or different segments of the same piece, they could control for the similarity or identity of the stimuli and tasks. This allowed them to distinguish between*stimulus-related effects* and *brain-related effects*.

Stimulus-related effects concern those neural similarities between different subjects' neural activities that can be traced back to the subjects' exposure to the same stimuli. In contrast, brain-related effects refer to those neural similarities between different subjects' neural activities that can be traced back to the brain itself—these effects reflect an active contribution from their brain's spontaneous activity rather than the exposure to the same stimulus material (e.g., stimulus-induced activity).

The study by Saenger et al. (2012) controlled well for stimulus-related effects. They included thirty-two guitarists with sixteen overlapping duets and, using EEG, measured their neural activity while playing together. Unlike in the previous study by Lindenberger et al. (2009), they also manipulated the roles of both leader and follower across the sixteen pairs of guitarists. As in the previous study they measured PLI and IPC (and other whole brain measures such as small network organization, which I only peripherally touch on here).

They showed more or less the same results as in the previous study. There was again increased phase locking between electrodes (PLI) in the theta range in the brains of the single subjects during both preparatory and playing periods. Moreover, as in the previous study, such intrasubject phase locking was accompanied by interbrain phase coherence. There was phase coherence between the different subjects' brains (IPC) in fronto-central electrodes with strong phase locking or coherence in especially the delta range. As in the previous study, this suggests that intersubject phase coherence occurs mainly in lower frequency ranges, namely, delta ranges, when compared to intrasubject phase locking in the theta range.

Importantly, the results show differences between leaders and followers in both measures, phase locking index (PLI) and inter brain phase coherence (IPC). The leader showed theta phase locking increase between electrodes, that is, PLI already in the preparatory period, while in the follower that increase occurred later in the playing period. Moreover, the delta phase coherence between subjects' brains (i.e., the IPC) was particularly strong in the leader when compared to the followers.

These differences suggest that the followers synchronized their intra- and interneuronal phases (i.e., PLI and IPC) in relation to the leader and her or his phase onsets and coherence. Since the followers have no direct access to the leader's brain, the former must have perceived the latter during the preparatory and initial playing period. Neuronal synchronization between the different subjects' brains thus went along with perceptual synchronization of the followers to the leader. Accordingly, neuronal synchronization between brains is related to consciousness as it was accompanied by both conscious perception and action.

One may now be inclined to argue that the data presented above only concerned the social world but not the world as such. The data concerned only spatiotemporal alignment to another person as part of the social world and did not concern spatiotemporal alignment to other events or objects independent of persons. However, the same kind of spatiotemporal alignment with phase shifting, neuronal synchronization, and cross-frequency coupling has also been observed with regard to tones, and music (as shown here) as well as with respect to other objects and events (as demonstrated in various studies) (Nang et al., 2014; Schroeder & Lakatos, 2009, 2010; Stefanics et al., 2010). Hence, taken altogether, these data suggest that spatiotemporal alignment can be conceived of as a basic principle of how the brain's neural activity aligns itself to the world in general, including both social and nonsocial worlds (see figure 8.1).

Spatiotemporal Model Ia: Social Cognition and Consciousness—Attention Schema Theory (Graziano)

What do these findings tell us about consciousness? One may be inclined to suggest a core role for social perception and cognition in consciousness.

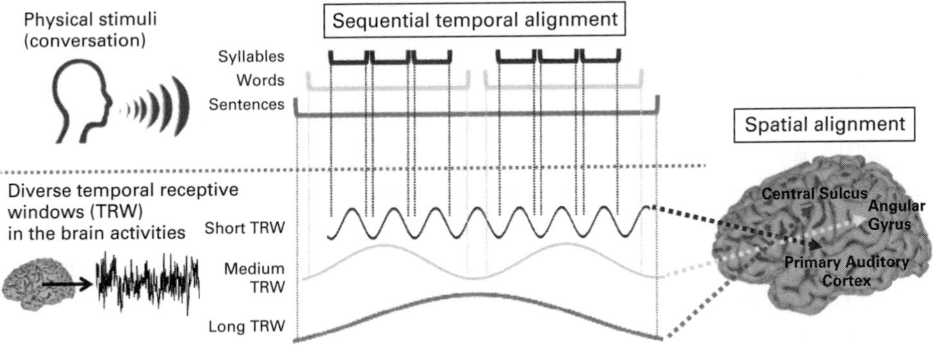

Figure 8.1
Temporal alignment of the brain to body and world.

The link between social cognition and consciousness has indeed been suggested by several authors (Carruthers, 2009; Frith, 1995; Saxe & Kanwisher, 2003; Saxe & Wexler, 2005; Saxe, 2006). I here discuss one of the most outstanding theories in this respect, the *attention schema theory*, as suggested by Graziano (Graziano, 2013; Graziano & Kastner, 2011; Webb & Graziano, 2015), that links social and cognitive functions.

According to the attention schema theory, consciousness is a perceptual model of attention directed toward either the external social world or one's own inner world. More specifically, our brain processes various visual stimuli from the external social environment, all of which compete with each other. If, for instance, stimulus B wins, we will attend to stimulus B rather than stimulus A in the same way that we will attend to the person standing on the left rather than the one on the right. This amounts to pure attention, that is, social attention. Taken in this sense, attention is a feature or attribute of the stimulus itself. However, to be conscious of that very same stimulus, something else needs to be added. The attention schema theory suggests that this additional process consists in the reconstruction of the attention of a specific stimulus in terms of a model, a so-called attention schema.

The attention schema is a simplified model of the attention of stimulus A that leaves out many of the mechanistic details of the attentional process itself. Most importantly, the attention schema includes one's own self (like the body) in reconstructing and modeling the attention of a specific stimulus: the model (i.e., the attention schema) includes stimulus, the attention itself of that stimulus, and one's own self. Such model of the attention toward a specific stimulus provides us with consciousness of the attention to the stimulus—we then associate our attention to the stimulus with consciousness (which is used synonymously with the terms "subjective awareness" and "subjective experience"; see Webb & Graziano, 2015, p. 4).

How about the neural basis of consciousness in the context of the attention schema theory? Graziano suggests that regions like superior temporal sulcus, temporoparietal junction, and superior temporal gyrus as well as specific neurons like the mirror neurons provide the "machinery for social perception and attention" (Webb & Graziano, 2015, p. 4; see also Graziano & Kastner, 2011). By reconstructing the attention of other people to a specific stimulus using one's own brain and its "machinery for social perception and attention," one develops a model of another person's attention. That, in turn, inclines us to attribute consciousness to the other person.

The same holds for one's own inner mental states. We attend to our own inner states, such as thought Z. The very same neural basis, that is, "machinery for social perception and attention," does then reconstruct a model of that attention to thought Z—we consequently attribute consciousness to ourselves. Hence, consciousness of both inner and outer events or objects can be traced to one and the same underlying neural basis, the "machinery for social perception and attention," and processes, that is, the reconstruction of attention in terms of an attention schema.

One may now want to argue that consciousness in this sense is a second-order presentation of attention, which leads ultimately to theories that conceive consciousness in terms of higher-order cognitive functions such as higher-order thoughts (Lau & Rosenthal, 2011) or metacognition (Bayne & Owen, 2016; Carruthers, 2009). That is rejected, however, by Graziano and his assumption of a "machinery for social perception and attention."

True indeed, the attention schema theory is based on a second-order representation of attention. However, unlike in cognitive approaches, that reconstruction is not cognitive, abstract, and semantic but rather sensory, perceptual, and concrete. The attention schema thus suggests a perceptual rather than a cognitive model of consciousness. Therefore, Graziano (Graziano & Kastner, 2011) compares it to Ned Block's concept of phenomenal consciousness (as the property of consciousness itself) as distinguished from access consciousness (Block, 1996, p. 456)—the latter holds only if we access the attention schema cognitively by reporting it.

Spatiotemporal Model Ib: Spatiotemporal Alignment and Expansion versus Attention Schema and Social Extension

How do the attention schema theory and its determination of consciousness as a model of social attention (i.e., attention schema) stand in relation to the characterization of consciousness by spatiotemporal alignment and expansion?

Graziano supposes that attention comes with the stimulus and that we only need to reconstruct that very same attention. However, attention does not come solely and exclusively with the stimulus itself. Instead, as based on the various findings by Lakatos (Lakatos et al., 2008, 2013), it is also the degree to which we phase align our brain's spontaneous activity to the stimulus and thus the degree of entrainment that first and foremost initiates and determines our attention. If we can phase align and thus entrain well, the stimulus will yield high degrees of attention from us; if, in contrast, phase shifting and entrainment are low, attention to the stimulus will be low too. The same can be said about the findings in the musicians discussed above (Lindenberger et al., 2009; Sänger, Müller, & Lindenberger, 2012): consciousness of and subsequently attention to the other musician may be driven here by brain–brain relationship (i.e., brain-to-brain coupling) as manifested in their degree of phase alignment and synchronization.

What does this imply for attention? Attention may be hybrid, resulting from the interaction between the brain's spontaneous activity and the stimuli; that interaction, as phase entrainment and spatiotemporal alignment suggest, takes place on spatiotemporal rather than cognitive grounds. Hence, while Graziano may describe medium-order processes, he seems to neglect the most basic and fundamental lower-order processes ranging between world and brain, that is, spatiotemporal alignment processes, which first and foremost make possible consciousness and subsequently attention.

Moreover, by neglecting those basic and fundamental spatiotemporal processes between world and brain (i.e., world–brain relation), Graziano reverses the relationship between consciousness and attention: he seems to conceive attention as more basic than consciousness (see also Prinz, 2012) while the spatiotemporal model suggests the reverse, namely, that consciousness drives and is hence more basic than attention. I therefore conceive attention in primarily spatiotemporal terms rather than in either sensory, that is, perceptual, or cognitive terms; such spatiotemporal approach to attention needs to be further investigated and more clearly defined in the future.

More generally, Graziano neglects spatiotemporal expansion of the brain's spontaneous activity beyond the brain itself to the world (i.e., spatiotemporal alignment). Because he neglects spatiotemporal alignment as the most basic and fundamental process, he cannot but conceive consciousness in terms of social perception and cognition. For that reason, he must revert to some medium-order perceptual and attentional processes to allow for accessing the other person and her or his consciousness. He consequently must assume expansion to social function rather than spatiotemporal features—one may therefore speak of *social expansion* that is primarily sensory and/or cognitive as distinguished from spatiotemporal expansion that is primarily spatiotemporal.

Note that I do not argue against social expansion per se. I am very happy to acknowledge social expansion and its relevance for consciousness as it is well supported by the musician study described above. Instead, I only argue against the assumption that social expansion is the basis and fundament for consciousness. As evidenced by the findings above, I suggest that social expansion is based on and can be traced to spatiotemporal features, that is, spatiotemporal alignment of the brain to the world. I consider such spatiotemporal alignment of the brain to the world as a necessary condition of possible consciousness (i.e., a prerequisite). Consciousness is consequently by default not only neuronal but, at the same time, ecological, that is, to be more precise, neuro-ecological.

Spatiotemporal Model IIa: Spatiotemporal Alignment versus Content-Based Integration

How can we conceptually describe spatiotemporal alignment in more detail? First and foremost, the data show that there is a direct relationship between world and brain. Their relationship is temporal and spatial: the brain aligns its spontaneous activity to the temporal and spatial features of its respective environmental context. Analogous to the case of the relation between body and brain, I therefore speak of spatiotemporal alignment of the brain to the world.

As in the case of body and brain, spatiotemporal alignment must be distinguished from other forms of their possible relationship. World and brain are also related in terms of sensorimotor, affective, cognitive, and social contents: the brain, as based on its respective functions, can integrate and generate sensorimotor, affective, cognitive, and social contents by means of which it can impact and modulate the world (see below for details). The relationship between world and brain is then determined by specific contents, that is, sensorimotor, affective, cognitive, or social. As these contents are based on integration, one can speak of *content-based integration* (see also chapter 7).

Spatiotemporal alignment must be distinguished from such content-based integration. Instead of integrating different contents (i.e., sensorimotor, affective, cognitive, and/or social), spatiotemporal alignment is based on the brain's alignment to the world's temporal and spatial features. This is clearly illustrated in our empirical examples: the brain aligns the temporal and spatial features of its own spontaneous activity to the temporal and spatial features of the world.

How are spatiotemporal alignment and content-based integration related to each other? I suppose that the former provides the background, if not the necessary condition, of the latter—content-based integration may be based on spatiotemporal alignment. The study by Lindenberger et al. (2009) provides some empirical evidence for that though indirectly: perception of the contents was dependent upon and thus modulated by the structure of the background tones (i.e., rhythmic or nonrhythmic), which induced different degrees of spatiotemporal alignment.

Yet another difference between spatiotemporal alignment and content-based integration is the location of their operation. Spatiotemporal alignment operates across the boundaries of world and brain—it crosses them in temporal and spatial terms. In contrast, content-based integration is restricted to and thus located within the confines of the brain. Note, however, that spatiotemporal alignment does not take place outside the brain. Instead, spatiotemporal alignment constitutes a continuum between world and brain, a continuum between ecological and neuronal spatiotemporal features. One can therefore speak of a *neuro-ecological continuum*.

Spatiotemporal Model IIb: Neuro-ecological Continuum between World and Brain

What do I mean by the concept of neuro-ecological continuum? The concept of neuro-ecological continuum is first and foremost an empirical term—it describes the empirical relationship between the brain's neuronal activity and the world's ecological activity. Moreover, that very same continuum is based on spatiotemporal features rather than specific contents, that is, sensorimotor, cognitive, affective, social—the neuro-ecological continuum is first and foremost a *spatiotemporal continuum* between world and brain.

The empirical and spatiotemporal nature of the neuro-ecological continuum implies that it comes in degrees: it is not a matter of all-or-nothing but can rather exhibit different degrees in the spatiotemporal continuum. Thereby the relation between world and brain, including their respective spatiotemporal features, is dynamic and bidirectional. The neuro-ecological continuum can either shift more strongly toward the brain's neural activity at the expense of the world's ecological activity—this amounts to what Schroeder and Lakatos describe as a "continuous mode of brain activity." Or, alternatively, the neuro-ecological continuum can shift more toward the opposite pole, the world, which occurs at the expense of the brain's neuronal activity—this amounts to what Schroeder and Lakatos describe as a "rhythmic mode of brain activity."

Taken in this sense, the neuro-ecological continuum allows for a vast range of various spatiotemporally based constellations between neuronal and ecological activities in brain and world. The healthy brain and its neural activity are usually balanced, more or less, in their relation to the world—they can thus be located around the middle of the neuro-ecological continuum. This is different in psychiatric disorders where the brain's neuro-ecological balance is shifted toward the extreme neuronal and ecological poles of brain and world (see figures 8.2a and 8.2b).

For instance, behavioral autism can be characterized by almost complete detachment from the world as reflected in the subjects' social isolation and disinterest in others. Such behavior can be traced to their brains' neural activity that is primarily neuronally rather than neuro-ecologically determined—this shifts neuronal activity toward the neuronal pole of the brain and away from the ecological (and social) pole of the world on the neuro-ecological continuum (Damiano et al., submitted).

Analogous though somewhat different detachment from the world can be observed in schizophrenia. These patients often show social isolation and thus autistic behavior. Neuronally, their brain is no longer able to align the phase onsets of their spontaneous activity to the onsets of external stimuli (Lakatos et al., 2013), which can interfere with their ability to couple and align to the spatiotemporal structure of the world (Northoff & Duncan, 2016). The opposite seems to be the case in mania, where patients show extremely strong behavior directed toward the external world (they are quasi "glued" to various stimuli in the external world). Their brains' neuronal activity is shifted toward the ecological pole of the neuro-ecological continuum (Martino et al., 2016; Northoff et al., 2017).

The neuro-ecological continuum may thus describe the balance between world and brain in both neural activity and associated behavior. As that balance can be characterized by temporal–spatial features, that is, spatiotemporal alignment of the brain to the world, one may characterize the

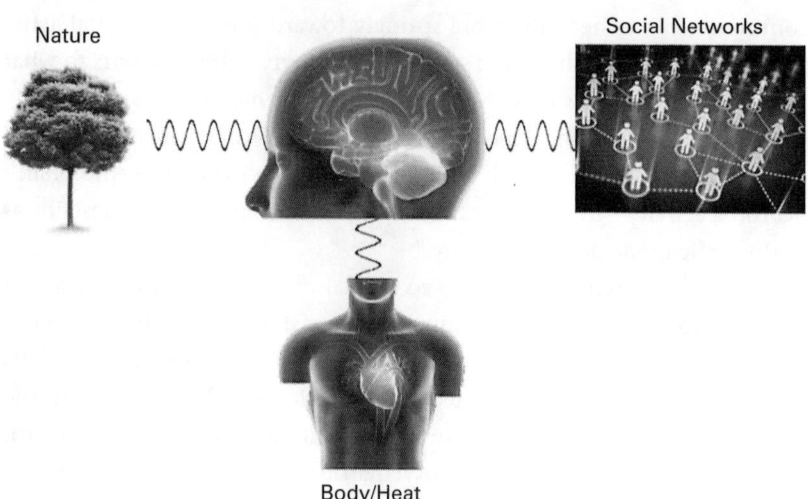

Figure 8.2a
Brain between body and world.

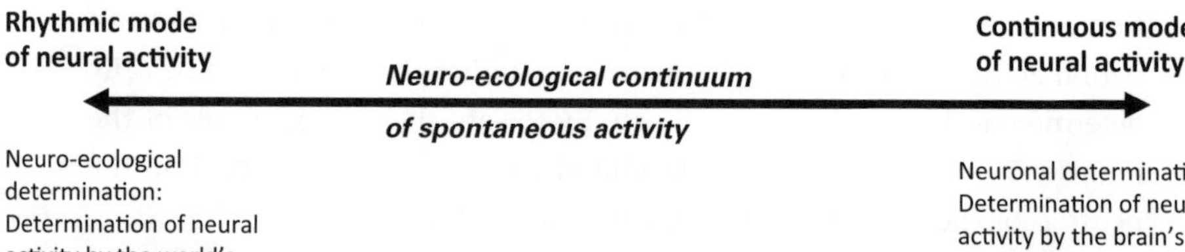

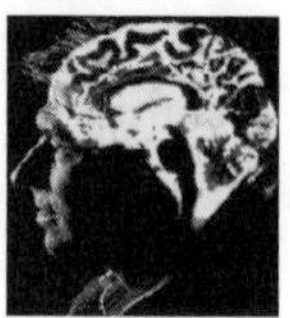

Figure 8.2b
Neuro-ecological continuum and world–brain relation.

balance by spatiotemporal structure and organization. This amounts to what I described as the "form" of consciousness, the spatiotemporal organization and structure of consciousness (Northoff, 2013, 2014b). The concept "form" of consciousness refers thus to a third dimension that complements the contents and level/state as other dimensions of consciousness (chapter 7).

Spatiotemporal Model IIc: Relation between World and Brain—World–Brain Relation

The neuro-ecological continuum is characterized by the balance between neuronal and ecological features in the brain's neural activity. Therefore, the brain's neural activity can be described as hybrid in that it is neither purely neuronal nor purely ecological. On a more general level, the hybrid neuro-ecological nature of the brain's neural activity means that it relates world and brain—this amounts to what I call the *world–brain relation.*

What do I mean by world–brain relation? First, the concept of world–brain relation is here understood in an empirical sense. It denotes the relation between world and brain that is constituted by the brain's spatiotemporal alignment in its interaction with the world. This is empirically exemplified by the example of the perceptual–social synchronization between the musicians (Lindenberger et al., 2009; Sänger et al., 2012) that, neuronally, can be traced to specific neuronal mechanisms such as phase coherence and so forth (see above).

Note that, in addition to this empirical sense, the concept of world–brain relation can also be understood in an ontological sense. Rather than concerning specific empirical mechanisms such as spatiotemporal alignment, the concept of world–brain relation does then refer to existence and reality. As will become clear in chapter 9, I will characterize the brain's existence and reality by world–brain relation.

Second, the concept of world–brain relation, as understood in an empirical sense in this chapter in the following, describes bilateral or mutual interaction between world and brain. The brain must show the capacity or predisposition to exert and recruit certain neuronal mechanisms such as spatiotemporal alignment that allow it to align its neural activity to the stochastic structure of the world. More generally, the brain must be predisposed for developing a possible rhythmic mode of neural activity as distinguished from a continuous mode (see above).

At the same time, the world itself must show a certain spatiotemporal structure (see chapter 3 for more detail on that point) to which the brain and its neural activity can possibly align. If, for instance, the musicians do not play any kind of rhythmic structure, spatiotemporal alignment of the single musician's brain to the other musicians' brains would remain impossible. Accordingly, in addition to the brain's predisposition for the rhythmic mode, the world itself must predispose possible spatiotemporal alignment by the brain. Therefore, I characterize the concept of world–brain relation by bilateral interaction between both brain and world.

Third, the characterization of world–brain relation by bilateral interaction shifts the conceptual focus from world and brain themselves to the concept of relation. The concept of world–brain relation denotes specifically the relation between world and brain rather than world and brain themselves independent of their relation. When I speak of world–brain relation in both empirical (here in this chapter) and ontological (chapters 9–11) contexts, my focus is on this relation rather than world and brain themselves. Specifically, the relation between world and brain adds something that cannot be reduced to either world or brain: their relation makes it possible to integrate, that is, nest and contain, world and brain in a commonly shared spatiotemporal framework, that is, relational time and space (chapter 9).

Spatiotemporal Model IIIa: World–Brain Relation—Spatiotemporal Nestedness of Brain within World

How can we describe the relation between world and brain (i.e., world–brain relation) in more detail? The world–brain relation is primarily spatiotemporal. The different spatiotemporal scales or ranges of world and brain are linked and integrated in their relation. Specifically, the smaller spatiotemporal scale or range of the brain is aligned and thus related to the much larger one of the world: the former (i.e., the brain) is thereby nested within the latter (i.e., the world). We can therefore describe the world–brain relation as *spatiotemporal nestedness*. In the same way that, in a set of Russian nesting dolls, the smaller doll is nested within the next larger one, the brain is nested within the world.

How are different (i.e., larger and smaller) spatiotemporal scales related to each other? We saw in the case of the brain's spontaneous activity that, purely empirically, the phase of slower frequencies is coupled to and thus contains or nests the amplitude of faster frequencies—this is described as cross-frequency coupling (chapter 7). Taking the different frequencies together results in an elaborate temporal structure where slower frequencies contain or nest the next faster one and so on—one can thus speak of a *slow–fast nestedness* or, better, spatiotemporal nestedness, which indicates a certain directedness, that is, from slow to fast, in the brain's spontaneous activity.

I now assume an analogous slow–fast nestedness with spatiotemporal nestedness in the relation between world and brain. The world includes much slower frequencies, such as seismic earth waves, than does the brain. Therefore, those slower frequencies nest and contain the brain's faster frequencies—taken in purely spatiotemporal terms, the brain is thus nested and contained within the world. For that reason, I speak of world–brain relation rather than brain–world relation (see below for details).

Note that we already encountered the concept of spatiotemporal nestedness in the previous chapter: it described how the smaller spatiotemporal scale or range of single stimuli or tasks is integrated, that is, nested, within the relatively larger spatiotemporal scale or range of the brain's spontaneous activity. Taken in this sense, spatiotemporal nestedness must be understood in a purely neuronal sense as confined to the boundaries of the brain.

I here extend the use of the same concept beyond the boundaries of the brain to the brain's relationship with the world. Spatiotemporal nestedness is now no longer purely neuronal but neuro-ecological, referring to the neuro-ecological continuum between world and brain. That very same neuro-ecological continuum consists in the degree to which different spatiotemporal scales or ranges are linked and integrated and thus nested within each other: the better the brain's smaller spatiotemporal scale is integrated and thus nested within the much larger one of the world, the more continuous the neuro-ecological continuum.

Spatiotemporal Model IIIb: World–Brain Relation—Triple Spatiotemporal Expansion of the Brain's Neural Activity

Taken in such neuro-ecological sense, spatiotemporal nestedness operates across the boundaries of brain and world including their respective spatiotemporal scales. The brain and its neural activity thus expand beyond their own boundaries to the world when aligning to and including the world's much larger spatiotemporal scale or range. I therefore speak of the *spatiotemporal expansion* of the brain to the world. Such spatiotemporal expansion can be understood in a threefold way.

First, spatiotemporal expansion described how the brain's spontaneous activity expands the single stimulus or task beyond their own spatiotemporal scales, that is, the duration and extension of stimulus or task (chapters 2, 5, and 7). This can be described empirically as a rest–stimulus interaction and can, conceptually, be phrased as *rest–stimulus relation* (chapters 2 and 7).

Second, I described how the body and its spatiotemporal scale expand the brain's spontaneous activity beyond itself to the body. That was made possible by what I described empirically as spatiotemporal alignment of brain to body, which conceptually was phrased as *body–brain relation*. Third, we now encounter the expansion of the brain's spontaneous activity by its spatiotemporal alignment to the world. This is empirically accounted for by the brain's spatiotemporal alignment to the world, which conceptually is phrased as *world–brain relation*.

Taken altogether, one can speak of *triple spatiotemporal expansion*: the brain's stimulus-induced activity is expanded by the brain's spontaneous activity (first expansion), which, in turn, is itself expanded by its spatiotemporal alignment to body (second expansion) and world (third expansion). Such triple spatiotemporal expansion allows for spatiotemporal nestedness between brain, body, and world: the brain's stimulus-induced activity is spatiotemporally nested within the brain's spontaneous activity, which itself is spatiotemporally nested within body and world (i.e., world–brain relation).

Spatiotemporal Model IIIc: World–Brain Relation—Triple Spatiotemporal Expansion and Consciousness

Why is the triple spatiotemporal expansion of the brain relevant for consciousness? The data presented in this (and the previous) chapter show that the degree to which the brain's spontaneous activity is nested within body and world strongly impacts consciousness. The better and the higher the degree to which the brain's spontaneous activity is spatiotemporally aligned to the spatiotemporal structure of body and world, the more likely the respective stimulus or content can be associated with consciousness.

I consider spatiotemporal alignment of the brain to the world and subsequently the triple spatiotemporal expansion a necessary condition of consciousness, that is, a neural prerequisite of consciousness. Without the spatiotemporal alignment of our brain's spontaneous activity to body and world, we can no longer associate consciousness to the stimuli and their contents. This is supported by the above presented data. Moreover, it is in line with the data on the loss of consciousness where such spatiotemporal alignment is disrupted (chapter 4). Once the brain and its spontaneous activity are no longer expanded beyond themselves to body and world and thus spatiotemporally nested within the latter, consciousness becomes impossible—this is the case in disorders of consciousness (chapter 4).

Taken on a more conceptual level, this implies that world–brain relation (and body–brain relation) is a necessary condition of possible consciousness (i.e., a predisposition). Loss of world–brain relation entails the loss of consciousness. Note that I explicitly focus on the relation between world and brain. Both world and brain may still be present even during the absence of consciousness. Instead, it is the presence of specifically their relation, the world–brain relation, that is central for the possible presence of consciousness.

Accordingly, the absence of the relation between world and brain leads to the absence of consciousness even if both world and brain remain present. Therefore, it is the *relation* itself, that is, the relation between world and brain, rather than world and brain themselves, that is, independent of their relation, that makes possible consciousness—the world–brain relation. This is what I mean when I say that the world–brain relation is a necessary condition of possible consciousness—the world–brain relation is thus what I describe as a "predisposition of consciousness."

Note that, as already indicated above, the concept of relation can be understood in both empirical and ontological senses. Throughout this chapter I understand the concept of relation in an empirical sense as characterized by specific empirical mechanisms such as spatiotemporal alignment of the brain to the world, while later (in chapters 9–11), I will shift from the empirical to the ontological realm. Ontologically, the concept of relation in world–brain relation denotes existence and reality, that is, a basic unit of existence and reality as suggested in structural realism. More specifically, I will suggest that the world–brain relation accounts for the existence and reality of the brain (chapter 9), which, in turn, renders possible (i.e., predisposes) the existence and reality of consciousness (chapter 10).

Spatiotemporal Model IIId: World–Brain Relation—Brain–World Relation? Given the bilateral nature of their interaction, one may now wonder why I speak of world–brain relation rather than brain–world relation. After all, it is the brain that aligns to the world—this would make the case for the reverse concept, namely, brain–world relation. That is to neglect the difference in spatiotemporal scale or range between world and brain though. The brain shows a much smaller spatiotemporal range than the world, which is much larger and thus includes a wider range (such as ultrasonic frequencies and the aforementioned extremely slow frequencies of seismic earth waves). The concept of world–brain relation thus spans across and integrates different spatiotemporal scales. However, that by itself is not yet a reason to prefer the concept of world–brain relation over that of brain–world relation.

I characterized world–brain relation by spatiotemporal nestedness and expansion. Both imply directionality (i.e., spatiotemporal directionality). Faster frequencies are nested within slower ones, which allows expanding the former by the latter. Hence, slower frequencies must be predisposed to allow for nesting and expanding of faster frequencies: without slower frequencies, spatiotemporal nestedness and expansion remain impossible. An analogous spatiotemporal directionality can now be observed in the relation between world and brain: the world shows slower frequencies and thereby makes possible the faster frequencies of the brain—the brain is thus nested and contained within the world (i.e., world–brain relation).

To characterize the spatiotemporal relation between world and brain by the concept of brain–world relation would be to simply reverse spatiotemporal directionality: the faster frequencies of the brain would then contain or nest the slower frequencies of the world. True, the concept of brain–world relation is certainly conceivable on purely conceptual–logical grounds. However, brain–world relation with reverse spatiotemporal directedness (i.e., nesting of slower within faster frequencies) is not supported on empirical grounds, that is, it remains empirically implausible. Therefore, conceived in purely spatiotemporal terms, I deem the concept of world–brain relation to be more empirically plausible than brain–world relation.

In addition to their empirical plausibility, the concepts of world–brain relation and brain–world relation can also be characterized by different roles for consciousness and cognition. I claim that world–brain relation is a necessary empirical (this chapter) and ontological (chapter 10) condition of possible consciousness—world–brain relation is both a neural and ontological predisposition of consciousness. Accordingly, put in a nutshell, I deem world–brain relation including its spatiotemporal characterization as essential for consciousness in both an empirical and an ontological regard.

In contrast, I do not suppose analogous relevance of brain–world relation for consciousness. Rather than predisposing consciousness, brain–world relation is central for sensory, motor, cognitive, affective, and social function with subsequent brain-based perception and cognition of the world. Without elaborating the details here, I therefore deem brain–world relation to predispose cognition rather than consciousness. To now replace world–brain relation by brain–world relation is to confuse consciousness and cognition.

As already discussed previously (chapters 3 and 6), consciousness cannot be traced or reduced to specific contents and our cognition of those very same contents. This is further supported by the fact that consciousness itself cannot be reduced to or fully explained by cognitive functions such as attention, working memory, or higher-order cognitive functions (Lau & Rosenthal, 2011; Prinz, 2012; Tsuchiya et al., 2012). While these various cognitive functions may well account for the cognitive component of consciousness, that is, reporting with access to the contents of consciousness (chapter 7), they do not account for the phenomenal features of consciousness as targeted here (chapter 7). Taken in the present context, I suppose that brain–world relation can well account for the cognitive features of consciousness while world–brain relation is necessary for the phenomenal features of consciousness.

Spatiotemporal Model IVa: Four E's—Embodiment and Body–Brain Relation

There is much conceptual (i.e., philosophical) discussion about the role of body and world in consciousness—this can be characterized by the four E's, embodiment, enactment, extendedness, and embeddedness. Without going into thorough detail, I will discuss the four E's briefly in the present spatiotemporal context.

Let us start with embodiment. The advocate of the body and embodiment may now wonder about the role of the body. After all, the brain is part of the body and the body "locates" us in the world. One would consequently assume a more central role for the body than the world in consciousness. This conforms well to what is described as embodiment (Gallagher, 2005; Rowland, 2010) and enactment (Noe, 2004; Rowland, 2010) in the current philosophical discussion.

How does the spatiotemporal model account for the seemingly special role of the body? We saw above that there is no principal difference between body and world when it comes to spatiotemporal alignment, nestedness, and expansion. In both cases, one and the same mechanism, that is, spatiotemporal alignment, allows spatiotemporal expansion of the brain beyond itself to body and world with the result that the brain is nested within both. This suggests no special role of the body when compared to the world.

However, there is a difference in degree. The body is continuously present and therefore presents a much more stable and continuous presence for the brain's spatiotemporal alignment. The world, in contrast, is much more unstable and not as continuously present—the degree of the brain's spatiotemporal alignment to the body may therefore be much stronger than its alignment to the world. Moreover, the world includes a much larger spatiotemporal range than the body, which differs much more from the spatiotemporal range of the brain—the larger spatiotemporal discrepancy may make it more difficult for the brain to align itself to the world than to the body. Therefore, it is only in exceptional cases (as, for instance, in extreme forms of meditation when one detaches one's own cognition and ultimately one's own body from their alignment to the brain's neural activity; see Tang et al., 2015; Tang & Northoff, 2017) that the brain's spatiotemporal alignment to the world may override its spatiotemporal alignment to the body.

Accordingly, the spatiotemporal model acknowledges the difference between body and world. However, that difference between body and world is merely quantitative and thus empirical. There is a difference in the degree of spatiotemporal alignment of the brain to body and world. The spatiotemporal model thus considers the body to be only quantitatively and thus empirically different from the world. In contrast, there is no qualitative and ultimately ontological difference between world and body in general and with regard to consciousness in particular (see chapters 10 and 11 for more details on the ontological issue).

This carries major implications for the relation between the concepts of body–brain relation and world–brain relation. I subsume the concept of body–brain relation under the umbrella of the more basic and fundamental concept of world–brain relation: the body is part of the world for the brain and its spatiotemporal alignment with subsequent spatiotemporal nestedness and expansion. Hence, the concept of world–brain relation, as understood here, includes that of body–brain relation. The concept of embodiment as specified by body–brain relation can consequently be subsumed under the umbrella of the concept of world–brain relation.

Spatiotemporal Model IVb: Four E's—Embeddedness and Spatiotemporal Scaffolding

One may now wonder how the concept of spatiotemporal expansion stands in relation to those of extendedness, embeddedness, and enactment as used in current philosophical discussion (Clark, 1997, 2008; Clark & Chalmers, 2010; Gallagher, 2005; Lakoff & Johnson, 1999; Noe, 2004; Rowland, 2010; Shapiro, 2014; Thompson, 2007; Varela et al., 1991). Specifically, one may want to argue that what I mean by "spatiotemporal expansion" is much better expressed and covered by the concepts of embeddedness, extendedness, and enactment; for that reason, I had better use the latter rather than my own concept. I will show that both are quite compatible and that the concepts of embeddedness, extendedness, and enactment need to be specified in spatiotemporal terms.

How about the concept of embeddedness? The concept of embeddedness points out that consciousness and cognition are dependent upon the respective situational constellation. Certain events or objects in the environment can be used as resources for consciousness to minimize the load for the brain—the world thus provides an "external scaffolding" for consciousness (Shapiro, 2014). Presupposing external scaffolding, embeddedness implies that consciousness can be understood in a relational sense—it allows for relation between internal states and external events or objects.

The spatiotemporal model supposes that such scaffolding is possible on spatiotemporal grounds. The world and its various objects or events provide a certain spatiotemporal structure as in the case of music. Our empirical example (Lindenberger et al., 2009; Sänger et al., 2012) demonstrated that the brain's spontaneous activity can align itself to the rhythmic structure of music in spatiotemporal terms. That, in turn, makes it possible to relate and thus scaffold the brain's internal state to the external events or objects in the world (i.e., the music piece).

I consequently specify the concept of scaffolding as *spatiotemporal scaffolding*. The concept of spatiotemporal scaffolding means that the spatiotemporal features of the world are those features to which the brain can align, which, in turn, makes it possible to use the world and its various objects and events for external scaffolding. Spatiotemporal scaffolding is possible only when there is some relation between world and brain (i.e., world–brain relation). Without spatiotemporal alignment of the brain to the world, the world and its various objects or events, any kind of external scaffolding remains impossible. Therefore, I consider world–brain relation as based on spatiotemporal alignment as a necessary condition of external scaffolding in terms of spatiotemporal scaffolding and ultimately of embeddedness.

Spatiotemporal Model IVc: Four E's—Extendedness/Enactment and Spatiotemporal Expansion

The concept of spatiotemporal expansion is also quite compatible with the concepts of *extendedness* and *extended mind* (Clark, 2008; Clark & Chalmers, 2010). For example, consciousness can well extend to external contents beyond one's own internal contents. For instance, the piano and its keys may become part of the body in the consciousness of the professional pianist. The same occurs when we listen to music with its rhythms' becoming part of our consciousness. Consciousness is thus distributed and social rather than being nondistributed or focalized and merely neuronal.

How is such extendedness possible? Our empirical example of the guitarists showed such extendedness: the single musician and her or his playing was extended beyond that musician and her or his brain to the other musician and her or his brain (Lindenberger et al., 2009; Sänger et al., 2012). This was made possible by spatiotemporal alignment of the one brain's spontaneous activity to the other person's brain. Due to spatiotemporal alignment and expansion of the brain's spontaneous activity to the world including other persons and their brains, consciousness becomes distributed and social just as described in the concept of extendedness.

Taken in this sense, consciousness is extended and thus distributed and social by default: spatiotemporal alignment and expansion with world–brain relation are a necessary condition of possible consciousness without which the latter becomes impossible. Extendedness of consciousness is thus not an accidental secondary feature of consciousness but a necessary and most basic feature as it is based on world–brain relation. Hence, the spatiotemporal model of consciousness is not only quite compatible with extendedness but makes the latter even stronger by showing its necessity for possible consciousness on both empirical and conceptual grounds. Spatiotemporal expansion of the brain to the world and thus extendedness must be considered necessary conditions of possible consciousness (i.e., they are a predisposition of consciousness).

The central importance of the world is also pointed out in the concept of enactment (Noe, 2004; Thompson, 2007; Varela et al., 1991). Beyond the body, the world itself is here taken into account in constituting consciousness. Specifically, it is the way in which we relate to and thereby enact the world in our actions and perception that first and foremost makes possible sense and ultimately consciousness. By enacting the world, we transform the world into our environment, the "life world," as some say (Merleau-Ponty, 1963, p. 235).

How does the concept of enactment stand in relation to the spatiotemporal model of consciousness? The proponent of enactment is right. We and our brains are enacting the world. However, such enacting should not be understood in a literal sense, that is, in terms of action and perception. Instead, enacting may better be understood in a spatiotemporal sense: our brain aligns itself to the spatiotemporal structure in the world by means of which it constitutes a neuro-ecological continuum that, in turn, makes possible consciousness that allows us to subsequently perceive and act in that very same world.

It may therefore be better to speak of *spatiotemporalizing* rather than enacting: by aligning itself to the world in a spatiotemporal way, the brain links and integrates the spatiotemporal features of the world to itself and our body, which, in turn, makes it possible to enact the world. Hence, the brain spatiotemporalizes the world (Northoff, 2014a) for us by linking and integrating the world's spatiotemporal features to our brain's neuronal activity and its own spatiotemporal features. Therefore, I consider spatiotemporal alignment a necessary condition of possible enactment.

Spatiotemporal Model IVd: Four E's—Concept of World and Argument of Inclusion

One may now be interested to know what exactly I mean by the concept of world. Besides other meanings, one can understand the term "world" in an empirical, phenomenological, and ontological sense. The empirical concept of world consists in the world as we observe it—that world is presupposed in empirical investigation as in neuroscience. The world understood in a phenomenological sense is the world as we experience it in consciousness—this is the world referred to in phenomenology. Finally, the concept of world can also be understood in an ontological sense in terms of its existence and reality as it remains independent of us including our brains.

The concept of world, as understood in this section, demarcates the border between empirical and ontological realms. It goes beyond the purely observational and thus empirical sense in that it conceives the world by itself independent of our observation. That wider meaning is, for instance, reflected in my use of the term *ecological* that includes both social and nonsocial features. Such concept of world reaches out toward the ontological meaning of world, that is, its existence and reality by itself independent of us. That will be fully discussed in chapters 10 and 11.

In contrast, the concept of world, as understood here, does not amount to the phenomenological meaning of world, that is, the way we experience the world in our consciousness. That would be to confuse the necessary condition of possible consciousness with the phenomenal features of consciousness itself: the world–brain relation is a necessary condition of possible consciousness, which precludes its characterization by consciousness itself. Therefore, the concept of world as in world–brain relation is not meant in a phenomenological sense as, for instance, used in phenomenology. I refer the reader to chapter 11 as well as chapters 12–14 for a more detailed account of the concept of world.

We are now ready to address the second part of the argument of inclusion, that is, the need to include the world in our model of consciousness. The argument of inclusion, we recall, points out the need to include both body and world in our model of consciousness. The spatiotemporal model can well include the world, giving it a central role in consciousness—that role of the world for consciousness is much stronger than in most other accounts, including both neuroscientific and philosophical ones. Rather than just including the world as an additional modulatory factor (i.e., as context or external scaffold), the spatiotemporal model supposes that the world in terms of its relation to the brain, the world–brain relation, is a necessary condition of possible consciousness.

How can we support the assumption that the world in terms of world–brain relation is a necessary condition of possible consciousness (i.e., a predisposition)? The data presented here show that that holds in an empirical way: spatiotemporal alignment of the brain's neural activity to the world and thus its neuro-ecological continuum is an NPC (Northoff, 2013, 2014b; Northoff & Heiss, 2015). The same holds, analogously, on the ontological level where the world–brain relation can be regarded an ontological predisposition (of the possible existence and reality) of consciousness (chapter 10).

Finally, the spatiotemporal model can account not only for the inclusion of body and world but also for their close and intimate relationship in consciousness. By assuming a similar mechanism (i.e., spatiotemporal alignment) in body–brain relation and world–brain relation, brain, body, and world are integrated and intimately linked with each other. That very same intimate linkage is well reflected in spatiotemporal nestedness that includes and operates across all three, brain, body, and world.

Conclusion

Is consciousness limited to the confines and boundaries of the brain? Neuroscientists point out the central role of the brain while philosophers emphasize the role of body and world in consciousness (when assuming extendedness, embodiment, enactment, and embeddedness). The present chapter aimed to reconcile these seemingly contradictory positions in the spatiotemporal model of consciousness. I reviewed various empirical findings that show how the brain and its spontaneous activity align themselves to the spatiotemporal features of body and world. I therefore speak of spatiotemporal alignment of the brain to the world (subsuming the body under the concept of world) that makes possible a neuro-ecological continuum that is based on and corresponds to world–brain relation.

The concept of world–brain relation (with body–brain relation being a subset) describes a spatiotemporal relation with a neuro-ecological continuum between world and brain. The smaller spatiotemporal scale of the brain is nested within the larger one of the body, which, in turn, is by itself nested and contained within the even larger spatiotemporal scale of the world. World–brain relation thus amounts to what I describe as spatiotemporal nestedness.

The empirical findings suggest that world–brain relation and its spatiotemporal nestedness are necessary conditions of, possible consciousness—they are predispositions of consciousness. I therefore conclude that the spatiotemporal model of consciousness can well address the argument of inclusion in that it allows for integrating the brain, body, and world into a coherent framework, that is, a spatiotemporal framework. Such spatiotemporally based integration of brain, body, and world allows also for transitioning from the empirical to the ontological level—that shall be the focus in the third part of this book (chapters 9–11).

III World–Brain Problem

9 Ontology I: From Brain to World–Brain Relation

Introduction

Background and Argument

I discussed different models that conceive the brain mainly in an empirical context (chapters 1–3). That was complemented by developing a spatiotemporal model of consciousness (chapters 4–8). The spatiotemporal model of consciousness emphasized the central role of the world–brain relation. How the world–brain relation characterizes the existence and reality of brain and consciousness remains unclear though.

The brain is usually considered the subject of empirical observation in neuroscience. In contrast, the brain as such is not considered the subject of philosophy. For example, there is no well-established "philosophy of brain" (Northoff, 2004) as distinguished from, for instance, "philosophy of mind" (Searle, 2004). Unlike the mind, the brain has not yet been intensely scrutinized in epistemology and ontology. Instead of following the traditional path and starting with the mind, I here aim to do the opposite—namely, to develop an *ontology of brain*. Such an ontology of brain can, in a second step, serve as stepping-stone for an *ontology of consciousness* (chapter 10).

The main aim in this chapter is to develop an ontology of brain that is empirically plausible, that is, in accordance with the empirical data as discussed in Parts I and II of the book. I will argue for an ontological definition of the brain's existence and reality by relation and structure as developed in structural realism (SR). It shall be noted that I use the concept of ontology in a certain sense as will be outlined briefly in the next section within this introduction.

I will develop the structural-realist characterization of the brain in the first part of this chapter. Hence I will discuss two arguments against such structural-realist view of the brain, the argument of individuation and the argument of time and space, and I will reject both. That allows me to maintain and support my claim of a structural-realist ontological characterization of the brain through world–brain relation. Such structural-realist characterization of the brain must be distinguished from its traditional ontological determination by elements such as physical or mental properties.

Definition of Ontology

What do I mean by ontology? Ontology is the study of being, and it deals with the categories of existence and reality. Ontology in this sense is often subsumed under or taken to be more or less equivalent with metaphysics, the question of Being (Tahko, 2015; van Inwagen, 2014). However, I do not take such a stance here. I carefully distinguish ontology from metaphysics—existence and reality, as understood here, are not mere instances of the more general "Being as such" as dealt with in metaphysics.

One distinguishing feature for now is that I use empirical data to support my ontological assumptions, something that is usually rejected in metaphysics as in analytic metaphysics (MacLaurin & Dyke, 2012) and metametaphysics (Tahko, 2015). Accordingly, unlike metaphysics, ontology is here not understood as operating on purely a priori, analytic, and conceptual grounds. Instead, my use of ontology includes a posteriori, synthetic, and empirical elements as being linked and coupled with the traditional a priori, analytic, and conceptual strategy. Importantly, that does not amount to a reductive methodological strategy though (as, e.g., in Anglo-American neurophilosophy; Churchland, 1986, 2002)—I focus on the linkages and transitions between, for instance, empirical and ontological domains (Northoff, 2014).

The clear distinction of ontology from metaphysics entails that I remain within the realm of the phenomenal as distinguished from the noumenal (as understood in a Kantian sense; Kant, 1781/1998; see chapter 13 for more details). Metaphysics targets the noumenal realm while ontology, as understood here, remains within the phenomenal domain. The distinction between metaphysics and ontology thus finds its analogue in the one between noumenal and phenomenal realms. All I am interested in is the phenomenal realm, that is, the world we live in and how the brain as part of that world is related to that very same world (i.e., the world–brain relation) and can thereby yield mental features such as consciousness.

What exactly do I mean by the concept of *world*? I determine the concept of world in a phenomenal sense through space and time. The world we live in is essentially spatiotemporal. That leaves open the exact nature of time and space as they determine our world. Therefore, in this chapter, I will put considerable effort into developing and outlining a proper concept of time and space—this is important in order to determine not only the concept of world itself but also the existence and reality of brain as a fundamental part of that very same world and its time and space. In contrast to the phenomenal world and its spatiotemporal features, I am happy to leave open the search for the noumenal realm (in a Kantian sense), that is, what is behind our world and its world–brain relation—this is the territory of metaphysics in general and the metaphysics of mind and mind–body relation in particular (see chapter 13 for more details).

My concept of ontology must also be distinguished from what is described as cognitive ontology (Poldrack & Yarkoni, 2016; Smith, 1995). In a nutshell, cognitive ontology takes features of human cognition (rather than language) as a starting point to characterize existence and reality. In contrast to such cognitive ontology, I here do not consider cognition as an ontological starting point—I therefore speak of *spatiotemporal ontology*.

Such spatiotemporal ontology integrates the brain within the world in spatiotemporal terms, that is, in terms of world–brain relation. Ontology of brain is consequently closely coupled to spatiotemporal ontology with both taking an intermediate position between metaphysics and cognitive ontology.

Finally, I shall briefly mention the notion of brain per se. The ontology of brain suggested here concerns the brain as a whole. The focus on the brain as a whole must be distinguished from the development of a taxonomy of specific mental and cognitive functions in cognitive ontology that focuses on specific parts and functions of the brain (Poldrack & Yarkoni, 2016). Accordingly, I detach my ontological determination of the brain from its cognitive functions and mental features (i.e., consciousness), as well as from specific parts of the brain. Hence, the ontological focus in this chapter is exclusively on the brain as a whole and its relation to the world, the world–brain relation, prior to and independent of its different parts or regions and their respective cognitive and mental features.

Part I: Ontology of Brain—Structural Realism

Structural Realism Ia: Ontological Priority of Relation over Elements

What is structural realism (SR)? SR highlights the central role of relations and structure. Either relata are included in conjunction with relations (moderate SR; Beni, 2017; Esfeld & Lam, 2008, 2011; Floridi, 2008, 2009, 2011) or relata are eliminated completely in favor of relations (eliminativist SR; French, 2014; French & Ladyman, 2003). SR has been discussed mainly in the context of physics (Esfeld & Lam, 2008, 2011; French, 2014; French & Ladyman, 1998) but has also recently been applied to information (Floridi, 2008, 2009, 2011; see also responses by Beni, 2017; Berto & Tagliabue, 2014; Fresco & Staines, 2014; Sdrolia & Bishop, 2014), cognitive science (Beni, 2016), the brain (Beni, 2016), and secondary qualities (Isaac, 2014). Finally, SR comes in an epistemic and ontological version. The epistemic version of structural realism (ESR) is the more modest one when claiming that all we can know are structure and relations. Importantly, this epistemic claim is not accompanied by ontological assumptions. ESR remains agnostic to the question of whether what we know really corresponds to ontological existence and reality independent of ourselves (i.e., ontic structural realism; OSR).

Structural realism highlights the notions of relation and structure. How can we define the concepts of relation and structure? Let us start with determining the concept of relation. One may want to distinguish two determinations of relation. In the first case, relation is supposedly constituted by the combination of and connection between different elements such as mental or physical properties.

Existence and reality are here ultimately traced to the basic elements rather than the relations themselves—this presupposes what I describe as *element-based ontology* with the supposition of, for instance, specific properties (or substances) such as mental or physical properties. Even if element-based ontology considers the notion of relation, it still claims ontological priority of elements, with relations remaining ontologically secondary at best. This is the most traditional form of ontology.

That is not the notion of relation as presupposed in SR, however. Here relations themselves are constitutive of reality and existence—there is ontological priority of relation over elements with the latter remaining ontologically secondary. SR claims that relations themselves are constitutive of existence and reality and are therefore ontologically most basic. Hence, the traditional element-based ontology is here replaced by what I describe as *relation-based ontology*. Relation-based ontology can be characterized by ontological priority of relation over elements—I will argue that such ontological characterization of relation is central for describing the existence and reality of brain.

Structural Realism Ib: Moderate OSR and Structure

How does OSR conceive the relationship between relation and elements or relata? Different versions of OSR have been distinguished with, for instance, noneliminativist or moderate versions on the one hand and eliminativist ones on the other (Esfeld & Lam, 2008, 2010). The eliminativist version of OSR claims that the relation itself is the sole basis and fundament of existence and reality with no role at all for the relata anymore (see, e.g., French & Ladyman, 1998; Ladyman, 2014).

In contrast, the noneliminativist or moderate version of OSR claims that relata still have a role but cannot be defined as such (and their properties) independent of their relation to each other—the relata thus no longer show any intrinsic properties (Esfeld & Lam, 2008, 2010). I here presuppose the moderate version of OSR, namely, that the relata themselves do not show intrinsic features, for example, elements or properties that, independent of their relations, define their existence and reality. However, at the same time, the relata still have a role besides the relation itself: the difference between relata (as between world and brain) is considered, which, unlike in traditional element-based ontology, is not traced to some intrinsic properties within the relata themselves (i.e., within world and brain) but to the relation holding between them (i.e., world–brain relation).

What about the concept of structure? The concept of structure can be determined as the combination and organization of different relations. There can be relation with distinct degrees of spatiotemporal extension. The concept of structure describes how the different relations, including their distinct spatiotemporal extensions, are related to each other and thus organized. Briefly, structure concerns the organization of relations (see chapter 11 for a more detailed definition of structure).

One empirical example of structure in this sense is the brain's spontaneous activity and its spatiotemporal structure. For instance, one frequency (such as 10 Hz) is based on the relation (i.e., differences) between peaks and troughs across time. That very same frequency and its difference-based relation is now coupled to other frequencies (such as 0.01 Hz; i.e., cross-frequency coupling [CFC]; see chapter 1)—CFC organizes the different frequencies and thus provides structure in the brain's spontaneous activity. Note that structure in the current context does not pertain to what is empirically described as anatomical structure and the different regions. Instead, structure is here understood in a strictly functional sense that determines the different parts (as empirically manifest in the determination of single regions' neural activities by their functional connectivity).

Taken in this sense, the concept of structure needs to be distinguished from that of aggregate. The concept of aggregate refers to the mere addition or collection of different elements or relations without any organization between them. For example, one would then encounter a brain with different frequencies (i.e., difference-based relation) that are no longer coupled with each other (i.e., without CFC). There would still be relation but no structure anymore; that is, for instance, the case during the loss of consciousness as in a vegetative state, sleep, or anesthesia (see chapter 5).

Structural Realism IIa: Moderate SR and Brain—Difference-Based Coding

How can we apply SR to the brain? I will argue that the brain's existence and reality can be defined by relation and, more specifically, the world–brain relation, rather than elements or properties within the brain itself. For that, we need to understand the brain's coding strategy (i.e., difference-based coding) and its ontological implications.

I characterized the brain's coding strategy by difference-based coding (see chapter 2). Briefly, *difference-based coding* refers to the encoding of neural activity in terms of statistically based differences between different stimuli. Taken in this sense, difference-based coding must be distinguished from stimulus-based coding, which refers to the encoding of neural activity in terms of single stimuli remaining independent of other stimuli. Empirical evidence, as discussed in chapter 2 (see also Northoff, 2014a, for more details), speaks in favor of difference-based coding rather than stimulus-based coding. Therefore, I consider difference-based coding as the brain's coding strategy that constitutes and shapes its neural activity, including both stimulus-induced and spontaneous activity.

What does difference-based coding imply in an ontological regard for the brain's existence and reality? I so far considered difference-based coding in a purely empirical sense. The concept of difference-based coding as stochastic coding strategy depends on observation (i.e., indirect observation) as related to our models of brain (see chapter 2). Taken in this sense, the concept of difference-based coding does not seem to carry any ontological implications, that is, concerning the brain's existence and reality. That is not so as I will argue in the following.

The brain's existence and reality can be defined by its neural activity. If there is no neural activity anymore, the brain is considered dead. That is empirically the case if one can observe a zero line in EEG, in which case one speaks of "brain death" (see chapter 5 and Northoff, 2016a,b). Accordingly, even if the brain as mere anatomical gray mass (i.e., as physical substance) is still present, the absence of the brain's neural activity goes along with the absence of the brain. The brain's existence and reality, as functionally meaningful, are thus determined by the presence of its neural activity rather than its presence as gray matter or physical substance.

How does such definition of the brain's existence and reality stand in relation to difference-based coding? The brain's existence and reality are defined by neural activity. That very same neural activity is based on and constituted by difference-based coding. Therefore, the brain's existence and reality are determined by difference-based coding and, more generally, the differences as encoded into the brain's neural activity during difference-based coding. Difference-based coding is thus not only empirically relevant in characterizing the brain's coding strategy (Northoff, 2014a) but also ontologically relevant in that it determines the brain's existence and reality.

Difference-based coding is based on the encoding of statistically based differences in terms of the relation between different stimuli; that is distinguished from the encoding of single stimuli as single elements as in stimulus-based coding. This presupposes ontological priority of relation over elements. Difference-based coding is thus quite compatible with the assumption of relation as a basic ontological feature as suggested in SR.

Accordingly, difference-based coding is relevant for the ontology of brain. This becomes even more clear when considering that difference-based coding allows us to encode the brain's neural activity in relation (i.e., difference) to both body and world. The brain encodes the world's events or objects in their relation to the brain itself (i.e., its spontaneous activity) into its neural activity. Difference-based coding thus allows us to establish a relation between world and brain, the world–brain relation, which, in turn, constitutes the brain's existence and reality (i.e., its neural activity). This is compatible with the assumed ontological priority of relation over elements as claimed in SR.

Structural Realism IIb: Moderate SR and Brain—Threat of Logical Circularity?

One may now want to argue that the presumed ontological relevance of difference-based coding for the brain's existence and reality amounts to logical circularity. Difference-based coding is a feature of the brain, and for that to hold the brain must already exist—difference-based coding presupposes the brain's existence and reality. At the same time, I suppose that difference-based coding establishes the existence and reality of the brain by constituting its relation to the world, the world–brain relation. That is logically circular though: the brain's existence and reality must be already presupposed (as the basis of the brain's difference-based coding) to establish it at the same time (i.e., through difference-based coding in relation to the world).

To avoid such a threat of logical circularity, we need to define the brain by specific elements prior to and independent of its relation to the world as established by then merely empirical difference-based coding—we must thus revert to element-based ontology. Element-based ontology presupposes specific single elements such as physical or mental properties to underlie and determine existence and reality. Presupposing element-based ontology, the brain's existence and reality would then need to be determined by specific elements rather than relation as in SR.

More specifically, the brain's neural activity would need to be traced to single elements such as specific stimuli in body and world. That ultimately presupposes stimulus-based coding on the empirical level. Instead of encoding the differences between different stimuli and ultimately the difference between world, body, and brain into its neural activity, the brain would then encode single stimuli by themselves: it would encode the world independent of its relation to the brain into its neural activity. This amounts to what I described as stimulus-based coding as distinguished from difference-based coding (chapter 2). In a nutshell, element-based ontology of brain implies stimulus- rather than difference-based coding.

That is contrary to empirical evidence though. The brain shows difference-based coding rather than stimulus-based coding (chapter 2 and Northoff, 2014a). We therefore need to reconcile element-based ontology on the ontological level with difference-based coding holding on the empirical level. The relation between world and brain established by difference-based coding would then remain ontologically secondary at best while elements would still attain ontological priority by defining the existence and reality of both world and brain independent of their relation. This avoids logical circularity while at the same time considering empirical evidence.

However, we are then confronted with discrepancy between ontological presupposition (i.e., element-based ontology) and empirical characterization (i.e., difference-based coding). Though avoiding logical circularity and thus being logically plausible, the assumption of element-based ontology is not empirically plausible given that difference-based coding entails relation-based ontology (i.e., SR). I argue that we need to suppose SR rather than element-based ontology in order to allow for empirically plausible ontological assumptions that are in accordance with the empirical data (i.e., difference-based coding). However, this raises the threat of logical circularity.

Structural Realism IIc: Moderate SR and Brain—Relational View of the Brain

How can we avoid the threat of logical circularity? The threat of logical circularity is based on the assumption that difference-based coding cannot hold at the same time and co-occur with the constitution of the brain's existence and reality by relating it to the world (i.e., world–brain relation). I suggest using the notion of *difference* in an ontological rather than empirical sense. By encoding its relation to the world in terms of differences (i.e., difference-based coding), the brain constitutes its existence and reality.

Difference in this ontological sense constitutes existence and reality rather than presupposing it (as is the case when using the notion of difference in a merely empirical sense). Such ontological determination of difference avoids the threat of logical circularity (which therefore is ultimately based on confusing empirical and ontological understandings of the concept of difference). Most important, the ontological notion of difference allows us to determine the brain's existence and reality in a logically noncircular way by world–brain relation as constituted by difference-based coding. This amounts to what I describe as a *relational view* of the brain.

Such a relational view of the brain is quite compatible with moderate OSR. As with moderate OSR, I argue that the brain's existence and reality depend on its relation to the world, the world–brain relation. The relation (i.e., the world–brain relation) is thus constitutive of the existence and reality of the functioning brain—this is made possible by difference-based coding that entails the concept of difference in an ontological (rather than merely empirical) sense.

At the same time, the concept of world–brain relation entails and acknowledges the distinction between world and brain: world and brain show distinct spatiotemporal scales, which, as I propose, is the very basis of their relation. Therefore, the ontological determination of the brain by world–brain relation and its relational view of brain is quite compatible with moderate SR. Moderate SR gives a role to both relation (i.e., world–brain relation) and relata (i.e., world and brain). In contrast, the relational view of the brain is not compatible with eliminativist SR that denies any role by the relata themselves (i.e., world and brain) and would therefore disregard the spatiotemporal distinction between world and brain.

Structural Realism IIIa: Conflation of the Notion of Difference

How can we determine the notion of "difference" in an ontological rather than merely empirical sense? This is even more important given that a possible counterargument about false inference from empirical to ontological levels may be raised. Let me detail this.

One may now want to argue that I so far did not really provide any argument for moderate OSR of the brain in terms of world–brain relation. Rather I merely stated my assumption and distinguished it from the alternative supposition, namely, the determination of the brain's existence and reality by elements or properties. Even worse, the philosopher may want to accuse that I infer from the empirical level to the ontological determination of the brain.

This amounts to what can be called the *empirical–ontological fallacy* that historically can be traced to Kant and his characterization of Locke as a "physiologist of reason" (Kant, 1781/1998). Thereby, the concept of the empirical strictly conforms to observation as in science independent of whether any knowledge is acquired; hence the notion of the empirical is distinguished from that of the epistemic. The fallacy pointed out thus amounts to an empirical–ontological fallacy (rather than an epistemic–ontological fallacy; see chapter 14 for the latter).

Specifically, one may say that I infer from the empirical observation of difference as in the brain's difference-based coding to the ontological level of relation that can also be determined by difference. I thus conflate two notions of difference: the empirical concept of difference as the difference between different stimuli in difference-based coding and the ontological notion of difference as inherent in relation. One and the same concept, that is, the concept of difference, is thus used and applied in both contexts, that is, empirical and ontological.

I suggested that the brain's difference-based coding implies the ontological determination of its existence in terms of relation (i.e., world–brain relation). Those who take an opposing view may now want to argue that I inferred the ontological concept of difference as inherent in the notion of relation from the empirical one as in difference-based coding. Since the empirical level of observation and the ontological level of existence and reality are not identical, any inference from the brain's difference-based coding to the brain's existence and reality must be considered fallacious. That amounts to nothing less than an empirical–ontological fallacy (see figure 9.1).

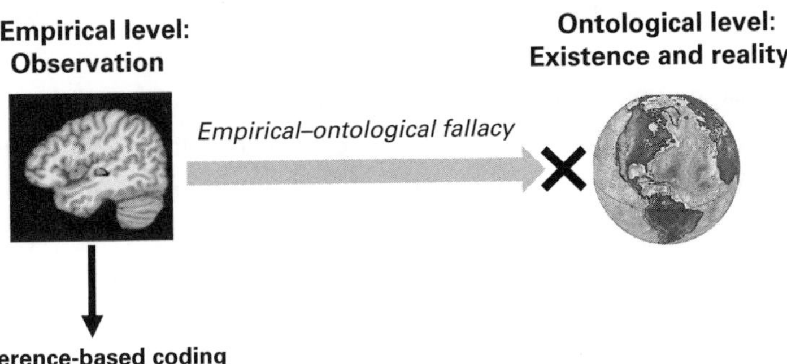

Figure 9.1
Empirical–ontological fallacy.

In order to avoid such empirical–ontological fallacy, I must refrain from characterizing the brain's existence and reality by difference and thus relation (i.e., world–brain relation). The ontological determination of the brain by world–brain relation must thus be rejected on conceptual or logical grounds. How can we escape the conflation between empirical and ontological notions of difference and consequently the empirical–ontological fallacy? I will argue that we need to distinguish two different concepts of difference, empirical and ontological; for that, I turn to Floridi (2008), who distinguishes between two distinct concepts of difference, the empirical notion of *difference per se* and the ontological concept of *difference de re*.

Structural Realism IIIb: Difference De Re versus Difference Per Se

What is meant by the concepts of *difference per se* and *difference de re*? Floridi determines the concept of difference per se in a purely empirical sense as the difference we can observe. For instance, we can observe a difference between two different brain regions and their neural activities—this amounts to difference per se. Yet another example of a difference per se would be that we can observe neural differences between spontaneous and task-evoked activity. Hence, the notion of difference in difference per se is understood in a purely empirical sense without any ontological connotations.

How can we determine the ontological meaning of difference (i.e., difference de re)? Difference de re means that existence and reality are based on difference rather than unity (or identity) of elements (i.e., nondifference). Taken in this sense, differences de re are the basic constituents of reality and existence and are thus ontological rather than empirical (or epistemic; Floridi, 2008). Therefore, the ontological concept of difference de re must be distinguished from its empirical counterpart, that is, difference per se.

How does Floridi describe his ontological concept of difference de re? He illustrates the ontological concept of difference de re using the example of marriage. Without the difference between two people (man and woman, woman and woman, or man and man) marriage would not exist—one cannot marry oneself. The existence and reality of marriage are thus based on difference (difference de re), that is, the difference between two people whose existence and reality as wife and husband are determined by their relation.

The ontological concept of difference de re is well reflected in the following quote by Floridi (2008):

However, the relation of difference is binary and symmetric. In the example, the white sheet of paper is not just the necessary background condition for the occurrence of a black dot as a datum; it is a constitutive part of the datum itself, together with the fundamental relation of inequality that couples it with the dot. In this specific sense, nothing is a datum per se, without its counterpart, just as nobody can be a wife without there being a husband. It takes two to make a datum. So, ontologically, data (as still unqualified, concrete points of lack of uniformity) are purely relational entities. (p. 220)

Note that Floridi's ontological concept of difference is akin to the notion of differences as suggested by other philosophers in the European-continental tradition. This includes the Heidegger (1927/1962) (who introduces difference as distinguished from identity), Derrida (1978) (who speaks of "différance"), and Deleuze (1994, in his work *Difference and Repetition*). However, the exact details of such ontological notion of "difference," including the differences between the different authors, are beyond the scope of this book.

Structural Realism IVa: Difference De Re and the Brain

How can we apply the ontological notion of difference de re to the brain? We can observe differences (i.e., difference per se) between two regions' neural activities. If, now, the neural activity of each region is determined by its relation to the respective other, the regions' neural activities are constitutively dependent on each other—this is indeed empirically supported by the data (see chapters 1 and 2). In that case the observable difference per se can be traced to and is based on an underlying difference de re in the spatial domain of the brain.

The same holds analogously in the temporal domain. The difference frequencies in the brain are determined in their power by their relationship to each other (i.e., CFC; chapter 1). If, for instance, their relation (CFC) is strong, the power of the single frequency is low while the power of the single frequency is high in the case of low CFC. Hence, the power of the single frequency is determined by and in dependence on its relation to others (i.e., CFC).

Yet another example is the relationship between spontaneous and task-evoked activity. As described in chapters 1 and 2, we can observe differences (i.e., difference per se) between both forms of neural activity. Moreover, the empirical data suggest that the task-evoked activity is constituted in dependence on and relation to the spontaneous activity that, conversely, is dependent on the former (see chapters 1 and 2 for details). Constitutively, spontaneous and task-evoked activity are thus mutually or reciprocally dependent upon each other—it is their difference (i.e., difference de re) that determines their respective neural activity levels.

One may now want to argue that I use the concept of difference de re in a merely empirical rather than ontological way. To use the concept of difference de re in a truly ontological sense, I would need to apply it to the brain as a whole, to its existence and reality, and its relation to the world, the world–brain relation. That is easily done. The measures cited above (i.e., functional connectivity, CFC, and the spectrum of relation between spontaneous and stimulus-induced activity) constitute not only the brain's neural activity but, at the same time, its relation to the world, the world–brain relation (chapters 3 and 8). They can consequently be considered the empirical manifestations of the ontological existence and reality of brain in terms of difference de re.

If, in contrast, these measures were not reflecting the brain's relation to the world, the world–brain relation, difference-based coding would no longer be ontologically relevant. The notion of difference de re would then no longer be distinguished from and thus collapse into that of difference per se. However, that is contrary to empirical evidence. That evidence shows the relevance of functional connectivity, CFC, and the spectrum of relation between spontaneous and stimulus-induced activity for establishing and constituting the brain's relation to the world (as, e.g., in a rhythmic or continuous mode; chapter 8).

How can we illustrate the roles of world and brain in world–brain relation analogous to Floridi's example of marriage? Marriage is defined by the difference between two people who, on the basis of their relation in marriage, are subsequently determined as wife and husband (or wife and wife or husband and husband). Analogously, world–brain relation is constituted by the difference between world and brain. The spatiotemporal difference between world and brain first and foremost makes possible their relation, the world–brain relation. That very same relation, the world–brain relation, determines, at the same time, the existence and reality of world and brain (in a noncircular way; see above), that is, as world as distinct from the brain as well as brain as distinct from the world. This is analogous to the way the two people are determined as wife and husband (or wife and wife or husband and husband) by their relation (i.e., the marriage).

Taken together, the ontological characterization of the brain in terms of SR presupposes difference de re as it features world–brain relation. The difference between world and brain, the world–brain relation, determines the brain's existence and reality. Without that very same relation, the brain would not exist. The concept of relation in world–brain relation must thus be understood in terms of difference de re's entailing an ontological rather than empirical meaning (as in difference per se).

Structural Realism IVb: Empirical–Ontological Plausibility versus Empirical–Ontological Fallacy

The introduction of two different concepts of difference, that is, empirical and ontological, makes any inference from the empirical to the ontological level futile and superfluous. We presuppose different independently generated concepts of difference in both empirical and ontological contexts (i.e., difference per se and difference de re). This allows us to feature the ontological level in an independent way by a specific concept of difference (i.e., difference de re) that distinguishes and makes it independent of the difference as understood on the empirical level (i.e., difference per se). The independence of the two concepts precludes a fallacious inference, that is, an empirical–ontological fallacy.

Those who take an opposing view may nevertheless want to argue that we still rely on empirical data to decide the ontological determination of the brain in favor of OSR. Though we no longer use the same concept, we nevertheless use empirical data to opt for OSR rather than element-based ontology in our ontological determination of the brain. The ontological determination of the brain thus remains empirically based. Such an empirical basis of the ontological determination of the brain must be rejected, though: the ontological determination of the brain must remain independent of its empirical characterization.

I argue that this argument needs to be rejected. The proponent of such argument presupposes that we cannot use any empirical data in our ontological determination of the brain. I reject this assumption: we can use empirical data in order to test whether our ontological determination of

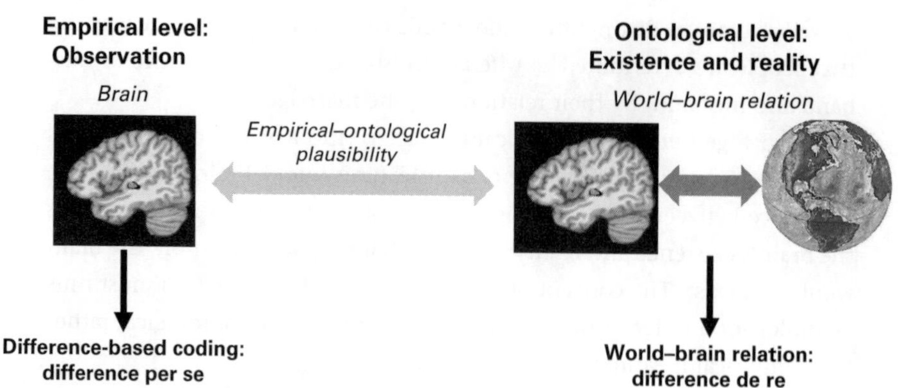

Figure 9.2
Empirical–ontological plausibility.

the brain is empirically plausible or not, amounting to what I describe as empirical–ontological plausibility (see figure 9.2).

The advocate of this argument confuses the concept of empirical–ontological fallacy with what I describe as empirical–ontological plausibility. She or he considers that any use of empirical data in ontological determination of the brain amounts to an inference from the empirical to the ontological level (i.e., empirical–ontological fallacy). However, such inference (empirical–ontological fallacy) occurs only when one uses one and the same concept on both the empirical and ontological levels in the same way—this is indeed the case when one does not distinguish empirical and ontological concepts of difference.

This, in contrast, is no longer the case if one uses different concepts and meanings of difference such as difference de re and difference per se to describe the ontological and empirical levels. In that case, one can investigate whether both concepts hold and are plausible on their respective levels—that is, empirical and ontological—independent from each other. If both concepts hold on their respective levels, one may consider the ontological concept of difference de re as empirically plausible while the empirical concept of difference per se can be regarded as ontologically plausible. Given the strong empirical evidence for difference per se in terms of difference-based coding, I argue that the ontological characterization of the brain by difference de re in terms of OSR is empirically plausible.

How about the opposite scenario with a discrepancy between ontological and empirical levels? In that case, the empirical data show stimulus- rather than difference-based coding entailing that there is no empirical evidence in favor of difference per se. One could nevertheless still characterize the brain ontologically by difference de re in terms of OSR, which, taken by itself (i.e., independent of the empirical data), may still be ontologically plausible. However, given the empirical data speaking against difference per se, such ontological characterization of the brain in terms of difference de re would no longer be empirically plausible. One would then rather revert to element-based ontology to account for the brain's existence and reality in an empirically plausible way.

Part II: Ontology of Brain—Argument of Individuation and Argument of Time and Space

Argument of Individuation Ia: Individuation of Relata—Individuation by Spatiotemporal Structure

One of the arguments against OSR is that it fails to account for the individuation of objects or relata (Esfeld & Lam, 2008, 2010). A particular relatum must possess some intrinsic properties in order to allow for its ontological distinction from other relata. For instance, the brain must possess some specific properties that are intrinsic to the brain which allow us to distinguish its existence and reality from those of nonbrains within the world. More generally, this means that one must suppose element-based ontology to allow for individuation while that remains impossible in the case of relation and structure and thus OSR. I therefore speak of the "argument of individuation."

The argument of individuation rests on the presupposition that individuation requires elements or properties, for example, element- and property-based individuation. In contrast, individuation on the basis of relation and structure as in OSR remains impossible. I reject the argument of individuation by showing that relation and structure and thus OSR can well account for individuation.

How can we counter the argument of individuation? Presupposing OSR, Esfeld and Lam (2008, 2010) reject this argument by postulating that the position of objects within the "web of structure" (Esfeld & Lam, 2006, p. 28; as analogous to Quine's "web of beliefs," Quine, 1969, p. 134) can identify their particular existence and reality, including their distinction from other objects. Individuation in this sense entails a central role for space and time: the individuation of the object by its position within the web of structure must be determined in spatial and temporal terms.

The conceptualization of "individual" may presuppose specific discrete points in time and space. However, these discrete points in time and space may be dependent upon spatiotemporal relations and thus the overall spatiotemporal structure. If so, any particular discrete point in time and space featuring a particular individual can only be individuated by its spatiotemporal relation to others and therefore by the overall spatiotemporal structure.

This individuation by spatiotemporal structure is reflected in the following quote about space and time in general relativity theory (GR) by Esfeld and Lam (2010):

> On the other hand, the physical description of space-time within GR (and in particular the principle of active general covariance) makes meaningless any individuation of space-time points (with the help of intrinsic properties or of primitive thisness for instance) independently of the space-time relations they enter into or independently of the space-time structure they are part of—both being represented by the metric. (p. 22)

Argument of Individuation Ib: Spatiotemporal Individuation—Individuation of Brain by World–Brain Relation

How does the argument of individuation apply to world–brain relation? First and foremost, I am here considering the individuation of the brain as a whole and its distinction from the rest of the world, including nonbrains. Hence, I understand individuation in a strictly ontological sense. This must be distinguished from individuation of different parts within the brain such as its different regions and frequencies; that would concern individuation in a neuronal and thus empirical way rather than in an ontological sense as it is targeted here.

More generally, we must distinguish between two different forms of individuation with regard to the brain as a whole, empirical and ontological. "Empirical individuation" allows for individuation between different individual subjects, including their brains—the brain of subject A is individuated and distinguished from the brain of subject B within a particular species (such as the human species). In contrast, "ontological individuation" makes possible the individuation and distinction of brains from nonbrains within the world across different species. I now argue that OSR can account for both empirical and ontological individuation.

Let us start with empirical individuation. Empirical data suggest that the spontaneous activity's spatiotemporal structure is highly individual for a particular subject and distinguishes it from other subjects (chapter 8). For instance, different individual subjects experiencing different degrees of early childhood trauma show different degrees of entropy, that is, dissimilarity or chaos, in their spontaneous activity's spatiotemporal structure (see chapter 3 and Duncan et al., 2015, for details). Thus, entropy of the spontaneous activity's spatiotemporal structure can individuate the individual subjects' brains on the basis of their brains' relation to the world and its (potentially traumatic) early life events, the world–brain relation. In a nutshell, the brain's spontaneous activity and its spatiotemporal relation to the world, the world–brain relation, can account for empirical individuation.

How about ontological individuation? Let us take the example of brains and nonbrains. Brains and nonbrains have different spatiotemporal features. Both brains and nonbrains are part of one and the same world. This by itself makes impossible any ontological individuation and distinction of brains and nonbrains unless one wants to characterize them by different elements or properties. However, that is to neglect that both brains and nonbrains are related to one and the same world in different ways: the brain may be related to the world in a much broader spatiotemporal scale or range than nonbrains such as stones—world–brain relation and world–stone relation can thus be distinguished on spatiotemporal grounds. I therefore speak of *spatiotemporal individuation*.

How can we further characterize such spatiotemporal individuation on ontological grounds? We recall that relation and structure can ontologically be traced to and are based on difference (i.e., difference de re or differentiating de re). Brains and nonbrains such as stones are "differentiating de re" from the world and thereby from each other in different ways on mainly spatiotemporal grounds: the brain is individuated and distinguished from stones by including differences de re of a much larger spatiotemporal scale or range in its relation to the world (i.e., the world–brain relation) when compared to the world–stone relation. Accordingly, true to its name, spatiotemporal individuation is based on the spatiotemporal features of differences de re in the relation of brain and nonbrains to the world (i.e., world–brain relation and world–stone relation).

Ontological individuation in terms of spatiotemporal individuation is quite compatible with the account of individuation in OSR as suggested by Esfeld and Lam (2008, 2010). What Esfeld and Lam (2008, 2010) describe as "web of structure" can well be specified as "spatiotemporal structure," as it features the world as a whole, including its relation to the parts, such as brains and nonbrains: in the same way the web of structure is determined by spatiotemporal features, the world, including its relation to brains and nonbrains, is signified by spatiotemporal features.

Moreover, Esfeld and Lam's talk about a position within the web of structure corresponds to what I describe as relation in world–brain relation and world–nonbrain relation: the spatiotemporal scale or range of its relation to the world (i.e., the world–brain relation) situates the brain in a different position on the spatiotemporal trajectories within the world's spatiotemporal structure when compared to the relation of nonbrains (i.e., stones). Accordingly, brains and nonbrains are distinguished in their existence and reality in an indirect way, namely, by means of their different relation to the world (i.e., world–brain relation and world–nonbrain relation). The relation to the world thus allows for ontological individuation.

In sum, individuation, including both empirical and ontological individuation, is not tied to the supposition of elements and element-based ontology. Structure and relation can well account for both empirical and ontological individuation—since such individuation occurs on spatiotemporal grounds, I speak of *spatiotemporal individuation*. Spatiotemporal individuation allows us to individuate the brain in both empirical and ontological regards. We can therefore reject the argument of individuation as it is based on the presupposition that individuation is possible only on the basis of elements or properties.

Most importantly, spatiotemporal individuation on both empirical and ontological levels is quite compatible with empirical evidence (see Parts I and II of this book). For that reason, I favor spatiotemporal individuation over individuation by elements or properties and therefore reject the argument of individuation as argument against the ontological determination of the brain in terms of OSR.

Argument of Time and Space Ia: Determination of Time and Space

How can we more clearly distinguish relation and OSR as relation-based ontology from element-based ontology? Proponents of OSR such as Esfeld and Lam (2008, 2010) make a strong case for characterizing the concept of relation in terms of spatial and temporal features—OSR consequently amounts to what I describe as spatiotemporal ontology (see also Northoff, 2016b). The concept of spatiotemporal ontology entails that time and space themselves are the basic units of existence and reality—this, as I will argue, is quite compatible with the focus on structure and relation in OSR.

Esfeld and Lam (2008) mainly draw on physics, for example, GR and quantum physics in particular, when featuring OSR in spatiotemporal terms. This is, for instance, reflected in the following quote:

> Moreover, the *space-time structure* described by GR is such that the *space-time relations* and the objects that stand in the relations (the space-time points or events) are on the same (fundamental) ontological footing. On the one hand and in an analogous way to the general case discussed in the first section, it makes no sense to consider an actual (that is, instantiated in the physical world) space-time relation without relata standing in the relation—*space-time points or events* in the pure gravitational cases. (Esfeld & Lam, 2010, p. 22; emphasis added)

My overall argument is that, analogous to GR in physics, the brain must also be characterized by space-time relations rather than space-time points or events. "Space-time relation" specifies and lends further support to relation-based ontology of brain in terms of OSR. To understand the notion of the space-time relation, we need to distinguish between different concepts of time and space, namely, *relational* time and space and *observational* time and space.

The proponent of element-based ontology may want to put forward the following argument against OSR. Relation and structure are temporal and spatial and must therefore ultimately be traced to and are based on single discrete points in time and space (i.e., space-time points or events). This opens the door for supposing elements as basic units of existence and reality (i.e., element-based ontology): elements such as physical or mental properties are determined by discrete points in time and space (i.e., space-time points or events) rather than space-time relation. We consequently need to reject OSR as relation-based ontology while, at the same time, embracing element-based ontology. Because the notion of time and space is central in this line of reasoning, I describe this argument as the *argument of time and space*.

The rejection of OSR may be further aggravated by considering that the notions of time and space are rather trivial. The brain and its neural activity are spatial and temporal by default; this is empirically reflected and manifest in functional connectivity and the fluctuations in different frequencies. That makes any ontological characterization of the brain in terms of time and space superfluous at best and trivial at worst (see chapter 7 for the argument of triviality in the context of consciousness). The argument of time and space can thus also be understood as an argument against the trivial characterization of the brain by time and space in an ontological (rather than empirical; see chapter 7) sense.

Argument of Time and Space Ib: Observational Time and Space

The argument of time and space is primarily an argument against relation-based ontology. However, I will reject that argument by disputing its presupposition. In a nutshell, my rejection is as follows. Structure and relation as presupposed in relation-based ontology such as OSR are indeed temporal and spatial. However, structure and relation in an ontological sense cannot be traced to and are not based on single discrete points in time and space (i.e., space-time points or events) but presuppose a different notion of time and space as defined by space-time relation. Space-time points or events reflect what I will describe as *observational time and space* while space-time relation presupposes *relational time and space.*

Accordingly, to reject the argument of time and space, we need to describe and distinguish the notions of observational and relational time and space. That shall be the focus in the following. It should be noted that I cannot go into full detail about the metaphysics of time and space (see, e.g., Dainton, 2010), which would deserve a book by itself. Instead, I only focus on time and space as they are relevant in the current context of the brain. Let us first start with observational time and space.

We observe the brain and its relation to the world. For instance, we observe the brain and its neural activity when applying specific tasks or stimuli to probe the brain's stimulus-induced or task-evoked activity at discrete and single points in time and space. The brain and its neural activity, for example, stimulus-induced activity, is then framed and put within the time and space of the observer and her or his discrete points in time and space she or he presupposes when applying specific stimuli or tasks. The time and space attributed to the brain and its neural activity are thus based on the time and space of the observer—time and space in this sense are dependent upon the observer. I therefore speak of observational time and space, which, epistemically, must be characterized as mind dependent or brain dependent.

Observational time and space can be characterized by space-time points or events. We observe the brain and its neural activity in terms of "here" and "now" and thus in terms of specific discrete points in time and space. For instance, neural activity is located in a certain region, that is, "here," at a specific point in time, that is, "now," which distinguishes it from neural activity in other regions, that is, another "here," and other points in time, that is, another "now." In contrast, we remain unable to directly observe the relationship between the different points in time and space. We cannot link and relate the different "now" points with each other nor the various "here" points in our observation. Observational time and space thus presuppose space-time points or events rather than space-time relation.

Argument of Time and Space Ic: Relational Time and Space

How about time and space as they remain independent of our observation? I argue that this leads us to a different notion of time and space, relational time and space as based on space-time relation rather than space-time points or events. Such relational time and space characterizes the brain itself, including its relation to the world, the world-brain relation, independent of our observation of brain and world (in terms of observational time and space with space-time points or events). Therefore, space-time relation with relational time and space must be conceived epistemically as mind independent or brain independent. Historically, the concept of relational time and space as advocated here stands in close relationship to specifically dynamic concepts of time as have been suggested by Leibniz and Clarke (2000), Whitehead (1929/1978), Bergson (1904), and more recently Dainton (2010) when claiming for presentism. Future investigation is required for detailed comparison of my structural-realist approach to time in terms of relational time with the ones discussed in the metaphysics of time in philosophy.

How can we characterize the time and space of the brain itself, including its relation to the world, the world–brain relation? I demonstrated in Part I (chapters 1–3) that the brain's spontaneous activity shows spatiotemporal structure—this amounts to what Esfeld and Lam describe ontologically as *space-time relation.* I now argue that the concept of space-time relation can ontologically be specified by those of *duration* and *extension.* Let us start with duration.

The concept of duration refers to the time the brain and its neural activity construct by themselves, the brain's *inner time.* Empirically, duration is related to the time it takes for neural activity, and thus a neural event, to occur by itself independent of any external stimuli, including their "here" and "now"—that is manifest in the brain's spontaneous activity and its various frequency ranges that define the brain's inner duration (see chapters 1–3). This is well reflected in the following quote by D. Griffin (1998) in his description of process philosophy: "Having an inside would mean that they [objects or events such as the brain] can have an inner duration, which is the time it takes each event to occur—the time between its reception of information and its transmission of this information into subsequent events" (p. 144).

Taken in an ontological sense, duration determines the existence and reality of the brain in terms of its relation to the world. The world–brain relation can then ontologically be characterized by time in the sense of duration, that is, *inner duration,* that describes its extension in time across different points in time and distinguishes from other durations, that is, *outer durations,* in the rest of the world.

Analogous to duration, I speak of *extension* to characterize the spatial features of the brain. The brain and its neural activity show a certain spatial extension as is empirically manifest in, for instance, its functional connectivity (chapters 1–3). Functional connectivity makes it possible that the single region's neural activity is extended to others, which constitutes an *inner extension* that is specific to the brain and remains independent of the observer. Analogous to duration, I therefore suggest using the term *extension* in an ontological sense to characterize the existence and reality of brain in terms of space, that is, its inner extension. The world–brain relation can then be characterized by a certain spatial extension, an inner extension, that distinguishes it from the outer extension in the rest of the world.

How can we illustrate the concepts of inner duration and extension in further detail? Inner duration and extension are not defined by single discrete points in time and space (i.e., "here" and "now"). Instead, as based on empirical evidence, inner duration and extension of the brain's spontaneous activity are based on the relation between different regions, that is, functional connectivity, and frequencies, that is, CFC with scale-free activity (chapters 1–3, 5, and 6). Both inner duration and extension can therefore be signified by space-time relation rather than space-time points or events. Moreover, as empirical evidence shows, the brain aligns to and integrates itself within the world on the basis of its own inner duration and extension when constituting space-time relation with the world (i.e., world–brain relation; chapters 4 and 8).

Argument of Time and Space IIa: Spatiotemporal Spectrum Model

One may now want to raise the question of the relationship between relational and observational time and space with regard to the brain. Relational time and space can be characterized by space-time relation while observational time and space are characterized by space-time points or events. Are both mutually incompatible and exclusive, or are they compatible with each other? This depends on the version of OSR one presupposes.

If one presupposes eliminativist OSR (see above), they are not compatible with each other since then space-time points or events do not exist at all, not even by themselves (not even as abstractions from the more concrete space-time relation). If, in contrast, one presupposes a moderate or noneliminativist stance in OSR, space-time points or events can exist but only in dependence on space-time relation. This is what Esfeld and Lam (2010) suggest:

> Space-time points do not possess any independent existence (they are not atoms in the philosophical sense), but only exist in virtue of their standing in relation to other space-time points. There is no ontological priority, but rather a mutual ontological dependence between space-time relations and space-time points. (p. 22)

Presupposing moderate or noneliminativist OSR, observational time and space are a specific instance of relational time and space. That is central in explaining the paradox that observational time and space is based on the observer and her or his brain that by itself can be characterized by relational time and space. How can observational time and space be based on something, that is, the brain with its world–brain relation, that by itself shows a different notion of time and space, that is, relational time and space?

First and foremost, I suggest that, put into an empirical context, observational and relational time and space are related to different forms of neural activity, that is, spontaneous and stimulus-induced activity. The brain's relational time and space is manifest in its spontaneous activity and its relation to the world (i.e., world–brain relation) with its space-time relation as described by inner duration and extension—while the observer's observational time and space is based on her or his brain's stimulus-induced or task-evoked activity and its various perceptual and cognitive functions that allow for observing space-time points or events.

We demonstrated that there is no sharp and clear-cut empirical distinction between spontaneous and stimulus-induced activity—this amounted to the spectrum model on the empirical level of the brain's neural activity (chapter 1). Analogously, I now suppose that there is no sharp and clear-cut distinction between relational and observational time and space and hence between space-time relation and space-time points or events. This amounts to an analogous spectrum model on the ontological level of time and space, a *spatiotemporal spectrum* model.

How can I determine the spatiotemporal spectrum model? What we describe as *spatiotemporal points or events* in observational time and space may ontologically be an extreme instance of an extremely short extension and duration of space-time relation in relational time and space. That is, rather than being different in principle and mutually exclusive, relational and observational time and space can be characterized by a continuum or spectrum of different spatiotemporal scales or ranges: relational time and space entail a longer spatiotemporal scale or range which configures as space-time relation, while the one in observational time and space is extremely short and surfaces as space-time points or events. Relational and observational time and space can consequently be "positioned" or "located" on different ends of a commonly shared spatiotemporal spectrum.

Note that the concept of spectrum is here understood in a truly ontological sense concerning the spectrum of different notions of time and space within the world. That must be distinguished from the more empirical use of the notion of spectrum as in the "spectrum model of brain" as developed in the first chapter. Here time and space are limited to the brain as well as to our observation of time and space. That is different in the ontological notion where time and space are considered within the world rather than the brain as well as independent of observation.

Argument of Time and Space IIb: Rejection of the Argument of Time and Space

The spatiotemporal spectrum model also characterizes time and space of the brain. From the world over the brain's spontaneous activity to the brain's stimulus-induced activity, a spectrum of different temporal and spatial scales or ranges is recruited and implicated. When the brain and its spontaneous activity align themselves to and integrate within the world (i.e., world–brain relation), a large scale or range of time and space is involved—this is manifest in space-time relation and relational time and space.

If, in contrast, the brain's stimulus-induced or task-induced activity is recruited during observation, the spatiotemporal scale or range becomes smaller and shifts toward space-time points or events as in observational time and space. Observational time and space with its space-time points or events may thus be conceived as an abstraction from the spatiotemporally more extended relational time and space.

However, stimulus-induced or task-evoked activity is dependent upon spontaneous activity (see chapter 2), which, in turn, is dependent upon its relation to the world, the world–brain relation. This also means that space-time points or events as in observational time and space are dependent and based upon space-time relation as in relational time and space.

This is obviously quite compatible with Esfeld and Lam's noneliminativist version of OSR in which space-time points or events do not exist independently of space-time relation. Their stance can now be extended and complemented by the spatiotemporal spectrum model that, as an ontological model of time and space, suggests a continuum between different spatiotemporal extensions of different notions of time and space such as relational and observational time and space. The space-time points or events are then a continuum of space-time relations on an extremely small spatiotemporal scale—the former are thus an abstraction of the latter.

We are now ready to address the argument of time and space. The argument of time and space is based on the presupposition that relation and structure are spatiotemporal and must therefore be based on space-time points or events (see above). However, this presupposition is rendered wrong by the spatiotemporal spectrum model. The spatiotemporal spectrum model argues that space-time points or events are based and dependent upon space-time relation rather than the latter being dependent upon the former. Such spatiotemporal spectrum model is not only ontologically plausible but also empirically supported given that it rests on the spectrum model of brain (chapter 1). I am thus able to reject the argument of time and space as an argument against moderate OSR of the brain in terms of world–brain relation and space-time relation on both ontological and empirical grounds.

Moreover, the ontological characterization of the brain by time and space is not trivial at all. One can characterize the brain ontologically by observational time and space; in that case, there would be no distinction between empirical and ontological determination of the brain. Alternatively, one can ontologically describe the brain by relational time and space as distinguished from observational time and space; in that case, one would need to distinguish between ontological and empirical characterization of the brain.

We can then also address the argument of triviality. We already rejected the empirical version of that argument in chapter 7 by hinting at different spatiotemporal mechanisms (chapter 7). This is complemented now by rejecting its ontological version, namely, that the ontological characterization of world and brain including world–brain relation by time and space is trivial. Because we are confronted with two alternative ontological options, that is, relational versus observational time and space, the ontological determination of the brain by time and space cannot be considered trivial at all.

Most important, this carries major ontological implications. In the case of observational time and space, the brain's existence and reality are determined independent of those of the world, entailing element-based ontology. In contrast, that is no longer the case with regard to relational time and space where the brain's spatiotemporal determination entails world–brain relation, which presupposes relation- rather than element-based ontology. We will see in the next chapter that both world–brain relation and relation-based ontology are central for the ontological determination of consciousness.

Conclusion

I characterize the brain ontologically by relation and structure. This amounts to SR and, more specifically, moderate OSR of the brain. Moderate OSR determines the brain's existence and reality by relation and thus world–brain relation. The brain is its relation to the world; in short, the brain is world–brain relation. Without its relation to the world, the brain does not exist. Such relational view of the brain must be distinguished from its ontological definition by elements such as mental or physical properties as in element-based ontology. The discussion of the ontological determination of brain can be regarded as a first step toward a "philosophy of brain" (Northoff, 2004).

How can the relation in the concept of world–brain relation be defined in more ontological detail? Following OSR, the relation can be defined in temporal and spatial terms, that is, by space-time relation rather than space-time points or events. This led me to distinguish relational time and space with duration and extension from observational time and space, which I then applied to the brain and world–brain relation. The world–brain relation remains independent of our observation and thus observational time and space. Instead, the world–brain relation can be characterized by relational time and space that determines the brain's existence and reality. Most important, based on empirical evidence (see chapters 7 and 8), I propose that the world–brain relation, including its relational time and space, is a predisposition of consciousness. This shall be the focus in the next chapter.

10 Ontology II: From World–Brain Relation to Consciousness

Introduction

General Background—Ontology of Consciousness

I have characterized the brain's existence and reality as *world–brain relation*. This is compatible with structural realism and, more specifically, ontic structural realism (OSR; chapter 9). Rather than presupposing basic elements such as physical or mental properties, OSR presupposes relation and structure as basic units of existence and reality. The brain can thus ontologically be defined by relation as in world–brain relation and structure specified as spatiotemporal structure.

That very same spatiotemporal structure is characterized as space-time relation with relational time and space as distinguished from space-time points as in observational time and space (chapter 9). How such determination of the brain in terms of world–brain relation and space-time relation can account for the ontological characterization of consciousness (and mental features in general) remains unclear, however.

The empirical findings on consciousness suggest a spatiotemporal model (chapters 7 and 8). The spatiotemporal model characterizes consciousness by spatiotemporal mechanisms such as spatiotemporal expansion and nestedness (chapter 7) as well as spatiotemporal alignment to body and world (chapter 8). These spatiotemporal mechanisms concern the constitution of time and space by the brain itself, that is, its "intrinsic" time and space (chapter 7), as well as their relation to the world's time and space (chapter 8). Ontologically, such construction of time and space amounts to what I described as *relational time and space* (chapter 9). Presupposing such relational time and space allows me now to go beyond the empirical to the ontological frame and, more specifically, to investigate the question of the basic existence and reality of consciousness, that is, mental features.

Aim and Argument—Spatiotemporal Model of Consciousness

The main aim in this chapter is to suggest a spatiotemporal model of consciousness on the ontological level. Note that I am mainly concerned with the phenomenal features of consciousness as distinguished from neuronal features (while I leave aside cognitive and rational features of consciousness; chapter 7). My main argument is that the world–brain relation as defined in terms of OSR can ontologically account for consciousness (see the Introduction in chapter 9 for my understanding of ontology). Specifically, I will argue that the world–brain relation can be considered a necessary nonsufficient ontological condition of possible consciousness, an *ontological predisposition of consciousness* (OPC), as I say.

I will first introduce and sketch the spatiotemporal model of consciousness—this is the focus in the first part (part I). The second part (part II) focuses on the core problem, the quest for a necessary (a posteriori) ontological connection between brain and consciousness, the *contingency problem*, as I describe it. I argue that the assumption of world–brain relation as OPC renders it possible to conceive the relationship between brain and consciousness in a necessary (a posteriori) rather than contingent way: as world–brain relation provides the necessary ontological condition of possible consciousness (i.e., OPC), the brain, as ontologically defined by world–brain relation, is also necessarily (rather than contingently) connected to consciousness (part II).

Importantly, the brain alone, that is, independent of its relation to the world as defined in element-based ontology (chapter 9), does not have a necessary but only contingent connection to consciousness. This makes it possible to disentangle the concepts of consciousness and mind: we no longer need the concept of mind to account for the necessary connection between consciousness (i.e., phenomenal features) and brain (i.e., world–brain relation) as the underlying ontological basis. We can establish a necessary (a posteriori) connection of consciousness and its phenomenal features to the brain (through world–brain relation), which makes the concept of mind superfluous. I therefore conclude that, ontologically, world–brain relation can take on the role of the concept of mind in our search for the existence and reality of consciousness. Therefore, I suggest that what I call the *world–brain problem* can replace the mind–body problem (part III).

Part I: Ontology of Consciousness—Spatiotemporal Model

Spatiotemporal Model Ia: Spatiotemporal Mechanisms—Spatiotemporal Structure

I characterized consciousness by a spatiotemporal model that is empirically based on different spatiotemporal mechanisms (chapters 7 and 8). These included spatiotemporal expansion, nestedness, and alignment. Despite empirical differences, they all share their essentially spatiotemporal nature, that is, they reflect distinct ways of how the brain itself constructs its own time and space, that is, intrinsic time and space.

Spatiotemporal expansion allows for extending the specific space-time points or events of single stimuli (or contents) beyond themselves to a larger spatiotemporal scale while spatiotemporal nestedness entails the integration of the stimuli/contents' smaller spatiotemporal scale within the larger range of the brain's spontaneous activity (chapter 7). Finally, spatiotemporal alignment concerns the linkage or coupling of the brain's smaller spatiotemporal scale to and within the world's overall spatiotemporal range (chapter 8).

Taken altogether, the spatiotemporal mechanisms underlying consciousness share the integration of different spatiotemporal scales or ranges. Consciousness, as we have seen, is about such *spatiotemporal integration*: its phenomenal features are based on integrating different spatiotemporal scales from brain, body, and world by and within the brain's neural activity (chapters 7–8).

The central relevance of spatiotemporal integration for consciousness is further supported by findings about disorders of consciousness and psychiatric disorders. Disorders of consciousness leading to loss of consciousness such as sleep, anesthesia, or vegetative state show loss of spatiotemporal integration in the brain's neural activity (chapters 4, 5, and 7). Moreover, abnormal spatiotemporal integration also characterizes psychiatric disorders such as schizophrenia or depression (chapters 2 and 3). That spatiotemporal abnormalities in the brain result in abnormal mental features, that is, loss of consciousness (as in disorders of consciousness) or abnormal consciousness (as in psychiatric disorders), illustrates the central relevance of spatiotemporal integration for consciousness.

What does spatiotemporal integration imply for the ontological characterization of consciousness? Spatiotemporal integration allows for constituting spatiotemporal structure. The spatiotemporal model of consciousness, as developed in chapters 7 and 8, emphasized the central relevance of spatiotemporal structure for consciousness in an empirical sense. Specifically, spatiotemporal structure describes here the relation and organization between the various temporal and spatial features of the brain's spontaneous activity (as measured in scale-free activity, cross-frequency coupling, etc.; chapters 7 and 8).

Spatiotemporal Model Ib: Spatiotemporal Structure—Ontological Features

How can we now transition from the empirical to the ontological level and raise the question of the ontological determination of consciousness? For that, we need to conceive the concept of spatiotemporal structure in an ontological rather than empirical sense. I already prepared such ontological ground in the last chapter (chapter 9) when conceiving the brain's existence and reality. Summarizing that account, I determine the concept of spatiotemporal structure by four ontological features:

(i) Relation as distinguished from elements. Spatiotemporal structure can ontologically be determined by relation. Relations are conceived here as the basic units of existence and reality without any prior and more basic underlying primary ontological features—this amounts to OSR. This distinguishes the ontological notion of relation from that of elements such as physical or mental properties or substances. Even if such element-based ontology considers relation, it only considers it in a secondary sense as the relation between primary and independently existent elements or properties including mental or physical properties. In addition, relation-based ontology must also be distinguished from other forms of ontology such as process- and capacity-based ontology (chapter 9).

(ii) Organization as distinguished from collection. Spatiotemporal structure can ontologically be characterized by organization of relation. The organization of relation describes the coupling and linkage between different relations which, most notably, are established in a systematic way. Importantly, organization is spatiotemporal in that it allows for linking and coupling different space-time relations. Such spatiotemporal organization of relation must be distinguished ontologically from mere collections of elements or collections of processes that are usually conceived as only secondary and nonsystematic (chapter 9).

(iii) Difference as distinguished from unity. Spatiotemporal structure is based on difference rather than unity. Specifically, following Floridi (2008), differences de re (chapter 9) can be taken to be the basic unit of existence and reality of spatiotemporal structure. Taken in such an ontological sense, differences de re must be distinguished from their empirical counterpart, that is, differences per se, as they are, for instance, manifest in the brain's difference-based coding (chapters 1, 2, and 9).

(iv) Space-time relation as distinguished from space-time points or events. Spatiotemporal structure is defined by space-time relations that feature relational time and space (chapter 9)—they must be distinguished from our perception and cognition of time and space in terms of space-time points or events as in observational time and space (chapter 9). Hence, space-time relation as well as relational time and space can be considered truly ontological, whereas space-time points or events, including observational time and space, remain empirical (and/or epistemic at best) (but not ontological).

Spatiotemporal Model IIa: Ontology of Consciousness—Relation and Organization

I suppose that spatiotemporal structure in such ontological sense can also account for the existence and reality of consciousness and mental features in general. The spatiotemporal model of consciousness as developed so far in a purely empirical sense (chapters 7 and 8) is now extended to the ontological level. Consciousness is not only spatiotemporal in an empirical sense, as supported by the empirical data, but also intrinsically spatiotemporal in an ontological sense.

Put briefly, the existence and reality of consciousness, that is, of its phenomenal features, are spatiotemporal and structural and therefore entail OSR. Specifically, the existence and reality of consciousness can be defined by relational time and space with spatiotemporal structure as it spans between world and brain and defines their relation (i.e., world–brain relation). This shall be explicated as follows:

(i) Consciousness is relational. The existence and reality of consciousness can be determined by relations. These relations are neither physical nor mental but spatiotemporal, consisting in space-time relation. Importantly, such a relational view of consciousness must be distinguished from any kind of property-based ontology that assumes mental, physical, or neutral properties to underlie consciousness. The traditional ontological alternative between monism versus dualism that is based on the question of the relationship between mental and physical properties must consequently be discarded (chapter 9). Additionally, any substance-based ontology of consciousness as well as other ontologies such as process ontology (as in Whitehead, 1929/1978; see also Northoff, 2016a,b) or capacity-based ontology (chapters 5 and 9; Cartwright, 1989; McDowell, 1994) of consciousness must be replaced by the assumption of the relational nature of consciousness.

The relational claim considers relation in such ontological sense a necessary condition of possible consciousness (i.e., an OPC; see below for details on the concept of OPC). Hence, the absence of relation in such ontological sense entails the absence of consciousness. For instance, element-based ontology remains incompatible with consciousness. If there were indeed elements or properties defining the basic units of existence and reality as when assuming mental or physical properties, consciousness would nevertheless remain impossible and thus absent—the OPC would simply be no longer given.

(ii) Consciousness consists in organization. The existence and reality of consciousness consist in complex organization of relation, that is, the linkage and coupling between different space-time relations such as those of the existence and realities of world and brain (chapter 9). The notion of organization taken in such ontological sense bears some resemblance to the notion of synthesis as used by Kant (1781/1998) and Cassirer (1944); future investigation may detail such resemblance further.

The absence of organization may consequently entail the absence of consciousness. If, for instance, there is no linkage and coupling between the different space-time relations between the existences and realities of world, body, and brain, consciousness remains absent. Hence, mere addition or collection of world, body, and brain is not compatible with the presence of consciousness. Accordingly, without the spatiotemporal ontological organization of world, body, and brain in terms of spatiotemporal structure, consciousness and its phenomenal features cannot come into existence and reality.

Spatiotemporal Model IIb: Ontology of Consciousness—Difference and Relational Time and Space

What are the basic ontological building blocks of consciousness? This leads us back to the question of the most basic units of existence and reality that first and foremost make possible consciousness. Based on prior chapters, I determine difference, that is, difference de re, and relational time and space as the most basic ontological building blocks of consciousness:

(iii) Consciousness is ontologically based on difference, that is, difference de re. (See also Northoff, 2014b, for details.) Difference is understood here in an ontological sense, that is, difference de re, rather than empirically, that is, difference per se. Difference de re constitutes consciousness that therefore is difference based in an ontological sense, which, empirically, is manifest in difference-based coding (chapters 1 and 2; Northoff, 2014a) and thus in what is conceptually described as difference per se (chapter 9).

The claim of the difference-based existence and reality of consciousness contrasts with the traditional claim of unity as being the most basic and fundamental ground of consciousness. The assumption of the unity-based nature of consciousness has a long philosophical history that can be traced at least to Descartes and Kant and is still prevalent today (see Bayne, 2010; Searle, 2004). My claim of the difference-based rather than unity-based nature of consciousness breaks with that tradition which, philosophically, converges with European-continental philosophers such as Heidegger and Deleuze.

However, the notion of difference, that is, difference de re, as used here, is closely related to the concept of relation as understood in OSR. Both relation and difference de re can be used interchangeably on a purely conceptual level, whereas ontologically, one may consider difference de re as an ontological construction feature by means of which relation is established (i.e., constructed).

(iv) Consciousness is ontologically characterized by relational time and space. The existence and reality of consciousness consist in the spacetime relation that characterizes relational time and space (chapter 9).

Taken in such sense, consciousness cannot be characterized by space-time points or events as a hallmark of observational time and space. This excludes any ontological characterization of consciousness by specific physical or mental properties as well as a merely empirical determination: since physical or mental properties presuppose space-time points or events, consciousness would remain impossible in either of these cases.

The spatiotemporal characterization of consciousness by relational time and space makes it possible to account for its phenomenal features on the basis of spatiotemporal relation and structure. Phenomenal features can then ontologically be characterized by specific forms of spatiotemporal organization and configuration and their relation to the spatiotemporal features of world–brain relation while empirically one can then develop what I described earlier as neurophenomenal hypotheses (Northoff, 2014b, 2015).

Note that such spatiotemporal account of consciousness and its phenomenal features must be sharply distinguished from the reductive and eliminative account of consciousness in current neurophilosophy (Bickle, 2003; Churchland, 2002, 2012; Mandik, 2006). As consciousness (and mental features) are here conceived in merely empirical terms, they are characterized by what I describe as observational time and space (chapter 9). This, in turn, makes it possible to eliminate consciousness and mental features altogether in favor of the brain, which, ontologically, leads to eliminative materialism (Churchland, 1988). Such elimination of consciousness and mental features stands square to the present approach. I do not aim to eliminate mental features but only trace them back to world–brain relation as their ontological predisposition (rather than as an ontological correlate; see chapter 13 for a more detailed discussion of eliminative materialism).

Spatiotemporal Model IIc: Ontology of Consciousness—Mind versus World–Brain Relation and Internalism versus Externalism

(v) The determination of consciousness by relational time and space also stands square to the traditional aspatial and atemporal characterization of consciousness when it is associated with the possible existence and reality of mind (see chapter 13 for a more detailed discussion of the concept of mind). The present account considers consciousness and its phenomenal features as intrinsically spatiotemporal, that is, in terms of relational time and space (Northoff, 2014b for details of spatiotemporal approach to phenomenal features); this excludes its aspatial and atemporal determination: without space and time, that is, relational time and space, consciousness, that is, its phenomenal features, would remain impossible.

Note that the present characterization of consciousness in terms of world–brain relation renders superfluous the concept of mind. We simply no longer need or require the concept of (the possible existence and reality of) mind and its aspatial and atemporal features to account for the existence and reality of consciousness as the latter can now be traced to world–brain relation and its relational time and space.

Therefore, I suggest disentangling consciousness, that is, its phenomenal features and, more generally, mental features, from the concept of mind as such. We can address the question of the existence and reality of mental features independent of and without presupposing the possible existence and reality of mind; that, in turn, renders impossible the subsequent question of the mind's relationship with the body, that is, the mind–body problem, which then can be replaced by the world–brain problem (see chapter 13 for details).

(vi) The existence and reality of consciousness are based on the existence and reality of the world and its relation to one of its part, that is, the brain, as in our human case. This suggests some form of externalism of consciousness, that is, the necessary reference of consciousness (and mental features in general) to the world. However, externalism in the present context is relational and ontological as it is based on world–brain relation and OSR. Such relational and ontological externalism must be distinguished from the more empirical biological externalism (which, ontologically, is more property- rather than relation-based) as it is, for instance, claimed for by Millikan (1984), Tye (2009), and Dretske (1995). At the same time, the present approach also defies internalism (in the usual sense) of consciousness as the latter necessarily requires relation to the world (i.e., world–brain relation) as OPC.

More generally, the ontological characterization of consciousness (and mental features in general) in terms of world–brain relation complements and traces the distinction between internalism and externalism of consciousness and its contents to a more basic and fundamental level, that is, the level of relation and structure (as in OSR): contents are no longer conceived as either internal or external but are traced to the more fundamental level of relation and its spatiotemporal features (see also chapter 6 for discussion of the role of contents in consciousness).

Part II: Ontology of Consciousness—Contingency Problem, or Necessary Ontological Connection between Brain and Consciousness

Contingency Problem Ia: Internal Relation—Double Necessary Ontological Connection

How can the world–brain relation account for the existence and reality of consciousness and mental features? To address that question, we need to investigate, first, the relationship between world and brain (i.e., world–brain relation) and, second, the relation of world–brain relation to consciousness and mental features.

Let me start with the relationship between world and brain. For that, I turn to Thomas Nagel and the example of H_2O and water. Nagel says that we must investigate the behavior of molecules, including the "geometry of their spatiotemporal structure," to understand how the microlevel with the different molecules of H_2O as parts entails water on the macrolevel as whole. H_2O is defined by molecules, that is, H and O, that show an "internal relation" (Nagel, 2000, p. 14) and therefore are necessarily (a posteriori) connected with each other. That internal relation, in turn, makes possible the internal relation of H_2O to water, that is, their necessary (a posteriori) connection with *upward entailment* of water by H_2O (see below for details on the concept of upward entailment).

I now argue that world and brain are necessarily (a posteriori) connected to each other as well as to consciousness in a way that is more or less analogous to the relationship between H_2O and water. In the same way that H and O as molecules are internally related to each other, that is, necessary (a posteriori), world and brain show a necessary and thus internal relation with each other—this is what I describe as world–brain relation. Moreover, as H_2O is necessarily connected to water, world–brain relation is necessarily (a posteriori) connected to consciousness and mental features.

We have to be careful though. The analogy between H_2O–water and world–brain relation can be understood only in a figurative rather than a literal way. That is because there is spatiotemporal discrepancy. H_2O shows a much smaller spatiotemporal scale or range than water—upward spatiotemporal entailment and a necessary connection operate here thus from a smaller (i.e., H_2O) to a larger (i.e., water) spatiotemporal scale. The spatiotemporal scale is different in the case of world–brain relation though as, unlike H_2O, it does not operate on a molecular level and its small spatiotemporal scale. However, one may argue that consciousness and its phenomenal features "go beyond" the brain in spatiotemporal terms (chapters 7 and 8); this puts consciousness on a somewhat analogous spatiotemporal footing as water that also goes beyond H_2O on spatiotemporal grounds.

Let me make the analogy more explicit. What Nagel describes as the geometry of their spatiotemporal structure on the microlevel of H_2O may correspond in our case to world–brain relation and its spatiotemporal structure as constituted on the basis of relational time and space—the world–brain relation may thus be characterized by "geometry of spatiotemporal structure between world and brain." As in the case of the relation between H and O, this makes possible "internal relation" between world and brain. That internal relation is intrinsically spatiotemporal as it is based on space-time relation with relational time and space (chapter 9), which entails a necessary rather than contingent relation between world and brain. In short, the relation in world–brain relation is necessary rather than contingent.

The necessary world–brain relation, in turn, makes possible necessary ontological connection between brain and consciousness as will be explicated in the third part in this chapter. Without the necessary connection between world and brain, the brain could not be connected necessarily to consciousness. That is more or less analogous to the fact that the internal relation between H and O makes possible the necessary connection between H_2O and water: without the necessary connection between H and O, neither H alone nor O alone could be necessarily connected to water.

In sum, I propose a twofold necessary ontological connection. The first necessary ontological connection is between world and brain, resulting in world–brain relation, while the second necessary ontological connection consists in the necessary ontological connection of the world–brain relation, including brain and consciousness. Taken both together, the necessary world–brain relation is an ontological predisposition for the necessary ontological connection between brain and consciousness.

Contingency Problem Ib: External versus Internal Relation—Causal versus Constitutive Relation

How can we describe the necessary connection between world and brain, that is, their internal relation, in more detail? The traditional philosopher may now want to argue that these are causal relationships: the world causes the brain, which, in turn, causes consciousness. Without being able to go into full detail about, especially, the concept of causality, I here briefly indicate that this does not hold; I reject the characterization of the internal relations as causal relations—internal relations are noncausal and constitutive.

Causal relation presupposes an *external relation* where world and brain can be distinguished and separated from each other, which, in turn, allows them to link in a causal way. That is not the case in the internal relation of world–brain relation though. Here, world and brain are related to each other by default, implying that they cannot be clearly distinguished and separated from each other on ontological and ultimately also on empirical (chapter 8) grounds. Analogously, H and O cannot be distinguished and separated from each other within H_2O—to consider them in terms of an external or causal relation within H_2O would simply be nonsensical as it would make H_2O impossible.

Accordingly, to characterize the internal relation between world and brain (i.e., world–brain relation), as well as the internal relation between brain (i.e., world–brain relation) and consciousness as causal relation is to confuse internal relation and external relation and consequently necessary and contingent connection. Instead, we may want to characterize the internal relation of world–brain relation as constitutive rather than causal: the relation between world and brain constitutes the existence and reality of the brain in a relational and, more specifically, in difference, that is, difference de re (chapter 9), to the world. However, future investigation is needed to characterize such constitutive rather than causal relation in more detail.

Contingency Problem IIa: Brain and Consciousness—Necessary versus Contingent Connection

I am now ready to address the second step, the relationship between world–brain relation and consciousness. I will argue that the world–brain relation is a necessary ontological condition of possible consciousness (i.e., an OPC). How can the ontological connection between world–brain relation and consciousness be necessary rather than contingent? For that, I turn to a paper by Thomas Nagel (2000). Note that I will mainly focus on discussing the necessary versus contingent connection between brain and consciousness. In contrast, I will leave out the discussion of the a priori versus a posteriori nature of the necessary connection—I will simply follow Nagel (who, in turn, bases his account on Kripke, 1972) when assuming a necessary a posteriori connection between brain and consciousness.

Nagel argues that a solution to the mind–body problem must address and challenge the problem of the contingent connection between brain and consciousness: "It appears at first blush that we have a clear and distinct enough grasp on both phenomenological consciousness and physical brain processes to see that there can be no necessary connection between them" (Nagel, 2000, pp. 3–4). Following Kripke, Nagel states that we need to draw a necessary connection between brain and consciousness, that is, a necessary connection between mental and physical processes, to address and ultimately solve the mind–body problem. This necessary connection between mental and physical processes will be the focus in the remainder of this chapter.

How can we conceive or take into view the potentially necessary connection between brain and consciousness? We observe the brain and its neural activities in the brain scanner. We observe various changes in the brain's neural activity, but none of that tells us anything about consciousness—the brain's neural activity, as we observe it, does not entail consciousness. Hence, we cannot observe consciousness in the brain and do therefore remain unable to draw any necessary connection between them—the relation between brain and consciousness remains opaque and thus contingent.

Despite all their empirical progress, the various neuroscientific theories of consciousness such as global neuronal workspace theory and integrated information theory (chapters 5 and 7) cannot overcome the problem of contingency between brain and consciousness. We are thus confronted with the problem of contingency between brain and consciousness—the *contingency problem*. The contingency problem is a conceptual–logical problem that concerns the nature of connection between brain and consciousness that can be either contingent or necessary. As such, the contingency

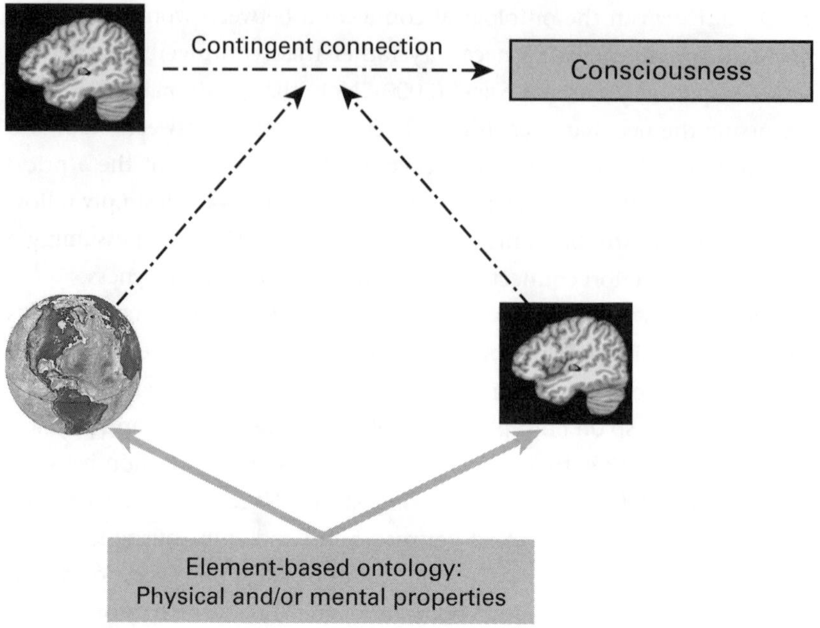

Figure 10.1
Contingency problem of connection between brain and consciousness.

problem is prevalent in both the empirical domain of neuroscience and the ontological domain of philosophy (see figure 10.1).

Contingency Problem IIb: Introduction of Mind—Mind–Body Problem

How can we resolve the contingency problem? One way to address the contingency problem is to claim that there just is a necessary connection between brain and consciousness, as posited by identity theory (see Searle, 2004, for an overview). However, the necessity of such a connection between brain and consciousness remains rather intuitive and hence problematic. To escape these problems, one may want to simply eliminate mental features on an ontological level, which renders superfluous and eliminates the contingency problem—this is the strategy suggested in eliminative materialism (Churchland, 1998). However, as with identity theory, such eliminative materialism remains at best intuitive and raises several problems by itself (see chapter 13 for extensive discussion). Therefore, without going into detail, both identity theory and eliminative materialism have to be discarded as feasible candidate answers to the contingency problem.

We may thus revert to the traditional way to address the contingency problem. We may want to go beyond brain/body themselves and introduce the concept of mind. Instead of the brain, the concept of mind can address the contingency problem: by its very definition as mind, the concept of mind shows a necessary rather than contingent connection to mental features such as consciousness, that is, the mind, unlike the brain, entails by default mental features in a necessary (a priori) way (see chapter 13 for more details on the concept of mind). The contingency problem between brain and consciousness is thus resolved by introducing the mind and its necessary a priori connection with consciousness (see figure 10.2).

Nothing is free, though. The introduction of the possible existence and reality of mind raises yet another question, namely, that of the mind's ontological relationship to the actual existence and reality of the body, including the brain, that is, the mind–body problem. Accordingly, the introduction of the concept of mind as an ontological (or metaphysical) basis of consciousness turns out to be a Pyrrhic victory. One solves one

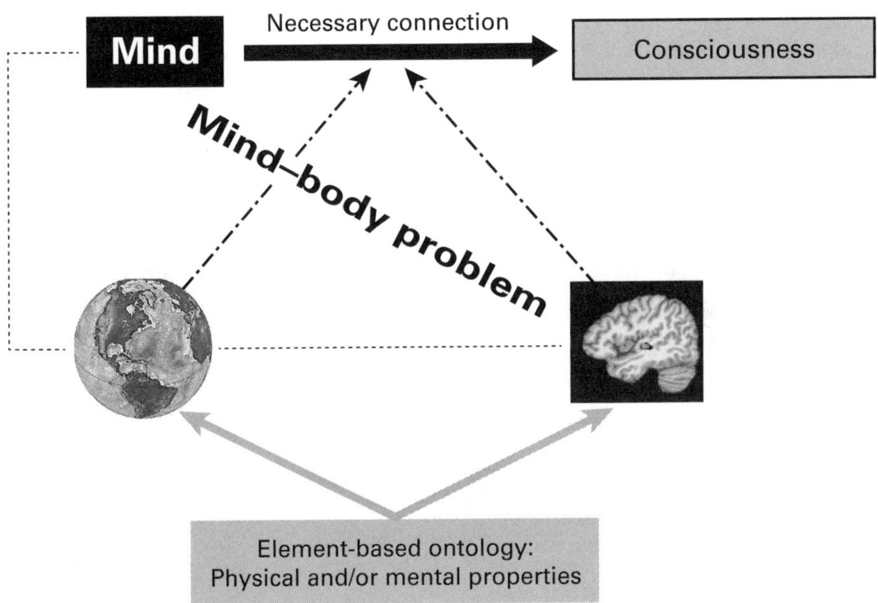

Figure 10.2
Contingency problem—necessary connection between mind and consciousness.

problem by introducing another one: it solves the contingency problem of a necessary connection between brain and consciousness by linking the latter to the mind, which introduces the mind–body problem.

How can we deal with this situation? One way is that one can now pursue the mind–body problem and discuss different solutions as is done in philosophy of mind. That, as I claim, cannot resolve its original birth defect though, namely, the shift from brain to mind for taking into view a necessary connection to consciousness. Alternatively, one may go back to brain and consciousness themselves and investigate how we can conceive their necessary connection in a way that is different from both identity theory and eliminative materialism (and related solutions)—that shall be the focus in the following.

Note that the concept of mind, as understood here, is not considered identical to or synonymous with the concept of consciousness or mental features. While both mind and mental features are necessarily and a priori connected with each other, that does nevertheless not entail that we cannot consider them separately and thus dissociate mental features from the concept of mind. That is, for instance, possible by showing a necessary connection of mental features to a concept that is different from that of mind—this is exactly the strategy I will pursue here.

Contingency Problem IIIa: Brain and Consciousness—Upward Spatiotemporal Entailment

Why is it so difficult to draw a necessary connection between brain and consciousness? Nagel, relying on Kripke, compares the relationship between brain and consciousness to that between H_2O and water. We can draw a necessary connection between H_2O and water while, because of their spatiotemporal differences, we remain unable to do so in the case of brain and consciousness. There is no upward entailment of consciousness by the brain as there is of water by H_2O.

Let us cite a quote by Nagel (2000):

> But to reach this conclusion, we must see that the behavior of H_2O provides a true and complete account, with nothing left—an approximate entailment—of the features that are conceptually essential to water, and that this account is in fact true of the water around us. *It is this "upward entailment" that is so difficult to imagine in the case of the corresponding psychophysical hypothesis, and that is the nub of the mind-body problem.* We understand the entailment of the liquidity of water by the behavior of

molecules through geometry, or more simply micro-macro or part-whole relation. Something analogous is true of every physical reduction even though the spatiotemporal framework can be very complicated and hard to grasp intuitively. But nothing like this will help us with the mind–body case, because we are not dealing here merely with larger and smaller grids. *We are dealing with a gap of a totally different kind, between the objective spatiotemporal order of the physical world and the subjective phenomenological order of experience. And here it seems clear in advance that no amount of physical information about the spatiotemporal order will entail anything of a subjective phenomenological character.* (p. 13; emphasis added)

Why is there a lack of upward entailment? Nagel argues that the objective spatiotemporal order of the physical world and the subjective phenomenological order of experience are different in principle when it comes to spatiotemporal features: the former is objective and spatiotemporal while the latter is subjective and phenomenological and thus nonspatiotemporal (if not aspatiotemporal; see above). This principal difference precludes their necessary connection, that is, the brain by default, cannot entail anything about consciousness, which renders their connection contingent rather than necessary.

Nagel formulates it very clearly. We can conceive upward entailment between H_2O and water while that remains impossible in the case of brain and consciousness. He argues that the objective spatiotemporal order of the physical world is in principle different from and does not entail the subjective phenomenal order of experience. I will argue that he is right and wrong at the same time.

Nagel is right in that our current definition of time and space in general, which conceives the brain's time and space in terms of the objective spatiotemporal order of the physical world, does indeed not allow us to consider upward entailment of consciousness by the brain. In contrast, Nagel is wrong in his assumption that both orders, that is, spatiotemporal and phenomenological, are mutually exclusive: once one presupposes a different concept of time and space, that is, relational rather than observational time and space, one can draw a necessary connection with upward entailment between brain and consciousness. I will argue that the lack of upward entailment between brain and consciousness is due to the way the brain is traditionally defined in ontological and, more specifically, spatiotemporal terms.

Contingency Problem IIIb: Ontological Redefinition of Brain—Structural Realism and Relational Time and Space

Traditionally, the brain is defined by physical properties as presupposed in element-based ontology (chapter 9). Such definition of the brain by physical properties goes hand in hand with its definition by space-time points or events as we can observe them—this amounts to the objective spatiotemporal order of the physical world Nagel refers to. Those very same space-time points or events define the brain (as well as the world) and its objective spatiotemporal order. Most important, they cannot be related to the space-time relation with relational time and space that characterize consciousness.

Unlike space-time points or events characterizing the supposed existence and reality of the brain (as part of the physical world), space-time relations as they signify consciousness cannot be observed. Because of their different spatiotemporal orders, that is, space-time points or events versus space-time relation, brain and consciousness cannot be connected to each other in a necessary way. Instead, brain and consciousness can spatiotemporally only be connected in a contingent way—the brain's time and space (i.e., space-time points or events) do not entail consciousness (i.e., space-time relation) in an upward way in the way H_2O entails water. Accordingly, lack of upward spatiotemporal entailment (as I say) of consciousness by the brain renders impossible their necessary connection.

However, that changes once one ontologically defines time and space of the brain in a different way. Now the brain's existence and reality are no longer defined by physical properties with space-time points or events but rather by a relation with space-time that intrinsically relates the brain to the world (i.e., world–brain relation; chapter 12). Instead of presupposing element-based ontology with space-time points or events and observational time and space, one may rather define the brain by relation-based ontology, that is, OSR with world–brain relation and space-time relation with relational time and space.

Contingency Problem IIIc: Ontological Redefinition of Brain—Necessary Connection to Consciousness in Terms of Upward Spatiotemporal Entailment

How does such determination of the brain by world–brain relation change our view on the connection between brain and consciousness? The world–brain relation is featured by space-time relation rather than space-time points or events. That puts the world–brain relation on the same spatiotemporal and ultimately ontological ground as consciousness that, as in the spatiotemporal model outlined above, can also be defined by space-time relation. If so, the world–brain relation entails consciousness in an upward way in the same way H_2O entails water—one can thus speak of *upward spatiotemporal entailment*. Upward spatiotemporal entailment implies that world–brain relation is necessarily (a posteriori) connected to consciousness.

So far, I have only demonstrated a necessary (a posteriori) connection between world–brain relation and consciousness. In contrast, I left open a necessary connection between brain and consciousness. That is easy though. As the brain is ontologically defined by world–brain relation (chapter 9), the latter's necessary connection to consciousness implies a necessary connection of the brain to consciousness. We must thus presuppose relational, and, more specifically, ontic structural realist, determination of the brain to conceive its necessary connection to consciousness. If, in contrast, one presupposes element-based ontology with ontological determination of the brain by either physical or mental properties, the necessary relation of the brain to the world (i.e., world–brain relation) will no longer be conceivable; that, in turn, renders it impossible to take into view a necessary connection between brain and consciousness, which then remains contingent by default (see figure 10.3).

In sum, the contingency problem of a necessary connection between brain and consciousness can be resolved without reverting to the concept of mind. This is possible by presupposing a different ontological determination of brain, that is, relation-based rather than element-based ontology, and a different concept of time and space, that is, relational rather than observational time and space (which distinguishes my approach from both identity theory and eliminative materialism and related theories). The ontological determination of brain in terms of both relation-based ontology and relational time and space makes it possible to conceive its necessary rather than contingent connection to consciousness: consciousness and its relational time and space are entailed by the brain's relational time and space, including their relation to the world's time and space—this amounts to upward spatiotemporal entailment between brain and consciousness.

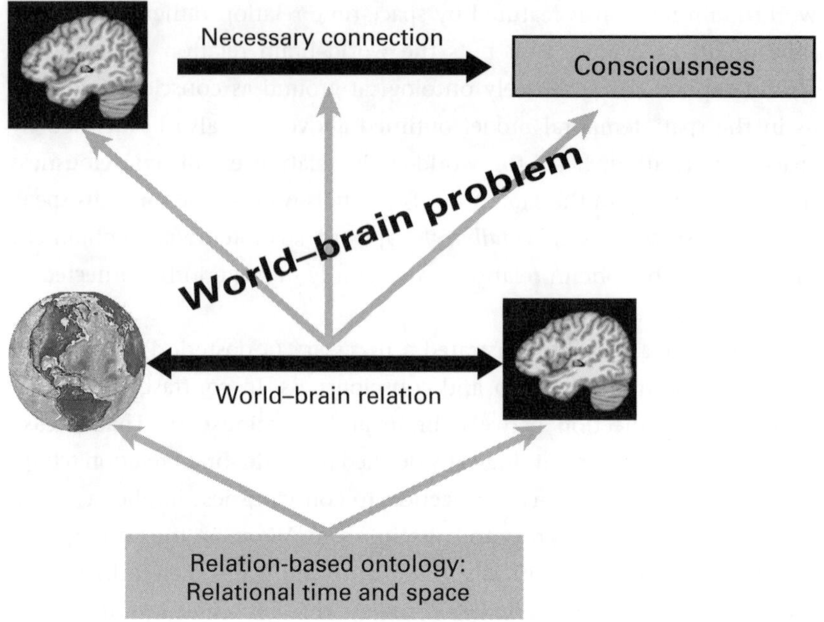

Figure 10.3
Contingency problem—necessary connection between brain and consciousness.

Such an ontological redefinition of the brain fits well with Nagel, who argues in exactly this way, namely that we need to shift our conceptual (or ontological) definitions in order to account for the necessary (a posteriori) connection between two concepts (such as brain and consciousness) that otherwise seem to be merely contingently (a posteriori) connected:

> The greatest scientific progress occurs through conceptual change which permits empirically observed order that initially appears contingent (a posteriori) to be understood at a deeper level as necessary (a posteriori), in the sense of being entailed by the true nature of the phenomena. (Nagel, 2000, p. 22)

Contingency Problem IVa: Criteria of Necessity—Spatiotemporal Fit into the World

What are the criteria that must be met and fulfilled for that connection to be necessary? For that, I turn again to Nagel, who touches on the question of such criteria for the necessary (rather than contingent) character of the ontological (rather than merely empirical) connection between mental features and their potential ontological origin, that is, ontic origin. I will focus on three such criteria: spatiotemporal fit into the world, transparency through world–brain relation, and spatiotemporal subjectivity.

The first criterion consists in what I call *spatiotemporal fit* into the world. I discuss how the existence and reality of world can be characterized by space and time (chapters 9 and 11). At the same time, we are part of that very same world and its spatiotemporal features—I demonstrated that that becomes possible by means of our brain: our brain relates us to the world (i.e., world–brain relation) by means of which we become part of that very same world.

How is it possible for the world–brain relation to integrate us into the world such that we become part of the wider world? Since the world is by itself spatiotemporal, the world–brain relation must allow for linking and integrating the brain within the world's time and space, that is, its relational time and space (chapter 9). The brain must thus relate to the world's relational time and space in a spatiotemporal way by establishing spatiotemporal relation with the world—the world–brain relation is intrinsically spatiotemporal, that is, it is defined by its spatiotemporal features without which it would not exist.

The world–brain relation integrates us into the world by spatializing and temporalizing us and our existence as part of the wider spatiotemporal scale of the world. Taken in this sense, the brain and its relation to the world (i.e., world–brain relation) can be taken as marker of our fit into the world, a *spatiotemporal fit into the world,* as I say. Such spatiotemporal fit into the world comes close to what Nagel (2012) describes as "*systematic understanding of how we and other living things fit into the world*" (p. 128); this is also well expressed in the following quote:

> The hope is not to discover a foundation that makes our knowledge unassailably secure but to find a way of understanding ourselves that is not radically self-undermining, and that does not require us to deny the obvious. The aim would be to offer a plausible picture of *how we fit into the world.* (Nagel, 2012, p. 25; emphasis added)

How does this spatiotemporal fit into the world establish a necessary ontological connection between world–brain relation and consciousness? The world itself can ontologically be characterized by relational time and space (chapter 9), which also characterizes the brain and its relation to the world (i.e., world–brain relation). As the world–brain relation is a necessary

OPC, consciousness itself must be characterized by relational time and space and thus "fit" spatiotemporally into the world. Spatiotemporal fit of consciousness into the world consequently entails a necessary connection between world–brain relation and consciousness—the former can thus be regarded as a criterion of the latter.

Contingency Problem IVb: Criteria of Necessity—Third Shared and Commonly Underlying Feature

The critic, however, may not want to relent yet. The spatiotemporal fit of consciousness into the world characterizes consciousness as spatiotemporal. However, the assumption of the spatiotemporal nature of consciousness conflicts with our preconception that mental features are aspatial and atemporal, which distinguishes them from physical features that are spatial and temporal (see chapter 13 for a more detailed discussion of this point).

The critic may thus want to argue that we lose the distinction of mental features from physical features by characterizing them in a spatiotemporal way. To escape the critic's argument, we need to show how consciousness and mental features in general can be spatiotemporal rather than aspatial and atemporal without collapsing them into physical features. Importantly, that argument needs to concern specifically mental features themselves and must thus be separate from the argument for the spatiotemporal nature of world–brain relation as OPC.

How can we provide such argument for the spatiotemporal nature of mental features? When conceiving mental and physical features themselves, we cannot but state their essential difference in spatiotemporal terms. Physical features can be observed in time and space, entailing observational time and space (chapter 9). In contrast, mental features cannot be observed at all in time and space—consciousness can neither be observed in the brain nor elsewhere. Mental features show neither any spatial extension nor temporal duration—they are aspatial and atemporal. As spatiotemporal and aspatial/atemporal features are mutually exclusive, physical and mental features are not compatible with each other. This, in turn, makes it impossible to draw a necessary ontological connection between physical and mental features.

How can we establish a necessary ontological connection between physical and mental features? Because of spatiotemporal discrepancy between physical and mental features, claims of a necessary and direct connection between brain and consciousness as in identity theory and eliminative materialism (and related suggestions) remain at best intuitive. As a direct way seems to be impossible for spatiotemporal reasons (and others; see chapter 13), we may want to search for indirect ways. Nagel suggests exactly that. He proposes that we may want to seek some third feature that is shared between and thus commonly underlies both mental and physical features:

> What will be the point of view, so to speak, of such theory? If we could arrive at it, it would render transparent the relation between mental and physical, not directly, but through the *transparency of their common relation to something* that is not merely either of them. (Nagel, 2000, p. 45; emphasis added)

I now postulate that the third shared and commonly underlying feature, as I describe it, consists in world–brain relation and its spatiotemporal features. Following Nagel, I now need to show that world–brain relation provides a common relation, that is, a necessary ontological connection, to both brain (as placeholder for what Nagel describes as "physical") and consciousness (as placeholder for what Nagel describes as "mental"). That, in turn, renders transparent the necessary ontological connection between brain and consciousness, that is, the relation between mental and physical.

Contingency Problem IVc: Criteria of Necessity—Spatiotemporal Transparency through World–Brain Relation

I argue that world–brain relation is an ideal candidate to account for such third shared and commonly underlying feature in the sense of Nagel. Let me explicate that in the following.

I demonstrated that the brain is necessarily connected to world–brain relation (chapter 9). The existence and reality of brain are necessarily dependent upon its relation to the world—without world–brain relation, the brain simply does not exist and is not real. There is thus a necessary (a posteriori) ontological connection between brain and world–brain relation. Thereby, the emphasis is put on relation (as in world–brain relation), which precludes equivocation of the concept of brain as included in both "brain" and "world–brain relation." The same holds with regard to consciousness and mental features. I showed in this chapter that mental features such as consciousness are necessarily dependent upon world–brain relation—the world–brain relation is an OPC.

The world–brain relation shows a necessary ontological connection with both brain and consciousness. This makes the world–brain relation an ideal ontological candidate for the third shared and commonly underlying feature (in the sense of Nagel) as it is shared between and commonly underlies both brain and consciousness. Following Nagel, this renders transparent the necessary ontological connection between brain and consciousness on spatiotemporal grounds: as both are based on world–brain relation, brain and consciousness share the former's relational time and space, which renders transparent their necessary ontological connection within that very same relational time and space. I consequently claim that the necessary ontological connection between brain and consciousness, that is, between physical and mental features, becomes transparent by conceiving world–brain relation—I thus speak of the *transparency of brain–consciousness connection through world–brain relation.*

If, in contrast, one neglects world–brain relation (as in both identity theory and eliminative materialism), one can only apply observational time and space, which renders opaque the necessary ontological connection between brain and mental features on spatiotemporal grounds: the brain can now be determined only by observational time and space while mental features are then characterized as aspatial and atemporal in order to distinguish them from physical features and the brain. In that case, transparency is replaced by opacity of the relation between brain and consciousness—the *transparency of brain–consciousness connection through world–brain relation* is here replaced by *opacity of brain–consciousness connection.*

The critic may now want to argue that the claim of transparency of brain–consciousness connection through world–brain relation does indeed provide an answer to Nagel's question. However, it does not provide an answer to the critic's argument, that is, the spatiotemporal nature of mental features as distinct from physical features. That can be addressed easily though.

World–brain relation can be characterized by space and time and, more specifically, relational time and space as distinguished from observational time and space (see above and chapter 9). By being necessarily connected to world–brain relation, mental features are ontologically connected to relational time and space and must therefore be characterized in this way—mental features are spatiotemporal in terms of relational time and space. That distinguishes them from physical features that are characterized by observational time and space. For instance, the phenomenal features of consciousness such as qualia, intentionality, and so forth may then be determined by relational time and space (see Northoff, 2014b, for details).

We can now address the critic's argument. We are well able to characterize mental features in spatiotemporal terms in such way that distinguishes them from both physical features and aspatial/atemporal features. Hence, the world–brain relation "renders transparent" not only the necessary ontological connection between brain and consciousness but also the spatiotemporal nature of mental features in terms of relational time and space—I therefore speak of *spatiotemporal transparency through world–brain relation.*

The critic neglects the possibility of such spatiotemporal transparency through world–brain relation. Therefore, both the necessary ontological connection between brain and consciousness as well as the spatiotemporal nature of mental features remain opaque to her or him and cannot be rendered transparent. According to Nagel (as implied by the first sentence of his quote), the critic simply applies the "wrong" point of view. What does the "right" point of view look like? That, as I suggest in later chapters, requires nothing less than a Copernican revolution in neuroscience and philosophy (chapters 12–14).

Part III: Ontology of Consciousness—World–Brain Problem

World–Brain Problem Ia: Subjectivity and Spatiotemporal Structure

The critic may not be satisfied yet though. The hardest nut to crack with regard to the existence and reality of consciousness and mental features is their subjectivity (Nagel, 1974; Searle, 2004). Mental features are intrinsically subjective, which distinguishes them from physical features that are nonsubjective and thus objective. How is it possible that something as subjective as consciousness or other mental features can occur in a world characterized by brains and bodies that are objective rather than subjective?

What does the quest for subjectivity imply for world–brain relation and its spatiotemporal features? If the world–brain relation serves as OPC, it must also provide the necessary condition of the subjective nature of consciousness and mental features in general. The spatiotemporal features of world–brain relation must thus predispose the subjective nature of consciousness. There must thus be an intrinsic linkage, that is, a necessary ontological connection between spatiotemporal and subjective features in world–brain relation.

The necessity of such intrinsic linkage between spatiotemporal and subjective features is well reflected in the following quote by Nagel (2000):

> The right point of view would be one which, contrary to present conceptual possibilities, *included both subjectivity and spatiotemporal structure from the outset,* all its descriptions implying both these things at once, so that it could describe inner states and their functional relations to behavior and to one another from the *phenomenological inside and the physiological outside simultaneously*—not in parallel. (pp. 45–46; emphasis added)

Extending Nagel, I now argue that such intrinsic linkage, that is, a necessary ontological connection between subjectivity and spatiotemporal structure is included "from the outset" in the ontological concept of world–brain relation. My argument includes two steps. I first determine the concept of subjectivity in a novel way, that is, in spatiotemporal terms (in a brief way though without going into the myriads of literature on this topic). That, in turn, serves as a basis for the second step, that is, showing the necessary ontological connection between subjectivity and spatiotemporal structure within world–brain relation, including the necessary connection to mental features. Let me start with the first step, the determination of subjectivity.

World–Brain Problem Ib: Spatiotemporal Subjectivity versus Mental Subjectivity

We traditionally determine subjectivity in reference to mental features such as consciousness—everything that is mental is subjective as distinguished from that which is nonmental and thus objective rather than subjective. When determining the concept of subjectivity, we usually presuppose (most often in an implicit and tacit way) consciousness and mental features and, more generally, the mind as such as our reference, that is, as epistemic reference (see chapters 12–14 for more detailed determination of this concept). This renders subjectivity by default mental—I therefore speak of mental subjectivity. This, for instance, renders it rather paradoxical if not incoherent to determine something that is nonmental and observable like the brain as subjective. Hence, mental subjectivity is the wrong frame or epistemic reference to characterize the brain in a subjective way.

How about taking the world itself and its spatiotemporal features rather than mental features as the epistemic reference for determining the concept of subjectivity? In that case, we no longer reference subjectivity against mental features and the mind but, alternatively, compare and set it against the spatiotemporal framework of the world. For instance, when comparing the smaller spatiotemporal scale or range of both world–brain relation and brain against the much larger one of the world itself (i.e., independent of world–brain relation and brain), the former can be characterized as subjective when compared to the objective nature of the latter.

Subjectivity is here determined on spatiotemporal grounds, that is, in reference to the spatiotemporal scale or range of the world itself. Such spatiotemporal determination of subjectivity can be described as *spatiotemporal subjectivity*. The concept of spatiotemporal subjectivity determines subjectivity on purely spatiotemporal rather than mental grounds for which reason it must be distinguished from mental subjectivity. Specifically, spatiotemporal subjectivity is determined on the grounds of *spatiotemporal discrepancy* to the world that is objective (on spatiotemporal grounds) and therefore serves as an epistemic reference for determining spatiotemporal subjectivity.

The concept of spatiotemporal subjectivity fulfills Nagel's requirement of a concept that "included both subjectivity and spatiotemporal structure from the outset, all its descriptions implying both these things at once." Let me specify that in both directions, from space and time to subjectivity as well as from the latter to the former.

The concept of "spatiotemporal" in spatiotemporal subjectivity refers to relational time and space (chapter 9). As it is relational, relational time and space imply relation between world and its parts such as the brain (i.e., world–brain relation), which show different, that is, smaller, spatiotemporal scales or ranges than the world itself. Relational time and space thus imply what I described as spatiotemporal discrepancy. As spatiotemporal discrepancy defines spatiotemporal subjectivity, relational time and space and, more specifically, their "spatiotemporal structure" (to use Nagel's term) cannot but include spatiotemporal subjectivity right from the outset.

What about the reverse, namely, that spatiotemporal subjectivity includes time and space, that is, spatiotemporal structure, from the outset?

When setting and comparing subjectivity against mental features and mind as the epistemic reference, we cannot draw any necessary connection to spatiotemporal features. Since the mind is traditionally determined in an aspatial and atemporal way (see above and chapter 13), mental subjectivity is not conceived in spatiotemporal terms at all and therefore shows no necessary connection to spatiotemporal features.

That changes once one shifts the epistemic reference from mind to world though. As the world itself can be characterized by time and space, we can now set and compare subjectivity against the spatiotemporal features of the world, that is, relational time and space, including its respective spatiotemporal scale or range. That renders transparent the necessary connection between subjectivity, that is, spatiotemporal subjectivity, and time and space, that is, relational time and space. This, in turn, makes it possible that, unlike the concept of mental subjectivity, spatiotemporal subjectivity (as in its name) includes reference to time and space right "from the outset."

World–Brain Problem Ic: Spatiotemporal Subjectivity as Necessary Condition of Mental Subjectivity

The critic may now want to argue that I showed very well the necessary connection between subjectivity and spatiotemporal structure as it is suggested by Nagel. In contrast, I have not shown that the necessary connection between subjectivity and spatiotemporal structure is related to both world–brain relation and mental features. This is the easy part, which leads me to the second part of my argument, the hard part.

World–brain relation is essentially spatiotemporal—it consists in the spatiotemporal relation between the world's larger spatiotemporal range and the smaller one of the brain. That includes spatiotemporal discrepancy and therefore entails spatiotemporal subjectivity (see above). Hence, when compared to the world itself, that is, independent of its relation to the brain, world–brain relation cannot be but subjective (rather than objective) in a spatiotemporal sense. In short, world–brain relation entails and can therefore be characterized by spatiotemporal subjectivity.

How is the spatiotemporal subjectivity of world–brain relation related to mental features and their mental subjectivity? I showed that world–brain relation provides the necessary OPC which is possible on spatiotemporal grounds (see above). I now argue that world–brain relation can provide the OPC by means of the subjective nature of its spatiotemporal features (i.e., spatiotemporal subjectivity). Because its spatiotemporal features are subjective (in a spatiotemporal sense), the world–brain relation can predispose the mental subjectivity of consciousness and mental features.

World–Brain Problem Id: Self-Mediation between Spatiotemporal Subjectivity and Mental Subjectivity

Without providing a separate argument, I postulate that the relationship between spatiotemporal and mental subjectivity is mediated by the self: the self is intrinsically relational (as based on world–brain relation), spatiotemporal (as based on relational time and space), and subjective (as based on spatiotemporal subjectivity; see Northoff, 2016, 2017, for the concept of self in the realm of neuroscience). At the same time, the self is not necessarily mental, that is, conscious or experienced as such, while it enables consciousness—the self is thus preconscious or prephenomenal (or protoconscious, as philosophers might want to say) rather than nonconscious or nonphenomenal (see Northoff, 2014b, for the concept of prephenomenal). This makes the self an ideal candidate to mediate between spatiotemporal and mental subjectivity by providing the bridge between the nonphenomenal world and the phenomenal consciousness of a specific subject with its mental subjectivity.

In sum, I postulate that the spatiotemporal subjectivity of world–brain relation is a necessary condition of its role as OPC, which, through mediation by the self, makes possible mental subjectivity. Put simply, spatiotemporal subjectivity of world–brain relation is an ontological predisposition of mental subjectivity. This makes it possible for world–brain relation to simultaneously (rather than in parallel) predispose "the phenomenological inside and the physiological outside" (as described by Nagel, 2000, quoted above) of mental features: both "phenomenological inside" and "physiological outside" can be traced to one and the same underlying spatiotemporal structure, that is, relational time and space, that features world–brain relation by spatiotemporal subjectivity.

Finally, note that the concept of spatiotemporal subjectivity is tied neither to a first-person perspective (FPP) nor to a second- or third-person perspective (SPP, TPP). True, mental subjectivity can be featured by FPP and physical objectivity by TPP. However, as it provides the basis for both, including their distinction, spatiotemporal subjectivity itself cannot be characterized by either FPP or TPP as it would be to confuse the necessary condition with what it conditions. Instead, spatiotemporal subjectivity as based on world–brain relation is by itself nonperspectival or preperspectival as it provides the necessary ontological condition of possible epistemic distinction between FPP and TPP.

This carries major reverberations for consciousness. As I characterize consciousness by spatiotemporal subjectivity, consciousness itself cannot be characterized by either FPP or TPP—FPP only provides the epistemic access to consciousness that ontologically remains nonperspectival (or preperspectival). Hence, to characterize consciousness by FPP (or TPP) is to confuse ontological (i.e., non- or preperspectival) and epistemic determination of consciousness (which I would, for instance, charge against the distinction between first- and third-person ontology as suggested by Searle, 2004).

World–Brain Problem IIa: Brain—Subjective or Objective?

The critic may now be inclined to argue that the ontological redefinition of the brain in terms of world–brain relation renders the brain subjective and conscious rather than objective and nonconscious. The only way for the brain to account for its necessary connection to consciousness is that the brain is by itself subjective and conscious. Otherwise, following Nagel, the brain could not bridge the gap between objective spatiotemporal order and subjective phenomenological order. However, the ontological characterization of the brain as subjective entails some sort of panpsychism, which ultimately would undermine my own approach in terms of OSR.

Such an ontological determination of the brain as subjective and conscious has indeed been assumed by some authors. These include the nineteenth-century philosopher Arthur Schopenhauer, who spoke of the brain as subjective (Schopenhauer, 1818–1819/1966), and more recently Colin McGinn (1991), who assumes specific mental properties in the brain. Finally, Nagel himself seems to tend in this direction when speaking of a "conscious brain" (Nagel, 1993, p. 6). The concept of a conscious brain is also somewhat entailed by John Searle (2004) in his concept of first-person ontology (as distinguished from third-person ontology), even though he does not explicitly characterize the brain itself as conscious or subjective (Searle, 2004): first-person ontology accounts for the FPP of consciousness (see chapter 8 for discussion of FPP vs. TPP with regard to consciousness) and its underlying neuronal mechanisms in the brain that thereby must be subjective and conscious (or at least pre- or proto-conscious).

I reject any such ontological definition of the brain as subjective and/or conscious (or as given by first-person perspective as related to first-person ontology). The ontological redefinition of the brain in terms of world–brain relation can be considered neither subjective nor objective. It pertains to neither the objective spatiotemporal order nor the subjective phenomenological order. That, as I argue, would be to confuse the world–brain relation as a necessary condition, that is, as an OPC, with what it conditions, that is, the brain as we observe it within the objective spatiotemporal order and its necessary connection to and upward spatiotemporal entailment of consciousness as featured by its subjective phenomenological order. Let me explain in more detail.

To regard the brain as either subjective and conscious or as objective and nonconscious is to simply confuse world–brain relation and brain on ontological grounds. The brain's existence and reality can only be defined by its relation to the world, the world–brain relation (chapter 9). If one now conceives the brain by itself, that is, as separate and detached from the world (as when characterizing it as subjective and conscious), one replaces world–brain relation by what can ontologically be described as *world–brain isolation*. Such world–brain isolation is possible only by presupposing a particular conception of time and space though: the brain could then longer be defined by space-time relation with relational time and space but only by space-time points or events as in observational time and space.

World–Brain Problem IIb: Brain Paradox—Dissolution

The characterization of the brain in terms of world–brain isolation provides the necessary condition of the possible distinction between world and brain and their subsequent characterization as objective and subjective: the world is objective while the brain is subjective and as both are isolated from each other, there is no necessary connectivity between objective physical and subjective mental features. The isolation between world and brain thus entails the dissociation and segregation between objectivity and subjectivity including their determination as physical and mental.

Moreover, world–brain isolation provides the presupposition for the "brain paradox" (Northoff, 2004; Schopenhauer, 1818–1819/1966). In a nutshell, the brain paradox consists in the fact that one and the same brain cannot be objective (i.e., physical) and subjective (i.e., mental) at the same time. Because both determinations of the brain, that is, subjective/conscious and objective/nonconscious, are opposite and mutually exclusive, the connection between subjective/conscious and objective/nonconscious brain remains contingent by default. The mind–body problem thus resurfaces in what can be called the *brain–brain problem*, the problem of the relationship between subjective and objective brain.

We can avoid both the brain paradox and the brain–brain problem by shifting our ontological presuppositions. Instead of presupposing world–brain isolation as based on element- or property-based ontology (chapter 9), one can account for world–brain relation as based on OSR. The latter renders impossible any segregation between world and brain, including the brain paradox, while it makes possible the introduction of spatiotemporal subjectivity. The brain can then ontologically be characterized by spatiotemporal subjectivity as based on its spatiotemporal relation to the (spatiotemporally) objective world, the world–brain relation.

This undermines the paradoxical dichotomy between subjective/conscious and objective/physical brain by putting it into the larger spatiotemporal framework of world and world–brain relation. That, in turn, makes it possible to dissolve the brain paradox: the characterization of the brain as both subjective and objective is at best epistemic or even better empirical but not ontological anymore—the paradoxical nature of double determination of the brain is thus dissolved.

World–Brain Problem IIIa: World–Brain Relation—Ontological Predisposition of Consciousness

I demonstrated two necessary connections, the one between world and brain (i.e., world–brain relation), as well as the one between brain and consciousness through world–brain relation and its spatiotemporal subjectivity. Moreover, I argued that the second necessary connection, that is, the one between world–brain relation and consciousness, is based on the first one, that is, the necessary connection between world and brain in terms of world–brain relation. This was specifically reflected in the assumption that mental subjectivity is based on and presupposes spatiotemporal subjectivity.

This carries major implications for consciousness. Taken both necessary connections together, this amounts to the claim that the necessary (a posteriori) connection between world and brain (i.e., world–brain relation) is a necessary ontological condition of possible consciousness. Formulated in a converse way, without the necessary (a posteriori) connection between world and brain (i.e., the world–brain relation), consciousness remains altogether impossible. Therefore, world–brain relation is a necessary condition of possible consciousness, an OPC, as I say.

How can we describe the notion of ontological predisposition in more detail? The notion of predisposition in OPC refers to the necessary (rather than sufficient) ontological conditions of possible (rather than actual) consciousness (i.e., OPC). Conceived in this way, the concept of predisposition mirrors to a certain extent Kant's concept of the transcendental as distinguished from the empirical. Following Kant (in in a loose sense), transcendental conditions (i) cannot be directly accessed, (ii) operate in the background and are, at the same time, (iii) indispensable. That holds well for the world–brain relation: (i) it cannot be accessed as such in a direct way but only indirectly, (ii) it remains in the background, and (iii) it is nevertheless indispensable for the existence and reality of consciousness. I consequently postulate that the world–brain relation is a necessary condition of possible consciousness (i.e., OPC) by means of which it takes on a transcendental role (in the sense of Kant) or, as I would say, a neurotranscendental role.

World–Brain Problem IIIb: World–Brain Relation as OPC—Panpsychism or Neutral Monism?

The critic may now want to argue that the introduction of world–brain relation as OPC implies panpsychism (Strawson, 2016) or, at least, proto-panpsychism (Chalmers, 1996). Briefly, the world–brain relation can only serve as OPC if the world can be characterized by the existence and reality of some kind of psychic elements or properties or, at least, psychic proto-properties. Otherwise, in the absence of such psychic properties in the world, the world–brain relation could not serve as OPC. I reject the assumption of panpsychism, however.

The advocate of panpsychism is certainly right that the world itself must show certain ontological features that make possible and ultimately necessary its relation to the brain, the world–brain relation. However, those ontological features do not need to be psychic or proto-psychic elements by themselves. That would mean to take something as a sufficient ontological condition of actual consciousness (i.e., ontological correlate of consciousness; OCC) that is only a necessary condition of possible consciousness (i.e., OPC). Instead, the world and its relation to the brain only need to provide those spatiotemporal features that predispose or make possible consciousness—neither the world nor world–brain relation are conscious by themselves. As we will see in the next chapter (chapter 11), in more detail, we can indeed ontologically define the world by spatiotemporal features that predispose consciousness.

Most importantly, these spatiotemporal features entail relational time and space, which goes hand in hand with relation-based ontology (chapter 9). Relation-based ontology stands square to the panpsychist or proto-psychic assumption of psychic or proto-psychic properties or elements. Therefore, the assumption of world–brain relation as OPC is not compatible with any form of panpsychism or proto-psychism. Instead, one may rather want to ontologically presuppose what I describe as spatiotemporalism of world and world–brain relation. Such spatiotemporalism can, ontologically, be considered as a necessary condition of possible consciousness (i.e., an OPC).

The assumption of world–brain relation as OPC bears some superficial similarity to yet another approach in the realm of possible mind–body relation, that is, neutral monism (NM). NM assumes that mind and body can ontologically be traced to some more basic and fundamental ontological existence and reality that are neutral, that is, they are neither mental nor physical by themselves. The proponent of NM may now be inclined to argue that my concept of world–brain relation can be considered a candidate for such neutral ontological basis: the world–brain relation provides the OPC while, at the same time, it is closely related to physical features.

The analogy to NM is only superficial though as there are some basic differences. First, the assumption of such neutral ontological basis in NM provides the answer to the question of how we can link mind and body. That is different in my case. The world–brain relation and its role as OPC provides the answer to the question of the existence and reality of consciousness and mental features. Hence, NM still presupposes the concept of mind whereas that is no longer the case in world–brain relation.

The difference in starting point, that is, presupposition versus nonpresupposition of mind, carries major implications. Because it still presupposes the (possible existence and reality of) mind, NM must provide a necessary relation of the neutral ontological basis to both mind and body. That is no longer necessary in my case. There is no need to provide a necessary connection of world–brain relation to the mind as the latter is simply no longer presupposed. Moreover, unlike in NM, the relationship to the body is already entailed in world–brain relation as the body is part of the world for the brain (chapter 8 for details). Taken together, this relieves the world–brain relation of establishing a necessary connection to both mind and body, which is one of the major puzzles in NM. Therefore, the similarity of my assumption of world–brain relation as OPC with NM is at best superficial with major differences becoming apparent once one compares both in more depth.

World–Brain Problem IVa: Mind–Body Problem versus World–Brain Problem

The ontological redefinition of the brain in terms of world–brain relation carries far-reaching implications for the concept of mind and subsequently the mind–body problem. We recall the concept of mind was introduced to address the question of the lacking necessary connection between brain/body and consciousness (or mental features in general). (See chapter 13.)

To establish a necessary connection of consciousness (and mental features in general) to its underlying ontological substrate, philosophers introduced the concept of mind: they assumed the possible existence and reality of mind that is connected necessarily and a priori to consciousness (and to mental features in general). However, that turned out to be a Pyrrhic victory. While solving one problem, that is, that of the necessary connection between body/brain and consciousness, another one was created, that is, that of the ontological relationship between mind and body, the mind–body problem.

I now argue that the concept of mind becomes superfluous for establishing a necessary connection to consciousness and mental features as this role can be taken over by world–brain relation. The world–brain relation is an OPC. As an OPC, the world–brain relation makes possible consciousness, implying that neither world alone nor the brain itself could account for a necessary connection to consciousness. Therefore, to understand the necessary (a posteriori) ontological connection between brain and consciousness, we need to go back to the relationship between world and brain (the world–brain relation).

This shifts the ontological focus away from the mind–body problem to a novel problem that I call the *world–brain problem*. We need to understand the relation between world and brain (the world–brain relation) to account for the necessary (a posteriori) ontological connection between brain and consciousness. Specifically, we first need to investigate the necessary ontological connection between world and brain to understand the necessary connection between world–brain relation and consciousness. Therefore, I speak of a world–brain problem that must be raised to address the question of the existence and reality of consciousness and mental features. As such, the world–brain problem renders the mind–body problem simply superfluous as the question raised by the latter can well be addressed by the former.

World–Brain Problem IVb: World–Brain Problem—Brain–World Problem?

What is the world–brain problem? The world–brain problem is an ontological problem that concerns the ontological relationship between world and brain. Specifically, the world–brain problem concerns the question of how the existence and reality of the world are related to those of the brain. The concepts of world and brain are understood in a strictly ontological sense rather than either an epistemic or an empirical sense: the world–brain problem is about existence and reality of world and brain rather than our knowledge or observation as related to either world or brain. The world–brain problem is thus about the ontological rather than epistemic or empirical relationship between world and brain.

The world–brain problem as ontological problem intentionally puts the terms *world* and *brain* in this sequence, as distinguished from *brain–world problem*. The brain is part of the world as a whole. Conceived in purely logical–conceptual terms, the assumption that the brain is part of the world as a whole comes close to trivial as there is no brain outside or beyond the world (see below for more details on the argument of triviality). This changes once one conceives their relationship in empirical and ontological terms, however. Instead of mere passive entailment on a logical–conceptual basis, there are active construction processes, both empirically and ontologically, that first and foremost make it possible for the brain to become part of the world as a whole. Using a term from Sellars (1963), the brain as part of the world as a whole is not a "given" (Sellars 1963, p. 128).

Empirically, such active construction processes were, for instance, manifest in specific coding mechanisms, that is, difference-based coding (chapter 2), and spatiotemporal mechanisms such as spatiotemporal alignment of the brain's rhythmic structure to the one of the world (chapter 8). While ontologically, such active construction is provided by differences de re that constitute relation and structure with relational time and space (chapter 9) which make possible integration of the brain as a part within the world as a whole. If one were now locating these active construction processes within the brain itself, one would indeed better change the sequence of terms and speak of the brain–world problem rather than the world–brain problem. That is not the case, though. Relation and structure as postulated in OSR operate across the observational divide between world and brain by aligning and integrating the latter as part (i.e., brain) within the former as a whole (i.e., world). Therefore, ontologically conceived, we would better speak of the world–brain problem rather than the brain–world problem.

While the concept of world–brain problem is ontological, the reverse sequence as in brain–world problem may be understood in epistemic and empirical terms. The brain–world problem may epistemically concern how we can obtain knowledge of the world on the basis of our brain on the basis of first-, second-, and/or third-person perspective. Empirically, the brain–world problem describes the various ways in which our brain can process and interact with events in the world (chapter 2). As my main focus in this book is on the ontological question of the relationship between brain and consciousness, I concentrate on the world–brain problem while, in contrast, I leave open the epistemic issues related to the brain–world problem.

The critic may now want to argue that the world–brain problem may be just a mereological problem about the relationship between whole and part rather than being a genuine ontological problem. I reject that argument though. True, the brain is indeed part of the world as a whole. However, OSR defines the world by relation and structure that, by definition, include its parts such as the brain in a necessary (a posteriori) way.

As that very same connection remains contingent when one presupposes element-based ontology, the world–brain problem is not just merely mereological but concerns a much deeper ontological problem (see chapters 13 and 14 for discussion of mereological issues). Specifically, the world–brain problem raises the question of how relation and structure must be defined such that they can link world and brain necessarily, in such a way that their relation entails consciousness and mental features. Therefore, the question of world–brain relation is not just a mereological question but rather a basic ontological issue about relation and structure and, more generally, relationship.

World–Brain Problem IVc: World–Brain Problem—Two Halves

That is only half of the world–brain problem, however. The other half consists in the question of the existence and reality of mental features such as consciousness—that shall be explicated in the following.

What must the ontological relationship between world and brain be like to serve as an OPC? I argued that the characterization of the ontological relationship between world and brain in terms of elements (i.e., element-based ontology) is not plausible. Specifically, the definition of world and brain in terms of element-based ontology leaves the connection between brain and consciousness contingent (see above) and therefore fails to account for the existence and reality of consciousness. Therefore, defined by element-based ontology, neither the world nor the brain alone (nor their mere combination or addition) can serve as OPC. Instead, we need to presuppose an alternative ontology, that is, relation-based ontology (i.e., OSR), where structure and relation (rather than elements) constitute world and brain including their relation (i.e., world–brain relation). That allows for the necessary connection between world–brain relation and consciousness with the former serving as OPC.

Taken together, I suppose that the ontological redefinition of the brain in terms of OSR leads to an ontological shift from the mind–body problem to the world–brain problem. Instead of raising the question of the ontological relationship between mind and body, we better question how the world is related to the brain (the world–brain problem) when addressing the question of the existence and reality of consciousness and mental features.

Unlike the mind–body problem, the world–brain problem can well address the original problem of the lack of a necessary connection and upward entailment between brain and consciousness without reverting to either the concept of mind or intuitive relation (as in identity theory or eliminative materialism; see above). This puts the world–brain problem in a superior position when compared to the mind–body problem, which therefore can be replaced by the former.

World–Brain Problem IVd: World–Brain Problem—World–Body Problem? Finally, one may argue that the world–brain problem can be identified with or even be replaced by what may be called the world–body problem as it may, for instance, be postulated in embodiment approaches (Park et al., 2014; Thompson, 2007; see chapter 8 for more details). I reject that, though. As discussed in chapter 8, the body is transformed from a merely objective body into a lived body by the brain's alignment to body and world. Ontologically, the lived body presupposes the constitution of consciousness on the basis of world–brain relation as OPC since otherwise there would be no experience of the body as lived body.

Specifically, this means that the body is related to the world on the basis of the brain's active construction of time and space in terms of the world's relational time and space. Therefore, the brain and its relation to the world (i.e., world–brain relation) must be considered a necessary condition of transforming the merely physical or objective body into a lived body, the body as we experience it (chapter 8). I therefore speak of the world–brain problem rather than the world–body problem.

However, the proponent of embodiment may not yet be satisfied. We do not experience world–brain relation at all while we do experience our body as lived body and its relation to the world (i.e., world–body relation). Therefore, the world–body problem must be more basic and foundational than the world–brain problem. This is to confuse phenomenal and ontological realms though. True indeed, we do not experience world–brain relation by itself as it is only a predisposition but not a correlate of consciousness (i.e., OPC rather than OCC).

However, to infer from experience of the body and the concomitant lack of experience of world–brain relation to the ontological primacy of the world–body problem over the world–brain problem is to confuse phenomenal and ontological realms. The fact that we do not experience world–brain relation as such in our consciousness does not entail that it cannot serve as OPC of consciousness. More generally put, we cannot infer from the phenomenal realm of consciousness, that is, the experience of the body as lived body, to its ontological basis, world–body relation. This amounts to what I describe as the *phenomenal–ontological fallacy*. The proponent suggesting the ontological primacy of the world–body problem over the world–brain problem can make that claim only by committing such phenomenal–ontological fallacy. Therefore, her or his argument can be rejected.

The inference from the phenomenal realm of the lived body to the ontological primacy of world–body relation is more or less analogous to the following scenario. Imagine we were inferring from our lacking consciousness of H_2O to the claim that H_2O cannot constitute the molecular basis of water. This would be considered absurd given our current knowledge. In contrast, this is not considered absurd in the case of world–brain relation by at least the proponent of embodiment. Let us put things straight. In the same way that H_2O provides the molecular basis of water, world–brain relation constitutes the ontological basis of consciousness including our experience of the body as lived body. Therefore, as with H_2O with respect to water, world–brain relation must be ontologically more basic and foundational for consciousness than the lived body including world–body relation.

The critic may want to argue that the concept of world–brain relation is way too abstract as we can neither observe it nor experience it as such. Even if ontologically valid, the concept of world–brain relation is too abstract to serve as OPC for something as concrete as our consciousness. This is to neglect the history of science though. As pointed out in chapter 2, several discoveries in science including quantum theory and the genetic code are rather abstract and not directly accessible as such in both observation and experience. However, that neither hinders quantum theory in serving as an ontological predisposition of physical reality nor the genetic code in providing the ontological basis of inheritance. Hence, the *argument of abstraction* as an argument that world–brain relation is too abstract to serve as OPC must be rejected on scientific and ontological grounds (see also chapter 14 for a similar argument).

World–Brain Problem Va: World–Brain Problem—Argument of Triviality

One may now want to argue that the world–brain problem is trivial. The argument of triviality posed here with regard to the world–brain problem can be considered an ontological extension of the argument of triviality I raised in the empirical context of the spatiotemporal model of consciousness (chapter 7). Specifically, the world–brain problem may be regarded as trivial on empirical, conceptual, and ontological grounds.

First, the world–brain problem is empirically trivial in that it refers back to the brain and its neuronal mechanisms. Therefore, conceived empirically, the world–brain problem really turns out to be a "brain problem" rather than world–brain problem. Second, the world–brain problem is trivial on conceptual grounds. The addition of the brain does not add anything new to the concept of world, which includes the brain by default since the latter is part of the former. Therefore, considered conceptually, we could replace the world–brain problem by what can be called the *world problem*.

Third, the world–brain problem is ontologically trivial. The existence and reality of the world must also characterize the existence and reality of the brain as the latter is part of the former. For instance, the physical or mental properties that characterize the world, as in materialism or panpsychism, also apply to the brain and must thus characterize its existence and reality. Therefore, the inclusion of the brain in the world–brain problem is rather trivial on ontological grounds.

However, I reject all three claims of triviality. First, I demonstrated that a specific neuronal mechanism, that is, spatiotemporal alignment, accounted for the brain's empirical relation to the world (chapter 8). The absence of such spatiotemporal alignment renders impossible, on empirical grounds, world–brain relation, which is then replaced by world–brain isolation. Hence, considered empirically, the world–brain problem includes different kinds of empirical options, that is, mechanisms by means of which the brain's neural activity could position itself in regard to the world, that is, world–brain relation versus world–brain isolation. Therefore, the assumption of the world–brain problem is far from trivial on empirical grounds.

Second, the world–brain problem is not conceptually trivial. The world–brain problem contains different options with respect to the relationship between world and brain. For instance, there can be a necessary or a contingent connection between world and brain. If the connection between world and brain is necessary, the world–brain problem can account for the necessary connection between brain and consciousness. If, in contrast, the connection between world and brain remains contingent, the world–brain problem cannot account for the necessary connection between brain and consciousness and remains therefore unable to address the question of the existence and reality of mental features. Since the world–brain problem includes different conceptual options, that is, necessary versus contingent, for the relationship between world and brain, it cannot be considered trivial on conceptual grounds.

Third and finally, the world–brain problem is not ontologically trivial. One can presuppose different ontological frameworks such as element-, relation-, process-, and capacity-based ontology. We have already seen that the relationship between world and brain will be different when presupposing either element- or relation-based ontology. Other ontological options for their possible relationship emerge when presupposing either process-based ontology (Northoff, 2016a,b) or capacity-based ontology (chapters 5 and 9). Since the ontological characterization of world and brain, including their relationship, depends on the presupposed ontological framework that entails different ontological options, the world–brain problem cannot be conceived as ontologically trivial.

World–Brain Problem Vb: World–Brain Problem versus World–Brain Relation—Question versus Answer

The critic may now want to argue that we did not really define the various terms included in the notion of world–brain problem. We defined neither the concept of world nor that of relation; only the concept of brain was defined somewhat as it relied on the previous chapter (chapter 9). I will define the concept of world in an ontological sense in more detail in the next chapter, chapter 11. Here I shall focus on the concept of *relation*. We can distinguish between at least two (possible) distinct concepts of relation in world–brain relation, for example, narrow and wide.

"Relation" in "world–brain relation" can be understood in a narrow sense. In that case, "relation" refers to the ontological definition of relation in terms of OSR. Empirically, the narrow meaning of relation is determined by spatiotemporal alignment (chapter 8) while, conceptually, it implies a necessary (rather than contingent) and therefore intrinsic (rather than extrinsic) connection between world and brain. Hence, the narrow meaning of relation is determined in a specific way on empirical, conceptual, and ontological grounds. Such determination, and consequently the narrow meaning of "relation," is presupposed when I consider world–brain relation as the answer to the world–brain problem (as the underlying question).

What about the wide concept of relation in world–brain relation? The wide meaning of "relation" refers to relationship in general, that is, the commonsense notion of relationship, which includes all possible ontological, conceptual, and empirical options. Thus, the wide meaning of "relation" in "world–brain relation" remains empirically, conceptually, and ontologically undetermined. This is the notion of relation I presuppose when I speak of the world–brain problem. Since it includes several empirical, conceptual, and ontological options with regard to the relation between world and brain, the world–brain problem cannot be considered trivial at all on any of these grounds (i.e., empirical, conceptual, and ontological).

In conclusion, my rejection of the trivial nature of the world–brain problem on all three levels, that is, empirical, ontological, and conceptual, presupposes the wide meaning of the concept of relation in my concept of world–brain relation. The world–brain problem must therefore be distinguished from world–brain relation: the former raises the question of the possible relationship between world and brain by adopting a wide meaning of relation while the latter provides an answer by determining relation in a specific and thus narrow meaning. If, in contrast, one presupposes the narrow meaning of relation in the concept of the world–brain problem, the latter will indeed be rendered trivial—that is to confuse answer (i.e., the world–brain relation with its presupposed narrow meaning of relation) and question (i.e., the world–brain problem presupposing the wide meaning of relation).

Conclusion

How can we determine the existence and reality of consciousness? As based on the ontological determination of the brain in terms of world–brain relation and OSR, I suggest the world–brain relation as a necessary, nonsufficient ontological condition of possible consciousness (i.e., as OPC). Most important, because of its constitution of spatiotemporal structure with space-time relation, the world–brain relation allows us to take into view and thus conceive a necessary ontological connection between brain and consciousness. That must be distinguished from the contingent relationship between brain and consciousness that plagues most past and present philosophical and neuroscientific approaches to consciousness and mental features in general.

To allow for a necessary rather than contingent ontological connection between brain and consciousness, we have to revise our standard ontological presuppositions though. Instead of element-based ontology with mental and physical properties, we rather need to presuppose OSR with structure and relation as basic units of existence and reality. This makes possible the ontological redefinition of the brain in terms of relation, that is, world–brain relation, rather than by some intrinsic features within the brain itself such as physical or mental properties.

How and why can world–brain relation allow for a necessary ontological connection between brain and consciousness? I propose that it is connected with its spatiotemporal characterization by relational time and space. Relational time and space make necessary the ontological relation between world and brain (i.e., world–brain relation). That, in turn, puts the brain, through its world–brain relation, in a necessary ontological connection to consciousness as defined by its phenomenal features, which I propose are characterized by space-time relation (reflecting relational time and space).

Hence, time and space and, more specifically, relational time and space provide the missing glue or missing link between brain and consciousness and, even more generally, between world and consciousness. The proposed empirical spatiotemporal theory of consciousness (chapter 7) can thus be complemented on the ontological side by an analogous spatiotemporal model of consciousness.

Such spatiotemporal model of consciousness provides a new view on some of the problems discussed in philosophy of mind such as the explanatory gap problem (Levine, 1998), which shall be briefly indicated here (awaiting further detailed discussion in the future). The explanatory gap problem argues that there is an explanatory gap between physical and mental features which, applied to the case of the brain, can be reframed as the gap between neuronal and phenomenal features (Northoff, 2014b). Within the current ontological framework of structural realism, the concept of such an explanatory gap is not plausible and therefore can no longer be sustained. The role of world–brain relation as OPC implies the necessary ontological connection between brain and consciousness. Such a necessary connection stands counter to the assumption of a gap between neuronal and phenomenal features, which in turn renders the assumption of an explanatory gap implausible and even nonsensical in the present framework.

Most important, characterization of world–brain relation in terms of spatiotemporal ontology renders superfluous the need to introduce the concept of mind for drawing the necessary connection to consciousness and mental features. The role of the mind can now be taken over by world–brain relation, which serves as OPC. This renders the concept of mind and subsequently the mind–body problem superfluous in our account of consciousness and mental features. All that we aim to answer by the concept of mind and the mind–body problem can now be addressed in a much more empirically and ontologically plausible way by the world–brain problem. In short, we can replace the mind–body problem with the world–brain problem.

Several issues remain open, however. First, I identified the necessary ontological conditions, that is, predisposition of consciousness (OPC); this left open the sufficient ontological conditions of actual consciousness though, the OCCs. Second, I left open the nature of phenomenal features of consciousness and how they are related to world–brain relation as OPC. Third, one may wonder about the sequence of the terms "world" and "brain" in "world–brain relation." One may, alternatively, suggest brain–world relation, which I reject though as the latter is at best epistemic or empirical rather than ontological. Finally, I left open the exact determination of the concept of world in my account of world–brain relation. These issues shall be addressed in the next chapter.

11 Ontology III: From the World to Consciousness

Introduction

World and Consciousness

Where are we now? I first discussed the existence and reality of brain, that is, ontology of brain (chapter 9). That let me to define the existence and reality of brain in the sense of ontic structural realism (OSR), that is, by structure and relation as realized and manifest in world–brain relation (chapter 9). The existence and reality of brain thus consists in world–brain relation—the brain is world–brain relation. That very same world–brain relation is of central importance for consciousness (and mental features in general). Specifically, the world–brain relation serves as a necessary ontological condition of possible consciousness, that is, as an ontological predisposition of consciousness (OPC; chapter 10).

However, despite all emphasis on brain and world–brain relation, the ontological characterization of the world itself, including its role for consciousness, remains open. The world as considered so far is important for consciousness only through its relation to the brain, the world–brain relation, that serves as OPC. That leaves the world by itself (i.e., independent of brain) ontologically underdetermined though: the world's existence and reality extend and reach far beyond its relation to the brain. There is thus "more" to the world than world–brain relation, and this "more" may be central for the existence and reality of mental features such as consciousness.

Main Aim and Argument

The main aim in the present chapter is to characterize the existence and reality of world itself and its relevance for consciousness. Thereby, I focus specifically on the phenomenal features of consciousness and how they are related to the ontological, that is, spatiotemporal features of world and world–brain relation. Moreover, it shall be noted that I here presuppose the concept of world in the ontological terms of OSR—the world is ontologically characterized by structure and relation with relational time and space (chapter 9).

Such structural–relational ontological determination of the world must be distinguished from other meanings of world such as empirical, for example, physical (as in science), phenomenal (as in phenomenology), mental (as in idealism), and cognitive–representational (as most often in cognitive neuroscience) characterizations. Moreover, I clearly distinguish such ontological meaning of world from any metaphysical determination as I sharply distinguish metaphysics and ontology (see the introduction to chapter 9). Finally, note that I presuppose the concept of world in a phenomenal rather than noumenal sense (as in the meaning of Kant) as the world in a noumenal sense may not be accessible to us (which, as I argue, is due to world–brain relation; see chapters 13 and 14).

My main argument in this chapter is that the world itself is ontologically indispensable for the existence and reality of consciousness. This is specified by three ontological features of the world, including "calibration process" (part I), "constitution of structure" (part II), and "complex location" (part III), that are all necessary for the existence and reality of consciousness. I therefore conclude that the world itself must be included in our ontology when addressing the question of the existence and reality of mental features such as consciousness.

Part I: World and Consciousness—Argument of Calibration

Argument of Calibration Ia: World—Superfluous, Trivial, and Nonnecessary?

Why do we need to include the world when addressing the question of the existence and reality of consciousness? We have already seen in the empirical part that the brain's spatiotemporal alignment to the world is a necessary empirical condition of actual consciousness, that is, a neural prerequisite of consciousness (chapter 8). However, the empirical relevance of world for consciousness does not imply its ontological relevance. Ontologically, brain or mind may be fully sufficient by themselves to account for the existence and reality of mental features such as consciousness. Let us detail that in the following.

One can, for example, define and trace the existence and reality of consciousness to the brain (as most often in materialism and physicalism). In that case, the world itself, that is, independent of the brain, does not take on any role in consciousness—the world itself thus remains irrelevant if not superfluous in this case. One may now want to argue that the here suggested world–brain relation gives at least some role to the world. However, that role is merely indirect as it is based on the brain and how it relates to the world. One may, for instance, argue that the relation between world and brain, the world–brain relation, is sufficiently dependent upon the brain itself—this renders superfluous the world itself, that is, independent of the brain, for consciousness.

Does the world itself really remain irrelevant? Another argument for the world could be mereological, pointing out that the brain is part of the world as whole. One can therefore not avoid including the world in at least an indirect way as the part implies the whole. Such mereological inclusion is rather trivial though (as it is implied by the concepts of world and brain) and, even more important, it does not change anything in our ontological determination of consciousness (when compared to its definition by the brain as part independent of the world as whole). Therefore, the hint toward mereological part-whole relationship between brain and world does not really render the world itself (i.e., independent of the brain) relevant for consciousness beyond mere triviality.

How is the role of world when defining mental features such as consciousness by mind rather than brain? In that case, the world is not even included in either an indirect (as through mind–world relation as analogous to world–brain relation) or mereological (as a whole including the brain as a part) sense. In contrast, determination of mental features by the mind even excludes world to sharpen its distinction from the physical features of the world (including brain and body). Accordingly, ontological determination of mental features by mind excludes the world almost by default, that is, in a necessary way.

Taken together, the critic may want to argue that, ontologically, the world has no role in our ontological determination of mental features. Mental features can be sufficiently determined ontologically by either brain or mind without considering the world itself (i.e., independent of brain and mind). I will argue against this argument. Contrary to the argument, I will argue that the inclusion of world is necessary for the ontological determination of mental features; this is based on the central role of the world for what I describe as the "calibration process" which is essential for consciousness. I therefore speak of an "argument of calibration."

Argument of Calibration Ib: World—Spatiotemporal Frame versus Spatiotemporal Baseline

I presuppose OSR that characterizes the basic units of existence and reality by relation and structure. I so far applied OSR to brain (chapter 9) and consciousness (chapter 10). However, as it concerns the basic units of existence and reality, OSR must also apply to the world itself, that is, its existence and reality, as it remains independent of both brain and consciousness. Specifically, as I characterized OSR in a spatiotemporal way, one would claim that the world can ontologically be characterized by what I described as "relational time and space" (chapter 9). I now aim to develop OSR of the world in order to understand how that makes possible phenomenal features of consciousness.

How can we now characterize relational time and space in more detail? Spatiotemporal relation and structure are characterized by a certain spatiotemporal scale or range: within the boundaries of the world's spatiotemporal scale or range, the world exists and is real whereas outside the boundaries of its spatiotemporal range, the world, that is, the world we live in, does not exist. That does not exclude that another world or even another universe exists that shows a different spatiotemporal scale or range. The spatiotemporal range thus provides a boundary or frame for the world—I therefore speak of "spatiotemporal frame." Presupposing OSR in a spatiotemporal sense, the notion of spatiotemporal frame is an ontological concept that characterizes existence and reality of world in a spatiotemporal way.

Why and how is the spatiotemporal frame of the world related to consciousness? For that, we need to first introduce yet another concept. I considered world–brain relation as OPC (chapter 10). Specifically, the world–brain relation can be characterized by the coupling of the world's larger spatiotemporal range to the smaller one of the brain (chapter 9).

Such spatiotemporal coupling between world and brain in the world–brain relation constitutes the basis for subsequent consciousness: as the world–brain relation provides the OPC, its spatiotemporal features provide the baseline for possible consciousness. As the baseline is determined by the spatiotemporal scale or range of world–brain relation, I speak of "spatiotemporal baseline." The concept of spatiotemporal baseline is an ontological concept that describes the spatiotemporal features of world–brain relation and, more generally, the spatiotemporal relation between the world as whole and its parts such as the brain.

Let me illustrate the concept of spatiotemporal baseline by the example of the bat as put forward by the philosopher Thomas Nagel in his famous paper "What Is It Like to Be a Bat?" (Nagel, 1974). The bat can process ultrasonic frequency waves that are not included in the spatiotemporal frequency range of the human brain. Therefore, the bat's world–brain relation shows a different spatiotemporal range than the world–brain relation in humans—humans and bats thus exhibit different spatiotemporal baselines. As the world–brain relation and its spatiotemporal baseline provide the OPC, the spatiotemporal range of consciousness will also be different between bats and humans. Accordingly, the answer to Nagel's (1974) famous question "What Is It Like to Be a Bat?" consists in investigating the species-specific spatiotemporal range of the bat's spatiotemporal baseline, that is, its species-specific world–brain relation.

Argument of Calibration Ic: World—Divergence between Spatiotemporal Frame and Spatiotemporal Baseline

How does the concept of spatiotemporal baseline stand in relation to that of spatiotemporal frame? First and foremost, both are ontological concepts that describe different spatiotemporal features of the world within the context of OSR. Specifically, the concept of spatiotemporal frame concerns only the world itself independent of our experience or consciousness of the world including the underlying world–brain relation. This distinguishes spatiotemporal frame from spatiotemporal baseline.

Unlike spatiotemporal frame, the concept of spatiotemporal baseline refers to the relation between the world's spatiotemporal range and that of the brain, that is, the world–brain relation. Therefore, to equate or identify spatiotemporal frame and spatiotemporal baseline would be to confuse world itself, that is, as it remains independent of its parts such as the brain, and the world's relation to the brain as one of its parts, that is, world–brain relation.

The distinction between the two concepts makes it possible for "spatiotemporal baseline" and "spatiotemporal frame" to diverge from each other. It is, for instance, well conceivable that two different spatiotemporal baselines like those of humans and bats refer to one and the same "spatiotemporal frame" as they are "located" and situated within a commonly shared world. Whereas their "spatiotemporal baseline" apparently differ from each other as indicated above. Such possible divergence between "spatiotemporal frame" and "spatiotemporal baseline" lend further support to the assumption that both concepts cannot be identified with each other.

Finally, the difference between spatiotemporal frame and spatiotemporal baseline does not preclude that the latter is dependent upon the former. The spatiotemporal range of the spatiotemporal frame predisposes the spatiotemporal difference between world and brain, that is, the spatiotemporal baseline: the larger the spatiotemporal range of the spatiotemporal frame, the larger the spatiotemporal difference that the spatiotemporal baseline needs to bridge to couple, that is, relate, world and brain. Accordingly, the spatiotemporal baseline is dependent upon the world's spatiotemporal frame (while the reverse dependence does not hold, i.e., the spatiotemporal frame remains independent of the spatiotemporal baseline).

Argument of Calibration IIa: Consciousness—Spaces of Experience and Their Calibration Processes

I so far characterized the world ontologically by spatiotemporal frame and spatiotemporal baseline. However, that leaves open why and how both spatiotemporal frame and spatiotemporal baseline are relevant for consciousness. That shall be the focus in the following. For that, I turn to Isaac (2014), who suggests a structural realist account of experience and, more specifically, of secondary qualities. While he focuses exclusively on secondary qualities, I enlarge his focus by applying his ideas to phenomenal features of consciousness in general.

Isaac (2014) compares the occurrence of secondary qualities such as the experience of heat to a measurement or calibration process. When we, for example, measure temperature, we measure temperature not in an absolute way but rather in a relative way since we compare it against our thermometer and its scale. Depending on the scale or calibration of the measurement device (e.g., the thermometer), one obtains a certain value for the temperature. This is, for instance, well reflected in the difference between Celsius and Fahrenheit as the temperature scales used in Europe and the United States, respectively: the same room with the same absolute temperature will be characterized by different temperatures in Europe and the United States since in both instances different scales are used. We thus obtain a relative rather than absolute value of temperature as depending on the calibration of the measurement device, the thermometer (Isaac, 2014).

The same holds now analogously, according to Isaac (2014), in the case of secondary qualities. The physical causes of heat are set and compared against a baseline that is calibrated in a certain way. Depending on the calibration of that very same baseline, we may experience one and the same temperature as either hot or cool. Based on its calibration, the "baseline" may allow for a certain scope or range within which the temperatures can be experienced in various ways, that is, degrees—the experience of temperature, including its secondary qualities, is thus dependent upon the presupposed baseline and its subsequent calibration process.

Argument of Calibration IIb: Consciousness—Prephenomenal versus Phenomenal and Nonphenomenal Spaces of Experience

I now extend Isaac's notion of "calibration process" from secondary qualities to phenomenal features of consciousness in general. For that, we need to characterize such calibration process in more detail. Following Isaac (2014), there are three ingredients in the calibration process when it comes to secondary qualities. There is (i) a "space of possible experience" that, for instance, may include possible experience of hot or cold, and therefore serves as the "baseline" of possible experience; (ii) a "space of possible external correlates to experience" that, for instance, may include temperature; and (iii) a process by which the two are linked that allows for calibrating the latter with respect to the former, that is, "calibration process," as I say.

What exactly is meant by the concept of "space" in the first two ingredients, that is, the space of possible experience and the space of possible external correlates to experience? Though Isaac himself does not really discuss the concept of space, it is clear that it is not meant in a purely physical and observational sense. This is more or less excluded by characterizing such space by experience and, as I say, consciousness and its phenomenal features. However, to identify the concept of space as phenomenal would be to confuse possible and actual experience. Isaac is talking about a "space of possible experience" and a "space of possible external correlates to experience" rather than "actual experience" or "actual external correlates to experience."

The distinction between "possible" and "actual" makes it impossible to characterize Isaac's concept of space in a phenomenal sense by itself. However, at the same time, Isaac clearly indicates that the two spaces are relevant for experience and its external correlates as they determine the possible ranges of both. Both spaces thus provide the necessary condition of possible experience and its external correlates—they are predispositions of experience and thus of consciousness for which reason I characterize them as "prephenomenal" (rather than phenomenal; see Northoff, 2014b, for extensive discussion and usage of the concept of prephenomenal).

The characterization of both spaces as prephenomenal must be also distinguished from their nonphenomenal determination. Even though they are not yet phenomenal by themselves, both spaces can nevertheless not be characterized as nonphenomenal—that would be to cut their relationship to possible experience and its external correlates, which ultimately would render the latter two impossible. Therefore, I characterize the concept of space in both "space of possible experience" and "space of possible external correlates to experience" as prephenomenal rather than as either phenomenal or nonphenomenal.

How can the two spaces serve as a necessary condition of consciousness? I propose that, following Isaac's third ingredient, they allow for the calibration process. The comparison and calibration between both space of possible experience and space of external correlates of experience can by itself not be experienced—it is not accessible for us in consciousness. However, experience and thus consciousness nevertheless are based and thus depend on such calibration process, which therefore can by itself by characterized as prephenomenal (rather than either phenomenal or nonphenomenal).

Argument of Calibration IIc: Consciousness—Space of Possible Experience and Spatiotemporal Baseline

How is the prephenomenal realm of the two prephenomenal spaces related to the ontological realm of world–brain relation? More specifically, I raise the question of how the prephenomenal space of possible experience is related to the ontological characterization of the world in terms of spatiotemporal baseline and spatiotemporal frame. I will argue that the prephenomenal features, as postulated by Isaac, are closely related to and can be traced to the ontological determination of the world in terms of spatiotemporal frame and spatiotemporal baseline. Let me start with the first prephenomenal feature, the space of possible experience.

The spatiotemporal baseline is ontologically determined by world–brain relation and its spatiotemporal features (see above). At the same time, both world–brain relation and its role as spatiotemporal baseline serve as a necessary condition of possible consciousness, that is, OPC. In contrast, the world–brain relation and its spatiotemporal baseline cannot be considered sufficient conditions of actual (rather than possible) consciousness (chapter 10). This is mirrored also on the prephenomenal side where the "space of experience" refers to "possible experience" rather than "actual experience."

I now argue that what Isaac describes as "space of possible experience" in the prephenomenal realm is directly related to what is ontologically referred to as the "spatiotemporal baseline" as constituted by world–brain relation. The spatiotemporal baseline constituted by world–brain relation provides the necessary ontological condition of the prephenomenal space of possible experience. The prephenomenal space of possible experience is thus ontologically dependent upon the spatiotemporal scale or range of the world–brain relation and its spatiotemporal baseline.

This entails a rather radical consequence. If the prephenomenal space of possible experience is ontologically dependent upon world–brain relation as spatiotemporal baseline, phenomenal features of consciousness must by themselves be characterized in spatiotemporal terms (see Northoff, 2014b, for details on that point). We should be careful about the concepts of time and space, however. The concept of spatiotemporal refers here to relational time and space and thus to structure and relation as distinguished from observational time and space (chapter 9). Therefore, the spatiotemporal characterization of the phenomenal features of consciousness does not entail their scientific and ultimately merely physicalistic determination in terms of observational time and space.

In sum, I suppose that the spatiotemporal baseline of world–brain relation provides the necessary ontological condition of the prephenomenal space of possible experience. The range of possible experiences and thus consciousness (with both terms being used synonymously for the sake of simplicity) is thus predisposed ontologically by the spatiotemporal range of the spatiotemporal baseline as constituted by world–brain relation. This not only links and relates ontological and prephenomenal levels of consciousness but also makes it necessary to characterize phenomenal features in spatiotemporal terms, that is, relational time and space.

Argument of Calibration IIIa: Consciousness—Space of Possible External Correlates to Experience and Spatiotemporal Frame

How about the second feature of experience in the sense of Isaac, the "space of possible external correlates to experience"? This refers to the objects or events that can possibly be associated with consciousness. The events or objects with which consciousness can possibly be associated are part of the world and its spatiotemporal frame. Therefore, the events or objects themselves must be characterized by specific spatiotemporal features which relate them in a particular way to the world and its spatiotemporal frame, that is, "world–object/event relation," as I say.

How can we characterize the concept of world–object/event relation? As with world–brain relation, the concept of world–object/event relation can be described in spatiotemporal terms: the objects or events, including their specific spatiotemporal features, stand in a certain spatiotemporal relationship to the world and its spatiotemporal frame. The spatiotemporal frame is thus explicitly present in world–object/event relation in that it shapes the relation between world and object/event in a spatiotemporal way. Importantly, that very same world–object/event relation remains independent of the spatiotemporal baseline as provided by world–brain relation as that is distinct from world–object/event relation.

I now argue that the world–object/event relation, including its dependence upon the world's spatiotemporal frame, is a necessary ontological condition of the prephenomenal space of possible external correlates to experience. The way the objects and events stand in spatiotemporal relation to the world and its spatiotemporal frame determines whether they can be included or excluded within the space of possible external correlates to experience. As in the case of the space of possible experience, I determine the space of possible external correlates of experience in a spatiotemporal way, that is, in relation to the world's spatiotemporal frame.

The prephenomenal space of possible external correlates to experience is not solely determined by the world's spatiotemporal frame and world–object/event relation, however. Additionally, we need to consider the world–brain relation and its spatiotemporal baseline. More specifically, we need to consider the degree to which world–object/event relation and world–brain relation overlap spatiotemporally: the more the spatiotemporal baseline of world–brain relation overlaps with the spatiotemporal frame of world–object/event relation, the more likely the respective objects or events will be included in the space of possible external correlates to experience. If, in contrast, their spatiotemporal overlap is minimal or absent, the respective events or objects will not be included in, and thus excluded from, the space of possible external correlates to experience.

Argument of Calibration IIIb: Consciousness—Phenomenal versus Empirical Meanings of "Internal" and "External"

I discussed how the world–object/event relation provides the ontological condition of the prephenomenal space of possible external correlates of experience. In contrast, I left open the meaning of the notion of "external"—that shall be the focus in the following.

The concept of "external" obviously stands in contrast to the notion of "internal." There are external correlates as well as internal correlates in the prephenomenal space of experience. I characterized the world–object/event relation and its spatiotemporal overlap with world–brain relation as an external correlate of experience. In contrast, the internal correlate of experience may consist in the world–brain relation that provides the spatiotemporal baseline (and necessary ontological condition) for the prephenomenal space of possible experience.

We need to be careful, though. The meanings of "internal" and "external" are here understood in a prephenomenal or phenomenal sense as distinguished from their empirical meaning. Empirically, the meaning of "internal" refers to brain and body as distinguished from the world as "external": everything that happens inside brain and body is internal while events or objects outside in the world are considered external.

However, that is to be distinguished from the prephenomenal or phenomenal meaning of "internal" and "external." In that case, the notion of "external" refers to the objects or events of experience, that is, those objects or events which are associated with experience. Importantly, this can include events or objects outside in the world as well as events or objects inside in brain (such as spontaneous thoughts) or body (such as the heartbeat or heart palpitations). Hence, the prephenomenal or phenomenal meaning of "external" includes both notions "internal" and "external" as understood in an empirical sense.

What about the concept of the internal in the prephenomenal or phenomenal sense? This refers to the experience itself, that is, experience as such, independent of the objects or events, that is, the "external" correlates, with which it is associated. Experience itself is thus internal while the objects or events with which it is associated are its external correlate. One may now be inclined to argue that the prephenomenal or phenomenal meaning of "internal" corresponds more or less to the empirical determination of "internal": in the same way, the empirical notion of the "internal" is restricted to the inside of brain and body, the prephenomenal or phenomenal determination of the "internal," that is, experience, takes place within the inside of brain and body.

That is not true, though. Experience and thus consciousness is not limited to the inside of brain and body. Consciousness extends beyond both brain and body as well as beyond our person as a whole—it links us to and "anchors" us in the world as part of the world. When we experience something, that is, an event or object, as an "external" correlate, we do not experience that event or object within our brain or body. Instead, we experience that event or object as well as its relationship to ourselves as part of the wider world—consciousness thus aligns us to the world.

Accordingly, the internal character of experience, that is, consciousness, cannot be restricted to and thus compared with the notion of internal as understood in an empirical sense. As in the case of external, the prephenomenal or phenomenal concept of internal does not obey the boundaries between brain, body, and world. Instead, it operates across those boundaries that are therefore empirical but not phenomenal. Ontologically, such phenomenal (rather than empirical) operation across the boundaries between brain, body, and world is predisposed by the relationship between world–brain relation and world–object/event relation—their relationship first and foremost makes possible the prephenomenal or phenomenal concepts of internal and external as distinguished from their empirical siblings.

Argument of Calibration IIIc: Consciousness—Spatiotemporal Calibration as Ontological Correlate of Consciousness

What about the third feature in Isaac's structuralist account of experience, the calibration process, which links the space of possible experience and the space of possible external correlates to experience? I suppose that such linkage is provided by the calibration process as mentioned above. The calibration process consists in comparing and matching the "external correlates to experience" with and against the space of possible experience. The central question here concerns the comparison and matching—what exactly happens here, and how does it calibrate our experience?

I traced the prephenomenal space of possible experience ontologically to world–brain relation while the space of possible external correlates to experience is predisposed by world–object/event relation (and its relationship to world–brain relation; see above). How, now, can both world–brain relation and world–object/event relation be compared and matched with each other in such way that the former calibrates the latter?

We recall that the world–brain relation provides a spatiotemporal baseline while the world is characterized as a spatiotemporal frame. Both world–brain and world–object/event relation share two ontological features. First, both are relations and can therefore be directly compared with each other (which otherwise would remain impossible as when, for instance, one were a property and the other a relation). Second, both world–brain relation and world–object/event relation include the world as a commonly shared spatiotemporal frame that provides a common reference for both brain and objects/events, including their relation to the world.

Because of the world's spatiotemporal frame as common reference, world–brain relation and world–object/event relation can be compared and matched with each other in terms of their spatiotemporal features. Specifically, the world–brain relation provides the spatiotemporal baseline against which world–object/event relation is set, compared, and matched and thus calibrated. The calibration process is thus spatiotemporal for which reason I speak of "spatiotemporal calibration."

What exactly do I mean by the concept of spatiotemporal calibration? First and foremost, the concept of spatiotemporal calibration is an ontological concept. As such, it must be distinguished from an empirical concept. Spatiotemporal calibration describes the ontological comparison of different spatiotemporal scales and, more specifically, the comparison of the spatiotemporal ranges of world–object/event relation against those of the world–brain relation that serves as a spatiotemporal baseline. By serving as a spatiotemporal baseline, the world–brain relation can conform and adjust, that is, "calibrate," the possible objects/events (including their world–object/event relation) according to its own spatiotemporal range.

Such conformation and adjustment of the spatiotemporal features of the objects or events of the world to those of world–brain relation, in turn, make it possible to associate the former with consciousness. Let me detail that. The conformation allows for integration of the spatiotemporal features of the objects or events, including their world–object/event relation, within the spatiotemporal range of world–brain relation—that, in turn, is central for consciousness (chapters 6–8 and 10). Hence, what I describe by "spatiotemporal calibration" provides the sufficient ontological condition of the actual linkage between the two prephenomenal spaces, that is, the space of possible experience and the space of possible external correlates to experience. Their linkage, in turn, allows for transforming the prephenomenal realm of possible experience (including its possible external correlates) into the phenomenal realm of actual experience of objects or events.

Taken together, spatiotemporal calibration can be considered a sufficient ontological condition of actual consciousness and thus what I describe as an "ontological correlate of consciousness" (OCC). Spatiotemporal calibration as OCC must be distinguished from world–brain relation as OPC (chapter 10): without spatiotemporal calibration, world–brain relation as the ontological basis of the two prephenomenal spaces, that is, the space of possible experience and the space of possible external correlates to experience, cannot yield consciousness and mental features. At the same time, world–brain relation is also necessary, since without world–brain relation as OPC, there would be no ontological capacity (see chapter 5 for the concept of capacity in a more scientific context) to render possible spatiotemporal calibration as OCC.

Argument of Calibration IVa: Consciousness—Spatiotemporal Calibration versus Neuronal Calibration

The neuroscientist and empirically minded philosopher may now be confused. Why not take the brain itself rather than world–brain relation as the spatiotemporal baseline for the calibration process? That is, for instance, suggested in an implicit way by Raichle (2015), who considers the default-mode network (DMN) as such spatiotemporal baseline against which neural activity in the resting state of the brain is calibrated. The term "default-mode" within "default-mode network" already includes reference to some kind of baseline and calibration process—he even speaks of a "default-mode function" (Raichle, 2015).

However, the concept of the DMN or default-mode function indexes a merely empirical (rather than ontological) concept of the calibration process. In that case, the calibration process concerns only the brain itself and consequently remains within the confines of the brain itself and its neuronal activity—I therefore speak of neuronal calibration. Neuronal calibration remains merely empirical whereas, unlike spatiotemporal calibration, it is not ontological. Such merely empirical neuronal calibration may be relevant for the brain itself whereas it remains insufficient for consciousness.

To account for consciousness, we need to go beyond the brain and consider the world–brain relation as a spatiotemporal baseline that makes possible spatiotemporal calibration as distinguished from neuronal calibration. Accordingly, I suppose that we need an ontological (rather than empirical or neuronal) calibration, that is, spatiotemporal calibration, to link the two prephenomenal spaces, that is, the space of possible experience and the space of external correlates to experience, and thus to make possible consciousness.

Argument of Calibration IVb: Consciousness—From Ontological Correlate of Consciousness to Neural Predisposition of Consciousness

How does neuronal calibration stand in relation to spatiotemporal calibration? As mentioned above, neuronal calibration concerns only the brain, independent of the world, for which reason it remains merely empirical. In contrast, spatiotemporal calibration explicitly includes the world and reaches therefore beyond the confines of the brain; it is thus ontological rather than empirical (see chapter 14 for a more detailed discussion of the concept of "beyond the confines of the brain"). However, despite their differences, neuronal and spatiotemporal calibration are not incompatible with each other.

Usually, neuronal calibration of the brain's neural activity by the DMN is based on and builds on spatiotemporal calibration by world–brain relation. However, in extreme cases such as schizophrenia (chapters 3 and 8), spatiotemporal calibration by world–brain relation is disrupted, which leaves neuronal calibration by the DMN without an underlying spatiotemporal ground within the world.

That, in turn, radically changes the spatial and temporal organization and structure of these patients' consciousness, which leads to major perceptual, motor, affective, and cognitive changes (Northoff & Duncan, 2016, as well as Northoff, 2015, 2016, for such spatiotemporal approach to schizophrenia). Such possible divergence between neuronal calibration and spatiotemporal calibration in schizophrenia further underlines the importance of distinguishing these concepts from one another.

However, the difference between the ontological concept of spatiotemporal calibration and the more empirical one of neuronal calibration does not preclude their linkage and transition. Together with world–brain relation as OPC, spatiotemporal calibration as OCC provides the ontological basis for the necessary empirical, that is, neuronal, conditions of possible consciousness, that is, the neural predispositions of consciousness (NPC; chapters 7 and 8). The NPC can be found in spatiotemporal alignment of the brain to the world as well as in DMN, serving as neuronal calibration for the brain's neural activity. We can thus see how spatiotemporal calibration as OCC provides the ontological basis for neuronal calibration as NPC. Hence, there is distinction and transition between ontological and empirical realms, that is, from OCC to NPC.

Argument of Calibration IVc: Consciousness—Neuro-ecological/Ontological Intimacy

Why and how is spatiotemporal calibration so important for consciousness? By calibrating objects or events, including their spatiotemporal features, against world–brain relation as a spatiotemporal baseline, both objects/events and world–brain relation are set in an intimate relation to each other that crosses the internal–external boundary between brain, body, and world (see above for a discussion of the concepts of internal vs. external). One can thus speak of what I describe as "neuro-ecological intimacy." Such neuro-ecological intimacy makes possible the phenomenal notions of "internal" as "external" as distinguished from their empirical determination (see above).

The concept of neuro-ecological intimacy (which may also be formulated as "neuro-ontological intimacy") borrows from and adapts what Thomas Nagel describes as "physico-mental intimacy," that is, the "apparent intimacy between the mental and its physical conditions" (Nagel, 1986, p. 20). I postulate that what Nagel refers to as "physico-mental intimacy" can be traced ontologically to neuro-ecological intimacy as based on world–brain relation and spatiotemporal calibration.

Following Nagel, "physico-mental intimacy" provides the brain with "insideness" that accounts for its foundational character for subjective experience:

> It [the brain] can be dissected, but it also has the kind of inside that can't be exposed to dissection. There's something it is like from the inside to taste chocolate because there's something it's like from the inside to have your brain in that condition that is produced when you eat a chocolate bar. (Nagel, 1987, pp. 34–35)

Most interestingly, Nagel traces such "insideness" of the brain to a "fundamental essence" (Nagel, 1979, p. 199) which can be defined by complex forms of organization and combinations of matter, that is, "unusual chemical and physiological structure" (Nagel, 1979, p. 201).

What Nagel describes as "insideness" of the brain can now be specified. Due to its ontological definition by world–brain relation, the brain shows an "insideness" with regard to the world: what appears as mere "outsideness" when considering the brain alone by itself (i.e., independent of the world) is transformed into "insideness" when defining the brain's existence and realty by its relation to the world (i.e., world–brain relation).

The world–brain relation thus allows the brain to constitute an "insideness" with regard to the world—that very same "inside" is manifest in "neuro-ecological/ontological intimacy" as well as in spatiotemporal calibration of objects or events in the world by world–brain relation. Taken in such sense, world–brain relation may account for what Nagel describes as "fundamental essence": the latter's description by "unusual chemical and physiological structure" can now be specified ontologically by "spatiotemporal structure" and, more generally, OSR.

Part II: Structure and Consciousness—Argument of Structure

Argument of Structure Ia: World and Consciousness—No Structure and Dynamics?

The spatiotemporal model determines the existence and reality of consciousness by spatiotemporal structure. That stands square to the so-called structure and dynamics argument (Chalmers 2003, p. 247; see also Alter, 2016; Pereboom, 2011; Stoljar, 2006). In a nutshell, the structure and dynamics argument (i.e., the "argument of structure," as I call it) points out that the microphysical world with quanta and Hilbert space can be described in terms of abstract structure and dynamics. In contrast, that very same abstract structure cannot be found on the macroscopic and phenomenal level of consciousness, which therefore cannot be described in terms of structure and dynamics.

The argument of structure relies on and is based on the dichotomy between structure and nonstructure; however, I reject such dichotomy on the grounds of OSR and the spatiotemporal model of consciousness. Rather than being nonstructural and nondynamic, consciousness is highly structural and dynamic as reflected in its spatiotemporal structure. This, as I suggest, can be traced to the world–brain relation and its constitution of relational time and space. Following OSR, that very same spatiotemporal structure is pervasive throughout the whole world, including all its parts such as body and brain, as well as at all levels such as microphysical, macrophysical, and phenomenal levels. Therefore, the dichotomy between structure and nonstructure must be rejected, which, in turn, makes it possible to rebut the argument of structure.

The aim in this second part is to show that there is strong structure on both the macroscopic level of world and the phenomenal level of consciousness. Note that I understand the concept of "structure" in an ontological sense, which allows me to rely on OSR. In the following I will specify OSR with respect to the world by showing its spatiotemporal structure. Importantly, relation and structure as basic units of existence and reality transgress the boundaries between micro- and macrolevels and phenomenal levels. To better understand such ontological transgression, we need to determine the concept of structure in more ontological detail.

Argument of Structure Ib: World—Spatiotemporal Nestedness

How can we describe the world–brain relation in more specific spatiotemporal terms? First and foremost, world and brain can be characterized by different spatiotemporal ranges or scales and thus in their degree of spatiotemporal extension. The brain shows a smaller spatiotemporal scale or range when compared to that of the world: the "inner durations" and "inner extensions" (see chapters 7 and 12 for these terms) of the world are much larger when compared to those of the brain. World and brain can thus be characterized by different degrees of "spatiotemporal extension."

How can the brain's smaller spatiotemporal scale or range be related to the larger one of the world? We encountered the same problem of linking different spatiotemporal scales in the empirical domain. The empirical data show, for instance, that different frequencies (with different temporal scales) are linked in terms of "cross-frequency coupling" (CFC; chapters 1 and 7). Specifically, the phase of slower frequencies is linked to the amplitude of the faster frequencies. This means that the shorter time scale of the faster frequency is contained by and nested within the longer time scale of the slower frequency. One can therefore speak of "nestedness" which encompasses different frequencies and thereby also different regions—this amounts to "spatiotemporal nestedness" (chapters 5 and 7).

Spatiotemporal nestedness in that context is understood in an empirical sense as being restricted to the brain. However, as the data show, spatiotemporal nestedness may extend and operate across the boundaries of brain, body, and world. We discussed data showing CFC from stomach to brain that nested the amplitude of the brain's faster frequencies (i.e., alpha) within the phase of the stomach's slower frequency (chapter 8). One may therefore want to speak of "spatiotemporal nestedness" of the brain within the body. The same can be observed in the case of brain and world: the brain's frequencies can be aligned to and thus nested within the larger frequency range of the world (see chapter 8)—the brain is thus spatiotemporally nested within the world.

Taken together, these data demonstrate that CFC and spatiotemporal nestedness operate across the boundaries between brain, body, and world. There are not only different frequencies nested within each other within the brain itself, that is, its spontaneous activity, but the brain itself is nested and contained within the spatiotemporal features of body and world. The existence and reality of the brain can consequently no longer be determined by the brain alone—instead, the basic units of existence and reality featuring the brain operate across the boundaries between brain, body, and world. I therefore determine the existence and reality of world by spatiotemporal nestedness between world, body, and brain, which is then understood in an ontological (rather than merely empirical) sense (see figure 11.1).

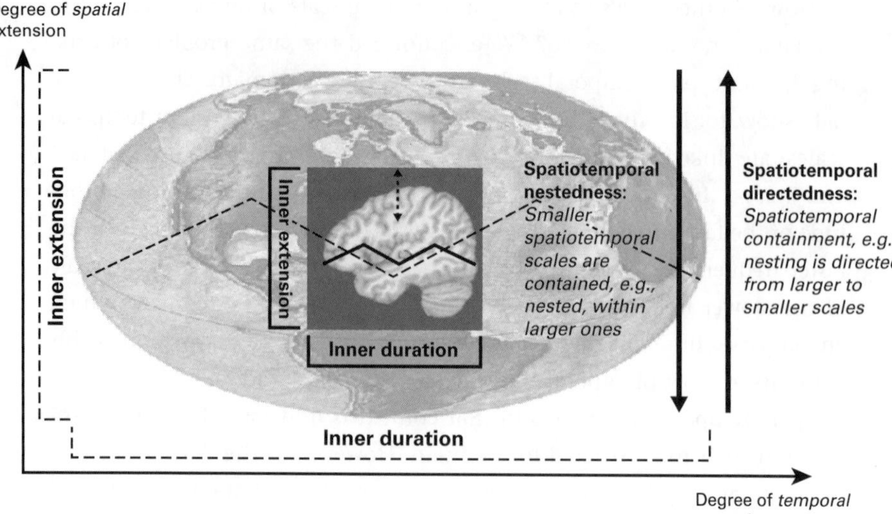

Figure 11.1
Spatiotemporal nestedness and spatiotemporal directedness between world and brain.

Argument of Structure Ic: World—Spatiotemporal Directedness

Let us briefly compare the brain's spatiotemporal nestedness to the example of the Russian dolls. In the same way the smaller Russian doll is nested or contained within the next larger one, the spatiotemporally smaller brain is nested and contained within the larger spatiotemporal scale or range of the world. Most importantly, we cannot determine the existence and reality of the smaller doll independent of the larger ones—the shape and spatiotemporal extension of the smaller doll are dependent upon the next larger doll. Analogous to this, the spatiotemporal structure of the brain's spontaneous activity is dependent upon the larger spatiotemporal scales of body and world. The spatiotemporal nestedness of the smaller Russian doll within the larger ones thus corresponds well to how the brain is spatiotemporally nested within body and world.

Let us further dwell on our example of the Russian dolls. We would never conceive that the smaller Russian doll includes and harbors the next larger one and so forth. Instead, we take it for granted that the larger one contains or nests the next smaller one. Spatiotemporal nestedness thus goes hand in hand with a certain directionality, that is, "spatiotemporal directedness," as I describe it. There is spatiotemporal directedness from the larger to the smaller doll rather than from the smaller to the larger one.

The same applies to the relation between world and brain. The larger spatiotemporal scale or range of the world makes it possible for the world to contain or nest the brain and its smaller spatiotemporal scale—this is what I mean by "world–brain relation." In contrast, the reverse scenario remains spatiotemporally impossible: the smaller spatiotemporal scale of the brain makes it impossible for the brain to contain or nest the world with its larger spatiotemporal scale—"brain–world relation," as one may say, remains spatiotemporally impossible on an ontological level as it would violate spatiotemporal directedness (see figure 11.2).

In sum, I characterize the existence and reality of world in spatiotemporal terms and, more specifically, by spatiotemporal nestedness and spatiotemporal directedness. This allows for the concept of world–brain relation on ontological grounds as distinguished from the reverse one, that is, brain–world relation. Unlike world–brain relation, the concept of brain–world relation cannot be regarded as an ontological concept: due to the impossible nesting of the world's larger spatiotemporal scale within the smaller one of the brain, the concept of brain–world relation cannot be determined ontologically as, for instance, by spatiotemporal nestedness and directedness. Note that this does not exclude the possible determination of brain–world relation in epistemic terms—that is beyond the scope of this chapter though.

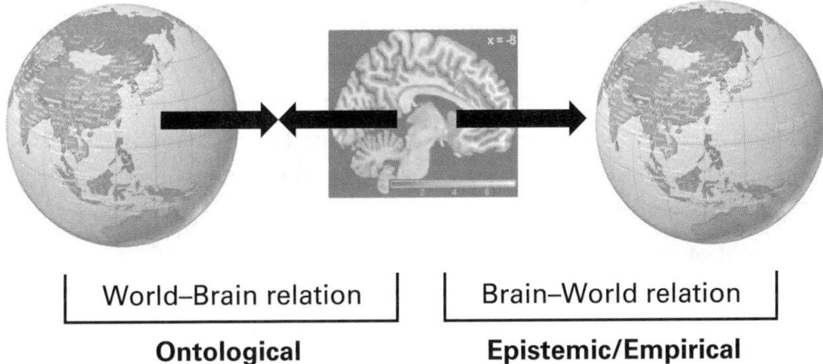

Figure 11.2
World–brain relation versus brain–world relation.

Argument of Structure Id: Rejection of the Argument of Structure

How do spatiotemporal nestedness and directedness stand in relation to the argument of structure? We recall that the argument of structure rests on the distinction between micro- and macrophysical levels with only the former being structural and dynamical. This can now be refuted. Micro- and macrophysical levels reflect different spatiotemporal scales or ranges and may therefore be ontologically nested or contained within each other, entailing spatiotemporal nestedness. Spatiotemporal nestedness makes it possible for smaller scaled features to be nested and contained within larger scaled features and their spatiotemporal structure.

What seems to look nonstructural on the macrophysical level may be intrinsically structural (and dynamical) when considered in the context of spatiotemporal nestedness. Compare that once more to the Russian doll. If one only sees the largest Russian doll from the outside but not its inside, one is indeed inclined to suppose that the Russian doll is not structured at all. However, once one opens the large Russian doll, one sees the various smaller ones. Moreover, it becomes clear then that the shape and size of the largest doll is strongly determined, that is, predisposed, by the smaller ones. Hence, what looks unstructured from the outside reveals itself as highly structured from the inside.

The same holds analogously in the case of consciousness. Taken by itself, that is, from the outside, consciousness looks unstructured without any spatiotemporal features. That changes once one conceives consciousness from the inside, that is, from the brain and world–brain relation. We can then see how much world–brain relation shapes and configures consciousness by providing it with a complex spatiotemporal structure. Consciousness, as signifying the macrolevel and phenomenal level, is thus highly structured and spatiotemporal. Therefore, we can refute the argument of structure as it simply neglects the spatiotemporal context and highly structured nature of consciousness as it can be traced to world–brain relation.

Argument of Structure IIa: Spatiotemporal Nestedness and Consciousness

How do mental features stand in relation to the ontological characterization of the brain in terms of spatiotemporal nestedness? I will argue that, based on the empirical data, spatiotemporal nestedness plays a central role in yielding consciousness (chapters 4, 5, and 7). I will briefly recount some of the empirical data in the following.

The brain's scale-free activity can be characterized by the inclusion of different temporal scales or ranges, implying spatiotemporal nestedness in an empirical sense (chapters 4, 5, and 7). Moreover, the brain's degree of scale-free activity is central for consciousness: states such as anesthesia or sleep where one loses consciousness show decreased levels of scale-free activity with loss of nestedness (chapters 4 and 5). The spatiotemporal nestedness of the brain's spontaneous activity is thus central for consciousness.

Moreover, a recent study conducted by my colleagues and myself also showed that the degree of scale-free activity predicts yet another mental feature like self-consciousness (Huang et al., 2016). Though the exact neuronal mechanisms mediating the relation between the brain's scale-free activity and consciousness remain to be clarified, the data show that spatiotemporal nestedness of the brain's spontaneous activity is central (see also Northoff & Huang, 2017, as well as Northoff, 2017). Even more relevant, the data show that spatiotemporal nestedness of the brain's neural activity within body (Park et al., 2014) and world (Monto et al., 2008) is directly related to consciousness (chapters 7 and 8).

What does this imply for the ontological determination of consciousness? The basic unit of the existence and reality underlying consciousness can ontologically not be "localized" within the brain and thus is not restricted to the confines and boundaries of the brain. Instead, consciousness needs to be characterized ontologically by a basic unit of existence and reality that, analogous to the empirical data, crosses the boundaries of the brain and makes possible the latter's spatiotemporal nestedness within body and world.

I postulate that spatiotemporal nestedness is central for rendering world–brain relation as OPC (chapter 13). To predispose consciousness, the underlying predisposition, that is, world–brain relation, must transgress the boundaries of the brain. Otherwise, if restricted and limited to the confines of brain, body, or world, the respective ontological feature (such as elements or properties) remains unable to predispose consciousness. Importantly, spatiotemporal nestedness makes possible integration of different time and space scales, which, in turn, is central for consciousness: spatiotemporal nestedness between world, body, and brain provides the kind of spatiotemporal structure that makes possible consciousness (see above).

Argument of Structure IIb: Spatiotemporal Directedness and Mereological Fallacy

In addition to spatiotemporal nestedness, world–brain relation can also be characterized by spatiotemporal directedness (see above). Spatiotemporal directedness points out that there is directionality from the larger spatiotemporal range to the smaller one and thus from world to brain. I therefore speak of world–brain relation and distinguish it from brain–world relation (see above). That very same spatiotemporal directedness is central for the ontological definition of the brain in that it is related to the world by being nested within the latter's larger spatiotemporal extension.

How about consciousness? I now argue that the same holds for consciousness. The empirical findings show that the directionality in CFC from the slower to the faster frequencies is central in mediating consciousness (chapters 7 and 8) while that very same directionality is disrupted during the loss of consciousness (chapters 5 and 7). The empirical findings thus support a central role of spatiotemporal directedness in consciousness.

Something analogous holds true on the ontological level. Spatiotemporal directedness, as based on spatiotemporal relation, makes it possible for consciousness to experience ourselves as part of the world. In contrast, the reverse direction, namely, that we experience the world as part of us, remains impossible. There is thus spatiotemporal directedness from world to consciousness with the latter integrating us as part of the former as a whole.

The ontological characterization of consciousness by spatiotemporal directedness also carries major conceptual implications. Spatiotemporal directedness makes it impossible to "locate" consciousness in the brain and thus to confuse the brain as part with the conscious person as whole. Bennett and Hacker (2003) pointed out that brain as part and person as whole are often confused in current neuroscience and philosophy of mind—they therefore speak of a "mereological fallacy" (Bennett and Hacker 2003, p. 2).

Such mereological fallacy is ruled out when determining consciousness by spatiotemporal directedness: consciousness can no longer be located in the brain but must instead be traced to world–brain relation. The person who, as whole, experiences the world as whole in consciousness can consequently no longer be conflated with her or his own brain as part. Instead, the person's consciousness is rather based on her or his brain's relation to the world, the world–brain relation—the risk of a mereological fallacy is precluded. Moreover, it excludes possible confusion between consciousness and brain, which, following Bergson, can lead to either empiricism or idealism of consciousness (Bergson, 1904; Northoff, 2016b).

How about the argument of structure with regard to consciousness? Consciousness is characterized ontologically by spatiotemporal nestedness and directedness from world to brain. This means that, spatiotemporally, the macrophysical level of consciousness contains or nests the microlevel of abstract physical description. Hence, the microphysical structure and dynamics are contained and nested within the macrophysical structure of world–brain relation and consciousness.

The argument of structure supposes that structure only exists on the micro- but not macrophysical level. That is to neglect spatiotemporal directedness and nestedness though. Any structure, independent of how abstract it is, is nested and contained within the next larger and more concrete one. That also holds for consciousness that is contained or nested within the world–brain relation as its underlying larger spatiotemporal structure, which, in turn, is nested and contained within the even more concrete structure of the world itself, that is, its spatiotemporal frame. The argument of structure claiming for the absence of structure on the macrolevel of brain and the phenomenal level of consciousness can thus be rebutted on spatiotemporal grounds.

Part III: Location and Consciousness—Argument of Location

Argument of Location Ia: Can We Locate Brain and Consciousness in Time and Space?

One of the major gaps between brain and consciousness consists in their location in time and space. We can locate the brain at the "here" and "now" of specific space-time points or events within the world. This, in contrast, remains impossible for consciousness. We cannot locate consciousness at a particular here or now of specific space-time points or events within the world. Instead, consciousness must be characterized by "nonlocation." The problem we are facing when linking brain and consciousness is thus to bridge the gap between location and nonlocation.

How about location in the context of the ontological determination of brain and consciousness in terms of OSR? One may argue that this makes matters even worse. Defining the brain by relation and structure makes it impossible even to locate the brain at the "here" and "now" of specific space-time points or events within the world. The brain must consequently be characterized by nonlocation, which puts it on an equal footing with consciousness. That does not bring us any further toward linking brain and consciousness though.

Instead of "nonlocating" the brain, one may therefore better aim to locate consciousness, which makes it possible to link consciousness to the brain and its location. That is, for instance, possible by suggesting mental or physical properties that can be located at specific space-time points or events in an ontological sense. The specific space-time points or events at which the brain is located can then be linked to the specific space-time points or events of mental or physical properties.

However, as OSR defies any such location of consciousness, it remains unable to link brain and consciousness; for that reason, that is, its inability to locate both brain and consciousness, OSR needs to be rejected. I therefore speak of an "argument of location" that can be considered an ontological argument against OSR. I will counter that argument by showing that it conflates the specific kind of location implied by OSR, that is, "complex location," with both "simple location" and "nonlocation."

Argument of Location Ib: Simple Location—Empirical Meaning

We usually locate the brain at a particular discrete point in time and space. The anatomist sees the brain "here" and "now" in front of her or him while the brain imager locates stimulus-induced activity and even spontaneous activity at specific points in time and space within the brain. In either case, the brain is located in the time and space of the observer, that is, observational time and space, that the observer herself or himself imposes and employs during her or his observation. Location in this sense is characterized by specific points in time and space, that is, space-time points or events, which presupposes observational time and space (chapter 12).

Moreover, such "localization" at different space-time points or events does not consider any other or additional space-time points or events. The localization of the brain at specific space-time points or events remains independent of its respective spatiotemporal context—the dependence of space-time points or events on "space-time relation," as postulated in OSR (see above) is completely neglected. Because "localization" here is restricted to specific space-time points or events independent of others with the neglect of the respective spatiotemporal context, I speak of "simple location."

Simple location is based on observational time and space, which renders it primarily empirical (chapter 12). For instance, neuroscience considers the brain in purely observational terms and thus characterizes it by observational time and space. For that reason, neuroscience locates the brain and its neural activity at specific space-time points or events in the world. In contrast, neuroscience neglects the brain's relation to other space-time points or events outside the brain as in the world—that neglect renders it impossible to consider, for example, world–brain relation as it is based on relational time and space.

Argument of Location Ic: Simple Location—Ontological Meaning

How about simple location in an ontological sense? In that case, one would locate the basic units of existence and reality at specific space-time points or events. Such location is, for instance, presupposed in element-based ontology: elements such as physical or mental properties are supposedly located at specific space-time points or events in the world. That very same location at specific points in time and space remains completely independent of the other space-time points or events in the world. For example, physical properties may show a location that is different and remains independent from that of mental properties. One can therefore speak of "simple location" of elements or properties in element-based ontology.

How are empirical and ontological concepts of simple location related to each other? One may want to argue that simple location is simply transferred from the empirical, that is, observational, to the ontological level: one infers from the simple location of our observations to the simple location of the underlying elements or properties. For instance, from the observation of the simple location of the brain's neural activity, one infers to the simple location of its physical or mental properties. Since such inference from the empirical to the ontological level is fallacious, one can speak of an "empirical–ontological fallacy" as I call it (see chapter 9 for details) in the case of simple location in an ontological context.

The process philosopher Alfred North Whitehead argues that the empirical–ontological fallacy of simple location can be traced to the modern period. This is well reflected in the following quote:

> One such assumption underlies the whole philosophy of nature during the modern period. It is embodied in the conception which is supposed to express the most concrete aspect of nature. The Ionian philosophers asked, What is nature made of?

> The answer is couched in terms of stuff, or matter, or material—the particular name chosen is indifferent—which has the property of simple location in space and time, or, if you adopt the modern ideas, space-time. What I mean by matter, or material, is anything which has this property of *simple location*. By simple location I mean one major characteristic which refers equally both to space and time, and other minor characteristics which are diverse as between space and time. The characteristic common to both space and time is that material can be said to be *here* in space and *here* in time, or *here* in space-time, in a perfectly definite sense which does not require for its explanation any reference to other regions of space-time. (Whitehead, 1925, pp. 48–49; see also Whitehead, 1925, p. 58, as well as Griffin, 1998, p. 119)

Following Whitehead, I postulate that an analogous empirical–ontological fallacy is still prevalent today. The attempt to locate the basic units of existence and reality at specific space-time points or events, as presupposed in element-based ontology, is modeled after and based on the empirical concept of simple location. Elements such as physical or mental properties are supposedly located in a simple way at space-time points or events, which defines their very existence and reality. Hence, the empirical meaning of simple location of the brain is simply transferred to the ontological level of consciousness. However, that falls short for both brain and consciousness as we will see in the following.

Argument of Location IIa: Complex Location versus Distributed Location

Simple location is based on space-time points or events and neglects the respective spatiotemporal context. I now argue that we need to contrast simple location with what I describe as complex location (I owe this distinction to Da Dong, who is a student of mine in Hangzhou, China).

How can we characterize such complex location? Unlike in simple location, we can no longer "localize" different existences and realities such as brain and nonbrains at one specific space-time point or event independent of each other and their respective spatiotemporal context. Instead, brains and nonbrains may be located on different positions of an underlying commonly shared spatiotemporal spectrum, a "spatiotemporal trajectory," as I say (chapter 12).

Let me give an empirical example of such complex location in terms of spatiotemporal trajectories. Take the brain's spontaneous activity. The brain's spontaneous activity shows continuous activity changes across time and space, that is, in different regions and frequency ranges. One can now locate each activity change by itself at each specific space-time point or event—this amounts to simple location. Alternatively, one can consider the different activity changes in relation to each other: the degree of change in space-time points or events from one activity to another and so forth. One then locates the different activity changes in dependence on each other along the line of an ongoing spatiotemporal trajectory—this amounts to complex location in an empirical sense.

Taken in an ontological context, complex location allows us to locate the brain in relation to and dependence on its respective spatiotemporal context as constituted by body and world. More specifically, the brain and its neural activity can be located in relation to the spatiotemporal features of body and world in terms of space-time relation. Complex location thus locates the brain ontologically in a way that operates across the observable space-time points or events of brain, body, and world. This distinguishes complex location from simple location that remains within the confines and boundaries of the brain and its space-time points or events.

The proponent of simple location may now be inclined to argue that complex location amounts to nothing but "distributed location." Instead of being located at one specific space-time point or event, one now simply supposes several space-time points or events that are distributed across time and space. For instance, Schechtman (1997) speaks of a "distributed view" where the mind is distributed across the whole body; she distinguishes that from a "standard view" where the brain is conceived as the locus of the mind.

That is to neglect that complex location is determined by space-time relation with relational time and space rather than space-time points or events though. The mere addition or collection of different space-time points or events does not constitute any kind of relation between the distributed space-time points or events. The mere "collection of space-time points" must therefore be distinguished from "relational space and time." For that reason, location in terms of space-time relation, that is, complex location, cannot be identified with distributed location.

I suppose that the space-time relation of the brain with the world defines its existence and reality rather than its involvement of different distributed space-time points or events. The brain thus presupposes complex location rather than either simple location or distributed location. Finally, it shall be noted that the brain's complex location is not "complex" because it involves a high number of distributed space-time points or events. Instead, the brain's location is "complex" because of its space-time relation with body and world, which "position" the brain on their spatiotemporal trajectories across the empirical boundaries of brain, body, and world.

Argument of Location IIb: Complex Location versus Nonlocation

The proponent of simple location may want to put forward yet another argument, however. Specifically, she or he may want to say that complex location amounts to nonlocation. If the brain cannot be located at specific space-time points or events, it is "everywhere at all times" (Whitehead, 1925, p. 91; see also Whitehead, 1968, pp. 3–4, as well as Griffin, 1998, p. 144)—this amounts to nonlocation rather than complex location.

This is to neglect that there are different space-time relations though. Space-time relation can show different spatiotemporal scales or ranges. For instance, the space-time relation between world and brain extends over a much larger spatiotemporal scale than the one between body and brain. The brain can thus be located in different ways relative to world and body—hence, the distinction between world–brain relation and body–brain relation (with the latter being a specific instance of the former; chapters 8 and 13). This contrasts with nonlocation in which case the brain should be "everywhere at all times" and thus in both world and body in the same way at all time.

Taken together, we need to distinguish complex location from simple location and distributed location as well as nonlocation. Complex location is based on space-time relation with relational time and space; this distinguishes it from both simple location and distributed location that presuppose space-time points or events with observational time and space. At the same time, "complex location" refers to location in terms of positioning on spatiotemporal trajectories, which distinguishes it from nonlocation, where "everything is everywhere at all times."

Argument of Location IIc: Complex Location of Consciousness

What about the location of consciousness and other mental features? Historically, consciousness could not be located in terms of simple location for which reason it was characterized by nonlocation. This opened the gap between simple location of brain and body, on the one hand, and nonlocation of consciousness, on the other. The assumption of mental properties as analogous to physical properties can be seen as an attempt or remedy to overcome this gap: simple location of physical properties is now simply doubled on the mental level with mental properties showing analogous simple location.

I reject both assumptions, that is, nonlocation and simple location, of consciousness, however. Instead, I suppose that consciousness (and mental features in general) can be located in a complex way, that is, complex location, which can be traced to the complex location of the brain in the world in terms of world–brain relation.

How can we illustrate the complex location of consciousness? For that, I briefly turn to the empirical findings. The various neuroscientific investigations show that mental features such as consciousness cannot be located in the "here" of one particular region or network in the brain (chapters 5 and 6). Instead, the neural activity must be integrated and globalized across several regions and networks to yield consciousness (Koch et al., 2016)—this is highlighted in both integrated information theory and the global neuronal workspace theory (chapters 5 and 7). The same holds analogously on the temporal side. Consciousness cannot be associated with one specific frequency in the brain; rather it involves the different frequency ranges and their coupling as in CFC and scale-free activity (chapters 5–7).

What do these empirical data tell us about the "ontological location" of consciousness in the brain? First and foremost, they tell us that we cannot locate consciousness in specific space-time points or events in the brain—simple location of consciousness in an empirical sense remains simply impossible.

The same holds analogously on the ontological level. Consciousness cannot be located in the world at its various space-time points or events such as body or brain—this precludes simple location of consciousness in the world. The failure of simple location does not imply nonlocation, though. The dichotomy of simple location versus nonlocation is misplaced in the present ontological framework. To avoid such a misplaced dichotomy, I speak of complex location. The term 'location" refers now to spatiotemporal relation rather than to space-time points. Consciousness can then be "located" in a complex way in and through the spatiotemporal relation and trajectories featuring the world–brain relation.

The possible location of consciousness in terms of complex location renders futile and superfluous the ontological assumption of physical and mental properties. These properties are, in part, introduced to overcome the gap between simple location of brain and the presumed nonlocation of consciousness. If consciousness can now be located in terms of complex location, we no longer need to introduce physical and/or mental properties to close the ontological gap between simple location and nonlocation.

In sum, consciousness (and mental features in general) can be located, though not in terms of simple location but complex location as distinguished from nonlocation. This is based on OSR with the ontological characterization of both brain and consciousness by world–brain relation. Importantly, OSR allows us to completely close the gap between simple location of brain and nonlocation of consciousness; this is possible by ontologically characterizing both brain and consciousness by complex location as distinguished from simple location and nonlocation. The argument of location as argument against the spatiotemporal model and OSR of brain and consciousness can thus be refuted.

Conclusion

We need to consider the world. More specifically, the world and its large spatiotemporal scale take on an important and indispensable ontological role for consciousness. First, the world, as in world–brain relation, serves as a spatiotemporal baseline that makes possible spatiotemporal calibration and defines the space of possible experience. Second, the world and its large spatiotemporal scale allows for nesting and containing the smaller spatiotemporal scales, including the ones of the brain—that very same spatiotemporal nestedness is central for consciousness in both empirical (chapter 8) and ontological (this chapter) terms. Finally, third, the world allows for complex location of consciousness and brain in the world as distinguished from simple location and nonlocation.

What does this imply for our ontology of consciousness? We cannot reduce the ontology of consciousness to the question of the existence and reality of the brain, an ontological "brain problem," as one may say. Nor can we conceive consciousness in terms of "brain–world problem" in which case one would assume ontological primacy of brain over world (see chapter 10 for details). In either case, one neglects that the world takes on multiple roles for consciousness, that is, as spatiotemporal baseline for spatiotemporal calibration, as spatiotemporal frame for complex location, and as structure providing spatiotemporal nestedness of consciousness.

Instead, we need to approach the question of the existence and reality of consciousness in terms of the world and its relation to the brain, that is, "world–brain problem" (chapter 10). Importantly, in the same way that we cannot reduce the world–brain problem to brain or brain–world relation, we cannot reduce the world–brain problem to the world alone and thus to what ontologically can be described as "world problem." Though not argued explicitly for in the present chapter, the world itself, that is, independent of its relation to the brain (or an analogue of the brain), remains unable to take on an ontological role in predisposing consciousness (i.e., as OPC).

Why is there consciousness rather than nonconsciousness in the world? This amounts (more or less) to what Chalmers defined as the "hard problem" (Chalmers 1995, p. 210). Briefly, the hard problem consists in the metaphysical question of why there is consciousness rather than nonconsciousness. The answer I give is ontological (while leaving the respective metaphysical issues open; see the introduction to chapter 9 for their distinction) and consists in the following: there is consciousness because the world shows spatiotemporal structure and relation that make possible world–brain relation as OPC.

If, in contrast, there would be no spatiotemporal structure and relation in the world but, for instance, elements such as physical properties, consciousness would remain impossible—in that case, the neural and ontological predispositions of consciousness are no longer given—consciousness would thus remain absent while nonconsciousness would prevail. The hard problem is thus resolved by shifting from an element- to a relation-based ontology of the world.

Can consciousness occur independently of the brain in, for instance, artificial intelligence or neuromorphic computers? The criteria for the possible existence and reality of consciousness are clear. Empirically, such artificial creature would need to show spatiotemporal mechanisms such as spatiotemporal alignment, nestedness, and expansion (chapters 7 and 8) as well as difference- rather than stimulus-based coding (chapters 2 and 12). Ontologically, the existence and reality of such artificial creature need to be based on differences rather than elements and consequently on structure and relation, that is, spatiotemporal structure and relation with the inclusion of a wider spectrum of different spatiotemporal scales (chapters 12 and

13). That makes possible world–machine relation, which then, analogously to world–brain relation, could be conceived as OPC.

In sum, we need to include both the brain's relation to the world and the world's relation to the brain in our question concerning the existence and reality of consciousness. We cannot reduce the existence and reality of consciousness to either the world alone (i.e., independent of the brain) or the brain by itself (i.e., independent of its relation to the world). Therefore, I speak of a world–brain problem as distinguished from both the brain problem and the world problem. I consider the world–brain problem an empirically, conceptually, and ontologically more coherent, that is, more plausible problem than both the brain problem and the world problem for addressing the question of the existence and reality of consciousness (and mental features in general).

IV Copernican Revolution

12 Copernican Revolution in Physics and Cosmology: Vantage Point from beyond Earth

Introduction

Mind-Body Problem versus World–Brain Problem

No doubt, mental features such as consciousness must be attributed to the mind as their underlying ontological origin. We usually take that for granted and thus as given. This is the standard (most often tacit or implicit) background assumption of the mind–body problem, that is, the question of how the existence and reality of mind are related to those of the body. However, is it really evident and necessary that the existence and reality of mental features must be attributed to the mind? I suggested an alternative strategy in the third part of this book. Instead of considering the mind as their potential ontological origin, I attributed mental features to world–brain relation—this led me to what I call the *world–brain problem* (chapters 10 and 11).

The concept of mind is pervasive. Common sense speaks of mind and attributes all mental features such as consciousness to the mind. Neuroscience investigates the mind empirically in terms of cognition as in "cognitive neuroscience" (see Parts I and II of this book) while philosophy even developed a separate discipline concerning specifically the mind, that is, philosophy of mind, to investigate its ontological and epistemic features (Searle, 2004). Hence, the assumption of mind is seemingly taken for granted. All we need to do is search for the empirical and ontological underpinnings of mind in both neuroscience and philosophy. That, as tacitly presupposed, will ultimately resolve the current questions revolving around mind, including the mind–body problem.

However, unlike common sense as well as current neuroscientific and philosophical discussions, I do not take the mind for granted. Instead of providing yet another answer to the question of the empirical and ontological underpinnings of mind, I questioned the question itself. I demonstrated that the question of mind and its relationship to the body, the mind–body problem, is superfluous and thus no longer necessary. Mental features can be necessarily connected to the brain through world–brain relation that then serves as an ontological predisposition of consciousness (OPC; chapter 10). We thus no longer need to introduce the concept of mind to account for the necessary connection of mental features to their underlying ontological substrate—the role of mind can now be taken over by world–brain relation (chapters 10 and 11). This shifts the focus from mind–body to world–brain problem with the former being replaced by the latter.

Mind versus World–Brain Relation—Intuition of Mind

The philosopher of mind may now want to argue that the world–brain problem may nevertheless remain rather counterintuitive. We have no direct access to our brain, let alone to the brain's relation with the world (i.e., the world–brain relation), in our knowledge—we suffer from what I described earlier as "auto-epistemic limitation" (Northoff, 2004, 2011). Because we cannot access brain and world–brain relation by themselves, world–brain relation is not an option for our knowledge, that is, a possible *epistemic option* (see below for details)—this renders the world–brain problem rather counterintuitive on epistemological grounds.

In contrast, we have direct access to the mind in our knowledge—the mind, unlike world–brain relation, is thus a possible epistemic option which, as I will argue, is the basis for what philosophers describe as an "intuition pump" (Dennett, 2013, p. 5) or "sympathetic imagination" (Nagel, 1974, p. 445; see also Papineau, 2002) of mind. The "intuition of mind" may pull us toward the mind and the mind–body problem when addressing the question of the existence and reality of mental features. How can we counter the intuition of mind, including mind–body problem, and, at the same time, render the world–brain problem more intuitive? That is the central question in this and the next two chapters in this final part.

Intuition of Mind—Aim and Argument

The main aim in this chapter is to provide the ground for derailing the intuition of mind, including mind–body problem. At the same time, I aim to render the world–brain problem as an ontological problem for addressing mental features more intuitive on epistemic grounds. My main argument is that we need to modify the possible epistemic options that are included in our presupposed *logical space of knowledge* (see below for definition). That, as I argue, is possible by shifting our *vantage point* (see below for definition), that is, the viewpoint we take, when investigating the existence and reality of mental features.

The first part in the present chapter focuses on defining the concepts of logical space of knowledge and vantage point while the second part describes the Copernican revolution in cosmology and physics as a paradigmatic example of how we can change and modify our possible epistemic options as they are included in our presupposed logical space of knowledge: that, as I argue, was possible for Copernicus by shifting our geocentric vantage point from within Earth to a heliocentric vantage point from beyond Earth (see below for details).

Why do I revert to the Copernican revolution? The Copernican revolution in physics and cosmology provides the epistemic template for an analogous shift in our current vantage point that includes mind as a possible epistemic option in our logical space of knowledge as the basis of our intuition of mind and mind–body problem (chapters 13 and 14). We need to replace such vantage point with a different vantage point that allows for the world–brain relation as a possible epistemic option in our logical space of knowledge while, at the same time, excluding mind and mind–body problem as an impossible epistemic option (chapter 13). I will argue in the final chapter (chapter 14) that such shift in vantage point requires nothing less than a Copernican revolution in neuroscience and philosophy.

Part I: Logical Space of Knowledge—Epistemic Options and Vantage Point

Logical Space of Knowledge Ia: Logical Space of Knowledge—Definition

How can we define the concept of logical space of knowledge? I adopt the concept of logical space of knowledge from the concepts of the logical space of nature and the logical space of reason as suggested by Sellars (1964) and McDowell (1994). Put in a nutshell, the concepts of logical spaces of nature and reason provide what I describe as *operational background spaces* (i.e., as a necessary or transcendental condition in a Kantian sense) for science, that is, logical space of nature, and philosophy, that is, logical space of nature. I shall not go into detail here about how the logical spaces of nature and reason provide the operational background spaces for the world–brain and the mind–body problem—that shall be subject of future investigation.

We need to consider the operational background space of our intuition of mind though. That leads us back to our epistemic presuppositions, namely, to that which we claim to know. We presuppose that we can know the mind when intuiting the mind—otherwise, if we were not presupposing to possibly know the mind, we could not intuit the mind at all. The intuition of mind thus presupposes the mind as what I describe as a possible *epistemic option*. To rule out the intuition of mind, we therefore need to render the mind an impossible epistemic option (see below for details): as long as the mind is still a possible epistemic option, we are in danger of falling prey to the intuition of mind.

How can we change our epistemic options and, more specifically, render the mind an impossible epistemic option? For that we need to go back to the operational background space we (most often tacitly or implicitly) presuppose, which I describe as *logical space of knowledge*. What do I mean by this concept? As its siblings, that is, the logical spaces of nature and reason, the logical space of knowledge remains in the realm of what is conceivable and possible as distinguished from what is actual. More specifically, the logical space of knowledge concerns our possible knowledge, that is, what we can possibly know, which reflects what I describe by the term *possible epistemic options*.

Taken in such sense, the logical space of knowledge describes our possible epistemic options for knowing the world. The logical space of knowledge includes certain possible epistemic options while excluding others, that is, impossible epistemic options. What about the mind? The strong pulling forces of our intuition of mind suggest that the mind is included as a possible epistemic option in our logical space of knowledge (see below for detail). In contrast, the counterintuitive nature of world–brain relation may be related to, as I argue, its exclusion as an impossible epistemic option from our logical space of knowledge.

Finally, as with the logical space of nature (McDowell, 1994), the boundaries of the logical space of knowledge are malleable. They can be shifted by us, which changes our epistemic options, that is, those that are included as possible epistemic options and excluded as impossible epistemic options. For example, what is excluded as an impossible epistemic option in one particular conception of the logical space of knowledge may be included as a possible epistemic option in another one. I will argue that that is, for instance, the case in the Copernican revolution in physics and cosmology.

Logical Space of Knowledge Ib: Phenomenal versus Noumenal Features

Let me detail those epistemic options that are excluded from our logical space of knowledge, that is, impossible epistemic options. For instance, Kant argued that we cannot know noumenal features, which limits our knowledge to phenomenal features—noumenal features are thus excluded as an impossible epistemic option from our logical space of knowledge. In contrast, Kant argued that we can know the world in a phenomenal way—our logical space of knowledge thus includes phenomenal features as a possible epistemic option. Alternatively to Kant, one may argue that the boundaries of the logical space of knowledge are malleable, which can then be conceptualized in such a way as to include noumenal features as a possible epistemic option.

The staunch Kantian may reject such move though and argue for a special kind of impossible epistemic option. Noumenal features cannot be known in principle; they are intrinsically unknowable. Thus, it remains in principle impossible to include noumenal features as possible epistemic options in the logical space of knowledge: the intrinsic unknowability of noumenal features renders it in principle impossible to include them as possible epistemic options. Therefore, the logical space of knowledge is not malleable when it comes to noumenal features—the assumption of the malleability of the boundaries of the logical space of knowledge must hence be rejected. Noumenal features are thus not only impossible epistemic options but, even stronger, *epistemic nonoptions* (see below for details).

The critic is right and wrong. She or he is right in that there are limits to the malleability of the logical space of knowledge. However, that does not exclude the possibility that the boundaries of the logical space of knowledge are nevertheless malleable within certain limits. This requires me to distinguish different types of impossible epistemic options, that is, impossible epistemic options and epistemic nonoptions.

Logical Space of Knowledge Ic: Impossible Epistemic Options versus Epistemic Nonoptions

First, we may need to consider those impossible epistemic options that are excluded from our logical space of knowledge but are nevertheless knowable for us (rather than unknowable). This concerns phenomenal features (in a Kantian sense). We may, for instance, exclude certain phenomenal features as impossible epistemic options from our logical space of knowledge that are knowable for us. Let us consider a concrete example.

The world–brain relation as OPC is apparently excluded as an impossible epistemic option from the logical space of knowledge we currently presuppose in philosophy of mind while, at the same time, the world–brain relation can be known by us in phenomenal (rather than noumenal) terms (as taken in the epistemic sense of Kant). However, world–brain relation is apparently not included as a possible epistemic option in the logical space of knowledge we presuppose when investigating the existence and reality of mental features. We may therefore need to change the boundaries of our logical space of knowledge in such a way that we can include world–brain relation as a possible epistemic option.

Second, we need to consider those impossible epistemic options that neither are included in our logical space of knowledge nor can be known by us in principle, thus remaining intrinsically unknowable. These impossible epistemic options concern, for instance, noumenal features in the sense of Kant. As they remain intrinsically unknowable to us, these impossible epistemic features can never be included as possible epistemic options in our logical space of knowledge for which reason they are noumenal (rather than phenomenal). No matter how we define the boundaries of our logical space of knowledge, it will never include these epistemic options as possible epistemic options. As these epistemic options thus remain impossible by default, that is, in principle, I describe them as *epistemic nonoptions*.

Taken together, the boundaries of the logical space of knowledge are malleable with regard to the first type of impossible epistemic option, that is, the phenomenal features. I conceive world–brain relation as a paradigmatic example of such impossible epistemic option for which reason it is considered counterintuitive. In contrast, there is a limit to the malleability of the boundaries of the logical space of knowledge when it comes to the second type of impossible epistemic option that, by default and in principle can never be included as a possible epistemic option in our logical space of knowledge. To distinguish both types of epistemic options on conceptual grounds, I will describe the second type of impossible epistemic option as an epistemic nonoption.

My focus in this and the subsequent chapters is on those impossible epistemic options that can, in principle, be included as epistemic options in our logical space of knowledge—these are phenomenal rather than noumenal features (to use Kantian language). My focus is not on the epistemic nonoptions that, as being noumenal rather than phenomenal (in a Kantian sense), can, in principle, not be included as possible epistemic options in our logical space of knowledge.

Logical Space of Knowledge IIa: Possible Epistemic Option—Mind

What about the logical space of knowledge we presuppose in our investigation of the existence and reality of mental features? For that, we need to shed an even more detailed light on what is included as a possible epistemic option and excluded as an impossible epistemic option in our logical space of knowledge.

Let me start first with what is included as a possible epistemic option. The epistemic options included in the logical space of knowledge may be subdivided in two. First, there are epistemic options which correspond to something that, ontologically, exists and is real. For instance, the brain is an epistemic option in our logical space of knowledge, that, as verified by empirical investigation, is real and existent. Second, there are possible epistemic options included in our logical space of knowledge that do not correspond to something that is ontologically real and existent. Hallucinations are such an example: the hearing of voices is a possible epistemic option that is included in our logical space of knowledge (as manifest actually in the schizophrenic patient) even though those voices do not correspond to something that is shared with other subjects in the world.

More generally put, the possible epistemic options that are included in the logical space of knowledge may either correspond to or diverge from the ontological options included in the logical space of existence that describes the different options to describe existence and reality (as, for instance, in terms of properties or relation; chapter 9). If both epistemic and ontological options correspond with each other, we know something about the world itself, that is, independent of us. If, in contrast, our epistemic options cover something that is not included in the possible ontological options of the logical space of existence, we do not know the world itself as it remains independent of us, that is, mind-dependent.

I now argue that an example of the latter case concerns the mind. The mind is an epistemic option in our logical space of knowledge—otherwise, we would not be able intuit and subsequently assume the mind as a possible ontological origin of mental features. The intuition of mind is ultimately based on our inclusion of mind as a possible epistemic option in our logical space of knowledge. Such inclusion of the intuition of mind as a possible epistemic option of our logical space of knowledge is, as I argued, based on our ability to draw a necessary connection between mind and mental features (chapter 10).

However, as empirical and ontological evidence shows (see Parts I–III of this book), that very same epistemic option, that is, the intuition of mind, does not correspond to something real and existent in the world, we could not find any support for the assumption of mind in the world. There is thus a discrepancy between logical space of knowledge and logical space of existence: what is included as an epistemic option in our logical space of knowledge is at first excluded as an impossible ontological option from our logical space of existence. However, as the mind is included as a possible epistemic option in our logical space of knowledge, it exerts strong impact, that is, pulling forces, on the ontological options of the logical space of existence. The inclusion of mind as a possible epistemic option in our logical space of knowledge forces us to include mind as a possible ontological option in our logical space of existence. Most important, that very same inclusion of mind as a possible ontological option in the logical space of existence is based solely on its inclusion as an epistemic option in our logical space of knowledge.

In contrast, there is no independent empirical or ontological evidence for including mind as a possible ontological option in our logical space of existence—the existence and reality of mind as a possible ontological option remain consequently a mere "intuition," the "intuition of mind," as I say. Accordingly, the inclusion of the mind as an epistemic option in our logical space of knowledge exerts pulling forces on us to include the mind as an ontological option in our logical space of existence—the intuition of mind is ultimately merely epistemic rather than ontological.

How can we escape the pulling forces of the intuition of mind? We need to render impossible the pulling forces of the intuition of mind and exclude the mind as an epistemic option from our logical space of knowledge. I argue that for that, we need to shift the boundaries of the logical space of knowledge—that shall be the main focus in this and the next chapters.

Logical Space of Knowledge IIb: Impossible Epistemic Option—World–Brain Relation

Which epistemic options are excluded from the logical space of knowledge we presuppose in our investigation of the existence and reality of mental features? I argue that world–brain relation is excluded as an impossible epistemic option from our logical space of knowledge. Why? We can only perceive and thus know contingent connection between brain and consciousness when considering the brain in isolation from the world (chapter 10). Moreover, we remain unable to draw a necessary connection between world and consciousness—we can only account for a necessary connection between mind and mental features but not a necessary connection between either world or brain and mental features (chapter 10).

Because of our apparent inability to account for a necessary connection of brain and world to mental features, we exclude world, brain, and world–brain relation as epistemic options from our logical space of knowledge in our investigation of mental features. Specifically, world–brain relation is not included as a possible epistemic option in the logical space of knowledge we presuppose when addressing the question of the existence and reality of mental features. Therefore, supposing world–brain relation to underlie mental features and, more generally, the world–brain problem seems counterintuitive to those who take the mind for granted as a possible epistemic option in their respective logical space of knowledge.

The critic may now want to argue that world–brain relation is noumenal and thus intrinsically unknowable (see above). If so, world–brain relation can in principle not become an epistemic option at all, which makes it impossible by default to include it as a possible epistemic option in our logical space of knowledge. In short, world–brain relation is an epistemic nonoption rather than an impossible epistemic option (see above). However, that is to confuse noumenal and phenomenal features. The world–brain relation can be known by us and, relying on Kantian terms, is phenomenal rather than noumenal (see above). Therefore, world–brain relation is an impossible epistemic option rather than epistemic nonoption. It consequently depends on us and how we configure our logical space of knowledge whether we include world–brain relation as a possible epistemic option or exclude it as an impossible epistemic option.

Taken in such sense, world–brain relation must be distinguished from the kind of noumenal properties McGinn (1991) assumes when he characterizes the brain by mental properties, that is, property P. Following McGinn, property P is in principle unknowable for us and thus noumenal (in a Kantian sense). Therefore, property P is an epistemic nonoption rather than an epistemic option for which reason it can never be included in any kind of logical space of knowledge no matter how we shift and configure its boundaries.

Logical Space of Knowledge IIIa: Vantage Point—Transparency versus Opaqueness

How can we demarcate and restrict the logical space of knowledge in such a way that it excludes the mind as an impossible epistemic option and incudes world–brain relation as a possible epistemic option? Knowledge presupposes a certain point of view, viewpoint, or, *vantage point*, as I say in the following. By presupposing and taking a certain vantage point, we can know certain things while, at the same time, we remain unable to know others. This leads us to the definition of the concept of vantage point.

What is a vantage point? I here consider the concept of vantage point in its original definition as a "position or stand point from which something is viewed or considered" (*Oxford Dictionary*). Taken in this sense, the concept of vantage point comes close to those of point of view or viewpoint. The chosen vantage point may provide a specific view that includes a wide range of phenomena. For instance, being on the top of a mountain at the edge of the city provides us with a "vantage point from beyond the city," as I say. We can then perceive and ultimately know the city as a whole, which thereby is rendered transparent to us. The vantage point thus allows us to include the whole city as a possible epistemic option in our logical space of knowledge.

That very same epistemic option is excluded when one takes a different vantage point though. If, in contrast, one remains within the city itself, one can only take a vantage point from within the city itself. This, for instance, allows us to perceive some details such as the door mosaic of the cathedral that we were unable to perceive when taking a vantage point from beyond the city. However, nothing is free. The city as a whole, including its boundaries, remains opaque to us—the vantage point from within the city renders opaque the city as a whole, which is thus excluded (rather than included) as an impossible epistemic option from the logical space of knowledge.

Accordingly, the concept of vantage point or viewpoint (I use both terms synonymously) implies that we can take something into view by means of which it becomes transparent to us. However, at the same time, that very same vantage point precludes us from taking something else into view, which therefore remains opaque to us. Hence, the vantage point we presuppose may impact what is transparent and included as a possible epistemic option as well as what remains opaque and thus excluded as an impossible epistemic option from our knowledge—the vantage point frames and determines the boundaries of the logical space of our possible and impossible epistemic options, that is, the logical space of knowledge.

Logical Space of Knowledge IIIb: Vantage Point—Malleability of Boundaries of the Logical Space of Knowledge

What does our example about the different vantage points with regard to the city tell us about the logical space of knowledge? The logical space of knowledge is malleable, we have an impact on it and can thus, in part, determine which possible epistemic options we want to include and which ones we prefer to exclude, that is, impossible epistemic options.

By shifting the vantage point, we also change the boundaries of the logical space of knowledge, which, in turn, may render something transparent that was opaque before. A vantage point from within the city itself renders transparent the detailed view of the cathedral door (which is included as a possible epistemic option) while the city as a whole remains opaque (and thus excluded as an impossible epistemic option). The reverse happens in the case of a vantage point from beyond the city that renders transparent the city as a whole (and is thus now included as a possible epistemic option) and renders opaque the detailed view of the cathedral (which thereby is excluded as an impossible epistemic option).

Why is that relevant in the present context? I will argue in the next chapter that we need to shift our vantage point from within mind (or brain) to a vantage point from beyond brain to render transparent the world–brain relation as a possible epistemic option for consideration as an ontological predisposition of mental features. However, at the same time, that renders opaque the mind as an impossible epistemic option of our possible knowledge.

Accordingly, I will argue that our vantage point determines whether world–brain relation is included as a possible epistemic option or excluded as an impossible epistemic option within our logical space of knowledge. The inclusion of world–brain relation as a possible epistemic option will, as I postulate, render our assumption of the world–brain relation as the ontological origin of mental features intuitive. In contrast, because of its exclusion as an impossible epistemic option from our logical space of knowledge, the assumption of mind as ontological origin of mental features will now appear rather counterintuitive.

Logical Space of Knowledge IVa: Distinction—Vantage Point versus God's-Eye View

The concept of vantage point as understood here needs to be distinguished from both "God's-eye view" and the concept of perspective as in first-, second-, and third-person perspective. Let us start with the former, a God's-eye view or an Archimedean point.

The vantage point can be characterized by a specific balance between transparency and opaqueness. The vantage point from within the city renders transparent the cathedral and its door while it renders opaque the city as a whole, including its boundaries. In contrast, the vantage point from beyond the city makes transparent the city as a whole, including its boundaries, whereas now the cathedral door remains opaque. There is thus a balance between transparency and opaqueness which determines the epistemic options that are included and excluded in the logical space of existence.

That is different in the case of a God's-eye view or an Archimedean point. In that case, the totality can be taken into view at one and the same time so that nothing remains opaque. For instance, a God's-eye view renders transparent both the city as a whole as well as the cathedral door at one and the same time—there is no opaqueness at all since otherwise it would not be a view of totality as implied by a God's-eye view or an Archimedean point. Accordingly, unlike the vantage point, any kind of view of totality such as a God's-eye view or an Archimedean point no longer presupposes balance between transparency and opaqueness. There are thus no epistemic options excluded in the respective logical space of knowledge.

How can the view of totality include all possible epistemic options in the logical space of knowledge at one and the same time? That is possible by the fact that there is no specific stance. The vantage point takes a specific stance, such as "from within the city" or "from beyond the city." That very same stance implies balance between transparency and opaqueness with the subsequent inclusion and exclusion of epistemic options in the logical space of knowledge. In contrast, such stance is no longer presupposed in the view of totality—the view of totality presupposes a view that resembles what Thomas Nagel described as a "view from nowhere" (Nagel, 1986).

Logical Space of Knowledge IVb: Distinction—Vantage Point versus Perspective

We also need to distinguish the concept of vantage point from the concept of perspective as in first-, second-, and/or third-person perspectives.

The vantage point concerns the world as a whole, that is, which parts of the world as a whole are transparent and which ones remain opaque to us. This remains independent of the specific way in which we perceive and cognize the world. That, in contrast, is relevant in the case of perspectives. We can perceive the world through consciousness (first-person perspective), social context (second-person perspective), and observation (third-person perspective). Accordingly, the notion of perspective can be characterized as a specific mode of perceiving the world, as in first-, second-, or third-person perspective. The concept of vantage point refers to a more basic way of approaching the world by taking a certain view, such as a perspectival versus a nonperspectival view.

Finally, I here understand the vantage point in a purely methodological or operational sense: it provides a methodological or operational tool that allows us to shape our epistemic options and thus the respectively presupposed logical space of knowledge. Analogous to the characterization of the logical space of knowledge as an operational background space (see above), one may describe the vantage point as an "operational background tool" that helps and allows us to shape the former. Put into Kantian terms, one may want to characterize both logical space of knowledge and vantage point as transcendental features in a methodological sense (rather than empirical, as understood in a Kantian way; see also Sullivan, 2000).

Note that the purely methodological or operational determination of the vantage point does not carry any ontological implications. When we take a vantage point from either within or beyond the city, the vantage point itself remains completely independent of the existence and reality of the city itself—the city is a possible (or impossible) epistemic option but must not necessarily be an ontological option. The vantage point itself thus remains indifferent to any ontological assumptions—it is an operational background tool that provides us with epistemic options to describe existence and reality but should not be confused with ontological assumptions themselves about existence and reality by themselves, that is, independent of our epistemic options.

Part II: Copernican Revolution in Physics and Cosmology—Vantage Point from beyond Earth

Vantage Point from beyond Earth Ia: Geo- versus Heliocentric Views—Copernican Revolution

I first discuss the shift in vantage point or viewpoint suggested by Copernicus in his attempt to understand the relationship between sun/universe and Earth. It shall be noted that I do not intend to reconstruct the Copernican revolution in full historical detail nor to point outs its implications for philosophy of science (see Kuhn, 1957). Instead, I only aim to schematically sketch the Copernican revolution to illustrate how a shift in vantage point can render something transparent that remained opaque before. In other terms, the Copernican revolution changed our epistemic options and thus our logical space of knowledge. This, as we will see in the next chapter, can serve as a blueprint for shifting our vantage point with respect to mind and brain.

The ancient Greeks and the medieval people considered the Earth the center of the universe around which the sun and the rest of the universe revolves. This was stated by the Greek cosmologist Ptolemy. He suggested that the heavens and thus the universe are spherical and show movements (see below for details) that revolve around the Earth: the only way to explain our observation of movement or motion in the universe as, for instance, the movement of the sun from east to west is to assume that the Earth lies at the very center of the universe and does not move by itself. The so-called Ptolemaic view is geocentric where the Earth is the center of the universe around which the sun revolves. Because the Earth is considered the center of the universe in the Ptolemaic view, one can speak of a *geocentric view* (see figure 12.1).

The geocentric view was doubted by Nicolaus Copernicus, however. In his famous book *On the Revolution of the Celestial Spheres* (Copernicus, 1543/1952), he suggested the reverse relationship between sun and Earth, namely, that the sun (rather than the Earth) is the center of the universe (and the solar system) with the Earth revolving around the sun (rather than the sun revolving around the Earth). The Earth is no longer considered the center of the universe (or solar system); instead, the sun is now the center around which the Earth revolves—the geocentric view is thus replaced by a heliocentric view (see figure 12.2).

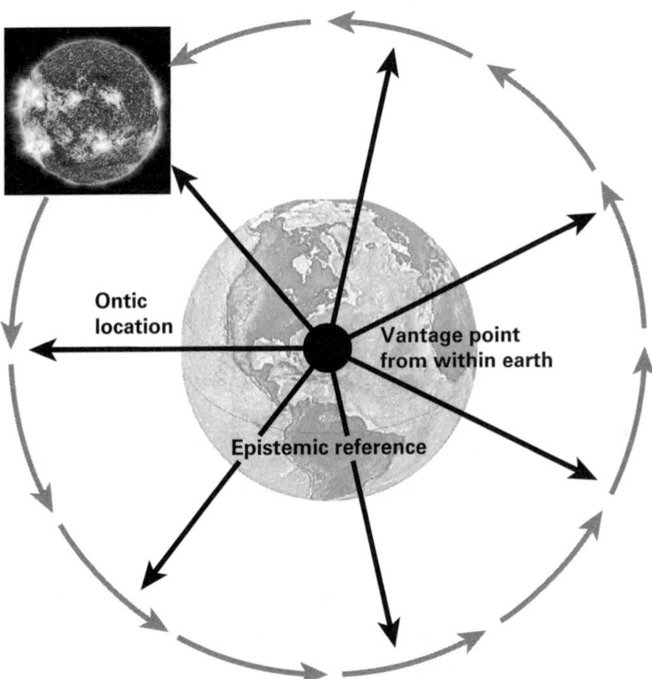

Figure 12.1

Geo- versus heliocentric models and their vantage points. Geocentric model with a vantage point from *within* Earth (the black arrows indicate the observed movements and their attribution to the sun).

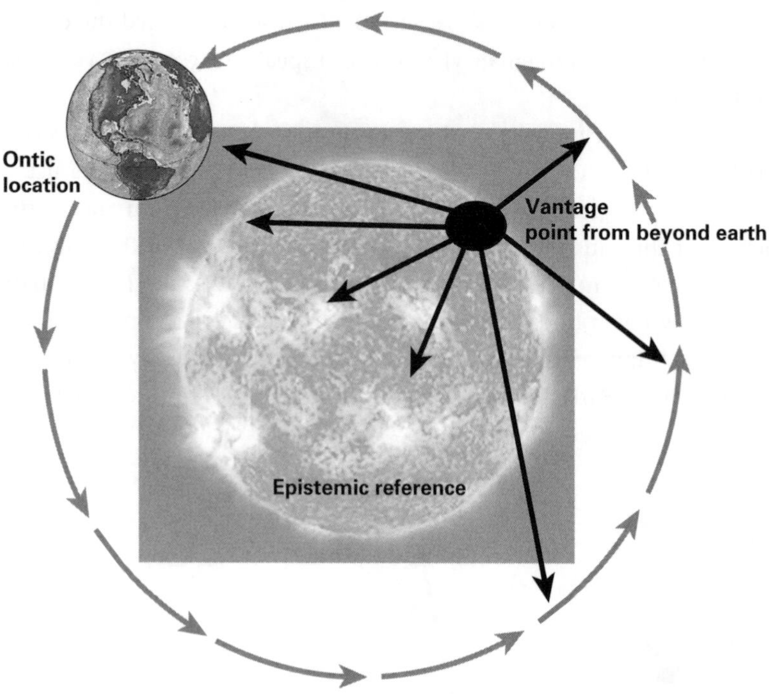

Figure 12.2
Heliocentric model with a vantage point from *beyond* Earth (the black arrows indicate the observed movements and their attribution to the Earth).

The Copernican shift marks the geocentric view as pre-Copernican while the heliocentric view can be characterized as post-Copernican. Subsequent empirical observations and mathematical formalization by Kepler, Bruno, Galileo, and Newton lend further empirical and mathematical credibility and support to the heliocentric view. Our current well-established view of the relationship between universe and Earth, the universe–Earth relation, was thus made possible by a shift from the pre-Copernican geocentric to a post-Copernican heliocentric view. The shift from a geo- to heliocentric view changed the epistemic options of our possible knowledge and thus the logical space of knowledge: it included now the heliocentric view as an epistemic option while excluding the geocentric view. I will argue in the following that such a change in the epistemic options of our logical space of knowledge was made possible by shifting the vantage point.

Vantage Point from beyond Earth Ib: Geocentric View—Spatiotemporal and Mereological Confusion

How can we further illustrate the difference between geo- and heliocentric views? Let us start with the geocentric view. The geocentric view takes the Earth itself as the vantage point or viewpoint from which the rest of the universe, including the sun, is conceived. For that reason, I speak of a *vantage point from within Earth*. Let us explicate such vantage point from within Earth in the following.

A vantage point from within Earth can take into view the universe including the sun—universe and sun are transparent and thus an epistemic option in our logical space of knowledge. In contrast, the Earth itself does not come into view when taking a vantage point or viewpoint from within Earth. We simply remain unable to see the Earth itself (including its own movements) when taking a vantage point from within Earth—the Earth itself remains opaque and is thus not an epistemic option in our logical space of knowledge.

Such vantage point from within Earth also precludes our taking into view how the Earth itself is related to its respective context or environment, that is, the universe, including the sun, the *universe–Earth relation*, as I say. The universe–Earth relation, and, more specifically, how the Earth stands in relation to the universe, remains opaque and is therefore not an epistemic option in our presupposed logical space of knowledge.

As we remain unable to take into view the universe–Earth relation, we can view the connection between universe and Earth as contingent at best while we remain unable to see their necessary connection. Accordingly, the vantage point strongly impacts how and in which way we can conceive the relationship between universe and Earth. Specifically, the lack of transparency of the universe–Earth relation, including its merely contingent connection, may thus be related to our presupposed vantage point, the vantage point from within Earth.

How does the geocentric view allow us to conceive the universe–Earth relation? In the context of a geocentric view, the Earth is the center (see below for details on the concept of center) and is therefore supposed to nest or contain the universe including the sun. That is paradoxical though as it implies confusion between two different spatiotemporal scales, that is, *spatiotemporal confusion*: the geocentric view implies that something spatiotemporally smaller (i.e., the Earth) nests or contains something that is spatiotemporally larger (i.e., sun/universe). However, something smaller (i.e., the Earth) cannot contain or nest something larger (i.e., the universe)—this amounts to spatiotemporal confusion.

Such spatiotemporal confusion goes along with the confusion between part and whole: the Earth as part is confused with the universe as whole when supposing that the former nests or contains the latter rather than the latter nesting or containing the former. I therefore speak of *mereological confusion* (which is somewhat akin to Bennet and Hacker, who speak of a *mereological fallacy* [Bennet & Hacker 2003, p. 6] in the relationship between mental features and brain).

Vantage Point from beyond Earth Ic: Heliocentric View—No Spatiotemporal and Mereological Confusion

How about spatiotemporal and mereological confusion in the heliocentric view? I argue that the heliocentric view does not suffer from either spatiotemporal or mereological confusion, which renders it more plausible than the geocentric view (on conceptual–logical grounds).

Instead of presupposing a vantage point from within Earth as the geocentric view, the heliocentric view conceives Earth in a different way, for example, from beyond itself—this entails what I describe as a *vantage point from beyond Earth*. Because of such vantage point from beyond Earth, one is now able to conceive of how the Earth is related to the universe, the universe–Earth relation, in a more transparent way without spatiotemporal and mereological confusion. Let me detail that in the following.

Specifically, the Earth as center was supposed to contain the spatiotemporally larger world—this amounts to a mereological confusion between part and whole. Instead of the Earth itself (as part) nesting or containing the universe (the whole), the spatiotemporally smaller Earth (i.e., the part) can now be conceived as being nested or contained within the spatiotemporally larger universe (i.e., the whole).

Put conversely, the whole and its larger spatiotemporal scale (i.e., the universe) contain the part with its smaller spatiotemporal scale (i.e., the Earth)—this precludes spatiotemporal confusion. Because it cannot avoid both spatiotemporal and mereological confusion, the vantage point from beyond Earth must be conceived as more plausible than its sibling, the vantage point from within Earth.

Vantage Point from beyond Earth IIa: Ontic Location versus Ontic Center

What exactly led Copernicus to suppose the reverse relationship between Earth and sun when shifting from a geocentric to a heliocentric view? Following him, there are three types of movements that need to be explained: (i) the circuit of day and night, which implies movement from west to east that is not a movement of the heavens around Earth but rather a movement of the Earth itself; (ii) the annual movement of the Earth around the sun, which is inferred from the movement of the ecliptic; and (iii) the declination that must be assumed on the basis of change in the length of day and night throughout the year.

Copernicus argued that all three movements must be attributed to Earth as their origin rather than the sun. To see this, that is, to take this into view, requires a shift from a geocentric to a heliocentric view. The shift from a geocentric to a heliocentric view puts the sun rather than the Earth into the center. What exactly is meant by the concept of *center* here? I argue that this concept can be understood in two different ways, ontic and epistemic. Let us start with the ontic meaning.

First, the concept of center can be understood in an ontic sense in that it denotes our *location* within the universe: our existence and reality are *located* in the universe with the Earth's providing that very same location—I therefore speak of *ontic location* (see chapter 11 for such ontic location when distinguishing between simple and complex location).

When supposing that the Earth is the center of the universe, as in the vantage point from within Earth, one assumes that our ontic location on Earth puts us into the *ontic center* of the universe. Our ontic location is then identical with the ontic center of the universe. If, in contrast, one denies the Earth to be at the ontic center of the universe, as in the vantage point from beyond Earth, one dislodges or dislocates us from our presumed position or location as ontic center within the universe. In that case, our ontic location diverges from the ontic center of the universe: our ontic location on Earth is no longer identical with the ontic center of the universe that now is supposed to consist in the sun rather than the Earth.

Such dislodgment from the ontic center of the universe does not imply that we completely "fall outside" the universe, however. The fact that our ontic location is no longer identical with the ontic center of the universe does not imply that we are "located" outside the universe. Instead, it only means that our ontic location on Earth is part of the universe rather than being its ontic center. Our ontic location consists then in the universe–Earth relation as it is, for instance, manifest and reflected in the movements of the Earth within the universe. Copernicus's shift in vantage point from within to beyond Earth thus made possible divergence between our ontic location within the universe (i.e., Earth as related to the universe) and the ontic center of the universe itself (i.e., the sun).

Importantly, such divergence between our ontic location and ontic center of the universe enabled Copernicus to take into view the necessary relation between universe and Earth: by moving and revolving around the sun as center of the universe, the Earth is necessarily rather than contingently related to the universe. The shift in vantage point from within to beyond Earth thus rendered transparent the necessary connection between universe and Earth, the universe–Earth relation, that remained opaque before, that is, when taking a vantage point from within Earth.

Vantage Point from beyond Earth IIb: Epistemic Reference—Earth versus Universe

In addition to its ontological meaning, the concept of center can also be understood in an epistemic sense as an epistemic reference. The concept of center now denotes a baseline or standard against which we set and compare and ultimately calibrate our possible knowledge (see also chapter 14 for the concept of calibration)—the center is now understood in an epistemic sense as reference for our knowledge, that is, *epistemic reference.*

Copernicus shifted the epistemic reference. Instead of Earth itself serving as an epistemic reference for our possible knowledge about the universe, it is now the universe itself that provides the baseline or standard against which our knowledge, that is, our observation of the movements (see above), is set and compared (i.e., calibrated). Such shift in epistemic reference, that is, from Earth to universe, enabled him to take into view that the observed movements have their origin in the Earth itself rather than in the universe, that is, the sun.

The novel epistemic reference allowed Copernicus to include novel epistemic options within our logical space of knowledge in a more extended way. When presupposing the Earth as an epistemic reference, the logical space of knowledge is restricted to the Earth itself and thus to ourselves—any possible relation between universe and Earth, that is, necessary universe–Earth relation, as well as the origin of the movements of the Earth remain opaque and are thus excluded as epistemic options from the logical space of knowledge.

That very same logical space of knowledge is reconfigured once one shifts the epistemic reference from the Earth to the universe though. Now, the observed movements and the Earth itself can be set and compared (i.e., calibrated) against the universe rather than the Earth—the universe–Earth relation and the origin of the observed movements are no longer opaque but transparent. That, in turn, allows one to take into view the necessary connection between the universe and the Earth, which therefore can be included as an epistemic option in our logical space of knowledge.

Vantage Point from beyond Earth IIIa: Ontic Location and Epistemic Reference—Complete Dependence

The critic may now want to argue that ontic location and epistemic reference must be identical. We can only take something as an epistemic reference which conforms to our ontic location: only what is ontologically within our reach, that is, our own ontic location, can serve as an epistemic reference since otherwise we know something that is beyond the reach of ourselves and our ontic location. Since we are ontologically located on Earth, only the Earth itself (i.e., alone, independent of sun and universe) can serve as an epistemic reference. In contrast, the sun or the universe cannot serve as an epistemic reference since they do not conform to but rather reach beyond the Earth as our ontic location.

Let us rephrase the argument in a more formal way. Our ontic location must serve as a necessary and sufficient condition of epistemic reference—hence, the Earth as ontic location is by itself necessary and sufficient for epistemic reference. This amounts to *complete dependence* between ontic location and epistemic reference. One can conceive other possible relationships between ontic location and epistemic reference though—among others, these include complete independence and partial dependence, which I shall discuss in more detail below. As it is about the possible dependence between ontic location and epistemic reference, I speak of an *argument of dependence*.

The argument of dependence is a primarily conceptual–logical argument about the relationship between ontic location and epistemic reference. As such, the argument of dependence may be considered to raise the conceptual implications of the Copernican revolution in physics and cosmology, which (as we will see in the next chapters) do also apply to the supposed Copernican revolution in neuroscience and philosophy (chapter 14).

More specifically, the argument of dependence, as conceived here, argues for the complete dependence between ontic location and epistemic reference. Any possible divergence between both as in complete independence and partial dependence (see below) is thus excluded by the argument of dependence—that shall be discussed in the following.

Vantage Point from beyond Earth IIIb: Ontic Location and Epistemic Reference—Complete Independence

One may opt for the opposite extreme, namely, that the ontic location is neither a necessary nor a sufficient condition of epistemic reference. This amounts to complete independence between ontic location and epistemic reference. We would then need to choose an epistemic reference that, unlike the sun, is not related at all to and therefore remains completely independent of Earth as our ontic location. Even the universe, including the sun, could then no longer serve as an epistemic reference since both are still related to our ontic location on Earth. To allow for complete independence between ontic location and epistemic reference, we must thus search for an epistemic reference that lies outside the universe and thus remains completely independent of our ontic location on Earth.

What would such epistemic reference look like? It must lie outside or beyond the universe within which our Earth is ontically located. That also means that it must be different from the world we live in, the logical space of nature, as the philosopher may want to say. This excludes the logical space of nature as a possible epistemic reference. In contrast, the logical space of reason may then serve as an epistemic reference for our possible knowledge about Earth and the world we live in.

However, the logical space of reason lies outside or beyond the world we live in, that is, the logical space of nature. Therefore, presupposing the logical space of reason as an epistemic reference will render possible metaphysics (rather than merely ontology; see chapter 9 for details on their relationship). Such metaphysics remains without or better beyond the boundaries of our empirical, epistemic, and ontological evidence though. Let me explicate that point in more detail.

Empirical, epistemic, and ontological evidence is bound and tied to the world we live in (i.e., the logical space of nature). If now we take something, that is, the logical space of reason, as an epistemic reference that lies beyond that very same world and thus the logical space of nature, the various lines of evidence, as based on the world itself as logical space of nature, are rendered futile and invalid. The lack of applicable empirical, epistemic, and ontological evidence means that metaphysics becomes open to the "excesses of reason and speculation," as Kant would have said, or "fictional forces," as Sacks (2000, p. 312) says. As made clear, I reject any such metaphysics when opting for clear-cut distinction between metaphysics and ontology (chapter 9).

How does such scenario of complete independence stand in relation to the Copernican revolution? I postulate that complete independence between ontic location and epistemic reference amounts to neither a pre-Copernican nor a post-Copernican stance but a *non-Copernican stance*, as I say. It is not pre-Copernican because it assumes complete independence, rather than complete dependence, between ontic location and epistemic reference.

At the same time, the scenario of complete independence is not post-Copernican either. Copernicus did not shift the epistemic reference outside or beyond the boundaries of the universe; instead, he only shifted them outside the boundaries of Earth, that is, beyond Earth, while remaining within the bounds of the universe. Therefore, I consider the case of complete independence as non-Copernican (rather than either pre- or post-Copernican). The distinction between non-Copernican and post-Copernican approaches will become highly relevant when it comes to mind and the vantage point we presuppose when investigating the existence and reality of mental features (chapters 13 and 14).

Vantage Point from beyond Earth IIIc: Ontic Location and Epistemic Reference—Partial Independence

How can we counter the argument of dependence? The revolutionary move of Copernicus consisted in taking into view or seeing that our epistemic reference does not need to be identical with our ontic location. He diverged epistemic reference and ontic location: despite the fact that we are ontologically located on Earth (as in complete dependence), he nevertheless suggested taking an epistemic reference, that is, the sun as ontic center of the universe, that is different from the Earth as our ontic location within that very same universe.

One can thus speak of a divergence between ontic location and epistemic reference in the Copernican revolution. However, that dissociation is not complete but only partial. The sun as an epistemic reference is still related to the Earth since both are part of one and the same universe—there is thus still partial (rather than complete) dependence between epistemic reference and ontic location. Let us conceive that in more formal terms.

The universe is a necessary condition of our epistemic reference. In contrast, it is not sufficient by itself as it needs to be related to the Earth to serve as an epistemic reference. Conversely, the Earth by itself is not sufficient either (though necessary) for serving as an epistemic reference: the Earth must be related to the universe to serve as an epistemic reference. Accordingly, neither universe nor Earth are sufficient by themselves to serve as an epistemic reference—instead, it is the universe–Earth relation that is sufficient for epistemic reference. As neither universe nor Earth is sufficient by itself, we can characterize such a case as partial dependence as distinguished from both complete dependence and independence.

Vantage Point from beyond Earth IIId: Ontic Location and Epistemic Reference—Rejection of Metaphysics

What does the logical space of knowledge look like in the case of partial dependence? Because the epistemic reference is not supposed to be identical anymore with our ontic location, the logical space of knowledge is no longer restricted to knowledge about ourselves, that is, about Earth. Instead, the logical space of knowledge can now include epistemic options that reach beyond Earth itself to the universe and, more specifically, to the universe–Earth relation. The epistemic options and thus the logical space of knowledge itself are thus extended in the case of partial dependence: they are wider than in complete dependence while they are more restricted than in complete independence.

Why is the extension or expansion of epistemic options and thus of the logical space of knowledge relevant? The expansion of the logical space of knowledge, for instance, makes it possible to attribute the origin of the observed movements to the Earth rather than the sun. This, in turn, enables us to take into view the necessary connection between the universe and Earth, the universe–Earth relation, and subsequently also the necessary connection between Earth and movements. Accordingly, both necessary connections, that is, between universe and Earth as well as between

Earth and movements, are rendered transparent when presupposing partial dependence between ontic location and epistemic reference.

This distinguishes the case of partial dependence from that of complete dependence, where both connections remain opaque and are thus not included as epistemic options in the logical space of knowledge. Moreover, unlike in the case of complete independence, the case of partial dependence allows for the epistemic reference to remain within the same universe within which the Earth as our ontic location is located and part of.

That opens the door for empirical, epistemic, and ontological evidence while it closes the door for metaphysical speculation and excesses including the "fictional forces." Copernicus did not go down that road, however. Instead, he opted for partial dependence for which reason his revolution is not compatible with any form of metaphysics reaching beyond ontology. This, as we will see in the next two chapters, carries major implications for our question of intuition of mind and my aim to replace the mind–body problem with the world–brain problem.

Conclusion

Why are we so attached to the mind? Despite contrary empirical, epistemic, and ontological evidence, we nevertheless cling to the assumption of mind in our philosophical discussion. Philosophers such as Nagel (1974), Papineau (2000), or Dennett (2013) speak of imagination or intuition that pulls us toward assuming the mind. To completely replace the mind–body problem by the world–brain problem, we therefore need to eliminate our *intuition of mind*, as I call it.

I claim that the intuition of mind, including its strong pulling forces, can ultimately be traced to the fact that we include the mind as a possible epistemic option within our logical space of knowledge. Analogous to "logical spaces of reason and nature" (McDowell, 1994; Sellars, 1963), I therefore speak of a *logical space of knowledge*. Like its siblings, the logical space of knowledge is an operational background space that, most often implicitly or tacitly, demarcates or delineates which epistemic options we include (i.e., possible epistemic options) and which ones we exclude (i.e., impossible epistemic options) from our possible knowledge.

Why is the logical space of knowledge relevant in the present context of mind? I postulate that we include the mind as a possible epistemic option in our logical space of knowledge—this renders intuitive addressing our question of the existence and reality of mental features in terms of mind and mind–body problem. In contrast, we exclude world–brain relation as an impossible epistemic option from our logical space of knowledge. This renders both world–brain relation and world–brain problem counterintuitive. Therefore, I argue that we need to include world–brain relation as a possible epistemic option in our logical space of knowledge while, at the same time, we need to exclude mind and the mind–body problem as impossible epistemic options.

How can we modify and change our logical space of knowledge in such a way that it includes world–brain relation and excludes mind as a possible epistemic option? That, as I argue, is possible by choosing the "right" vantage point. A paradigmatic example in this respect is the Copernican revolution in physics and cosmology. Copernicus shifted the geocentric vantage point from within Earth to a heliocentric vantage point from beyond Earth: that made it possible to include the heliocentric view of the universe as a possible epistemic option in the logical space of knowledge while it excluded the geocentric view as an impossible epistemic option.

What can we learn from the example of the Copernican revolution in physics and cosmology that can be applied to understanding the intuition of mind? This example shows that we can change our possible and impossible epistemic options and thus our logical space of knowledge by shifting our vantage point. That, in turn, renders something transparent which hitherto, as in the previous vantage point, remained opaque and was not included as a possible epistemic option in the logical space of knowledge.

Accordingly, I suggest that we can use the Copernican revolution in physics and cosmology as a template for shifting our vantage point in such a way that it allows for including the world–brain relation as a possible epistemic option while, at the same time, excluding mind as an impossible epistemic option from our logical space of knowledge. That, as I will argue, requires an analogous Copernican revolution in neuroscience and philosophy—this will be the focus in the next two chapters.

13 Pre-Copernican Stance in Neuroscience and Philosophy: Vantage Point from within Mind or Brain

Introduction

Aim and Argument—Origin of Intuition of Mind

How can we free us from the chains of our intuition of mind, including its pulling forces? I am now ready to get to and demonstrate the origin of our intuition of mind (see chapter 12 for details). This is the focus in the present chapter. My aim consists in demonstrating that our intuition of mind is related to a specific vantage point, that is, the vantage point from within mind that remains pre-Copernican (part I). Moreover, the various escape strategies, that is, other vantage points such as the vantage point from within reason or from within brain or body, do not really yield a truly post-Copernican vantage point.

My main argument is that we need to shift our pre-Copernican vantage point from within mind (or from within brain or body) to a post-Copernican vantage point from beyond brain to free ourselves from both intuition of mind and the mind–body problem. That, in turn, opens the door for taking into view both world–brain relation and the world–brain problem when addressing the question of the existence and reality of mental features. This amounts to nothing less than a Copernican revolution in neuroscience and philosophy as will be developed in full detail in the next chapter.

Concept of Copernican Revolution

What do I mean by the concept of *Copernican revolution*? I propose an analogy between the Copernican revolution in physics/cosmology and the one suggested here in neuroscience and philosophy. We need to distinguish between a "weak" and "strong" analogy, however.

In the strong analogy, the Copernican revolutions in physics/cosmology and neuroscience/philosophy correspond to each other in almost a one-to-one way, coming close to one-to-one correspondence. In contrast, the weak analogy implies that there are analogous features in both Copernican revolutions without claiming a one-to-one correspondence between them. As there are essential differences in their respective frameworks (such as that the question of Earth–universe relation does not correspond one-to-one to the question of mind–body relationship), I here opt for the latter, the weak analogy between the Copernican revolution in physics/cosmology and the one suggested here in neuroscience/philosophy. Because of such weak analogy, I use the concept of Copernican revolution in a figurative rather than literal (as in the case of strong analogy) way.

Kant was the first to claim that a Copernican revolution is needed in philosophy (Kant, 1781/1998). Instead of questioning the relation between mind and brain, Kant's supposed Copernican revolution concerned the relationship between subject and object—he, as I say, shifted the Humean vantage point from within object to a vantage point from within subject. However, commentators demonstrated that Kant's Copernican revolution remained ambivalent at best or failed at worst (Allison, 1973; Bencivenga, 1987; Blumenberg, 1987; Broad, 1978; Cleve, 1999; Cohen, 1985; Cross, 1937; Engel, 1963; Gerhardt, 1987; Gibson, 2011; Guyer, 1987; Hahn, 1988; Hanson, 1959; Langton, 1998; Lemanski, 2012; Miles, 2006; Palmer, 2004; Patson, 1937; Robinson, 1990; Russel, 1948, 2004). Therefore, I will not discuss his Copernican revolution in more detail.

Yet another philosopher who has been connected to a Copernican revolution in philosophy is Alfred North Whitehead (see Sherbourne, 1983, p. 368; Wiehl, 1990). These commentators argue that Whitehead, because of his supposed inversion of the Kantian subject (Whitehead, 1929/1978, p. 88; see also Northoff, 2016a and b), puts the subject back into nature, that is, the world—he, as I say, may have replaced the Kantian ambivalent vantage point from within subject by a truly post-Copernican vantage point from beyond subject. As in the case of Kant, a detailed investigation of Whitehead's supposed Copernican revolution remains beyond the scope of this book. Thus, future investigations are needed to specifically compare the Copernican revolution suggested here and its vantage point from beyond brain with those concerning the vantage point from beyond subject as based on Kant and Whitehead.

Part I: Pre-Copernican Stance—Vantage Point from within Mind

Vantage Point from within Mind Ia: Mind—Ontic Origin and Ontic Location

We experience ourselves and the world in our consciousness. In addition to consciousness, there is also an experience of other mental features such as self, emotional feeling, free will, ownership, agency, and so forth (Searle, 2004). These various mental features are often considered hallmark features of our existence. We are not merely physical machines but mental creatures. Where are these mental features coming from, and what is their ontological origin? We usually take it almost for granted that they can be traced to mind as their underlying ontological origin the—mind is the "ontic origin" of mental features.

Since mental features characterize our existence in the world, we also assume that the mind "locates" us ontologically in the world—the mind is our *ontic location* within the world. The mind as ontic origin of mental features and our ontic location in the world provides the basis for what I describe as a *vantage point from within mind.* The mind provides the basis of our vantage point or viewpoint: we take into view ourselves and the world from the viewpoint of the mind—this amounts to a vantage point from within mind. Compare this to the vantage point from the summit of a mountain. We stand on the summit of the mountain and take into view everything else, that is, mountain and valleys, from that viewpoint. The mind as ontic center and ontic location is analogous to the summit we stand on, and it is from there that we take into view body and world (as more or less analogous to mountain and valleys; see figure 13.1).

The vantage point from within mind is more or less analogous to the vantage point from within Earth. Like the former with regard to the mind, the latter suggests that Earth is our ontic origin and, at the same time, provides our ontic location within the universe. As we are based and find ourselves on Earth, we assume that the Earth locates us ontically in the universe. Analogously, the mind is supposed to ontically locate ourselves within the world—this provides us with a vantage point through which we can take a view onto the world. Just as Earth ontically locates us in the universe, the mind is our ontic location in the world.

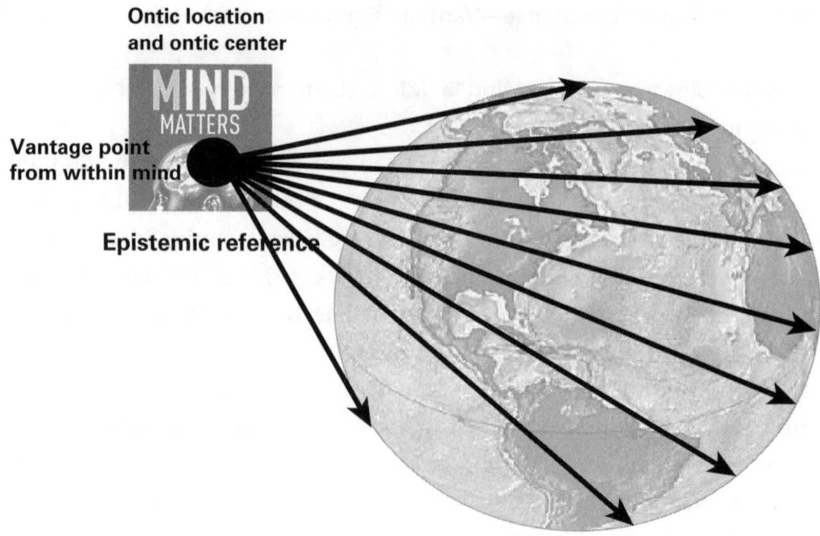

Figure 13.1
Vantage point from within mind and its mento-centric view.

The assumption of the mind as ontic location is especially striking given that we often suppose the world as merely physical. How can the mind as something that is purely mental and therefore different in principle from the rest of the merely physical world locate us ontically in that very same world? For the mind to locate us ontically in the world, one would suppose that it should share at least some basic features with the physical features that define the world. That seems to be not the case, though, as mind is mental and body is physical.

Let me explicate that in more detail. If the mind and its mental features do not share some basic features with the supposedly physical world, the mind cannot be part of the physical world. Therefore, the vantage point from within mind seems to locate us beyond or outside the physical world. Such an ontic location of the mind and its mental features beyond the supposedly physical world provides the basis for the mind–body problem: how can the mind and its mental features be related to the physical features of the world?

Vantage Point from within Mind Ib: Mind and World—Mereological and Spatiotemporal Exclusion

The vantage point from within mind confronts us with major spatiotemporal problems. The vantage point from within mind only allows us to postulate mental features as aspatial and atemporal: since it is tied to the mind (as distinguished from the physical world), the vantage point from within mind does not allow us to take into view the spatial and temporal features of the physical world. This puts mental features into conflict with physical features that are spatiotemporal rather than aspatial and atemporal.

The ascription of different mutually exclusive features dissolves any part–whole relationship between mind and world. Something like the mind that is aspatial and atemporal cannot be part of something like the physical world that is spatiotemporal. We can reconcile both mind and world only if we characterize the world itself either as mental or, alternatively, as both mental and physical. That results in either panpsychism or dualism—but neither position is supported on empirical or ontological grounds. Moreover, either position dissolves the part–whole relationship between mind and world: panpsychism assimilates the part (mind) into the whole (world), while dualism separates mind (part) and world (whole) into two wholes.

The dissolution of the part–whole relationship goes hand in hand with the the mutual exclusion of mind and world on spatiotemporal grounds. Presupposing a vantage point from within mind, mind cannot but be characterized as aspatial and atemporal while the world is spatiotemporal. Since aspatial/atemporal and spatiotemporal features entail different frames, mind and world are not spatiotemporally included within a commonly shared frame but excluded—there is spatiotemporal exclusion rather than spatiotemporal inclusion of mind and world. Accordingly, taken together, the vantage point from within mind entails both mereological and spatiotemporal exclusion of mind from world.

How does such mereological and spatiotemporal exclusion of mind and world stand in relation to mereological and spatiotemporal confusion (chapter 12)? Mereological and spatiotemporal exclusion presuppose that mind and world no longer share a common frame. This makes it impossible to even raise or conceive the question of the part–whole relation between mind and world as that presupposes some commonly shared frame, that is, mereological inclusion. That, in turn, makes impossible any possible answer including mereological confusion: if there is no question anymore, any answer becomes subsequently impossible—mereological confusion is not even an epistemic option in the logical space of knowledge.

The same holds on the spatiotemporal level. Because mind is supposedly aspatial and atemporal, any relationship with the spatiotemporal world is rendered impossible from the very beginning—such spatiotemporal exclusion excludes spatiotemporal confusion as a possible epistemic option in the logical space of knowledge. Taken together, I claim that mereological and spatiotemporal exclusion of mind and world renders impossible their spatiotemporal and mereological confusion as the latter is not even included as an epistemic option in the logical space of knowledge entailed by the vantage point from within mind.

In sum, I characterize the vantage point from within mind by (i) assumption of the mind as ontic location; (ii) mereological exclusion, which renders impossible any mereological confusion as an epistemic option; and (iii) spatiotemporal exclusion, which renders impossible any spatiotemporal confusion as an epistemic option.

Taken in this sense, the vantage point from within mind can be somewhat compared to the vantage point from within Earth that, analogously, also suffers from mereological and spatiotemporal problems, that is, mereological and spatiotemporal confusion (chapter 12). However, as mereological and spatiotemporal exclusion are much stronger than mereological and spatiotemporal confusion (which are possible only on the basis of mereological and spatiotemporal inclusion), the vantage point of mind is even stronger pre-Copernican than its sibling, the vantage point from within Earth.

Vantage Point from within Mind Ic: Mind as Ontic Center of the World—Mento-centric and Ego- and Anthropocentric View

How can we characterize such vantage point from within mind? The main problem in the pre-Copernican view and its vantage point from within Earth consisted in the fact that Earth as our ontic location within the universe was also considered the supposed ontic center of that very same universe. Our ontic location and the ontic center of the universe were thus identical, which marked the pre-Copernican view as a geocentric view (chapter 12). I now claim an analogous *mento-centric view* when we presuppose a vantage point from within mind.

Imagine again the situation of the mountain summit. You stand on the mountain summit—this provides your "stance" within the world, that is, your ontic location. That very same ontic location, that is, the mountain summit, also provides the vantage point or viewpoint from which you perceive the valleys, their various villages, and thus the rest of the world—this amounts to a vantage point from within mountain summit. Now, while perceiving the valleys and their villages, you suppose to stand at the center of the rest of the world—you assume the mountain summit to be the ontic center of the world.

The same applies analogously to the vantage point from within mind. The mind does not only provide your ontic location within the world and your vantage point or viewpoint from which you perceive and conceive the world. Additionally, the mind is also supposed as the ontic center of the world. The mind thus takes on a triple role for us, that is, as ontic location, vantage point, and ontic center.

Because we consider the mind as the ontic center of the world, our view of the world becomes mento-centric when taken to an extreme. This compares well to the geocentric view in pre-Copernican times: in the same way that the pre-Copernican cosmologists conceive the Earth as the ontic center of the universe, we conceive ourselves as the ontic center of the world. Hence, our view of the world with ourselves as ontic center is as much mento-centric as our pre-Copernican view of the universe with the Earth as ontic center is "geocentric."

Moreover, such mento-centric view of the world is, at the same time, egocentric or anthropocentric rather than allocentric or eco-centric (see below for the latter). Since we suppose that the mind as ontic center of the world also provides our own ontic location within that very same world, the mento-centric view of the world cannot be but egocentric or anthropocentric: we conceive the world in terms of our own mental features and thus our mind. The identification of mind as both ontic center and ontic location excludes any possible allocentric or eco-centric view of the world—the latter views are simply not included as epistemic options in the logical space of knowledge as entailed by a vantage point from within mind.

Vantage Point from within Mind IIa: Mind as Epistemic Reference—Exclusion of Necessary Ontological Connection

The main aim of Copernicus was to locate the origin of the different types of movements we observe in the universe. The pre-Copernican cosmologists attributed these movements to the universe itself that was supposed to move around the Earth as ontic center. That, as stated in chapter 15, was possible only by supposing that the Earth itself served as the baseline, standard, or reference, that is, as the *epistemic reference*, for calibrating our knowledge, that is, the observation of the movements.

Why is the choice of epistemic reference so important? The pre-Copernican cosmologists referenced their observations, that is, the observed movements, against the Earth itself—that very same reference renders it impossible to attribute the observed movements to the Earth itself: something (i.e., the Earth) that serves as reference for something else (i.e., observed movements) cannot be connected and thus related in a necessary way to that for which it serves as reference (i.e., the observed movements). The necessary ontological connection between Earth and the observed movements is thus not a possible epistemic option within the logical space of knowledge as entailed by the vantage point from within Earth—the vantage point from within Earth renders it impossible for us to take into view the necessary ontological connection between the Earth and the movements as a possible epistemic option.

Note that my argument does not concern whether the connection between the Earth and the movements is actually necessary (and a posteriori) or not. It only concerns our possible knowledge, that is, whether our possible knowledge of the world includes a necessary connection between the Earth and the movements as a possible epistemic option within the logical space of knowledge. I argue that the vantage point from within Earth renders impossible such epistemic option: the logical space of knowledge as presupposed by the vantage point from within Earth is such that it does not allow us to take into view a necessary ontological connection between the Earth and the movements as a possible epistemic option.

The same holds, in a more or less analogous way, in the case of the vantage point from within mind. In the same way that the Earth is taken as the epistemic reference in the vantage point from within Earth, the mind also serves as the epistemic reference for our possible knowledge about the world in the vantage point from within mind. We set, match, and compare and thus calibrate our knowledge about the world, including ourselves, against the mind as a baseline, reference, or standard (i.e., epistemic reference). However, this excludes a necessary ontological connection between mind and body/world as a possible epistemic option: something that serves as reference (i.e., mind) cannot be taken into view to show a necessary connection to something else (i.e., world) for which it serves as an epistemic reference for our knowledge about their ontological relationship.

Accordingly, the choice of mind as the epistemic reference is comparable to the situation in which the pre-Copernican cosmologists set and calibrated their knowledge (i.e., the observed movements) against the Earth as an epistemic reference. However, such choice of epistemic reference confronts both pre-Copernican cosmologists and current philosophers with a problem, namely, a conflict between epistemic reference and ontological necessity—that is, *epistemic–ontological conflict*—that shall be explicated in the following.

Vantage Point from within Mind IIb: Mind as Epistemic Reference—Epistemic–Ontological Conflict

What do I mean by epistemic–ontological conflict? I claim that something like mind or Earth that serves as epistemic reference cannot be ontologically related or connected to something like body or world for which it serves as reference. The role of mind or Earth serving as epistemic reference is not compatible with their ontological characterization—this amounts to an epistemic-ontological conflict. Such a conflict can be avoided only by keeping the epistemic reference ontologically independent of that for which it serves as reference. The need for independence of the epistemic reference makes it impossible to include its (i.e., the epistemic reference) necessary ontological connection (to what for which it serves as reference) as a possible epistemic option in the respective logical space of knowledge.

How does that apply to the mind as an epistemic reference? Specifically, as the mind serves as an epistemic reference, the mind's necessary ontological connection to what it serves as reference or standard, that is, body and world, remains impossible. A necessary ontological connection between mind and body/world is simply excluded as an impossible epistemic option from the logical space of knowledge when presupposing mind as an epistemic reference.

Taken altogether, we are confronted with a conflict: on the one hand, the choice of mind as the epistemic reference renders impossible a necessary ontological connection between mind and body/world while, on the other hand, we are searching for exactly that, namely, the necessary ontological connection between mind and body/world. As this conflict plays out between epistemic reference and ontological necessity, I speak of an *epistemic–ontological conflict*.

The concept of epistemic-ontological conflict means that epistemic and ontological assumptions are incompatible with each other. It describes contradiction with mutual exclusion between epistemic requirement, that is, no possible necessary ontological connection between mind and body/world, and ontological demand, that is, the need for a necessary ontological connection between mind and body/world. I postulate that our current discussion of mind and the mind–body problem suffers deeply from that very same epistemic–ontological conflict.

The epistemic–ontological conflict renders it impossible for us take into view the possible necessary (a posteriori) connection between mind and body as it is excluded as an impossible epistemic option in our logical space of knowledge. This is analogous to the way in which it remained impossible for the early cosmologists to take into view the necessary connection between the Earth and the movements as it was excluded as an impossible epistemic option from their logical space of knowledge.

Vantage Point from within Mind IIc: Mind as Epistemic Reference—Shift in Vantage Point

What does the epistemic–ontological conflict tell us about our choice of epistemic reference? We cannot take into view the necessary ontological connection between mind and body as long as we take the mind itself as the epistemic reference. To take into view the ontologically necessary (a posteriori) connection between mind and body as a possible epistemic option, we require an epistemic reference that is different from, and at least partially independent of, mind (as well as, conversely, different from the body). As soon as we take (either) mind (or body) as the epistemic reference, we remain unable to take into view any necessary ontological connection between mind and body as this is simply not a possible epistemic option within the respectively presupposed logical space of knowledge.

How did Copernicus solve the problem? We saw that, by shifting his vantage point from within to beyond the Earth, he could change his epistemic reference from the Earth to the universe (chapter 15). This allowed him to take into view the necessary ontological connection between the Earth and movement as a possible epistemic option in his now modified logical space of knowledge—that made it possible for him to attribute the origin of the latter to the Earth rather than the universe (chapter 15). His shift in vantage point thus allowed him to include (rather than exclude) the necessary ontological connection between the Earth and movement as a possible (rather than impossible) epistemic option into his now modified logical space of knowledge.

This is analogously so in our case. We will see in the next chapter that the shift in vantage point from within mind to beyond brain allows for exactly that, namely, a shift in epistemic reference from mind to world (chapter 14). This allows us to take into view as a possible epistemic option the necessary ontological connection between brain and consciousness through world–brain relation (chapter 10). Accordingly, presupposing a vantage point from beyond brain allows us to include the necessary ontological connection between brain and consciousness as a possible epistemic option within our logical space of knowledge.

Vantage Point from within Mind IIIa: Necessary Ontological Connection between Mind and Mental Features—Inclusion but Superfluous?

The proponent of mind may now want to argue that such radical changes in both vantage point and our logical space of knowledge are not necessary. The logical space of knowledge as entailed by the vantage point from within mind includes the necessary ontological connection of mind to mental features as an epistemic option. We want to explain mental features such as consciousness as we observe them in the world. By attributing them to the mind, we establish the necessary ontological connection between mind and mental features—the mental features are necessarily (a priori) connected ontologically to the mind, which accounts for their origin, that is, ontic origin (see above).

Accordingly, the mind provides the answer to the question of the ontological origin of mental features. As the necessary connection between mind and mental features is an epistemic option within the logical space of knowledge as entailed by the vantage point from within mind, we do not need to change either our vantage point or our logical space of knowledge. More generally, unlike in the case of the vantage point from within Earth, we do not require a Copernican revolution of our vantage point from within mind.

True, the mind is indeed necessarily connected ontologically to mental features. The necessary ontological connection between mind and mental features is indeed an epistemic option in the logical space of knowledge as entailed by the vantage point from within mind. However, the necessary ontological connection between mind and body (as well as the one between mind and world) is not included as an epistemic option in that very same logical space of knowledge.

This carries major implications. Because the necessary ontological connection between mind and body is excluded as an epistemic option in the logical space of knowledge, the mind–body problem remains completely unsolvable: its possible solution, that is, the necessary ontological connection between mind and body, is not included as an epistemic option in the logical space of knowledge as entailed by the vantage point from within mind. We therefore can develop all kinds of possible answers to the mind–body problem—none of them will include the necessary ontological connection between mind and body, however, as that is not included by itself as an epistemic option within our presupposed logical space of knowledge.

Taken together, the mind–body problem does indeed include a necessary ontological connection of mental features to their ontic origin as an epistemic option in its logical space of knowledge. However, that necessary ontological connection is the wrong one: instead of including the necessary ontological connection between mind and body as an epistemic option, it only includes the one between mind and mental features in the logical space of knowledge of the vantage point from within mind. As the necessary ontological connection between mind and mental features cannot account for the one between mind and body, inclusion of the former as an epistemic option in the logical space of knowledge is basically useless if not superfluous.

Vantage Point from within Mind IIIb: Intuition of Mind—Four Different Intuitions

The proponent of mind may want to argue that I did not really explain the intuition of mind. I, at best, demonstrated the analogy between the vantage point from within mind and the vantage point from within Earth, which marks both as pre-Copernican. In contrast, I did not demonstrate why, where, and how the intuition of mind comes into play. I reject that claim as it neglects four intuitions of mind as ontic origin, ontic location, ontic center, and epistemic reference.

The first time we intuit the mind is when we assume the mind as the ontic origin of our mental features such as consciousness, self, and so forth (see above)—we suppose that the mind provides the ontic origin, that is, existence and reality, that underlies our mental features. That is based on an inference from our observation of mental features to the existence and reality of a mind on purely intuitive grounds—this is the first intuition of mind. That is the most basic and fundamental intuition of mind as it provides the ground for all other intuitions of mind.

We are often not even aware of this very first intuition of mind—we take it for granted that we need to address the existence and reality of mental features in terms of mind. Though it seems as if the assumption of mind is a given, this is not the case. Instead, the assumption of mind as ontic origin of mental features is related to us and, more specifically, our choice of our vantage point and its logical space of knowledge.

The second intuition of mind occurs when we assume that that very same mind also provides our ontic location within the world (see above). The third intuition of mind happens when we assume that the mind as our ontic location within the world also provides the ontic center of that very same world. Finally, the fourth intuition of mind occurs when we take the mind as the epistemic reference for our knowledge of the world—the mind thus shapes our logical space of knowledge.

Despite being distinct, all four intuitions of mind share that they are all based on one and the same vantage point, that is, the vantage point from within mind. Because of the vantage point from within mind, we intuit the mind as ontic origin and location, which, in turn, pulls us toward intuiting the mind as both the ontic center of the world and the epistemic reference of our knowledge of that very same world. Accordingly, it is the vantage point itself, the vantage point from within mind, that exerts a pulling force to intuit the mind in all four instances.

Why does the vantage point from within mind exert such pulling force toward intuition of mind? As it is taken from within mind and presupposes mind as the epistemic reference, the vantage point from within mind does not allow us to take anything into view independent of the mind. This allows us to view both body and world as well as mental features only and solely in terms of mind as they are compared and set and thus referenced against mind as the epistemic reference. We are consequently pulled toward intuiting mind as ontic origin, ontic location, ontic center, and epistemic reference.

What can liberate and free us from the chains of mind? The only way to be freed from the chains of the intuition of mind is to detach ourselves from the vantage point from within mind and to replace it with a vantage point that no longer exerts such pulling forces toward intuition of mind. This is exactly what Copernicus did when he shifted the vantage point from within Earth to beyond Earth—this freed him from the intuition of Earth as center and allowed him to take into view the necessary ontological connection between the Earth and movements as an epistemic option within his then modified logical space of knowledge. We thus need to do the same and shift our vantage point, which will allow us to presuppose an epistemic reference that is different from the mind—that will be explained further below. First, however, we need to discuss some other escape strategies.

Part II: Escape Strategies—Vantage Point from within God, Reason, Consciousness, or Brain

Vantage Point from within Brain Ia: Escape Strategies—God's-Eye View

One of the main problems in the vantage point from within mind consists in the fact that the mind itself is taken as the epistemic reference and ontic location at the same time—this amounts to *complete dependence* (see above and chapter 12): the mind is not only a necessary condition of our epistemic reference (as related to its role as ontic location) but also, at the same time, a sufficient condition of our epistemic reference. Such complete dependence renders it impossible to include the necessary connection between mind and body as a possible epistemic option in our logical space of knowledge.

Why not claim the opposite, namely, *complete independence* between ontic location and epistemic reference (chapter 12)? In that case, one would choose an epistemic reference that remains completely independent of our ontic location, that is, of our mind. This opens up two different options, first, we could take God as the epistemic reference and, alternatively, we could take reason as the epistemic reference. Let us start with the first option, that is, God as the epistemic reference.

Taking God as the epistemic reference presupposes a vantage point from within God. We have to be careful, though. As God is almighty, his view cannot be described by a vantage point or point of view anymore—he "stands everywhere" and "views everything" at the same time; a vantage point is thus no longer appropriate or needed. Therefore, I speak of a *God's-eye view* rather than a vantage point from within God (see chapter 12 for details on this point).

How can we describe the God's-eye view in more detail? The God's-eye view renders opaque for us the necessary connection between mind and body and consequently the one between brain and consciousness. Anything, including mind, body, and consciousness, remains contingently connected when compared to and calibrated against God as the epistemic reference: for us, when compared to God, the necessary connection between mind and body as well as between brain and consciousness remains (necessarily) opaque and thus contingent—it is not a possible epistemic option that is included within our logical space of knowledge. Only God herself or himself can take into view the necessary connection between mind and body and consequently the one between brain and consciousness—it is only a possible epistemic option in her or his logical space of knowledge, whereas it remains an impossible epistemic option for us that is excluded from our logical space of knowledge.

Moreover, presupposing God as the epistemic reference reaches beyond the universe and our world (including world–brain relation) and thus exceeds the boundaries of our ontic location and the world itself. The presupposition of a God's-eye view amounts to complete independence between ontic location and epistemic reference: the mind as our ontic location remains completely independent of God as the epistemic reference. Such complete independence, however, renders the God's-eye view non-Copernican rather than pre- or post-Copernican (chapter 12).

Accordingly, the vantage point from within God (i.e., God's-eye view) does not solve our problem, namely, to include the necessary connection between mind and body (and also the one between brain and consciousness) as a possible epistemic option in our logical space of knowledge. Instead of solving the problem, it rather accentuates it in that it leads us beyond the world—this opens the door for metaphysics with its "fictional forces" toward speculation (Sacks, 2000). We therefore need to search for yet another vantage point. One such vantage point could consist in reason, amounting to a *vantage point from within reason*, as I call it.

Vantage Point from within Brain Ib: Escape Strategies—Vantage Point from within Reason I

What do I mean by vantage point from within reason? The vantage point from within reason presupposes reason as the epistemic reference for our knowledge about that very same world. Such vantage point from within reason combines both mind as ontic location and reason as the epistemic reference, which allows for complete independence between ontic location and epistemic reference.

Such vantage point from within reason is, for instance, paradigmatically presupposed by McDowell (1994, 2009). Without going into the details, he presupposes mind as our ontic location in the world and, at the same time, sets, compares, and thus references the mind against reason (and concepts) as the epistemic reference. However, many other approaches in current mind–body discussion (such as the one by David Chalmers and others) and past philosophy (including Kant) also presuppose such vantage point from within reason as for many philosophers it is almost evident or natural to consider reason as an epistemic reference.

Can such vantage point from within reason account for the necessary connection between mind and body as well as between brain and consciousness? No. When taking reason as the epistemic reference, mind is located in the logical space of reason while the body is associated with the logical space of nature (see McDowell, 1994, 2009; Sellars, 1963, for the distinction between these two logical spaces). As mind and body are different in principle, the vantage point from within reason remains unable to include the necessary ontological connection between mind and body as a possible epistemic option in our logical space of knowledge (chapter 12).

Vantage Point from within Brain Ic: Escape Strategies—Vantage Point from within Reason II

What is the role of the world in the vantage point from within reason? Reason as an epistemic reference remains completely outside and thus beyond the boundaries of both mind as our ontic location and the world within which it locates us. Because of the "location" of the epistemic reference outside or beyond the boundaries of both our mind as ontic location and the world itself, the necessary ontological connection between mind and body cannot be included as a possible epistemic option in the respective logical space of knowledge.

The relation between brain and consciousness is set and compared against something as the epistemic reference that lies completely outside and beyond the world in which both brain and consciousness are located; this renders impossible the necessary ontological connection between brain and consciousness, which is thus no longer included as a possible epistemic option in the respective logical space of knowledge. In short, the vantage point from within reason cannot but fail by default (i.e., necessarily) and therefore cannot solve our problem either.

Why can the vantage point from within reason not include the necessary ontological connection between mind and body as a possible epistemic option in its logical space of knowledge? This is so because here, as in the case of the God's-eye view, the epistemic reference remains completely independent of our ontic location: reason as the epistemic reference remains independent of the mind as our supposed ontic location within the world (chapter 12).

This puts the vantage point from within reason on somewhat the same par or ground as the vantage point from God that also remains completely independent and thus outside or beyond our ontic location and the world within which we are located (see above). Therefore, as with the vantage point from within God, the vantage point from within reason must also be characterized as non-Copernican rather than pre- or post-Copernican. One may now speculate that Kant's attempted Copernican revolution failed for exactly that reason: he may have presupposed the wrong vantage point, namely, a vantage point from within reason that is non-Copernican rather than post-Copernican—I leave that open for future discussion.

Vantage Point from within Brain IIa: Escape Strategies—Vantage Point from within Consciousness I

One may now reject the vantage point from within reason and shift the vantage point to consciousness. One may then want to take the view from experience, that is, from within consciousness. Such vantage point from within consciousness is, for example, presupposed in phenomenology. By conceiving the world as it appears through consciousness, phenomenology presupposes a vantage point from within consciousness. For instance, the body is conceived in the way it is experienced, that is, as *lived body*, rather than as it is observed, that is, as *objective body* (chapters 8 and 10). Moreover, everything that is experienced and surfaces in our consciousness may be considered real and existent whereas this may not hold for that which is not accessible in consciousness.

The vantage point from within consciousness puts consciousness in the center of philosophical investigation. Once we understand consciousness, we will know the world—experience and ultimately consciousness is presupposed as our epistemic reference for our knowledge about the world. Our ontic location within the world is closely related to consciousness and thus falls somewhat together with the choice of consciousness as the epistemic reference. Such vantage point from within consciousness amounts ultimately to a consciousness-centric and thus rather ego- and anthropocentric view of the world. This marks the vantage point from within consciousness as distinctively pre-Copernican rather than post-Copernican.

What about ontological assumptions? Presupposing the vantage point from within consciousness leaves us no choice but to frame those ontological assumptions in mental terms. One example is the body: since the vantage point from within consciousness only allows us to take into view mental or conscious features, the body can only be considered as the body of our experience, the lived body. The body as lived body is then considered as the phenomenological (and ultimately ontological) basis of mental features—this entails the phenomenological and ontological primacy of the world–body problem over the world–brain problem (chapters 10 and 11).

I reject that claim. The claim presupposes inference from the phenomenal realm of our experience of the body as lived body to the ontological realm of the body as an ontological basis of consciousness and mental features. However, nothing in our experience precludes that something more basic and foundational such as the world–brain relation that cannot be experienced as such can nevertheless serve as an ontological predisposition of that very same experience (i.e., as an ontological predisposition of consciousness; OPC). Therefore, the inference from phenomenal features of experience to their ontological basis remains problematic at best and fallacious at worst, amounting to what I called the phenomenal–ontological fallacy (see chapter 10).

The vantage point from within consciousness is very much prone to the phenomenal–ontological fallacy as, by its very nature, the vantage point from within consciousness remains unable to go beyond consciousness and its phenomenal realm to their underlying neuronal and neuro-ecological conditions and ultimately to their underlying ontological substrates (that, by themselves, may not be accessible to consciousness). Therefore, the vantage point from within consciousness cannot, for instance, take into view the role of world–brain relation as OPC (chapter 10). This renders the vantage point from within consciousness problematic and insufficient.

Vantage Point from within Brain IIb: Escape Strategies—Vantage Point from within Consciousness II

The phenomenologist may now want to defend her or his vantage point from within consciousness. Because we can approach and know the world, including ourselves, only in terms of experience, that is, consciousness, we remain unable to go beyond the boundaries of consciousness. We are enclosed in our consciousness without any escape from it. Therefore, as we cannot go beyond the boundaries of our own consciousness, we cannot but presuppose a vantage point from within consciousness. As the argument is based on our enclosure within consciousness, I speak of an *argument of enclosure* (see, e.g., Dietrich & Gray-Hardcastle, 2010).

How can we escape the argument of enclosure? The proponent of the argument of enclosure is certainly right when we consider the phenomenal domain alone. Because of its very nature as phenomenal, the phenomenal domain, including the vantage point from within consciousness, is closed by default with us being enclosed by it. When presupposing a vantage point from within consciousness, we are indeed enclosed within consciousness and remain unable to go beyond the boundaries of our consciousness.

However, the argument of enclosure is a phenomenal or phenomenological (I here use both terms synonymously for the sake of simplicity) argument that only pertains to the phenomenal realm of consciousness. In contrast, it does not apply to the underlying ontological realm that can go beyond consciousness itself. For instance, consciousness in general and, more specifically, the experience of the lived body may be traced to their underlying ontological conditions, that is, the OPC, which by themselves may not be accessible to consciousness (chapter 10).

Let us consider some of the conceptual distinctions we made between phenomenal and ontological realms in previous chapters (chapters 9–11). First, there is the distinction between phenomenal and ontological realms, which is important as we cannot directly infer from the former to the latter since otherwise we commit a phenomenal–ontological fallacy (chapter 10). Second, there is the distinction between prephenomenal and phenomenal levels (chapter 11). The world–brain relation may well be prephenomenal (chapter 11) in that it serves as an OPC even if it is by itself not accessible to experience and thus the phenomenal realm. Third, we need to distinguish OPC and ontological correlates of consciousness (OCC; chapters 10 and 11). While OCC are open to experience, that is, consciousness, OPC are not directly accessible in consciousness.

In sum, the vantage point from within consciousness can only take into view phenomenal features while remaining somewhat blind to their underlying ontological features, including prephenomenal features and OPC. To take into view these ontological features, we require a vantage point that is different from and goes beyond the vantage point from within consciousness. That, as I suggest, is possible only by shifting from the pre-Copernican vantage point from within consciousness to a truly post-Copernican vantage point from beyond brain (chapter 14).

Vantage Point from within Brain IIIa: Escape Strategies—Vantage Point from within Brain and Intuition of Brain

One may now want to suggest that we simply resist the pulling forces of our intuition of mind and no longer intuit the mind as the ontic origin and location of our mental features and existence in the world. Instead, we can replace the mind with the brain: the brain provides the ontic origin of our mental features and our ontic location within the world. Going even more extreme, one may then also assume the brain as ontic center of the world as well as the epistemic reference for our knowledge about the world. In short, the brain takes over the role of the mind (see figure 13.2).

Does the vantage point from within brain really abolish the intuition of mind? True, the vantage point from within brain resists the intuition of mind. However, that does not imply that it also resists intuition as such. I claim that the intuition of mind is simply replaced by yet another intuition, an "intuition of brain." Only the content of our intuition changes, from mind to brain, whereas the intuition itself, independent of any content, remains. Specifically, I suggest that the brain takes over the role of the mind in the above-described four intuitions—let me explicate that in the following.

Let us assume that the brain as ontic origin of mental features is purely intuitive as there is no necessary connection between both included as an epistemic option in the respective logical space of knowledge entailed by the vantage point from within brain. This leads ontologically to what is

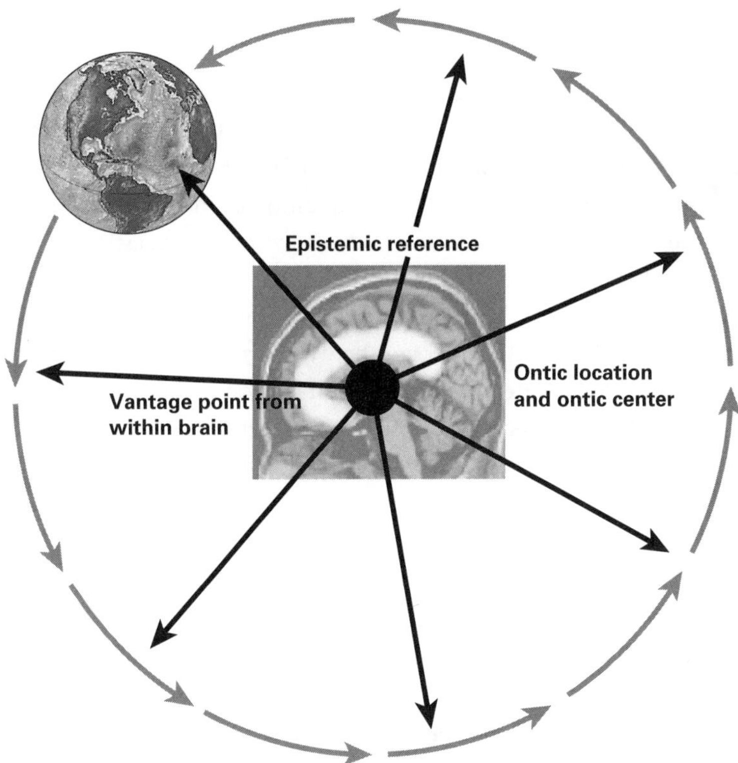

Figure 13.2
Pre-Copernican vantage point from within brain and its neuro-centric view (the black arrows indicate that the world is supposed to "move around" the brain as center).

described as materialism and/or physicalism. Moreover, taking the brain as our ontic location in the world is again purely intuitive as there is no necessary connection between world and brain either (as a possible epistemic option as included in our logical space of knowledge).

The intuitive component becomes even stronger when supposing that the brain provides the ontic center of the world and an epistemic reference for our knowledge of the world. Accordingly, taken together, the vantage point from within brain simply replaces one intuition, the intuition of mind, with another one, the intuition of brain. Therefore, the vantage point from within brain and subsequently physicalism/materialism stand on more or less the same ground as those approaches they aim at escaping from, that is, those that are based on a vantage point from within mind.

Vantage Point from within Brain IIIb: Escape Strategies—Vantage Point from within Brain and Its Neuro-centric View

How about the necessary ontological connection between mind and body? Once one presupposes the vantage point from within brain, the mind is no longer included as a possible epistemic option within the logical space of knowledge. That renders impossible the question of the necessary ontological connection between mind and body. However, the question of the necessary ontological connection of mental features to their underlying ontological origin remains. That question now resurfaces in the question of the necessary ontological connection between brain and consciousness (and mental features in general): does the vantage point from within brain allow for including the necessary ontological connection between brain and consciousness as a possible epistemic option in its logical space of knowledge?

The answer to that question is clear: No. The vantage point from within brain renders impossible and thus opaque the necessary ontological connection between brain and consciousness—it is simply not included as a possible epistemic option in the logical space of knowledge (see also chapter 12). There is nothing in the brain itself and its merely physical features that could provide the necessary ontological connection to mental features such as consciousness—the necessary ontological connection between brain and consciousness is simply not included as a possible epistemic option in the logical space of knowledge for which reason it remains opaque (rather than transparent).

How can we take into view the necessary ontological connection between brain and mental features? Only when one assumes mental features within the brain itself, as McGinn (1991) does, can the necessary ontological connection between brain and consciousness be taken into view and thus be included as a possible epistemic option within the logical space of knowledge. As the brain itself is now conceived in mental terms, such vantage point from within brain can no longer be properly distinguished from the vantage point from mind, however. We are thus confronted with more or less the same problems as when presupposing a vantage point from within mind—characterizing the brain by mental properties thus amounts to nothing more than a "pseudo-solution."

How about the brain as the ontic center of the world? As the brain is now considered the ontic origin of mental features as well as the ontic location of our existence within the world, the vantage point from within brain also predisposes us toward assuming the brain as the ontic center of the world. This amounts to a *neuro-centric view* that then replaces the mento-centric view. Replacing our mind with our brain as the ontic center of the world renders the neuro-centric view as ego- and anthropocentric as the mento-centric view.

That puts the vantage point from within brain on the same par and ground as the geocentric view of the pre-Copernican cosmologists—the vantage point from within brain and its neuro-centric view of the world are as much pre-Copernican as the vantage point from within Earth with its geocentric view of the universe. Like its geocentric sibling, the neuro-centric view makes it impossible for us to take into view and thus render transparent the necessary ontological connection of the brain to something that extends beyond the brain itself, that is, mental features such as consciousness.

Vantage Point from within Brain IIIc: Escape Strategies—Vantage Point from within Body and Intuition of Body

How we can escape such neuro-centric view? The proponent of embodiment (see chapter 8 for more details on that) may want to argue that we need to presuppose a vantage point from within body rather than from within brain. The body rather than the brain provides the ontic origin of mental features, and it is the body (and not the brain) that anchors us within the world as our ontic location. Moreover, the body may be the ontic center of the world and thus also provide the epistemic reference for our knowledge about the world.

However, without going into detail, the assumption of body as ontic origin, ontic location, ontic center, and epistemic reference remains as intuitive as when intuiting either mind or brain. As in the case of the vantage point from within brain, the vantage point from within body simply replaces one intuition, that is, intuition of brain, with yet another one, that is, *intuition of body*. The neuro-centric view is simply replaced by a body-centric view. This puts the vantage point from within body on the same par or ground as the vantage point it aims to escape from, that is, the vantage point from within brain.

Moreover, without going into detail, the vantage point from within body still does not allow us to include the necessary ontological connection between brain and consciousness as a possible epistemic option in our logical space of knowledge. Why? Because, as in the case of the brain, there is simply no necessary conceptual connection between the physical features of the body and mental features such as consciousness. Therefore, the necessary ontological connection between body and consciousness is still not included as a possible epistemic option within the logical space of knowledge as entailed by the vantage point from within body.

How can we include the necessary ontological connection between brain or body and consciousness as a possible epistemic option in our logical space of knowledge? Thomas Nagel already pointed out well that neither a vantage point from within mind (i.e., mental point of view) nor a vantage point from within brain or body (i.e., physical point of view) will render transparent the necessary ontological connection between brain/body and consciousness:

> Neither the mental nor the physical point of view will do for this purpose. The mental will not do because it simply leaves out the physiology, and has no room for it. The physical will not do, because while it includes the behavioral and functional manifestations of the mental, this doesn't enable it, in view of the falsity of conceptual reductionism, to reach to the mental concepts themselves. (Nagel, 2000, p. 45)

What does Thomas Nagel tell us with regard to the vantage point? We require a vantage point that allows us to take into view that which extends or reaches beyond both mental and physical, that is, "something that extends beyond its grounds of application" (Nagel, 2000, p. 46). How is that possible? That is the moment we can turn to Copernicus and learn from his revolution in physics and cosmology. He shifted the vantage point from within to beyond Earth. This allowed him to include the universe as an epistemic reference which, reaching beyond Earth as our ontic location, rendered transparent the necessary ontological connection between the Earth and movements.

Analogously, we can shift our vantage point from within mind (or brain or body) to a vantage point from beyond brain. This, as I hope, allows us to reach beyond our own brain as ontic location within the world and to subsequently include the world itself in our epistemic reference. That, in turn, should render transparent the necessary ontological connection between brain and consciousness—this will be the focus in the next chapter.

Conclusion

I demonstrated that our intuition of mind and its pulling forces toward the assumption of the mind as ontic origin of mental features can be traced to our vantage point. Specifically, by presupposing a vantage point from within mind, we include mind as an epistemic option in our logical space of knowledge. This amounts to a pre-Copernican stance in neuroscience and philosophy as it is comparable to the vantage point from within Earth in physics and cosmology prior to Copernicus.

How can we escape our intuition of mind and its pulling forces toward assuming the mind as ontic origin of mental features? We first and foremost need to escape the vantage point from within mind. I demonstrated various escape strategies, including the vantage point from within reason and from brain (or body). However, they all failed in their endeavor to overcome our intuition of mind, which, as in the case of the vantage point from within brain, was simply replaced by yet another intuition, the intuition of brain.

I postulate that we require a much more radical shift in our vantage point to render the intuition of mind impossible to sustain. Analogous to Copernicus in physics and cosmology, we require a radically different vantage point, a vantage point from beyond brain, that is analogous to his vantage point from beyond Earth (chapter 15). Such a vantage point from beyond brain will render it impossible for us to sustain the concept of mind. That, in turn, will open the door for replacing mind and the mind–body problem with world–brain relation and the world–brain problem. This amounts to nothing less than a Copernican revolution in neuroscience and philosophy—that will be the focus in the next chapter.

Conclusion

[illegible]

14 Copernican Revolution in Neuroscience and Philosophy: Vantage Point from beyond Brain

Introduction

Mental Features—Extension beyond Ourselves to the World

Why are mental features so special? Mental features link and connect us to the world. For example, consciousness allows us to experience ourselves as part of the world. If we lose consciousness (chapters 4 and 5), we can no longer experience ourselves as part of the world and instead remain isolated from it—this, for instance, renders impossible communication with others as we can no longer participate in and share the world with others. The same applies to other mental features such as self, emotional feeling, agency and ownership, free will, and so forth that also allow us to participate in the world by becoming part of it. In a nutshell, consciousness and mental features are about the world and, more specifically, our relation to the world—mental features relate us to the world by means of which we can become part of the world.

How can mental features establish our relation to the world? They must make it possible for us to extend "beyond" our brain and body to the world—they reach *beyond ourselves*, as I will say in the following. I already pointed out that that very same "beyond ourselves" of our mental features can be traced to our brain's empirical (chapters 7 and 8) and ontological (chapters 9–11) integration within the world, that is, world–brain relation—the world–brain relation is an ontological predisposition of consciousness (OPC; chapter 10). In contrast, I left open how we can take into view that very same "beyond ourselves," that is, the world–brain relation as OPC—that shall be the focus in this chapter.

Main Aim and Argument

The main aim in the present chapter is to complement the empirical (chapters 7 and 8) and ontological (chapters 9–11) account of "beyond ourselves" and thus of world–brain relation as OPC on the methodological and epistemological level. I argue that we methodologically need to radically shift our vantage point from within mind or brain to a vantage point from "beyond brain" to take into view the role of world–brain relation as OPC. Such vantage point from beyond brain will allow us to include the role of world–brain relation as OPC as a possible epistemic option within our logical space of knowledge (chapter 12) while, at the same time, it excludes mind as an impossible epistemic option from our logical space of knowledge.

I conclude that the exclusion of mind renders impossible the mind–body problem, which therefore can be completely replaced by the world–brain problem. As such ontological replacement of the mind–body problem by the world–brain problem is methodologically based on a radical shift in our vantage point, it amounts to nothing less than a Copernican revolution in neuroscience and philosophy (see introduction in chapters 12 and 13 for the concept of Copernican revolution).

Part I: Post-Copernican Stance—Vantage Point from beyond Brain

Vantage Point from beyond Brain Ia: Ontic Origin and Ontic Location—Mental Features Reach beyond Ourselves to the World

How can we take into view our relation to the world? We discussed different vantage points such as those from within mind, brain, and body. None allowed us to take into view our relation to the world though. All three vantage points assumed that mind, brain, or body provide the ontic origin of mental features as well as our ontic location within the world (chapter 13). However, that only allows us to take into view mind, body, or brain while it excludes the world itself, including its relation to our body and brain. We thus require a different vantage point. That vantage point should allow us to take into view the world itself, including our relation to the world, and thus what extends beyond our brain and body, that is, beyond ourselves.

Copernicus encountered an analogous challenge. He searched for a vantage point that allowed him to take into view how we, as bound to the Earth, can reach and extend beyond the Earth to the universe, that is, beyond ourselves. Specifically, the pre-Copernican vantage point from within Earth did not allow us to take into view our relation to the universe (i.e., universe–Earth relation), which rendered it impossible to account for what extends beyond Earth, that is, beyond ourselves (chapter 12). Hence, like us with respect to mind, body, and brain, he was confronted with the challenge of developing a vantage point that allowed him to take into view the universe beyond ourselves, that is, beyond our ontic location on Earth.

What exactly extends beyond ourselves, that is, beyond Earth, in the case of Copernicus? Copernicus searched for the ontic origin of the movements that could be observed. As they take place within the universe, those movements reach and extend beyond Earth—they can be characterized by what I described as "beyond ourselves." How could Copernicus take into view that very same "beyond ourselves"? By shifting the vantage point from within Earth to a vantage point from beyond Earth, Copernicus was able to take into view that very same "beyond ourselves," that is, how the observed movements could extend and reach beyond ourselves and take place within the universe as a whole with the Earth as its part (chapter 12).

I now argue that we require an analogous shift in vantage point with respect to mental features. Like the movements in the case of Copernicus, mental features confront us with the problem of taking into view something that reaches beyond ourselves, that is, beyond our body and brain to the world. Learning from Copernicus, I therefore suggest shifting our vantage point from within mind, body, or brain to a *vantage point from beyond brain* (I owe the suggestion of the term "beyond" in the context of vantage point to Kathinka Evers in Uppsala, Sweden; see figure 14.1).

Vantage Point from beyond Brain Ib: Ontic Origin and Ontic Location—World–Brain Relation as beyond Ourselves

What do I mean by the vantage point from beyond brain? The vantage point from beyond brain allows us to take into view that which extends beyond our brain and body, that is, beyond ourselves. Specifically, it allows us to take into view that our brain relates us to the world (i.e., world–brain relation) by means of which we become part of the world. That can be compared to the vantage point from beyond Earth. Analogously, the vantage point from beyond Earth allowed us to take into view how we, as based

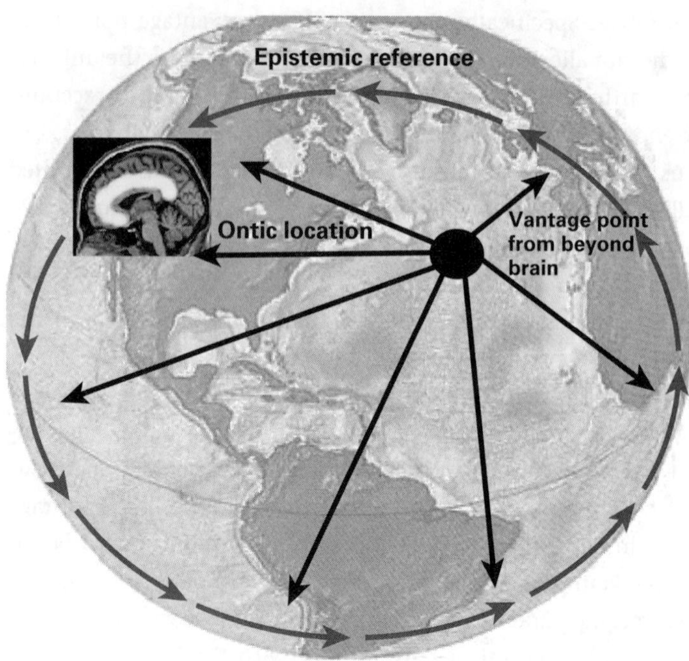

Figure 14.1
Post-Copernican vantage point from beyond brain and its allo- and eco-centric view (the black line indicates that the brain "moves around" the world).

ourselves on Earth, can become part of the universe. We were now able to take into view how the Earth, as on the basis of its movements, can relate us to the universe (i.e., universe–Earth relation; chapter 12).

How can the vantage point from beyond brain account for the ontic origin of mental features and our ontic location within the world? We recall, in the case of the vantage point from within mind, brain, or body, we could only take into view mind, brain, or body as both the ontic origin of mental features and the ontic location of ourselves within the world. That is different in the case of the vantage point from beyond brain. The vantage point from beyond brain renders impossible determining mind, brain, or body as the sole and single ontic origin of mental features and our ontic location within the world.

As it extends our view beyond ourselves to the world, that is, beyond brain and body, the vantage point from beyond brain renders it impossible to determine both ontic origin and ontic location solely by mind, body, or brain alone, that is, independent of the world. Instead, as the vantage point from beyond brain allows us to take into view that which is beyond ourselves, that is, the world, we can now include the world in our determination of both ontic origin and ontic location.

Let me detail that. The shift from a vantage point from within brain to a vantage point from beyond brain allows us to take into view that which extends and reaches beyond our brain, that is, beyond ourselves. What extends beyond ourselves, that is, beyond brain and body, is the world and how it relates to us including our brain (i.e., the world–brain relation). That, in turn, makes it possible for us to determine world–brain relation (rather than the brain itself or, alternatively, body or mind) as the ontic origin of mental features and our ontic location within the world.

Taken together, the vantage point from beyond brain allows for a wider view of both ontic origin of mental features and our ontic location within the world. Rather than restricting both ontic origin and ontic location to mind, body, or brain alone, that is, independent of the world, we can now take into view the world itself and how it relates to, for instance, the brain (i.e., world–brain relation). The vantage point from beyond brain thus makes it possible to take into view that which lies beyond ourselves, namely, world and world–brain relation.

In a nutshell, the vantage point from beyond brain provides us with a wider view of ourselves that reaches beyond ourselves to the world. That, in turn, makes it possible for us to take into view how we are integrated within the world by means of our brain (i.e., world–brain relation) and can thereby become part of the world as a whole.

Vantage Point from beyond Brain IIa: Vantage Point from beyond Mind—Beyond World

The proponents of mind or body may now want to argue that they fully share the need to go beyond ourselves, that is, beyond brain or body, when determining both the ontic origin of mental features and our ontic location within the world. However, that can best be done by employing a vantage point from beyond mind or a vantage point from beyond body rather than a vantage point from beyond brain: instead of world–brain relation, we can then take into view mind–world relation or body–world relation and how they serve as the ontic origin of mental features and our ontic location within the world. In short, mind–world relation or body–world relation replace world–brain relation.

I reject both suggestions though. Let us start with the vantage point from beyond mind. The vantage point from beyond mind does indeed allow for taking into view that which extends beyond the mind. However, that very same "beyond mind" targets a world that is different from the one we live in. Put into the terms of the logical spaces of nature and reason (chapter 15), one may say that the vantage point from beyond mind targets the logical space of reason as distinguished from the logical space of nature. This carries major implications for our determination of ontic origin and ontic location.

The ontic origin of mental features is now found in those features, that is, conceptual relations, that characterize the logical space of reason (McDowell, 1994; Sellars, 1963), while our ontic location, even if in the logical space of nature, may then be determined in the conceptual–logical terms of the logical space of reason (chapter 15). As it relies primarily on reason, the vantage point from beyond mind converges with (and, even stronger, may be identical with) what I described as the *vantage point from within reason* in chapter 13.

However, the determination of the ontic origin of mental features and our ontic location within the world in the conceptual–logical terms of reason must be rejected as it extends the "beyond ourselves" too far: it reaches not only beyond ourselves, that is, beyond brain and body, but also beyond the world within which brain and body are "located," that is, "beyond world." One is then confronted with the question of the relation between the two "beyonds," that is, "beyond ourselves" and "beyond world."

Vantage Point from beyond Brain IIb: Vantage Point from beyond Mind—Beyond Ourselves versus beyond World

How do the two "beyonds," that is, "beyond ourselves" and "beyond world," stand in relation to each other? The critic may want to argue that they are identical in their extension—beyond ourselves reaches as far as beyond world. That is not the case though. The concept of beyond world entails an extension beyond both ourselves and world. In contrast, the concept of beyond ourselves only includes an extension "beyond body and brain." That very same "beyond body and brain" does not entail an extension beyond the world itself within which body and brain are located, though—beyond ourselves thus does not extend as far as beyond world. Therefore, we can easily reject the proponent's argument of identical extension of beyond ourselves and beyond world.

Let me rephrase the distinction between beyond ourselves and beyond world in terms of the logical space of nature and reason (McDowell, 1994; Sellars, 1963). As it remains within the boundaries of world, beyond ourselves is quite compatible with the presupposition of the logical space of nature in a spatiotemporally extended version. In contrast, as it extends beyond the world itself and relies on conceptual relation and reason, beyond world requires us to presuppose the logical space of reason (rather than the logical space of nature). This opens the door for speculation with metaphysics and its "fictional forces" (Sacks, 2000, p. 312) including the intuition of mind.

Most important, the need of "beyond world" to presuppose the logical space of reason (rather than the logical space of nature) renders it distinctively non-Copernican rather than post-Copernican (chapters 12 and 13). Therefore, as it entails beyond world (rather than beyond ourselves), the supposition of a vantage from beyond mind simply misses its aim, namely, to provide a truly post-Copernican vantage point as alternative to the pre-Copernican vantage point from within mind.

Vantage Point from beyond Brain IIIa: Vantage Point from beyond Body—Beyond Observation versus beyond World

How about the vantage point from beyond body? The vantage point from beyond body allows us to extend our view beyond our body and thus beyond ourselves. In contrast, it does not allow us to extend our view beyond the world we live in, that is, beyond world. The view we can take when presupposing the vantage point from beyond body thus remains within the bounds of the world without reaching beyond world. Therefore, unlike the vantage point from beyond mind, the vantage point from beyond body is not confronted with the problem of the discrepancy between beyond ourselves and beyond world.

What does this imply for our determination of the ontic origin of mental features and our ontic location within the world? As the vantage point from beyond body does not extend our view beyond world, we can determine both ontic origin and ontic location in the terms of the world. This raises the question of what such determination looks like in methodological terms.

The vantage point from beyond body allows us to take into view that which is beyond ourselves in the world. As beyond ourselves also includes extending beyond our own methodological tools such as observation, the vantage point from beyond body allows us to go beyond our own observation (i.e., "beyond observation"). More specifically, we can now take into view that which we cannot observe (i.e., that which is beyond observation) but which is nevertheless part of the world (i.e., beyond ourselves), as distinguished from that which extends beyond the world itself (i.e., beyond world).

Put into the terms of the concept of the logical space of nature (McDowell, 1994; Sellars, 1963), the vantage point from beyond body allows us to take into view a conception of the logical space of nature that extends beyond observation. This makes it possible for us to distinguish a spatiotemporally extended logical space of nature as in ontic structural realism (chapter 9) from the traditional observationally restricted logical space of nature as in science (Sellars, 1963). Most importantly, as beyond observation only implies beyond ourselves but not beyond world, that very same distinction can be made without the need to reach beyond the logical space of nature itself and thus beyond the world to the logical space of reason.

In sum, the vantage point from beyond body allows us to take a view that extends beyond ourselves without extending too far, that is, beyond the world we live in (i.e., beyond world). This renders the vantage point from beyond body distinctively post-Copernican as distinguished from both the pre-Copernican vantage point from within body and the non-Copernican vantage point from beyond mind. Because it is truly post-Copernican (rather than either pre- or non-Copernican), I consider the vantage point from beyond body superior to both the vantage point from beyond mind and the vantage point from within body.

Vantage Point from beyond Brain IIIb: Vantage Point from beyond Body—Scope of View

How does the vantage point from beyond body stand in relation to the vantage point from beyond brain? Its truly post-Copernican stance puts the vantage point from beyond body on the same par or ground as the vantage point from beyond brain. Both allow for extending our view beyond ourselves and beyond observation without reaching beyond the world itself (i.e., beyond world). That distinguishes both the vantage point from beyond body and brain from the vantage point from beyond mind, which extends our view not only beyond ourselves and beyond observation but also beyond world.

This raises yet another question though, namely, that of the distinction between the vantage point from beyond body and the vantage point from beyond brain. How can we distinguish these two vantage points? This is especially important given that I opt for the vantage point from beyond brain (rather than the vantage point from beyond body). On a purely conceptual–logical level, both vantage points can indeed not be distinguished from each other as both allow for taking into view the same world, that is, the world we live in as characterized by spatiotemporal features, as well as one and the same conception of the logical space, that is, the spatiotemporally extended logical space of nature.

In contrast to the conceptual–logical realm, both vantage points lead to differences on the ontological level when it comes to determining ontic origin and ontic location. The vantage point from beyond body will determine world–body relation as the ontic origin of mental features and our ontic location within the world, whereas the vantage point from beyond brain allows us to take into view the brain, including its relation to the world (i.e., world–brain relation), as the ontic origin of mental features and our ontic location within the world.

Why do both vantage points lead to different ontological determinations? I argue that the scope of their respective view is different. The vantage point from beyond body can only take into view all that which is beyond the body—this includes the body's relation to the world (i.e., world–body relation). In contrast, the vantage point from beyond brain can include all that which lies beyond the brain—this includes the brain's relation to the world (i.e., world–brain relation), as well as how that impacts the body and its relation to the world, that is, "beyond body." I will specify that difference in the scope of their views in the following section.

Vantage Point from beyond Brain IIIc: Vantage Point from beyond Body—Beyond Body versus beyond Brain

The proponent of the vantage point from beyond body may now want to argue that there is indeed a difference in scope but that this speaks in favor of the vantage point from beyond body. The vantage point from beyond body can well take into view the brain as the brain is included as part of the body as a whole—beyond body thus entails beyond brain. Therefore, as it includes both beyond brain and beyond body, the vantage point from beyond body shows a wider scope than the vantage point from beyond brain that only includes beyond brain but not beyond body. I reject that argument, though, and suggest instead the reverse, namely, that beyond brain includes beyond body for which reason the scope of the vantage point from beyond brain is wider than that of the vantage point from beyond body.

True indeed, the vantage point from beyond body allows us to take into view the brain. However, the brain can be taken into view only as part of the body and thus in dependence on the body, including its relation to the world (i.e., world–body relation). In contrast, the brain itself, with its own relation to the world (i.e., the world–brain relation) does not come into view at all. In short, the vantage point from beyond body excludes world–brain relation from its view.

This is obviously different in the vantage point from beyond brain. The vantage point from beyond brain can take into view all that which is beyond the brain. However, the exact meaning of "beyond brain" remains unclear, as we need to define the scope of what "beyond" refers to. That shall be discussed in the following. Beyond brain includes the brain's relation to the world (i.e., world–brain relation), as well as the body's relation to the world (i.e., world–body relation). I thus argue that beyond brain includes beyond body. As it includes beyond body, beyond brain shows a wider scope and extension when compared to those of beyond body that are limited to the body while excluding the brain.

How can beyond brain include beyond body? Put into empirical terms, I demonstrated that the brain's spontaneous activity receives inputs from both body, that is, interoceptive stimuli, and world, that is, exteroceptive stimuli. Most importantly, both inputs are integrated within the brain's spontaneous activity and its spatiotemporal structure, which, in turn, makes it possible to align brain and subsequently the body to the world (chapter 8). The same holds, analogously, on the ontological level: the brain constitutes the relational time and space by means of which brain itself and subsequently body can be integrated within and thus related to the world (chapter 10)—the world–body relation can thus be traced to the world–brain relation (chapter 10).

What does this imply for the relationship between beyond brain and beyond body? Beyond body, that is, the extension of the body to the world, is empirically and ontologically dependent upon beyond brain. Therefore, beyond brain implies or entails beyond body. In contrast, beyond body only focuses on the body's relation to the world (i.e., world–body relation) while neglecting the brain's own relation to the world (i.e., world–brain relation). As beyond body does not consider the brain's own relation to the world, the scope of the world–body relation remains limited. For instance, it remains unable to account for why and how the objective body is transformed into the lived body—for that, the world–brain relation is central as it allows for the brain's spatiotemporal alignment to the world, which, in turn, transforms the objective into the lived body (chapter 8).

In sum, I argue that the vantage point from beyond brain provides us with a wider scope, that is, including both beyond brain and beyond body, in our view of the beyond ourselves when compared to the scope of the vantage point from beyond body that is limited to beyond body. Thus, the vantage point from beyond brain allows us to take into view that which extends beyond both brain and body whereas we can only take into view that which reaches beyond body in the vantage point from beyond body.

Vantage Point from beyond Brain IVa: Ontic Center of the World—Three Criteria

We have so far focused on the ontic origin of mental features and our ontic location within the world. That leaves aside yet another feature of a vantage point, namely, that it allows us to make assumptions about the "ontic center" (chapters 12 and 13). For that, I again turn back briefly to Copernicus.

Copernicus shifted the vantage point from within Earth to a vantage point from beyond Earth. This allowed him to determine the sun rather than the Earth as the ontic center of the universe and thus to replace the geocentric view with a heliocentric one (chapter 12). This strongly affected the supposed ontic center of the universe. The geocentric view is rather ego- and anthropocentric, as it puts us (i.e., humans) right into the ontic center of the universe (chapter 12). That changed though with the shift from the geo- to heliocentric view. This made it possible to establish an "allocentric view" rather than egocentric view, which considered the sun as the ontic center of the universe (chapter 12). I now claim that the same holds analogously in the case of the vantage point from beyond brain. We recall from the previous chapter (chapter 13) that, analogous to the geocentric view, the vantage point from within mind, body, or brain puts us as humans right into the ontic center of the universe—this amounts to an ego- and anthropocentric view of the world. That changes when shifting the vantage point from within mind, body, or brain to a vantage point from beyond brain.

As it reaches and extends beyond brain and body (see above), the vantage point from beyond brain allows us to take into view the world itself, that is, beyond ourselves. We therefore no longer need to identify our own ontic location within the world with the ontic center of the world itself. Specifically, we can now determine the ontic center of the world in a way that is different and somewhat independent of ourselves, that is, body and brain. We can thus take into view that which is beyond ourselves which may define the ontic center of the world by itself (i.e., as it remains independent of us).

What is the ontic center of the world? Let us consider some criteria that must be fulfilled for determining the ontic center of the world. First, the ontic center of the world must allow for determining the world independent of us: it should remain independent of body, brain, world–brain relation, and, most importantly, also of our mental features (such as consciousness). Second, the ontic center of the world must allow for including its relation to brain and body (i.e., world–brain and world–body relation) as they provide the ontic origin of mental features and our ontic location within the world. Third, the ontic center must be a necessary condition of the existence and reality of the world as such: without the ontic center, the world could not exist in the same way the universe could not exist without the sun as the ontic center.

Vantage Point from beyond Brain IVb: Ontic Center of the World—Time and Space

What is now the ontic center of the world? I suppose that space and time constitute the ontic center of the world as they fulfill all three criteria. Let us start with the third condition. Time and space are the ontic center of the world as without them the world as such would no longer exist—time and space are thus a necessary condition of the existence and reality of the world itself. This fulfills the third criterion.

Moreover, time and space in this sense can include the relation of the world to ourselves like the world–brain relation—one would then assume time and space to exist in terms of what I described as *relational time and space* (chapters 9 and 11). More specifically, world–brain relation is an intrinsically spatiotemporal relation as it links the different spatiotemporal scales of world and brain to each other (chapters 9–11). Time and space as the ontic center of the world thus make possible our relation to the world (i.e., world–brain relation) as our ontic location within that very same world. This is very much analogous to Copernicus's cosmological assumption: the sun as the ontic center of the universe makes possible our ontic location, that is, universe–Earth relation, within that very same universe. Thus, the requirement of the second criterion, the relation between the ontic center and us, is well met.

Finally, time and space themselves remain completely independent of us and our existence and reality. Whether we, as humans, including our brain and body, exist or not does not matter for time and space, whose existence and reality are more encompassing and thus beyond ourselves. This meets the first criterion, the independence of time and space from us. Taken together, as time and space meet all three criteria, I consider them ideal candidates for being the ontic center of the world.

Vantage Point from beyond Brain IVc: Ontic Center of the World—Ego- and Anthropocentric View versus Allo- and Eco-centric View

What does the assumption of time and space as the ontic center of the world imply for our view of the world and ourselves? We recall that the vantage point from within brain resulted in an ego- and anthropocentric view, as it identified our ontic location within the world with the ontic center of the world itself. Such an ego- and anthropocentric view was manifest in a neuro-centric view of the world (which replaced the mento-centric view of the vantage point from within mind; chapter 13).

How about the vantage point from beyond brain? Unlike the vantage points from within mind, brain, or body, the vantage point from beyond brain allows for divergence between ontic location and ontic center: the world–brain relation is our ontic location within the world, while time and space constitute the ontic center of the world. This makes it possible for the vantage point from beyond brain to escape any kind of ego- and anthropocentric view of the world including neuro- and mento-centric views. Specifically, by taking the world beyond ourselves into view, the vantage point from beyond brain allows us to conceive ourselves as part of the wider world—the egocentric view is replaced by an allocentric view. Moreover, the vantage point from beyond brain allows us to detach ourselves from the view that we as humans are the center of the world—the anthropocentric view is replaced by an eco-centric view.

Let me summarize. The vantage point from beyond brain allows for divergent determination of both our ontic location within the world and the ontic center of the world. The ontic center of the world can now be determined as independent of us and our ontic location within the world. That makes it possible to abandon an ego- and anthropocentric view of the world and replace it with an allo- and eco-centric view. Rather than inferring the ontic center of the world from our own ontic location within the world, we can now make an inference in the opposite direction from, ontic center to ontic location: we can determine our ontic location within the world in dependence on the ontic center of the world. This allows us to replace neuro- and mento-centric views with a novel view of the world.

What does such novel view of the world look like? We recall that time and space were determined as the ontic center of the world. Our view of the world is consequently spatiotemporal, entailing a *spatiotemporal view*, as I say. I therefore suppose that our current neuro- and mento-centric view of the world must be replaced by a spatiotemporal view of the world. Specifically, the spatiotemporal view determines the world in terms of relational time and space: the latter constitute spatiotemporal relation and structure as the ontic center of the world itself, which includes world–brain relation as our ontic location within that very same world.

Vantage Point from beyond Brain Va: Ontic Center of the World—Spatiotemporal and Mereological Confusion

The critic may now want to argue that the characterization of both ontic center and ontic location by space and time leads to mereological and spatiotemporal confusion. Let us return briefly to Copernicus. The vantage point from within Earth could be characterized by mereological and spatiotemporal confusion in that it locates the universe as a spatiotemporally larger whole within Earth as its spatiotemporally smaller part (chapter 13).

An analogous argument may now be put forward against the vantage point from beyond brain: it locates the spatiotemporally more extended world as a whole in the brain as its spatiotemporally smaller part. The vantage point from beyond brain thus suffers from mereological and spatiotemporal confusion, for which reason it must be rejected as conceptually incoherent. However, that argument confuses the vantage point from beyond brain with a vantage point from within brain. The vantage point from within brain does indeed locate the spatiotemporally more extended world as a whole within the brain as its spatiotemporally more restricted part—this amounts to *spatiotemporal and mereological confusion* (see chapter 13 for details).

That does not apply to the vantage point from beyond brain though. By extending the view beyond the brain itself, the vantage point from beyond brain can take into view how the brain as a spatiotemporally smaller part is related to and integrated within the spatiotemporally larger world as a whole. Rather than locating the spatiotemporally larger world as a whole within the brain as a spatiotemporally smaller part, the vantage point from beyond brain allows us to take into view the reverse, namely, to consider how the brain, as a less spatiotemporally extended part, is related to and integrated within the spatiotemporally more extended world as a whole.

Vantage Point from beyond Brain Vb: Ontic Center of the World—Spatiotemporal Boxing versus Spatiotemporal Nestedness

Let us consider the relation between brain and world in a slightly different way. Instead of locating or "boxing" the world within the brain (i.e., "spatiotemporal boxing"), the brain is *integrated* or *nested* within the world—we can thus account for what ontologically I described as *spatiotemporal nestedness* (chapter 11. Importantly, spatiotemporal boxing and spatiotemporal nestedness entail different relationships between world and brain. In the case of spatiotemporal boxing, the brain and its smaller spatiotemporal scale must relate to the larger one of the world in order to include the latter—this amounts to what I describe as *brain–world relation*. That entails indeed spatiotemporal and mereological confusion as the spatiotemporally larger world is boxed within the spatiotemporally smaller brain.

The converse holds in the case of spatiotemporal nestedness. In that case, the world and its larger spatiotemporal scale must relate to the smaller one of the brain in order to contain and nest the latter—this amounts to what I describe as world–brain relation. There is no spatiotemporal and mereological confusion in this case as something larger (the world) can well contain and nest something smaller (the brain).

We are now ready to reject the argument of mereological and spatiotemporal confusion against the vantage point from beyond brain. I claim that the argument itself is based on the confusion between spatiotemporal boxing (of the world within the brain) through brain–world relation on the one hand and spatiotemporal nestedness (of the brain within the world) through world–brain relation on the other. Only spatiotemporal boxing with brain–world relation suffers from mereological and spatiotemporal confusion whereas that is not the case in spatiotemporal nestedness as featured in the world–brain relation.

Taken together, the argument of mereological and spatiotemporal confusion must be rejected. Moreover, I return the favor of confusion. I claim that the proponent of this argument herself or himself suffers from confusion as she or he confuses different spatiotemporal relations, that is, spatiotemporal boxing versus spatiotemporal nestedness, and consecutively different relationships between world and brain (i.e., brain–world relation vs. world–brain relation).

Part II: Post-Copernican Stance—Exclusion of Mind

Post-Copernican Stance Ia: Epistemic Reference—Mind/Body/Brain versus World

Copernicus was confronted with the problem of determining the ontic origin of the different types of movements that could be observed in the universe (chapter 12). More specifically, the pre-Copernican cosmologists remained unable to take into view the necessary ontological connection between the movements and the Earth. Therefore, they attributed the movements to the universe as their ontic origin when they assumed that the universe supposedly circulates around Earth as the ontic center of the universe. That changed with Copernicus though. By shifting his vantage point, he, unlike the pre-Copernican cosmologists, was able to take into view the necessary ontological connection between the movements and the Earth. Why did the shift in vantage point made it possible for him to take into view the necessary ontological connection between the movements and the Earth?

I postulate that this was made possible by a change in "epistemic reference," that is, the standard or baseline against which he compared or set his knowledge (see chapter 12 for details). Instead of the Earth's serving as the epistemic reference, the observed movements could now be set and compared against the universe itself as the epistemic reference. This, in turn, made it possible to draw the necessary ontological connection between the Earth and the movements and thus to attribute the ontic origin of the movements to the Earth rather than to the universe (chapter 12).

We are now confronted with a problem analogous to that of the pre-Copernican cosmologists when it comes to mental features. Like Copernicus's predecessors in their search for the ontic origin of movements, we are confronted with the question of the ontic origin of mental features. Moreover, as in their case of the relation between the Earth and the movements, we remain unable to take into view the necessary ontological connection between brain and consciousness.

How can we change that? We can do in our case of mental features exactly what Copernicus did in his case of the movements. We can change our epistemic reference. Analogous to Copernicus's shift of his epistemic reference from the Earth to the universe, we may want to shift our epistemic reference from mind/body/brain to the world: instead of mind, body, or brain serving as the epistemic reference, we can now set and compare our knowledge against the world itself as the epistemic reference. That, in turn, should allow us to take into view the necessary ontological connection between brain and mental features.

Post-Copernican Stance Ib: Epistemic Reference—Partial Dependence between Ontic Location and Epistemic Reference

How can we change our epistemic reference from mind, body, or brain to the world itself though? For that, we require a vantage point that allows us to take into view the world. Let me explicate that in more detail. The world is that which is beyond ourselves (see above). That very same "beyond ourselves" concerns what is beyond our own body and brain (i.e., beyond brain and body)—this amounts to nothing but the world itself as it remains independent of us including our brain and body. Accordingly, by conceiving "beyond brain and body," we can take into view the world itself which, in turn, makes it possible to compare and set our knowledge against the world (rather than brain or body) as the epistemic reference.

How does the world as the epistemic reference stand in relation to our ontic location within that very same world? The pre-Copernican cosmologists took the Earth as both ontic location and epistemic reference—this amounted to what I described as *complete dependence* (chapter 12). In contrast, Copernicus's shift in vantage point allowed him to take an epistemic reference, that is, the universe, that remained partially independent of our own ontic location on Earth within the universe (i.e., partial independence; chapter 12).

The same holds analogously in our case of the vantage point from beyond brain. The world as an epistemic reference remains partially independent of world–brain relation as our ontic location within that very same world (see above). Let me explicate such partial independence between world and world–brain relation. The world itself can well be conceived without the brain whereas it remains impossible to conceive the world without relation and structure—the brain itself is not necessary for the world to exist and be real in terms of relation and structure (chapter 11). The world thus remains independent of the brain while it remains dependent upon relation and structure as signified in world–brain relation.

Taken together, this amounts to *partial independence* between world–brain relation as ontic location and world as epistemic reference, which must be distinguished from both complete dependence and complete independence (chapters 12 and 13). Moreover, such partial independence can be characterized as post-Copernican rather than pre-Copernican or non-Copernican (chapters 12 and 13). Accordingly, the change in epistemic reference from mind, body, or brain to world, as engineered by the shift in vantage point from beyond brain, allows us to take a true post-Copernican stance. More radically put, changing our epistemic reference to the world amounts to nothing less than a Copernican revolution in our investigation of mental features in neuroscience and philosophy.

Post-Copernican Stance Ic: Epistemic Reference—Necessary Ontological Connection between Brain and Mental Features

How does the world as the epistemic reference allow us to take into view the necessary ontological connection of mental features to their ontic origin? Presupposing the world as the epistemic reference makes it possible to set, compare, and match mental features, including their spatiotemporal range, against the world and its larger spatiotemporal range. We can then take into view that the "beyond ourselves" that characterizes mental features (see above) consists in exactly that, namely, the degree to which the spatiotemporal range of the world extends beyond ourselves, including our brain and body (see above).

As that spatiotemporal difference, that is, "beyond brain and body," can be ontologically traced to world–brain relation (chapter 10), we can now match, set, and compare mental features against world–brain relation and, ultimately, the world and its larger spatiotemporal range as the epistemic reference. This, in turn, allows us to take into view the necessary ontological connection between world–brain relation and mental features as it consists in spatiotemporal relation and structure (chapter 10). More specifically, we can now determine world–brain relation as the ontic origin of mental features, that is, as OPC (chapter 10); that, in turn, allows us to take into view the necessary ontological connection between brain and consciousness (chapter 10).

The critic may now want to argue that all this can already be achieved by a vantage point from within brain. The vantage point from within brain allows us to take the brain as an epistemic reference (chapter 13). That, in turn, makes it possible to take into view the necessary ontological connection between brain and consciousness. We therefore need to change neither our vantage point, that is, the vantage point from within brain, nor our epistemic reference, that is, the brain itself, to account for the necessary ontological connection of mental features to the brain as their ontic origin.

I reject that argument as it confuses different origins, that is, *empirical origin* and *ontic origin*. True, the vantage point from within brain allows drawing a connection between brain and mental features: this is possible by taking the brain as the epistemic reference for our empirical observations. The brain may thus be determined as the empirical origin of mental features. However, as we remain completely within the empirical realm of the brain while neglecting the ontological domain of the world, we cannot take into view any ontological connection between brain and mental features, let alone their necessary ontological connection. That is required though if one wants to determine the brain as ontic origin rather than mere empirical origin of mental features.

Post-Copernican Stance Id: Epistemic Reference—Ontic Origin versus Empirical Origin

We are now ready to reject the critic's argument. She or he confuses the empirical origin—that is, brain—and the ontic origin—that is, world–brain relation—of mental features: she or he falsely assumes that we can determine the ontic origin of mental features (as in world–brain relation) solely on the basis of their empirical origin (as in the brain). I suppose that such confusion is due to the fact that the presupposed vantage point from within brain only allows us to take into view the latter (i.e., the empirical origin) but not the former (i.e., the ontic origin). The only way to escape such confusion is thus to shift the vantage point from within brain to beyond brain. As this undermines, if not contradicts, the critic's presupposition, her or his argument must be rejected.

In sum, I argue that we need to change our epistemic reference from mind, body, or brain to the world to take into view the necessary ontological connection between brain and mental features. Such change in epistemic reference can be engineered by shifting our vantage point from within mind, brain, or body to a vantage point from beyond brain—this allows us to take into view that which is beyond ourselves, that is, the world.

Once we can take into view the world as the epistemic reference, we can set and compare mental features as characterized by "beyond ourselves" against the larger spatiotemporal range of the world, including its relation to the brain (i.e., world–brain relation). We can subsequently determine world–brain relation as the ontic origin of mental features, that is, as OPC; this, in turn, makes it possible for us to take into view the necessary ontological connection between brain and consciousness.

Post-Copernican Stance IIa: Intuition of Mind—Exclusion of Mind from Our View

Our initial starting point was the intuition of mind (chapter 12). To avoid the pulling force of the intuition of mind, we require a logical space of knowledge that no longer includes the mind as a possible epistemic option. As the logical space of knowledge, including its possible and impossible epistemic options, depends upon our vantage point (chapter 15), we need to develop a vantage point that no longer allows us to take into view the mind at all.

I claim that the vantage point from beyond brain is such vantage point. Specifically, I argue that the vantage point from beyond brain allows us to exclude the mind as an impossible epistemic option from our logical space of knowledge. This makes it impossible to sustain the concept of mind, including its pulling forces, that lets us suppose the mind as the ontic origin of mental features. However, we did not yet demonstrate any of that. I only showed how the vantage point from beyond brain allows us to change our epistemic reference to the world; that, in turn, makes it possible to take into view the necessary ontological connection between brain and consciousness. In contrast, I have not yet shown how we can abolish the intuition of mind—that shall be the focus in the reminder of this chapter.

Can the vantage point from beyond brain exclude the intuition of mind as a possible epistemic option within our logical space of knowledge? We recall the fourfold intuition of mind (chapter 13). The mind was intuited as the ontic origin of mental features as well as our ontic location within the world. Moreover, we intuited the mind as the ontic center of the world and the epistemic reference for our knowledge about that very same world. All four intuitions of mind are, as I propose, based on the vantage point from within mind that allows for including the mind as a possible epistemic option within the respective logical space of knowledge.

Does the logical space of knowledge as entailed by the vantage point from beyond brain still include the intuition of mind as a possible epistemic option? I argue that this is not the case—the intuition of mind is no longer included as a possible epistemic option in the logical space of knowledge as entailed by the vantage point from beyond brain. Let me specify this in the following.

First, the mind, that is, the possible existence and reality of mind, does not come into view at all in the vantage point from beyond brain: all we can see and take into view beyond ourselves (see above) is the world itself and how it relates to us, including our brain and body (i.e., world–brain relation). Moreover, we can take into view just how such world–brain relation provides the ontic origin of mental features as, for instance, in terms of OPC.

The advocate of mind may now want to argue that which is beyond ourselves is not just the world itself but includes the mind. That is to confuse beyond ourselves and beyond world though. The vantage point from beyond brain allows us to take into view that which is beyond ourselves within the world—we can now take into view what else there is in the world beyond our brain and body.

However, that very same world does not include the mind: to take into view the mind requires one to take into view that which is beyond our world rather than just that which is beyond ourselves, including our brain and body. In short, beyond ourselves does not entail beyond world. Therefore, the vantage point from beyond brain does not include the mind as a possible epistemic option in its logical space of knowledge.

Post-Copernican Stance IIb: Intuition of Mind—Spatiotemporal Exclusion of Mind

The critic may not want to relent yet though. We cannot know whether the mind is really excluded from the view beyond ourselves and thus from our world. Therefore, the vantage point from beyond brain remains unable to exclude the mind as an impossible epistemic option in its logical space of knowledge. I again reject that argument. That which is beyond ourselves in the world and thus the world itself must be as spatial and temporal as we are since otherwise we would not be part of that world. The world itself, including beyond ourselves, must thus be spatiotemporal.

This is different in the case of mind. The mind is intrinsically aspatial and atemporal (chapters 10 and 13). Therefore, the mind can only be taken into view by a vantage point that extends beyond our spatiotemporal world, that is, beyond world that can thus be specified as *beyond time and space*. As it is still related to the brain (and its spatiotemporal features), the vantage point from beyond brain cannot but remain within the boundaries of time and space of the spatiotemporal world. Therefore, the vantage point from beyond brain only allows us to take into view that which is spatiotemporal and beyond ourselves whereas it cannot take into view that which is aspatial and atemporal, that is, beyond time and space, as it specifies the mind as being beyond world.

In sum, the vantage point from beyond brain necessarily excludes mind as an impossible epistemic option from its logical space of knowledge. As the mind is excluded as an impossible epistemic option on spatiotemporal grounds, I speak of "spatiotemporal exclusion" of mind from the logical space of knowledge that is associated with a vantage point from beyond brain.

Post-Copernican Stance IIc: Intuition of Mind—Exclusion of Mind as Impossible Epistemic Option

How is the exclusion of mind as an impossible epistemic option from our logical space of knowledge related to the intuition of mind? What is no longer included as a possible epistemic option in the logical space of knowledge can no longer be assumed at all—the intuition of mind is simply no longer a possible epistemic option. That carries far-reaching consequences in that it renders impossible all four intuitions of mind. The main argument is that the aspatial and atemporal nature of mind that is beyond time and space and thus beyond world conflicts with the spatiotemporal nature of ontic origin, ontic location, ontic center, and epistemic reference as they all remain within the spatiotemporal bounds of the world. Let me explicate that.

We can no longer conceive the mind as the ontic origin of mental features. Assuming the ontic origin of mental features as characterized in spatiotemporal terms requires one to conceive above something that is spatiotemporal rather than aspatial and atemporal since otherwise it could not serve as their ontic origin. Moreover, this also makes it impossible to intuit the mind as the ontic location of ourselves within the world: if that which is beyond ourselves remains within the spatiotemporal bounds of the world (see above), we can no longer take into view and thus assume the mind as our aspatial and atemporal ontic location within a spatiotemporal world.

Moreover, the vantage point from beyond brain no longer allows taking into view the mind as the ontic center of the world—how can something that is aspatial and atemporal be the ontic center of something, that is, the world, that is inherently spatiotemporal? The vantage point from beyond brain can only view the world in terms of space and time, that is, *spatiotemporal world*, and therefore can only take into view an ontic center that shares time and space with the world—time and space themselves are then the ontic center of the world, which excludes the assumption of the aspatial and atemporal mind as a possible epistemic option.

Finally, the same holds for the fourth intuition of mind, that is, the mind as the epistemic reference. True, the vantage point from beyond brain reaches and extends our view beyond both brain and body. However, that does not imply that the vantage point from beyond brain also reaches and extends beyond world, including its time and space (i.e., beyond time and space). The distinction between both extensions, that is, beyond brain/body and beyond world, is important. Once one claims to reach and extend beyond the world, one abandons the vantage point from beyond brain and replaces it with a completely different vantage point such as a vantage point from within or beyond mind. This brings us back to the intuition of mind and the mind–body problem, however. Therefore, we need to distinguish carefully between the extension beyond brain/body as related to the vantage point from beyond brain and the extension beyond world that is associated with a vantage point from within or beyond mind. In sum, the logical space of knowledge entailed by the vantage point from beyond brain excludes the mind as an impossible epistemic option for all four intuitions of mind, the ontic origin of mental features, our ontic location in the world, the ontic center of world, and the epistemic reference of our knowledge about the world. As it is no longer included as a possible epistemic option in our logical space of knowledge, any intuition of mind remains impossible too, right from the very beginning. Something, that is, the mind, that is no longer included as a possible epistemic option within our logical space of knowledge cannot be conceived anymore nor can it exert any pulling forces on us in our ontological assumptions.

Post-Copernican Stance IIIa: Intuition of Relation—Spatiotemporal Discrepancy versus Spatiotemporal Relation

The critic may now want to argue in the following way. True, the vantage point from beyond brain does indeed render impossible the intuition of mind for ontic origin, ontic location, ontic center, and epistemic reference. That indeed puts the vantage point from beyond brain in a superior position when compared to the vantage point from within mind.

However, the vantage point from beyond brain seems to equally rely on intuition when it determines (i) world–brain relation as the ontic origin of mental features, (ii) world–brain relation as our ontic location within the world, (iii) time and space with spatiotemporal relation as the ontic center of the world, and (iv) the world with its spatiotemporal relation as the epistemic reference for our knowledge about the world.

While spatiotemporal features themselves and, more generally, time and space as such do not require intuition, the notion of relation itself seems to be based on intuition as it amounts to mere apprehension of the world without concepts or schema as well as without empirical support. We cannot but conceive relation including world–brain relation. Hence, though admittedly we no longer assume mind, we nevertheless are still assuming something, namely, relation—the intuition of mind is thus replaced by the "intuition of relation." Let me explicate such intuition of relation in more detail.

We can well take into view the spatiotemporal features of body and world when presupposing a vantage point from beyond brain. We can, for example, take into view that the spatiotemporal scale or range of the world is much larger than that of both body and brain as well as that the body exhibits a larger spatial and temporal scale than the brain. We can thus take into view what I described as *spatiotemporal discrepancy* as, for instance, the spatiotemporal discrepancy between world and brain (chapter 10).

However, that very same spatiotemporal discrepancy does not entail spatiotemporal relation. When taking into view spatiotemporal discrepancy between world, body, and brain, we do not view anything about their relation, that is, spatiotemporal relation. All we can view are spatiotemporal discrepancies that extend beyond ourselves, that is, beyond brain and body. In contrast, we do not take into view how world, body, and brain are related to each other—spatiotemporal relation, like world–brain relation, thus remains beyond that which we can take into view when presupposing a vantage point from beyond brain.

We must thus distinguish between spatiotemporal discrepancy and spatiotemporal relation as only the former but not the latter can be taken into view by the vantage point from beyond brain. The critic may want to argue that I simply confused both. I falsely assumed that the vantage point from beyond brain can take into view spatiotemporal relation whereas, in truth, it allows only for spatiotemporal discrepancy. This carries major consequences, which shall be detailed in the following.

The critic's claim amounts to the assumption that the vantage point from beyond brain only allows taking into view spatiotemporal discrepancy but not spatiotemporal relation. Any claim for being able to take into view spatiotemporal relation consequently reaches and extends beyond the epistemic options that are associated with the vantage point from beyond brain. Therefore, the claim for spatiotemporal relation ultimately rests on intuition, that is, an "intuition of relation." Since the vantage point from beyond brain only allows to take into view spatiotemporal relation on the basis of an intuition of relation, the critic may want to discard and reject the vantage point itself as insufficient.

Post-Copernican Stance IIIb: Intuition of Relation—Does the Vantage Point Matter at All?

The critic may now want to further strengthen her or his point by arguing that world–brain relation and spatiotemporal relation do not remain within the bounds of our world, that is, beyond ourselves, but that they extend beyond our world, that is, beyond world. As they extend beyond world, they cannot be taken into view by the vantage point from beyond brain as its view remains within the spatiotemporal bounds of the world. How then can we account for relation as in world–brain relation? Since we cannot take world–brain relation and spatiotemporal relation into view in our vantage point from beyond brain, we can only intuit them—this amounts to an intuition of relation.

The critic may extend her or his argument even further though. The fact that the vantage point from beyond brain can account for relation only by intuition (i.e., intuition of relation) puts it ultimately on the same ground as the vantage points from within mind and brain that also suffer from intuition (i.e., intuition of mind and intuition of brain; chapter 12). Therefore, as it still relies on intuition, there is no reason to abandon the vantage point from within mind in favor of the vantage point from beyond brain.

That is especially so as it seems that there is no escape from intuition at all. No matter which vantage point one presupposes, we are apparently always confronted with some intuition including intuition of mind, intuition of brain, and intuition of relation (or some other possible forms of intuition not yet discussed). Hence, it may not really matter which vantage point one presupposes as none provides an escape from intuition.

Post-Copernican Stance IIIc: Intuition of Relation—Different Conceptions of the Logical Space of Nature

I reject the argument of intuition of relation. Why? I argue that the proponent of that argument confuses different conceptions of the logical space of nature, that is, an observationally restricted versus spatiotemporally extended logical space of nature. Let me detail my reply.

True indeed, we cannot directly observe spatiotemporal relation between world and brain in the same way we can observe the apple in front of us. Spatiotemporal relation is not subject to observation. Therefore, spatiotemporal relation in world–brain relation is not included as a possible epistemic option in the logical space of knowledge of the vantage point from within brain (or body) as it does not extend beyond observation (chapter 13).

The vantage point from within brain presupposes a rather restricted logical space of nature though, that is, an observationally restricted logical space of nature (see above and chapter 13). As the restriction to observation renders it impossible to take into view spatiotemporal relation, we cannot but intuit world–brain relation and spatiotemporal relation. The charge of intuition of relation is consequently well justified when presupposing a vantage point from within brain (or body) and its observationally restricted logical space of nature.

We need to be careful though. The fact that we cannot observe relation, that is, world–brain relation, in a direct way by ourselves does not mean that we, in principle, cannot take into view spatiotemporal relation, including world–brain relation, when presupposing a different concept of the logical space of nature. The vantage point from beyond brain, for instance, presupposes a spatiotemporally extended logical space of nature rather than an observationally restricted logical space of nature (see above).

As the spatiotemporally extended logical space of nature is by itself characterized by spatiotemporal relation (see above), we can now include world–brain relation and spatiotemporal relation as possible epistemic options within our logical space of knowledge. This, in turn, makes it possible for us to take into view spatiotemporal relation like world–brain relation: we can, for instance, see that the world with its larger spatiotemporal scale is related to the brain with its smaller spatiotemporal scale by containing and nesting it (i.e., spatiotemporal nestedness; see above and chapter 11).

Most importantly, we do not require any intuition to account for such spatiotemporal nestedness as we can take it into view by itself in the same way we can take into view the various Russian dolls with their spatiotemporal nestedness. Thus, we only need to presuppose the "right" vantage point with the "right" logical space of nature, that is, spatiotemporally extended logical space of nature, to take into view world–brain relation and spatiotemporal relation.

We are now ready to reject the critic's argument. What the critic describes as intuition of relation may simply be related to the "wrong" logical space of nature, that is, observationally restricted logical space, as distinguished from the "right" one, that is, spatiotemporally extended logical space of nature. The critic thus confuses different conceptions of the logical space of nature when she or he charges the vantage point from beyond brain with intuition of relation. Moreover, this also shows that the vantage point strongly matters and, contrary to the critic's claim, is thus far from being irrelevant.

Post-Copernican Stance IVa: Intuition of Relation—Phenomenal versus Noumenal?

The critic may now want to argue that even if we claim that we can take into view spatiotemporal relation as in world–brain relation, it nevertheless remains rather abstract and may therefore border on, if not transgress into, the realm of the unknowable. Opting for a Kantian-like formulation, the critic may want to argue that spatiotemporal relation as in world–brain relation remains unknowable for us and thus noumenal. I will designate such noumenal meaning of relation in the following by designating it as *relation*.

Therefore, any claim of being able to take into view relation must be rejected as noumenal as it remains beyond our epistemic reach. The only way to account for relation as in world–brain relation is consequently to intuit relation, resulting in intuition of relation. I reject that argument chiefly for two reasons. First, the critic infers from the abstract nature of spatiotemporal relation to its noumenal character—this is fallacious though. Second, the critic confuses abstraction and intuition.

True, relation in world–brain relation is rather abstract as it is not as concrete as something that can be directly observed as the apple in front of us. Instead of being directly observable, relation in world–brain relation can, at best, only be postulated and thus accounted for in an indirect way in both empirical (chapter 8) and epistemic (chapter 10) domains. Specifically, we can only indirectly observe world–brain relation in the empirical realm by inferring it from the direct observation of, for instance, entrainment and phase shifting as in spatiotemporal alignment of the brain to the world (chapter 8). The same holds in the epistemic domain. We required a rather abstract line of transcendental reasoning to take into view world–brain relation and thus to justify its ontological rather than merely epistemic nature (chapter 11).

However, the abstract nature of spatiotemporal relation, including world–brain relation, does not justify our inferring its noumenal character. The distinction between abstract and concrete is a methodological distinction in that it tells us about how we can or cannot access features like spatiotemporal relation. In contrast, the distinction between phenomenal and noumenal concerns the relationship between epistemic and ontological domains, that is, whether spatiotemporal relation like world–brain relation concerns just our knowledge (i.e., epistemic) or existence and reality itself (i.e., ontological) as spatiotemporal relation (including world–brain relation) remain independent of us and our knowledge of them.

To infer from the abstract nature of spatiotemporal relation like world–brain relation to the relation's noumenal character (i.e., relation) is consequently to confuse the two distinctions and thus methodological and epistemic–ontological domains. The fact that something is abstract in terms of our methodological access does not imply anything about how our knowledge of it stands in relation to its existence and reality, that is, whether it is mind-dependent or mind-independent, and thus whether it is phenomenal or noumenal.

The critic thus confuses the question of methodological access to spatiotemporal relation like world–brain relation with the question of its phenomenal or noumenal nature. The critic fallaciously infers from the first question of methodological access to the second one of phenomenal–noumenal distinction. As such inference is fallacious, her or his argument of intuition of relation must be rejected as it is based on that very same inference.

Post-Copernican Stance IVb: Intuition of Relation—Existence versus Intuition

How can we make sure that abstract features like spatiotemporal relation reflect and thus correspond to existence and reality in the world? Let us compare the situation to Copernicus. He extended the logical space of knowledge by including a heliocentric view as an epistemic option. This was possible by shifting the vantage point from within Earth to a vantage point from beyond Earth. However, in his time, he did not know whether the heliocentric view was true or not, that is, existent and real. He could only rely on abstract mathematical evidence but was missing concrete empirical evidence. That was provided later by his successors such as Kepler, Bruni, Galileo and Newton—based on empirical evidence, they could show that the heliocentric view corresponds to the existence and reality of the universe.

We are encountering an analogous situation in the case of the spatiotemporal relation suggested here including world–brain relation. We currently do not know whether world–brain relation is existent and real and, most importantly, we do not know whether it is indeed the OPC. However, based on the different lines of empirical evidence (chapters 4–8) and ontological argumentation (chapters 9–11), I argue that world–brain relation, including its ontological predisposition of mental features, is existent and real by itself, independent of us and our brains.

In sum, the different lines of empirical and ontological evidence discussed in the previous parts suggest that spatiotemporal relation, including world–brain relation, is beyond ourselves but not beyond world. Moreover, as pointed out above, the post-Copernican vantage point from beyond brain can well take into view that very same "beyond ourselves" including world–brain relation. This makes it rather unlikely that my assumption of spatiotemporal relation including world–brain relation does not correspond to existence and reality as it is by itself independent of me and my brain. Most importantly, this makes it rather unlikely that my assumption of world–brain relation by itself, including its role as OPC, is just based on intuition, that is, intuition of relation. Accordingly, the various lines of evidence speak in favor of the existence and reality of world–brain relation rather than mere intuition. In short, I assume "existence" rather than "intuition" of world–brain relation.

Post-Copernican Stance IVc: Intuition of Relation—Need for Mathematical Formalization

However, as in the case of Copernicus, I will have to wait for the ultimate proof. That proof, as in the case of Copernicus, may be rather abstract. We cannot expect that something directly observable and concrete provides the ontic origin of something as complex as mental features. The history of science shows that the ontic origins of phenomena (such as genes as well as space and time themselves) that cannot be directly accessed in our observation is usually highly abstract (as in DNA and relativity theory) rather than concrete and can therefore often only be captured by mathematical formalization.

I suppose that exactly that will also hold in the case of world–brain relation. To prove and demonstrate the rather abstract nature of world–brain relation and especially its central role in mental features as ontological predisposition will require mathematical formalization. That is, for instance, possible in the mathematical terms of category theory that strongly emphasizes and formalizes relational features.

The assumption of such abstract nature of the ontic origin of mental features, including the need for mathematical formalization, is well expressed by Thomas Nagel:

> There is a sense in which the progress of science depends on the development of a common point of view. However, this development involves moving progressively away from the natural viewpoint of human perception, toward a mathematical description of a world which is increasingly not just not perceptible, but even not

perceptually imaginable. In any case, such a view has no special connection with the way things look or feel to a particular organism. (Nagel, 1993, p. 4)

Conclusion

Copernicus shifted the vantage point from within Earth to a vantage point from beyond Earth—this made it possible to free us from and abandon the intuition of Earth as the ontic center of the universe. Analogously, I suggest shifting our pre-Copernican vantage point from within mind (or from within brain) to a post-Copernican vantage point from beyond brain. That frees and unchains us from the pulling forces of our intuitive assumptions of the concept of mind as it excludes the mind as an impossible epistemic option from our logical space of knowledge.

Importantly, the shift in vantage point allows us to replace the "old" theory of mind and mind–body relation by a novel one, that is, world–brain relation. Unlike the old theory, the novel one enables us to take into view how the brain, as ontologically determined by its relation to the world (i.e., world–brain relation), shows a necessary ontological connection with mental features such as consciousness. That makes it possible for us to replace mind with world–brain relation, which, as the underlying ontic origin, can now account for the necessary ontological connection to mental features. That, in turn, shifts the focus from mind and the mind–body problem to world–brain relation and the world–brain problem.

Is the world–brain problem a plausible problem for addressing the question of the existence and reality of mental features? I argued that the world–brain problem is more plausible than the mind–body problem on empirical (chapters 1–8), phenomenal (chapters 7 and 8; see also Northoff, 2014b), epistemic, and ontological (chapters 9–11) grounds. The mind–body problem as the old theory becomes consequently superfluous and can therefore be replaced by the more plausible novel theory, the world–brain problem. Following the subtitle of my book, I therefore suggest moving on from the mind–body problem to the world–brain problem (see figure 14.2).

How can we engineer such shift from mind–body problem to world–brain problem? I argued that the shift from mind–body problem to world–brain problem is ultimately possible only by shifting our vantage point from within mind (or brain or body) to a vantage point from beyond brain. This amounts to nothing less than a Copernican revolution in neuroscience and

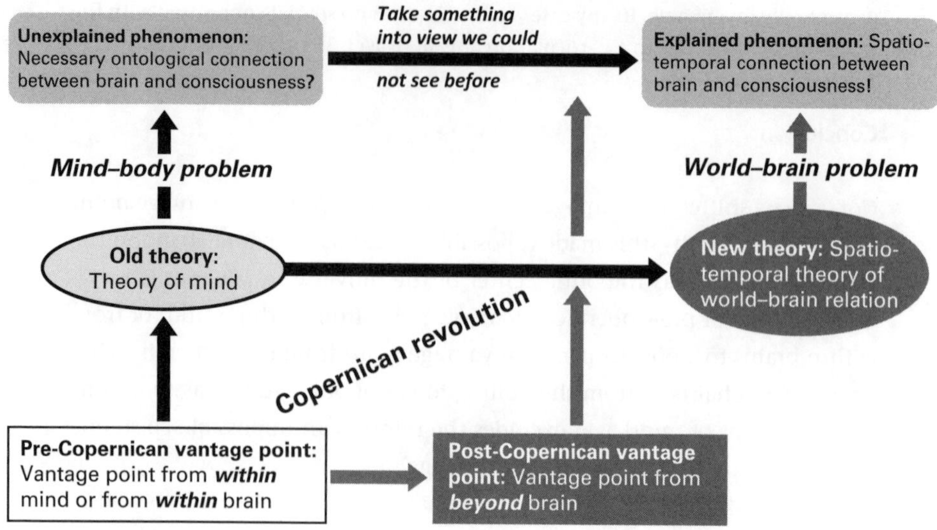

Figure 14.2
Shift in vantage point—Copernican revolution in neuroscience and philosophy.

philosophy. However, like Copernicus in his time, I will need to wait and be patient. My spatiotemporal theory of world–brain relation as the ontic origin of mental features will need to wait for future empirical and mathematical evidence to render fully transparent how world–brain relation can predispose mental features. Anticipating the future, I expect such evidence to speak in favor of the world–brain problem rather than the mind–body problem.

Conclusion: Copernican Revolution—Is the Brain's Spontaneous Activity an Empirical, Epistemic, and Ontological Game Changer in Neuroscience and Philosophy?

Are the brain and its spontaneous activity a "game changer" in our pursuit of the question of the existence and reality of mental features? A game changer is something that allows to take something into view that hitherto remained invisible and was not yet discovered. That, for instance, makes it possible to raise a novel question or problem replacing the previous one. I argue that the brain's spontaneous activity is indeed a game changer in this sense, an "empirical and ontological game changer" in that it allows us to replace the mind–body problem with the world–brain problem.

Let us start with the empirical domain. The discovery of the brain's spontaneous activity leads us to different views or models of the brain in neuroscience (chapters 1–3 as well as Northoff, 2014a). Even more important, the brain's spontaneous activity, due to its spatiotemporal structure, also provides a novel empirical approach to mental features such as consciousness. Though not yet fully conclusive, empirical data do indeed suggest that the brain's spontaneous activity and its spatiotemporal structure are central, if not indispensable, for yielding mental features such as consciousness (chapters 4–8 as well as Northoff, 2014b).

This allows for a spatiotemporal model of consciousness that is based on the brain's relation to the world, the world–brain relation (chapters 7–8; Northoff & Huang, 2017; Northoff, 2014b). Taken together, the brain and its spontaneous activity can be regarded as a gamer changer in neuroscience, that is, an empirical game changer: it allows for a spatiotemporal (rather than cognitive) model of brain and consciousness with a central role for world–brain relation (rather than the brain alone independent of the world or, alternatively, the brain being the center as in brain–world relation).

What about the ontological characterization of brain and mental features? I argued that the spontaneous activity's characterization by an elaborate spatiotemporal structure is most compatible with an ontological definition by relation and structure—this presupposes structural realism (SR) rather than property-based ontology (chapters 9–11). Importantly, SR defines the brain no longer by intrinsic properties like physical or mental properties that are supposedly "located" within the brain itself. Instead, SR defines the brain through its relation to the world, the world–brain relation, as I say.

That very same world–brain relation is a necessary condition of possible mental features such as consciousness, an ontological predisposition of consciousness (chapters 10 and 11). Taken together, the brain's spontaneous activity proves to be an ontological game changer for both brain and mental features: it allows us determining the existence and reality of brain and consciousness by relation and structure, that is, world–brain relation, rather than physical or mental properties.

Even more dramatically, the shift from mind–body problem to world–brain problem requires a novel methodological or epistemological approach in both neuroscience and philosophy. Presupposing a vantage point from within mind or brain, we could not but understand ourselves in a rather ego- and mento- or neuro-centric way—our mind or brain defines mental features, ourselves, and our position within the world. I refer to this view as "pre-Copernican" because it is analogous to the pre-Copernican geocentric view that considered the Earth as the center of the universe (chapters 12 and 13).

Such pre-Copernican mento- or neuro-centric view can now be abolished when shifting the vantage point from within mind or brain to a vantage point from beyond brain (chapter 14). That allows us to take into view how our brain is part of the world by being related to it (i.e., world–brain relation) and thus how we are part of the world rather than being its center. Even more important, such novel viewpoint renders transparent how that very same relation (i.e., world–brain relation) can account for the existence and reality of mental features. Our traditional rather ego- and mento- or neuro-centric view can thus be replaced by an allo- and eco-centric view of mental features, ourselves, and our position within the world (chapter 14). The brain's spontaneous activity is thus not only an empirical and ontological but also an epistemic gamer changer in our view of ourselves, mental features, and the world.

Taken together, the shift from mind–body problem to world–brain problem is much more than just a shift from one problem to another. In the same way that Copernicus shifted our view of the Earth and the universe in a major way, the shift from mind–body problem to world–brain problem shifts the framework within which we view ourselves, our mental features, and the world. Therefore, I conclude that the shift from mind–body problem to world–brain problem amounts to nothing less than a Copernican revolution in neuroscience and philosophy (chapter 14).

We need to be careful, though. The revolution initiated by Copernicus in physics and cosmology had to wait for subsequent empirical discoveries by Galileo, Kepler, Bruno, and Newton to be confirmed as a true revolution. This is analogously so in neuroscience and philosophy. The Copernicus revolution suggested here, including the world–brain problem, needs to be confirmed by future generations of both neuroscientists and philosophers. They will know whether I am right or wrong in my claim of the brain's spontaneous activity as an empirical, epistemological-methodological, and ontological game changer. Accordingly, they will be able to tell whether the world–brain problem (rather than the mind–body problem) is the the most plausible and thus the "right" problem for addressing the question of the existence and reality of mental features.

Glossary

Brain: Concept of brain in different domains (empirical, epistemological, ontological, methodological) Typically identified as the gray mass observable once the skull is opened. Such direct observation is complemented by indirect observation by various technologies including functional magnetic resonance imaging (fMRI). Both direct and indirect observation yield testable hypotheses that can be verified (or falsified) by experiments. Investigating the brain in such a way presupposes an empirical approach to the brain. Taken in this way, the brain's neuronal activity can be characterized by both spontaneous activity and stimulus-induced or task-evoked activity (chap. 1). Taken together, the various empirical data, suggest models of the brain's neural activity (chaps. 1–3, on the *spectrum model, interaction model,* and *prediction model* of brain).

One can also investigate the brain in other domains such as *ontology* (concerning existence and reality), *epistemology* (concerning knowledge), and *methodology* (as in our *vantage point* or viewpoint). This requires a theoretical approach to the brain rather than empirical as in science. The theoretical approach is often neglected in traditional philosophy, where the brain is considered merely empirical. However, recent empirical advances in neuroscience suggest that the brain is also theoretically relevant in the ontological and epistemological domains (chap. 9).

Ontologically, the brain's existence and reality cannot be inferred from (and thus accounted for) by observation and verifiable empirical evidence (see chap. 9 for the empirical-ontological fallacy). Different kinds of *ontology,* including property-based ontology or relation-based ontology, may characterize the brain's existence and reality (chaps. 9–11). The ontological determination of the brain may concern either its mere anatomical features, that is, its gray matter, or, alternatively, the brain's neuronal activity and its spatiotemporal structure (see *Structural realism*). Finally, we can also consider the brain in a methodological context. One can, for instance, take the brain as center of one's *viewpoint* as in a *vantage point* from *within* the brain (chap. 13). Alternatively, one may take a *vantage point* from *beyond* the brain (rather than from within the brain) (chap. 14).

Brain–world relation See *World–brain relation.*

Calibration The act of measuring or referencing something against something else so that the second serves as baseline or default for the first. Calibration is relevant for yielding consciousness on both empirical and ontological grounds. Empirically, the default-mode network (DMN) serves as baseline or default for the brain's neural activity against which any neural activity changes within the rest of the brain are set, compared, and matched, which is highly relevant for yielding consciousness (chaps. 1–2, 4–8). I therefore speak of "neuronal calibration" (chap. 11). Ontologically, the world and its large spatiotemporal scale serves as baseline or reference and thus as default for the brain's neuronal activity and its smaller spatiotemporal scale. I therefore speak of "spatiotemporal calibration," an ontological correlate of consciousness (OCC) as it is central for yielding the phenomenal features of consciousness (chap. 11).

Capacity- vs. law-driven The concept of capacity, as used in the present context, is based on Nancy Cartwright (1989), who takes it to be central to scientific models. Capacity-driven models are characterized by causal powers and causal structures that serve as necessary conditions of the possible realization of the target phenomenon (consciousness, in our case; chap. 5). By contrast, law-driven models focus on the causes underlying the actual (rather than possible) realization and manifestation of the target phenomenon. However, without capacities as the necessary conditions of the possible (rather than actual) realization of the target phenomenon, that target phenomenon cannot be understood. Based on empirical evidence, I argue that consciousness requires a capacity- rather than law-driven model of brain. Empirically, the capacities of the brain are specified as the neural predispositions of consciousness (NPC) (chap. 4) that signify the necessary conditions of possible (rather than actual) consciousness as distinguished from the sufficient conditions of actual (rather than possible) consciousness, that is, the neural correlates of consciousness (NCC) (chaps. 5, 7–8). Note that the concept of capacity is here meant in an empirical and ontological context, that is, within the context of the brain's neuronal activity and its existence and reality. For that reason, the concept of capacity needs to be distinguished from the more metaphysical concept of disposition that is understood in a more logical rather than naturalistic context.

Consciousness A pervasive and ever-present phenomenon, typically taken for granted and as a result difficult to define. The concept of consciousness has long been investigated in philosophy in mainly ontological, metaphysical, phenomenological, and epistemological terms. This has changed recently in the last 30 to 40 years where consciousness has also begun to be investigated empirically and experimentally in psychology and neuroscience. The investigation of consciousness in empirical, ontological, phenomenological, and epistemological domains leads to different definitions. Empirically, consciousness is characterized by neuroscientists by the two dimensions of state/level (chap. 4) and content (chap. 6) to which I add a third, namely its form (chap. 7). Philosophers often characterize consciousness with property-based ontology and, specifically, physical or mental properties (chaps. 9–10). In contrast, I determine the existence and reality of consciousness by relation and structure (chaps. 10–11) thus presupposing *structural realism* (chaps. 9–11). Based on structural realism and the empirical data, I propose a spatiotemporal and relational model of consciousness in both empirical (chaps. 7–8) and ontological (chaps. 9–11) contexts or domains. Phenomenologically, consciousness is characterized by experiences as manifest in various features such as qualia ("What it is like"), intentionality, self-perspectival organization, ipseity, etc. (chap. 11). Finally, consciousness can also be determined epistemologically as related to our knowledge. Consciousness may, for instance, demarcate the boundaries of our possible knowledge, that is, the logical space of knowledge (chap. 12).

Copernican revolution (and pre- and post-Copernican stance) The concept of the Copernican revolution is used to describe the change in viewpoint that physicist, mathematician, and cosmologist Nicolaus Copernicus proposed to account for the movement of the Earth: Copernicus suggested replacing the geocentric view of the universe with a heliocentric view (chap. 12). Kant attempted an analogous revolution in philosophy that, according to commentators, remained insufficient at best and failed at worst (chap. 12). I propose that we require an analogous change in vantage point in current neuroscience and philosophy. I base my analogy on different criteria that are based on the Copernican revolution in physics and cosmology (chap. 12) and apply, analogously, to the proposed Copernican revolution in neuroscience and philosophy (chap. 14). Applying these criteria allows me to distinguish between pre-Copernican vantage points (e.g., vantage points from within mind or within brain; chap. 13) and post-Copernican vantage points (e.g., vantage points from beyond brain; chap. 14). Most important, the shift from a pre-Copernican vantage point from within mind or brain to a post-Copernican vantage point from beyond brain excludes the *intuition of mind* as a possible epistemic option in the associated *logical space of knowledge* (chap. 14). At the same time, the post-Copernican vantage point from beyond brain makes it possible, and thus transparent, for us to take the view that the world–brain relation can serve as ontological predisposition of consciousness (OPC; chap. 14). The vantage point from beyond brain should not be confused with a vantage point from beyond world that leads us back into metaphysics with the *intuition of mind* and subsequently the *mind–body problem.* Rather than being post-Copernican, such a metaphysical stance is distinctively non-Copernican.

Default-mode network (DMN) A neuronal network located in the middle of the brain. The DMN shows specific features that distinguishes it from other networks in the brain. For instance, the DMN shows extremely stronger and slower frequencies and extensive connections to almost all other regions in the brain (chapter 1); this may account for the default-mode functionality of the DMN for the rest of the brain (chapter 1 and 11). Empirical evidence shows that the DMN has a central yet unclear role for consciousness (chaps. 4–5) and, as I claim, for its phenomenal features (chap. 11).

Difference-based coding (vs. stimulus-based coding) First and foremost, an empirical concept that describes a specific coding strategy in the biological world and thus in nature. I raise the question for the brain's neural code, that is, the format in which the brain processes stimuli and information. As its name suggests, difference-based coding describes how the brain uses the format of difference to encode and process stimuli and information. More specifically, what the brain encodes and processes in its neural activity are not single stimuli independent of each other (as in stimulus-based coding) but rather the relative (stochastically or probability-based) differences between different stimuli (chaps. 2–3). Taken in such a way, difference-based coding may be regarded a fundamental principle of the brain's neural activity. Though primarily empirical, difference-based coding carries major ontological implications for how we should characterize the existence and reality of the brain in an empirically plausible way. To mark the distinction between the concept of difference in empirical and ontological contexts, I speak of difference per se in the empirical context and difference de re in the ontological context (chap. 9). This allows me to ontologically characterize the brain by difference, i.e., difference de re, and consequently by relation and structure (as they are based on and intrinsically connected to difference). I therefore speak of *relational brain* (chap. 9).

Embodiment, embeddedness, extendedness, and enactment (Four E's) Embodiment states that mental features are dependent not only on the brain but also on the body ("consciousness is embodied") while embeddedness refers to the relevance of the environment for mental features ("consciousness is embedded") (chap. 8). Extendedness claims that consciousness and other mental features extend beyond ourselves to the world that scaffolds consciousness ("consciousness is extended") (chap. 8). Finally, enactment refers to the fact that we rely on our motor functions and actions to constitute consciousness, that is, we enact consciousness (chap. 8) ("consciousness is enacted"). I argue that all four concepts, that is, embodiment, embeddedness, extendedness, and enactment, must be put in a larger and more basic foundational framework, a spatiotemporal framework that ultimately can be traced to the spatiotemporal features of the world—brain relation (chap. 8).

Global neuronal workspace theory (GNWT) A neuroscientific theory of consciousness that considers the extension or globalization of neuronal activity to specific brain regions (e.g., prefrontal and parietal cortex) and event-related potentials (e.g., P300) with access to various cognitive functions (as related to prefrontal cortex) central to consciousness (chaps. 4–5). Based on empirical evidence, I argue that the GNWT must be considered in a wider spatiotemporal framework (chap. 7).

Integrated information theory (IIT) A neuroscientific theory of consciousness that postulates integration by the brain's neuronal activity to be central to consciousness. Integration itself is defined as a "sum that is more than the addition of its parts." I discuss the IIT (chaps. 4 and 5) but argue that it needs to be put into a wider spatiotemporal context to account for the phenomenal features of consciousness (chap. 7).

Interaction model of brain A theoretical model of the empirical relationship between spontaneous and stimulus-induced activities within the brain that can modulate each other in what can be described as rest-stimulus and stimulus-rest interaction (chap. 2). The interaction model must be distinguished from segregation and parallelism between spontaneous and stimulus-induced activity in which case there is no rest-stimulus or stimulus-rest interaction. There can be different forms of interaction, that is, additive and nonadditive, between spontaneous activity and stimulus-induced activity. Importantly, empirical evidence shows that the nonadditive nature of rest-stimulus interaction is central to consciousness: loss of consciousness is characterized by loss of nonadditive rest-stimulus interaction, which becomes merely additive when consciousness is lost (chap. 5).

Intuition of mind An intuition that the mind exists, even despite contrary empirical evidence that only the brain exists. How is this intuition possible? I argue that we intuit the mind, that is, we have an "intuition of mind" (chap. 12), and that such intuition is pervasive in our thinking about the ontological determination of mental features. That intuition of mind is included as possible option in a logical space of knowledge that presupposes a pre-Copernican vantage point from within mind (chap. 13); the replacement of such a vantage point by a post-Copernican vantage point from beyond brain makes it possible for us to abandon the intuition of mind as the concept of mind is then no longer included as possible epistemic option in our *logical space of knowledge* (chap. 14). Once we abandon the intuition of mind, we no longer need to connect mental features to the mind as underlying ontological substrate in a necessary way, which, in turn, opens the door to discarding the *mind—body problem* (chap. 14).

Logical space of knowledge An operational background space, that demarcates the possible knowledge options. Taken in this sense, the logical space of knowledge is an epistemological concept that is somewhat analogous to the concepts of logical space of nature and logical space of reason as introduced by Sellars (1963) and McDowell (1994). Specifically, the concept of the logical space of knowledge refers to possible epistemic options, that is, what we can possibly know and what we cannot know within our presupposed methodological framework (chap. 12). Depending on the methodological framework, the logical space of knowledge may include different epistemic options. One such methodological presupposition concerns the *vantage point*; I argue that different vantage points demarcate the logical space of knowledge in different ways with different possible epistemic options (chaps. 12–14). For instance, the vantage point from within mind includes the *intuition of mind* as one possible epistemic option (chap. 13), whereas the vantage point from beyond brain no longer includes the *intuition of mind* as a possible epistemic option (chap. 14).

Mental features Phenomena such as consciousness, self, free will, emotional feeling, and the like. I take consciousness as paradigmatic for mental features in general. Despite their differences, mental features are usually marked by first-person perspective as distinguished from third-person observation. Mental features have long been discussed in philosophy in ontological and epistemological contexts but have recently also been investigated empirically in neuroscience. Therefore, we can define the concept of mental features in different ways according to the respective context or domains, that is, in empirical, phenomenological, and ontological ways. Empirically, mental features refer to all those features that, unlike physical features, cannot be observed by a third-person perspective as in scientific investigation. Instead, mental features are characterized by experience in a first-person perspective (which does not imply that they cannot be investigated scientifically by a third-person perspective; chaps. 7–8). Ontologically, mental features have typically been associated with the mind: the mind is assumed to provide the existence and reality that supposedly underlies mental features. Mental features are thus assumed to be necessarily connected to the mind (chaps. 10, 13–14). I argue that the assumption of a necessary connection between mind and mental features is related to a specific viewpoint, that is, a vantage point from within mind (chap. 13). Once one takes a different viewpoint, say, a vantage point from beyond brain, one can no longer take into view the necessary connection between mental features and mind (chap. 13). I consequently postulate that we need to detach mental features from the mind to account for their existence and reality in an empirically, ontologically, and epistemic-methodologically plausible way (chap. 14, conclusion). The vantage point from beyond brain allows us to take into view the world–brain relation including its necessary connection to mental features. This, in turn, makes the assumption of mind superfluous; therefore, I propose to replace the traditional mind–body problem with the world–brain problem (chaps. 10–14).

Mind Typically considered in ontological or metaphysical domains or contexts in terms of existence and reality (see *Ontology*) and/or being (metaphysics) that underlies mental features (introduction). This establishes a necessary connection between mind and mental features in ontological and/or metaphysical contexts or domains (chap. 10), which, in turn, renders it possible for us to conceive the question for the relationship between mind and body, the *mind–body problem* (introduction, chap. 10). I argue that the necessary connection between mind and mental features is not plausible, given empirical (chaps. 7–8), ontological (chaps. 9–10), conceptual-logical (chap. 10), and epistemic-methodological (chaps. 13–14) evidence. I therefore argue that we need to reject the assumption of the necessary connection of mental features to the mind as their underlying ontological basis and foundation. As mental features are now detached from the mind, the *mind–body problem* including its various solutions (e.g., dualism, monism, panpsychism) become nonsensical.

The rejection of mind (and the *mind–body problem*) as the ontological substrate of mental features opens the door for considering another ontological substrate that is supported by stronger empirical, ontological, and epistemic-methodological evidence. Based on empirical (chaps. 4–8), ontological (chaps. 9–11), and epistemic-methodological (chaps. 12–14) evidence, I postulate that the world–brain relation provides the ontological substrate of mental features, as both are necessarily connected with each other (chap. 10). We can consequently replace the *mind–body problem* with a different more plausible problem, the world–brain problem (chaps. 10–14).

Mind–body problem The question of how the existence and reality of the body, including the brain, can be related to the existence and reality of mind. Taken in this way, the mind–body problem is an ontological (and metaphysical) problem. However, some authors consider it to be an epistemic or empirical problem. I here consider the mind–body problem an ontological problem as it concerns the existence and reality of mind and body. Importantly, I focus my discussion on the presuppositions of the mind–body problem rather than on arguing for and against specific solutions to the mind–body problem itself.

The question of the mind's relationship to the body rests on the assumption of the possible existence and reality of mind: without presupposing this, one cannot even raise the question of the mind's possible relationship to the body anymore. The main argument in this book is that the presuppositions of the possible existence and reality of mind are not plausible on empirical (chaps. 4–8), ontological (chaps. 10–11), and epistemic-methodological (chaps. 13–14) grounds. Therefore, I argue that we can discard the assumption of the possible existence and reality of mind and, consequently, the mind–body problem: the question of the mind–body relationship is nonsensical as it rests on an assumption that by itself is implausible on various grounds (introduction, chaps. 10–14, conclusion). All possible answers or solutions to the mind–body problem, such as dualism, monism, physicalism, supervenience, panpsychism, and the like, must consequently be discarded as nonsensical too as they are answers to a nonsensical question.

Neural correlate and predisposition of consciousness (NCC, NPC) The concept of the neural correlate of consciousness (NCC) refers to the sufficient neural conditions underlying the actual realization and manifestation of consciousness (chaps. 4–5). The concept of the neural predisposition of consciousness (NPC) describes the necessary neural conditions of the possible (rather than actual) realization and manifestation of consciousness (chaps. 4–8). Both NPC and NCC are empirical concepts and therefore belong to neuroscience. I designate NCC and NPC as strictly empirical. It therefore must be distinguished from what I describe as *ontological correlates and predispositions of consciousness* (chaps. 10–11), as these are ontological rather than empirical concepts. The distinction between neural and ontological correlates/predispositions is new in the current discussion about consciousness. Note that the concept of predisposition is here meant in a purely empirical context, that is, within the context of the brain's neuronal activity. For that reason, the concept of neural predisposition needs to be distinguished from the more metaphysical (and ontological) concept of disposition.

Neuro-ecological continuum An empirical concept that describes how the brain's neuronal activity is continuous with the activity in its respective ecological context (chap. 8). The neuro-ecological continuum is based on space and time: there is a continuum between the spatiotemporal structure of the brain's spontaneous activity and the spatiotemporal structure of the ecological context, the world (chap. 8). This spatiotemporally based neuro-ecological continuum between world and brain is based empirically on the mechanisms of spatiotemporal alignment that are central for consciousness (chap. 8). Together, spatiotemporal alignment and the neuroecological continuum provide the empirical ground, that is, the necessary empirical conditions, of what on a more conceptual and ontological level can be described as the world—brain relation (chaps. 8–9).

Neuronal-phenomenal correspondence An empirical concept that describes similarities between the brain's neuronal states and phenomenal features of consciousness (chap. 7). Based on empirical evidence, I argue that such similarities do not concern specific contents that are represented in the brain's neuronal activity (chap. 6). Instead, I propose that the similarities between neuronal states and phenomenal features consist in spatiotemporal features: neuronal states and phenomenal features show similar and corresponding spatiotemporal features as in their "inner extension and duration" (see *Time and space*; chap. 7). The concept of correspondence could be understood in either a weak or a strong sense: spatiotemporal features in neuronal and phenomenal states could correspond in a weak sense as in certain forms of isomorphism or, taken in a strong sense, could be identical as assumed in *integrated information theory*. Future investigation is thus needed to specify the concept of neuronal-phenomenal correspondence in more empirical and conceptual detail.

Neurophilosophy (narrow/reductive vs. wide/nonreductive) A philosophical investigation of the brain that focuses on the role of the brain in addressing traditional philosophical questions. The concept of neurophilosophy can be understood in both a narrow and a wide sense. Neurophilosophy taken narrowly is characterized by a strongly reductive if not eliminative tendency, as ontological and epistemological concepts, originating in philosophy, are supposed to be reduced to and replaced by empirical concepts from neuroscience (chap. 13). Methodologically, such a narrow and reductive concept of neurophilosophy presupposes a specific viewpoint, a vantage point from within brain (chap. 13). In neurophilosophy, taken in a wide sense, the reduction and/or elimination of philosophical, i.e., ontological and epistemological concepts, to empirical concepts of neuroscience is replaced by testing these concepts' empirical plausibility: one then tests, for instance, which ontological concept, relation, or property is better compatible with the empirical data and thus empirically more plausible, entailing what I call empirical-ontological plausibility (chap. 9 and Northoff 2014c, 2016). Methodologically, the notion of reduction/elimination is here replaced by plausibility/compatibility between philosophical and neuroscientific concepts (introduction, chaps. 9, 13). This nonreductive methodological strategy presupposes a different vantage point. The vantage point from within brain in the reductive/eliminative approach (chap. 13) is here replaced by a vantage point from beyond brain that allows for a nonreductive methodological strategy (chap. 14). The investigation in this book can be understood as neurophilosophy in the wide sense, that is, nonreductive.

Ontological correlate and predisposition of consciousness (OCC, OPC) The concept of the ontological correlate of consciousness (OCC) refers to the sufficient ontological conditions underlying the actual realization and manifestation of consciousness (chapter 11). The concept of the ontological predisposition of consciousness (OPC) describes the necessary ontological conditions of the possible (rather than actual) realization and manifestation of consciousness (chapter 10). Both OPC and OCC are ontological concepts. As such, they must be distinguished from the neural correlates and predispositions of consciousness (NCC, NPC) (chaps. 4–8), which are strictly empirical rather than ontological. Note that the concept of predisposition is here meant in a purely ontological context, that is, within the context of the natural world, i.e., the logical space of nature. This distinguishes the concept of ontological predisposition from the more metaphysical concept of disposition that presupposes the logical world, i.e., the logical space of reason, rather than the natural world, i.e., the logical space of nature.

Ontology (vs. metaphysics) Ontology refers to the discipline within philosophy that concerns the question of existence and reality, usually considered to be a subset of the larger and more comprehensive question of being as dealt with in metaphysics. Metaphysics, such as analytic metaphysics and metametaphysics, is characterized by a theoretical rather than empirical approach and more specifically by a priori, analytic, and conceptual methodological strategy (chap. 9). This, as in my view, is different from ontology, which can also include and use a posteriori, synthetic, and empirical elements; this is apparent when I compare ontological assumptions for their concordance with empirical data, i.e., empirical plausibility. Therefore, contrary to the current usage of ontology as subset of metaphysics in current philosophy, I sharply distinguish ontology and metaphysics (chap. 9); my focus in this book is only on ontology, not metaphysics. For instance, I consider the world—brain problem an ontological problem but not a metaphysical problem (chaps. 9–11). Distinguishing ontology from metaphysics allows me to develop a "spatiotemporal ontology" (chaps. 9 and 11) that features the logical space of nature and, as suggested by its name, is intrinsically spatiotemporal as distinguished from metaphysics that, as it presupposes the logical world and the logical space of reason, is intrinsically a-temporal and a-spatial (chap. 9).

Phenomenal vs. noumenal I use the terms *phenomenal* and *noumenal* in an epistemological sense (as suggested by Kant), to demarcate the epistemological boundary between what we can possibly know and what we remain unable to know in principle. Taken in this way, the concepts of the phenomenal vs. noumenal mirror the epistemic options that are included and excluded within the presupposed *logical space of knowledge*. I argue that the boundary of demarcation between phenomenal and noumenal is closely related to the *vantage point* one takes (chap. 12). Different vantage points presuppose different boundaries and subsequently different epistemic options in the *logical space of knowledge*, as for instance with regard to the *intuition of mind* (chaps. 13–14).

Prediction model of brain A theoretical model about the brain's neuronal activity in empirical terms. Specifically, the prediction model proposes that the brain's neuronal activity anticipates or predicts its own neuronal activity related to stimuli or contents of cognition. This is the theory of predictive coding (chap. 3). Predictive coding is characterized by predicted input and prediction error: the degree to which predicted input and actual input match each other determines the degree of actual stimulus-induced activity, the prediction error. If predicted and actual input do not match, prediction error is high, which leads to high amplitude in stimulus-induced activity. If, in contrast, the match between predicted and actual input is high, prediction error is low with low amplitude in stimulus-induced activity. Predictive coding is well supported by the empirical data and can be considered a well-established theory of the brain's neuronal activity (chaps. 3, 6). Predictive coding can well account for the contents of consciousness, whereas it remains unable to account for the phenomenal features that are associated with the contents of consciousness (chap. 6). Therefore, I propose to complement predictive coding with the spatiotemporal model of consciousness that allows us to bridge the gap between neuronal and phenomenal features (chaps. 7–8).

Relation and structure The concepts of relation and structure can be considered in both empirical and ontological domains. Empirically, *relation* refers to observable relations that can be measured; for instance, we can measure how the ongoing phases of the brain's spontaneous activity align and thus relate to the rhythm of music (chaps. 3, 8). The term *structure* in the empirical context refers to specific ways or forms of how spatial and temporal features are organized; the brain's spontaneous activity, for instance, shows an elaborate well-observable spatiotemporal structure with cross-frequency coupling, scale-free activity, etc. (chaps. 1–2). Such spatiotemporal structure amounts to what, empirically, I describe as form of consciousness (chaps. 7–8).

Ontologically, relation and structure can be understood in two ways. They may characterize the relationship between ontological properties: for instance, there may be a relation between physical and mental properties as discussed in the *mind—body problem* (chap. 9). In that case, properties are ontologically prior to relation and structure. Alternatively, relation and structure can by themselves be considered the most basic units of existence and reality; relations are then ontologically prior to properties, which is the central claim of *structural realism* (chap. 9). I here understand relation and structure in this latter sense. Moreover, extending *structural realism*, I specify relation and structure in spatiotemporal terms, that is, spatiotemporal relation and structure (chaps. 9, 11).

Spatiotemporal alignment, nestedness, and expansion Empirical concepts that describe neuronal mechanisms that, based on empirical evidence, are relevant to bringing about consciousness (chaps. 4–5, 7–8). Spatiotemporal alignment describes a neuronal mechanism that allows the brain and its spontaneous activity's spatiotemporal structure to follow, that is, to align to the spatiotemporal structure in its respective environmental context (chap. 8). Spatiotemporal nestedness is here understood in an empirical sense that refers to the scale-free nature of neuronal activity with stronger power in slower frequencies than faster frequencies (chaps. 4, 7). Moreover, spatiotemporal nestedness in this scale-free sense includes fractal features as characterized by self-affinity or self-similarity; that is, the structure of spatiotemporal features is manifest and thus self-similar or self-affine in and across different spatiotemporal scales (chaps. 4, 7). Finally, spatiotemporal expansion refers to integration, i.e., expansion, of stimuli of limited and small spatiotemporal scale beyond itself to a larger spatiotemporal scale by the brain's spontaneous activity—this, as based on empirical evidence, is considered central for associating consciousness to the stimulus (chaps. 4–5, 7–8). Taking all neuronal mechanisms together amounts to a spatiotemporal theory of consciousness in neuroscience, i.e., temporo-spatial theory of consciousness (TTC) that extends and complements other neuroscientific theories such as the *Integrated information theory* (IIT) and the *Global neuronal workspace theory* (GNWT).

Spatiotemporal nestedness and directedness Ontological concepts that describe ontological relations with regard to time and space (chap. 11). Spatiotemporal nestedness refers to the containment of a smaller spatiotemporal scale within a larger one: for instance, the brain and its relatively smaller spatiotemporal scale are nested or contained within the larger spatiotemporal scale of the world. Spatiotemporal directedness refers to the relationship between different spatiotemporal scales where the larger spatiotemporal scale, e.g., the one of the world, is directed toward the smaller one, e.g., the one of the brain; thus I speak of world–brain relation as distinguished from brain–world relation (with the latter entailing reversed directedness as from the smaller to the larger spatiotemporal scale) (chap. 11).

Spectrum model of brain A theoretical model of the brain that describes the brain's neural activity empirically with regard to its dependence on either internally or externally generated activity. Externally generated activity is associated with specific stimuli such as sensory stimuli resulting in stimulus-induced activity that has been described by a passive model and can be featured as a Humean-like model of brain (chap. 1). By contrast, internally generated activity in the brain is described as spontaneous activity (or resting state activity), which, philosophically, can be described by an active model and features as a Kantian like model of brain (introduction, chap. 1). The spectrum model of brain now postulates that, based on empirical evidence, the brain's neural activity is neither purely active, i.e., internally generated, nor purely passive, i.e., externally generated. Instead, the brain's neuronal activity can be characterized by a neuronal continuum between passive and active components and thus between internally and externally generated activity (chap. 1). Specifically, stimulus-induced activity is not purely passive and thus externally generated as it is impacted and modulated by the internally generated brain's spontaneous activity; this is manifest in what I describe as rest-stimulus interaction (chap. 1). Conversely, the internally generated spontaneous activity is not purely active, as it is modulated by the externally generated stimulus-induced activity; this is manifest empirically in what I describe as stimulus-rest interaction (chap. 1). The spectrum of different active-passive constellations in the brain's neuronal activity is extremely reduced during the loss of consciousness (chap. 4): neuronal activity is merely passive, i.e., externally generated, rather than active, i.e., internally generated.

Spontaneity and spontaneous activity The concept of spontaneity can be understood in the sense of Kant who characterized it as intrinsic and independent of any extrinsic activity (as, for instance, related to sensory input). Taken in this context, the concept of spontaneity has been closely associated with the concept of active as distinguished from passive (chap. 1). Since the brain also shows neuronal activity that remains independent of any specific externally applied sensory input or cognitive task, that very same neuronal activity has been described as spontaneous activity (or intrinsic activity or resting state activity) (introduction, chap. 1). Based on empirical evidence, I postulate that the brain's spontaneous activity can be characterized by a spatiotemporal structure that is central for yielding mental features like consciousness. I postulate that the empirical features of the brain's spontaneous activity carry major ontological implications for ontology in general (chap. 9) and the question of the ontological basis of mental features like world-brain relation vs mind (chaps. 10–11) as well as for methodological-epistemological issues like the *vantage point* (chaps. 13–14).

Structure and spatiotemporal structure See *Relation and structure.*

Structural realism (SR) A theory of a given phenomenon that highlights the central role of relations and structure. Either relata are included in conjunction with relations (moderate SR) or relata are eliminated completely in favor of relations (eliminativist SR). SR has been discussed mainly in the context of physics but has also recently been applied to information, cognitive science, the brain, and secondary qualities. Finally, SR comes in an epistemic and ontological version. The epistemic version of structural realism (ESR) is the more modest one, claiming that all we can know are structures and relations. Importantly, such an epistemic claim is not accompanied by ontological assumptions. ESR remains agnostic regarding the question of whether what we know really corresponds to ontological existence and a reality independent of ourselves (i.e., ontic structural realism; OSR).

I here use the ontological version of SR to characterize the existence and reality of the brain. As the brain's existence and reality is based on structure and reality, the brain must ontologically be determined by world–brain relation. The relation to the world and its structure is an intrinsic ontological feature of the brain without which the brain would not exist. I define the brain's existence and reality here by its neuronal activity as featured by a particular spatiotemporal structure. That must be distinguished from the definition of the brain's existence and reality by its anatomical structure, i.e., its gray matter that remains more or less independent of the brain's neuronal activity and its spatiotemporal structure. The mere presence of the brain's gray matter consequently remains insufficient to define the brain's existence and reality. Therefore, any property-based ontology that defines the brain in terms of its gray matter and anatomical structure by either mental or physical properties remains insufficient for determining the brain's spatiotemporal structure.

Time and space Notions much discussed in philosophy but usually taken for granted in the sciences, including neuroscience. I here emphasize that one cannot take time and space for granted in neuroscience as it strongly affects how we conceive the brain and its relationship to consciousness. Time and space must be considered separate and distinct in empirical and ontological contexts or domains. Empirically, we can observe discrete points in time and space—as such this view on time and space is based on observation, I speak of observational time and space (chap. 9). Observational time and space are related to us as observers and how we perceive and cognize time and space. Such observational time and space needs to be distinguished from the time and space the brain itself constructs in its own neuronal activity that characterizes the brain's existence and reality (chap. 7). We thus need to distinguish between perception/observation/cognition of time and space in the brain on the one and construction of time and space by the brain itself. I postulate that the latter, i.e., construction of time and space by the brain, is central for consciousness (chap. 7).

As we cannot infer directly from the empirical to the ontological domain (chap. 9), the existence and reality of time and space need not conform to the way we observe time and space, that is, in terms of discrete points in time and space. Based on empirical and ontological evidence, I postulate that the existence and reality of time and space consists in relation and structure. I therefore speak of relational time and space (chap. 9). The existence and reality of such relational time and space can, for instance, be characterized by inner duration and extension (chapters 7 and 9), which characterizes both world (chap. 11) and brain (chap. 7). Ontologically, inner duration and extension can be specified by *spatiotemporal nestedness and directedness* and complex location rather than simple location (chap. 11).

Vantage point Here understood as point of view or viewpoint, which needs to be distinguished from the notion of perspective including first-, second-, and third-person perspective as well as God's eye view (chap. 12). The chosen vantage point may provide a specific view that includes a wide range of phenomena. For instance, being on the top of a mountain at the edge of the city provides us with a vantage point from beyond the city. We can then perceive and ultimately know the city as a whole, which thereby is rendered transparent to us. The vantage point thus allows us to include the whole city as a possible epistemic option in our logical space of knowledge. If, in contrast, one stands in the midst of the city itself, one remains unable to perceive the city as whole. Accordingly, the vantage point determines the possible epistemic options in our *logical space of knowledge* by rendering certain epistemic options transparent and others opaque (chap. 12 for details, chaps. 13–14 for application). Thus I consider the concept of vantage point in an epistemic-methodological way. That allows me to distinguish different vantage points like the more pre-Copernican vantage points from within mind or brain (chap. 13), the post-Copernican vantage point from beyond brain (chap. 14), and the metaphysical non-Copernican vantage point from beyond world (see *Copernican revolution* as well as chaps. 12–14).

World A concept that is usually taken for granted and often not explicitly discussed and defined. I postulate, however, that we need to define and determine the concept of world in a detailed way in order to avoid fallacious inferences between the conception of world in different domains; therefore, I determine the concept of world differently in empirical, phenomenological, ontological, metaphysical, and epistemic-methodological contexts or domains. Empirically, the concept of world refers to what we can observe as in scientific investigation. Taken in this empirical sense, the world is characterized by discrete points in time and space (chap. 9). Phenomenologically, the concept of world refers to the way we experience the world as conscious beings. The world in this phenomenological sense is then characterized by temporal continuity as described in the concepts of "inner time consciousness" by E. Husserl and "stream of consciousness" by W. James (chaps. 4–7). Ontologically, the concept of world can be understood in different ways in terms of properties or relations (chap. 9). For instance, based on empirical plausibility, I characterize the world's existence and reality in a spatiotemporal way, that is, by relational time and space for which reason I speak of spatiotemporal ontology (chap. 9). The world as spatiotemporal in an ontological sense must be distinguished from the world in a metaphysical sense that requires the world to be strictly a-temporal and a-spatial (chap. 9). Finally, the term world can be understood in an epistemic-methodological context as different concepts of world are related to different vantage points (chaps. 12–14).

World–brain problem The question of the relationship between world and brain that can be considered in empirical, ontological, and epistemic-methodological domains, where it replaces the *mind–body problem*. Empirically, there is strong evidence that the brain and its spontaneous activity align and thus relate to their respective environmental context (chaps. 3, 8) which, as the data show, is relevant for consciousness (chap. 8). Ontologically, the world—brain problem raises the question for the existence and reality underlying the relation between world and brain; this can be answered by, for instance, properties or, alternatively, *relation and structure*: the existence and realty of world and brain including their relationship is characterized by relation or structure as the most basic unit of existence and reality in the world including the brain (chap. 9). Taken by itself, the world—brain problem is a separate ontological (and also empirical) problem and therefore not necessarily connected to the question for the existence and reality of mental features like consciousness (chap. 9). However, I propose that the world—brain problem provides an empirically (chaps. 7–8) and ontologically (chaps. 10–11) plausible approach to address the question for the existence and reality of mental features. Therefore, I argue that the world—brain problem can replace the *mind—body problem* in our quest for the existence and reality of mental features such as consciousness (chaps. 10–11, 13–14). Finally, one may also consider the world-brain problem in an epistemic-methodological context from a vantage point beyond brain (chap. 14).

World–brain relation (vs. brain–world relation) A relation between world and brain that can be understood in a bi-directional way as well as in both empirical and ontological domains. Empirically, the brain can relate to the world on the basis of its task- or stimulus-induced activity that is related to the brain's cognitive, sensory, motor, social, and affective functions—this can be described as brain–world relation (chaps. 8–11). However, the brain can relate to the world also by its spontaneous activity that shows strong spatiotemporal alignment to the environmental context (chap. 8). As the brain adapts and aligns to the world as the primary origin of the world's relation to the brain, I speak of world–brain relation rather than brain–world relation (chaps. 8–11).

Ontologically, the brain's adaptation and alignment to the world is accounted for by the concepts of *spatiotemporal nestedness and directedness*: the spatiotemporally smaller brain is nested and contained within the spatiotemporally larger world (chap. 11). I therefore characterize the concept of world–brain relation in an ontological sense which, as in the empirical context (chap. 8), must be distinguished from brain–world relation (chaps. 9–11). Finally, both brain–world and world–brain relation must also be distinguished on methodological grounds: brain–world relation presupposes a vantage point from within brain (chap. 13), whereas world–brain relation can only be taken into view by presupposing a vantage point from beyond brain (chap. 14).

References

Acquadro, M. A., Congedo, M., & De Riddeer. D. (2016). Music performance as an experimental approach to hyperscanning studies. *Frontiers in Human Neuroscience, 10*, 242. doi:10.3389/fnhum.2016.00242.

Adams, R. A., Stephan, K. E., Brown, H. R., Frith, C. D., & Friston, K. J. (2013). The computational anatomy of psychosis. *Frontiers in Psychiatry, 4*, 47. doi:10.3389/fpsyt.2013.00047.

Alderson-Day, B., Diederen, K., Fernyhough, C., Ford, J. M., Horga, G., Margulies, D. S., et al. (2016). Auditory hallucinations and the brain's resting-state networks: Findings and methodological observations. *Schizophrenia Bulletin, 42*(5), 1110–1123. doi:10.1093/schbul/sbw078.

Alink, A., Schwiedrzik, C. M., Kohler, A., Singer, W., & Muckli, L. (2010). Stimulus predictability reduces responses in primary visual cortex. *Journal of Neuroscience, 30*(8), 2960–2966. doi:10.1523/JNEUROSCI.3730-10.2010.

Allison, H. (1973). Kant's critique of Berkeley. *Journal of the History of Philosophy, 11*, 51.

Alter, T. (2016). The structure and dynamics argument against materialism. *Noûs, 50*(4), 794–815.

Ameriks, K. (1982). *Kant's theory of mind: An analysis of the paralogisms of pure reason.* Oxford: Oxford University Press.

Andersen, L., Pedersen, M., & Sandberg, K. (2016). Occipital MEG activity in the early time range (<300 ms) predicts graded changes in perceptual consciousness. *Cerebral Cortex, 26*, 2677–2688. doi:10.1093/cercor/bhv108.

Andreasen, N. C., O'Leary, D. S., Cizadlo, T., Arndt, S., Rezai, K., Watkins, G. L., et al. (1995). Remembering the past: Two facets of episodic memory explored with positron emission tomography. *American Journal of Psychiatry, 152*(11), 1576–1585.

Andrews-Hanna, J. R., Irving, Z., Fox, K., Spreng, N., & Christoff, C. (Forthcoming). The neuroscience of spontaneous thought: An evolving interdisciplinary field. In K.

C. R. Fox & K. Christoff (Eds.), *The Oxford handbook of spontaneous thought: Mind-wandering, creativity, dreaming, and clinical conditions*. New York: Oxford University Press.

Andrews-Hanna, J. R., Kaiser, R. H., Turner, A. E., Reineberg, A. E., Godinez, D., Dimidjian, S., et al. (2013). A penny for your thoughts: Dimensions of self-generated thought content and relationships with individual differences in emotional wellbeing. *Frontiers in Psychology, 4*.

Andrews-Hanna, J. R., Smallwood, J., & Spreng, R. N. (2014). The default network and self-generated thought: Component processes, dynamic control, and clinical relevance. *Annals of the New York Academy of Sciences, 1316*(1), 29–52.

Apps, M. A., & Tsakiris, M. (2013). Predictive codes of familiarity and context during the perceptual learning of facial identities. *Nature Communications, 4*, 2698. doi:10.1038/ncomms3698.

Apps, M. A., & Tsakiris, M. (2014). The free-energy self: A predictive coding account of self-recognition. *Neuroscience and Biobehavioral Reviews, 41*, 85–97. doi:10.1016/j.neubiorev.2013.01.029.

Arieli, A., Sterkin, A., Grinvald, A., & Aertsen, A. (1996). Dynamics of ongoing activity: Explanation of the large variability in evoked cortical responses. *Science, 273*(5283), 1868–1871.

Aru, J., Bachmann, T., Singer, W., & Melloni, L. (2012). Distilling the neural correlates of consciousness. *Neuroscience and Biobehavioral Reviews, 36*(2), 737–746.

Aru, J., Aru, J., Priesemann, V., Wibral, M., Lana, L., Pipa, G., et al. (2015). Untangling cross-frequency coupling in neuroscience. *Current Opinion in Neurobiology, 31*, 51–61. doi:10.1016/j.conb.2014.08.002.

Azouz, R., & Gray, C. M. (1999). Cellular mechanisms contributing to response variability of cortical neurons in vivo. *Journal of Neuroscience, 19*(6), 2209–2223.

Baars, B. J. (2005). Global workspace theory of consciousness: Toward a cognitive neuroscience of human experience. *Progress in Brain Research, 150*, 45–53. doi:10.1016/S0079-6123(05)50004-9.

Baars, B. J., & Franklin, S. (2007). An architectural model of conscious and unconscious brain functions: Global Workspace Theory and IDA. *Neural Networks, 20*(9), 955–961.

Babiloni F. (2014). Astolfi L2.Social neuroscience and hyperscanning techniques: Past, present and future. *Neuroscience and Biobehavioral Reviews, 44*, 76–93. doi:10.1016/j.neubiorev.2012.07.006.

Babiloni, F., & Astolfi, L. (2014). Social neuroscience and hyperscanning techniques: Past, present and future. *Neuroscience and Biobehavioral Reviews, 44*, 76–93. doi:10.1016/j.neubiorev.2012.07.006.

Babo-Rebelo, M., Richter, C. G., & Tallon-Baudry, C. (2016). Neural responses to heartbeats in the default network encode the self in spontaneous thoughts. *Journal of Neuroscience, 36*(30), 7829–7840. doi:10.1523/JNEUROSCI.0262-16.2016.

Babo-Rebelo M, Wolpert N, Adam C, Hasboun D, & Tallon-Baudry C. (2016). Is the cardiac monitoring function related to the self in both the default network and right anterior insula? *Philosophical Transactions of the Royal Society of London B: Biological Sciences, 371*(1708). doi:10.1098/rstb.2016.0004.

Bachmann, T., & Hudetz, A. G. (2014). It is time to combine the two main traditions in the research on the neural correlates of consciousness: C = L × D. *Frontiers in Psychology, 5*, 940. doi:10.3389/fpsyg.2014.00940.

Baird, B., Smallwood, J., Lutz, A., & Schooler, J. W. (2014). The decoupled mind: Mind-wandering disrupts cortical phase-locking to perceptual events. *Journal of Cognitive Neuroscience, 26*(11), 2596–2607.

Barlow, H. B. (1972). Single units and sensation: A neuron doctrine for perceptual psychology? *Perception, 1*(4), 371–394. http://www.ncbi.nlm.nih.gov/pubmed/4377168.

Barlow, H. (2001). The exploitation of regularities in the environment by the brain. *Behavioral and Brain Sciences, 24*(4), 602–607.

Barlow, H. B. (2009). Single units and sensation: A neuron doctrine for perceptual psychology? *Perception, 38*(6), 795–798. http://www.ncbi.nlm.nih.gov/pubmed/19806956.

Barry, R. J., Clarke, A. R., Johnstone, S. J., Magee, C. A., & Rushby, J. A. (2007). EEG differences between eyes-closed and eyes-open resting conditions. *Clinical Neurophysiology, 118*(12), 2765–2773.

Barttfeld, P., Uhrig, L., Sitt, J. D., Sigman, M., Jarraya, B., & Dehaene, S. (2015). Signature of consciousness in the dynamics of resting-state brain activity. *Proceedings of the National Academy of Sciences of the United States of America, 112*, 887–892. doi:10.1073/pnas.1418031112.

Bassett, D., & Sporns, O. (2017). Network neuroscience. *Nature Neuroscience, 20*, 353–364. doi:10.1038/nn.4502.

Bayne, T. (2010). *The unity of consciousness*. Oxford: Oxford University Press.

Bayne, T., & Chalmers, D. (2003). What is the unity of consciousness? In A. Cleeremans (Ed.), *The unity of consciousness* (pp. 23–58). Oxford: Oxford University Press.

Bayne, T., Hohwy, J., & Owen, A. M. (2016). Are there levels of consciousness? *Trends in Cognitive Sciences, 20*(6), 405–413. doi:10.1016/j.tics.2016.03.009.

Becker, R., Reinacher, M., Freyer, F., Villringer, A., & Ritter, P. (2011). How ongoing neuronal oscillations account for evoked fMRI variability. *Journal of Neuroscience, 31*(30), 11016–11027.

Bencivenga, E. (1987). *Kant's Copernican revolution.* New York: Oxford University Press.

Beni, M. (2016). Structural realist account of the self. *Synthese, 193*(12), 3727–3740.

Beni, M. (in press). Epistemic informational structural realism. *Minds and Machines.*

Bennett, M. R., & Hacker, P. M. S. (2003). *Philosophical foundations of neuroscience.* Oxford: Blackwell.

Berger, H. (1929). About the electroencephalogram of humans/Über das Elektrenkephalogramm des Menschen. *Archiv für Psychiatrie und Nervenkrankheiten, 87,* 527–570.

Bergson, H. (1904). Le paralogisme psycho-physique. Paper presented at the international congress of philosophy, Genova, Italy.

Berto, F., & Tagliabue, J. (2014). The world is either digital or analogue. *Synthese, 191*(3), 481–497. doi:10.1007/s11229-013-0285-1.

Bickle, J. (2003). *Philosophy and neuroscience: A ruthlessly reductive account.* Norwell, MA: Kluwer Academic Press.

Bickle, J. (Ed.). (2009). *The Oxford handbook of philosophy and neuroscience.* New York: Oxford University Press.

Bickle, J., Mandik, P., & Landreth, A. (2012). The philosophy of neuroscience. In Edward N. Zalta (Ed.), *The Stanford Encyclopedia of Philosophy* (Summer 2012 Edition), https://plato.stanford.edu/archives/sum2012/entries/neuroscience/.

Bishop, G. (1933). Cyclic changes in excitability of the optic pathway of the rabbit. *American Journal of Physiology, 103,* 213–224.

Biswal, B., Yetkin, F. Z., Haughton, V. M., & Hyde, J. S. (1995). Functional connectivity in the motor cortex of resting human brain using echo-planar MRI. *Magnetic Resonance in Medicine, 34*(4), 537–541.

Block, N. (1996). How can we find the neural correlate of consciousness? *Trends in Neurosciences, 19*(11), 456–459.

Blumenberg, H. (1987). *The genesis of the Copernican world.* Cambridge, MA: MIT Press. Originally appeared in German as *Die Genesis der Kopernikanischen Welt* (Frankfurt: Suhrkamp, 1975).

Boden, M. A. (2006). *Mind as machine: A history of cognitive science.* Oxford: Clarendon.

Boly, M., Balteau, E., Schnakers, C., Degueldre, C., Moonen, G., Luxen, A., et al. (2007). Baseline brain activity fluctuations predict somatosensory perception in humans. *Proceedings of the National Academy of Sciences of the United States of America, 104,* 12187–12192. doi:10.1073/pnas.0611404104.

Bonnefond, M., Kastner, S., & Jensen, O., 2017. Communication between brain areas based on nested oscillations. *eNeuro, 4*.

Britz, J., Landis, T., & Michel, C. M. (2009). Right parietal brain activity precedes perceptual alternation of bistable stimuli. *Cerebral Cortex, 19*(1), 55–65. doi:10.1093/cercor/bhn056.

Broad, C. D. (1978). *Kant: An introduction*. Cambridge: Cambridge University Press, 1978.

Brown, J. (2012). What is consciousness. *Process Studies, 41*(1), 21–41.

Buckner, R. L., Andrews-Hanna, J. R., & Schacter, D. L. (2008). The brain's default network: Anatomy, function, and relevance to disease. *Annals of the New York Academy of Sciences, 1124*, 1–38.

Bueno, O., French, S., & Ladyman, J. (2002). On representing the relationship between the mathematical and the empirical. *Philosophy of Science, 69*, 497–518.

Bullmore, E., Long, C., Suckling, J., Fadili, J., Calvert, G., Zelaya, F., et al. (2001). Colored noise and computational inference in neurophysiological (fMRI) time series analysis: Resampling methods in time and wavelet domains. *Human Brain Mapping, 12*, 61–78.

Buzsáki, G. (2006). *Rhythms of the brain*. Oxford: Oxford University Press.

Buzsáki, G., & Draguhn, A. (2004). Neuronal oscillations in cortical networks. *Science, 80*(304), 1926–1929. doi:10.1126/science.1099745.

Buzsáki, G., Logothetis, N., & Singer, W. (2013). Scaling brain size, keeping timing: Evolutionary preservation of brain rhythms. *Neuron, 80*(3), 751–764. doi:10.1016/j.neuron.2013.10.002.

Cabral, J., Kringelbach, M. L., & Deco, G. (2013). Exploring the network dynamics underlying brain activity during rest. *Progress in Neurobiology, 114*, 102–131.

Canolty, R. T., Cadieu, C. F., Koepsell, K., Ganguly, K., Knight, R. T., & Carmena, J. M. (2012). Detecting event-related changes of multivariate phase coupling in dynamic brain networks. *Journal of Neurophysiology, 107*(7), 2020–2031. doi:10.1152/jn.00610.2011.

Canolty, R. T., & Knight, R. T. (2010). The functional role of cross-frequency coupling. *Trends in Cognitive Sciences, 14*(11), 506–515.

Carhart-Harris, R. L., Leech, R., Erritzoe, D., Williams, T. M., Stone, J. M., Evans, J., et al. (2013). Functional connectivity measures after psilocybin inform a novel hypothesis of early psychosis. *Schizophrenia Bulletin, 39*(6), 1343–1351.

Carruthers, P. (2009). How we know our own minds: The relationship between mindreading and metacognition. *Behavioral and Brain Sciences, 32*(2), 121–138, discussion 138–182. doi:10.1017/S0140525X09000545.

Cartwright, N. (1989). *Nature's capacities and their measurement.* Oxford: Clarendon Press.

Cartwright, N. (1997). Where do laws of nature come from? *Dialectica, 51*(1), 65–78.

Cartwright, N. (2007). *Hunting causes and using them: Approaches in philosophy and economics*. Cambridge: Cambridge University Press.

Cartwright, N. (2009). If no capacities, then no credible worlds, but can models reveal capacities? *Erkenntnis, 70*(1), 45–58.

Cartwright, N., & Hardie, J. (2012). *Evidence-based policy: A practical guide to doing it better.* New York: Oxford University Press.

Casali, A. G., Gosseries, O., Rosanova, M., Boly, M., Sarasso, S., Casali, K. R., et al. (2013). A theoretically based index of consciousness independent of sensory processing and behavior. *Science Translational Medicine, 5,* 198ra105. doi:10.1126/scitranslmed.3006294.

Cassirer, E. (1944). The concept of group and the theory of perception. *Philosophy and Phenomenological Research, V*(1), 1–36.

Cerullo, M. A., Metzinger, T., & Mangun, G. (2015). The problem with phi: A critique of integrated information theory. *PLoS Computational Biology, 11*(9), e1004286. doi:10.1371/journal.pcbi.1004286.

Chalmers, D. J. (1995). Facing up to the problem of consciousness. *Journal of Consciousness Studies, 2,* 200–219.

Chalmers, D. J. (1996). *The conscious mind.* Oxford: Oxford University Press.

Chalmers, D. J. (2003). Consciousness and its place in nature. In S. Stich & T. Warfield (Eds.), *Guide to the philosophy of mind.* Cambridge: Blackwell. Reprinted in D. J. Chalmers (Ed.), *Philosophy of mind: Classical and contemporary readings,* 247–272 (New York: Oxford University Press, 2002).

Chalmers, D. (2012). *Reconstructing the world.* New York: Oxford University Press.

Chang, C., Metzger, C. D., Glover, G. H., Duyn, J. H., Heinze, H. J., & Walter, M. (2013). Association between heart rate variability and fluctuations in resting-state functional connectivity. *NeuroImage, 68,* 93–104. doi:10.1016/j.neuroimage.2012.11.038.

Changeux, J. P. (2017). Climbing brain levels of organisation from genes to consciousness. *Trends in Cognitive Sciences, 21*(3), 168–181. doi:10.1016/j.tics.2017.01.004.

Chemero, A. (2009). *Radical embodied cognitive science.* Cambridge, MA: MIT Press.

Chen, J., Hasson, U., & Honey, C. J. (2015). Processing timescales as an organizing principle for primate cortex. *Neuron, 88,* 244–246. doi:10.1016/j.neuron.2015.10.010.

Christoff, K. (2012). Undirected thought: Neural determinants and correlates. *Brain Research, 1428*, 51–59.

Christoff, K., Gordon, A. M., Smallwood, J., Smith, R., & Schooler, J. W. (2009). Experience sampling during fMRI reveals default network and executive system contributions to mind wandering. *Proceedings of the National Academy of Sciences of the United States of America, 106*(21), 8719–8724. doi:10.1073/pnas.0900234106.

Christoff, K., Irving, Z. C., Fox, K. C. R., Spreng, R. N., & Andrews-hanna, J. R. (2016). Mind-wandering as spontaneous thought: A dynamic framework. *Nature Reviews: Neuroscience*, 17, 718–731. doi:10.1038/nrn.2016.113.

Churchland, M. M., Yu, B. M., Cunningham, J. P., Sugrue, L. P., Cohen, M. R., Corrado, G. S., et al. (2010). Stimulus onset quenches neural variability: A widespread cortical phenomenon. *Nature Neuroscience, 13*(3), 369–378. doi:10.1038/nn.2501.

Churchland, P. M. (1988). *Matter and consciousness*. Cambridge, MA: MIT Press.

Churchland, P. M. (1989). *A neurocomputational perspective: The nature of mind and the structure of science*. Cambridge, MA: MIT Press.

Churchland, P. M. (2012). *Plato's camera: How the physical brain captures a landscape of abstract universals*. Cambridge, MA: MIT Press.

Churchland, P. S. (1986). *Neurophilosophy*. Cambridge, MA: MIT Press.

Churchland, P. S. (2002). *Brain-wise*. Cambridge, MA: MIT Press.

Clark, A. (1997). *Being there: Putting brain, body, and world together again*. Cambridge, MA: MIT Press.

Clark, A. (2008). *Supersizing the mind: Embodiment, action, and cognitive extension*. Cambridge: Cambridge University Press.

Clark, A. (2012). Embodied, embedded, and extended cognition. In K. Frankish & W. Ramsey (Eds.), *The Cambridge handbook of cognitive science*. Cambridge: Cambridge University Press.

Clark, A. (2013). Whatever next? Predictive brains, situated agents, and the future of cognitive science. *Behavioral and Brain Sciences, 36*(3), 181–204.

Clark, A., & Chalmers, D. J. (2010). The extended mind. In Richard Menary (Ed.), *The extended mind*. Cambridge, MA: MIT Press.

Cleve, J. Van. (1999). *Problems from Kant*. Oxford: Oxford University Press.

Cohen, I. B. (1985). *Revolution in science*. Cambridge: Cambridge University Press.

Copernicus, N. (1543/1952). On the revolution of the heavenly spheres. C. G. Wallis (Trans.). In R. M. Hutchins (Ed.), *Great Books of the Western World*, Vol. 16, *Ptolemy, Copernicus, Kepler*. Chicago: Encylcopedia Britannica.

Corlett, P. R., Honey, G. D., Krystal, J. H., & Fletcher, P. C. (2011). Glutamatergic model psychoses: Prediction error, learning, and inference. *Neuropsychopharmacology, 36*(1), 294–315. doi:10.1038/npp.2010.163.

Corlett, P. R., Taylor, J. R., Wang, X. J., Fletcher, P. C., & Krystal, J. H. (2010). Toward a neurobiology of delusions. *Progress in Neurobiology, 92*(3), 345–369. doi:10.1016/j.pneurobio.2010.06.007.

Coste, C. P., Sadaghiani, S., Friston, K. J., & Kleinschmidt, A. (2011). Ongoing brain activity fluctuations directly account for intertrial and indirectly for intersubject variability in Stroop task performance. *Cerebral Cortex, 21*(11), 2612–2619.

Craig, A. D. (2003). Interoception: The sense of the physiological condition of the body. *Current Opinion in Neurobiology, 13*(4), 500–505.

Craig, A. D. (2009). How do you feel—now? The anterior insula and human awareness. *Nature Reviews. Neuroscience, 10*(1), 59–70. doi:10.1038/nrn2555.

Craig, A. D. (2011). Significance of the insula for the evolution of human awareness of feelings from the body. *Annals of the New York Academy of Sciences, 1225*, 72–82. doi:10.1111/j.1749-6632.2011.05990.x.

Craver, C. (2007). *Explaining the brain mechanisms and the mosaic unity of neuroscience.* Oxford: Oxford University Press.

Crick, F., & Koch, C. (2003). A framework for consciousness. *Nature Neuroscience, 6*(2), 119–126. doi:10.1038/nn0203-119.

Cross, F. L. (1937). Kant's so-called Copernican revolution. *Mind, 46*(182), 214–217.

Dainton, B. (2010). *Time and space.* 2nd ed. Durham: Acumen.

Damiano, S., Zhang, J., Huang, Z., Wolff, A., & Northoff, G. (submitted). Increased scale-free activity in salience network in autism.

D'Argembeau, A., Stawarczyk, D., Majerus, S., Collette, F., Van der Linden, M., Feyers, D., et al. (2010a). The neural basis of personal goal processing when envisioning future events. *Journal of Cognitive Neuroscience, 22*(8), 1701–1713. doi: 10.1162/jocn.2009.21314

D'Argembeau, A., Stawarczyk, D., Majerus, S., Collette, F., Van der Linden, M., & Salmon, E. (2010b). Modulation of medial prefrontal and inferior parietal cortices when thinking about past, present, and future selves. *Social Neuroscience, 5*(2), 187–200.

David, S. V., Vinje, W. E., & Gallant, J. L. (2004). Natural stimulus statistics alter the receptive field structure of V1 neurons. *Journal of Neuroscience, 24*(31). doi:10.1523/JNEUROSCI.1422-04.2004.

DeCharms, R. C., & Zador, A. (2000). Neural representation and the cortical code. *Annual Review of Neuroscience, 23*, 613–647.

Deco, G., Jirsa, V. K., & McIntosh, A. R. (2013). Resting brains never rest: Computational insights into potential cognitive architectures. *Trends in Neurosciences, 36*(5), 268–274.

Deco, G., Tononi, G., Boly, M., & Kringelbach, M. L. (2015). Rethinking segregation and integration: Contributions of whole-brain modelling. *Nature Reviews. Neuroscience, 16*, 430–439. doi:10.1038/nrn3963.

de Graaf, T. A., Hsieh, P. J., & Sack, A. T. (2012). The "correlates" in neural correlates of consciousness. *Neuroscience and Biobehavioral Reviews, 36*(1), 191–197. doi:10.1016/j.neubiorev.2011.05.012.

de Greck, M., Enzi, B., Prosch, U., Gantman, A., Tempelmann, C., & Northoff, G. (2010). Decreased neuronal activity in reward circuitry of pathological gamblers during processing of personal relevant stimuli. *Human Brain Mapping, 31*(11), 1802–1812.

Dehaene, S., & Changeux, J. P. (2005). Ongoing spontaneous activity controls access to consciousness: A neuronal model for inattentional blindness. *PLoS Biology, 3*(5), e141.

Dehaene, S., & Changeux, J. P. (2011). Experimental and theoretical approaches to conscious processing. *Neuron, 70*(2), 200–227. doi:10.1016/j.neuron.2011.03.018.

Dehaene, S., Changeux, J. P., Naccache, L., Sackur, J., & Sergent, C. (2006). Conscious, preconscious, and subliminal processing: A testable taxonomy. *Trends in Cognitive Sciences, 10*(5), 204–211. doi:10.1016/j.tics.2006.03.007.

Dehaene, S., Charles, L., King, J. R., & Marti, S. (2014). Toward a computational theory of conscious processing. *Current Opinion in Neurobiology, 25*, 76–84. doi:10.1016/j.conb.2013.12.005.

Deleuze, G. (1994). *Difference and repetition* (Paul Patton, Trans.). New York: Columbia University.

Dennett, D. C. (1981). *Brainstorms*. Cambridge, MA: MIT Press.

Dennett, D. C. (2013). *Intuition pumps and other tools for thinking*. New York: W. W. Norton.

den Ouden, H. E., Friston, K. J., Daw, N. D., McIntosh, A. R., & Stephan, K. E. (2009). A dual role for prediction error in associative learning. *Cereb Cortex, 19*(5), 1175–1185. doi:10.1093/cercor/bhn161.

den Ouden, H. E., Kok, P., & de Lange, F. P. (2012). How prediction errors shape perception, attention, and motivation. *Frontiers in Psychology, 3*(548). doi: 10.3389/fpsyg.2012.00548.

de Pasquale, F., Della Penna, S., Snyder, A. Z., Lewis, C., Mantini, D., Marzetti, L., et al. (2010). Temporal dynamics of spontaneous MEG activity in brain networks. *Proceedings of the National Academy of Sciences, 107*(13), 6040–6045.

de Pasquale, F., Della Penna, S., Snyder, A. Z., Marzetti, L., Pizzella, V., Romani, G. L., et al. (2012). A cortical core for dynamic integration of functional networks in the resting human brain. *Neuron, 74*(4), 753–764.

Derrida, J. (1978). *Writing and difference* (A. Bass, Trans.). Chicago: University of Chicago Press.

Dietrich, E., & Hardcastle, V. G. (2004). *Sisyphus's boulder: Consciousness and the limits of the knowable*. Amsterdam: John Benjamins.

Ding, N., Melloni, L., Zhang, H., Tian, X., & Poeppel, D. (2016). Cortical tracking of hierarchical linguistic structures in connected speech. *Nature Neuroscience, 19*(1), 158–164. doi:10.1038/nn.4186.

Dixon, M. L., Fox, K. C. R., & Christoff, K. (2014). A framework for understanding the relationship between externally and internally directed cognition. *Neuropsychologia, 62*, 321–330. doi:10.1016/j.neuropsychologia.2014.05.024.

Dominguez Duque, J. F., Turner, R., Lewis, E. D., & Egan, G. (2010). Neuroenthropology: A humanistic science for the study of culture-brain nexus. *Social Cognitive and Affective Neuroscience, 5*, 138–147.

Doucet, G., Naveau, M., Petit, L., Zago, L., Crivello, F., Jobard, G., et al. (2012). Patterns of hemodynamic low-frequency oscillations in the brain are modulated by the nature of free thought during rest. *NeuroImage, 59*(4), 3194–3200.

Doya, K., Ishii, S., Pouget, A., & Rao, R. P. N. (Eds.). (2011). *Bayesian brain: Probabilistic approaches to neural coding*. Cambridge, MA: MIT Press.

Dretske, F. (1988). *Explaining behavior: Reasons in a world of causes*. Cambridge, MA: MIT Press.

Dretske, F. (1995). *Naturalizing the mind*. Cambridge, MA: MIT Press.

Drevets, W. C., Burton, H., Videen, T. O., Snyder, A. Z., Simpson, J. R., & Raichle, M. E. (1995). Blood flow changes in human somatosensory cortex during anticipated stimulation.

Duncan, N. W., Hayes, D. J., Wiebking, C., Tiret, B., Pietruska, K., Chen, D. Q., et al. (2015). Negative childhood experiences alter a prefrontal-insular-motor cortical network in healthy adults: A preliminary multimodal rsfMRI-fMRI-MRS-dMRI study. *Human Brain Mapping, 36*(11), 4622–4637. doi:10.1002/hbm.22941.

Edelman, G. M. (2003). Naturalizing consciousness: A theoretical framework. *Proceedings of the National Academy of Sciences of the United States of America, 100*(9), 5520–5524. doi:10.1073/pnas.0931349100.

Edelman, G. M. (2004). *Wider than the sky*. New Haven, CT: Yale University Press.

Edelman, G. M., & Tononi, G. (2000). *A universe of consciousness: How matter becomes imagination*. New York: Basic Books.

Egner, T., Monti, J. M., & Summerfield, C. (2010). Expectation and surprise determine neural population responses in the ventral visual stream. *Journal of Neuroscience, 30*(49), 16601–16608. doi:10.1523/JNEUROSCI.2770-10.2010.

Eliasmith, C. (2012). *How to build a brain*. Oxford: Oxford University Press.

Ellamil, M., Fox, K. C. R., Dixon, M. L., Pritchard, S., Todd, R. M., Thompson, E., et al. (2016). Dynamics of neural recruitment surrounding the spontaneous arising of thoughts in experienced mindfulness practitioners. *NeuroImage, 136*, 186–196.

Engel, A. K., & Singer, W. (2001). Temporal binding and the neural correlates of sensory awareness. *Trends in Cognitive Sciences, 5*(1), 16–25.

Engel, A. K., Gerloff, C., Hilgetag, C. C., & Nolte, G. (2013). Intrinsic coupling modes: Multiscale interactions in ongoing brain activity. *Neuron, 80*(4), 867–886.

Engel, M. S. (1963). Kant's Copernican analogy: A re-examination. *Kant-Studien, 54*, 243–251.

Esfeld, M. (2004). Quantum entanglement and a metaphysics of relations. *Studies in History and Philosophy of Modern Physics, 35*, 601–617.

Esfeld, M. (2009). The modal nature of structures in ontic structural realism. *International Studies in the Philosophy of Science, 23*(2), 179–194.

Esfeld, M. (2011). Structures and powers. In A. and P. Bokulich (Eds.), *Scientific structuralism*. Dordrecht: Springer.

Esfeld, M. (2013). Ontic structural realism and the interpretation of quantum mechanics. *European Journal for Philosophy of Science, 3*(1), 19–32.

Esfeld, M., & Lam, V. (2008). Moderate structural realism about space-time. *Synthese, 160*, 27–46.

Esfeld, M., & Lam, V. (2010). Holism and structural realism. In R. Vanderbeeken & B. D'Hooghe (Eds.), *Worldviews, science and us: Studies of analytical metaphysics. A selection of topics from a methodological perspective* (pp. 10–31). Singapore: World Scientific.

Esfeld, M., & Lam, V. (2011). Ontic structural realism as a metaphysics of objects. In A. and P. Bokulich (Eds.), *Scientific structuralism*. Dordrecht: Springer

Esfeld, M., & Lam, V. (2012). The structural metaphysics of quantum theory and general relativity. *Journal for General Philosophy of Science, 43*(2), 243–258.

Faber, R., & Henning, B. G. (2010). Whitehead's other Copernican turn. In R. Faber, B. G. Henning, & C. Combo (Eds.), *Beyond metaphysics? Explorations in Alfred North Whitehead's late thought* (pp. 1–10). Amsterdam: Rodopi.

Faivre, N., & Koch, C. (2014). Temporal structure coding with and without awareness. *Cognition, 131*(3), 404–414. doi:10.1016/j.cognition.2014.02.008.

Faivre, N., Mudrik, L., Schwartz, N., & Koch, C. (2014). Multisensory integration in complete unawareness: Evidence from audiovisual congruency priming. *Psychological Science, 25*(11), 2006–2016. doi:10.1177/0956797614547916.

Fazelpour, S., & Thompson, E. (2015). The Kantian brain: Brain dynamics from a neurophenomenological perspective. *Current Opinion in Neurobiology, 31*, 223–229. doi:10.1016/j.conb.2014.12.006.

Fell, J. (2004). Identifying neural correlates of consciousness: The state space approach. *Consciousness and Cognition, 13*(4), 709–729.

Fell, J., & Axmacher, N. (2011). The role of phase synchronization in memory processes. *Nature Reviews: Neuroscience, 12*(2), 105–118.

Fell, J., Elger, C. E., & Kurthen, M. (2004). Do neural correlates of consciousness cause conscious states? *Medical Hypotheses, 63*(2), 367–369.

Ferrarelli, F., Massimini, M., Sarasso, S., Casali, A., Riedner, B. A., Angelini, G., et al. (2010). Breakdown in cortical effective connectivity during midazolam-induced loss of consciousness. *Proceedings of the National Academy of Sciences of the United States of America, 107*(6), 2681–2686. doi:10.1073/pnas.0913008107.

Ferri, F., Costantini, M., Huang, Z., Perrucci, M. G., Ferretti, A., Romani, G. L., et al. (2015). Intertrial variability in the premotor cortex accounts for individual differences in peripersonal space. *Journal of Neuroscience, 35*, 345–359.

Fingelkurts, A. A., Fingelkurts, A. A., Kivisaari, R., Pekkonen, E., Ilmoniemi, R. J., & Kähkönen, S. (2004a). Enhancement of GABA-related signalling is associated with increase of functional connectivity in human cortex. *Human Brain Mapping, 22*(1), 27–39. doi:10.1002/hbm.20014.

Fingelkurts, A. A., Fingelkurts, A. A., Kivisaari, R., Pekkonen, E., Ilmoniemi, R. J., & Kähkönen, S. (2004b). The interplay of lorazepam-induced brain oscillations: Microstructural electromagnetic study. *Clinical Neurophysiology, 115*(3), 674–690.

Fingelkurts, A. A., Fingelkurts, A. A., Kivisaari, R., Pekkonen, E., Ilmoniemi, R. J., & Kähkönen, S. (2004c). Local and remote functional connectivity of neocortex under the inhibition influence. *NeuroImage, 22*(3), 1390–1406. doi:10.1016/j.neuroimage.2004.03.013.

Fingelkurts, A. A., Fingelkurts, A. A., & Neves, C. F. H. (2013). Consciousness as a phenomenon in the operational architectonics of brain organization: Criticality and self-organization considerations. *Chaos, Solitons, and Fractals, 55,* 13–31. doi:10.1016/j.chaos.2013.02.007.

Fletcher, P. C., & Frith, C. D. (2009). Perceiving is believing: A Bayesian approach to explaining the positive symptoms of schizophrenia. *Nature Reviews: Neuroscience, 10*(1), 48–58. doi:10.1038/nrn2536.

Fliessbach, K., Weber, B., Trautner, P., Dohmen, T., Sunde, U., et al. (2007). Social comparison affects reward-related brain activity in the human ventral striatum. *Science, 318*(5854), 1305–1308.

Floridi, L. (2008). A defence of informational structural realism. *Synthese, 161*(2), 219–253.

Floridi, L. (2009). Against digital ontology. *Synthese, 168*(1), 151–178. doi:10.1007/s11229-008-9334-6.

Floridi, L. (2011a). A defence of constructionism: Philosophy as conceptual engineering. *Metaphilosophy, 42*(3), 282–304. doi:10.1111/j.1467-9973.2011.01693.x.

Floridi, L. (2011b). *The philosophy of information.* Oxford: Oxford University Press. 10.1093/acprof:oso/9780199232383.001.0001.

Floridi, L. (2013). What is a philosophical question? *Metaphilosophy, 44*(3), 195–221. doi:10.1111/meta.12035.

Florin, E., & Baillet, S. (2015). The brain's resting-state activity is shaped by synchronized cross-frequency coupling of neural oscillations. *NeuroImage, 111,* 26–35. doi:10.1016/j.neuroimage.2015.01.054.

Fogelson, N., Litvak, V., Peled, A., Fernandez-del-Olmo, M., & Friston, K. (2014). The functional anatomy of schizophrenia: A dynamic causal modeling study of predictive coding. *Schizophrenia Research, 158*(1–3), 204–212. doi:10.1016/j.schres.2014.06.011.

Ford, J. M., Palzes, V. A., Roach, B. J., & Mathalon, D. H. (2014). Did I do that? Abnormal predictive processes in schizophrenia when button pressing to deliver a tone. *Schizophrenia Bulletin, 40*(4), 804–812. doi:10.1093/schbul/sbt072.

Fox, K. C. R., Spreng, R. N., Ellamil, M., Andrews-Hanna, J. R., & Christoff, K. (2015). The wandering brain: Meta-analysis of functional neuroimaging studies of mind-wandering and related spontaneous thought processes. *NeuroImage, 111,* 611–621. doi:10.1016/j.neuroimage.2015.02.039.

Fox, M. D., Snyder, A. Z., Zacks, J. M., & Raichle, M. E. (2005). Coherent spontaneous activity accounts for trial-to-trial variability in human evoked brain responses. *Nature Neuroscience, 9*(1), 23–25.

Freeman, W. J. (2003). The wave packet: An action potential for the 21st century. *Journal of Integrative Neuroscience, 2*(01), 3–30.

Freeman, W. J. (2007). Indirect biological measures of consciousness from field studies of brains as dynamical systems. *Neural Networks: The Official Journal of the International Neural Network Society, 20*(9), 1021–1031. doi:10.1016/j.neunet.2007.09.004.

Freeman, W. J. (2011). Understanding perception through neural "codes." *IEEE Transactions on Biomedical Engineering, 58*(7), 1884–1890. doi:10.1109/TBME.2010.2095854.

French, S. (2010). Keeping quiet on the ontology of models. *Synthese, 172*(2), 231–249. doi:10.1007/s11229-009-9504-1.

French, S. (2014). The structure of the world metaphysics and representation. *Journal of Chemical Information and Modeling, 53.* http://doi.org/ 10.1017/CBO9781107415324.004

French, S. (2015). (Structural) realism and its representational vehicles. *Synthese, 194,* 3311–3326. doi:10.1007/s11229-015-0879-x.

French, S., & Ladyman, J. (2003). Remodelling structural realism: Quantum physics and the metaphysics of structure. *Synthese, 136*(1), 31–56. doi:10.1023/A:1024156116636.

French, S., & Ladyman, J. (2011). Defence of ontic structural realism. In *Scientific structuralism* (Vol. 281, pp. 25–42). New York: Springer. 10.1007/978-90-481-9597-8_2.

Fresco, N., & Staines, P. J. (2014). A revised attack on computational ontology. *Minds and Machines, 24*(1), 101–122. doi:10.1007/s11023-013-9327-1.

Fries, P. (2009). Neuronal gamma-band synchronization as a fundamental process in cortical computation. *Annual Review of Neuroscience, 32,* 209–224.

Friston, K. J. (1995). Neuronal transients. *Proceedings of the Royal Society of London B: Biological Sciences, 261*(1362), 401–405.

Friston, K. J. (2008). Hierarchical models in the brain. *PLoS Computational Biology, 4*(11), e1000211. doi:10.1371/journal.pcbi.1000211.

Friston, K. J. (2010). The free-energy principle: A unified brain theory? *Nature Reviews: Neuroscience, 11,* 127–138.

Friston, K. J., & Frith, C. D. (2015). Active inference, communication and hermeneutics. *Cortex, 68,* 129–143. doi:10.1016/j.cortex.2015.03.025.

Frith, C. D., & Frith, U. (1999). Interacting minds—a biological basis. *Science, 286*(5445), 1692–1695.

Gallagher, S. (2005). *How the body shapes the mind.* Oxford: Oxford University Press.

Ganzetti, M., & Mantini, D. (2013). Functional connectivity and oscillatory neuronal activity in the resting human brain. *Neuroscience, 240,* 297–309.

Garfinkel, S. N., Minati, L., Gray, M. A., Seth, A. K., Dolan, R. J., & Critchley, H. D. (2014). Fear from the heart: Sensitivity to fear stimuli depends on individual heartbeats. *Journal of Neuroscience, 34*(19), 6573–6582. doi:10.1523/JNEUROSCI .3507-13.2014.

Garfinkel, S. N., Seth, A. K., Barrett, A. B., Suzuki, K., & Critchley, H. D. (2015). Knowing your own heart: Distinguishing interoceptive accuracy from interoceptive awareness. *Biological Psychology, 104,* 65–74. doi:10.1016/j.biopsycho.2014.11.004.

Gerhardt, V. (1987). Kants kopernikanische Wende. Friedrich Kaulbach zum 75. Geburtstag. *Kant-Studien, 78,* 133–153.

Gibson, M. I. (2011). A revolution in method, Kant's "Copernican hypothesis," and the necessity of natural laws. *Kant-Studien, 102,* 1–21.

Giere, R. N. (1999). *Science without laws.* Chicago: University of Chicago Press.

Giere, R. N. (2004). How models are used to represent reality. *Philosophy of Science, 71*(5), 742–752.

Giere, R. N. (2008). *Explaining science: A cognitive approach.* Chicago: University of Chicago Press.

Globus, G. (1992). Toward a noncomputational cognitive neuroscience. *Journal of Cognitive Neuroscience, 4*(4), 299–310.

Goldstein, K. (1934/2000). *The organism: A holistic approach to biology derived from pathological data in man.* New York: Zone Books.

Gorgolewski, K. J., Lurie, D., Urchs, S., Kipping, J. A., Craddock, R. C., Milham, M. P., et al. (2014). A correspondence between individual differences in the brain's intrinsic functional architecture and the content and form of self-generated thoughts. *PLoS One, 9*(5), e97176.

Gotts, S. J., Saad, Z. S., Jo, H. J., Wallace, G. L., Cox, R. W., & Martin, A. (2013). The perils of global signal regression for group comparisons: A case study of autism spectrum disorders. *Frontiers in Human Neuroscience, 7.*

Graziano, M. S. A. (2013). *Consciousness and the social brain.* Oxford: Oxford University Press.

Graziano, M. S. A., & Kastner, S. (2011). Human consciousness and its relationship to social neuroscience: A novel hypothesis. *Cognitive Neuroscience, 2*(2), 98–113.

Graziano, M. S. A., & Webb, T. W. (2015). The attention schema theory: A mechanistic account of subjective awareness. *Frontiers in Psychology, 6,* 500. doi:10.3389/fpsyg.2015.00500.

Greicius, M. D., Krasnow, B., Reiss, A. L., & Menon, V. (2003). Functional connectivity in the resting brain: A network analysis of the default mode hypothesis.

Proceedings of the National Academy of Sciences of the United States of America, 100(1), 253–258.

Griffin, D. R. (1863/1998). *Unsnarling the world-knot: Consciousness, freedom, and the mind–body problem*. Eugene, OR: Wipf and Stock.

Grimm, S., Boesiger, P., Beck, J., Schuepbach, D., Bermpohl, F., Walter, M., et al. (2009). Altered negative BOLD responses in the default-mode network during emotion processing in depressed subjects. *Neuropsychopharmacology, 34*(4), 932–943. doi:10.1038/npp.2008.81.

Grimm, S., Ernst, J., Boesiger, P., Schuepbach, D., Hell, D., Boeker, H., et al. (2009). Increased self-focus in major depressive disorder is related to neural abnormalities in subcortical-cortical midline structures. *Human Brain Mapping, 30*(8), 2617–2627.

Gusnard, D. A., & Raichle, M. E. (2001). Searching for a baseline: Functional imaging and the resting human brain. *Nature Reviews. Neuroscience, 2*(10), 685–694.

Guyer, P. (1987). *Kant and the claims of knowledge*. Cambridge: Cambridge University Press.

Hagmann, P., Cammoun, L., Gigandet, X., Meuli, R., Honey, C. J., Wedeen, V. J., et al. (2008). Mapping the structural core of human cerebral cortex. *PLoS Biology, 6*(7), e159. doi:10.1371/journal.pbio.0060159.

Hahn, R. (1988). *Kant's Newtonian revolution in philosophy*. Journal of the History of Philosophy Monograph Series. Chicago: Southern Illinois University Press.

Hamilton, J. P., Farmer, M., Fogelman, P., & Gotlib, I. H. (2015). Depressive rumination, the default-mode network, and the dark matter of clinical neuroscience. *Biological Psychiatry, 78*(4), 224–230. doi:10.1016/j.biopsych.2015.02.020.

Hanson, R. N. (1959). Copernicus' role in Kant's revolution. *Journal of the History of Ideas, 20*, 274–281.

Hasselman, F., Seevinck, M. P., & Cox, R. F. A. (submitted). Caught in the undertow: There is structure beneath the ontic stream. http://fredhasselman.com/pubs/MAN_CaugthintheUndertow.pdf.

Hasson, U., Chen, J., & Honey, C. J. (2015). Hierarchical process memory: Memory as an integral component of information processing. *Trends in Cognitive Sciences, 19*(6), 304–313.

Hasson, U., & Frith, C. D. (2016). Mirroring and beyond: Coupled dynamics as a generalized framework for modelling social interactions. *Philosophical Transactions of the Royal Society of London B: Biological Sciences, 371*(1693), pii: 20150366. doi: 10.1098/rstb.2015.0366.

Hasson, U., Ghazanfar, A. A., Galantucci, B., Garrod, S., & Keysers, C. (2012). Brain-to-brain coupling: A mechanism for creating and sharing a social world. *Trends in Cognitive Sciences, 16*(2), 114–121. doi:10.1016/j.tics.2011.12.007.

Haynes, J.-D. (2009). Decoding visual consciousness from human brain signals. *Trends in Cognitive Sciences, 13*(5), 194–202. doi:10.1016/j.tics.2009.02.004.

Haynes, J.-D. (2011). Decoding and predicting intentions. *Annals of the New York Academy of Sciences, 1224*, 9–21. doi:10.1111/j.1749-6632.2011.05994.x.

He, B. J. (2011). Scale-free properties of the functional magnetic resonance imaging signal during rest and task. *Journal of Neuroscience, 31*(39), 13786–13795. doi:10.1523/JNEUROSCI.2111-11.2011.

He, B. J. (2013). Spontaneous and task-evoked brain activity negatively interact. *Journal of Neuroscience, 33*(11), 4672–4682.

He, B. J. (2014). Scale-free brain activity: Past, present, and future. *Trends in Cognitive Sciences, 18*(9), 480–487. doi:10.1016/j.tics.2014.04.003.

He, B. J., & Raichle, M. E. (2009). The fMRI signal, slow cortical potential and consciousness. *Trends in Cognitive Sciences, 13*(7), 302–309.

He, B. J., Zempel, J. M., Snyder, A. Z., & Raichle, M. E. (2010). The temporal structures and functional significance of scale-free brain activity. *Neuron, 66*(3), 353–369. doi:10.1016/j.neuron.2010.04.020.

Heidegger, M. (1927/1962). *Being and time* (J. Macquarrie & E. Robinson, Trans.). Oxford: Blackwell.

Hesselmann, G., Kell, C. A., Eger, E., & Kleinschmidt, A. (2008). Spontaneous local variations in ongoing neural activity bias perceptual decisions. *Proceedings of the National Academy of Sciences of the United States of America, 105*(31), 10984–10989. doi:10.1073/pnas.0712043105.

Hesselmann, G., Kell, C. A., & Kleinschmidt, A. (2008). Ongoing activity fluctuations in hMT+ bias the perception of coherent visual motion. *Journal of Neuroscience, 28*(53), 14481–14485. doi:10.1523/JNEUROSCI.4398-08.2008.

Hipp, J. F., Hawellek, D. J., Corbetta, M., Siegel, M., & Engel, A. K. (2012). Large-scale cortical correlation structure of spontaneous oscillatory activity. *Nature Neuroscience, 15*(6), 884–890. doi:10.1038/nn.3101.

Hobson, J. A., & Friston, K. J. (2012). Waking and dreaming consciousness: Neurobiological and functional considerations. *Progress in Neurobiology, 98*(1), 82–98. doi:10.1016/j.pneurobio.2012.05.003.

Hobson, J. A., Hong, C. C., & Friston, K. J. (2014). Virtual reality and consciousness inference in dreaming. *Frontiers in Psycholology, 5*(1133). doi: 10.3389/fpsyg.2014.01133.

Hohwy, J. (2007). Functional integration and the mind. *Synthese, 159*(3), 315–328.

Hohwy, J. (2013). *The predictive mind.* Oxford: Oxford University Press.

Hohwy, J. (2014). The self-evidencing brain. *Noûs, 50*(2), 259–285.

Hohwy, J. (2017). Priors in perception: Top-down modulation, Bayesian perceptual learning rate, and prediction error minimization. *Consciousness and Cognition, 47,* 75–85. doi:10.1016/j.concog.2016.09.004.

Honey, C., Sporns, O., Cammoun, L., Gigandet, X., Thiran, J.-P., Meuli, R., et al. (2009). Predicting human resting-state functional connectivity from structural connectivity. *Proceedings of the National Academy of Sciences of the United States of America, 106*(6), 2035–2040.

Honey, C. J., Thesen, T., Donner, T. H., Silbert, L. J., Carlson, C. E., Devinsky, O., et al. (2012). Slow cortical dynamics and the accumulation of information over long timescales. *Neuron, 76,* 423–434. doi:10.1016/j.neuron.2012.08.011.

Horga, G., Schatz, K. C., Abi-Dargham, A., & Peterson, B. S. (2014). Deficits in predictive coding underlie hallucinations in schizophrenia. *Journal of Neuroscience, 34*(24), 8072–8082. doi:10.1523/JNEUROSCI.0200-14.2014.

Huang, Z., Dai, R., Wu, X., Yang, Z., Liu, D., Hu, J., et al. (2014). The self and its resting state in consciousness: An investigation of the vegetative state. *Human Brain Mapping, 35*(5), 1997–2008. doi:10.1002/hbm.22308.

Huang, Z., Wang, Z., Zhang, J., Dai, R., Wu, J., Li, Y., et al. (2014). Altered temporal variance and neural synchronization of spontaneous brain activity in anesthesia. *Human Brain Mapping, 35*(11), 5368–5378.

Huang, Z., Zhang, J., Duncan, N. W., & Northoff, G. (submitted). Is neural variability a neural signature of consciousness? Trial-to-trial variability and scale-free fluctuations during stimulus-induced activity in different stages of anesthesia.

Huang, Z., Zhang, J., Longtin, A., Dumont, G., Duncan, N. W., Pokorny, J., et al. (2017). Is there a nonadditive interaction between spontaneous and evoked activity? Phase-dependence and its relation to the temporal structure of scale-free brain activity. *Cerebral Cortex, 27*(2), 1037–1059. doi:10.1093/cercor/bhv288.

Huang, Z., Zhang, J., Wu, J., Qin, P., Wu, X., Wang, Z., Dai, R., Li, Y., Liang, W., Mao, Y., Yang, Z., Zhang, J., Wolff, A., & Northoff, G. (2015). Decoupled temporal variability and signal synchronization of spontaneous brain activity in loss of consciousness: An fMRI study in anesthesia. *Neuroimage, 124*(Pt. A), 693–703. doi:10.1016/j.neuroimage.2015.08.062.

Hudetz, A., Liu, X., & Pillay, S. (2015). Dynamic repertoire of intrinsic brain states is reduced in propofol-induced unconsciousness. *Brain Connectivity, 5,* 10–22. doi:10.1089/brain.2014.0230.

Hume, D. (1739/2000). *A treatise of human nature*. Oxford: Oxford University Press.

Hunter, M., Eickhoff, S., Miller, T., Farrow, T., Wilkinson, I., & Woodruff, P. (2006). Neural activity in speech-sensitive auditory cortex during silence. *Proceedings of the National Academy of Sciences of the United States of America, 103*(1), 189–194.

Hyafil, A., Giraud, A., Fontolan, L., & Gutkin, B. (2015). Neural cross-frequency coupling: Connecting architectures, mechanisms, and functions. *Trends in Neurosciences, 38*, 725–740. doi:10.1016/j.tins.2015.09.001.

Hyder, F., Fulbright, R. K., Shulman, R. G., & Rothman, D. L. (2013). Glutamatergic function in the resting awake human brain is supported by uniformly high oxidative energy. *Journal of Cerebral Blood Flow and Metabolism, 33*(3), 339–347.

Hyder, F., Patel, A. B., Gjedde, A., Rothman, D. L., Behar, K. L., & Shulman, R. G. (2006). Neuronal—glial glucose oxidation and glutamatergic—GABAergic function. *Journal of Cerebral Blood Flow and Metabolism, 26*(7), 865–877.

Hyder, F., Rothman, D. L., & Bennett, M. R. (2013). Cortical energy demands of signaling and nonsignaling components in brain are conserved across mammalian species and activity levels. *Proceedings of the National Academy of Sciences of the United States of America, 110*(9), 3549–3554.

Isaac, A. M. (2014). Structural realism for secondary qualities. *Erkenntnis, 79*(3), 481–510.

Jacob, S. N., Vallentin, D., & Nieder, A. (2012). Relating magnitudes: The brain's code for proportions. *Trends in Cognitive Sciences, 16*(3). doi:10.1016/j.tics.2012.02.002.

Jardri, R., & Denève, S. (2013). Circular inferences in schizophrenia. *Brain, 136*(Pt 11), 3227–3241. doi:10.1093/brain/awt257.

Jardri, R., & Denève, S. (2014). Erratum. *Brain, 137*(Pt 5), e278.

Jennings, J. R., Sheu, L. K., Kuan, D. C., Manuck, S. B., & Gianaros, P. J. (2016). Resting state connectivity of the medial prefrontal cortex covaries with individual differences in high-frequency heart rate variability. *Psychphysiology, 53*, 444–454.

Jensen, O., Gips, B., Bergmann, T. O., & Bonnefond, M. (2014). Temporal coding organized by coupled alpha and gamma oscillations prioritize visual processing. *Trends in Neurosciences, 37*(7), 357–369. doi:10.1016/j.tins.2014.04.001.

Johnston, M. (2004). The obscure object of hallucination. *Philosophical Studies, 120*, 113–183.

Johnston, M. (2006). Better than mere knowledge? The function of sensory awareness. In J. Hawthorne & T. Gendler (Eds.), Perceptual experience (pp. 260–290). Oxford: Oxford University Press.

Johnston, M. (2007). Objective mind and the objectivity of our minds. *Philosophy and Phenomenological Research, 75*(2), 233–268.

Johnston, M. (2009). *Saving god: Religion after idolatry*. Princeton, NJ: Princeton University Press.

Kant, I. (1781/1998). *Critique of pure reason*. P. Guyer & A. W. Wood (Eds.). Cambridge: Cambridge University Press.)

Kay, K. N., Naselaris, T., Prenger, R. J., & Gallant, J. L. (2008). Identifying natural images from human brain activity. *Nature, 452*(7185), 352–355. doi:10.1038/nature06713.

Khader, P., Schicke, T., Röder, B., & Rösler, F. (2008). On the relationship between slow cortical potentials and BOLD signal changes in humans. *International Journal of Psychophysiology, 67*(3), 252–261.

Kilner, J. M., Friston, K. J., & Frith, C. D. (2007). Predictive coding: An account of the mirror neuron system. *Cognitive Processing, 8*(3), 159–166.

Kitcher, P. (1989). Explanatory unification and the causal structure of the world. In P. Kitcher & W. Salmon (Eds.), *Scientific explanation: Minnesota studies in philosophy of science* (Vol. 13, pp. 410–505). Minneapolis: University of Minnesota Press.

Klein, C. (2014). The brain at rest: What it's doing and why that matters. *Philosophy of Science, 81*(5), 974–985.

Kleinschmidt, A., Sterzer, P., & Rees, G. (2012). Variability of perceptual multistability: From brain state to individual trait. *Philosophical Transactions of the Royal Society of London B: Biological Sciences, 367*(1591), 988–1000.

Klimesch, W., Freunberger, R., & Sauseng, P. (2010). Oscillatory mechanisms of process binding in memory. *Neuroscience and Biobehavioral Reviews, 34*(7), 1002–1014. doi:10.1016/j.neubiorev.2009.10.004.

Koch, C. (2004). *The quest for consciousness: A neurobiological approach*. San Francisco: W. H. Freeman.

Koch, C. (2012). *Consciousness: Confessions of a romantic reductionist*. Cambridge, MA: MIT Press.

Koch, C., Massimini, M., Boly, M., & Tononi, G. (2016). Neural correlates of consciousness: Progress and problems. *Nature Reviews: Neuroscience, 17*(5), 307–321. doi:10.1038/nrn.2016.22.

Koch, C., & Tsuchiya, N. (2012). Attention and consciousness: Related yet different. *Trends in Cognitive Sciences, 16*(2), 103–105. doi:10.1016/j.tics.2011.11.012.

Koivisto, M., Mäntylä, T., & Silvanto, J. (2010). The role of early visual cortex (V1/V2) in conscious and unconscious visual perception. *NeuroImage, 51*(2), 828–834. doi:10.1016/j.neuroimage.2010.02.042.

Koivisto, M., & Rientamo, E. (2016). Unconscious vision spots the animal but not the dog: Masked priming of natural scenes. *Consciousness and Cognition, 41*, 10–23. doi:10.1016/j.concog.2016.01.008.

Koike, T., Tanabe, H. C., & Sadato, N. (2015). Hyperscanning neuroimaging technique to reveal the "two-in-one" system in social interactions. *Neuroscience Research, 90*, 25–32. doi:10.1016/j.neures.2014.11.006.

Kok, P., Brouwer, G. J., van Gerven, M. A., & de Lange, F. P. (2013). Prior expectations bias sensory representations in visual cortex. *Journal of Neuroscience, 33*(41), 16275–16284. doi:10.1523/JNEUROSCI.0742-13.2013.

Kripke, S. (1972). *Naming and necessity*. Cambridge, MA: Harvard University Press.

Kuhn, T. (1957). *The Copernican revolution: Planetary astronomy in the development of western thought*. Cambridge, MA: Harvard University Press.

Kutas, M., & Hillyard, S. A. (1984). Brain potentials during reading reflect word expectancy and semantic association. *Nature, 307*, 161–163.

Ladyman, J. (1998). What is structural realism? *Studies in History and Philosophy of Science, 29*(3), 409–424. doi:10.1016/S0039-3681(98)80129-5.

Ladyman, J. (2014). Structural realism. In Edward N. Zalta (Ed.), *The Stanford encyclopedia of philosophy*, https://plato.stanford.edu/archives/win2014/entries/structural-realism

Lakatos, P., Karmos, G., Mehta, A. D., Ulbert, I., & Schroeder, C. E. (2008). Entrainment of neuronal oscillations as a mechanism of attentional selection. *Science, 80*, 320–325.

Lakatos, P., Schroeder, C. E., Leitman, D. I., & Javitt, D. C. (2013). Predictive suppression of cortical excitability and its deficit in schizophrenia. *Journal of Neuroscience, 33*(28), 11692–11702. doi:10.1523/JNEUROSCI.0010-13.2013.

Lakatos, P., Shah, A. S., Knuth, K. H., Ulbert, I., Karmos, G., & Schroeder, C. E. (2005). An oscillatory hierarchy controlling neuronal excitability and stimulus processing in the auditory cortex. *Journal of Neurophysiology, 94*(3), 1904–1911.

Lakoff, G., & Johnson, M. (1999). *Philosophy in the flesh: The embodied mind and its challenge to western thought*. New York: Basic Books.

Lamme, V. A. (2006). Towards a true neural stance on consciousness. *Trends in Cognitive Sciences, 10*(11), 494–501.

Lamme, V. A. (2010a). How neuroscience will change our view on consciousness. *Cognitive Neuroscience, 1*(3), 204–220. doi:10.1080/17588921003731586.

Lamme, V. A. (2010b). What introspection has to offer, and where its limits lie. *Cognitive Neuroscience, 1*(3), 232–240. doi:10.1080/17588928.2010.502224.

Lamme, V. A., & Roelfsema, P. R. (2000). The distinct modes of vision offered by feedforward and recurrent processing. *Trends in Neurosciences, 23*(11), 571–579.

Langner, R., Kellermann, T., Boers, F., Sturm, W., Willmes, K., & Eickhoff, S. B. (2011). Modality-specific perceptual expectations selectively modulate baseline activity in auditory, somatosensory, and visual cortices. *Cerebral Cortex, 21*(12), 2850–2862. doi:10.1093/cercor/bhr083.

Langton, R. (1998). *Kantian humility: Our ignorance of things in themselves*. Oxford: Oxford University Press.

Lashley, K. (1951). The problem of serial order in behavior. http://faculty.samford.edu/~sfdonald/Courses/cosc470/Papers/The%20problem%20of%20serial%20order%20in%20behavior%20(Lashley).pdf.

Lau, H., & Rosenthal, D. (2011). Empirical support for higher-order theories of conscious awareness. *Trends in Cognitive Sciences, 15*(8), 365–373. doi:10.1016/j.tics.2011.05.009.

Laureys, S. (2005). The neural correlate of (un)awareness: Lessons from the vegetative state. *Trends in Cognitive Sciences, 9*(12), 556–559.

Laureys, S., & Schiff, N. D. (2012). Coma and consciousness: Paradigms (re)framed by neuroimaging. *NeuroImage, 61*(2), 478–491. doi:10.1016/j.neuroimage.2011.12.041.

Lechinger, J., Heib, D. P., Gruber, W., Schabus, M., & Klimesch, W. (2015). Heartbeat-related EEG amplitude and phase modulations from wakefulness to deep sleep: Interactions with sleep spindles and slow oscillations. *Psychophysiology, 52*(11), 1441–1450. doi:10.1111/psyp.12508.

Lee, T. W., Northoff, G., & Wu, Y. T. (2014). Resting network is composed of more than one neural pattern: An fMRI study. *Neuroscience, 274*, 198–208. doi:10.1016/j.neuroscience.2014.05.035.

Leibniz, G. W., & Clarke, S. (2000). *Correspondence* (R. Ariew, Ed.). Indianapolis: Hackett.

Lemanski, J. (2012). Die Königin der Revolution. Zur Rettung und Erhaltung der Kopernikanischen Wende. *Kant-Studien, 103*, 448–471.

Lewicki, M. S. (2002). Efficient coding of natural sounds. *Nature Neuroscience, 5*(4), 356–363. doi:10.1038/nn831.

Lewis, L. D., Weiner, V. S., Mukamel, E. A., Donoghue, J. A., Eskandar, E. N., Madsen, J. R., et al. (2012). Rapid fragmentation of neuronal networks at the onset of propofol-induced unconsciousness. *Proceedings of the National Academy of Sciences of the United States of America, 109*(49), E3377–E3386. doi:10.1073/pnas.1210907109.

Li, Q., Hill, Z., & He, B. (2014). Spatiotemporal dissociation of brain activity underlying subjective awareness, objective performance and confidence. *Journal of Neuroscience, 34*, 4382–4395. doi:10.1523/JNEUROSCI.1820-13.2014.

Limanowski, J., & Blankenburg, F. (2013). Minimal self-models and the free energy principle. *Frontiers in Human Neuroscience, 7*, 547. doi:10.3389/fnhum.2013.00547.

Lindenberger, U., Li, S. C., Gruber, W., & Müller, V. (2009). Brains swinging in concert: Cortical phase synchronization while playing guitar. *BMC Neuroscience, 10*, 22. doi:10.1186/1471-2202-10-22.

Linkenkaer-Hansen, K., Nikouline, V. V., Palva, J. M., & Ilmoniemi, R. J. (2001). Long-range temporal correlations and scaling behavior in human brain oscillations. *Journal of Neuroscience, 21*, 1370–1377.

Liu, X., Ward, B. D., Binder, J. R., Li, S.-J., & Hudetz, A. G. (2014). Scale-free functional connectivity of the brain is maintained in anesthetized healthy participants but not in patients with unresponsive wakefulness syndrome. *PLoS One, 9*, e92182. doi:10.1371/journal.pone.0092182.

Llinás, R. R. (1988). The intrinsic electrophysiological properties of mammalian neurons: Insights into central nervous system function. *Science, 242*(4886), 1654–1664.

Llinás, R. (2001). *I of the vortex: From neurons to self.* Cambridge, MA: MIT Press.

Llinás, R. R., Leznik, E., & Urbano, F. J. (2002). Temporal binding via cortical coincidence detection of specific and nonspecific thalamocortical inputs: A voltage-dependent dye-imaging study in mouse brain slices. *Proceedings of the National Academy of Sciences of the United States of America, 99*(1), 449–454.

Llinás, R., Ribary, U., Contreras, D., & Pedroarena, C. (1998). The neuronal basis for consciousness. *Philosophical Transactions of the Royal Society of London B: Biological Sciences, 353*(1377), 841–849.

Logothetis, N. K., Murayama, Y., Augath, M., Steffen, T., Werner, J., & Oeltermann, A. (2009). How not to study spontaneous activity. *NeuroImage, 45*(4), 1080–1089. doi:10.1016/j.neuroimage.2009.01.010.

Maandag, N. J., Coman, D., Sanganahalli, B. G., Herman, P., Smith, A. J., Blumenfeld, H., et al. (2007). Energetics of neuronal signaling and fMRI activity. *Proceedings of the National Academy of Sciences, 104*(51), 20546–20551.

MacDonald, A. A., Naci, L., MacDonald, P. A., & Owen, A. M. (2015). Anesthesia and neuroimaging: Investigating the neural correlates of unconsciousness. *Trends in Cognitive Sciences, 19*(2), 100–107. doi:10.1016/j.tics.2014.12.005.

MacDougall, D. M. D. (1907). Hypothesis concerning soul substance together with experimental evidence of the existence of such substance. *Journal of the American Society for Psychical Research, 1*(5), 237–244.

Machamer, P., Darden, L., & Craver, C. (2000). Thinking about mechanisms. *Philosophy of Science, 57*, 1–25.

MacLaurin, J., & Dyke, H. (2012). What is analytic metaphysics? *Australasian Journal of Philosophy, 90*(2), 291–306.

Magioncalda, P., Martino, M., Conio, B., Escelsior, A., Piaggio, N., Presta, A., et al. (2014). Functional connectivity and neuronal variability of resting state activity in bipolar disorder-reduction and decoupling in anterior cortical midline structures. *Human Brain Mapping*. doi:10.1002/hbm.22655.

Malone-France, D. (2007). *Deep empiricism: Kant, Whitehead, and the necessity of philosophical theism*. Lanham, MD: Lexington Books.

Mandik, P. (2006). The neurophilosophy of consciousness. In M. Velmans & S. Schneider (Eds.), *The Blackwell companion to consciousness* (pp. 418–430). Oxford: Blackwell.

Mantini, D., Corbetta, M., Romani, G. L., Orban, G. A., & Vanduffel, W. (2013). Evolutionarily novel functional networks in the human brain? *Journal of Neuroscience, 33*(8), 3259–3275.

Mantini, D., Perrucci, M. G., Del Gratta, C., Romani, G. L., & Corbetta, M. (2007). Electrophysiological signatures of resting state networks in the human brain. *Proceedings of the National Academy of Sciences of the United States of America, 104*(32), 13170–13175. doi:10.1073/pnas.0700668104.

Martino, M., Magioncalda, P., Huang, Z., Conio, B., Piaggio, N., Duncan, N. W., et al. (2016). Contrasting variability patterns in the default mode and sensorimotor networks balance in bipolar depression and mania. *Proceedings of the National Academy of Sciences of the United States of America, 113*(17), 4824–4829. doi:10.1073/pnas.1517558113.

Marx, E., Deutschländer, A., Stephan, T., Dieterich, M., Wiesmann, M., & Brandt, T. (2004). Eyes open and eyes closed as rest conditions: Impact on brain activation patterns. *NeuroImage, 21*(4), 1818–1824.

Mason, M. F., Norton, M. I., Van Horn, J. D., Wegner, D. M., Grafton, S. T., & Macrae, C. N. (2007). Wandering minds: The default network and stimulus-independent thought. *Science, 315*(5810), 393–395. doi:10.1126/science.1131295.

Massimini, M., Ferrarelli, F., Murphy, M. J., Huber, R., Riedner, B. A., Casarotto, S., et al. (2010). Cortical reactivity and effective connectivity during REM sleep in humans. *Cognitive Neuroscience, 1*, 176–183. doi:10.1080/17588921003731578.

Mathewson, K. E., Gratton, G., Fabiani, M., Beck, D. M., & Ro, T. (2009). To see or not to see: Prestimulus α phase predicts visual awareness. *Journal of Neuroscience, 29*, 234–245.

McDowell, J. (1994). *Mind and world.* Cambridge, MA: Harvard University Press.

McDowell, J. (2009). *The engaged intellect: Philosophical essays.* Cambridge, MA: Harvard University Press.

McGinn, C. (1991). *The problem of consciousness.* London: Blackwell.

Menon, V. (2011). Large-scale brain networks and psychopathology: A unifying triple network model. *Trends in Cognitive Sciences, 15*(10), 483–506. doi:10.1016/j.tics.2011.08.003.

Merleau-Ponty, M. (1945/2012). *Phenomenology of perception* (D. Landes, Trans.). London: Routledge.

Miles, M. (2006). Kant's "Copernican revolution": Toward rehabilitation of a concept and provision of a framework for the interpretation of the *Critique of Pure Reason. Kant-Studien, 97,* 1–32.

Millikan, R. G. (1984). *Language, thought, and other biological categories.* Cambridge, MA: MIT Press.

Mitra, A., Snyder, A. Z., Tagliazucchi, E., Laufs, H., & Raichle, M. E. (2015). Propagated infraslow intrinsic brain activity reorganizes across wake and slow wave sleep. *eLife, 4,* e10781. doi:10.7554/eLife.10781.

Molotchnikoff, S., & Rouat, J. (2012). Brain at work: Time, sparseness and superposition principles. *Frontiers in Bioscience—Landmark, 17.* doi:10.2741/3946

Montague, P. R., King-Casas, B., & Cohen, J. D. (2006). Imaging valuation models in human choice. *Annual Review of Neuroscience, 29,* 417–448.

Monti, M. M., Vanhaudenhuyse, A., Coleman, M. R., Boly, M., Pickard, J. D., Tshibanda, L., et al. (2010). Willful modulation of brain activity in disorders of consciousness. *New England Journal of Medicine, 362*(7), 579–589. doi:10.1056/NEJMoa0905370.

Monto, S. (2012). Nested synchrony—a novel cross-scale interaction among neuronal oscillations. *Frontiers in Physiology, 3.*

Monto, S., Palva, S., Voipio, J., & Palva, J. M. (2008). Very slow EEG fluctuations predict the dynamics of stimulus detection and oscillation amplitudes in humans. *Journal of Neuroscience, 28*(33), 8268–8272. doi:10.1523/JNEUROSCI.1910-08.2008.

Morcom, A. M., & Fletcher, P. C. (2007a). Cognitive neuroscience: The case for design rather than default. *NeuroImage, 37*(4), 1097–1099.

Morcom, A. M., & Fletcher, P. C. (2007b). Does the brain have a baseline? Why we should be resisting a rest. *NeuroImage, 37*(4), 1073–1082. doi:10.1016/j.neuroimage.2007.06.019.

Morganti, M. (2011). Is there a compelling argument for ontic structural realism? *Philosophy of Science, 78*(5), 1165–1176.

Mossbridge, J. A., Tressoldi, P., Utts, J., Ives, J. A., Radin, D., & Jonas, W. B. (2014). Predicting the unpredictable: Critical analysis and practical implications of predictive anticipatory activity. *Frontiers in Human Neuroscience, 8*(146). doi: 10.3389/fnhum.2014.00146.

Moutard, C., Dehaene, S., & Malach, R. (2015). Spontaneous fluctuations and non-linear ignitions: Two dynamic faces of cortical recurrent loops. *Neuron, 88*(1), 194–206. doi:10.1016/j.neuron.2015.09.018.

Mudrik, L., Faivre, N., & Koch, C. (2014). Information integration without awareness. *Trends in Cognitive Sciences, 18*(9), 488–496.

Mukamel, E. A., Pirondini, E., Babadi, B., Wong, K. F., Pierce, E. T., Harrell, P. G., et al. (2014). A transition in brain state during propofol-induced unconsciousness. *Journal of Neuroscience, 34*(3), 839–845. doi:10.1523/JNEUROSCI.5813-12.2014.

Mukamel, E. A., Pirondini, E., Babadi, B., Wong, K. F., Pierce, E. T., Harrell, P. G., et al. (2015). Erratum. *Journal of Neuroscience, 35*(22), 8684–8685.

Mukamel, E. A., Wong, K. F., Prerau, M. J., Brown, E. N., & Purdon, P. L. (2011). Phase-based measures of cross-frequency coupling in brain electrical dynamics under general anesthesia. In *Engineering in Medicine and Biology Society EMBC 2011 Annual International Conference of the IEEE,* 1981–1984. doi:10.1109/IEMBS.2011.6090558

Murray, J. D., Bernacchia, A., Freedman, D. J., Romo, R., Wallis, J. D., & Cai, X., Padoa-Schioppa, C., Pasternak, T., Seo, H., Lee, D., & Wang, X.-J. (2014). A hierarchy of intrinsic timescales across primate cortex. *Nature Neuroscience, 17,* 1661–1663. doi:10.1038/nn.3862.

Nagel, T. (1974). What it is like to be a bat? *Philosophical Review, 83*(4), 435–450.

Nagel, T. (1979). *Mortal questions*. Cambridge: Cambridge University Press.

Nagel, T. (1986). *The view from nowhere*. Oxford: Oxford University Press.

Nagel, T. (1987). *What does it all mean? A very short introduction to philosophy*. Oxford: Oxford University Press.

Nagel, T. (1993). What is the mind-body problem? and Summary. In *Experimental and Theoretical Studies of Consciousness, Ciba Foundation Symposium 174* (pp. 1–13, 304–306). Chichester: John Wiley & Sons.

Nagel, T. (1997). *The last word*. Oxford: Oxford University Press.

Nagel, T. (1998). Conceiving the impossible and the mind-body problem. *Philosophy, 73,* 337–352.

Nagel, T. (2000). The psychophysical nexus. In P. Boghossian & C. Peacocke (Eds.), *New essays on the a priori* (pp. 432–471). Oxford: Clarendon Press.

Nagel, T. (2012). *Mind and cosmos: Why the materialist neo-Darwinian conception of nature is almost certainly false*. Oxford: Oxford University Press.

Nakao, T., Matsumoto, T., Morita, M., Shimizu, D., Yoshimura, S., Northoff, G., et al. (2013). The degree of early life stress predicts decreased medial prefrontal activations and the shift from internally to externally guided decision making: An exploratory NIRS study during resting state and self-oriented task. *Frontiers in Human Neuroscience, 7*, 339. doi:10.3389/fnhum.2013.00339.

Naselaris, T., Prenger, R. J., Kay, K. N., Oliver, M., & Gallant, J. L. (2009). Bayesian reconstruction of natural images from human brain activity. *Neuron*, 63(6), 902–915.

Noe, A. (2004). *Action in perception*. Cambridge, MA: MIT Press.

Northoff, G. (1999). *Das Gehirn: Eine neurophilosophische Bestandsaufnahme* [The brain: A neurophilosophical "state of the art"]. Paderborn: Schoeningh.

Northoff, G. (2004). *Philosophy of brain: The brain problem*. Amsterdam: John Benjamins.

Northoff, G. (2011). *Neuropsychoanalysis in practice: Self, objects, and brains*. Oxford: Oxford University Press.

Northoff, G. (2012a). Autoepistemic limitation and the brain's neural code: Comment on "Neuroontology, neurobiological naturalism, and consciousness: A challenge to scientific reduction and a solution" by Todd E. Feinberg. *Physics of Life Reviews, 9*(1), 38–39. doi:10.1016/j.plrev.2011.12.017.

Northoff, G. (2012b). Psychoanalysis and the brain—why did Freud abandon neuroscience? *Frontiers in Psychology, 3*, 71. doi:10.3389/fpsyg.2012.00071.

Northoff, G. (2012c). Immanuel Kant's mind and the brain's resting state. *Trends in Cognitive Sciences, 16*(7), 356–359. doi:10.1016/j.tics.2012.06.001.

Northoff, G. (2013). What the brain's intrinsic activity can tell us about consciousness? A tri-dimensional view. *Neuroscience and Biobehavioral Reviews, 37*(4), 726–738.

Northoff, G. (2014a). *Unlocking the brain* (Vol. 1): *Coding*. Oxford: Oxford University Press.

Northoff, G. (2014b). *Unlocking the brain* (Vol. 2): *Consciousness*. Oxford: Oxford University Press.

Northoff, G. (2014c). How is our self altered in psychiatric disorders? A neurophenomenal approach to psychopathological symptoms. *Psychopathology*. doi:10.1159/000363351.

Northoff, G. (2014d). *Minding the brain: A guide to neuroscience and philosophy*. London: Palgrave Macmillan.

Northoff, G. (2015a). Do cortical midline variability and low frequency fluctuations mediate William James' "Stream of Consciousness"? "Neurophenomenal balance hypothesis" of "inner time consciousness." *Consciousness and Cognition, 30*, 184–200. doi:10.1016/j.concog.2014.09.004.

Northoff, G. (2015b). Spatiotemporal psychopathology II: How does a psychopathology of the brain's resting state look like? *Journal of Affective Disorder* (in revision).

Northoff, G. (2015c). Is schizophrenia a spatiotemporal disorder of the brain's resting state? *World Psychiatry, 14*(1), 34–35.

Northoff, G. (2015d). Resting state activity and the "stream of consciousness" in schizophrenia-neurophenomenal hypotheses. *Schizophrenia Bulletin*. doi:10.1093/schbul/sbu116.

Northoff, G. (2015e). Spatiotemporal psychopathology I: Is depression a spatiotemporal disorder of the brain's resting state? *Journal of Affective Disorder* (in revision).

Northoff, G. (2016a). Neuroscience and Whitehead I: Neuro-ecological model of brain. *Axiomathes*. doi:10.1007/s10516-016-9286-2.

Northoff, G. (2016b). Neuroscience and Whitehead II: Process-based ontology of brain. *Axiomathes*. doi:10.1007/s10516-016-9287-1.

Northoff, G. (2016c). Spatiotemporal psychopathology I: No rest for the brain's resting state activity in depression? Spatiotemporal psychopathology of depressive symptoms. *Journal of Affective Disorders, 190*, 854–866. doi:10.1016/j.jad.2015.05.007.

Northoff, G. (2016d). Spatiotemporal psychopathology II: How does a psychopathology of the brain's resting state look like? Spatiotemporal approach and the history of psychopathology. *Journal of Affective Disorders, 190*, 867–879. doi:10.1016/j.jad.2015.05.008.

Northoff, G. (2016e). *Neurophilosophy of the healthy mind: Learning from the unwell brain*. New York: Norton.

Northoff, G. (2017a). "Paradox of slow frequencies": Are slow frequencies in upper cortical layers a neural predisposition of the level/state of consciousness (NPC)? *Consciousness and Cognition, 54*, 20–35. doi:10.1016/j.concog.2017.03.006.

Northoff, G. (2017b). Personal identity and cortical midline structure (CMS): Do temporal features of CMS neural activity transform into "self-continuity"? *Psychological Inquiry, 28*(2–3), 122–131.

Northoff, G., & Bermpohl, F. (2004). Cortical midline structures and the self. *Trends in Cognitive Sciences, 8*(3), 102–107.

Northoff, G., & Duncan, N. W. (2016). How do abnormalities in the brain's spontaneous activity translate into symptoms in schizophrenia? From an overview of resting state activity findings to a proposed spatiotemporal psychopathology. *Progress in Neurobiology, 145–146*, 26–45. doi:10.1016/j.pneurobio.2016.08.003.

Northoff, G., Duncan, N. W., & Hayes, D. J. (2010). The brain and its resting state activity—experimental and methodological implications. *Progress in Neurobiology, 92*(4), 593–600. doi:10.1016/j.pneurobio.2010.09.002.

Northoff, G., Heinzel, A., Bermpohl, F., Niese, R., Pfennig, A., Pascual-Leone, A., & Schlaug, G. (2004). Reciprocal modulation and attenuation in the prefrontal cortex: An fMRI study on emotional-cognitive interaction. *Human Brain Mapping, 21*(3), 202–212. doi:10.1002/hbm.20002.

Northoff, G., Heinzel, A., de Greck, M., Bermpohl, F., Dobrowolny, H., & Panksepp, J. (2006). Self-referential processing in our brain—a meta-analysis of imaging studies on the self. *NeuroImage, 31*(1), 440–457.

Northoff, G., & Heiss, W. D. (2015). Why is the distinction between neural predispositions, prerequisites, and correlates of the level of consciousness clinically relevant? Functional brain imaging in coma and vegetative state. *Stroke, 46*(4), 1147–1151. doi:10.1161/STROKEAHA.114.007969.

Northoff, G., & Huang, Z. (2017). How do the brain's time and space mediate consciousness and its different dimensions? Temporo-spatial theory of consciousness (TTC). *Neuroscience and Biobehavioral Reviews, 80*, 630–645. doi:10.1016/j.neubiorev.2017.07.013.

Northoff, G., Magioncalda, P., Martino, M., Lee, H. C., Tseng, Y. C., & Lane, T. (2017). Too fast or too slow? Time and neuronal variability in bipolar disorder—a combined theoretical and empirical investigation. *Schizophrenia Bulletin*, May 19. doi:10.1093/schbul/sbx050.

Northoff, G., & Qin, P. (2011). How can the brain's resting state activity generate hallucinations? A "resting state hypothesis" of auditory verbal hallucinations. *Schizophrenia Research, 127*(1–3), 202–214.

Northoff, G., Qin, P., & Nakao, T. (2010). Rest-stimulus interaction in the brain: A review. *Trends in Neurosciences, 33*(6), 277–284.

Northoff, G., & Sibille, E. (2014a). Cortical GABA neurons and self-focus in depression: A model linking cellular, biochemical and neural network findings. *Molecular Psychiatry, 19*(9), 959.

Northoff, G., & Sibille, E. (2014b). Why are cortical GABA neurons relevant to internal focus in depression? A cross-level model linking cellular, biochemical and neural network findings. *Molecular Psychiatry, 19*(9), 966–977. doi:10.1038/mp.2014.68.

Northoff, G., & Sibille, E. (2014c). Why are cortical GABA neurons relevant to internal focus in depression? A cross-level model linking cellular, biochemical and neural network findings. *Molecular Psychiatry, 19*(9), 966–977. doi:10.1038/mp.2014.68.

Northoff, G., & Sibille, E. (2014d). Why are cortical GABA neurons relevant to internal focus in depression? A cross-level model linking cellular, biochemical and neural network findings. *Molecular Psychiatry, 19*(9), 966–977. doi: 10.1038/mp.2014.68.

Northoff, G., Wiebking, C., Feinberg, T., & Panksepp, J. (2011). The "resting-state hypothesis" of major depressive disorder-a translational subcortical-cortical framework for a system disorder. *Neuroscience and Biobehavioral Reviews, 35*(9), 1929–1945.

Notredame, C. E., Pins, D., Deneve, S., & Jardri, R. (2014). What visual illusions teach us about schizophrenia. *Frontiers in Integrative Neuroscience, 8*, 63. doi:10.3389/fnint.2014.00063.

Olshausen, B. A., & Field, D. J. (1996). Emergence of simple-cell receptive field properties by learning a sparse code for natural images. *Nature, 381*(6583), 607–609.

Olshausen, B. A., & Field, D. J. (1997). Sparse coding with an overcomplete basis set: A strategy employed by V1? *Vision Research, 37*(23), 3311–3325. http://www.ncbi.nlm.nih.gov/pubmed/9425546.

Olshausen, B. A., & Field, D. J. (2004). Sparse coding of sensory inputs. *Current Opinion in Neurobiology, 14*(4), 481–487. doi:10.1016/j.conb.2004.07.007.

Olshausen, B. A., & O'Connor, K. N. (2002). A new window on sound. *Nature Neuroscience, 5*(4), 292–294. doi:10.1038/nn0402-292.

Overgaard, M., & Fazekas, P. (2016). Can no-report paradigms extract true correlates of consciousness? *Trends in Cognitive Sciences, 20*(4), 241–242. doi:10.1016/j.tics.2016.01.004.

Owen, A. M., Coleman, M. R., Boly, M., Davis, M. H., Laureys, S., & Pickard, J. D. (2006). Detecting awareness in the vegetative state. *Science, 313*(5792), 1402.

Palmer, L. M. (2004). The systematic constitution of the universe. The constitution of the mind and Kant's Copernican analogy. *Kant-Studien, 95*, 171–182.

Palmer, C. J., Seth, A. K., & Hohwy, J. (2015). The felt presence of other minds: Predictive processing, counterfactual predictions, and mentalising in autism. *Consciousness and Cognition, 36*, 376–389. doi:10.1016/j.concog.2015.04.007.

Palva, S., Linkenkaer-Hansen, K., Näätänen, R., & Palva, J. M. (2005). Early neural correlates of conscious somatosensory perception. *Journal of Neuroscience, 25*(21), 5248–5258.

Palva, J. M., & Palva, S. (2012). Infra-slow fluctuations in electrophysiological recordings, blood-oxygenation-level-dependent signals, and psychophysical time series. *NeuroImage, 62*, 2201–2211. doi:10.1016/j.neuroimage.2012.02.060.

Palva, J. M., Zhigalov, A., Hirvonen, J., Korhonen, O., Linkenkaer-Hansen, K., & Palva, S. (2013). Neuronal long-range temporal correlations and avalanche dynamics are correlated with behavioral scaling laws. *Proceedings of the National Academy of Sciences of the United States of America, 110,* 3585–3590. doi:10.1073/pnas.1216855110.

Papineau, D. (2002). *Thinking about consciousness.* Oxford: Oxford University Press.

Park, H. D., Bernasconi, F., Salomon, R., Tallon-Baudry, C., Spinelli, L., Seeck, M., et al. (2017). Neural sources and underlying mechanisms of neural responses to heartbeats, and their role in bodily self-consciousness: An intracranial EEG study. [Epub ahead of print]. *Cereb Cortex,* 1–14. doi:10.1093/cercor/bhx136.

Park, H. D., Correia, S., Ducorps, A., & Tallon-Baudry, C. (2014). Spontaneous fluctuations in neural responses to heartbeats predict visual detection. *Nature Neuroscience, 17*(4), 612–618. doi:10.1038/nn.3671.

Park, H. D, & Tallon-Baudry, C. (2014). The neural subjective frame: from bodily signals to perceptual consciousness. *Philosophical Transactions of the Royal Society of London B: Biological Sciences, 369*(1641), 20130208. doi: 10.1098/rstb.2013.0208.

Patson, H. J. (1937). Discussion of "Kant's so-called Copernican revolution." *Mind, 46*(182), 365–371.

Pennartz, Cyriel M. A. (2015). *The brain's representational power: On consciousness and the integration of modalities.* Cambridge, MA: MIT Press.

Pereboom, D. (2011). *Consciousness and the prospects of physicalism.* New York: Oxford University Press.

Pitts, M. A., Metzler, S., & Hillyard, S. A. (2014a). Isolating neural correlates of conscious perception from neural correlates of reporting one's perception. *Frontiers in Psychology, 5,* 1078. doi:10.3389/fpsyg.2014.01078.

Pitts, M. A., Padwal, J., Fennelly, D., Martínez, A., & Hillyard, S. A. (2014b). Gamma band activity and the P3 reflect post-perceptual processes, not visual awareness. *NeuroImage, 101,* 337–350. doi:10.1016/j.neuroimage.2014.07.024.

Ploner, M., Lee, M. C., Wiech, K., Bingel, U., & Tracey, I. (2010). Prestimulus functional connectivity determines pain perception in humans. *Proceedings of the National Academy of Sciences of the United States of America, 107,* 355–360. doi:10.1073/pnas.0906186106.

Poincaré, H. (1905). *Science and hypotheses* (W. J. Greenstreet, Trans.). New York: Walter Scott.

Poldrack, R. A., & Yarkoni, T. (2016). From brain maps to cognitive ontologies: Informatics and the search for mental structure. *Annual Review of Psychology, 67,* 587–612. doi:10.1146/annurev-psych-122414-033729.

Ponce-Alvarez, A., He, B. J., Hagmann, P., & Deco, G. (2015). Task-driven activity reduces the cortical activity space of the brain: Experiment and whole-brain modeling. *PLoS Computational Biology, 11*(8), e1004445. doi:10.1371/journal.pcbi.1004445.

Prinz, J. (2012). *The conscious brain.* Oxford: Oxford University Press.

Purdon, P. L., Pierce, E. T., Mukamel, E. A., Prerau, M. J., Walsh, J. L., Wong, K. F., et al. (2013). Electroencephalogram signatures of loss and recovery of consciousness from propofol. *Proceedings of the National Academy of Sciences of the United States of America, 110*(12), E1142–E1151. doi:10.1073/pnas.1221180110.

Putnam, H. (2012). *Philosophy in an age of science: Physics, mathematics, and scepticism.* M. DeCaro & D. Macarthur (Eds.). Cambridge, MA: Harvard University Press.

Qin, P., Di, H., Liu, Y., Yu, S., Gong, Q., Duncan, N., et al. (2010). Anterior cingulate activity and the self in disorders of consciousness. *Human Brain Mapping, 31*(12), 1993–2002. doi:10.1002/hbm.20989.

Qin, P., Duncan, N. W., Wiebking, C., Gravel, P., Lyttelton, O., Hayes, D. J., et al. (2012). GABA(A) receptors in visual and auditory cortex and neural activity changes during basic visual stimulation. *Frontiers in Human Neuroscience, 6*, 337. doi:10.3389/fnhum.2012.00337.

Qin, P., Grimm, S., Duncan, N. W., Fan, Y., Huang, Z., Lane, T., Weng, X., Bajbouj, M., & Northoff, G. (2016). Spontaneous activity in default-mode network predicts ascription of self-relatedness to stimuli. *Social Cognitive and Affective Neuroscience, 11*, 693–702. doi:org/10.1093/scan/nsw008

Qin, P., Grimm, S., Duncan, N. W., Holland, G., Shen Guo, J., Fan, Y., et al. (2013). Self-specific stimuli interact differently than non-self-specific stimuli with eyes-open versus eyes-closed spontaneous activity in auditory cortex. *Frontiers in Human Neuroscience, 7*.

Qin, P., & Northoff, G. (2011). How is our self related to midline regions and the default-mode network? *NeuroImage, 57*(3), 1221–1233. doi:10.1016/j.neuroimage.2011.05.028.

Qin, P., Wu, X., Duncan, N., Bao, W., Tang, W., Zhang, Z., et al. (submitted). GABA(A) receptor deficits predict recovery in vegetative state—an exploratory flumazenil PET and fMRI investigations.

Qin, P., Wu, X, Wu, C., Zhang, J., Huang, Z., Duncan, N. W., Weng, X., Tang, W., Zhao, Y., Lane, T., Mao, Y., Hudetz, A. G., & Northoff, G. (in revision). Thalamus-SACC-Insula Functional connectivity is a central neuronal signature of consciousness—fMRI in sleep, anaesthesia and unresponsive wakefulness syndrome.

Quine, W. V. O. (1969). *Ontological relativity and other essays.* New York: Columbia University Press.

Raichle, M. E. (2009). A brief history of human brain mapping. *Trends in Neurosciences, 32*(2), 118–126.

Raichle, M. E. (2010). Two views of brain function. *Trends in Cognitive Sciences, 14*(4), 180–190. doi:10.1016/j.tics.2010.01.008.

Raichle, M. E. (2015a). The restless brain: how intrinsic activity organizes brain function. *Philosophical Transactions of the Royal Society of London B: Biological Sciences, 370*(1668), 20140172.

Raichle, M. E. (2015b). The brain's default mode network. *Annual Review of Neuroscience, 38*, 433–447. doi:10.1146/annurev-neuro-071013-014030.

Raichle, M. E., MacLeod, A. M., Snyder, A. Z., Powers, W. J., Gusnard, D. A., & Shulman, G. L. (2001). A default mode of brain function. *Proceedings of the National Academy of Sciences of the United States of America, 98*(2), 676–682.

Rao, R. P., & Ballard, D. H. (1999). Predictive coding in the visual cortex: A functional interpretation of some extra-classical receptive-field effects. *Nature Neuroscience, 2*(1), 79–87.

Rauss, K., Schwartz, S., & Pourtois, G. (2011). Top-down effects on early visual processing in humans: A predictive coding framework. *Neuroscience and Biobehavioral Reviews, 35*(5), 1237–1253. doi:10.1016/j.neubiorev.2010.12.011.

Rescher, N. (2000). *Process philosophy: A survey of basic issues*. Pittsburgh: University of Pittsburgh Press.

Revonsuo, A. (2006). *Inner presence: Consciousness as a biological phenomenon*. Cambridge, MA: MIT Press.

Rhodes, P. (2006). The properties and implications of NMDA spikes in neocortical pyramidal cells. *Journal of Neuroscience, 26*, 6704–6715.

Richter, C. G., Babo-Rebelo, M., Schwartz, D., & Tallon-Baudry, C. (2017). Phase-amplitude coupling at the organism level: The amplitude of spontaneous alpha rhythm fluctuations varies with the phase of the infra-slow gastric basal rhythm. *NeuroImage, 146*, 951–958. doi:10.1016/j.neuroimage.2016.08.043.

Robinson, H. (1990). Kant's Copernican revolution. *Journal of the History of Philosophy, 28*(3), 458–460.

Rodriguez, E., George, N., Lachaux, J. P., Martinerie, J., Renault, B., & Varela, F. J. (1999). Perception's shadow: Long-distance synchronization of human brain activity. *Nature, 397*(6718), 430–433.

Rolls, E. T., & Treves, A. (2011). The neuronal encoding of information in the brain. *Progress in Neurobiology, 95*(3). doi:10.1016/j.pneurobio.2011.08.002.

Rosanova, M., Gosseries, O., Casarotto, S., Boly, M., Casali, A. G., Bruno, M. A., et al. (2012). Recovery of cortical effective connectivity and recovery of consciousness in vegetative patients. *Brain, 135*(Pt 4), 1308–1320. doi:10.1093/brain/awr340.

Rosch, E., Thompson, E., & Varela, F. J. (1991). *The embodied mind: Cognitive science and human experience*. Cambridge, MA: MIT Press.

Rothman, D. L., De Feyter, H. M., Graaf, R. A., Mason, G. F., & Behar, K. L. (2011). 13C MRS studies of neuroenergetics and neurotransmitter cycling in humans. *NMR in Biomedicine, 24*(8), 943–957.

Rowlands, M. (2010). *The new science of the mind: From extended mind to embodied phenomenology*. Cambridge, MA: MIT Press.

Rozell, C. J., Johnson, D. H., Baraniuk, R. G., & Olshausen, B. A. (2008). Sparse coding via thresholding and local competition in neural circuits. *Neural Computation, 20*(10), 2526–2563. doi:10.1162/neco.2008.03-07-486.

Ruby, F. J., Smallwood, J., Engen, H., & Singer, T. (2013). How self-generated thought shapes mood—the relation between mind-wandering and mood depends on the socio-temporal content of thoughts. *PLoS One, 8*(10), e77554.

Ruby, F. J., Smallwood, J., Sackur, J., & Singer, T. (2013). Is self-generated thought a means of social problem solving? *Frontiers in Psychology, 4*.

Russell, B. (1948). *Human knowledge: Its scope and limits*. New York: Simon and Schuster.

Rutiku, R., Aru, J., & Bachmann, T. (2016). General markers of conscious visual perception and their timing. *Frontiers in Human Neuroscience, 10*, 23. doi:10.3389/fnhum.2016.00023.

Saad, Z. S., Gotts, S. J., Murphy, K., Chen, G., Jo, H. J., Martin, A., et al. (2012). Trouble at rest: How correlation patterns and group differences become distorted after global signal regression. *Brain Connectivity, 2*(1), 25–32.

Sacks, M. (2000). *Objectivity and insight*. Oxford: Oxford University Press.

Sadaghiani, S., Hesselmann, G., Friston, K. J., & Kleinschmidt, A. (2010). The relation of ongoing brain activity, evoked neural responses, and cognition. *Frontiers in Systems Neuroscience, 4*, 20. doi:10.3389/fnsys.2010.00020.

Sadaghiani, S., Hesselmann, G., & Kleinschmidt, A. (2009). Distributed and antagonistic contributions of ongoing activity fluctuations to auditory stimulus detection. *Journal of Neuroscience, 29*(42), 13410–13417. doi:10.1523/JNEUROSCI.2592-09.2009.

Sadaghiani, S., & Kleinschmidt, A. (2013). Functional interactions between intrinsic brain activity and behavior. *NeuroImage, 80*, 379–386. doi:10.1016/j.neuroimage.2013.04.100.

Sadaghiani, S., Poline, J. B., Kleinschmidt, A., & D'Esposito, M. (2015). Ongoing dynamics in large-scale functional connectivity predict perception. *Proceedings of the National Academy of Sciences of the United States of America, 112*(27), 8463–8468. doi:10.1073/pnas.1420687112.

Sadaghiani, S., Scheeringa, R., Lehongre, K., Morillon, B., Giraud, A. L., & Kleinschmidt, A. (2010). Intrinsic connectivity networks, alpha oscillations, and tonic alertness: A simultaneous electroencephalography/functional magnetic resonance imaging study. *Journal of Neuroscience, 30*(30), 10243–10250. doi:10.1523/JNEUROSCI.1004-10.2010.

Sänger, J., Müller, V., & Lindenberger, U. (2012). Intra- and interbrain synchronization and network properties when playing guitar in duets. *Frontiers in Human Neuroscience, 6*, 312. doi:10.3389/fnhum.2012.00312.

Sarà, M., Pistoia, F., Pasqualetti, P., Sebastiano, F., Onorati, P., & Rossini, P. M. (2011). Functional isolation within the cerebral cortex in the vegetative state. *Neurorehabilitation and Neural Repair, 25*, 35–42. doi:10.1177/1545968310378508.

Sauseng, P., & Klimesch, W. (2008). What does phase information of oscillatory brain activity tell us about cognitive processes? *Neuroscience and Biobehavioral Reviews, 32*(5), 1001–1013.

Saxe, R. (2006). Uniquely human social cognition. *Current Opinion in Neurobiology, 16*(2), 235–239.

Saxe, R., & Kanwisher, N. (2003). People thinking about thinking people: The role of the temporo-parietal junction in "theory of mind." *NeuroImage, 19*(4), 1835–1842.

Saxe, R., & Wexler, A. (2005). Making sense of another mind: The role of the right temporo-parietal junction. *Neuropsychologia, 43*(10), 1391–1399.

Schacter, D. L., Addis, D. R., Hassabis, D., Martin, V. C., Spreng, R. N., & Szpunar, K. K. (2012). The future of memory: Remembering, imagining, and the brain. *Neuron, 76*, 677–694. doi:10.1016/j.neuron.2012.11.001.

Schechtman, M. (1997). The brain/body problem. *Philosophical Psychology, 10*(2), 149–164.

Schneider, F., Bermpohl, F., Heinzel, A., Rotte, M., Walter, M., Tempelmann, C., et al. (2008). The resting brain and our self: Self-relatedness modulates resting state neural activity in cortical midline structures. *Neuroscience, 157*(1), 120–131.

Schölvinck, M. L., Friston, K. J., & Rees, G. (2012). The influence of spontaneous activity on stimulus processing in primary visual cortex. *NeuroImage, 59*, 2700–2708. doi:10.1016/j.neuroimage.2011.10.066.

Schölvinck, M. L., Maier, A., Ye, F. Q., Duyn, J. H., & Leopold, D. A. (2010). Neural basis of global resting-state fMRI activity. *Proceedings of the National Academy of Sciences of the United States of America, 107*, 10238–10243. doi:10.1073/pnas.0913110107.

Schopenhauer, A. (1818–1819/1966). *The world as will and idea*. London: Dover.

Schoot, L., Hagoort, P., & Segaert, K. (2016). What can we learn from a two-brain approach to verbal interaction? *Neuroscience and Biobehavioral Reviews, 68*, 454–459. doi:10.1016/j.neubiorev.2016.06.009.

Schroeder, C. E., & Lakatos, P. (2009a). Low-frequency neuronal oscillations as instruments of sensory selection. *Trends in Neurosciences, 32*(1), 9–18. doi:10.1016/j.tins.2008.09.012.

Schroeder, C. E., & Lakatos, P. (2009b). The gamma oscillation: Master or slave? *Brain Topography, 22*(1), 24–26. doi:10.1007/s10548-009-0080-y.

Schroeder, C. E., Lakatos, P., Kajikawa, Y., Partan, S., & Puce, A. (2008). Neuronal oscillations and visual amplification of speech. *Trends in Cognitive Sciences, 12*(3), 106–113. doi:10.1016/j.tics.2008.01.002.

Schroeder, C. E., Wilson, D. A., Radman, T., Scharfman, H., & Lakatos, P. (2010). Dynamics of active sensing and perceptual selection. *Current Opinion in Neurobiology, 20*(2), 172–176. doi:10.1016/j.conb.2010.02.010.

Schurger, A., Sarigiannidis, I., Naccache, L., Sitt, J. D., & Dehaene, S. (2015). Cortical activity is more stable when sensory stimuli are consciously perceived. *Proceedings of the National Academy of Sciences of the United States of America, 112*(16), E2083–E2092. doi:10.1073/pnas.1418730112.

Sdrolia, C., & Bishop, J. M. (2014). Rethinking construction: On Luciano Floridi's "Against Digital Ontology." *Minds and Machines, 24*(1), 89–99. doi:10.1007/s11023-013-9329-z.

Searle, J. (2004). *Mind: An introduction to philosophy of mind*. Oxford: Oxford University Press.

Sel, A., Harding, R., & Tsakiris, M. (2015). Electrophysiological correlates of self-specific prediction errors in the human brain. *NeuroImage, 125*, 13–24. doi:10.1016/j.neuroimage.2015.09.064.

Sellars, W. (1963). Empiricism and philosophy of mind. In *Science, perception, and reality* (pp. 127–197). Atascadero, CA: Ridgeview.

Seth, A. K. (2013). Interoceptive inference, emotion, and the embodied self. *Trends in Cognitive Sciences, 17*(11), 565–573. doi:10.1016/j.tics.2013.09.007.

Seth, A. K. (2014). A predictive processing theory of sensorimotor contingencies: Explaining the puzzle of perceptual presence and its absence in synesthesia. *Cognitive Neuroscience, 5*(2), 97–118. doi:10.1080/17588928.2013.877880.

Seth, A. K. (2015). Neural coding: Rate and time codes work together. *Current Biology, 25*(3), R110–R113. doi:10.1016/j.cub.2014.12.043.

Seth, A. K., Barrett, A. B., & Barnett, L. (2011). Causal density and integrated information as measures of conscious level. *Philosophical Transactions of the Royal Society A: Mathematical, Physical and Engineering Sciences, 369*(1952), 3748–3767.

Seth, A. K., & Critchley, H. D. (2013). Extending predictive processing to the body: Emotion as interoceptive inference. *Behavioral and Brain Sciences, 36*(3), 227–228. doi:10.1017/S0140525X12002270.

Seth, A. K., Dienes, Z., Cleeremans, A., Overgaard, M., & Pessoa, L. (2008). Measuring consciousness: Relating behavioural and neurophysiological approaches. *Trends in Cognitive Sciences, 12*(8), 314–321. doi:10.1016/j.tics.2008.04.008.

Seth, A. K., & Friston, K. J. (2016). Active interoceptive inference and the emotional brain. *Philosophical Transactions of the Royal Society of London B: Biological Sciences, 371*. doi:10.1098/rstb.2016.0007.

Seth, A. K., Izhikevich, E., Reeke, G. N., & Edelman, G. M. (2006). Theories and measures of consciousness: An extended framework. *Proceedings of the National Academy of Sciences of the United States of America, 103*(28). doi:10.1073/pnas.0604347103.

Seth, A. K., Suzuki, K., & Critchley, H. D. (2012). An interoceptive predictive coding model of conscious presence. *Frontiers in Psychology, 2*, 395. doi:10.3389/fpsyg.2011.00395.

Shapiro, L. (Ed.). (2014). *The Routledge handbook of embodied cognition*. London: Routledge.

Sherburne, D. (1966). Kant. In *A key to Whitehead's "Process and reality."* Chicago: University of Chicago Press.

Sherburne, D. (1983). Whitehead, categories, and the completion of the Copernican revolution. *Monist, 66*(3), 367–386.

Shulman, G. L., Astafiev, S. V., Franke, D., Pope, D. L., Snyder, A. Z., McAvoy, M. P., et al. (2009). Interaction of stimulus-driven reorienting and expectation in ventral and dorsal frontoparietal and basal ganglia-cortical networks. *Journal of Neuroscience, 29*(14), 4392–4407.

Shulman, G. L., Corbetta, M., Buckner, R. L., Fiez, J. A., Miezin, F. M., Raichle, M. E., et al. (1997). Common blood flow changes across visual tasks: I. Increases in subcortical structures and cerebellum but not in nonvisual cortex. *Journal of Cognitive Neuroscience, 9*(5), 624–647. doi:10.1162/jocn.1997.9.5.624.

Shulman, G. L., Fiez, J. A., Corbetta, M., Buckner, R. L., Miezin, F. M., Raichle, M. E., et al. (1997). Common blood flow changes across visual tasks: II. Decreases in cerebral cortex. *Journal of Cognitive Neuroscience, 9*(5), 648–663. doi:10.1162/jocn.1997.9.5.648.

Shulman, R. G. (2012). *Brain and consciousness*. Oxford: Oxford University Press.

Shulman, R. G., Hyder, F., & Rothman, D. L. (2009). Baseline brain energy supports the state of consciousness. *Proceedings of the National Academy of Sciences of the United States of America, 106*(27), 11096–11101.

Shulman, R. G., Hyder, F., & Rothman, D. L. (2014). Insights from neuroenergetics into the interpretation of functional neuroimaging: An alternative empirical model for studying the brain's support of behavior. *Journal of Cerebral Blood Flow and Metabolism, 34*(11), 1721–1735.

Shulman, R. G., Rothman, D. L., Behar, K. L., & Hyder, F. (2004). Energetic basis of brain activity: Implications for neuroimaging. *Trends in Neurosciences, 27*(8), 489–495.

Siegel, S. (2013). The contents of perception. In E. N. Zalta (Ed.), *The Stanford enyclopedia of philosophy* (Fall 2013). https://plato.stanford.edu/entries/perception-contents/.

Silverstein, B. H., Snodgrass, M., Shevrin, H., & Kushwaha, R. (2015). P3b, consciousness, and complex unconscious processing. *Cortex, 73*, 216–227. doi:10.1016/j.cortex.2015.09.004.

Simoncelli, E. P., & Olshausen, B. A. (2001). Natural image statistics and neural representation. *Annual Review of Neuroscience, 24*, 1193–1216. doi:10.1146/annurev.neuro.24.1.1193.

Simpson, J. R., Drevets, W. C., Snyder, A. Z., Gusnard, D. A., & Raichle, M. E. (2001). Emotion-induced changes in human medial prefrontal cortex: II. During anticipatory anxiety. *Proceedings of the National Academy of Sciences of the United States of America, 98*(2), 688–693.

Singer, W. (1999). Neuronal synchrony: A versatile code for the definition of relations? *Neuron, 24*(1), 49–65, 111–125.

Singer, W. (2009). Distributed processing and temporal codes in neuronal networks. *Cognitive Neurodynamics, 3*(3), 189–196. doi:10.1007/s11571-009-9087-z.

Sitt, J. D., King, J.-R., El Karoui, I., Rohaut, B., Faugeras, F., Gramfort, A., et al. (2014). Large scale screening of neural signatures of consciousness in patients in a vegetative or minimally conscious state. *Brain, 137*, 2258–2270. doi:10.1093/brain/awu141.

Smallwood, J., & Schooler, J. W. (2015). The science of mind wandering: Empirically navigating the stream of consciousness. *Annual Review of Psychology, 66*, 487–518.

Smith, B. (1995). Formal ontology, common sense and cognitive science. *International Journal of Human-Computer Studies, 43*, 641–666.

Smith, S. M., Fox, P. T., Miller, K. L., Glahn, D. C., Fox, P. M., & Mackay, C. E., et al. (2009). Correspondence of the brain's functional architecture during activation and rest. *Proceedings of the National Academy of Sciences, 106*(31), 13040–13045.

Snowdon, P. F. (2015). Philosophy and the mind/body problem. *Royal Institute of Philosophy*, (Suppl. 76), 21–37.

Sporns, O., & Betzel, R. F. (2016). Modular brain networks. *Annual Review of Psychology, 67*, 613–640. doi:10.1146/annurev-psych-122414-033634.

Spratling, M. W. (2011). A single functional model accounts for the distinct properties of suppression in cortical area V1. *Vision Research, 51*(6), 563–576. doi:10.1016/j.visres.2011.01.017

Spratling, M. W. (2012a). Unsupervised learning of generative and discriminative weights encoding elementary image components in a predictive coding model of cortical function. *Neural Computation, 24*(1), 60–103. doi:10.1162/NECO_a_00222.

Spratling, M. W. (2012b). Predictive coding as a model of the V1 saliency map hypothesis. *Neural Networks, 26*, 7–28. doi:10.1016/j.neunet.2011.10.002.

Spreng, R. N., Mar, R. A., & Kim, A. S. (2009). The common neural basis of autobiographical memory, prospection, navigation, theory of mind, and the default mode: A quantitative meta-analysis. *Journal of Cognitive Neuroscience, 21*(3), 489–510. doi:10.1162/jocn.2008.21029.

Stefanics, G., Hangya, B., Hernádi, I., Winkler, I., Lakatos, P., & Ulbert, I. (2010). Phase entrainment of human delta oscillations can mediate the effects of expectation on reaction speed. *Journal of Neuroscience, 30*(41), 13578–13585. doi:10.1523/JNEUROSCI.0703-10.2010.

Stein, B. E., Stanford, T. R., Ramachandran, R., Perrault, T. J., Jr., & Rowland, B. A. (2009). Challenges in quantifying multisensory integration: Alternative criteria, models, and inverse effectiveness. *Experimental Brain Research, 198*(2–3), 113–126. doi:10.1007/s00221-009-1880-8.

Stender, J., Gosseries, O., Bruno, M.-A., Charland-Verville, V., Vanhaudenhuyse, A., Demertzi, A., et al. (2014). Diagnostic precision of PET imaging and functional MRI in disorders of consciousness: A clinical validation study. *Lancet, 384*, 514–522. doi:10.1016/S0140-6736(14)60042-8.

Sterzer, P., & Kleinschmidt, A. (2007). A neural basis for inference in perceptual ambiguity. *Proceedings of the National Academy of Sciences of the United States of America, 104*(1), 323–328.

Sterzer, P., Kleinschmidt, A., & Rees, G. (2009). The neural bases of multistable perception. *Trends in Cognitive Sciences, 13*(7), 310–318. doi:10.1016/j.tics.2009.04.006.

Stoljar, D. (2006). *Ignorance and Imagination: The epistemic origin of the problem of consciousness*. Oxford: Oxford University Press.

Stoljar, D. (2009). Physicalism. In E. N. Zalta (Ed.), *Stanford encyclopedia of philosophy*. https://plato.stanford.edu/entries/physicalism/.

Strawson, G. (2006). Realistic monism: Why physicalism entails panpsychism. *Journal of Consciousness Studies, 13*(10–11), 3–31.

Strawson, G. (2017). Mind and being: The primacy of panpsychism. In G. Brüntrup & L. Jaskolla (Eds.), *Panpsychism: Philosophical essays*. New York: Oxford University Press.

Sugden, R. (2009). Credible worlds, capacities and mechanisms. *Erkenntnis, 70*(1), 3–27.

Sui, J., Chechlacz, M., Rotshtein, P., & Humphreys, G. W. (2015). Lesion-symptom mapping of self-prioritization in explicit face categorization: Distinguishing hypo- and hyper-self-biases. *Cerebral Cortex, 25*(2), 374–383.

Sullivan, R. J. (1989/2012). *Immanuel Kant's moral theory*. Cambridge: Cambridge University Press.

Summerfield, C., Egner, T., Greene, M., Koechlin, E., Mangels, J., & Hirsch, J. (2006). Predictive codes for forthcoming perception in the frontal cortex. *Science, 314*(5803), 1311–1314.

Summerfield, C., Trittschuh, E. H., Monti, J. M., Mesulam, M. M., & Egner, T. (2008). Neural repetition suppression reflects fulfilled perceptual expectations. *Nature Neuroscience, 11*(9), 1004–1006. doi:10.1038/nn.2163.

Tagliazucchi, E., Chialvo, D. R., Siniatchkin, M., Amico, E., Brichant, J.-F., Bonhomme, V., et al. (2016). Large-scale signatures of unconsciousness are consistent with a departure from critical dynamics. *Philosophical Transactions of the Royal Society of London, 13*, 244–267.

Tagliazucchi, E., & Laufs, H. (2014). Decoding wakefulness levels from typical fMRI resting state data reveals reliable drifts between wakefulness and sleep. *Neuron, 82*, 695–708. doi:10.1016/j.neuron.2014.03.020.

Tagliazucchi, E., von Wegner, F., Morzelewski, A., Brodbeck, V., Jahnke, K., & Laufs, H. (2013). Breakdown of long-range temporal dependence in default mode and attention networks during deep sleep. *Proceedings of the National Academy of Sciences of the United States of America, 110*(38), 15419–15424.

Tahko, T. E. (2015). *An introduction to metametaphysics*. Cambridge Introductions to Philosophy. Cambridge: Cambridge University Press.

Tang, Y., Holzel, B. K., & Posner, M. I. (2015). The neuroscience of mindfulness meditation. *Nature Reviews. Neuroscience, 16*, 213–225.

Tang, Y., & Northoff, G. (2017). Meditation and its different stages: A neurobiological framework. In preparation.

ten Oever, S., Schroeder, C. E., Poeppel, D., van Atteveldt, N., & Zion-Golumbic, E. (2014). Rhythmicity and cross-modal temporal cues facilitate detection. *Neuropsychologia, 63*, 43–50. doi:10.1016/j.neuropsychologia.2014.08.008.

Thagard, P. (2005). *Mind: Introduction to cognitive science* (2nd Ed.). Cambridge, MA: MIT Press.

Thagard, P. (Ed.). (2007). *Philosophy of psychology and cognitive science*. Amsterdam: Elsevier.

Thagard, P. (2009). Why cognitive science needs philosophy and vice versa. *Topics in Cognitive Science, 1*, 237–254.

Thagard, P. (2010). *The brain and the meaning of life*. Princeton, NJ: Princeton University Press.

Thagard, P. (2012a). Cognitive science. In Edward N. Zalta (Ed.), *The Stanford encyclopedia of philosophy* (Fall 2012), http://plato.stanford.edu/archives/fall2012/entries/cognitive-science/.

Thagard, P. (2012b). *The cognitive science of science: Explanation, discovery, and conceptual change*. Cambridge, MA: MIT Press.

Thompson, E. (2007). *Mind in life: Biology, phenomenology, and the sciences of mind*. Cambridge, MA: Harvard University Press.

Thompson, E. (2010). *The enactive approach*. Cambridge, MA: Harvard University Press.

Tononi, G. (2004). An information integration theory of consciousness. *BMC Neuroscience, 5*, 42. doi:10.1186/1471-2202-5-42.

Tononi, G. (2008). Consciousness as integrated information: A provisional manifesto. *Biological Bulletin, 215*(3), 216–242.

Tononi, G., Boly, M., Massimini, M., & Koch, C. (2016). Integrated information theory: From consciousness to its physical substrate. *Nature Reviews: Neuroscience, 17*(7), 450–461. doi:10.1038/nrn.2016.44.

Tononi, G., & Koch, C. (2008). The neural correlates of consciousness: An update. *Annals of the New York Academy of Sciences, 1124*, 239–261. doi:10.1196/annals.1440.004.

Tononi, G., & Koch, C. (2015). Consciousness: here, there and everywhere? *Philosophical Transactions of the Royal Society of London B: Biological Sciences, 370*(1668), 20140167.

Tsuchiya, N., Block, N., & Koch, C. (2012). Top-down attention and consciousness: Comment on Cohen et al. *Trends in Cognitive Sciences, 16*(11), 527, author reply 528. doi:10.1016/j.tics.2012.09.004.

Tsuchiya, N., Wilke, M., Frässle, S., & Lamme, V. A. (2015). No-report paradigms: Extracting the true neural correlates of consciousness. *Trends in Cognitive Sciences, 19*(12), 757–770. doi:10.1016/j.tics.2015.10.002.

Tye, M. (2009). *Consciousness revisited: Materialism without phenomenal concepts*. Cambridge, MA: MIT Press.

Uehara, T., Yamasaki, T., Okamoto, T., Koike, T., Kan, S., Miyauchi, S., et al. (2014). Efficiency of a "small-world" brain network depends on consciousness level: A resting-state fMRI study. *Cerebral Cortex, 24*, 1529–1539. doi:10.1093/cercor/bht004.

van Atteveldt, N., Murray, M. M., Thut, G., & Schroeder, C. E. (2014). Multisensory integration: Flexible use of general operations. *Neuron, 81*(6), 1240–1253. doi:10.1016/j.neuron.2014.02.044.

van Atteveldt N, Musacchia G, Zion-Golumbic E, Sehatpour P, Javitt DC, Schroeder C. (2015). Complementary fMRI and EEG evidence for more efficient neural processing of rhythmic vs. unpredictably timed sounds. *Frontiers in Psychology, 6*(1663). doi: 10.3389/fpsyg.2015.01663.

van Boxtel, J. J., Tsuchiya, N., & Koch, C. (2010a). Consciousness and attention: On sufficiency and necessity. *Frontiers in Psychology, 1*, 217. doi:10.3389/fpsyg.2010.00217.

van Boxtel, J. J., Tsuchiya, N., & Koch, C. (2010b). Opposing effects of attention and consciousness on afterimages. *Proceedings of the National Academy of Sciences of the United States of America, 107*(19), 8883–8888. doi:10.1073/pnas.0913292107.

van Dijk, H., Schoffelen, J.-M., Oostenveld, R., & Jensen, O. (2008). Prestimulus oscillatory activity in the alpha band predicts visual discrimination ability. *Journal of Neuroscience, 28*, 256–265.

van Eijsden, P., Hyder, F., Rothman, D. L., & Shulman, R. G. (2009). Neurophysiology of functional imaging. *NeuroImage, 45*(4), 1047–1054. doi:10.1016/j.neuroimage.2008.08.026.

van Gaal, S., & Lamme, V. A. (2012). Unconscious high-level information processing: Implication for neurobiological theories of consciousness. *Neuroscientist, 18*(3), 287–301. doi:10.1177/1073858411404079.

Vanhatalo, S., Palva, J. M., Holmes, M., Miller, J., Voipio, J., & Kaila, K. (2004). Infraslow oscillations modulate excitability and interictal epileptic activity in the human cortex during sleep. *Proceedings of the National Academy of Sciences of the United States of America, 101*(14), 5053–5057.

Vanhaudenhuyse, A., Demertzi, A., Schabus, M., Noirhomme, Q., Bredart, S., Boly, M., et al. (2011). Two distinct neuronal networks mediate the awareness of environment and of self. *Journal of Cognitive Neuroscience, 23*(3), 570–578. doi:10.1162/jocn.2010.21488.

Vanhaudenhuyse, A., Noirhomme, Q., Tshibanda, L. J., Bruno, M. A., Boveroux, P., Schnakers, C., et al. (2010). Default network connectivity reflects the level of consciousness in non-communicative brain-damaged patients. *Brain, 133*(Pt 1), 161–171. doi:10.1093/brain/awp313.

Van Inwagen, P. (2014). *Existence: Essays in ontology*. Cambridge: Cambridge University Press.

Varela, F. J., Thompson, E. T., & Rosch, E. (1991). *The embodied mind: Cognitive science and human experience*. Cambridge, MA: MIT Press.

Velmans, M. (2000). *Understanding consciousness*. London: Routledge.

Vetter, P., Sanders, L. L., & Muckli, L. (2014). Dissociation of prediction from conscious perception. *Perception, 43*(10), 1107–1113.

Vinje, W. E., & Gallant, J. L. (2000). Sparse coding and decorrelation in primary visual cortex during natural vision. *Science, 287*(5456), 1273–1276.

Vinje, W., & Gallant, J. (2002). Natural stimulation of the nonclassical receptive field increases information transmission efficiency in V1. *Journal of Neuroscience, 22*(7), 2904–2915.

Wacongne, C., Labyt, E., van Wassenhove, V., Bekinschtein, T., Naccache, L., & Dehaene, S. (2011). Evidence for a hierarchy of predictions and prediction errors in human cortex. *Proceedings of the National Academy of Sciences of the United States of America, 108*(51), 20754–20759. doi:10.1073/pnas.1117807108.

Wang, F., Duratti, L., Samur, E., Spaelter, U., & Bleuler, H. (2007). A computer-based real-time simulation of interventional radiology. *Annual International Conference of the IEEE Engineering in Medicine and Biology Society. IEEE Engineering in Medicine and Biology Society. Conference, 1742–1745*. doi:10.1109/IEMBS.2007.4352647.

White, B., Abbott, L. F., & Fiser, J. (2012). Suppression of cortical neural variability is stimulus-and state-dependent. *Journal of Neurophysiology, 108*(9), 2383–2392.

Whitehead, A. N. (1925). *Science and the modern world: Lowell Lectures*. New York: Macmillan.

Whitehead, A. N. (1929/1978). *Process and reality: An essay in cosmology*. D. R. Griffin & D. W. Sherburne (Eds.). New York: The Free Press.

Whitehead, A. N. (1927/1955). *Symbolism: Its meaning and effect*. New York: Fordham University Press.

Whitehead, A. N. (1933). *The adventures of ideas*. New York: The Free Press.

Whitehead, A. N. (1968). *Modes of thought*. New York: Simon & Schuster.

Wiebking, C., Duncan, N. W., Tiret, B., Hayes, D. J., Marjańska, M., Doyon, J., et al. (2014). GABA in the insula—a predictor of the neural response to interoceptive awareness. *NeuroImage, 86*, 10–18.

Wiehl, R. (1990). Whiteheads Kant-Kritik und Kants Kritik am Panpsychismus. In H. Holzhey, A. Rust, & R. Wiehl (Eds.), *Natur, Subjektivitaet, Gott: Zur Prozessphilosophie Alfred N. Whiteheads* (pp. 198–239). Frankfurt: Suhrkamp.

Willmore, B. D. B., Mazer, J. A., & Gallant, J. L. (2011). Sparse coding in striate and extrastriate visual cortex. *Journal of Neurophysiology, 105*(6). doi:10.1152/jn.00594.2010.

Yoshimi, J., & Vinson, D. W. (2015). Extending Gurwitsch's field theory of consciousness. *Consciousness and Cognition, 34*, 104–123. doi:10.1016/j.concog.2015.03.017.

Yu, B., Nakao, T., Xu, J., Qin, P., Chaves, P., Heinzel, A., et al. (2015). Resting state glutamate predicts elevated pre-stimulus alpha during self-relatedness: A combined EEG-MRS study on rest-self overlap. *Social Neuroscience, 11*, 249–263. doi:10.1080/17470919.2015.1072582.

Yuste, R., MacLean, J. N., Smith, J., & Lansner, A. (2005). The cortex as a central pattern generator. *Nature Reviews: Neuroscience, 6*(6), 477–483.

Zabelina, D. L., & Andrews-Hanna, J. R. (2016). Dynamic network interactions supporting internally-oriented cognition. *Current Opinion in Neurobiology, 40*, 86–93.

Zhang, J., Huang, Z., Wu, X., Wang, Z., Dai, R., Li, Y., et al. (Forthcoming). Breakdown in spatial and temporal organisation in spontaneous activity during general anesthesia. *Human Brain Mapping*.

Zhang, J., Zhanga, H., Huang, Z., Chenc, Y., Zhangc, J., Ghindaj, D., et al. (2018). Breakdown in temporal and spatial organization of spontaneous brain activity during general anesthesia. *Human Brain Mapping, 39*(5), 2035–2046.

Zhigalov, A., Arnulfo, G., Nobili, L., Palva, S., & Palva, J. M. (2015). Relationship of fast- and slow-timescale neuronal dynamics in human MEG and SEEG. *Journal of Neuroscience, 35*, 344–356.

Zmigrod, S., & Hommel, B. (2011). The relationship between feature binding and consciousness: Evidence from asynchronous multi-modal stimuli. *Consciousness and Cognition, 20*(3), 586–593.

Zuo, X.-N., Kelly, C., Adelstein, J. S., Klein, D. F., Castellanos, F. X., & Milham, M. P. (2010). Reliable intrinsic connectivity networks: Test-retest evaluation using ICA and dual regression approach. *NeuroImage, 49*(3), 2163–2177.

Index